To: Mel[illegible]

May th[illegible]
You move [illegible] your
life in the direction you
choose for yourself.

Love & Blessings,
Alice "Alicja" Jones

ALICE "ALICJA" JONES

Day by Day

Balboa Press books may be ordered through booksellers or by contacting:

Balboa Press
A Division of Hay House
1663 Liberty Drive
Bloomington, IN 47403
www.balboapress.com
1 (877) 407-4847

Printed in the United States of America.

ISBN: 978-1-5043-9942-5 (sc)
ISBN: 978-1-5043-9944-9 (hc)
ISBN: 978-1-5043-9943-2 (e)

Library of Congress Control Number: 2018902910

Balboa Press rev. date: 06/15/2018

Table of Contents

To
Wanda

Author's Note

Inspirational messages about God kept being downloaded into my psyche daily from 1999 through 2001; messages received from various Divine aspects of God. As I wrote, I grew not only in the development of my spirit, but in the expansion of my power, and started to *get it.* These were deeply personal, intensely private, completely consuming communiqués that spoke to the central core of my being, themes which fully impacted every area of my life. I soon realized these messages were also meant to be shared with others.

In 2000, when I was too wrapped up in material pursuits to stop and record my thoughts, I broke my wrist. There was not much I could do except to write. Thus, having fully committed to Spirit, I sat with my yellow pad each day as words flowed through me. It felt as though I was listening to "internal dictation"; three hours every morning, starting in the predawn hours.

I filled fifteen yellow tablets. Sorting the writings into any proper category seemed like a daunting task. When I complained internally, *That's a lot of work,* the answer I heard was, *Yeaaahhh?* Spirit had no sympathy.

During 2002, over a period of seven months, I was awakened in the middle of the night with a "phrase" streaming through my head; a different phrase each month, each as insistent as the last. The phrase *would not quit* repeating itself until I wrote it down. Only then would the message stop. I did not know what was going on, except that I had received so many messages from Spirit up to that point that I just blindly accepted this as yet another one of Spirit's idiosyncrasies, the meaning of which would be made clear to me eventually. The only thing handy for this middle of the night sojourn was a piece of semi-stiff filler paper, easy to find, save and retrieve when I was groping in the semi-darkness. Eventually, there were seven simple phrases, seven truths from Spirit, seven simple gifts: *The Outer Reflects the Inner, Make Different Choices, Believe That It Is Possible,*

Write It Down, *Choose Your Self*, *Cocoon,* and *Connect to Your Divine Source*. Only after I received the seventh phrase in the seventh month did I understand that everything I had been writing fit into one of the seven categories. Soon, the tablets were organized into their proper heading, then entered into the computer, then edited, re-edited, and edited again.

Sarah Ban Breathnach, author of *Simple Abundance,* was the inspiration for the format of this book. She experienced not knowing the exact book she was writing, but rather allowed it to evolve. In exactly the same manner, I did not know how the book would look as a finished product, thinking it might simply be a book of short essays. I soon realized there was a meditation for each day, but many needed to be expanded. My writing grew from being sporadic in 2003 to daily in 2005. Then, I worked on revising the material through October, 2006. From that point, the work was edited and re-edited until 2014, when it received its final touches. Whenever I received words from Spirit that I did not edit at all, I *italicized the entire paragraph or page(s).*

The book "rested" until it was ready to be released. This ultimately became a twenty year endeavor.

One purpose for writing this book is to assist us with accepting our Higher Self and to teach us how to communicate with it. Another purpose is to shed some light on the *mystery* of our life. Spirit always knows what it wants from us and acts in our best interest, even when we do not know what our best interest is. Spirit teaches us that forgiveness is one of the three major reasons for incarnating on this planet; the other two are to learn how to love unconditionally and to be of service to others. This book covers all three reasons.

I offer this book as a gift to you, just as it was offered to me.

S. Alice "Alicja" Jones
Fairfax Station, VA

Step 1

The Outer Reflects the Inner

January

Real Power, the power of Love, is kind, gentle, and thorough, honors all life visible and invisible, speaks with Inner Authority, respects and accepts all things because it respects and accepts its Self.

Real Power, the power of Love, honors the "Be"-ing that we are, honors the Sacred within each of us as a fellow traveler on this planet, sees us as another soul passing through this plane, and applauds all our steps toward spiritual mastery,

Real Power, the power of Love, is patient, never forces a bud to open before its time, giving us all the time we need to express our self, and in doing so, allows us to express our Self.

Real Power, the power of Love, is totally non-judgmental, clears all judgment out of our life, does not look to divide and conquer, and never cloaks hurtful statements as Love.

Real Power, the power of Love, is not something we have. Rather, it is something we are. It comes from knowing that we are One with all things, from knowing we are not separate from God, from knowing there is nothing outside of Self. What appears outside of us reflects what is inside of us since the outer reflects the inner.

January 1

"Out There" Reflects What Is "Inside" of Us

The months of January and February are dedicated to the phrase: *The Outer reflects the Inner. Everything outside of us reflects what is inside of us: what we think, how we feel, how we act and how we react.*

The following statements all say the same thing: the Outer reflects the Inner. There is nothing out there. Everything out there reflects attitudes, beliefs, feelings or energy patterns we hold inside of us. When we are convinced our life is not working, the outer world simply presents the same situations to us over and over and over to validate our belief. Our life becomes a self-fulfilling prophecy.

This statement appears in many variations:
The kingdom of God is within you. (Jesus Christ)
You are a Creator Be-ing. (Neale Donald Walsch)
There is nothing outside of self. (Michael J. Roads)
Within the problem is the solution. (*A Course in Miracles*)
You create your own reality. (The 60's Generation)
Only Love is Real. (Brian L. Weiss, M.D.)
Do onto others as you would have it done onto you.
(The Golden Rule)

The same conditions, although they may be disguised as *different* conditions, present themselves to us until we recognize that, in order for a situation to change, we have to change. We have to let go of attitudes, belief systems, feelings or energy patterns that are not working for us. As we change our mind about circumstances which no longer serve us, then miraculously, everything else changes around us. As we change, it changes. If we stay the same, it stays the same. When events no longer serve the purpose for which they came in the first place, they leave.

Everything else mirrors the belief systems, attitudes, feelings or energy patterns we hold inside of us. Changing our circumstances by changing our mind is a minute fraction of the power we have that we may not be conscious of. We control what happens in our life.

We can start the process of change through resolutions for the New Year. If resolutions leave us in a quandary, still our mind and listen. Spirit will give us one theme for the year that is perfect for us. One of mine recently was *Live by the Light of Grace*.

Happy New Year.

What circumstances in your in your life
keep repeating themselves?
As we change, "it" changes.

January 2

The Different Voice of Higher Self vs. Ego Self

Our Higher Self, our Spirit Self (an aspect of us that is connected to the Divine), knows what is right for us. It usually speaks very softly, faintly above a whisper, so as not to usurp our freedom of choice. Higher Self constantly tries to get our attention but speaks quietly, in a *voiceless* voice which can take the form of *impressions* in our mind or a gentle nudge, a yearning, a tug, a gnawing feeling. It is relentless in pursuing us – this *hound of heaven* – continuing to get our attention in its own gentle way, so as not to override our free will.

Higher Self lets us know when something is right. How many times has our heart leapt for joy and we did not know why? How many times have we felt a lightness of being when we encountered a certain person for the very first time?

The voice of our Higher Self guides us through the "crisis points" in our lives. If we are fervently praying for a specific outcome to our life's circumstance, the answer to our prayers may come in an unconventional manner: in the form of a bird, a butterfly, a star, or a flower which can be symbols for what we need to know. Maybe a song on the radio has the exact words of advice we need to hear; a license plate we glance at has a number sequence that is meaningful to us which gives us direction; a book a friend recommends addresses the very issues troubling us; or the next conversation we have with family, friends, or co-workers grants us a solution to a vexing problem. Any one of these can be guidance from our Higher Self, who is attuned to Spirit, the Divine within us.

Sometimes a hole in our heart has to open before we hear the gentle quiet voice of Higher Self – another word for Spirit – our connection to the Divine. Sometimes we have to sink to our knees before we are receptive to the advice from our Higher Self. Sometimes, the pain in our heart has to be so great that there is nothing left except Spirit. We turn to Spirit because all else has failed.

Sometimes, our Higher Self takes the form of Angels or Archangels.

The first intuitive I went to see told me: "Alice, your Angels have been weeping. They have been trying to reach you since you were eight years old," emphasizing the relentless pursuit of the Voice of the Higher Self and our reluctance to listen.

We can be our own worst enemy and not even know it, because we have another voice within us, the voice of the *ego self.* This is the *personality self*; the self we present to the world, the spacesuit we call our body, our mind, and all our traits and characteristics. The ego self is the self we propel through each lifetime.

Our Higher Self relentlessly tries to get our attention, but all too often its voice is obliterated by the clatter of the noisy ego self.

The ego self speaks in a loud shrill voice, drowning out the Voice of the Higher Self. The ego self believes we are *separate* from our Creator. It constantly judges those outside of us – called the *other* – and relishes administrating punishment to the guilty. The ego self subscribes to scarcity, thus grabbing from others because it believes there is not enough to go around. It favors ridiculing and belittling others, causing discomfort, in order for its *self* to shine. Through its cunning use of savage power cloaked in secrecy, along with its insatiable greed, the ego self plies misery into every corner in the world. More savage behavior appears in "civilized" societies than appears in "primitive" societies. People in positions of power bow in homage to their ego selves, as the ego's bold shrill voice outshouts the small quiet Voice of the Higher Self.

The ego self is necessary from the time we are born to the time we come into young adulthood. Then, just as quickly as it peaks, it needs to be dismantled. It serves its purpose up to a certain point in our life, needs to be acknowledged up to this point, and then ignored. To continue living a life propelled only by the ego self is to life a life filled with anxiety and chaos. When we feel we are thrashing about, we need to do whatever it takes to quiet our mind to hear the still calm voice of our Higher Self.

Messages come to us from all around us. It is up to us which antenna we select to use, whether we choose to be "tuned in" and connected to the Source through our Higher Self or to the ego. Our antenna can be tuned into the ego's voice exclusively, into Spirit's voice exclusively, or to a combination of the two. Acknowledging the ego's voice is the quickest way to still it.

Ego's voice vies for our exclusive attention. Spirit's voice, the voice coming through our Higher Self, is much more patient. It waits until we are ready to hear it.

Can you discern whether Higher "Self"
or ego "self" is speaking to you?
The voice of Higher Self is very quiet
while ego self is very brash.

January 3

Listening to the Voice of the Higher Self vs. Ego Self

Instead of using the inner voice of Spirit, the Higher Self, for a guide or as the murmuring of the Divine most of humanity lets everyone else guide them. Well-meaning (but misguided) advice is rampant on this planet.

We need to train our self to hear the inner voice of our Higher Self. Hearing the inner voice of the ego self is not a problem, for we are tuned into its endless chatter continuously as its mindless tape runs through our head. Spirit Self, in the form of our Higher Self, is also there, albeit much quieter and much less assuming. It is that quiet nudge, that "great idea," that inner knowing, that instant recognition, that gentle push, that relentless force which propels us towards the good. The voice of our Higher Self knows what our soul's contract is and how to fulfill it.

How do we start distinguishing these two voices? The inner voice of our Higher Self always speaks quietly and calmly, always speaks for our highest good, as well as for the highest good of the "other." *It will never harm us, suggest harm to another, encourage harm on any level, or override our free will.* It is not the *easiest* voice to follow, nor will it necessarily make us feel comfortable, guarantee the outcome we have in mind, or fulfill our fantasies.

Ego's voice is just the opposite. It speaks loudly and brashly and is only interested in putting self "first," no matter what the "cost" is to the other. Its tone is self-righteous and intolerant. The voice of the ego is *always right* with no room for another opinion, path, belief, or choice. It is inflexible and unforgiving and *always* seeks retaliation and restitution for everything it perceives as an "injustice." Look around at the state of affairs on Earth to see where the ego has led us.

The voice of the ego has led the people of this planet from the moment the idea of separation from God occurred. Intermittently, God has sent messengers to this planet to remind us of the Voice of the Higher Self. These sages have appeared in every generation, in every age. Have we been listening?

Can you determine if the voice of the ego self or the Voice of the Higher Self is speaking to you? The voice of the ego self is brash and brazen, the Higher Self, quiet and gentle.

January 4

The "Corrections" We Feel

If our lives are not working, our Higher Self may be attempting to give us a message. It is important. Please listen! This "correction" may manifest itself as a *feeling* within our body: our *gut instinct* tells us something is wrong, our *sixth sense* alerts us to be vigilant, or our *intuition* kicks in with a sense of alarm. Our Higher Self taps us far more often than we realize. This "correction" may be a disease (a wake-up call for us to change), or it may even be insomnia if we are striving for an unattainable goal. A correction can be a warning to *Get out of there!* whether "there" is a job, a marriage, a relationship, a social encounter, a street corner, or the home we live in.

We can be experiencing great difficulty at work. We may be putting forth one-hundred-ten percent effort: we are bright and conscientious, we motivate our fellow employees, yet are thwarted in our endeavor to climb up the corporate ladder. We witness bad habits, bad attitudes and a bad work ethic by those around us, yet, they get promoted and we don't. We feel as if we are striving to ski uphill.

Is this the right job for us? Our Higher Self may be pointing us in an entirely different direction from the one our ego self has chosen. Because it knows our soul contract, our Higher Self knows when it is time for us to step into a new role that differs from our current position no matter how strongly the ego self holds our personality in its clutches.

Our Higher Self attempts to reach us by putting stumbling blocks in our way. For her fiftieth birthday, one of my sisters requested a picture as a gift. A fabulous sale was coming soon on a variety of "starving artists" pictures, but what complicated the matter was that I needed to be out of town when the sale occurred. So I enlisted the assistance of a good friend to use her best judgment to purchase the picture, then mailed this bulky gift upon my return. When the gift arrived, what my sister thought would be perfect was too large to fit her needs, but she found another place to use it. The original intent of the gift was not met.

If this truly was the *perfect* gift, the sale would *not* have occurred when I was out of town which forced me to make special arrangements to purchase it. Had I been in town, I might possibly have taken a picture of the intended gift, sent it to her, included the dimensions, and asked if it was appropriate. All the clues were there, I just needed to tune into them.

When Higher Self does not smooth the way, *Pay Attention!* Our Higher Self is always ready to assist us in making decisions in our life, but respectfully awaits our invitation. There is nothing outside of *Self,* because *Self* is all there is. Self with a capital "S" is our *Higher Self,* the Divine aspect of our self, the Self connected to the Divine Source, who we *really* are.

Our Higher Self corrects us when we are not on the right path and *gently* leads us *towards* the right path, by letting us know *something is wrong.*

Did you ever hear any "corrections"
coming from your Higher Self?
Guidance from the Higher Self comes gently
at first, then more forcibly later.

January 5

The "Roles" We Play

Nothing is what it seems. Do you know what your soul's contract is? Do you know what *role* you have agreed to play and who has agreed to *play* opposite you? Do you know, at the soul level, to whom you agreed to be the instrument of forgiveness? Many people sitting in prisons today agreed to play a role that had a higher purpose than what is immediately evident.

When Mother Theresa made the statement, "I could have been Hitler," her audience members looked at each other in disbelief. They did not know what she meant. She was referring to the fact that in this lifetime she *had chosen* a "saintly" role, but she could have just as easily *chosen* the opposite, the role of a heinous villain.

The *Law of Attraction*, by continuing to send us the same situation over and over again, helps us figure out why the role we have chosen for our self makes us feel so bad. While still in Spirit form, our Spirit chose the perfect role for each of us to play on this planet. When something about each role we play while we are here causes us distress, we discover the role we were *meant* to play.

We sort out how we fit into this world, shifting through many types of "roles" until we find one that seems appropriate. If we choose a role that is inherently opposed to our character, we line up our temperament, our personality, and our energy field into a vibration that does not fit. If we are born with a tender heart, are compassionate by nature, have a way of offering comfort to those no one else ever listens to, we cannot play the role of a "heavy." Mary Poppins cannot play a stripper and be credible. Buddha cannot be cast to play a gangster effectively. This is where we try on one role after another until we *get it*, until we remember that "we are Spirit having a human experience."

A judgmental society exists because of the soul's agreement to forget where it comes from. The ego judges. Spirit does not. It takes more courage to accept a heinous role than a saintly one. Abominable actions and the people who perpetrate them are described in books, movies, and in TV documentaries, which elucidate their character in minute detail, exposing all their wretchedness. This exposure succeeds in hatred being heaped upon the person and his or her nefarious acts by a judgmental society that cannot accept that there is a higher purpose for these villainous actions.

It takes a great deal of courage to incarnate on this planet. Many souls are afraid to come here because of the agreement to forget from whence we come. This is where the *games* begin. Fortunately, we have help. To assist us, advanced souls are encouraging and aiding the current souls on the planet to *wake up*. The newly-awakening souls *are* hearing, *are* believing, and *are* acting according to their beliefs.

We are being prepared for a state of transition where Spirit will be visible and accepted by all, but that is not yet a fact. Here, on planet Earth, matters of Spirit must be accepted "on faith" because we cannot "see" Spirit with our physical eyes, at least not yet. More and more venues are opening where faith is leading the way to peace, the faith that points to *unconditional Love.* More people are accepting that *Peace begins with me* and are learning first to resolve the differences within themselves in a peaceful manner before moving on to another.

If we still find it difficult to accept anything "on faith," we can ask our Higher Self to help us understand what we are to learn from the role we are playing in this lifetime.

The Source, another name for God, creates only Love. Love is who we are and love is what we learn to perfect on this planet; otherwise, we would not be here. Once we are able to put aside our ego passions, we open our eyes to the Infinity that surrounds us. We can *deny* who we really are, but we cannot *change* who we really are through our denial of it because who we really are is infinite and changeless.

Yes, the actions we engage in during this lifetime may be considered to "merit" punishment if we look at them from an "ego" perspective. However, looking at them through the lens of "eternity," looking at them through the lens of our Higher Self, they appear entirely different.

How has your Higher Self revealed to you what "role" you are to play on this planet? We each play a role that we select prior to coming here.

January 6

Our Subconscious Beliefs

Below the threshold of our conscious mind lies the belief system of our subconscious mind. We may not know it is there, but it influences the way we think, feel, and speak. We may have no awareness of this belief system that effectively controls every aspect of our life, determining that which we experience.

We create our negative outcomes because of our negative beliefs. The Universe is neutral. It reflects what we put there. If our life is not unfolding the way we want it to, then our subconscious beliefs are undermining us.

Subconscious beliefs control our thoughts. If we are *highly critical and judgmental* of an "other," since there is no "other," this reflects that we are highly critical and judgmental of *ourselves.* If we are into *self-pity,* those who enter into our life reinforce our subconscious belief that squeezing pity out of others is the *only* way to get support from the Universe. If we feel we are a *victim* and consider ourselves to be a *martyr,* we are surrounded by people who persecute us so as to support our idea of victimhood and martyrdom. If *loneliness* is our game, we set up every situation in our life to ensure that we are lonely.

We plant, nurture, and harvest the seeds of discontent and destruction to our peace of mind. When we believe we do *not* deserve happiness, or success, or contentment, or peace, or financial solvency, or comfort, or respect, or a decent home, then every circumstance we create in our existence reflects this belief. Every interaction with family, friends, business associates, school, work, or social engagements validates this belief.

Is it any wonder we are not happy?

If we believe that the Universe supports that which we do *not* want out of life, we can equally believe that the Universe can support that which we *do* want out of life. Why does the negative prevail and not the positive? If we have a firm belief in exactly what we *do* want – unless it is in our soul contract not to get it – we generally get *exactly* that which we want out of life. Our subconscious beliefs are in alignment with our conscious beliefs.

If we do not know what our subconscious beliefs are, how can we possibly change them? To get a handle on our subconscious beliefs, we examine what themes are playing out in our life and indulge our self in the luxury of picking out the subjects that repeat in our life. Take the time necessary for this period of introspection. We spend more effort picking out a movie than picking out the beliefs in our life. Reflection on the themes of our life takes time.

After we evaluate the themes that have followed us throughout our life, in order to change our subconscious beliefs, we are going to have to monitor our thoughts diligently. We seem to have all the time in the world to mess our lives up; now we must give ourselves some time to straighten out our thought patterns. The most important sound is the sound *Within our heads, our thoughts*. Every thought we think *creates* something on some level of existence. Every thought we think *changes* something on some level of existence. Typically, we think a great number of thoughts a day. What percentage of these thoughts is negative? What percentage is positive? What we *think* is going to determine what we *see* in our life. What we *see* in our life is determined *by what we think*.

Choose only those thoughts that create what *you* wish to experience. Since there is no “other” (there is only Self), *any thoughts we think about an "other" are thoughts we think about our own selves.*

We must learn to choose our thoughts carefully; to choose only that which *we* desire to experience, because, *eventually,* we will. Anything we do to an "other" is an experience that will be done unto us, *in some dimension, at some point in* "time." There is nothing outside of Self. Self is all there is. There is no "other" out there. All "other" beings are simply there to mirror something we need to know about our self. All "other" situations are there to reflect a belief we carry about our self. There is only "Self."

We come here to learn how to create as we are created. Taking responsibility for our creations has nothing to do with arrogance. Instead, it places us as the highest of God's creations endowed with the ability to create just as the Source does. Most of us create *unconsciously;* now we are learning to create *consciously.* The key to living consciously, in the moment, in the now, is to change our subconscious beliefs.

What subconscious beliefs have influenced what you have encountered? Our subconscious beliefs underlie everything we experience.

January 7

Changing Our Mind Instantly

We are who we *believe* we are, but we can change our Universe instantaneously by changing our belief systems. The *light bulb* moment, takes only an instant; the *Aha Moment! I get it; I really get it!* We can believe we are a victim during our entire lives, but we can also change our mind about being a victim *instantly.* The Universe follows suit, according to our beliefs.

Our beliefs come from memories of our earliest experiences. If our parents tell us how slow, shy, stupid, or sloppy we are when we are a child, we tend to believe them, no matter how devastating their words feel to us. However, as an adult, we can take their words just as we would a piece of exercise equipment; something against which we can flex the muscles of our intention. We can turn their negative messages around, and so become a softer, gentler, kinder, more understanding, and more compassionate person than we might have become, had we not had to stand up to such harsh and demeaning words.

Suppose our soul contract – items we choose to accomplish during our current lifetime while we are still in Spirit– is to motivate others to rise above their impoverished circumstances; to teach others to become self-reliant. We need to experience our own impoverished circumstances and to rise above them in order to empathetically present the information to others. Looking at our situation from this angle, we can change our mind instantly about what wretched, judgmental, or mistaken people our parents, spouses, or significant others are.

Suppose our future soul contract is to become a research scientist who uncovers the secret to healing neuro-immunological disorders. In preparation for this role as a world renowned scientist, we might choose a role where we are stricken, at an early age, with a neuro-immunological disorder in order to fully understand and evaluate how the body succumbs to the disease. During the lifetime where we are stricken and die as a young adult, we leave behind a devastated family who loves us dearly. The personalities of those left behind are shattered, but on a soul level, their Spirit soars. Mission accomplished!

Understanding the soul contract of a loved one does not *eliminate* the pain, but can help us *manage* the pain. What brought only grief into our life can be healed eventually, sometimes instantly, through our understanding of the purpose of the loved one's death.

Suppose that we are puzzled about a troubling relationship; for example, someone to whom we would like to be closer. We might ask ourselves a question, such as: *Why am I so distant from*

Jack? If the answer that we hear inside our heads is: *Because you blame him for all the disappointments in your life, large and small,* then we have an insight. The word "blame" puts the responsibility for our feelings squarely on our own shoulders.

When we ask, *What are those feelings trying to teach me? What theme is playing out in my life?* we begin accepting responsibility for our own creations, rather than continuing to seek an "outside" reason for our failure to achieve our goals. We harness Real Power, the power of Love, as we change our mind about what a miserable person the "other" has been.

We are only in charge of our own lives, through our choices. As a co-creator of another person's life, we are meant to be a guide only, just as the Supreme Creator guides us. We are temporary caretakers for another person's life: for the souls who agree to be our children, for the students under our tutelage, for those who are dependent upon us.

The only thing we need to do is to take responsibility for our own lives. If we attempt to live vicariously through another person, we will be derailed. Should we feel we must accept responsibility for another's creation, we will be stopped. Should we attempt to offer advice where it is not wanted, we will be thwarted. Advice is only to be given when it is asked for, just as Spirit helps us only when we ask them to.

Each of us may say to ourselves: *Since there is nothing outside of Self, God's greatness is reflected in me or hidden by me as I select.* With regard to another, we may say: *If you bring light into my world, this reflects the light I have within. If you bring darkness into my world, then that reflects the darkness within me that needs to be healed.*

The kingdom of God is within us as co-creators of our Universe. The world *does* revolve around us and can change instantly as we change.

Have you ever changed your mind instantly and watched as the circumstances of your life changed accordingly? We can change our mind about anything that has ever happened to us.

January 8

Using Scapegoats

If we believe that we exist *outside* of our creations, then we are not able to correct our actions; we seek to blame the "other" for everything that is "bad." We look for someone or something to become a scapegoat when we refuse to take responsibility for what we have created.

We resort to using scapegoats when the feeling behind the emotion is too painful to confront. We may remember our mother making a statement: "I never really loved your father. The only reason I stayed with him was because of you."

Our ego self might respond with feelings of guilt, remorse, anger, or contempt, while our Spirit Self taps into awareness that our mother felt a lack of conviction that she could support herself and her children. As our consciousness taps into the *knowing* that she felt this weakness, our Spirit Self helps us to forgive our mother's statement. This helps us to release any negative feelings harbored within our bodies. Our mother's unconscious determination to set us up as a scapegoat for her lack of courage is common. Many people do it.

When we feel thwarted in our ability to pursue that which we really desire, we cast about looking for a scapegoat for our lack of initiative. We may feel overwhelmed with the tasks that are necessary in order to get to the place that we desire. Most of us fear failure, but even more threatening to us is the fear of success. Thus, we often stay in situations that drown our Spirit, instead of taking the lead to go after that which we really desire.

Using a scapegoat as an excuse for our lack of initiative derails us, but cannot prevent us from moving forward permanently when we recognize that we *deserve* that which we really desire out of life. Just as an actor rarely gives an Oscar-winning performance the first time in front of the camera, our feelings of inadequacy need to be bolstered up while we are learning the skills necessary to bring our "great idea" to fruition. Just as actors must play minor roles first, we need to take care of each mundane step necessary to perfect and hone the skills needed to complete the ultimate goal. Our first step is to complete the "task at hand."

The people who populate this planet often tell us from birth that we are not worthy, that we are born into sin, that we come from dust and to dust we shall return, that we are sinners our entire life, and are basically inadequate. *So why even try?* we may ask ourselves. Fortunately, when each of us tunes into our Spirit Self, something within us thrusts up against these statements. Then, we regurgitate that with which we have been labeled, reject these false labels, and move forward. While our personality selves might temporarily cast about looking for a scapegoat (to explain why we cannot do something), our Spirit Self waits patiently until we finally decide that everything we have heard about being inadequate is rubbish.

Our Higher Self tells us to give up our need for a scapegoat and decide to go ahead and pursue our life's dream. We cannot expect to have all the details worked out immediately as we work towards our heart's desire, because there are so many pieces to each task that to be aware of all of them would overwhelm us. However, we can systematically work at one piece at a time.

If we do go after what our heart desires and experience some setbacks along the way, this acts to test our resolve; to test how firm we are about our convictions. If we continue to set our intent *each day* that we are resolved to be ____, to have ____, and to do ____, then no setback is going to stop us. What we wish to bring forth is part of our soul's contract and the entire Spiritual realm stands in assistance when we ask for their help. If we were not meant to complete the task, we would not have been given the idea in the first place.

We do not need to use scapegoats to continue explaining why we are not where we want to be. We can take one action *right now* that advances us toward our goal. The important thing is to start today! Take the first step toward what makes our heart sing. Spirit helps if we ask for it!

Rather than using a scapegoat as an excuse for why we cannot, we can attempt to do one thing that moves us in the direction of *why we can*. We can take on one thing each day. Every person on this planet is given twenty-four hours each day. What we do within those twenty-four hours is up to each of us. Some people use their time to become President of the United States. We may feel that such a goal is impossible, but becoming president of our own company is not.

In my case, my commitment to my soul's contract to become a published author and a public speaker is to get up each morning when awakened, come downstairs and type for three hours. That is the minimum requirement asked of me to fulfill my role as one of God's teachers on this planet.

Have you ever resorted to using "scapegoats" as the reason for not achieving your goal? We start by taking one action each day, every day, toward our goal.

January 9

Moving into Divine Will

Divine Will *is* our will – the Will of our Higher Self – and is activated when we are in alignment with our divine purpose for incarnating on this planet. We all have a reason to be here. Some of us are here to stir things up; others to smooth things over. Some of us are here to act as a catalyst for change, some to reveal the underbelly (the seamy side of life), and some to connect us to the greatest heights. Some of us are here just to observe.

Understanding the difference between the will of the Higher Self and the will of the ego self (the personality self) that exists within each of us is important. The will of the ego self is associated with an energy center within each of us. This energy center, called the third chakra, exists around our solar plexus area. The "will" associated with this energy center helps us to get through the issues of our lives. In contrast, the Will of the Higher Self is associated with an energy center that opens when we are ready to accept matters of Spirit. This energy center, called the fifth chakra, is placed at our throat. Not all who incarnate are able to differentiate between the will of the ego self (the personality self) and the Will of the Higher Self (our Divine Self). As with any other gift from Spirit, we have to be open to receiving it.

Because we achieve that which we create, if what we wish to achieve is in keeping with *Divine Will*, our achievements will be harmonious. If not, our achievements fall apart. When the will of the lower self (the personality self) is in harmony with the Will of the Higher Self, then our road through life gets smoother. The obstacles in our life may jolt us, but behind every "jolt" is wisdom. We can curse the jolt, or we can glean the wisdom. When we open to the Will of the Higher Self (Divine Will), we accept the wisdom behind every occurrence against which our ego selves would otherwise revolt.

So why do we experience so many irritations throughout a lifetime? The pebbles in our shoes and the cinders in our eye are a source of constant aggravation. Pebbles and cinders are the continuous small setbacks we encounter as tests of our resolve: *Is this truly what I desire? Is this the best way to* "invest" *my time?*

If our personal goals do not support the purpose of the Universe, the Spirit world will not support them. In keeping with Divine Will, "time" is speeding up and changing. A universal force is accelerating "time" into an eternal NOW, moving with screeching clarity toward unconditional Love.

Those who understand and have accepted the unconditional Love that Divine Will promotes into their hearts and minds will step into a New World that is waiting for them. Those who continue to stay mired in their egos (those who have not accepted the greater truth of unconditional Love into their hearts and minds) will find themselves in the same world in which they were before. It is filled with others of like will, and as such, it will not be a very pretty sight. Some think that it is *money* that makes the world go around. They will soon change their mind. It is not! It is LOVE. A world that is built on a foundation of money and greed will come to a dead standstill.

If you are willing to align yourself with Divine Will – to accept the highest state of consciousness known as unconditional Love as part of your "Be"-ing – you will ascend into the higher state of existence. If you decide to stay tied to the lower state of consciousness, the state motivated by fear, money, and greed, you will stay in a place run by fear, money, and greed.

For each of us, it is an individual choice. We must each ask ourselves: *Where do I wish to be?*

Have you ever asked Spirit to align you with Divine Will?
We can ask Spirit to help align us with
Divine Will; the will of our Higher Self.

January 10

Sharing the Wealth

To truly attract abundance, each person must be taught self-reliance. On an abundant planet such as ours, there is enough for all. No person here should lack for basic needs, but greed inhibits the distribution of this plenitude. Social programs that distribute goods to those in need deliver fleeting comfort to the downtrodden.

In the New World to which the Earth is ascending, war – the last indicator of a barbarian society – is eliminated in every culture, in every country, and on every continent; no matter what the justification for the conflict has been. Homelessness is eradicated as the first sign of compassion for the plight of the poor. Refugee camps are replaced with permanent settlements where people have "real" homes. The conditions that caused refugees to flee their homes are a distant memory and people are allowed back to where they originated from to live in peace with neighbors of different cultures, different religious beliefs, and different life styles. In the New World of Light and Love, there is no need for social programs, since there in no greed. There is no need to help the poor if there are no poor.

In the New World Order, people learn to live with the same harmony that Nature exhibits. Plants and animals that need tropical conditions do not attempt to survive in the desert. Plants and animals that need fertile ground do not inhabit rocky mountain slopes. Each one finds its own best way to survive. The same is possible for the different cultures around the world. Accepting unconditional Love, an aspect of Divine Will, makes it possible for different cultures to survive side by side in harmony and peace.

The Earth that supports our life is such a bountiful place, filled with abundance. Yet, in spite of the plethora of natural resources, the majority of the people of this planet are denied a "perfect" place to live due to the huge concentration of material wealth hoarded by the very few; enormous wealth mainly hidden from view by layers and layers of "Trust Agreements."

But even that is changing. Kuwait, one of the richest places in the world, spreads its wealth amongst all its inhabitants. Bill and Melinda Gates, one of the richest couples in the world, are among the most generous. They, along with Bono, received recognition as *Time Magazine's Persons of the Year – 2005.* Many in the entertainment industry are lending their celebrity status to publicize causes they feel passionate about; causes addressing the needs of the poorest of the poor.

Abundance is a state of mind. Most of those who control the physical wealth of this planet do not understand that what they do to an "other" is that which they do to their own selves. They despoil the Earth in order to accumulate their riches and ignore their responsibility to preserve the resources of the natural environment for the benefit of all. They would rather wage civil war, drop bombs, plant land mines, and impose unspeakable hardships on the unfortunate populace than share the wealth. Yet, they never have enough. No matter how huge the accumulation, they constantly want more, and spend their lives protecting their hoard and living in luxury while the masses starve.

Those who do not understand their responsibility to this planet will find themselves in a barren place. Mother Earth, this living being, is preparing her Self for ascension and will take with her only those who are capable of honoring her.

The planet is a living being, just as we are. Walk softly upon the Earth. Treat her with the same gentleness and the same kindness we wish to have extended to our Self. She is part of us, just as we are part of her. We cannot exist on this planet without her beneficence. She has been very tolerant of us and our foibles, but that is coming to an end. Only those who truly honor the Earth will go on to the Higher State with her.

We have the power to change the Universe in which we exist by sharing our wealth, by honoring the natural resources of the planet, and by keeping the planet pristine for future generation. That power is Light and its fuel is Love.

Do you share your abundance with
those less fortunate than you?
Disasters usually spur compassion
from every corner of the globe.

January 11

Flushing out Conditional Love

Love can either be *unconditional* or *conditional.* Unconditional Love is love given freely without conditions of any type: without expectations, without judgments, without requirements, provisions, stipulations, or modifications. Conditional love expects the aforementioned as a requisite for its love.

Conditional love no longer works on this planet. Almine, one of Earth's greatest spiritual teachers, presents a model of *conditional love* that is based on the pattern of Love, Control and Rage: "I love you, therefore I can control you. When I discover that I cannot control you, I fly into a rage." Most of what passes for "love" on this planet is based on this model. Most of the complaints about issues of "love" are in reality complaints about issues of "control."

Every attitude and every belief system we carry inside our heart that is part of *conditional love* must be flushed out. Every situation in which we find our self embroiled is part of this flushing process. When we always find ourselves involved in circumstances that have spun out of control due to something that happened *out there,* then we need only to look inside of ourselves to see what attitudes are keeping us stuck in this cycle.

Conditional love, manifested through the will of the ego, creates with limitation, restriction, and darkness. When we create only in alignment with our ego selves, we create with scarcity and fear. This is a result of creating with conditional love. Only when we tire of the darkness, can we step into the Light. Sooner is better than later!

We have had eons and eons of practice eradicating conditional love from our "Be"-ing. Now we are on the brink of another major shift in consciousness. Other shifts in consciousness were barely noticed, but this shift will be so massive that every living being on the planet will be impacted.

Unconditional Love will be required in the new paradigm. Love with no conditions literally means letting go of judgment, forgiving all "others" until we see that there is nothing to forgive, treating everything and everyone else as part of the Self that is One with all creation,.

We are creator "Be"-ings, just like the Creator Being from which we came. We will "be" part of the same world we create for ourselves. There will "be" two worlds; one of darkness and one of light. On the surface, both may look exactly the same. However, when we examine the inhabitants more closely, we will notice the difference. One plane of existence, filled with unconditional Love, will be much lighter and brighter than the other.

We "are" what we create. The inner reflects the outer, the outer reflects the inner. When we create in alignment with our Higher Self, we create as our Source creates, with unconditional Love, with illumination, with unlimited potential.

Are you practicing conditional love on those around you? We are Spirit having a human experience, learning about unconditional Love.

January 12

Forgiving All

Who do I need to forgive? At the top of my list is *myself.* If I do not forgive my own self for my shortcomings, real or imagined, I am not able to forgive anyone else. Since there is nothing outside of self, I come first. When I forgive myself, I am able to forgive others. After I forgive myself and forgive all others, only then can I see all "others" as my brothers and sisters.

Who do I need to forgive? Everyone! Everyone else reflects an aspect of who I am, so everyone else is an aspect of myself. Only after I see all others as myself am I able to release the blockages that keep me bound up energetically; blockages that wreck havoc in my body.

A Course in Miracles states: "Everything we need is given us." If we need a lesson in forgiveness, we will be given *many* opportunities to forgive. Incident after incident will appear in our life with reasons for why we *have to* forgive. Our ego, the little "i" in our life, may not *like* the lessons, but they will continue until we learn.

My first marriage ended as a personal lesson in forgiveness. There was nothing left to do except to forgive. For years I lamented the treatment I had endured, not comprehending that the "bad" treatment made me a more compassionate person. I learned to be patient with and show compassion for those who stayed in the grips of a disastrous marriage; those who had not yet gathered enough strength to leave.

Forgiveness helps us eliminate the place in our hearts where we have kept tally of all the injustices in our lives, and have planned how we were going to respond and retaliate. Forgiveness helps us let go of our insecurities, our feelings of being "small," and our feelings of inadequacy. Forgiveness helps us to release our bitterness, our resentment, our rage, our insomnia, and our dis-ease. Forgiveness helps us get on with our lives.

After we are hurt, we begin healing when we start with forgiveness. Forgiveness heals the NOW and all "time." Since all time is NOW, forgiveness cuts through eons to the past and towards the future; it heals the past, the present and the future. It frees us from karmic ties that keep us coming back to learn the same lessons over and over.

Forgiveness starts to heal the negative energy trapped in our energy field that blocks us mentally and hurts us physically. Since everything we perceive hurts, in order not to feel the pain, we construct shields within our energy field. These blockages, which affect our emotions, take form in our etheric field and ultimately wreck havoc with our physical body. We can free ourselves from emotional hangovers through forgiveness. Whether it takes a tremendous amount of effort, or is instantaneous, it can be done!

Forgiveness is one of the three major reasons for incarnating on this planet. The other two are learning unconditional Love, and learning to be of service to others. While most consider this planet to be a maze, filled with blind alleys, dead-ends, and pits that swallow us whole, everything on this planet is designed to guide us through a labyrinth leading us back to Source. And a labyrinth has only one way in and one way out.

A variety of techniques on learning how to forgive are available.

Why is forgiveness such an important release on this planet? We free ourselves of blockages, large and small, when we forgive.

January 13

The Big "I" vs. the Little "i"

There is both an ego self and a Higher Self that live within us; a little "i" and a big "I" inside of each of us. The little "i" (our ego self, our personality self) is what usually runs the show, until we wise up to it and learn to acknowledge it, but not allow it to take over our life. The Big "I" (our Higher Self, that part of us that is connected to the Divine) patiently waits our acknowledgment of its existence, if only on our deathbed.

How do we separate the little "i" from the big "I?"

The little "i" corresponds perfectly with other terms used in this book: the ego self, the personality self, the will of the ego or will of the personality. It lives in the same place as does all these other characteristics; in the solar plexus, the third chakra. The little "i" is activated upon birth and can survive throughout our entire lifetime, since it is the way we negotiate our way around this plane of existence; the way we function in this world.

The little "i" is the way most of humanity lives. It is concerned only with the little self; the ego self. The little "i" forgets from whence it came, and sees itself as a separate body; separate from the rest of all the other beings upon which it looks. The little "i" grasps and gasps for a space in the world; for food, for shelter, for clothing, for material goods to call its "own." The little "i" is convinced that information can be kept private and can be given shades of meaning to twist out representations that have nothing to do with the truth; that it can be "spun" in fabrications. The little "i" sees everything and everyone on this planet as suspect. It is involved in most of the social and educational training received on this planet.

The big "I" is concerned with the Higher Self; with Divine Self. The big "I" sees itself as part of the whole; part of the Oneness of All, part of the Source, part of a vast consciousness of "Be"-ing, part of *All That Is*. The big "I" considers its Self to be part of the group mind of God. It never leaves communication with the group mind of God and knows that our physical bodies are part of a grand experiment. Thus, the big "I" is unconcerned about the outcome of our actions, because it knows that eventually we return to the Source. The big "I" never hurts anything, because it knows that *it is all things*. The big "I" never hurts an "other," because it is the "other" and if it were to attempt to hurt, would only hurting its Self. There is no "other." There is only Self. The big "I" sees the whole as One.

The big "I" has no boundaries, because it encompasses every part of who we are. Generally, it corresponds with the Higher Self and Divine Will, and lives in the upper chakra regions above the heart. We have to be *open* to the big "I" in order for it to activate within our consciousness. It is always there, but we are free to deny its existence. Our denial of its existence in no way eliminates it or affects its presence in our life.

There is a vast consciousness of "Be"-ing into which the big "I" taps, called the *Christ Consciousness* or the Christ Mind; a giant matrix surrounding our energy fields both inside and outside of our bodies. The Big "I" taps into this matrix; an arena of unconditional Love that promotes the Christ Consciousness both within and outside our bodies. This giant communication grid opens when we are receptive towards it and have removed the blockages from our energy field.

Do not get hung up on labels. If the word "Christ" throws you into a tailspin, use another term. *Collective unconscious* is the term Carl Jung coined. *Vast panorama of consciousness* or *collective consciousness* is another possibility. Labels do not matter.

What is the difference between the big "I" and the little "i"?
We have to be open to activate the
big "I" within our "Be"-ing.

January 14

Opening Our Hearts from Within

Our willingness must come from within. All we have to do is give a little willingness to Spirit, who assists us in every way possible, but who also waits for our invitation to come in. It is up to us to open our hearts. But most of us are shut so tightly.

When we open our hearts a little and let the Light of Spirit shine in, the results are astonishing. We start to feel different than we ever felt before. As we start to *feel* differently, we *see* things differently. As we see things differently, we *think* differently. As we think differently, we *act* differently. As we act differently, we change. As we change, everything around us changes. The world changes because we change. Since our thoughts create our reality, as we change our thinking, we also change our reality. It all starts with our willingness to allow Spirit to help us change from within.

"The kingdom of God is within you," the Master stated two thousand years ago, thus heralding in the New Age. Reminders of our willingness to let Spirit in can be found everywhere. Impressive granite pillars, arches and grey stone walls grace the interior of St. Paul's Cathedral in London, a stark contrast to the massive bright dome that became a symbol of hope for the Londoners living through the blitzkrieg during World War II. In contrast to the heavy grayness inside, towards the back of the Cathedral, resting on the floor, is a large striking picture of Christ knocking on a door ... but there is no door knob. The figure of Christ is illuminated, as is the door; His look is one of serene acceptance. He awaits our invitation to open up to his knock. We control the doorknob to our heart.

A Chinese proverb states: "A man convinced against his will is of the same opinion still." We can never *be* convinced that something is true when we do not want to be convinced. Ultimately, we only convince ourselves. This includes the messages in this text or in any other book on spiritual truths. Only we can open our heart to accept these teachings.

The Light is within us, but what we do to bring forth our Light is entirely up to us. We are asked to be the Light. We are not told to look for the Light outside ourselves. It is not there. Everything "out there" is within us. Everything "out there" is a reflection of what we think, see, or feel within our own "Be"-ing. Our "Be"-ing is lit from within and we completely control the intensity or dimness of that light.

Be the Light.

Who holds the key to opening your heart to light?
Spirit's light shines within us.

January 15

Law of Attraction

The *Law of Attraction* says that we draw to ourselves *exactly* what we put out. Life is energy and energy can be high or low, light or dense, fast or slow, with a negative or positive charge. It is not *good or bad.* Only the ego places that judgment upon it.

Since the type of energy we put out is the type of energy we draw towards ourselves, accepting what is around us as part of *our creation* is one of the steps to self-mastery. All too often, we indulge in blaming someone or making something else responsible for the situations in which we find ourselves. Instead, we can take *full* responsibility for the situations in our lives. As we take responsibility for our creations, we gain freedom in knowing that we can always "choose otherwise." We are never permanently stuck in any situation, regardless of what we may think. We may have to lower our standard of living temporarily while we pursue another goal, but no condition is permanent *unless we make it so*.

What we see outside of ourselves is reflective of what is inside of us. When we look around, what do we see within our line of vision? Do we see chaos, disorder, ugliness, or filth? Clothes heaped high here and there, toys, gifts, papers, puzzle pieces peeking out of every bin and clutter in every closet? Or do we see peace, harmony, orderliness, neatness, calm, and beauty? Since the outer reflects the inner, we control whether our life is pleasing, soothing, comfortable and harmonious, or whether it is discordant, screeching, unsettling, and uncomfortable.

What kind of social experiences are we attracting into our life? Do we feel that the people with whom we do business are out to get us? Are they defensive when they converse with us, or are we on defensive turf? Does someone who says they "love" us make us account for every minute away from them because of their jealousy? In like manner, are we demanding the same from those we say we "love?" As a different approach, we can give each other the freedom that allows each of us to develop talents through unconditional Love enhanced with trust and compassion.

The *Law of Attraction*, by continuing to bring us the same situations over and over again, helps close the walls in around us and makes us feel enough discomfort to help us decide that we can create better than that which we are currently receiving. When we do *not* know *what to do,* and so choose to do *nothing,* that is a choice. If we stay in a physically, mentally, or emotionally abusive relationship, whether at work or at home, sometimes we do so because of inertia. Sometime, we may not want to give up the comfort of our home or our job, even when the people in our home or at work terrorize us. That is a choice. We are not helpless! The *Law of Attraction* can help us choose otherwise.

How does knowing about the Law of Attraction help you take responsibility for your choices? The Law of Attraction acts as a boomerang in our lives.

January 16

Healing Words in Self-Help Books

Self-help books and other spiritual reading material are meant to aid us on our path. They soothe, comfort, and heal the fragmented selves that we think we are. By helping us integrate our unique ego self into our Higher Self, spiritual reading materials assist us on the path of self-discovery, opening the way to the greatest echelons of our "Be"-ing.

I will always credit *The Power of Positive Thinking* by Dr. Norman Vincent Peale, for saving my sanity in 1981, during the lowest ebb in my life when I felt no hope. I will never forget what my thoughts were when I first picked it up: *Oh no! Not another Jesus book. I need something that will* really *help me.* Fortunately, my Higher Self ignored that remark and encouraged me to keep reading. I have smiled innumerable times at the thought of those words*, not another Jesus book.*

That book became my lifeline. Prior to going to sleep each night, I read a chapter, a page, or a paragraph of that special book, underlined it in pencil, ballpoint, and red ink, highlighted it, and put paper markers to note special passages, re-reading the book six different times. Each night, before I went to bed, I read as much as I could before I fell asleep. That book gave me *hope* when nothing else seemed to work. Along with hope came calmness, and within that calm, unique solutions to financial problems appeared. Miraculously, that year we had income from thirty-three different sources, one of them being our piggy bank. This still seems incredible to me, although I have kept that list just to remind me that God graces us with miracles when we need them.

That exceptional book pulled me through the lowest point of my life. Where might I be today if Dr. Norman Vincent Peale had never written that book because he was "too busy? What if he had never persisted in attempting to get it published when editor after editor first turned it down? He was on the verge of quitting when one editor suggested a name change to *The Power of Positive Thinking.* This book helped me to learn powerful principles that have had a great effect on my life.

Nothing can be *given* to us without, on some level, our *asking* for that which we bring into our lives. Spirit never violates our free will, no matter how desperate we think we are. If we want Spirit to help us, we have to *ask* for help. Generally, this takes the form of a prayer. Prayers are the most powerful thoughts we can send out to the Universe, yet most of us only pray for "things."

We are usually at crisis point before we pray for help When we pray for strength, we receive more than we ever thought possible. In answering our prayer for strength, one of the means Spirit uses is books, magazine articles, the internet, and other telecasts, including music. There are many and diverse ways in which Spirit offers us materials designed to heal the wounded heart and the burdened mind. Words intended to be a balm for the crushed soul are everywhere. Since all words carry a vibrational level, the energy in words can *crush* but they can also *heal.* Words reach into the farthest recesses, the smallest caverns, the most buried areas of our mind that have been completely blocked, barricaded, and hidden from view. Spirit directs us to words that can heal; this then helps us to heal ourselves.

Has a Self-help book assisted you with a special need? The proliferation of Self-help and spiritual books address any possible problems we may experience.

January 17

Releasing Negative Thoughts

If our body is filled completely with negative thoughts, there is no room for positive ones. They cannot stay. Just as even one drop of water flowing into a full cup overflows the cup, when our body is consumed with negative thoughts, our positive ones have no place on which to latch.

As *negative thought forms,* they take on a life of their own to hide within our energy field. These negative thought forms then cause us discomfort that defy discovery by traditional means. Negative thoughts are a disaster to our body. If we think them often enough, they will become negative thought forms embedded in our energy field.

Even though negative thought forms can take many shapes, they typically form a mass of clouded energy over the part of the body they are affecting. However, they also take many other forms. During a healing session, working with my teacher on another person, I felt squiggly pieces of energy moving through and out of my hands, releasing from the person on the table. The energy felt like small snakes slithering out of the way. I asked my teacher about the forms that were releasing. She said that they were exactly that. Energetically, they looked like small snakes. Negative thought forms are not pretty, nor are do they assuage our distress.

No amount of recounting our hurts will change them. Only we can change them. The power is within us. Real Power – the power of Love – can change anything. We can change any memory that gives us pain.

We free the past from hurting us by forgiving the past. We have all the power within our self to change our past through forgiveness, which is the key to re-aligning back to God. Forgiveness is the key to getting rid of negative thoughts, breaking the wheel of karma, and getting off the cycle of re-birth on this planet.

By releasing that which does *not* serve us, we provide room for that *which does.* By letting go of negative thoughts through forgiveness, we develop the ability to move forward as we clean out old debris left over from lifetimes of pain and suffering.

The first step in releasing negative thoughts is becoming *aware* of when we are thinking them. We can then stop ourselves cold with a mantra, a "magic" word as a reminder that this is not what we intend. A simple word, such as "Cancel! Cancel!" might work, as recommended by Mother Mary in *Mary's Message to the World* by Annie Kirkwood. The mantra can be any word we choose. It is just a word to help us remember. We may have to stop ourselves repeatedly throughout the day until we can let the negative thought go. When we have to do so, let us not judge ourselves, nor allow ourselves to get discouraged.

The next step is to make conscious effort to replace our negative thoughts with positive ones. The universal challenge is to stay positive. We may have to buck the current climate of "need to know" by cutting ourselves off from our daily habit of newspaper, TV and internet "news." We all know "what is." But when we are concerned with upgrading our lives to include that which we wish to materialize in our life, not that which is already there, we must make changes in our routine. Our negative thoughts have helped us put into place all that which is there already. Positive thoughts position us to receive a new paradigm.

Choose this instant to begin transforming your thought patterns. Do not wait until you have the time to devote to it. Start immediately.

Every time we are aware of negative thoughts flowing through us, we can each say our own "magic" word for getting rid of those thoughts. In the beginning, we may have to consciously repeat this process hundreds of times. We will prevail.

Release negative thoughts and let them go. They no longer serve you.

What "magic" word do you prefer to help you release negative thoughts? We hold the power within to free ourselves from negative thoughts.

January 18

Releasing Prejudice

When we feel prejudice towards something – whether an individual or a group, or even a collection of ideas – what better way to eradicate that prejudice than to have it manifest itself in our personal life? When our prejudice involves the core group of people around us, how can we ignore it?

The Universe sends us the lessons we need. If we are homophobic, we might see a beloved member of our family enter into a same-sex relationship. If we deeply love that member of our family, we can choose to accept the choice s/he makes. As we accept their freedom to choose a member of the same sex for a love relationship, we receive a better understanding of unconditional Love; the love endowed upon us by our Creator.

If bigotry or racism is our "game," one of our children or stepchildren might choose to marry a member of another race. We may be violently opposed to the marriage or merely tolerant of it. However, the offspring of that union may be the ones who reach into our heart and love *us* unconditionally. In accepting these babies, we learn how to accept members of another race. Because of our love for the little ones, our prejudice softens, our bigotry melts.

Circumstances sometimes lend themselves in unique ways to help rid people of prejudice. There is a great experiment going on now in the Balkan area and in the Middle East; in areas where wars, religious and other, are continuously fought. Hundreds of children from both sides of the conflict have been orphaned and left homeless. No matter what their physical condition, whether healthy or wounded, missing parts of their body or fully intact, blind or seeing, all of the children from the different cultures and religions are being *raised together* in orphanages, thus paving the way for the elimination of bigotry and bias based on religious differences.

The future of these countries will change as these children grow up and find their way into positions of power in their own society. Eventually, there will be a blending of attitudes, releasing the feelings of hatred and retribution that thousands of years of war have imbedded into the adult leaders of these countries.

What about our attitude toward the poor? How queasy do we feel anytime a homeless person approaches us? Do we hide behind our rolled up car window, or scurry past, while pretending to fumble in our purse or pocket for loose change until we have passed by and no longer need to find any money? Have we or members of our family been mired in the same welfare situation for generations?

The seamy underbelly of America's treatment of its poor was splashed across major headlines across the globe for the entire world to scrutinize. During the coverage of hurricane Katrina in New Orleans in 2005, the many problems of the "rescue" operation were visible for the entire world to view, day by dreary day. Interestingly enough, for every horror story about the lack of care, a story surfaced about the dramatic efforts made by people around the United States who sped to the area with their vehicles to lend their expertise to the helpless people as well as to the animals left behind by the evacuation. Many people made heroic efforts to rescue animals that were abandoned by family members because they could not take them to the shelters. The compassion of the people in the United States revealed itself throughout the world as those seeking shelter in other states were warmly accepted in their new cities, found jobs, and had the mercy of family as well as strangers extended to them.

Prejudice and bigotry wears many faces, but these different faces can be eradicated, sometimes by extraordinary means. The peace accord negotiated by Senator George Mitchell in Northern Ireland is nothing short of miraculous. People who bitterly fought each other for over thirty years have learned to mend their differences.

Since the outer reflects the inner, all peace on the outside of us reflects how we feel within. As we learn to lead more peaceful lives in our march towards peace, the world wears a mantle of hope.

Is it possible that prejudice may be leading you towards unconditional Love?
We can change the world to one of harmony and peace.

January 19

Clearing Out Negative Emotions

Only when we clear out the old do we leave room for the new. We cannot pour hot water into a cup of cold water and expect to get hot tea. It will be lukewarm at best. We cannot pour flat champagne into our glass and expect an exhilarating drink, unless we happen to like flat champagne. Most of us do not.

The same holds true for emotions. To have room for new positive emotions, we need to clear out old negative emotions. We cannot keep stuffing new, raw, negative emotions into our body that is already full of old, stale, negative emotions and expect to feel good. Unless we get a "pay-off" from being ill – extra attention, people waiting on us, the ability to get others to do our bidding – most of us wish to be healthy and self-sufficient.

When we feel that our life is out of control, deep-seated anger arises within us, and we lash out at anything in our path. We destroy relationships, homes, and the very foundation of our existence, all because we do not take the time to clear negative emotions out of our body.

One way in which we can bring our life back under control is to take twenty minutes each day to clear away negative emotions through our breath and through our thoughts. By coupling an exercise regime that helps our body stay flexible together with this twenty-minute period of meditation each day to calm our mind, we *will* bring our life back under control. One hour devoted to these exercises each day will do us more good than all the alcohol, food, or distractions with which we fill our lives.

With each deep breath in, visualize the emotion within softening; with each exhale, visualize each negative emotion leaving in a cloud of vapor, just as steam evaporates from a pot of boiling water.

By repeating this over and over, we bring calmness and serenity back into our bodies, when our egos might be raging for revenge. We can use any visualization we prefer when we do this exercise. The important thing is to do it for twenty minutes. That is usually how long it takes for emotions to course through our body.

Addictions serve to mask the attitudes of despair, prejudice, rage, bitterness, anger, hopelessness, victimhood, self-righteousness, and obsessive or compulsive behaviors, none of which are a path to unconditional Love. In order *not to address* negative emotions within their bodies, many on this planet substitute addictions: to work, sex, shopping, or eating. Some even succumb to a chemical dependency, such as to drugs, alcohol, nicotine, or caffeine.

All addictions, no matter what they are designed to cover up, need to be eradicated. They keep us limited and bound up. Get rid of them!

Addictions may have genetic causes, but if caused by a habit that has become ingrained, they can be changed by substituting new behavior over a twenty-one day period. Yes, this takes effort, but look at the reward. When we seek to heal our ailments, we satisfy our own need for good health. If we seek to mask our ailments, we stay in poor health.

The best way to clear out the old is through *forgiveness*. *Never,* you exclaim! Fine! Holding onto the old may cause your body to degenerate and deteriorate. You can keep the old and stay in that vague unsettled feeling, that tugging inside yourself, that knowing that *all is not right*. Or do something about it. The choice is yours.

Whatever negative stuff you are holding onto – LET IT GO!

Have old negative emotions crammed into you left room for anything positive in your life? We have to make space in our life for the new feelings we desire.

January 20

Pursuing Ego Self

Ego self is that part of our nature that is tied to materialism; that part of us that worries about what others think; that part of us that thinks we can be filled with satisfaction by something on the outside. We constantly look for something outside of Higher Self. There is nothing. It doesn't exist. *It is not there*. There is only Higher Self and the Divine Aspect of "Be"-ing that we are.

We can spend our entire productive adult life chasing dreams of glory and recognition from the "outside." These may never come. We chase harder and wear our ego selves out even more. No amount of effort we exert satisfies all the other demands from our ego selves, as *ego self* is concerned with what all the other "ego selves" are thinking. Typically, fifty percent of the people disagree with us, no matter what we say, so we are always up against a faction who feels our words or our efforts are not correct. Still, we chase after that elusive rainbow called "recognition" for a job well done. It may never come. Every accolade we receive is accompanied by yet another problem whose needs have not been addressed. And so, we feel defeated. The accolades are empty. They are not enough to propel us forward. They are *never* enough! They do not give us the satisfaction that we desire.

Ego self presumes that we are separate from each other because we each maintain separate bodies, which is the best way for our Creator to experience exponentially. When we are ready to let go of ego needs (which we do eventually), we move forward in small increments. We take tiny baby steps to a new beginning; a new awareness of Higher Self in our lives. We experience wholeness, completeness, a feeling of joy, contentment and peace within.

"Joy is your birthright," as noted in *A Course in Miracles*. Our Higher Self agrees wholeheartedly.

Why does pursuing the needs of ego self unsupported by Higher Self never seem to satisfy? When we can let go of the needs to satisfy only ego self, we can open to the limitless potential of Higher Self.

January 21

Nurturing Higher Self

When we nurture our Higher Self first, all else comes to us. When we nurture Higher Self, we nurture Soul. Only after we nurture Higher Self, can we nurture others. We cannot give what we do not have. Higher Self is the highest vibration that exists within us. Higher Self is the direct link back to the Creator; that part of "us" that is tied back to Source, which is in constant communication with God.

Most of us have misconceptions of what it means to nurture Higher Self. Since we have no concept of Higher Self, we think ego self is all there is. Ego self causes us to lose ourselves in our work, sacrificing all for the "company store." It causes us to lose ourselves in our children's lives, or in our spouse's career, or in the lives of celebrities. But ego self cannot keep our body from deteriorating. Ego self causes us to numb out: with drink, with drugs, with food, with mindless TV or internet viewing, or with violent outbursts of pent-up emotions. All of these distractions serve to keep us from addressing the issues towards which Higher Self is leading us, the most important of which is our divine purpose: *What did we come here to do?*

Higher Self is ever vigilant about our acceptance of its "clues"; clues which bring about our awareness of it in our lives. Higher Self is very patient and very kind. It waits until we have played out all the drama trauma roles which we have chosen to play. It then finds a way to wedge into our psyche the message that it wants our ego or personality selves to know. Higher Self always waits for an invitation from us, but lays clues along the way. It is in constant communication with us, but waits until we choose to become aware of those communications.

Our ego demands not only keep us from nurturing Higher Self, but also keep us from addressing negative issues that we keep stuffing back into our bodies, none of which enhance our life. Issues that we do not address fester and boil until there is an ultimate destruction of our bodies. We can go to our demise with no lesson learned. That is our choice.

Some of us are just plain mean. We throw away happiness with both hands by not appreciating anything that is being given to us through all the effort of others or Spirit, which constantly works on our behalf.

According to Spirit, we never hurt an "other." There is never an injury to anyone else. There is only injury to ourselves because, ultimately, there is only One of us – One of us fragmented into a great many personalities. Each personality self is an aspect of Higher Self – a little piece of the Divine. Not one of us is different from another in our essence (in our real Self, our Higher Self), but we do differ in our personality selves – all of us who live on this planet. Think of a mirror shattering into a great many pieces. No matter how small the fragment, each one is still a mirror.

Regardless of what we believe, Higher Self stands by patiently, alert and ready to assist us when we *ask* for it. We can eliminate all aspects of Higher Self from our awareness, but our non-awareness does not *extinguish* the existence of Higher Self. We can follow all avenues of self-doubt and self-defeating behavior as we wish. We believe whatever we create.

In this, the Era of the Common Man (or Common Era, EC), we awaken and recognize our own power to co-create, to be one with the Divine aspect of Higher Self, to be part of the higher order of What Is. Nurturing Higher Self is part of that higher order of "Be"-ing.

Why is it so important to nurture Higher Self first?
As we nurture Higher Self, we nurture all
other aspects of our personality.

January 22

All Is a Mirror to Us

"Life is a mirror of your consistent thoughts," states Napoleon Hill and many other leading New Age thinkers and teachers. It is time to quit *blaming* the *other* for everything that is wrong in our life and look instead at how our *thoughts* are creating the problems that we have manifested. Since most of us look through the lens of our *ego selves* instead of our Higher Self, we do not see our life as a mirror reflecting every thought we think and do not realize that every thought we think *creates* some *thing* on some level.

When we accept the fact that we create our own realities, we recognize that all "others" reflect a part of us. If we are loving, caring, and giving – without need of recognition for our services – then we will have other loving, caring, giving people in our sphere. If we come from a position of "need," where we feel we *must do* something because of what an "other" might think of us, or to fill some void that we feel, then our world will reflect that emptiness. If our service to others comes from "guilt" or other negative emotions, then that too is reflected in our lives and serves to deplete us.

There is no *other* out there. All *other* beings simply mirror something that we need to know about ourselves. All *other* situations reflect a belief we carry about ourselves. If our life is harmonious and we are where we want to be, then the situations and people that we encounter reflect that harmony. If suddenly harmony leaves us, then that change may signify that we are ready to go to the next level. We may go through this lifetime with no major calamities presenting themselves. However, that is highly unlikely, for growth and development comes in the form of major upheavals in our lives, which present challenges that open us to new belief systems that better serve us.

When we carry beliefs that undermine *who we really are* – beliefs that do *not* support the idea of unconditional Love – most of the situations and people in our lives will mirror *those* beliefs, and we will continue stumbling through life. If we feel that we are being battered by an "other" for no good reason, then we need to ask our Higher Self to reveal to us the underlying cause. What are we supposed to learn from this situation? What life lesson did we agree to? Where are our lives leading us, so that we need to go through such agony? This is possible if we remember that there is no "other"; everything and everyone else is a reflection of something that we think we believe.

Love exists in the sharing, but stems from loving self. If we think we love an "other," but cannot love ourselves, then we are still attempting to deceive our Higher Self. We cannot "give" what we do not "have." We must decorate our own soul before we decorate the soul of an "other." We cannot help an "other" without helping ourselves first. This is not as in being selfish, but as in being "Self"-ish; an aspect of God.

Two-thousand years ago, a Master instructed: "You shall love your neighbor as yourself" (Mark 12:31), and also, "whatever you did for one of the least of these brothers and sisters of mine, you did for me" (Matthew 25:40). We can accept these teachings when we accept that there is no "other;" there is only Self. If we can accept that there is no other, that there is only Self, then we have an easier time accepting that what we think is reflected in everything that we see around us.

Everything and everyone else is a reflection of us or something in which we believe. There is no "other." There is only Self. All "others" serve as a mirror to self. All "others" simply reflect to us something that still is not healed. All is Self. Self is One. One is All.

How do your thoughts mirror your situation?
Every thought we think mirrors
"something" we have created.

January 23

Going to the "Top"

Eventually, life taught me to go straight to the "top" when I had a problem; to go to the highest authority to help me with problems that seemed insurmountable. While active as a full-time real estate broker, I even "broke" into a bank once, insistently pounding on the door after the bank had closed until the puzzled janitor came and opened it for me. Incredibly enough, the name of the President of the bank was listed on a marquee on the wall. I found his address in the phone book and went to his home in Arlington to breathlessly plead my case to his slightly perplexed wife.

This bank held the resolution to a very simple problem that was about to hold up a settlement the following morning, in spite of having consistently promised to resolve it in a timely manner.

Even more disturbing was that, since this settlement involved one of our neighbors as the sellers and the son and daughter-in-law of one of our agents as the buyers, a successful outcome was critical. Unfortunately, no one slept that night; not the sellers and the buyers, nor any of the agents. All were wondering if the settlement was going to take place. The information that I needed arrived the next morning, in time for the settlement to proceed.

When I have *little* problems, I speak to people. When I have *big* problems, I speak to God. During the late seventies and early eighties, my problem was my *life*. It just was not working. Going straight to the top to get answers to my questions made the most sense. Fortunately, my mother always turned to "Boza" (the Polish word for God) and taught me to do the same. However, she had been taught to pray to a God *outside* of herself, which is what she taught me. I did too, but eventually learned to pray to a God within.

After many years of introspection, God took the form of my Higher Self. Somehow, I knew my Higher Self was always there for me. What my Higher Self revealed to me was not pretty. Inside my heart, I held hurts, anxieties, resentments, and feelings of injustice and bitterness that I *did not even know* were there. Because of all the introspective clearing work I had done, I thought all these negative issues were released. In some cases, I had not even started.

Sometimes my friends pointed out how disastrous my thinking or my actions were towards others, specifically, the people I loved. Their comments hurt my feelings. I did not see their point of view and felt justified in all the petty attitudes I was holding onto. In retrospect, all was part of a cleansing process.

Turning to the God within helped me ferret out the miscreation that I kept producing throughout my life. Eventually, my life started to take the form my Higher Self was leading me to, concentrating my activity on spiritual matters.

And the God within smiled.

When you are at a loss for direction,
do you go to the "top?"
The first "need" of each day is to
connect to the God within.

January 24

Releasing Regret

One issue that kept resurfacing in my personal life was regret. I would find myself complaining: *I wish I had... or I wish I did...* and seemed to be stuck in an endless cycle of repeated incidences that just amplified and increased my remorse, usually centering on money. As long as the feeling that *I always made the wrong choice* haunted me, I was paralyzed and could not move forward. This *force* called regret controlled me, kept me spinning my wheels, digging my trenches deeper and deeper, allowing me to go nowhere. What I did not know then was that my feeling of regret physically *weakened* me, and that my ego self, who kept harping about regret, was *not* my friend.

On the heels of regret came *bitterness.* These two emotions sucked all the joy out of my life, wrecked havoc with my interior life, and caused tremendous pain in my body. My Higher Self stood by and waited patiently until I had had "enough" and sought to correct the situation.

Desiring to be rid of regret and bitterness led me to the world of herbal healing, specifically to a group of flower essences developed by Edward Bach, M.D., a physician in England in the 1930's whose premise was that there was a remedy in Nature for every human ailment. Flower essences were specially formulated to counter emotional imbalances, of which I had plenty. I used them to rid my body of negative feelings and to this day have kept one of the essences, *Rescue Remedy,* to be used when any general, non-specific type of anxiety showed up in my day to day activities. Fortunately, the best remedy for me at that time came from Bach Flower Essences, which could be purchased at health food stores or stores that sell organic foods.

Regret, and all its companions of self-absorption (remorse, bitterness, anxiety, and depression), is a useless emotion. Why do we constantly *want* to live a life of regret? We give our power away to whatever scene keeps "replaying" itself in our mind. If we think that everyone else has all the opportunities or all the "luck," and we only get the crumbs, we are emotionally unbalanced. Whether we are haunted by feelings of inferiority, superiority, or perfectionism, we are emotionally unbalanced.

If we hate one or both of our parents, our siblings, our spouse or significant other, or any of our co-workers for all the injustices committed against us or if we regret having been born, we are emotionally unbalanced. Yes, we can spend a lifetime in a therapist's chair reviewing all the *he done me wrong* situations, but if we do not release all those feelings from our body, what we have in the end (besides a bunch of canceled checks as receipts for our therapy sessions), is less than *nothing,* because our bodies will be dis-eased.

Suppose, as an example, that you wanted to pursue a theatrical career when young, and then did not follow this inclination. Now, as a mature adult, you would then sit in envy of movie stars that the multitudes adulate. How would you know that you had not already done that: been a celebrity in a past life? At one time, any of us could have been the subject of an entire *country's* adoration!

Unearthing buried hurts is good *only* if we *release* them and *forgive* them. If we use them as an excuse to continue our own vendetta against an "other" or as regret and remorse or bitterness over everything that has happened to us, please remember, buried hurts only destroy the vessel they are stored in, which is our body. We must each uncover and release the buried hurts to get back to full health.

Please remember, there is no "other." There is only Self. What we do to an "other" we do to ourselves.

Are you able to release "regret" or "bitterness" to clear the space for something positive in your life? When we release regret and its related companions, we clear the room for other positive emotions to enter.

January 25

Pain as Our Teacher

Pain can be eliminated once negative emotions are eliminated. The Spirit world is ever vigilant about our "progress" and will use any means to reach us. We can live to be any age relatively pain-free if we make use of the suggestions that are given to us.

Throughout my life, people sought to confide in me. Part of it was the compassion I expressed in my professions; first as a teacher, then as a real estate broker. In the seventies, eighties and into the nineties, real estate brokers and agents "qualified" their clients, rather than having a financial officer of a bank or mortgage company involved. They ran the financial information and decided whether the prospective buyers could afford to buy a home and for how much. People tended to trust those with whom they shared their financial history. Since I was able to assist both buyers and sellers through some very complicated transactions, they, in turn, trusted me enough to share their personal, financial, and social problems.

Yet, I was blind to my own "issues." I continued to hold onto grudges, especially when someone close to me did their work in a manner I felt was "wrong." I set lofty goals, ambitious undertakings that I wanted for myself. Internally, I also insisted that those close to me share my vision. When that did not happen, my *exterior ego self* became *disillusioned,* but my *interior ego self* went into a *rage.* My ego was totally out of control.

My Guides never gave up trying to reach me, but it was the pain that finally brought me to my knees. During this period, I was hospitalized for hyperventilation, having never even *heard* of the condition until it happened to me. What petrified me further was the horrendous back pain, both upper and lower, due to continuing aggravation at work. This precipitated one crisis after another as my physical health declined. One day I bent down to pick up a piece of paper and could not straighten up again, then crept through the next two weeks – my body at a forty-five degree angle – going from specialist to specialist in an attempt to heal. A combination of adjustments by my chiropractor (who administered trigger point releases and mild electrical stimulation), along with the treatment of the osteopathic surgeon (who internally stretched my sciatic muscle), benefited me the most.

Determined to get back to health without having to turn to drugs, surgery, or alcohol, I turned to additional alternative treatments. I had some intense massages, but it was the commitment to Rolfing, a specific type of deep tissue massage, which made the difference in the way I was able to respond to the barrage of daily stresses in my life. Yoga, stretching exercises, and daily walks also became part of my routine. I *had to* change, because my health was deteriorating rapidly, but my responsibilities at home and at work never diminished. As *I* changed, everything else changed around me.

It has been a long and tedious journey filled with distractions and detours all meant to ferret out ego issue that I clutched to my chest; issues that manifested as pain in my physical body. Pain brought me to my knees. This became the vehicle my Higher Self used to get my attention. No physical age "has to" succumb to pain, but I do not begrudge pain, since pain was my path to wisdom.

Pain was my path to wisdom. It certainly can be yours, as well.

What is your pain trying to tell you?
Pain, as our greatest teacher, can be the path to wisdom.

January 26

Only Love Lasts Forever

Through all the discord and disharmony, one thing stands true – LOVE. We come *from* Love, we were created *in* Love, and we are seen through the eyes *of* Love. No matter how it appears to the ego self, *we* create *with* Love. There is nothing else. "The Kingdom of God is within us" states the Bible When we learn to have all aspects of our ego self respond to the suggestions of Higher Self then, truly, there will be peace on Earth. But it all starts with Self, for there is nothing outside of Self.

"The kingdom of God *is* us" states *A Course in Miracles*. Our Higher Self, our Spiritual Self, our ego self, our personality self, our physical self, our mental self, our emotional self, all interact together to create our experiences in line with our soul contract, which is designed by Love. Those we love in Spirit are always with us. They recycle back into every situation we experience each time we arrive on the planet. They come here as our brother, our sister, our husband, our wife, our mother, our father, our best friends, our co-workers, our caregivers, even our worst enemies, if we have chosen that lesson. Sometimes we find that those we considered our enemies in this lifetime were really our best friends in Spirit. Only they would love us enough to be willing to endure our wrath while in physical body.

On every dimension we exist, *only Love is real,* blending each level into one demonstrative whole. Only Love lasts forever. Since there are so many levels to our "Be"-ing, is it any wonder we feel confused? We are a multi-dimensional "Be-"ing playing a role in all the levels in all the dimensions *at the same time and in the same place*. To our ego selves, life may seem to be a giant cacophony of sight and sound which feels as if we have stumbled into an orchestra pit that perpetually tunes up. To our Spirit Self, every note plays a specific tune that is in harmony with every other note we are playing.

Instead of concentrating our actions around Love, we might bellow *I want what I want when I want it,* but we *get* what we create at the moment we create it. We claim we "love" our fellow man and want peace on Earth, yet have no peace in our heart. We think we can force "peace" on a culture by pointing a loaded machine gun at the people, with no regard for the factions in the culture who need to stand up to their own injustices. We accept differences, whether they are cultural, national, societal, or religious, and tolerate selectively; *some* things, but not others.

Our multi-national corporations undermine the efforts of the native people who wish to bring change into their own society if that change threatens the corporate profit margin.

We cannot accept the only fact that is true about who we are: creator "Be"–ings, creating our own reality. Everything we see around us is there because *we* put it there. On some level, we agreed to all of it, even that which brings pain and misery to our self or others. Eventually, we will tire of all the pain and misery, get out of the fear space, and move into Love, which is the essence of who we really are because only Love lasts forever, and we, as spiritual "Be"-ings, also last forever.

Have you thought about asking to stay in tune with Love throughout your day? We will see the loved ones we have lost in this lifetime over again since only Love lasts forever.

January 27

Life as an "Experience" We Choose

God truly is the *Biggest Joker of All*, and the joke is on us. Each of us can learn to lighten up, and to not take life so seriously. We always get another chance to play another role, and another, and another, *and another.* The king will be the pauper, the male will be the female, the control freak will be weak and submissive, the powerful and domineering will be the powerless, the sexually repressed will be the sexually uninhibited, and the tyrant will be the abused. How can it be otherwise?

There is no *judgment* from God/Christ/Allah/Buddha/Krishna/The Great Spirit/Prime Creator/Source, or *whatever* we call a

Higher Power, about what role we choose. There is only *karma and dharma,* which translates into a new *adventure* each time we come to this planet. We come here to *experience* all of this, and then we decide what it is that we *no longer* wish to or need to *experience.* We are making up all the events we consider "real" and get as many opportunities as we desire to experience as many more episodes as we choose.

Once we transition to Spirit, we meet with our Spirit Group consisting of our consciousness, our Higher Self, and our Teachers and Guides (members of our Council of Twelve). We meet together to discuss what lessons we wish to learn in our next lifetime, based on the lessons, or lack thereof, that we learned in the lifetime that just passed. What our ego thought was our greatest *successes* on Earth may be looked upon as our greatest *failings* by our Spirit Group. We may find that the most "important" thing we did on a given day was to *smile* at someone who was previously "invisible" to us, or to be kind to a family member or acquaintance that we have loathed.

The greatest of all the spiritual gifts given to us is free will, which allows us the freedom to choose and to choose again. Between lives, we select our parents and the major circumstances of our next life. What else we accomplish is up to us; all based on the choices we make from moment to moment. We have the free will to alter any and all circumstances once we are here, even the ones that we "pre-selected" for ourselves through our contract with the Divine.

All life is on a spiral moving upward. In order to advance in our spiritual life, we have to see an issue from all sides within our physical life. Each point on the spiral has four quadrants: the physical, the mental, the emotional, and the spiritual. To balance all four quadrants as we continuously advance up that spiral, we are given chance after chance to evaluate an issue from all sides before we move up. When one part of our self is balanced, we take on another issue in our movement up the spiral of life.

None of our "experiences" are either "good" or "bad." They are just "experiences" we have chosen for our self in order to advance up the spiral of life. If we have qualms about perfectionism in this lifetime and have a compulsion about cleanliness, we act the role of a "clean freak." However, in another lifetime we may choose to be an inordinate slob. In yet another lifetime, we may choose to come in as the spouse or significant other or child of the compulsive "clean freak," or the sibling sharing a room with the slob. If our issue is sexual prurience, in one lifetime we may come in as a prostitute and in another lifetime as a cloistered nun, denying the body any possibility of sexual expression.

For further insight about what the soul experiences between lives, and the choices the soul makes for its next incarnation, please read *Journey of Souls* and *Destiny of Souls* by Michael Newton, Ph.D. These books will enhance your entire perspective on the life you now lead and expand your vision of who you really are.

What are some outrageous situations you have created in this lifetime as "experiences" you have chosen for yourself?
We and our Spirit Group set up all the major experiences we wish to have.

January 28

Signs and Messages that Guide Us

Everything that happens to us, everything we witness – every animal or insect that crosses our path – means something. We are being given signs, guideposts, and messages every step of our way. When we hear, see, or feel something *more than once,* pay attention. What is the message? Asking for clarification from our Guides helps us to hear the message, especially when it is not what we expected to hear.

One summer day, a katydid kept crossing my path in the most unlikely places. By the third time, I finally remembered to ask my Guides what that meant. Their answer: *Just do it, just like katydid.* With their incredible sense of humor, they were prompting me to get back to my writings, for they sensed my discouragement with this manuscript for my second book.

Shortly before I sent out the manuscript for my first book for publication, *God is the Biggest Joker of All,* I had been given erroneous information. A previously published author told me that if a manuscript was held for longer than three weeks, it was a "shoo-in." I now know how incorrect that remark was, since the first editor held the manuscript four months, then rejected it, and the second held it five months, then rejected it also. My feelings sank when the two manuscripts came back after being held for so long. Eventually, I self-published the first book and learned from that experience.

What about the many signs that are given to us to get out of employment that is no longer suitable for the growth of our soul? Many of us are in jobs that no longer satisfy us. How productive is that? How validating to our "Be"-ing? What is the point in staying in a job that will ultimately cause us an ulcer or lead us to physical ruin, cause our nervous system to collapse, or deteriorate our organs as our body consumes itself out of frustration?

How many of us receive messages to move on instead of staying in relationships that no longer suit? How much good can come from staying with a partner we have outgrown? Though there are many good reasons to stay in a relationship, complacency is not one of them, neither is fear that we cannot make it on our own.

Even though I was considered a success in the real estate profession, after a while, it felt as if a huge hole was opening in my heart. No amount of earnings, accolades, awards, or praise from colleagues, clients, or family could make the emptiness go away.

When I met Barry Lee, an intuitive from England, he stated that our meeting had been set up by Spirit *prior to my incarnation* as a "warning" for me. He claimed, "If you kept ignoring Spirit's call to do God's work and continue to work solely in real estate, you will not die, but you will be very, very sick." Instinctively, I knew he was correct, because I was already very sick, but kept on working outrageous hours in spite of this. Could there have been a greater sign than that?

The stirrings of our Soul are not to be taken lightly. They are the stirring of *Who we really are*. They are the stirrings of that part of us that is connected to the Source, to Prime Creator, to All That Is, to the Oneness of the Universe; our Higher Self.

What are the signs from Spirit trying to tell you?
When the Universe sends us a message, we need to listen.

January 29

Releasing Judgment about Anger

When anger is a major force in our life, we cannot pretend it does *not* exist. Before long, we have to stare anger in the face and recognize it for what it is – *a force beyond our control.* On some level, we agreed to all the anger we are experiencing, and on this level we have to deal with it. When we find ourselves being challenged by anger, eventually, we have to confront it. It is not in our life for us to ignore. It is there for a reason and we cannot escape it. Whatever the reason is, we have to flush it out and face up to it.

Much of my life has been consumed trying to deal with anger – as expressed by some key people in my life. I took multiple approaches to dealing with any outburst of anger: ignoring it, baiting it, cajoling it, side-stepping it, forgiving it, crying over it, making excuses for it, feeling like a martyr over it, and burying myself in an avalanche of work to forget about it. All these were done in my attempt to eliminate anger from my life. No technique offered a permanent solution. Was there any good reason not to confront this anger and leave it behind? No, but *my* reason was that I did not want to walk away from a second marriage just because I could not deal with angry outbursts, so I dealt with them as best as I could, using all of the above strategies.

Many reasons exist for ignoring anger and the ensuing damage it causes. Parents say they feel an obligation to their children to raise them in a "stable" environment regardless of their personal needs. What they do not admit is that an explosive situation never nourishes a child's upbringing, and they are simply teaching the child abusive and aggressive behavior. As children mimic the behavior they witness growing up, they learn to become either perpetrator or victim. Staying married "for the sake of the children" while living in a hostile home environment causes problems down the line rather than solving them.

A friend, during *A Course in Miracles* study group, while listening to yet another recitation of an angry outburst in my life, asked me, "Alice, what is it about you that you have so much anger in your life?"

I was taken aback by her question, and replied, *I don't know. I will have to think about that.*

I thought about it for two days before it finally occurred to me: I had so much anger in my life because I had a *judgment* about anger. I thought it was "bad." I had to release that judgment and when I was able to let go of it, the anger lessened considerably.

Anger is neither "good" nor "bad." It just *is.* The best way to deal with it is to walk away from it and say, *This is not for me.* When the opposing party has no resistance to push up against, the wind of anger has no sails to fill.

Today, anger almost never appears in my life, but when it does, I do not take it personally. Everyone has the right to react to any situation the way they do. And if they react with an angry outburst, so be it. It is not my way, but I do not condemn them for reacting "their" way.

How can releasing judgment "about" anger release you "from" anger?
When anger flares up in our life, we can learn to step away from the emotional attachment to it.

January 30

Message from My Guides

People cope with anger in many different ways, some which are disastrous for their body. Some get liver cancer, some get breast cancer; both are related to unresolved anger. Some get nervous tremors. Some withdraw into a dream world where they are the ones in charge. Some put material goods over their own safety, which is neither safe nor smart, and yet others do not want to leave the "comfort" of their home. Some do not know what to do.

Given the energy "Be"-ing that each of you are, the body stresses when issues that it has been given are not addressed. This is a very efficient Universe. All misplaced energy goes somewhere. All thoughts create something on some level. You would not be very happy if you saw what your thoughts create, or miscreate, when anger surrounds your life.

You have such power to create a satisfying life for yourself, yet you give away your power so quickly. Then you wonder why you are depleted and have no energy. Instead of confronting and facing issues, you fill the holes in your life with food, drugs, work, sex, or any one of the other addictions.

Instead, you can tap into the power of the Universe, which is yours for the taking. This is where your future lies. Comprehend who you really are, recognize how to keep and accept your power as a creator "Be"-ing.

The belief system of the entire world needs to be switched around. You need to know that you create what you experience by your thoughts. You alone are responsible for everything you find in your life. You alone. No one else. All the details – you put there. You are not a victim. On some level, you "agreed" to experience everything that is "happening" to you. It is all there for your learning, to understand yourself as your Self – as a creator "Be"-ing.

And so it is!
I Am.
Amen.

How does accepting responsibility for what you "create" bring you one step closer toward personal freedom? As we accept responsibility for our creations, we can monitor them and change them when necessary.

January 31

Breathing Deeply

Our breath connects us to our Creator. We can use deep breathing every time we feel rising anger or any other debilitating emotion. Also, when we cannot go to sleep at night, we can choose to breathe deeply. Rather than lying awake rolling from side to side, turning from front to back, deep breathing will help us to still the myriad thoughts that arise during a state of anxiety. Breathing deeply will also help cleanse the toxins from our inner organs. As we do this, we can imagine each breath delivering oxygen to every cell in our body.

When anxiety strikes, breathing in to the count of eight, holding our breath, then exhaling to the count of eight calms us. Eight seconds in, hold, eight seconds out. If eight seconds is too long, start with less and work up to eight seconds. It is our breath that connects us to our Creator. It is through our breath that we can transmute whatever negative emotions we feel as we make deep breathing a pattern in our life.

As we breathe in, we imagine our body filling up with energy from the Earth through our root chakra (the energy center at the base of our spine), or filling up with energy from the Divine Source through our crown chakra (the energy center at the top of our head). As we breathe in, we fill our inner organs with light. As we breathe out, we release all the tension we store within our body. As we breathe in, we feel our bones regenerating with light. As we breathe out, we release all the toxins stored within our cells. As we breathe in, we fill our minds with light. As we breathe out, we relax the tension around our faces, eyes, and brows.

Whenever we feel uncomfortable in our own body, or are struggling with any low-grade anxiety, we can breathe deeply, in and out. The next time we feel emotionally scared, we can remember that FEAR is at the core. FEAR is the hidden culprit, the base, the root cause. All negative emotions, no matter how banal the justification, come from FEAR. Breathing deeply helps us to alleviate FEAR no matter its source.

If we can *own* the feeling, we can *change* the feeling. If we do not own something, we cannot return it. Anything we own can be changed, transmuted, or returned to its Maker (to go on to its next state of higher evolution). Thus, we can learn not to just stuff feelings back into our bodies, no matter how badly we may wish to be rid of them in that moment. The sensations of discomfort *will pass* if we allow ourselves to "feel" them.

The feelings that we stuff back into our bodies will not pass. They stay deeply buried inside us, and raise havoc with our energy field. We may bury them now, but they will erupt later, usually as a physical illness – the source of which often *cannot be found*. Breathing deeply helps us to sort out all those unnamed feelings we have floating through our energy fields. Breathing deeply helps us to release large amounts of anxiety.

Can you take the first few moments of each day to practice your deep breathing exercises? Deep breathing connects us to the Divine.

February

Real Power, the power of Love, is who we are. It is not given to us. It is not something we have to earn, nor is it something we have to master. It does not come to us when we reach a certain age. It is not something that can be taken away from us. Even if we are forced against our will to surrender our body, we still have Real Power.

Real Power, the power of Love, is who we are. It is something we bring with us when we agree to incarnate on this planet. It is not something that is awarded us, nor is it dependent on our status, our education, our age, our development, or our profession. It is our Birthright!

We will never stop being in Real Power. We will never stop being who we really are. We will always have consciousness of the essence of the Light that we truly are, even if we are not aware, or maybe dimly aware, of our true nature.

There are easier places in the Universe to incarnate; enlightened places, places where we experience no separation from our Creator and from each other. That is not the case here. Here we incarnate and agree to a state of total amnesia from the spiritual dimension we originate in. This planet, in the third dimension, is a Grand Experiment in the Mind of God. At the moment of separation, in the same instant the thought of separation occurred, the "answer" to the separation was also put into place. As stated in A Course in Miracles, the Atonement (pronounced At-one-ment), comes to us through the Voice of the Holy Spirit. The Voice of the Holy Spirit speaks to us constantly through our Higher Self, so that we never forget who we have helping us on our journey through this planet. We have only to listen.

February 1

Spiritual Mastery

We don't do anything to anyone else. We only do it to ourselves. There is no one "else." There is only Self. Understanding this concept is one tiny step toward spiritual mastery: that space in our lives where the gifts of Spirit guide our every action.

If each *perpetrator* could only begin to understand that *they,* at some "time" in the "future," come back as the *victim,* there would be fewer and fewer perpetrators. No one would be so available to hurt an*other* if they knew, with complete certainty, that to balance their life as a perpetrator, they choose a life where they are *hurt.*

We have only to witness perpetrators as predators, terrorists, rapists, molesters, pedophiles, sociopaths, those consumed by greed and monstrous egos in the corporate, financial and banking industry, in the political and legal arena – whether on a family, community, society, national, or international level – to see the next group of "victims."

Letting go of the need for *retribution* – punishment for a perceived evil – is one small step toward spiritual mastery, but it is an important step. Demand for retribution fuels most of the misery on this planet. Many of the wars fought on this planet center around retribution, whether they are "religious" wars, civil wars, wars instigated by one country who claims the right to dominate, or world-wide conflicts. Retribution has figured into every "personal vendetta" that has ever been waged.

Another step towards spiritual mastery is *finding courage* to do what is important to us. So much frustration is borne from the idea that we *cannot do* what our heart desires. Something deep inside of us spawns *rage* when we feel we cannot *have* what we so dearly long for. That rage boils over into physical ailments within our body as we settle for less of a life than we desire. This need not be.

Still another step toward spiritual mastery is to find the courage to do *what is right.* There is a connection to the Divine within each one of us that gives us warning bells. There is something within us that lets us *know* when a three-year old is telling the truth about a forty-year old who is lying, despite the adult's vehement protests that the child is making things up. We need to find the courage to stand up to the adult who is lying.

Listening to our own inner warnings is yet another step. There is something within us that warns us when we should not enter a building, continue with the same job, seek out the same friends, or stay in the same marriage – whether we call that "something" our intuition, our sixth sense, our gut feeling, or our instinct. Our connection to the Divine exists even if we deny its existence. It is there to guide us, but we are free to ignore its guidance in our life.

The biggest step toward spiritual mastery is *learning to forgive.* Our need to forgive is the foundation, the reason most of us incarnate on *this* planet, and we will be given opportunity after opportunity to learn how to do this. Those who have hurt us the most are the first who need to be forgiven by us since they are only part of a scenario that, *on some level,* we agreed to. The "sad sack," the one who we always feel sorry for, the "unlucky one," the one whose goals are constantly thwarted, the pessimist who perpetually depresses us, also need to be forgiven, for these individuals reflect within us the hidden defects onto which we hold; those parts of our personality selves which we choose not to address.

As we develop in spiritual mastery, we learn that we are all part of One Mind, that there is no such thing as a "wasted life." Every life has its purpose and is part of a Divine Plan, even when it looks otherwise.

What steps toward spiritual mastery are present currently in your life?
Endeavors that lead us towards spiritual mastery can be found in the most unlikely places.

February 2

A Wake-Up Call

Most of us who walk this Earth buy into the idea that we are separate from our Creator. We think we are a ship without an anchor, on a course without direction, with no inner compass to check or guide our movements. We continue to drift along, filling our life with busyness or with bitterness until one day, we collapse. Then, we become physically, mentally, emotionally and spiritually depleted; we find ourselves in such a state of mental dis-"ease" that our body is riddled with physical disease.

Suddenly, we brake to a stop. This jolt is our *wake-up call,* whether it be a life-threatening illness, or such emptiness in our lives that we can no longer function; not in our jobs, nor in our professions, nor with our families, and not even in our bodies. We know something is drastically wrong, yet we do not know what it is or how to fix it. The hollow feeling that begins as a little pinprick in our throats or in the pit of our stomachs is now a yawning cavern so great that no amount of "remedy" can fill it.

Addictions seem to offer a temporary solution. Addictions fill this cavern with their unique blend of "corrective treatment" which momentarily distracts, but the fix is only temporary. Whenever another disconcerting situation arises, the anxiety starts all over again. No amount of drink, drugs, travel, work, food, or sex fills the emptiness or eases the pain.

In extreme situations, we put coping mechanisms in place: neurosis and psychosis. We have all manners of defense and displacement techniques to keep ourselves from facing issues that confront us. I once heard a University of Michigan psychology professor state that all neurosis stems from our unwillingness to feel *twenty minutes* worth of pain.

Spirit patiently waits to show us the way to self-fulfillment as we take detours through all our ego "stuff." Are we really lost, or have we just taken a temporary detour? When every single avenue seems to be blocked for us, then we need to reassess what motivates us and makes us happy and why.

In the early 1980's, when I hungered for more time to pursue spiritual interests, I was invited to participate as an audience member for an instructor who was going to video tape her seminar series on empowering women. As I was led to the room where the session was to occur, the friend who invited me showed me her office. On her bookcase were the titles of many of the current popular self-help books of the day. I remember looking at the titles of the books and yearning to have the time to read them. That was my first wake-up call. Little did I know how important these books would be to my future.

When all exterior avenues are blocked to us, when all self-deception or self-protection fails us, then we turn to something deep within ourselves. We turn to a Higher Power: to *God, Allah, Buddha, Krishna, Prime Creator, Source, or Christ; to the Divine, or to whatever we call the Supreme Creator.* Labels do not matter, only the experience does.

Has a wake-up call entered your life and why is it there? Wake-up calls can be rather drastic or they can be mild, depending upon our resistance to Spirit's message.

February 3

Searching for Truth

As our personal paradigm expands, it also expands for the entire population of the planet. And thus, humanity evolves. The limitations which have been put in place in order to give structure to the "outer" world can no longer hold us. Instead, their constrictions lead us to that which expands our "inner" world. We *cannot* hold Spirit back.

"Ask, and it shall be given you," the Bible assures us. We continue to search for answers. When we ask for help from Spirit, we are given an assortment of answers, one of which makes a dent in our psyche. This is our starting point. We can act on the advice that makes sense to us, no matter how "outrageous" that advice seems to be to our ego.

People start by looking for God "outside" of themselves and go to churches, temples, synagogues, and mosques. To some, these offer a permanent solution and they look no further. To others, these offer a temporary solution and fill a need that suffices for awhile. If questions continue to arise within, but dissatisfaction with the answers received from "others" persists, people increase their efforts as spiritual seekers. They continue to look further. Their quest for answers is not satisfied.

One of the ways Spirit uses to reach us is through books. A series of books may appear all of which seem to have a *vein of gold,* or offer a *pearl of wisdom,* or reveal a *nugget of truth.* No single one of them offers the *whole* truth. It is up to us to discern from each book what *we* need the most to fill our quest as a spiritual seeker. We may find that we gravitate towards books on the Angelic realm, or on the faerie kingdom, or on Earth changes, or on the sacred sites of the Earth, or on environmental issues. Whatever our quest, there seems to be an author who has written about it.

As we attempt to fill our self with as much "truth" as we can uncover, if a yawning chasm opens within us which knows no boundaries but instead seems to expand, we need to look further. If no amount of reading material offers "enough" to satisfy the insatiable appetite of this chasm, which continues to widen, we need to look further.

My journey consisted of reading everything that was recommended to me and then perusing book shelves in the metaphysical section of large and small book stores to see which books "jumped out" at me. Some would literally fall into my hands. Other titles seemed as if they were beacons of light that drew me towards them. Only when I was led to books on energy healing did that yawning chasm seem to fill. Energy healing was the missing link in my understanding; the step that I needed for self-fulfillment. Mine was a commitment to be part of the healing of the world, not only through the words that I write – words given to me by the Spiritual realm – but also through healing, through using vibrational energy from the Universe.

Besides our personal quest, with the different recommended readings we receive from friends, each book leads us to yet more esoteric study. The "truths" keep coming and coming. Each book offers one or two more "truths" and validation for each "truth" is found in other books we read. We discover that since "truth" is the *same* for each person on the planet, many things are "true" that have nothing to do with "truth."

As we travel on the journey toward spiritual enlightenment, we discover that *God* is not *out there, God* is within. It cannot be otherwise.

Are you being led to spiritual offerings to help you find the God within? As we pay attention to the resources to which we are attracted, we recognize their "nuggets" of truth.

February 4

Offering Blessings

The most famous biblical story about a child seeking a blessing is the story of Esau and Jacob. Jacob deceived his nearly blind father, Isaac, into thinking he was the first-born by wearing the skin of newly-slain goat, since Esau had such a hairy body. Because of that deception, Jacob received the blessing that had been reserved for Esau, the first-born son. In that era, a father's blessing was a very prized gift that bestowed not only spiritual blessing on a person, but also material blessing. This blessing was reserved for the first-born son, who was heir to the father's estate. Jacob knew its meaning, its importance and determined that he would have it, no matter what the consequence.

Today, more than ever, we need to acknowledge blessing in our life. Today, very few cultures practice such a blessing. Slowly, the ages of time have dissipated its practice but not its importance.

As we give our children their goodnight kiss for the night, bless them before they go to sleep each night. We change the energy field around them by invoking a blessing upon them. As we invoke a blessing upon any person anywhere, living or dead, we change their energy field by adding the Light of Grace to it. This enhances what they do, how they feel, and how they are able to cope.

If we bless our food before we eat it, we change the vibrational pattern that has been picked up by the food prior to its coming into our sphere. We can think of all the people who are associated with the food we eat: those who produce the seed, the farmer or conglomerate who plants and grows the seed, the seasonal help who harvest the food, the packers who get it ready for market, the shippers, the truckers who deliver it, the store clerks who unload it, and the grocer who sells it. If any one of the people associated with this process is miserable, the vibrational pattern of that misery is picked up by the vibrational pattern of the food. Blessing our food changes the vibrational pattern to one of peace and harmony with the Universe.

When we bless our homes, they become the most sacred space of our lives. Our homes are the nests to which we retreat after a stressful day at work. Keeping our homes neat, clean, fragrant, organized, and updated keeps the energy alive, vibrant and harmonious; exactly the type of environment we need to renovate and rejuvenate our soul. Cluttered, disorganized, or dirty homes lower the vibrational field of everyone in them and add to the disharmony and confusion in our lives.

When we bless our work environments, our cars, and all the projects on which we are working, the same energy that keeps our homes vibrant applies to our work places and our cars. Keeping our desks free of clutter, and moving the paperwork off our desks in a timely manner, is also a form of blessing; a way of helping ourselves to change the vibrational pattern that is holding us back.

We can each let blessings shine throughout our lives. The more we bless, the more blessing we have. As we give, we get.

How does blessing everything intensify the vibrational energy of your life? Offering daily blessings changes everything around us.

February 5

The Gift of Sunshine

Our lives are surrounded by so much natural beauty that we do not see. So many of us get up and go to work in the dark and come home after dark. Natural beauty surrounds us everywhere and is absolutely free, but we flit by it without a passing glance. We hardly know that daylight exists, and dismiss the need to get outdoors as a total waste of time. Even when we manage to go outside in our hurry for a luncheon or dinner engagement, we are so preoccupied with our work that we are barely aware of the soothing warmth from the rays of the sun.

Noticing the natural beauty around us every single day and welcoming the gift of sunlight into our life brings joy into our life. Becoming cognizant of all the beauty around us may help us slowly remember that *everything we are is due to the sun.* Everything we own has its origin from the sun. Everywhere we seek shelter, from cave to the tallest skyscraper, traces its beginnings to the sun. Caves we might understand, but skyscrapers? Before they become skyscrapers, these structures of glass and steel began as silicon dioxide, melted at high temperatures to produce glass. These structures began as purified iron with traces of chromium, manganese, and nickel to produce steel. The windows began as sand. The concrete likewise began as sand, mortar, and water. None of these transformations would have been possible without the raw materials formed by the action of the sun on the earth.

The sun shines equally on all of us and is totally free of charge. Not a one of us is deprived. Technology which harnesses energy from the sun to heat our homes and our water, bringing our energy costs to a minimum, waits for us to make use of it. Those of us who are constructing new homes can apply all the latest techniques that have been developed. We just have to utilize them. Many of us lack vitamin D, while it radiates from the sky gratis, a gift from the Creator. Ten minutes each day with our face turned to the sunlight would benefit us immensely, and one-half hour is even better, if we can tolerate it.

Sunlight, rather than an option, is a necessity in our life. Even those who live in countries, cities, or states where the sun shines the least have remedies. Since the discovery of SAD (Seasonal Affect Disorder), many options for receiving strong artificial light are available. There is no reason to be without sunshine or its equivalent.

One heavily overcast day, I took my dog Taffy outside. He was a rambunctious corgi who equated going for a walk as one of his greatest joys. As we walked towards Burke Lake, I looked up and saw the sun peek out from behind this dense cloud cover, shine brilliantly, wink, and then retreat. It was almost as if it had come out to say: *Hello. Well done! Carry on!* That sun beamed joy within me and a contented feeling radiated throughout my day.

The Guides are not asking anyone to become sun worshipers. Far from it. They ask only for your awareness. Say hello to the sun each day. You may be surprised at the response.

How does sunlight impact you?
Sunlight reflects the Light that we hold within.

February 6

Thought Comes First

"In the beginning was the Word, and the Word was with God, and the Word was God." This biblical passage, from the Gospel of St. John (John 1:1), focuses on the importance of thought. Thought comes first, before anything else in creation. Thought is the first "Word" to exist: *thought in the Mind of God.* Words have such power behind them, for good reason. Words are the vocal expression of thought and thought creates.

Why is thought so important? Because everything we think creates some "thing" on some level. We may have a hard time understanding this concept because we do not see the "creations" of our thoughts quickly. While some of us may see our thoughts manifest into form instantly, many of us might think of something and never see our thoughts come into form until later, when the correlation from thought to form is not as easy to discern.

If we predominantly think negative thoughts, how satisfying will our "life" be if we *instantly experience* that which we think about? That is why it is so critical to monitor our thoughts on this dimension. If we are stuck in a rut of negative thinking, that negative thinking is going to wreck havoc with our "creations" once we transition from here.

Thought comes from that to which we *pay attention.* Each day offers us unlimited possibilities to pay attention to new situations and new opportunities, yet so many of us stay mired within the same thoughts we had the day before. Rarely do we think about something new, but instead continue to tread over the same territory. Thus, we feel stuck. This is where spiritual guidance comes in, to help us move out of a stuck position.

Attention influences our thoughts, which then determines what happens in our lives. However, attention can be programmed with *intention,* which can be conscious or subconscious. That to which we give attention is what manifests in our lives. It is from our *intentions* that we create *purposefully* each day. We can set our own intentions each day, or events can set it for us. Intention starts the forces of creation.

Life on Earth is such a gift to us because it gives us the opportunity to savor, at a much slower pace, the effects of our thoughts. Since we have time to change our mind about anything we think about, it is considered such a *prize* to come to this planet. There are many more souls waiting to incarnate here than there are bodies for them. But, there are also those souls who refuse to experience the third dimension, for they witness some of the difficulties which we encounter here.

However, life in other dimensions is not that easy either. When we transition to the *next* dimension to which we go, *the moment we think it, we experience it.* When we *instantly* place ourselves in the situation we think about, then – if we continue to think negative thoughts – we can generate nothing but chaos.

We can think of Planet Earth as a training ground, a teacher of "how to think positively." We can learn to monitor our thoughts to create that which will enhance our life.

How do your thoughts influence your "creations?"
As we change that to which we pay attention,
we can also change our thoughts

February 7

Do It NOW with Love

Within us are all the tools necessary to become whatever our heart desires. We come to this plane of existence with everything already in place; we are born with all the equipment that we need to fulfill our soul's contract. "If God has led us to it, God will lead us through it." There is nothing that our heart desires that we cannot have or do, if it is within our soul's contract. We have prepared over many lifetimes for this one. Everything we hold deep within the recesses of our heart is ours, if we ask for God's help as we take the necessary steps to fulfill our dream.

We often stand in awe of someone else's power, all the while denying our own. This exempts us from the responsibility of exercising *our* gifts. We say to ourselves: *I can't do that. I don't know enough. I need more practice. I need more education. I need more money. I don't have time. I have children to care for and rear. I'll do it, when I get around to it.* The list is endless.

Why not accept the motto: *Do It NOW with Love? Do it NOW* before we master it. *Do it NOW* before we know every minute detail of the task involved. *Do it NOW* before we feel ready. *Do it NOW* before we have all the "tools" needed to complete the job. *Do it NOW* even when we do not have the money or the time for it. *Do it NOW* in the midst of raising our family. *Do it NOW* even when we feel clumsy, unqualified, or self-conscious about it. As the Nike commercial states: "Just Do It."

If we make choices when we are young, before we hear our Higher Self speaking to us, we may choose a career out of a sense of duty or dependency; we may feel pressured by obligation, or forced into a career against our will. We allow our egos to control us. By responding to the demands of our egos, we allow our "little" self, our ego self, to take the place of our Higher Self. We act as if our Higher Self does not exist. That is not true. Our Higher Self waits patiently and never stops reaching out to us. Many of us can hear the guidance from our Higher Self about what to do next only after we are down on our knees because we have had "enough." Otherwise, the advice of the Higher Self falls on deaf ears. It speaks, but we do not listen.

We can use our *setbacks* to spur us forward. Setbacks are put into place to test our resolve: *Is this what we really want?* Setbacks help us alter our course of behavior when we are not on the correct path; they help guide us to another place where our talents are more needed. As my friend Willy Jolly says, "Set-backs are a set-up for a come-back."

How liberating it is to *Do it NOW with Love.* By seeing in our mind's eye the finished outcome, the *fait accompli,* we may find the inner drive to become the master healer, the published author, the public speaker, the business owner, the chef, the entrepreneur, or whatever goal it is that we wish to pursue. By *Doing it NOW with Love*, we are on our way to owning that elusive rainbow which we so deeply desire.

We can encourage ourselves to realize our dreams and desires by placing a picture of the finished outcome where we can see it every day. Our heart's desire has already been created on *some* level of existence and is in form there. We each have only to bring it down to this level. As we continue working toward our individual goals, we bring them into form on *this* level.

We are a work in progress, but we will *always* be a work in progress. That never ends, certainly not while we occupy the space known as the third dimension. When we *do it NOW, with Love,* we are our way to Self-Mastery.

We are continuously learning what it means to be a creator "Be"-ing.

Amen.

How can "Do it NOW with Love" change the direction of your life?
We need no excuse to keep ourselves from pursuing our heart's desire.

February 8

Different Paths to Power

I just experienced three oil leaks in my car today. To me, this situation represents a loss of essential fluids. Since the outer reflects the inner, I asked my Guides how this was related to my personal life.

Their answer was: *You are losing energy through your throat in three places:*

You are not saying what you mean.

You feel you have to hold back your words.

You feel you cannot be understood.

I thought about these words for awhile and reflected on what had recently happened to me. I had spoken to several people whose fundamentalist belief was to *condemn* all others who were not part of *their* religion. They pounced on my statement that *there are as many paths to God as there are people on this planet.* I stated that since there is nothing outside of self, if there are seven billion people on the planet, there are seven billion paths to God. They *vehemently* disagreed.

Because someone disagreed with my point of view did not mean I had to give away my power, yet that was exactly the way my ego self reacted. While they ravenously put forth their point of view, my ego self felt too bruised and too stymied to continue sharing my point of view. Spirit Self took over and helped me retreat into a corner of my mind to bring my peace back to center.

We can stay in our power by simply *acknowledging* the other person's point of view, but stating that *ours is different.* That allows each of us to *be* different, yet to co-exist in the same space without violating each other's rights. Each of us has the right to be exactly where we are on our path toward spiritual mastery. Our opinions are not always right for the "other." Their opinions count just as much as ours do. Their opinions simply reflect where they are in their evolution back to the Source.

The common modus operandi on this planet is: *I'm right. You're wrong. And I am going to kill you if you don't follow my way.*

So much trouble comes to Earth from people in power insisting on pressing their point of view on the rest of the populace. People with the lowest vibrational energy are the most violent and subject others to their violence, whether it is on a personal, state, national, or international level. Lower vibrational energies can amass great support because there are so many people still operating on that frequency.

That situation is now fast changing. There is hope. People with the highest vibrational energy honor the sacredness of all life. Humans may have started all the wars on this planet, but they have also been the ones to bring the greatest messages of peace, love, mindfulness, compassion and understanding in an attempt to change the paradigm of hatred and retribution that has been in vogue throughout the millennia.

For the previous four thousand years, masculine energies dominated during the Piscean Age. However, feminine energies will dominate the Aquarian age that we have just entered. Watch how many females will enter prominence on the world stage in the next decade. As the feminine energies become more entrenched, war as a viable option will be totally eliminated, for no mother would willingly send her son or daughter into war. When the consciousness of man changes to one in which war is no longer an option, neither as a desired course nor as a credible resolution to conflict, human kind will enter a place of Love on our path to God. When we come from a position of Real Power, the power of Love, we will have peace on Earth.

A young rock singer, Jimi Hendrix, before his brief life was cut short, stated: "When the power of love overcomes the love of power, the world will know peace."

I totally agree.

How many paths to power exist within your own family? We need to allow each other the" right" to exercise our own "valid" path to God.

February 9

Taking Responsibility for Our Creations

We say to ourselves; *I am going to change, but not just yet, not just now.* We want things, situations, people, and relationships, always the *other,* to be different, yet *we* do not want to be different. *We* want to stay exactly the same, not recognizing that *we* are *all that is.* As long as we stay bound to the concept that everyone else has to change, then we continue to experience exactly that which we have experienced in the past. According to Einstein, the definition of insanity is to *do the same thing but expect different results.* We set ourselves up for failure when we refuse to *own* our creations.

When *we* agree to be different, then things, situations, people, and relationships will all be different, because there is nothing outside of Self. *We* are All That Is. We change, then everything changes around us.

We are afraid of our power because with power comes *obligation*. We have to *act* on our power. It is more comforting to always be in a process of *seeking*. We search for yet another modality. We are open and curious to all manner of truth, but we do not wish to focus on any one of them. We would rather sample amongst a large smorgasbord of delights for the spiritual senses.

As long as I was playing *The Blame Game*, my life was in chaos. Fortunately, through my commitment to *A Course in Miracles,* I was able to let go of blaming everyone except myself for my miscreation, and to start looking at what I created and how it was showing up in my life.

What we create is what shows up in our life. *On some level*, we create *everything* that shows up in our life. That level may have come from a "time" past. Since there is no time in the Spirit realm, the thing we create in a time "past" is also being created in present time, and in future time.

The present is pre-"sent." It shows up in the present because it is pre-"sent" by us. Anything from a time past will show up in the present because that which is past is also NOW. We only have NOW, nothing more, nothing less. Our NOW is meted out to us in exactly the same manner that everyone else's NOW is given to them – one second at a time. What we do with each second is up to us.

When we forgive something from a time past, it is also forgiven in present time and in future time. It is forgiven in all time frames and in all dimensions. What a great relief to strive for!

What creations, or miscreation, are you experiencing in your life? Taking responsibility for our creations or miscreation can help us change them.

February 10

Clearing Our Personal Space

We need to learn to clear ourselves of all energy imbalances as soon as they occur. Clearing ourselves can be a mental exercise or can be done using physical items. Clearing energy imbalances can be done through the power of our mind, simply *intending* to let them go. We can ask Spirit to help *ground, clear, center, align, and balance* us. We can breathe deeply and quiet our mind until we feel a gentle calmness flowing over us. This exercise needs to be done daily (every time we feel unbalanced), for rarely does a day go by that does not unbalance us. When we are patient with ourselves we will get what we ask for. Again, it is our *intent to clear* that sets the clearing in motion.

There are certain commercial products to help clear ourselves and the space around us. One method is to use a **sage smudging stick**, a Native American tradition. White sage, sacred to Native Americans, is sold in health food stores, in specialty stores, and in grocery stores that feature organic foods and metaphysical products. Briefly light the bound leaves, extinguish, and gently waft the smoke around and into the areas we want cleared, making sure the closet doors, cupboards, or desk drawers are open.

Essential oils have wonderful properties for clearing, protecting and enhancing our well being. While there are many of them on the market, only a few of them are outstanding. We can check their life force with a pendulum or ask our intuitive sense to guide us as we smell them. They should smell strong, vibrant, and clear, with no bitter tinge to their odor. An assorted blend of essential oils can be diffused in distilled water and sprayed in our work or home environment. These oils are versatile, and their vibrational energy helps alter our vibrational energy. An excellent reference book on the properties of essential oils is *Essential Oils Desk Reference*, compiled by *Essential Science Publishing.*

When I needed peppermint oil, I smelled each one of the six products available. Only one of them smelled alive and vibrant; the rest had a weak, a sharp, or an "acid" scent. The one that had the most sparkling scent was not the most expensive.

Flower essences (the vital energy of the plant which is then mixed in water with brandy or vinegar added as a preservative) are also excellent tools for clearing our personal energy field. Practitioners specializing in essences can be found through word-of-mouth referrals, through advertising, through the internet or through the back of this book in the *Resource Guide*. Most qualified practitioners are on the internet and are able to ship their products world-wide.

Crystals, with their incredible array of size, shape and form, are yet another outstanding tool for clearing energy fields. Each variety addresses different characteristics and needs. The best crystals to use for general clearing are either clear or rose quartz. Exquisite crystals can be found in many stores, including the

Museum and Discovery stores, Angel stores, Native American stores, metaphysical gift shops, mineral stores, or Museums of Natural History. Some people are fortunate to live in areas where crystals are prolific and can dig them up in their own backyard. They are such sacred objects to have around. Honor them. Keeping them on the window sills of the rooms that need to be cleared perpetuates clear energy into the room.

There are a few outstanding books on the *spiritual* properties of crystals. One of my favorites is *Book of Stones: Who They Are and What They Teach*, by Robert Simmons and Naisha Ahsian, with contributions by Hazel Raven. While spading my front flower-bed to expand it, I unearthed a large peach quartz crystal in the shape of a heart. To honor its energy, I asked the heart whether it was okay for me to bring it out of the garden and into the house. When I heard *Yes* internally, it promptly went onto the window sill of my home office. I felt as if this crystal had rewarded me.

Another excellent clearing tool is a **set of chimes**, especially Tibetan chimes, although any clear crystal, glass, or metal chime can be effective. There is a certain sweetness to their sound. Use them by striking with a tool provided for that purpose, against each other, or ring them as a bell. Other forms of clearing occur when we go to a forested area or to the ocean. Each of us may recall how good we have felt after a trip to the ocean. There are negative ions in the air at the ocean, as there are in the air under pine trees. These negative ions help clear our energy fields. For those who can do so safely, flowing with strong water currents (such as the ocean) can be both clearing and exhilarating. For others, that same uplifted feeling comes from standing under a waterfall, taking a good brisk shower, or walking in pine groves, whether during a trip to the mountains or within our own backyards. The ion exchanges in these places is so very beneficial that all these options can be very clearing

Constantly paying attention to our energy fields, and keeping our intent to stay clear, will help us to realize our "clearing" intention. Fresh breezes, fresh scents, rainfall, waterfalls, all bodies of water, sunlight, and natural beauty everywhere conspire to make us feel as if we have touched a little bit of heaven on Earth. We have.

How often do you clear your energy imbalances throughout the day? Clearing our energy imbalances each time we feel incapacitated restores our life force.

February 11

Energy from the Source

We can be verbally assaulted or emotionally assaulted by an "other" or by our own "self," through our thoughts. Any time we are subjected to someone's bad temper, we are under emotional assault. Being verbally assaulted renders us feeling powerless, whether we are under verbal attack ourselves, or when we witness someone else (whether adult or child) or something else (such as an animal or pet) being verbally assaulted. Our own energy feels spent. The smallest chore becomes too difficult for us. Everything drains us. Any request looks like a monumental hurdle, no matter how essential it is to our physical, mental, emotional, or spiritual well-being.

We can overcome verbal and emotional assault, and we can do so without the process costing us anything more than our time and attention. We learn to take energy from the Source, from All That Is, from Prime Creator, from God. Forgetting to take energy from the Source is debilitating and keeps us in a state of weakness and exhaustion. Not replenishing energy from the Source weakens our subtle bodies, and eventually our physical body.

Taking energy from the unlimited Source of energy – God – is exhilarating, exciting, and freeing. The Source of energy is always there and it is ours for the taking. We do not need permission, a pass, a code word, a fee, a stipend, a token, or an exclusive right. It belongs to us free of charge! It is our birthright! It is given to us in Love and Joy. No questions asked, no monetary exchange necessary, and no bartering in return. It is totally, completely, and permanently FREE!

One way to receive energy from Spirit is through visualization. One of my favorites is the following, modified from several sources: a Buddhist meditation technique, a visualization process in *The Complete Ascension Manual* by Joshua David Stone, Ph.D., and from my own Reiki instruction.

Visualize a funnel of light the width of your head and connect to it through the dimensions to the place you call God. Bring this funnel of light back from God, send it down through your body to the center of the Earth, then bring it back up again. You are now connected between Heaven and Earth through this sign of infinity. Continue to breathe deeply and rhythmically while filling up your body with light: down from God, up from the Earth in a lovely figure eight. Mix both of the energies in your heart. Use this light to shine out of your eyes, out of your heart, and out of every cell of your body into the lives of those you touch.

It is that simple. The Source of energy is brought into our body through our breath and our thoughts. Learn to breathe deeply. Breathe so that each breath circulates from the soles of our feet, to our fingertips, to the top of our crowns. Breathe rhythmically, evenly, and with intent to heal.

When we breathe with purpose, we expand and heal our energy fields.

Have you tried to receive the endless supply of energy from the Source, which is always available to you? Sometimes the most effective techniques are the simplest ones.

February 12

Past Lives

Many of us feel that we have had past lives, whether we wish to admit it or not. We may instinctively feel camaraderie with someone whom we have just met, or feel fear or intense dislike for someone to whom we have just been introduced. There seems to be no rational reason for our feelings, but we know they are there. Exploring our past lives can explain those feelings, can free us from constraints of discomfort with certain people, or validate our happiness about other people. This can be a life-long process.

By asking our Guides to help us understand the karmic reasons for our experiences, we can gain insights that help clarify why certain "idiosyncrasies" exist in our lives. For this reason, knowledge of past lives is useful; they give explanations when none are available through any other means. Understanding a past life may help us see its connecting thread to a current life theme; it may help us illuminate that which we would never have known otherwise.

Those who like to flaunt past lives, bragging that we were someone "important," forget that *everyone* has had an "important" life at some point. Most of the time, during an "important" life, we usually learn the least. During these lives, we were too trapped by our egos and their demands on our material lives to pay any attention to Spirit. We let our most important lessons slide by, with scarcely a glance in their direction. We learn nothing if we do not allow Spirit in, because we believe that we have a *reputation* to protect. We tell ourselves that spiritual development just has to wait. More important earthly issues take precedence.

Hypnotherapy revealed the source of one of my greatest fears: the fear of deep water. A couple who became friends, both licensed hypnotherapists, offered regressive hypnotherapy to those willing to explore past lives. During my first regressive hypnotherapy session, a past life image emerged during which I was unjustly accused of stealing money, stabbed by the accuser, and thrown off a ship into the middle of the ocean. I saw myself floating downward in the water; a long flowing beard floating up over my face. I was not afraid to die, but cursed the man who stabbed me, knowing that I was innocent of his accusation. The impact of this regressive hypnotherapy session showed me that I had good reason to fear deep water, and explained why I always felt wary of the accuser from that lifetime; a man I recognized in my current lifetime.

Knowledge of certain past lives can bring clarification into our own lives. I could never comprehend why my heart just *melted* the first time I saw our little Corgi, Taffy, the pet we brought home for our children in 1992. He was the only one of a litter of nine who was interested in us and stayed by the fence licking our outstretched fingers. All the other puppies stayed momentarily, and then bounded away.

During a Rolfing session (similar to deep tissue massage but even more intense), I saw myself as an old man in a tiny cottage in the Swiss Alps, living a very humble, but productive and happy, life as a cobbler. I lived alone on the side of the mountain with a faithful companion; a little Corgi. Townspeople came up intermittently, requesting repairs on their shoes or leaving an occasional order for a new pair; stopping by to chat about the local events of the day. During many weeks I had few visitors, but my faithful little dog never left my side, and listened intently to everything I shared with him.

One evening, I choked on a chicken bone, could not dislodge it, bent over and fell to the floor and died. As my Spirit hovered over my body for three days, I witnessed my beloved pet resolutely lie by my side, his little face looking at me mournfully until someone came to the house and took us both away. As I watched this tender scene, I realized that this Corgi was the same pet that chose us in this lifetime. Yes, our pets can and do come back with us and, if they leave this dimension before we do, are there to greet us when we transition. No wonder we form such strong attachments to them.

To be born with the knowledge of all of our past lives would be senseless. We would be on overload, and would not be able to function properly in this (the third) dimension. Thus, we are given information only as we need it. We recycle back to the Earth, both as male and as female, taking part in every culture and every race, and living on every continent, until we achieve spiritual mastery.

Did you ever receive knowledge of a past life that cleared up confusion in your current life? Knowledge of a past life is meant to instruct, not to glorify.

February 13

Reflections on a Cold Winter Morning

Walk with me in my garden on a cold but beautiful winter morning. Each morning has its own particular beauty, but what an especially glorious morning today is! Look at those first snowdrops, the first bulb to bloom in the New Year. There has been a break in the weather for the past few days. The eastern sun has warmed the earth enough for the snowdrops to burst forth. Earlier, when I went to get the morning paper, their demure little heads were bent forward, closed to the fierce cold that came late in the night, but now they are gently raising their faces to capture the warmth of the sun.

I round the corner of my home and spy the Christmas rose in bloom, while the Lenten rose sprawls out dramatically in its own untidy tangle. Both are members of the Hellebore family, and both produce green flowers. (However, the Christmas rose has been coaxed to blossom with pink, white, purple, and a hint of lavender accenting the green.) How much pleasure they bring me. The Hellebore species, a member of the buttercup family, are evergreen perennials that spread widely and evenly. Unlike buttercups, which need full sun, they thrive in shade and do well as long as there is enough moisture to sustain them.

The Christmas rose stands fully in control, demands respect, and lets her compactness speak with authority. Her flowers are similar to large apple blossoms: their lovely petals, in multiple hues of lavender to green, curve inward and seem to last forever. Here they are, still in bloom and it is the middle of winter.

The Lenten rose sprawls and bends and is a little more foolhardy. She sends out her shoots in tentacle fashion, rests them against a bush for support, and then sends up stalks and stalks of genteel green flowers – not too brazen, not too compact – a gentler version of her companion, the Christmas rose. The green flowers are profuse enough to glorify the surrounding area. They always startle, and then delight me. Right now, only her foliage bursts forth in a lacy sunburst pattern, resembling the Japanese lace leaf maple. It is hard to believe that something that appears so delicate could survive the winter.

As you took this walk with me, I hope you enjoyed the flowers as much as I did; always possible when you are open to the beauty around you. Isolate yourself to gain access to the higher parts of your Soul.

Do you make a habit of walking around your home each day to see the new growth that has sprung forth? We need to invest time in ourselves to open to Spirit.

February 14

Our Solar Angel

On a higher level, "we" are an Angel. My teacher, when referring to our Higher Self, calls her our Solar Angel. Our current level of consciousness may not be aware of her, but that does not matter. Our lack of awareness does not preempt her existence.

Our Solar Angel has infinite patience with us because she comes from the *infinite part* of us. No creation has greater love for us than our Solar Angel, for she is the Divine aspect of us connecting us to the Divine Source of *unconditional Love*. She may not be concerned with our need to amass material possessions – how many teaspoons we wish to accumulate – but she steps in to warn us if our life is in danger. Our priorities rouse her attention when they concern matters of spirit.

As we take time to work, to play, to love, to pray, to sleep, and to be in the moment, we also need to take time to be with our Solar Angel. We can learn to listen within to the quiet of our Soul for her gentle whisperings. She accompanies our every waking minute on the Earth plane, and tenderly assists us when we think there is no hope; when we feel that everyone on this planet has abandoned us or misunderstood us, or when we feel totally unloved.

Higher Angelic Beings pay attention to us when we are ready for their messages. Regardless of the role we choose to play on this Earth plane, our Solar Angel knows what our soul's contract is. She knows that we are perfect, no matter what the outward appearance of the circumstances of our life demonstrate.

We can each learn to listen to our own Solar Angel. She is there. We receive the interventions of our Solar Angel as we respond to her entreaties to us.

My Solar Angel set up the circumstances of my first journaling "assignment." She knew I was ready to be awakened in the middle of the night to communicate with my Guides; that I was willing to come downstairs to the computer and record all the messages my Angels and Guides were communicating. These later became my *Angel Journal*. She called in reinforcements when needed.

For the first six months of communicating with Spirit, I credited my Guides as communicating with me. Only when I heard the words, “my child,” did I realize it was an Archangel who was transmitting a thought to me, then another and another. The words *my child* always preceded Angelic intervention; in my case, Archangel Michael.

We are each given *exactly* the same *spiritual* gifts. It is up to us to uncover them. What any Spiritual Master does, we can do. When we stand in awe of *anyone,* we give away our power. None of that is necessary, since “we” are all of it, all the way back to the Source.

On some level, in some dimension, “you” are your Solar Angel, “you” are an Ascended Master, “you” are an Archangel, and “you” are One with Source. “You” are not bound to any aspect of physicality, for some aspect of “you” – tied to the Source of All That Is, the great I AM – remembers exactly who “you” really are and from whence “you” really came.

When we are consumed with third dimension material accumulation, we have scant time for anything as lofty as spiritual pursuits. Some of us give all our attention to raising our families, and none to raising our consciousness. Only when crisis hits our lives, do most of us open to matters of Spirit. By opening to matters of Spirit NOW, before crisis swamps our life, we tune our senses to spiritual matters – to matters of Love – unencumbered by an overwhelming situation.

What better time to learn about our Solar Angel than on St. Valentine’s Day, the day celebrating Love. Happy Valentine’s Day!

Has your Solar Angel been trying to reach you?
As we listen to our Solar Angel’s promptings,
we increase in spiritual mastery.

February 15

Free Energy

A simple antenna to harness energy from the atmosphere – so that anyone, anywhere, could put up an antenna and have all the free energy that he or she wanted or needed – was invented by Nicola Tesla in the early 1900's. Tesla was a scientist, born in Croatia but living in the United States. He applied for and received a patent for his work. The rights to this patent were purchased by the major utility companies and swallowed by the corporate giants. Why were the people of this planet not given the opportunity to harness free energy from the Universe, by putting up a simple antenna on the roofs of their homes?

Wind, water, and electrical currents are so abundant on this planet that it is a very simple matter to harness them inexpensively for the use of every person. The technology already exists! Because man is part of a universal grid, in which all communication is shared, the technology for such an antenna is currently available as a home industry, and has been for quite some time. Doesn't that make us wonder why we never hear about *free* energy, or why there is no mass distribution of such antennae? Ask to be led to those who have the invention in place, so that we can partake in free energy instead of depleting the natural resources of the Earth.

In whose best interest is it, to keep us from understanding who we really are and what power we really have? Whose best interest is being served by keeping us small, doubtful, hesitant, cautious and – most of all – fearful? Who has trained us into giving our power away to that which makes no difference in the totality of our life? Who robs us of the joy that is our birthright, by keeping us concerned with so many pointless issues that consume our attention? Who wishes to keep us "poor," even when our masses make the highest incomes in the world?

Which factions of our lives take all of our allotted time, squandering it by keeping us tied up in irrelevancies? How many hours are we spending working on projects for which we have no real use and no real interest? What causes us to salivate over useless items that end up keeping us bound to mountains of bills as our reward? Only we can answer these questions, for only we know how we utilize the minutes of our days.

"Ask and you shall receive." For whatever new appears in your life – whether it is a new life partner, a new place to live, a change in careers, new educational opportunities, or *free energy* – ask to be led by wisdom to that which is necessary for your soul harmonics to bring peace to yourself.

Then, and only then, can we bring peace to the planet.

Are you being guided to bring "free energy" to the planet? All humans are part of a mass communication grid in which all information is shared.

February 16

Spirit Sees Only Perfection

Spirit sees only a world of perfection. What we see as "real," Spirit sees as a "dream." What we hold up as "real" – time, for example – Spirit merely smiles at, for Spirit exists where timelessness exists, always in a perpetual NOW.

When we remember *we are Spirit having a human experience,* we see how sad it is that we take ourselves so seriously. We miss the inherent beauty of each day as we tumble forward paying attention only to our list of grievances and complaints. By taking ourselves so seriously, we also miss the opportunity to evolve beyond our list of injustices. We keep ourselves from knowledge; a *knowing* that all is perfect in the total scheme of the Divine plan.

To see the world through the eyes of the ego is to see the world through the eyes of error. The ego sees blame around every corner and insists on retribution for all the injustice committed. There is no possible way that retribution is the answer. Nevertheless, the ego marches forward, holding its banner of righteous indignation, firmly demanding "an eye for an eye, a tooth for a tooth." That attitude did not work millennia ago, and does not work today. Yet the "need" for retribution is being demanded every day by someone from almost every nation on the planet.

Good things happening to bad people and bad things happening to good people can represent dharma, a cosmic order of law according to the Buddhist tradition. It can be what we set in motion millions of years ago, thousands of years ago, hundreds of years ago, or yesterday. When we evaluate how promptly the results of our actions are coming back to us, we realize that these days dharma comes quicker and quicker.

What the ego may consider the most heinous crime, we may have contracted for in Spirit as a lesson in forgiveness for the self or for the "other." When we forgive those *who trespass against us*, we are in effect forgiving ourselves, because – on some level – we set all this up. We did this to give ourselves the lessons that we desired. Nothing escapes the attention of Spirit. Nothing is hidden. Whatever we smash down deep within our psyche as "untouchable" is in bright view to Spirit. And Spirit *always* sees us as perfect.

Thanks to the astute advice of Dr. Andrew Weil, in his book, *8 Weeks to Optimum Health: A Proven Program for Taking Full Advantage of Your Body's Natural Healing Power,* I have put myself on a daily newspaper and TV news "diet." I do not watch news programming (save for partial attention to a few select PBS programs), nor do I read the newspaper, except for the few sections - *Style, Travel*, or *The Arts* in *The Washington Post* - that nourish my Soul. Whatever I have to know is given to me through other means. If it is truly important, I find out about it.

Stories from the daily newspapers and on TV news programs might cause us to ask: *When did all the brightness recede from our*

Soul? When did we become so hopelessly mired in total lawlessness? When did the morass of materialism take over our lives?

After perusing my favorite sections recently, an opposite thought occurred to me: *When did so much beauty continue to be explored, propagated, and protected? When did the good of the common man come to the forefront? When did everyone start to listen to the tug of Spirit in their heart and become so attuned to the needs of the environment and to the animals on this planet?* Even comic strips have been sharing a spiritual message.

The words *harmonic convergence* (originally identifying a measurement of light taken by the Spiritual realm from this planet during August 17-19, 1987) must have struck a chord in the collective consciousness, for those words are coming into common usage. The other day, *The Washington Post* featured an article about new varieties of home-grown tomatoes, which were likened to the *best of a harmonic convergence*. Another article used the same term when describing a decorator item. *Measuring the light quotient of our planet* is not exactly a topic that finds its way into *The Washington Post,* yet several times recently the phrase *harmonic convergence* has appeared.

Spirit makes a dent into our consciousness by any means possible; and those in the know smile.

Can you look beyond the demand for retribution and see the perfection in all things, the same way Spirit does? Where we see flaws, Spirit only sees perfection.

February 17

Balance

Life seeks balance. When a portion of us is out of balance, it affects both our body and our mind. If there is a part of us who feels unnoticed, we may seek a career that compensates for this feeling. Celebrity comes to mind. Rather than seeking the applause of one, we seek the adoration of millions. Sometimes, even though we may have the adulation of millions, this feeling of inadequacy cannot be squashed. When no amount of people telling us how great we are fully eliminates our discomfort; we turn to other means to keep from addressing our feelings; harmful things such as drugs, unsafe sex, clandestine relationships, or multiple partners. We become further and further removed from our center and act in a manner detrimental to our being. We are out of balance.

A past life revealed to me that during one lifetime as a male I was born with a physical deformity that kept me from even attempting an intimate relationship. I hid my shame by becoming an outstanding actor, adored by the masses. Unfortunately, the applause I heard each night offered me no comfort, and instead simply reinforced the feelings of inadequacy that had initially brought me into the entertainment industry. Both the need for applause and the feeling of inadequacy became a vicious cycle, which eventually became cell memory and kept me off balance.

In this lifetime, I have always striven to do my best. As a child and as a young adult, I sometimes felt that my person, my skill, and my work went unnoticed or unrewarded. As an adult, despite a sixty-hour work week as a real estate broker, putting my clients' needs first, giving them unlimited access to my time and knowledge, receiving accolades, awards, and tributes for my efforts, somehow I felt that I did not "deserve" the *monetary compensation* for my efforts. But the intangible rewards – the awards, the plaques, the million-dollar club standing – as well as the financial rewards kept me reaching for more, however out of balance I felt.

Since it was one of the feelings I incarnated with, feeling unbalanced was in my cell memory, and nothing I achieved *corrected* this feeling that I was inadequate and undeserving. When the past life as the actor revealed the *source* of my feelings of inadequacy, I could let those feeling go in the same manner an animal, insect, or reptile sheds a skin that it has outgrown – automatically. I no longer felt a need to hold on to those feelings.

We can incarnate onto this planet bringing "baggage" into our new life. This can make us feel ill and often does. Most of the time, this is tied to a lesson that we have chosen for ourselves in our current lifetimes. In the meantime, we do not feel so good. But wait. There is help. It is called energy balancing and those who are familiar with energy fields can help us. Practitioners – those who specialize in balancing energy - can see or feel the distortions in our energy field. Many specialties work with energy fields; some of the commonly known ones include chi or qi gong, Falun Gong, tai chi, and other martial arts. These are all excellent ways to bring balance into our energy field and to bring new energy into our body. Additionally, there are other healing methods: acupuncture, Chinese medicine, reflexology, Polarity Balancing, Zero Balancing, Healing Touch, Therapeutic Touch, Reiki, Rolfing, deep-tissue massage, and other modalities. These all work to balance our energy.

In the energy healing practice in which I participate, we have watched people valiantly struggle against the slimmest of odds to bring themselves back to health, and to maintain their balance, their sense of humor, and their peace of mind without any assistance from the outside. Some feel they need years of energy healing work, others feel a dramatic shift within a few short sessions. Each person decides for him or herself what treatment would be most appropriate.

Are feelings of inadequacy holding you back and affecting your balance? Finding the right energy healing modality can bring us back to balance.

February 18

Patterns, Precious Commodities, and Pitfalls

Unless our patterns are so ingrained that we are unwilling to change, eventually most of us come to the place called *forgiveness,* for this is the planet of forgiveness. We learn to forgive here, and the first person whom we learn to forgive is our ego self because our Higher Self is the one who set it all in motion initially. When our ego self learns to defer to unconditional Love, then our ego self incorporates into Higher Self. Ego self transforms into Higher Self: self becomes Self. As we learn to let it all go, we release the ties that bind us. When we can look at life through a *cosmic lens*, we come to the realization that there is nothing to forgive, since *we* set it all in motion in the first place.

Contrary to what we may have been told, *if we do not learn it here, we do not learn it elsewhere.* This is why "life" on the third dimension is considered such a precious commodity in the higher realms. This is the place where we can taste, savor, season, and salt however much we wish until we are satisfied. We are free to make a mess of our lives, to work ourselves up in a lather, to twist ourselves up in knots, to accuse the "other," to continue to see ourselves as victim, martyr, or slave. We are also free to change our minds instantly and let all those debilitating attitudes go.

For some, Earth seems to be a battleground; for others, a resting-place. Some of us cannot get the hang of surviving in the other dimensions and are in such a rush to come back here that we do not choose our parents wisely. On Earth, we need parents who will foster the lessons that our Souls have chosen for ourselves, so that our Higher Self can expand its awareness of the Divine. If we choose our parents too hastily, they may not be the right ones for us and we may end up hating them. This simply sets up another set of lessons for a future lifetime. Regardless of the pitfalls in this dimension, there are many more souls who wish to come here than there are bodies available for them.

This message came to me from Sananda expressing the Cosmic Christ: *In the other dimensions,* the moment you think it, you experience it. *The moment you wish to be someplace else, you are there. Think of the difficulty that would cause you in your current state. Many thoughts per minute race through your mind, and most of them are negative. What would the quality of your life be if you kept constantly placing yourself in a sea of negativity? And you think life on this planet is hard?*

Our thoughts and our actions generate karma. We get off the wheel of karma through forgiveness. For most, there is no other way. We need to be careful with our words and our actions. What karma are we engendering? We are free to choose to think, to do, and to be anything we want. However, we are subject to the consequence of our choices through the natural Law of Cause and Effect. Each time we self-righteously prevent an "other" from exercising their choice, we set up karma.

Please remember, there is no other. There is only Self. What we do to an "other" we do to our own selves, for the outer reflects the inner.

Is there is a pattern in your life requiring you to forgive?
Patterns, precious commodities, or pitfalls
in our lives reveal our lesson to us.

February 19

The Energy of Words in Spiritual Books

While exploring the world of spiritual books, I discovered that words had energy in them; something I had known all along, but had forgotten. After realizing that some books, even spiritual ones, made me feel sick after I finished reading them, I began using discretion in what I read. The books expounding a totally fundamentalist point of view weakened me.

Fundamentalists who would rather condemn or kill unless all believe in *their* book, which they express to be **The* Word* of* God** – whatever their name for God is – might benefit from a little cross-cultural exposure. How dull it would be for everyone to be identical. Positively boring! Fundamentalists point a loaded gun at anyone who disagrees with them, even when that gun shoots nothing but a missive of words, which are meant to energetically weaken the "opposition."

Different cultures and different belief systems add variety, texture, and interest to life. People who exhibit cross-cultural differences have the same inherent right to be as any other living species. Each species adapts itself for its own special place in the environment. Let us extend the same privilege to those who have different cultural habits as well as belief systems.

Dr. Masaru Emoto, a water researcher in Japan, through the ten thousand experiments he made photographing water crystals, showed the results of the energy of word hurtled at the water. Positive, upbeat words influenced crystals to display an exquisite crystalline structure. Negative words, even those that were slightly negative, contorted water crystals into the most grotesque forms. Parts of his work are replicated in his delightful book: *The Hidden Messages in Water.*

Authors of spiritual books come from their own perspectives and share the best they have to offer at the time they are writing the material. They write to expand the consciousness of their audience, just as their own consciousness has been expanded. They write to remind the populace of truths stated hundreds or thousands of years before. Most are concerned with universal truths; truths which carry within themselves an energy that resonates within the Divine matrix of each Soul on the planet.

We might be trapped in the idea that *a new truth* – no matter how many people proclaim it – if opposed to everything we were conditioned to believe, is dangerous. This reiterates the observation of George Bernard Shaw that "all great truths begin as blasphemies."

Those who study the Sacred Literature of the different world religions are struck by the similarities found in each book. The Masters who bring the various sacred writings to this planet, somewhere in their offering, state the same message – one of unconditional Love.

For almost twenty years, with each new spiritual book I picked up, I thought: *Is this the one? Is this the book that will finally help me break through this cloud of dust through which I continuously walk, this fog of nothingness? Will it help clear up any misunderstandings that I have?* During those years I kept thinking, If only I manage to read the right book, it will give me all the answers. Eventually I realized that each book that I picked up gave me only a nugget of truth; a part of the whole. There was no one book that could give me all the answers. That just did not exist for me.

All the answers could only come from one source: my Higher Self.

Have any spiritual books "dropped off"
the shelf you were perusing?
Spiritual books "call" us to read them.

February 20

Transmuting through the Light of Grace

Transmuting through the Light of Grace touched me intimately as, once again, I tried to deflect anger. Waking in the middle of the night, after I had struggled to get to sleep, I received a message. I was told that instead of deflecting anger, I was supposed to *transmute* it using the following techniques.

A point of light glows within our body at the solar plexus (called the Earth Star), and another point of light glows about six inches above our head (called the Soul Star). By combining the light of the Earth Star present within our solar plexus and the Soul Star above our head, we can increase the light to make it as big as we want. As we make the light grow, we are able to place any person, any spot on the planet, or the entire planet within this ball of light. Into this ball of light, we can even place the entire solar system, the entire galaxy, and finally, the entire Universe. We, as the progenitor, have the ability to transmute all ills through light.

Another technique is to expand the Soul Star and the Earth Star until we are standing in the middle of the two lights, and then see that image standing within a purple flame. The *Purple Transformational Flame of St. Germaine* – ranging from deep iridescence to the most intense shade of neon purple, glowing with embers of light alternating from light to dark – is also a new energy that has been dispensed to the Earth to help transmute negative energy. By combining the energies of the Earth Star, Soul Star and the *Purple Transformational Flame*, we are able to transmute anything that is hurtled at us. We do not have to worry about deflecting it. It leaves of its own accord.

Another technique to transmute through the Light of Grace is to visualize a *stream of twinkling lights cascading downward from the center of the galaxy* to the person or place which concerns us. In this manner we are always sending the Light of Grace to each person or each place about whom or which we are worried, instead of sending them worry-thoughts. Any time we feel the need to worry about a person, a "hot spot," or a place in conflict, we can instead send them the Light of Grace. This will help to transmute the negative energy given off by that person or the place.

A promise given to us in the Bible is that "the wolf also shall dwell with the lamb." (Isaiah 11:6) This can only be accomplished through the Light of Grace. Even a predator can have its "natural instincts" released and transmuted through the Light of Grace. Recently a picture published in the Washington Post illustrated this premise. A snake which refused to eat frozen mice was offered a lovely plump little hamster. Instead of devouring the hamster as the succulent meal that it was intended to be, the snake became the hamster's best friend, even allowing the hamster to sleep on its back. The hamster would curl up next to the snake as if sharing intimate secrets. It defied all odds of becoming just another tasty meal to its predator friend.

Amazing grace reached through the animal kingdom to share its light between man and a flock of wild cherry head parrots. They probably bred from what may have been escaped pets as recounted in *The Wild Parrots of Telegraph Hill*, a splendid documentary shot by Judy Irving. The parrot's main advocate, Mark Bittner, a modern day St. Francis of Assisi, spent a year befriending them, and has looked after them ever since.

The film described the relationships that Bittner formed within the flock, as well as the relationships they formed with each other. While nursing a badly injured little parrot that he named Tupelo, he described how tenderly he would take her outside to get her close to the flowers that are around his home. The video shows how gratefully she would look at the flowers, her head cocked to one side, her beady little eyes reflecting a smile.

One day, as he lay Tupelo down next to himself for five hours, he felt this tremendous outpouring of gratitude from her. He then placed her down on the floor when he was ready to go to sleep. He was afraid to leave her next to himself in the bed, in case he might roll over in the middle of the night and smother her. As soon as Mark put her down on the floor, he felt resignation and disappointment pour out of Tupelo. She so wanted to stay next to him.

Because his home was being sold, he had to leave the parrots behind. The tender way he bid farewell to the four birds he kept in two cages during his final goodbye to them brought tears to my eyes.

Just as with *Winged Migration,* another amazing documentary in which birds were the main focus, *The Wild Parrots of Telegraph Hill* video is a "must have" in your video library.

Have you noticed any change in the way "opposing" creatures are acting? The Light of Grace can transmute any opposing energy.

February 21

Idols: Why have them?

What is an idol? According to *A Course in Miracles*, an idol is "a false belief… a substitute for your reality … a false impression … a veil across the face of Christ because its purpose is to separate your brother from yourself."

An idol is something outside of ourselves to which we give away our power. Idols can be *personal*: our spouses, our significant others, the ones we love the most, or the ones who do not love us back. They can be *social*: our best friends, our worst enemies, those whom we criticize the most, those to whom we are attached, or those whom we feel need us the most or feel that we need the most. They can also be *material*: our cars, our homes, our bank accounts. They can be status symbols such as memberships in the country club, the right hairdressers, designer handbags, or our personal trainers. Idols can even be our jobs, or our government, our political party. They can be our affiliations, our profession, our outside activities, our fun stuff, our figures, our exercise regimes. They can be the activities from which we shrink the most, or those which we like to do the most, or even the food that we eat. The list goes on and on. Each of these persons, items, beliefs, or associations can be idols.

A Course in Miracles further states that the only two emotions existing on this planet are “love” and “fear.” All other emotions emanate from these two. We are driven by fear when we set up “idols” to govern our life. Our “idols” are that which we look to for protection, for safety, for acknowledgment, for strokes, for authentication, or for power. We set up idols in our lives in order to make ourselves more “perfect,” to help us feel that we “have” more than others, or to help us feel “good” about ourselves. This might work temporarily. Soon, however, the effect wears off and we still feel just as low as we did before.

How does an idol weaken us? We feel an emptiness that makes us uncomfortable, so we cast about to snare an “other” that will fill that emptiness in our life. We think that the “other” will complete us, take care of us, protect us, save us, and make us happy. We think something outside of ourselves will make us “whole.”

We do not know that *we are whole and complete just the way we are.* The only emptiness that we feel is that part of our Self whom we have shut down; the Divine Self. When we learn to access Higher Self, we do not have to turn to idols to complete ourselves. When we access the Divine within, we are able to access the power of that part of Self that is all-knowing, all-loving, and all-giving. *All the power is within us,* but we are not aware of it, so we give away our power to an idol.

You can give away your power to a *cookie* and not even know it. How many times have you heard: *You can’t eat only one.* Next time you are being encouraged to consume anything you do not want, stand in your power and refuse to be bullied. A treat is just that, a treat. It is not meant to be lunch. Yes, you *are* strong enough to resist.

Since all idols are external, all idols will disappoint us. We look to an "other" to guide us, protect us, honor us, love us, and lead us. We look to an "other" to *complete* ourselves, not understanding that, for each of us, Self is all there is. *There is nothing outside of Self.*

Our strength comes from within. Look for it there.

How are you giving away your power to the idols that govern your life? When we access the Divine within, we find the strength to give up our idols.

February 22

Release from the Ego Self

If we can view all life, seen and unseen, through the cosmic lens of Spirit, and have *reverence* for all life, we are on our way to becoming a self-actualized human; a human who is capable of combining body, mind, and spirit. The effects of the ego are left behind. We adhere *only* to the Voice of the Holy Spirit! We have neither the will nor the desire to continue staying gripped in the clutch of the ego self. As the talons of the ego self release and let go, we encounter joy and bliss. After we release from the grasp of our ego selves, we sense a freedom from constraint and wonder why we did not do this sooner.

According to *A Course in Miracles*, the ego's grasp is all so meaningless because it is *nothing*; that for which the ego grasps is not "real." This simply means that the ego's grasp does not come from Love. Anything that does not come from Love comes from fear. Our fear-based ego self, grasping and clutching at our personality, makes us feel uneasy. Only Love fills us, making us feel whole and nourishing us.

An unconditionally loving God put *no limitations* on what it is that we wish to experience. *God "allows" our ego selves to go after whatever it is that we desire.* Whatever we desire, God desires. Only when we learn to desire the highest good for the greatest number of people, do we then align our ego selves fully with the Divine Will. In the meantime, for as many lifetimes as we choose, we are free to experience that on which we focus and concentrate, regardless of the effects that our desires have on our lives or the lives of those around us.

If we could just remember that Spirit accompanies us on our routine throughout the day – that Spirit is there while we get dressed, shower, shave, make breakfast, get the children ready for school or day care, dash off to work, fight traffic, stress-out over our jobs, hassle with our co-workers, clients, or colleagues, run car-pools, hustle the children to and from practices, go out to eat, make dinner, go to volunteer meetings, exhaustively climb into bed, or make love – we could more easily align our ego selves with the Divine.

Spirit *is always there* patiently waiting for our acknowledgment, never leaving our side, staying with us every step of the way. It is hard to fathom that Spirit accompanies our every waking moment, good or bad, productive or ineffective, giving or indulgent, flush or insolvent. Spirit is always there, nudging us to accept the magnificence of who we really are, saying, WAKE UP! WAKE UP! WAKE UP! Only we can make the choice to pay attention to Spirit's urging; that still silent Voice for God within us.

Believing that we can both release ourselves from our ego selves and also come to know the Divine Will in our lives is not an idle dream. This is a reality that can be ours.

How can release from your ego self help you move forward in your life?

The power to release from our ego selves is within us.

February 23

Finding the Divine Within

When we start to question, *Who am I? Why am I here? What is my purpose?* we open the door to allow Spirit's entry. When we further question, *What is my role in the Divine Plan? How do I fit in? Where do all the pieces fit? How am I to be used to suit God's purpose? How am I ever going to be able to see God's purpose?* then we are on our way to self-actualization. We are willing to do whatever it takes to align with Higher Self.

One of my earliest memories was looking up at the sky and asking the question

Who am I? closely followed by *Why am I here*? The one thing I knew for certain was that I was "old" and I knew what "old" meant. I was only four at the time.

If you were asked what your highest good is on this planet, what role would you play if given the opportunity to be anything or anybody? Come and step forward and, using the U.S. Army's slogan for the early 2000's, *Be all you can be.* Come and be the person you really are. Who else can you be but who you really are? But do you know who you really are? Many clues are being revealed right now to give you that answer, which will give you back your power. Your power is infinite because the Source of your power in infinite.

Our greatest enemies are our greatest teachers. The people who "pinch" us – those who make us uncomfortable; those whom we wish to avoid – are the ones from whom we receive the greatest benefit. Our greatest lessons do not come to us when everything is going well, but rather, when everything is falling apart. Our greatest strengths are amassed at our lowest points. When we feel we can no longer continue, something breaks through for us. It is at these times that we find an inner strength and an inner reserve we did not know we had.

At one of my lowest points financially, when interest rates had hit 17% and earnings from real estate had dried up, the mortgage on our home – as well as our bills - were always paid. Money always appeared from "somewhere." During this period, I saw a picture of a home that I desperately wanted. It was listed at $300,000, but may as well have been three million. It was so far out of reach. After listening to a lecture called *The Promotable Woman* given by Jan Northrup, on her recommendation, I took the picture of that home and hung it on a window that overlooked my desk. It stayed there for three years. At the end of three years, we signed a contract for that very home, by that very same builder. We moved into it ten months later.

Financial disaster has been averted in our home more than once. The lesson to me has been that Spirit *knows* my most dire needs and *helps me* accordingly.

Believe the power of the Divine is within you, and that you can tap into its reserve.

What challenges have you experienced that have ultimately strengthened you? Spirit knows our every need and helps us fill our every need.

February 24

Sons of God

We are ALL Sons of God and we can immediately step forward to take our place beside our Master Teachers; not to elevate or deify them, but rather to walk beside them as co-creators. We are not simply a "maker" of creation, but are co-creators. As co-creators, we exercise our God-right to be who we really are; on equal footing with and equal in ability to those who have come before to teach us. We step forward to reclaim our Divine right – our Divine Power to be who we really are – *the most powerful creation who has ever existed.*

Fundamentalist religions teach that there is only one Son of God. There is not. People eventually discover that they can claim that status for themselves. When people find out who they really are, they reclaim their power as the Sons of God, rather than the sons of man. As Sons of God, they have unlimited power. As sons of man, they are chained to the laws of man. As Sons of God, they harness the power of the Universe, unlimited power, the power of who they really are. As Sons of God, they are whole; they want for nothing. As sons of man, they are always in need. As Sons of God, they see only Oneness. As sons of man, they see only separation. As Sons of God, they see their connection to all things, and nothing is impossible to them. As sons of man, they see only their limited little abilities that never seem to measure up to an "other."

Since the majority of the world religions promote that there is only "one" Son of God, the human populace has had to stand behind a very limiting paradigm. The human populace is tied to a wall of chains hung behind a curtain of fear. ***Dissolve that wall.*** If we view life from such a narrow bandwidth, we play into the hands of the institutions that wish to keep us small: our religious institutions, our governments, and our financial industries.

We are on the cutting edge of breaking loose from our limiting beliefs. We are being blasted with so much spiritual energy, that there is absolutely no reason to stay in our little limiting boxes. Not anymore. We have so many resources from which to choose, and so much excess baggage we are shedding, that our ego loads are getting lighter all the time.

We are as vast as the Universe. We put tiny fences around that aspect of ourselves that we call our bodies, and think *they are* our Universe. They are only the teeniest portion of who we really are – a minuscule fragment of the whole. We are encouraged to remember that *a crest of a wave is nevertheless part of the entire ocean.*

Believe that you are all the Sons of God.

How does belief that you are a Son of God strengthen your belief in your Divine Self? Know that we have each been given the same gifts as the greatest Masters who ever walked this Earth.

February 25

Changing What We "Really" Want

Somewhere during my late teens, I developed the idea that *I would never get what I really wanted so I should settle for what I could get.* This idea settled into my consciousness and became a part of my paradigm. I never realized that this particular paradigm controlled me well into my forties. It was only after years of introspection that I realized that this oh so limiting belief *was not true!*

Up until my early forties, I had felt that the goals that I had achieved where not the ones that I *really* wanted. Thus, what I had achieved brought me no real satisfaction. One morning, while coming into full consciousness, I made an inventory of the things I *really wanted* that I *had achieved:* graduating from the University of Michigan, marrying my second husband (a man with whom I had fallen madly in love, and still love deeply to this day), giving birth to two delightful children (a daughter and a son), acquiring lovely furniture and accessories, moving into our large colonial home, having a successful real estate career, and taking a family vacation to Hawaii. (This vacation had been a goal of mine since the age of fifteen.)

Basically, the big goals were all there; accounted for and standing tall. I did not lack in achieving that which *I had really wanted.* And for the first time in years, I felt at peace with myself. I ***had not*** settled for "second best." I ***had*** achieved all my "first choices."

After I turned fifty, I was pushed by Spirit to shift my priorities from material pursuits to spiritual pursuits. What I had achieved in the past was over. The first priorities I had set were accomplished. Now came Spirit's turn

Now, what I *really want* is just beginning to emerge. A new set of priorities is in place, and I am working towards them each day. Every single day sees me tending to these new goals in very specific and tangible ways.

Has "what you really want" changed over the years? As we re-evaluate our goals, we see if they reflect the person we are today.

February 26

Message from my Guides: The Power of Your Thoughts

"It doesn't matter. It's in the past."
Rafiki, speaking to Simba in *The Lion King*

If it happened a second ago, it qualifies as being in the "past." The only thing that matters is what is happening NOW! The world can change in an instant, or it can take three hundred thousand years. It is up to you. You can think the change through, or you can plod through it. It is all up to you. You are birthing the thirteenth Universe. How you do this is entirely up to you. You have the means to do it instantly, if only you believe, or you can take as long as you wish. That is the power of your free will.

We will work with you, we will help you, and we will support you. But we won't do your work for you. You have to do it alone.

That is why a "rescue mission" for the planet Earth – which was once anticipated – is not needed now. The Earth changes (those that have been predicted by many sources) are still taking place, but at a much slower pace, and with a much lower level of intensity.

You have all the tools necessary to effect a Great Global Society, not just for one nation, but for all nations under God. You have such a dynamic effort that is in place. You have all the power you need. You have all the means you need. You need nothing more than thought. It all starts with thought.

Thought, Word, Deed brings all into being. You can be anyone you wish to be. You have greatness and unlimited potential locked within each of you. See life from the perspective of the Cosmos; from out there to down here. See your thoughts, words, deeds reflected in the Cosmos.

Every thought you think goes somewhere. It creates something on some level. You have no idea how powerful your thoughts are. You are a creator "Be"-ing. There is never a time when you are not creating. You have all the means within you to change the world, and to do so in the twinkle of an eye. Just believe it is possible!

Know that your thoughts combined with the thoughts of like-minded others, bring together a force that is unlike any that has ever been known to man. Think only of that which you desire to experience. If you desire peace for the planet, think only of peace. Your combined thoughts will have a megaton energy force that is greater than anything you have ever known.

And so it is.

I am. Amen

How can you change your thoughts to help you birth exactly that which you wish to experience? The power of our thoughts is the greatest "force" in the Universe.

February 27

Message from My Guides: There Is Only NOW

Backwards or forwards in time means nothing outside of this, the third dimension. Outside of the third dimension, all is One – NOW. Everything that has happened millions of years ago is happening NOW. Everything that will happen millions of years in the "future" is happening NOW. There is no "future" outside the third dimension. There is only NOW! NOW is the only time you have. NOW is the creative force of the Universe. NOW is when birth occurs. NOW, everything is possible!

Don't think about it tomorrow. Think about it NOW! NOW! NOW! You are stepping into a new arena of "Be"-ing; an arena that has the possibility of an eternal NOW. "Time," as you know it, is compressing. A month now feels like two weeks. "Time" is changing; expanding or contracting, depending upon how intensely you are concentrating.

When you get a hunch NOT to do something, pay attention. Besides your internal guidance system (IGS), it can be a future aspect of your Self warning you, or a past aspect of your Self warning you. This is why forgiveness is so powerful. It heals the present, the past, and the future all at the same "time."

You are endowed with the creative force of your Creator. Create as your Creator does – with unlimited possibility. Create with that – not with limitation, not with restriction, not with conditions – but only with unlimited possibility. Then you have tapped into the Creative Energy of the Universe. See your Self as the unlimited "Be"-ing that you are, not as the little being you think you are.

I see you in all the glory of the Universe. All light. All power. All shine. No limitations. No restrictions. Pure joy, pure "Be"-ing, pure essence, pure Love, as is your Creator.

And so it is!
Amen!

How can focusing on the NOW reveal to you the "force" of creation? All time is NOW!

February 28

Message from My Guides: Developing Our Spiritual Side

The only "real" problem that you have on this level of existence (the third dimension) is that you feel, think, and believe you are separate from God. That is such bombastic audacity. Most other spheres of creation know that they are One with their Creator. You are on a plane of existence that believes that you created your selves; at least some of you do. In terms of descent into materiality, there is some truth in that: you created your "egos." In terms of your true essence, your essential Self, "who you really are," there is no truth in that whatsoever. You are part of a Divine Whole, a seamless Being that continues to expand.

The planet Earth, in the third dimension (one of the densest planes of existence) is a planet of duality. You see everything from two sides: up/down, good/bad, high/low, black/white, and you judge accordingly. The third dimension is a state of being that encourages you to measure and evaluate, to criticize and judge everything around you.

Give up judgment and learn to live in acceptance of a state of being known in the Buddhist tradition as "what is." "What is" represents a state of being that eventually leads you to a place of unconditional Love. "What is" can be understood after you start to do the internal work necessary to change from critical and judgmental thinking into loving and non-judgmental thinking.

Each person incarnating on this planet comes here in order to find and develop the spiritual side of its "Be"-ing. To allow Spirit to enter into your lives, you have to quiet your lives. There is no other way. You have to quiet your minds, your bodies, your efforts. You have to stop the seeking, the pushing, the busy-ness (business) that keeps you tied up in knots. The pressure you apply to yourselves to "get ahead" is all illusion, and you can let it all go.

You have the means to change the world overnight; in an instant. You have the means to bring peace to the planet; to bring joy, to bring fulfillment, to bring accomplishment, to bring well-being, to bring wholeness and satisfaction to every creature on the planet. In fact, you have no "job" other than that one. There is nothing you "have to do" except to recognize your Self as part of the Whole, part of the Oneness, part of All that is.

Believe that you are being led to your Spirit Self in order to recognize that you are part of the Oneness of creation.

Have you been "nudged" recently to give up your idea of separation from God? We are all part of the Oneness of Being

February 29

A Different Model of Love

According to Almine, a contemporary healer, teacher, and mystic, the current model of Love on this planet (one which repeats itself endlessly) is a triangle involving Love, Control, and Rage: "I love you. Therefore, I think I can control you. When you resist my control, I fly into a rage." This model repeats itself until someone cries *Enough!*

God's model for love is, I love you. Therefore, I trust you to do what is right for your Self and for the "other," because in truth, there is no "other." Thus, I grant you the power to create just as I do, with unconditional Love and with free will to create anything you desire. You will, however, experience the effects of your creations.

Negotiating through the Earth plane, through the restrictions of the power of the ego, is seen by most souls as a difficult challenge. Amnesia from our Source is so total when arriving on the Earth plane that few complete the passage through the birth canal with any memory from whence they came. Those who do are usually held up to ridicule and debasement by those in the grip of *ego* power, which is perceived by most of those who live on this plane as *real* power. This is not Real Power, since Real Power is the power of Love. However, most people on this planet have a convoluted idea of what the power of Love entails.

To know is to love. When we know something, we can love it. As we learn to love our inadequacies, they no longer stay buried deep within our cells. Our Soul is free to rise above that which drags it down. We are free to rise above our problems; above our pain, above our hurts, our anxieties, our inadequacies.

Loving unconditionally (with no concern for the outcome) releases us from our difficulties. It is very hard *not* to be attached to outcomes. Most of us have an idea about how we want things to turn out. God wants for us what our Higher Self wants for each of us. Not many of us have the wherewithal to release our judgment of what we want the outcome to be, but somehow we have to trust that God has it all under control.

To rid ourselves of anything, we need to release our judgment. We release it by letting it go and loving it. Love the cancer. Love the pain. Love the hurt, the agony, the grief; that which we find intolerable. In loving it, we bring light to it. In bringing light to it, we let it go. As we release to the Universe that which we love, our releasing it eliminates its control over us. This is a paradox of the first degree.

That which we hate, we draw to ourselves and increase, simply through our *attention.* The electromagnetic energy of our human energy field attracts more of that very thing we do not want. A good example of this is to reinforce good behavior in a child while ignoring the bad behavior. Control is a factor with each of us on the Earth. By surrendering control to the Source, we no longer have to spend so much energy attempting to keep everything as tightly corralled as possible.

We are all part of a Divine plan. There is no one who knows all the pieces of the plan except the Source. We are all part of a "majestic metaphysical multidimensional" tapestry of Love. That we all fit in somewhere is a given.

Is it possible for you to bring in God's model of unconditional Love as the guiding force in your life? As we learn to love that which we hate, we loosen its grip on us.

Step 2

Make Different Choices

March

Real Power, the power of Love, can never be taken away from us because Real Power is not something that is given to us. It is part of who we really are.

Real Power, the power of Love, does not come and go depending upon our circumstances, and does not need anyone else to validate it. It knows how to accept compliments in the spirit in which they are given, with love and generosity, and does not find a "hidden agenda" within the compliments.

Real Power, the power of Love, knows that the body we occupy on this plane is just a shell, a means to propel us through this dimension. The body is not who we are; it is only the outward casing of who we are. We are so much more than the shell we occupy. We are as vast as the Universe and even beyond that, the Multiverse.

Real Power, the power of Love, comes from the Source of Creation, which is infinite. There is never an instant when Real Power does not exist, although it has many expressions of its existence and uses the many levels and dimensions of the Universe as an expression of its existence.

From the highest to the humblest, Real Power, the power of Love, accepts all men as belonging to one race on this planet; it is called human. There are other races on other planets in this Universe: some of them are human, some are not.

There is an unlimited supply of Real Power, the power of Love, because it comes from the Source. It is not something we get from another; it is not something we give to another; it is not something we take from another; it is something we are!

March 1

Be, Have, Do

The road to happiness according to our current mode of thinking in our culture emphasizes *Do, Have, Be: Do* – work hard and responsibly, *Have* – enough money to buy an advertised product, and *Be* – our ultimate goal; loved, successful, sexy, desirable, accepted, cherished, valued, envied, and happy. Buy this – *do.* Own this – h*ave.* Achieve happiness – *be.* Every sales promotion emphasizes this model. Every commercial sells us this bill of goods.

Spirit's way is opposite the way of materialism. According to Spirit, first comes *Be,* then *Have,* then *Do.* This is a concept beautifully explained in *Conversations with God - Book 1* by Neale Donald Walsch. We are creator *"Be"*-ings – *Be.* We then elect to *choose* (from what we think about) – *Have.* Our results come from our choices – *Do.* We are *all that is,* All That Is; which is another name for God. We are not human *"Do"*-ings; we are human *"Be"*-ings. We are happy when we side with Love and are depressed when we side with Fear.

Is it any mystery that we feel out of sync with our Self? By attempting to live our life backwards, we feel out of sync because we *are* out of sync. As we become oblivious to media bombardment (to the thousands of commercials to which we are subjected) and listen to the feelings inside our own hearts (those feelings lead our hearts to a safe port), we become "in sync;" we come back to the place where we belong.

During my human "doing" period, I took great pride in my work ethic. In my twenties, to keep up with mounting bills from continuous moves during a very unstable first marriage, I worked three jobs and was proud of how many minutes were "booked." During my second marriage, while in my thirties and forties, in addition to having two children, a large home, and a dog, I still worked a sixty-hour week as co-owner (along with my husband) of a small real estate company. My health deteriorated steadily, but that was acceptable as long as I able to check off items daily on my "to do" list.

While I was in the "accumulation" mode, no sacrifice of my time was too great and no demand from my clients went unmet. I shunted family time – nights, weekends, each holiday – until all my joy was gone. Then a jolt from the universe brought to a halt all the unreasonable demands I placed on myself. I bent over to pick up a piece of paper and could not straighten up. That single action changed the direction of my life. I had to re-evaluate what I was doing to myself. So much *busyness* kept me from having to look at my priorities, kept me from pursuing spiritual matters, kept me from choosing those items that made my heart sing.

I was forced to re-evaluate every priority until it was in sync with the desires of my Soul. We cannot buy happiness, but we *can* choose it. Choosing to witness natural beauty, such as the changing phases of the moon, is free. Such a choice brings joy to our hearts, and is available continuously.

How can you incorporate Spirit's model of Be, Do, Have to guide your life? The choices of Be, Do, and Have free us from the grip of materialism.

March 2

Happiness and Kindness

Spirit's law states that we receive only that which we give, and what we *give* is what we *get*. Most of us claim that we *want to be* happy, yet many of us do everything in our power to repel happiness. When we *give* happiness away to others, we *receive* it for ourselves. Paradoxically, though, this only works if we have *no agenda* of our own. We have to give without expectation of receiving something else in return.

We can give happiness to others in the simplest way possible, through kindness: a kind word, a kind gesture, a loving caress, a caring touch, a compliment, a smile. Nothing lifts a body's spirit as much as a smile does. How do we feel when we receive a smile unexpectedly? Time is suspended while everything within us softens and melts. When a baby smiles at us, the tension within us releases: our shoulders relax, our stomachs distend, and the lines around our faces become less taut. As the glow from the eyes of this tiny creature finds us, we stand in awe. The baby's face breaks out into a cherubic smile. We smile and say, *Awwwhhh!*

After we transition to the next dimension, we may be surprised during our life review to find that the *most* important thing we did on any given day was to *smile* at someone, regardless of the significant earthly responsibilities we juggled or the level of "power" we held. Examples of this have been documented by those who do regressive hypnotherapy between lives, such as Michael Newton, Ph.D.

Let us consider displaying patience when exasperation is the way in which we would normally respond. Let us consider using a gentle tone of voice when a heated exchange is more to our liking, or allowing the "other" to have the last word when normally, we would reserve this province for ourselves.

Readjusting our point of view through the lens of kindness increases the amount of happiness coming our way. Acts of kindness, not only to those whom we know and love, but to total strangers – to our service personnel, and to others whom we rarely consider – enrich our lives. Practicing acts of kindness to those who may have become invisible to us enhances our lives in immeasurable ways. If we smile the next time we meet one of those people who support our existence – store clerks, gardeners, highway repair crews, delivery people, sanitation pick-up, phone service personnel, newspaper vendors, doormen, valets, restaurant employees – we may change the entire pattern of our day.

As we increase our awareness of those whom we never hitherto noticed, our awareness of all life around us increases exponentially. We start noticing a world we never knew existed. We may even start to have conversations with objects, flowers, plants, pets and minerals, because we have become so tuned to the Voice inside our head – a Voice that speaks without sound but with feeling, and that feeling is Love. We may become more attuned to the Love that is present in all things; the Love that drives the Universe. We may become attuned to the Oneness that is part of All That Is, all possible because we have chosen to be kind.

How can even one kind act per day change your life? Spreading kindness to whatever we encounter changes the energy around us.

March 3

Debilitating Beliefs

If our underlying belief is that the Universe *does not support* us, then that belief reflects itself not only in the circumstances which surround us but also in the shapes of our bodies as well as our mental conditions.

Any issues we have with support, whether they are financial, emotional, mental, or spiritual, are going to be found in problems with the skeletal frame. If our underlying belief is that the Universe does *not* support us, then somewhere along the way, we may experience a debilitating illness that changes our spinal column, which in turn changes the shape of our jaws, and results in further physical problems. Alternatively, we may find ourselves experiencing difficulties with our knees, or having other skeletal injuries. The skeleton provides the support for the soft muscle tissue that encases the organs.

Since I had issues about support in the financial, emotional, mental, and spiritual areas, it was no wonder that I had curvature of the spine both to the right and to the left. My scoliosis was so extreme that the first chiropractor I went to in Virginia made the diagnosis that I would never be able to carry a baby to term. I was twenty-six at that time and in a very rocky marriage, so a baby was not a priority.

Contrary to that prediction, I did give birth to two very healthy, full-term babies during my second marriage. However, I didn't explore the issues about what my spine represented until many years later. Because my spine was so badly curved, my neck was also out of line, which caused the bottom half of my jaw to move in one direction and the top half of the jaw to move in another. Eventually, my jaw started to unhinge and clicked when I chewed. The corrective measure (since I refused to allow surgery on my jaw) was to wear braces for five years in order to re-establish my bite. Ultimately, Rolfing (a form of deep tissue massage) worked miracles in correcting my spinal curvature. Now, my acupuncturist, during my monthly visit, claims that sometimes there is no curvature whatsoever.

If we find ourselves in circumstances in which a debilitating belief undermines our health, then we need to *choose a different belief system*. One way to do this is to state *affirmations* confirming that the Universe *does* sustain us. By taking the time to think about how the Universe supports us – how the many people in our life help us achieve what we desire – we change from having a debilitating belief to having an empowering one. We can do this no matter how impoverished our circumstances may be, and no matter how little money we earn, with or without a support system. It is all up to us.

Vocalizing affirmations without believing them is an empty gesture. It does not work! But vocalizing affirmations with *belief and feeling* does work. This applies to any set of circumstances in which we find ourselves. If we do not like what our choices have created, we can always choose differently.

Some people, believing that only that which their senses validate is "real," state: *I will believe it when I see it.* Unfortunately, the Universe does not work that way. The Law of the Universe, natural law, states: *You see it* because *you believe it.* Everything depends on our belief system.

What impossible thing do you believe you can accomplish?

What underlying belief is holding you back?
Debilitating beliefs can be changed.

March 4

Clearing Out Limiting Beliefs

If we are relentlessly pursuing goals that we have set for ourselves, and our lives are not working, we may choose to stop and question, *What is wrong? What is my purpose? Where am I supposed to be? Why is my life not working?*

When old debilitating beliefs no longer serve us, we can choose to clear them out of our energy fields. If we do not like what we experience in our lives, by changing our *underlying beliefs,* we change the conditions that magnetize the experience towards us.

Clearing out old limiting beliefs (those that keep us in fear) is similar to cleaning out anything: a car, a desk drawer, a purse, a home, an office, a closet, a cabinet, an attic, or a garage. The easiest way – perhaps the *only* way – to really rid ourselves of the entire jumble is to remove everything from the space that it occupies, look at each item we have removed, and put back only that which we wish to keep. This is easy to do with physical objects, and is harder to do with an energy field that is cluttered with emotional and mental debris.

Imagine what happens to our bodies when we start clearing out beliefs, emotions, attitudes, and attributes that no longer serve us. We like to credit our own creations as being someone else's creations, and to point fingers at others as the cause of our misery. We need to excavate deeper and deeper in order to release by-products of the stuff we keep hidden in the deepest crevices of our consciousness and sub-consciousness. What we have refused to release up until now *all has to go.*

This *is* going to be painful. Clearing out any wound is painful. Keeping the dirt in it, and putting a Band-Aid over it, is even more painful in the long run. Instead of just putting Band-Aids over our fears, we must clear out the fears. This means removing all the attitudes and beliefs that come from fear: blame, judgment, guilt, hate, bigotry, prejudice, debasement, ridicule, sarcasm. The list is endless. *It all has to go.* Is this easy? No. Is it necessary? Yes. We can no longer keep that which destroys our peace of mind.

To clear out fear, we tune into the *voiceless voice* within; we turn to the stillness of our Self, from which we can receive internal guidance. This *voiceless voice* attempts to reach us at all times, but we hear it only in the silence of our own heart. As we calm our minds, center our emotions, clear the churning of worldly concerns, and turn down the worries, we begin to tune into the silence of our own hearts to listen for answers. These answers then settle softly into our awareness.

We have compacted ourselves for eons with negativity. NOW is the time to let it all go. We can choose love or stay in fear. Choosing love causes more upheaval in our lives than staying in fear. Staying in fear preserves the status quo. Choosing love opens new venues for us. New is scary. Old is painful, but old is familiar. At least we know that which we must tolerate. New takes us into the unknown. We cannot have new without first releasing the old.

To clear out old debilitating beliefs, we need to identify them, and then make different choices from the ones we have made in eons past.

Which limiting belief can you identify and choose to release? Eliminate one debilitating belief at a time.

March 5

Find the Peace Within

We say that we want peace in the world. First, we must *make peace within ourselves.* We each must choose to create peace within. To *have* peace, we must first *be* peace. If we wish to witness others engaged in peaceful acts around us, we must first anchor peace in all the circumstances of our own lives. This means giving up the "normal" ways in which we react to stimuli that we consider to be "not peaceful."

When we begin bringing peaceful reactions to everything that we do, we witness others *do*ing things that bring peace into our own lives, not only on a personal and neighborhood level, but on a community, national, and global scale as well. Global transformation begins within.

It all starts with self; a self who makes different choices, led by the wisdom of Higher Self. We cannot cure ills "out there" while we hold onto ills within ourselves. If we claim that we want peace in the world, but react with wrath because someone does not load the dishwasher properly, then we break the chain reaction of gratitude and acceptance that comes from accepting peacefully someone else's assistance.

If we feel superior toward anyone, our distorted thinking pollutes our energy field. This applies to global as well as personal levels. The negative thinking of the people of this planet has long polluted the energy field of Mother Earth. Fortunately, positive thinking helps to clear it. Also, working with the *Purple Transformational Flame of St. Germaine* (an Ascended Master concerned with escorting negativity to its next place of evolution) helps to transform this planet into one of peace.

There is nothing that we *have to do,* except to change ourselves. Peace is not "out there." When we find peace *within,* then we will see it *out there*, because all is a reflection of what is within. It all starts with self, because the ego self is a stepped-down version of the Higher Self who is our direct connect to God. The denser energies of both our ego self and the finer energies of our Higher Self comprise layers of esoteric energy all the way back to the Source. Our lack of awareness of our connection to the Source does not affect the connection from whence we came, any more than closing our eyes affects the room we are in. We can be as aware of our connection to Source, or unaware of it, as we choose.

Eliminating negativity within us eliminates negativity outside of us. We cannot get rid of a boil on our body without bringing the puss to the surface. Holding onto negativity of any type keeps the puss within our body. All negative thoughts affect us. Our negative thoughts *go somewhere,* either within our energy field or within the energy field of Mother Earth, so we need to guard our thoughts carefully.

Mother Mary, in *Mary's Message to the World*, authored by Annie Kirkwood, said, "If you only knew what your negative thoughts look like, you would never think them."

What type of peaceful action can you implement each day? Peace begins within. Choose peace first.

Creations within Us

We have everything *within us* to master that which we need to do in this lifetime. If we are given an idea, then we are also given the means to bring that idea to fruition. Our "acre of diamonds," is within, as Earl Nightingale proclaims in his tape *Lead the Field.* We are not given a nudge to do something that is totally out of grasp for us, no matter how remote it may seem at first. Spirit does not tantalize us with ridiculous possibilities that cannot be achieved by us. Spirit does not work that way.

We are the ones who self-abort our creations before we give them a chance to birth. Not only do we abort our creations prematurely, but we also sabotage our creations after birthing them when we are not willing to put forth the effort to flesh them out. Julie Cameron, in *The Artist's Way,* comments, "You are willing to write your Oscar acceptance speech, but you are not willing to get up to go to acting class."

"If God brings us *to it,* God will bring us *through it*" (a quote from the wisdom shared on the internet) applies both to ideas as well as personal tragedies. Whatever major circumstances we find in our lives will be that to which, on some level, our Higher Self has agreed. Our personality-self "fills in the blanks" with the ways in which we choose to react to all the major and minor details of our life. Spirit never abandons us in our efforts to slog through our tragedies, neither are we abandoned in our efforts to flesh out our great ideas. We are *never* alone in whatever endeavors we pursue.

Choose to start by gathering your great ideas in a folder and separating them by topic. You may find that you already have the beginning of a magazine article, a pamphlet, or a book – even if it is based only on personal tragedy. There are some lives that are simply not funny, no matter how you look for the humor. Herbert Ross, one of the founders of *The New Yorker* magazine said, "If you can't be funny, be interesting." Maybe you fit into that category.

I have never considered the possibility of becoming a brain surgeon, but I have considered the possibility of becoming a writer, simply because I love to read great literature and the universal themes expounded in these substantial works. Similarly, poetry takes me into the outer reaches of my imagination and bathes my Soul with light. Finally, I have throughout my entire life always chosen to put my feelings or my thoughts down on paper.

The possibility of becoming a public speaker feels natural, because I love to talk. Talking, whether to one person or to a small group of people, has always energized me, and I am comfortable speaking in front of large groups. Every speech I give at *Service to Spirit* in the Rays of Healing Church helps me perfect the art of public speaking. Practice and consistency make my ability even better.

The first time I spoke to a general audience – one not related to a church or an energy healing group – brought out fear within me. My colleagues from the National Speaker's Association (DC Chapter) witnessed this when I gave my *first* speech to them, as part of the DC Chapter's Fast Track program. (This was an opportunity offered by them for those who were serious about jump starting a speaking career.) I shook so badly that I had to hold the microphone in both hands. In my effort to speak from the heart, I had not memorized my speech. As a result, I stumbled on some words and did not include others that were critical to the speech. I never saw the "One-minute left" time marker that was held up, but did see the one that said, "Cut your speech now!" That did not help my composure.

Fear welled within me because I was proclaiming my affinity for spiritual matters for the *first* time in a public arena. No longer was I speaking to a nice, safe, small group of like-minded people. My topic about Reiki and chakras was something I did not think my audience of over one hundred well-seasoned public speakers would find relevant. However, I was determined to speak on this topic, even though the audience might find me strange or even turn against me.

I received comments on my evaluation sheets ranging from: "You have an Angelic presence," to "Don't be afraid. You have a very important point to make!" to "What was your point?" Three people rushed up to me afterwards. One commented on the fact that he, too, had been a Reiki practitioner but no longer practiced actively, and two others asked about classes in Reiki, the energy healing modality which I had described in my talk.

Because I had birthed the idea that I, too, could become a public speaker on spiritual matters, the Universe rewarded me with support arriving from many sources. My public speeches continued to be on topics close to my heart, just as the things about which I write.

What creations within you are waiting to be birthed? The Universe supports us in our attempt to bring forth the best that is within us.

March 7

Moving On

It is not *what* happens to us that counts; it is our *reaction to* what happens to us that makes the difference. Stuff happens. Bad stuff. Horrible stuff. Really tragic stuff. Some of us allow it to roll off our backs, pick up the pieces, and go on. Others of us collapse under the weight of the slightest transgressions. Some of us drug ourselves so as not to feel what happens, or live our lives looking up from the bottom of a bottle. Some of us bury ourselves under mountains of work, so that we do not have the time to think about what happens. Still others of us find our solace in sameness, and cannot tolerate even the slightest alteration to routine.

While dealing with an utterly senseless tragedy, my father became one of the silent heroes of my life. Shortly after my parent's twenty-fifth wedding anniversary, at a time when they felt successful, happy, and fulfilled, and were looking forward to buying a cottage on a lake in Michigan, they were the victims of a land subsidence. The ground underneath their home collapsed three feet in ten seconds. Within days, a cavern appeared that was thirty feet deep and twenty feet wide. Long thick boards extended from solid ground to underneath their home to keep the house from falling into this pit. It took a year before they were able to save enough money to move the home to another lot and reconnect to public services.

The insurance company refused to pay for the damages since they considered it an *Act of God.* This was Grand Rapids, Michigan in 1966. Sinkholes *did not exist* in Grand Rapids, Michigan. No one was there to help them: not the city, nor the state, nor the insurance company, nor the attorneys. No attorney would take a case against the city of Grand Rapids or against Kent County. The church to which they belonged collected $1,000 to assist, while quiet whispers circulated amongst the parishioners that my parents must have done something horrible to "deserve" such a tragedy.

I had just started my junior year at the University of Michigan. The week before this subsidence, I became teary-eyed, started to pace in my apartment, and called home to find out if everyone was all right. I went down the list of family members and was assured by my mother that everyone was fine. It was just a normal quiet Sunday afternoon.

One week later, in the middle of the night, at 3:20 am, tragedy struck. A loud *CRACK* thundered and awakened everyone. My mother, rushing outside, nearly broke a leg stepping onto the front stoop that was three feet lower than it should have been.

Shortly after, I remember coming home, walking into the kitchen and looking at my father. He looked like a tired old lion. In 1965, he was only forty-nine years old, but that day he looked eight-nine. He just sat there quietly, drumming his fingers on the table and never saying a word, mulling over what to do next. Ultimately, they moved into temporary shelter for a year. They continued to shore up the home until the transport company felt it was safe to get close enough to move the home to another lot a few streets away. Then, my parents continued to maintain the empty lot. The sinkhole was filled, opened up again, and was refilled. The grass was cut every week, and year after year, the taxes on the lot were dutifully paid to the state of Michigan.

My parents moved one last time, in 1979, two years before my mother's death. This time the move was to a brand new, solid brick home which they had built in a beautiful neighborhood, framed by gently rolling hills on the northwest side of Grand Rapids. They never gave up. They continued to work, save, and move forward. My father lived until 1987. He died the same day Edsel Ford died; on Oct 19, 1987 – Black Monday, the single largest loss of stock value since the crash in 1929 – a fitting end to his life.

When my sister, the executor of my father's estate, went to "settle" with the county to "deed" the lot back to them after my father's death, the city executive could not look her in the eye. The lot, originally sold by the city to the developer for $1.00 "at your own risk," should have never been sold in the first place.

One of the women at my father's funeral told me that when she was a child, she and the neighborhood children who always played on that lot had called it the "mystery lot." They would leave something there, a mound of twigs, a pile of stones, or a discarded toy, and the next day it would be gone. The vacant land, used for construction refuse when the developer bought it, *originally had been a sinkhole.*

Obviously, my parents had been dealt a huge lesson in forgiveness. They were able to reclaim their lives because they *chose* to forgive and were *able* to forgive. They did not stay stuck and lament the past. They did not continue to live in a house of regret for what "should have" been. They forgave and moved forward; moved on with their life.

My parents, through their example, gave me one of the greatest gifts I have ever received. Whenever I have felt at an impasse, I too, have learned to forgive and move on.

Is there a forgiveness issue with which you need to deal; one that is keeping you from moving on? We free ourselves from the molasses of regret when we forgive.

March 8

Healing with Energy

Christ was a clear channel for Divine energy, and he used the same energy to heal that is used today. By aligning with the Christ Consciousness – a grid of consciousness in the sixth dimension that envelopes the Earth – we can learn to channel the same energy that Christ channeled.

My favorite story from the New Testament of the Bible about energy healing is in Mark 5:28-34. (This story, the *Woman with a Hemorrhage*, is actually a story within the larger story about the *Daughter of Jairus*.) Jesus, in midst of a large crowd, is summoned by a synagogue official whose daughter is critically ill. A woman in the throng, afflicted with a hemorrhage for a dozen years, thinks to herself: "If I just touch his clothing, I shall get well." She does so. Jesus, becoming conscious that healing power has gone *through* him, asks: "Who touched me?" The apostles are mystified by his question because of the multitude of people thronged around him; pressing against him.

Jesus knew, despite the number of people who pressed around him, that one of them touched him with *the intent to heal.* As he continued looking around, she came forward to tell him the truth. He answered: "Daughter, your faith has made you well; go in peace and be healed of your affliction." (Luke 8:48)

We find an identical attitude in the people who come to us for energy healing. What heals them *is their faith* that the energy which we channel through us *will* heal them. Without that faith, what happens? That depends on the soul's contract of the person to be healed. A person who does not believe in energy healing never asks for it for themselves. If a friend of a person who is ill is determined to send healing to an "other" who has not requested it, then the Higher Self of the person for which the healing is intended directs the healing. Free will is never violated, no matter how good the intention. If the person for whom the healing is intended would not choose to accept healing for themselves, then that healing is directed towards someone else who would benefit.

We have witnessed people who believed they could be healed but did not wish to change anything about their thinking that made them ill in the first place. As fast as we put the energy into their body, it leaked out and they were not healed.

We have much work to do on this planet. There is not a second to waste. The phrase, *time waits for no one*, simply means that we are to take this moment and allot it to our highest good. If we are drawn to energy healing, we could explore various sites on the internet that offer information: classes, places where people gather to do energy healing, or books on healing. If we do not own a computer, public libraries offer the service for free.

Resources abound once we seek them out: there are bookstores devoted entirely to metaphysical topics and major chains that carry a metaphysical section, as well as the public library. Free magazines devoted entirely to metaphysical themes and energy healing modalities, paid for by the advertisers, can be found in bookstores, in health food stores, and in gift shops devoted to spiritual matters. These all become resources for classes and healing.

We have so much power to channel energy – to be instruments of direct healing – we simply have to believe in our power and accept it. We *are* the most powerful beings ever created; the *only one* of God's creations who can pass *light* through our hands. (When those who have a *healing* pet take offense at this remark, please remind them that pets have paws, not hands.) We have *incredible abilities* to heal, and thus are healers if we *choose to be.* We come to this planet first in order to heal ourselves, and then to accept ourselves as the instruments of healing.

The most powerful words on the planet are *I Am*, since the words *I Am* have the power of the *Source* behind them. *I Am* – another name for the Source – creates with the same intensity that the Source uses. We need to carefully choose the words we place after saying *I Am.* If we can understand the power of these two words, we begin to understand the power of who we really are. When we say, *I am a healer,* we set our intent to channel energy from the Source in order *to* heal. We harness the energy from the Source, from God, to bring positive energy through us to the "other," while helping us clear out negative energy.

By understanding the power of these words, we begin to understand the power of who we really are. We are the most powerful "Be"-ing ever created, and thus need to choose our words carefully.

Do you feel that you have a "natural ability" to heal? Explore all the avenues that open that lead to energy healing.

March 9

Choose to Live in the NOW without Fear

Each thought brings with it a choice. I once spent an entire weekend at a seminar called *The Forum* learning the concept that even when I choose *not to choose,* I have made a choice – *the choice not to choose.* Every thought is a choice.

We can choose from a position of Love or from a position of Fear. It is all our choice. When we choose from a position of Love, we are more than just passive observers. We actively anchor the higher energies on this planet and interact with the Spiritual plane on a daily basis to guide our thoughts, words, and actions.

We say we are opposed to fear, yet never seem to get away from it – since fear knows no boundaries. We are afraid we are not physically attractive enough, handsome enough, thin enough, witty enough, bright enough, or financially secure enough. We are afraid of being exposed as a fraud. *Stop!* Enough already! By giving up our thoughts of fear, we let go of operating in a state of fear. We do not allow others to govern us through fear, nor can we be manipulated by fear. Thus, we free our Self to make other choices.

If my daily habits caused me to live in fear, breathe in fear, and ingest fear, this was all due to choices I made. I finally realized that when my ego led me through a path of fear, I was in a maze of my own making.

Trying to foresee all the possibilities is ludicrous and prevents us from any joy in our life. We think we can foresee all possibilities. We cannot. In that, our actions are not only irrational, they are insane, because our thinking is insane. Those of us who try to predict all possibilities are usually paralyzed with the fear; we think that we are forgetting something important. If it is truly important, Spirit reminds us of it when necessary.

We have no faith when we come from fear. Our lack of faith is exemplified by our lack of trust in the present; in fact, most of us *miss* the present since our actions are designed to keep us *soooo* busy providing for the future. We do not. We provide for the NOW! That is all we have. We create in the NOW! What we create in the NOW is what our future brings to us.

Taking action in the NOW – when we have a chance to do so – insures us that we will have no regret that opportunities have passed us by. If we see life as a "risk," we will not live our life with any degree of fullness and might not take opportunities that life offers us for pleasure, for enjoyment, for rest, for relaxation, for enrichment, or for grace. Rather, we may hold opportunities away from ourselves.

Time is an illusion. What helps us understand and make sense of our world moves us into a state of continuous NOW. Many times our ego causes us to live our life looking at the past or looking forward to the future, with scarcely a passing glance to the present. Unfortunately, there *is* only the present and it *is* an "everlasting moment;" an eternal NOW.

Eckhart Tolle, the author of *The Power of Now*, helps imbed this concept into our psyche. The total focus and concentration of his life is to teach us stay in the NOW, both through his written as well as his spoken words. He creatively provides an endless assortment of descriptions that exemplify the power of staying in the NOW.

Listen and learn.

What is the most gripping fear you can let go of NOW? Learn to live in the NOW, the only place we live.

March 10

Forgiving Old Wounds

To forgive is to break the cycle of karma that we inhabit. When we are able to look at our brother through a "cosmic lens" – when we are able to see that our brother *is* our *Self* – we also see that there is *nothing* to forgive, because in essence we are forgiving ourselves. That which we do not release through forgiveness is what binds us to the next cycle; thus history repeats itself. The power within us to change our past is through forgiveness.

Can you recall the most *important* thing you wanted to *have* ten, twenty, forty, sixty, or eighty years ago; the item you coveted above all others? Probably not. But you can recall what *traumatized* you, what hurt you; what you need to forgive from ten, twenty, forty, sixty, or eighty years ago.

No amount of "remembering" our hurts will make us whole again, or change the memory of their anguish. Unfortunately, we hold on to our old wounds, bring them out, re-examine them, even show them off, and then stuff them back in. We specialize in what Caroline Myss (author of *Why People Don't Heal and How They Can*) calls "woundology;" parading out old wounds as part of our identity. Yet, no amount of re-counting our hurts alters them in the least. No amount of re-airing our grievances dissolves the fact that they happened.

Only *we* can change the negative power they hold over us, for the power to change comes from within. We can change any memory from the past that gives us pain. We free the past from hurting us by *forgiving* the past. Forgiveness is the key to re-aligning ourselves back with God and back to Real Power.

We must forgive our hurts. They are *nothing!* They only have the power *we* give them. Forgive them and they will disappear. We need not hold on to old wounds, grudges, hatreds, misunderstandings, slights, injustices, or fears. We no longer need terror, remorse, guilt, or any other type of pain. When we hold on to old grievances, we shadow-box with memories.

When we build our wall of hurts around us, we build a house of regret. It has no more substance than our shadow does, yet it is very real to us. What can we do with it? What can it do for us? Yet, we constantly look to align ourselves with it. It is like trying to align with a puff of smoke: "there" for a few seconds, then gone.

We have been here before. We will come here again until we learn to forgive and *let go* of every thought we feel that is unloving. The greatest pain that anyone has inflicted on us is one that we *may have* inflicted on them in some previous "time." Those painful experiences may have been a quest for wisdom.

As we forgive ourselves, we forgive the world. We give birth to a new paradigm based on love which expands throughout the land.

Who is at the top of your forgiveness list?
Forgiveness takes us off the wheel of karma.

March 11

Advanced Souls

We are created perfect. Even if we have a birth defect, imperfection exists only in the mind of the ego. According to the mind of Spirit, only perfection exists.

The most enlightened souls take on the biggest burdens. The souls who agree to a mental, physical, or emotional challenge – and the parents or other caregivers who agree to nurture them – are all advanced souls. Advanced souls may wish to become teachers of the mentally, physically, or emotionally challenged in the next lifetime, thus are willing to endure the same challenge in this lifetime.

Parents experiencing extreme pain because of the suffering their children endure, parents who nurture a child through a coma, through cancer treatment, through a heart condition, paralysis, or muscular degeneration, are also advanced souls. Part of the perfection of the Divine plan is that only advanced souls agree to such a mission, for the spirit of a new soul or a young soul would be crushed.

Advanced souls access their cell memory when adjusting to living the life of an emotionally, mentally, or physically challenged person. There is that part of them, the part attached to the Divine, that rises to the challenge provided. Even though Timothy Ramie, in his exceptional book called *New Revelations,* states that we can access our entire cell memory through our bones, we would become too ungrounded and unable to function on this planet if all cell memory was available to us at all times. Memories released selectively to advanced souls help them to function when under crisis.

While caroling on the children's wing of one of our local hospitals, I once witnessed a baby clinging to her mother, resting her little head softly on her mother's shoulder, her sorrowful eyes looking hurt and bewildered. I could only imagine how abandoned this precious little one-year old felt when her mother had to leave her. Only an advanced soul would agree to do this. It is difficult enough to incarnate here without the additional trauma of being separated from a nurturing mother.

Fortunately, we are being deluged with advanced souls. "Every baby born into the world is a finer one than the last," as Charles Dickens astutely observed over one hundred years ago. Advanced souls are arriving in legion numbers on the planet, but are *sometimes* misdiagnosed as having ADD (Attention Deficit

Disorder) or ADHD (Attention Deficit and Hyperactive Disorder). Thus they are overmedicated to "slow them down." Sometimes those who genuinely need help might be denied it.

These tiny advanced souls are arriving on the planet in record numbers. Simply watching them move, barely twelve months old, as they explore their world, is wondrous. Their verbal skills are acute. Two-year-olds are using sentences that seem very clever in six-year-olds. Ask any three-year old who s/he was when s/he was "big," and listen to their answer without judgment and without correction of the "facts." We have the right to be astonished at their answers, for advanced souls have memory of from whence they came.

Although they are considered egocentric, these advanced souls – even as babies – have an innate sense of their own perfection and "know" they are perfect. Whether they laugh, follow colors or movement with their eyes, pacify themselves by poking a fist in their mouth, or bellow and cry, they have their own innate sense of perfection that endears them to us. Whether rolling around in their crib, looking up curiously from their carrier, delighting in any fraction of attention lavished on them, they exude precociousness.

Imagine looking at an infant in its cradle. Feel the peace that enters your body as you watch the small shudder that runs through their tiny shoulders. Imagine picking up the child. Watch a baby's head look down to one side before coyly looking up again, raising then lowering his or her head repeatedly, and then breaking into a soft smile.

We even become mesmerized just watching such babies sleep.

There is something so blessed about witnessing what a new life represents.

Can you see the perfection of a challenged child in a different light?
Only advanced souls take on mental, physical, or emotional challenges.

March 12

Harm No One or No Thing – Ever

Each soul has the right to evolve *in its own way* towards the Light. When we choose to control anything or anyone for our own personal gain, we activate the Universal Law of Cause and Effect. Whatever we sow, we reap. We cannot sow war and expect to harvest peace. We cannot sow greed and expect to harvest generosity. We cannot impose our political system on another culture, and expect to harvest harmony and lack of resistance. This is so, no matter how "right" we think we are, or whether we feel we are acting out of "Divine" right.

We each have the free will to create whatever we choose, but we do not have the right to impose our will on an "other" to do them harm, *no matter what our justification may be.* Far too often, we choose to harm an "other" in the name of God, saying that it is *God's will* to justify whatever atrocities we impose on the "other."

This applies to nations as well as to individuals. Anyone who points to their "sacred literature" as justification for their cruelties forgets that no God, by whatever name that energy is called, is interested in or demanding of any type of assault on the "other" for any reason whatsoever. *That is man's interpretation.*

Unconditional Love is just that; love with no strings attached. A God of unconditional Love *places no demands* on anyone for any special *needs.* A Supreme Being, no matter what this Being is called, *has no special needs.* Only man throughout the eons put those needs in place, usually to justify the most horrible atrocities. In his book, *The New Revelations: A Conversation with God,* Neale Donald Walsch goes into great detail about this concept. Well worth reading and digesting.

I am the type of person who escorts moths, spiders, and bugs outdoors because I take the phrase *harm no one or nothing ever* pretty seriously. Also, I'll have a serious talk with the Deva of Ants to let her know that the ants infesting my home have to leave because if they don't, they will be sprayed with pesticide. Most of the time, within a short time, they are gone. As I do this, I imagine a world where everyone does the same.

We do not live in a vacuum on this planet. We are tied to every living creature, as well as each "stationary" one. All of Nature is alive and is being threatened by the human. We are the caretakers of the Earth. However, our stewardship – to date – is a failure. Fortunately, many activist groups are awakening to the needs of the planet; to our responsibility to the Earth and all of her inhabitants.

As we learn about the consequences of our thoughts and our actions, we are more willing to make different choices.

How much peace do you bring to your current life? Foresee an era free from violence and war to make peace a reality.

March 13

Reasons to Come to This Planet

As President Lincoln said, "People are just about as happy as they make up their minds to be." Some people seem to lead such charmed lives. Every decision they make benefits them. Blessings trail them wherever they go. No matter what the circumstances, they are happy. If we take the time to question them, we find out that this is so because their underlying belief is to *be* happy.

Other people seem to have nothing but bad news that follows them from birth to death. A wall of tears surrounds them. Each new circumstance and every thought they think contributes to this wall, until it barricades their *personality self* and prevents them from accessing any higher knowing. These people become experts at burying emotions, which enlarges their wall of tears. They feel that nothing ever happens to them to cause them to *be* happy, no matter how pleasurable the event may be.

Some of us have a very good reason for our fatalistic thoughts. Certain ones of us may have brought very painful feelings into this incarnation, and do not know from whence these feelings come.

If you are one of those who look at life through a wall of tears, please know that you have a choice. You can choose to think otherwise.

Sometimes, painful occurrences exist to offer us a form of *resistance*; to help us meet and overcome the challenges of this lifetime. As we continue to search, our spiritual quest reveals to us the source of those feelings; we learn to access the memories that make the feelings comprehensible.

Some people incarnate on this planet simply to be observers. They are not here to fulfill any function other than that – just to *be*. They might be young souls, or they may be in (what is described by Spirit as) a "restful" life. Even in a restful life, people are free to choose whatever attitudes they wish to have as their guiding light. If they choose to *be* happy, then no matter what circumstances they are confronted with, they see life through the lens of happiness.

Each person has his or her role to play on this planet. Besides coming here just to observe, some are here to relax and rest. Others are here to toil and suffer – or so they think. Some are here to assist an "other" to learn spiritual lessons; others are here to lead. Some are here to guide, still others are here to be a catalyst for change. Each soul has a role and each role is "useful." No role is ever "wasted."

Sometimes, we can be more "useful" to our soul's spiritual advancement at the end of our life than at any other time, even if we have Alzheimer's disease, simply because we have less ego invested and more heart. During a period of dementia, none of the ego issues that drove our life are in the forefront. To the ego mind, we have reverted back into infancy. To the Spirit mind, we are given more opportunity to commune with Spirit, since there is little else we can do.

If we are an embittered "Be"-ing, only invested in ego issues, we will recycle again, in order to learn to lessen the grip of the ego on our personality. Only when we invest in matters of the heart, can we understand who it is that we really are and why we choose to incarnate on this planet. The Divine makes every attempt to reach us, but it is up to us to listen.

Are painful memories resurrecting painful feelings you cannot explain? Any feeling, no matter what the source, can be changed.

March 14

Expanding Our "Sight"

All come here to learn, to re-member, to become One with the whole, to join in union with every other Spirit. Every soul is an aspect of the Divine, but has agreed to *forget* about this part of its "Be"-ing when it arrives here. The challenge of this planet is for each soul to *reconnect* to that memory. This is a planet of healing. Souls from the entire Universe – their many varied experiences ranging from the very enlightened to the very dark – arrive here, where they continue to play out their respective roles; that which the ego judges to be either "good" or "bad."

We are never separate from the Light; we just think we are. The physical body we occupy is composed of the smallest parts of our being, whose properties are composed of particles of light. Light is who we are; light is where we came from; light is that to which we return. We come from light, and we return to light. We understand this concept once we leave this dimension, but are striving for understanding while still on this planet.

We think we are separate because we see separate bodies with our physical eyes; totally understandable since we *have* separate bodies. However, the physical senses reveal only the minutest portion of who we really are. Scientists have long touted that we use only a small portion of our brain. What about the rest? What does it do? If a large portion of our brain is lying fallow, is it not arrogant to say that the five sense reveal it all? What about the other portion? What might it reveal?

What we see now with our physical eyes is that which we think we are; however, only when we develop our *spiritual sight* will we be able to really "see" the fullness of what exists. Furthermore, what we think, we *think we see.* We put in place that which we *think* is there. This lesson became clear to me as I received acupuncture treatments a few years ago. The Chinese doctor always had a habit of putting me into an empty room after the treatment, even though each room contained two beds and, typically, other patients were doubled up. One morning, as he entered the room, I expected him to approach me, but instead, he walked *past* my bed. As I followed his direction, I was shocked to see a woman dressed in a bright red sweater and dark blue jeans – an outfit *no one could have possibly missed* – laying on the second bed. Yet, because I did not *expect* anyone to be in the room when I was brought in, I saw it as vacant.

Outside of this dimension, our Spirit overlaps with every other Spirit, just as the ripples on a stream overlap with each other. Ripples cannot separate themselves from the stream, no more than a wave can separate itself from the ocean. In the same manner, we cannot separate our Self from the creator "Be"-ing we are, or separate our Self from the Creator from Who we come.

There is no separation in Spirit. Each of us is part of each other and part of the Whole. We do nothing to an "other," for there is no "other"; there is only One. What we do to an "other" is that which we do to ourselves, for there is only Self. Why would we hurt an "other?" We are only hurting ourselves. We choose to help an "other" because we are only helping our Self, since there is no "other." We gain spiritual sight as we accept these concepts.

The opening to spiritual sight starts when we begin healing our idea of separation. When we first think, *Who am I? What is my purpose? Why am I here?* these questions give Spirit a wedge; an ability to enter our stream of consciousness in order to expand our *awareness* of Spirit. These questions lead us to question our higher purpose; to seek a reason for our existence other than that which is evident on the surface. As we open ourselves to this inquiry, we give Spirit the license to answer. Throughout our existence, our greatest gift – free will – is never going to be trampled on by the Divine aspect of our Self. Spirit waits for our invitation.

How we choose to think of each other is entirely up to us. When we choose to think we are part of a *whole*, we feel much better.

Did you ever "see" something that was not there? Choose to see the "whole" instead of separation.

March 15

The Power of Group Thought

The "collective unconscious," as Carl Jung calls it – the collective thoughts of every person on this planet – *lives* somewhere. It lives in the mental body of Mother Earth and guides group action on this planet.

Thought precedes deed. Group thought, or consensus reality – the group opinion of others – *precedes* group action. There is tremendous power in group thought. Just ask Madison Avenue. Companies are willing to spend over a million dollars to air a thirty-second ad on Super Bowl Sunday, so that they can convince as many people as possible, as quickly as possible, to purchase their product. They capitalize on the established *hunger* within the mass populace psyche in order to push their product towards filling that hunger. Unfortunately, the emptiness that most people feel cannot be filled with "things," no matter how great the status symbol may be. Further, as a new *hunger* is identified, a new status symbol is quickly put into place as the next *best thing* that we should seek. In the meantime, seventy percent of the American population is living beyond their means, drowning in credit card debt, escalating the fear that they feel.

Individual thought, linked together as group thought, is far more powerful than just the number of people involved, because its power increases exponentially. We can stop Madison Avenue's control of our psyche. Our models change because *individual thought changes*. Group thought changes our experience exponentially. Two people thinking the same thing is 2 to the 2nd power, the equivalent of *four* people thinking the same thing. But *eight* people thinking the same thing is 8 to the 8th power, or the equivalent of *sixteen million, seven-hundred seventy-seven-thousand, two-hundred sixteen (16,777,216)* people thinking similar thoughts. (To prove this to yourself, multiply 8x8x8x8x8x8x8x8.) *Like-minded people change group thought*. This is why a small number of people, meditating on a singular thought or purpose, can exert such a profound influence.

How do we change the paradigm of fear in which the world is trapped? We start with the individual. We change the world not only by changing our thinking, but also by aligning with people who share like-minded thoughts with us. By doing this, we tap into consensus reality; the group opinion of others who agree with us. As we do this, we exponentially increase the effect of our thinking. A good example can be found in government. The concept of democracy was amplified when the people of Athens brought it to the forefront. The Romans further expanded this concept before it moved from the Old World to the New World.

How hard is it to get eight people to think the same thought? Not very, but the established religions and governments are counting on inertia: the fact that we continue to think about the same restrictions as did our parents. But, we can fool them. We can choose to *think thoughts of peace* when nothing but talk of war swirls around us.

Our thoughts of peace, combined with thoughts of peace from other people around the world, do change the paradigm of fear to one of peace, for action follows thought.

Why is aligning with like-minded people so important to this planet? There is tremendous power in group thought.

March 16

An Exciting Time in Which to Live

This era will usher in a thousand years of peace, according to the beliefs of many indigenous peoples. For more than a millennium, many indigenous tribes have been given different "signs" which will predicate the start of a new era of peace. A white buffalo (the sign given to the Hopi tribe) was born a few years ago in the southwestern part of the United States. This gave the Hopi tribe hope that peace was indeed coming to the planet.

Many believe that we are living in the "end times," as predicted in the book of Revelations in the Bible: a prophecy of God's wrath, loathsome diseases, pestilence, doom and gloom. They point to the dysfunctional segments of society that are causing chaos on the planet and predict extensive Earth changes and massive loss of human life. While some clearing of the planet is taking place (as is evident by the violent outbursts of Mother Nature), the major shift has been one of a deepening level of consciousness. The function of a prophecy is to change the consciousness of humanity; to change the thinking and the ways of the inhabitants of the planet. "A fulfilled prophecy is a failed prophecy," states Mother Mary in *Mary's Message to the World*, by Annie Kirkwood.

Why is the idea of a thousand years of peace, related to a shift in consciousness, so fearful to some? Although a shift in consciousness need not be fearful, many existing societal structures would be impacted. Think of the major paradigm shift this planet would experience if the concept of *war* would be eliminated. Think of all the companies whose services would no longer be needed, should there be no use for all the equipment or personnel that support war. If there was no more war, there would be no need for the military. Huge segments of populations would be affected. Huge *profits* would be lost. Labor would have to be redistributed towards peaceful endeavors, rather than war-like endeavors. Disciplinary ways would change to reflect peace rather than war.

What would happen if everyone simply told the truth? Think of the careers that would be eliminated if there were no need for lawyers and judges, because there were no criminals and no criminal activity. Think of all the buildings rendered obsolete, if their function was no longer useful. Could these buildings be renovated and used to house the homeless? Think of how many communities could be set up where functions would be shared: meals and housing, supervision of children and the elderly. Such changes would positively affect both small and large towns across the globe. Can we envision a better way is there to live than for each person to go back to his or her own abode, as they do now?

My Guides chimed in with the following message: *It is very exciting to be on the planet at this time. You have so much power to bring about so much change; perhaps more power than ever before, because earlier you brought in too much doubt. That is why your earlier efforts collapsed. You experience success now as your beliefs are reinforced with an attitude of* "it can be done." *More and more of you see results from your ideas, and that gives you the impetus to go on.*

The new Universe will combine the best of all that came before it. All will live in harmony and honor their home, their planet, and each other. All will see themselves and everything else as an aspect of the Divine. There will be no sense of separation.

When you are able to bring your understanding to encompass the Whole, then you can be Whole. The greatest problem on this planet arises from the fact that you see yourselves as separate from God. That is not the case. When you are ready to step into the role of who you really are, then you can bring heaven to Earth!

And so it is.

I Am.

Amen.

Just for this moment, can you see your Self as both you and part of the One? Our paradigm shifts as we accept that we are One with our Creator.

March 17

Healing Mysterious Pain

Healing happens in layers. We heal one issue and then it resurfaces from a deeper level. We then heal that issue, and the process repeats. One of my healing sessions took an interesting twist along these lines. After visiting family in Michigan and arriving back home in Virginia, my body went into crisis. I came down with flu-like symptoms: tiredness, sore throat, cough, aches and chills. However, it felt more like a *cleansing* than an illness, as if my body was sloughing off emotions that had been stored in it for eons, emotions that no longer needed to be there. Fortunately, prior to visiting my family, I had already scheduled a healing session with my teacher and healer, Wanda Lasseter-Lundy, who always seemed to sense the exact needs of my body.

During this healing session, a vision comes forward: *I see the interior of a very opulent setting; private chambers filled with luxurious, genteel appointments, exhibiting the finest décor of the gaslight era. Lounging about on an assortment of lavishly upholstered couches are many beautiful young men. The older man, who owns all of this luxury, has enough money to buy anything or anybody he wants. He is bored with all of it. There is no satisfaction. He knows, in the deepest recesses of his heart, that one youth, the young man who is his constant companion, does not care for this opulence. The youth just wants to have a monogamous partner in the older man. The older man abuses his trust. The youth feels scorned, as if the love he holds for the older man has little value. He dies young, broken-hearted, never breaking through the barricades the older man set up around himself.*

Images appear and re-appear in my mind's eye, each image morphing into the next.

Wanda asks: "Are you ready to go deeper?"

As if in a dream, I answer "Yes."

"What does the bored, wealthy man reflect to you?" she queries.

"A wasted life; unfulfilled dreams," is my quiet – almost muffled – reply.

"Whose?"

"My own."

Resting for a moment, a new picture starts forming in my mind's eye along with new sensations and feelings.

I ask: "Did I ever have a homosexual relationship with my current brother in a past life?"

Wanda answers, "You were many things to him over many lifetimes."

I was that older man and my brother, the youth. Since the memory of that lifetime was stored in my cell memory, it had to be released and let go. By forgiving myself for the lascivious, bored, and calloused behavior I exhibited in that lifetime, I was able to release the pain it had trapped within my body.

That lifetime displayed one type of power: the power that money could buy and its control over other people. Unfortunately, that type of power brought little or no satisfaction, since it was based on not caring for anybody. That lifetime did not have Love as its foundation.

From this experience, I grew in understanding that only those who share their wealth for the betterment of their fellow man feel any real satisfaction from their monetary largess.

Do you experience mysterious ailments of an unknown origin? Healing comes from many places and takes many forms.

March 18

Past Life Recall

At the same healing session described in March 17th, the scene shifts. Another vision appears. I had seen this before, during a regressive hypnotherapy session in which I had partaken a few years earlier.

This is how it appears before my "mind's eye": *I am an officer on a tall sailing vessel in the 18th century, taking my watch in the middle of the night. Another sailor comes up totally miffed about some money that he claims I have stolen from him. I know I am not guilty, but no amount of protesting my innocence can sway him to change his mind. He stabs me in the shoulder and throws me overboard. I watch myself drown. I am not afraid to die, but I remember that I curse him before I slide under the water.*

During that session, the hypnotherapist asked me to look closely at the sailor accusing me. Who I saw again was my brother from this lifetime. This time, *I* was the victim, and he the "injured" one. Obviously, our two souls continued to reverse roles: *he who was victimized in one lifetime then became the victim in the next lifetime.* Moments prior to my regression, I told the hypnotherapist that, at the age of ten – when my brother was five-years old – I made what I thought was an ominous prediction. As the session progressed, the therapist asked if my statement was a *prediction* or a *curse*. The words that I swore during the scene on the sailing vessel before I drowned were clearly a curse.

Patterns repeat themselves lifetime after lifetime, until we forgive ourselves and forgive the "other." There are other ways to get off the wheel of karma, but the easiest way is to forgive. Understand this or not; it does not matter. Uncover the underlying issues or leave them buried; it does not matter. Forgiveness is the key to setting us free. Forgiveness brings the blessing, and dissolves the "sticky" energy that keeps us bound to the "past." This then allows us to move through the pain and move on with our lives.

My first regressive hypnotherapy session had increased my ability to recall prior lifetimes. Strong images had come before; usually in dreams. Some of these were lucid dreams enabling me to return to them the next night, as if the dream was part of a serial on television. After this session, my past lives were revealed to me, as needed, to heal a portion of my "self" that still was hurting.

Past life recall can present itself through a variety of venues: energy healing, deep tissue massage, Rolfing, regressive hypnotherapy or any type of energy movement such as yoga, Pilates, tai chi, qi gong, karate, judo, or tai kwon do. Past lives have a sneaky way of surfacing when we have deep tissue massage work done on our bodies, but can also appear during meditative states, or even during intense discussions of life issues.

Past life recall usually occurs in the silence of our own souls, especially during solitary communion with Nature: trekking up a mountain, sitting by the ocean or by the side of a lake, river, or stream, or during a solitary hike in the woods, walking through a pine grove. Perusing the perimeters of our own home and contemplating a flower – really seeing its various components – or sitting under a tree in our own backyard for thirty-minutes per day, or sitting silently observing the moon or stars can help us dissolve the edges of our consciousness, taking us into an altered space where past life memories can surface.

My Bio-energy instructor, Mietek Wurkus, taught us another ingenious way to see a multiple number of past lives. He suggested that we enter a small unlit room in which a mirror had been placed or hung on a wall. We should leave the door open about one foot, light a candle, and then stare at our image in the mirror for about twenty minutes.

The first time I did this, instantly a number of past lives appeared; each one flashing by in less than a second. Sometimes head gear appeared from the past life, or my sex or age changed dramatically – from very young to very old. Each time this happened, I felt an energy shift within myself, as if someone was cutting a piece of paper quickly.

Once, when I faced another person in a dimly lit room for a similar type of exercise, I felt the same energy shift. This time, though, the person across from me saw all my past lives flit by, one by one. I saw nothing change in her face, but did see a very deep sadness in her eyes, to which I sent healing. A fascinating exercise!

If you are interested in healing past life issues, choose a venue that feels right to you.

Has an image of a past life ever occurred while you silently communed with Nature? Past life recall occurs when we advance in spiritual understanding.

March 19

Clearing Past Life Trauma (1)

Recognizing that pain from past lives is *an aspect of us that still has a hold on us in this lifetime,* but not a permanent hold, can help us free the pain. Pain that is generated from past lives can be cleared, for just surfacing the memory effects a type of clearing. If we can recognize the pain's origin, we can clear it from our energy field by ourselves or with the help of an energy healer.

Both back problems and digestive imbalances related to constipation had plagued me throughout my adult life. Chiropractic treatment brought relief for my back, but constipation continued to be a struggle. I also experienced occasional bouts of laryngitis and flu, together with horrendous earaches, headaches, loss of vision around the periphery of my eyes, and fits of anger, all chalked off as "normal" for a busy real estate broker simultaneously running a business while raising a family. Stress from a sixty-hour work week, while trying to raise two children and maintain a large home with two pets, increased my health problems. I was told by one specialist to "slow down." This did not seem to be an option for me. I was adamant about not using drugs, having surgery, or taking any other drastic measures to heal myself. This led me to investigate alternative healing measures, one of which was to work on healing past lives.

Healing that occurred by releasing past life trauma was illustrated by Michael J. Roads, an author from Australia who taught with his wife, Treenie. During 1997, I attended a *Roadsway Retreat* offered by this couple during their United States visit. During this retreat, Michael spoke of a past life in which he was the victim of a murder to avenge an infidelity. In that lifetime, he was murdered by having a lance thrust through his stomach. As a "lesson" to other philanderers, he was buried with the lance still protruding from his stomach, sticking straight up through the casket.

Michael had suffered from stomach pain his entire life, but once he understood the *cause* of the pain, he time-travelled back to the same instant, and screamed to his best friend (who was in the room at that time) to "Remove the lance!" From that moment forward, he no longer suffered from stomach problems. Remember, *as spiritual "Be"-ings having a human experience, anything is possible.*

In a past life, we may have been a crusader who zealously defended our faith by killing everyone in the name of God. We may have become a casualty of battle by having a spear thrust into our back or a sword pierce through our stomach. That past life experience could be the source of our back or stomach problems in this lifetime.

Sometimes, very normal and "ordinary" events can trigger an important past life memory. I became extremely anxious and started to fidget uncontrollably while watching one of the recent versions of *Joan of Arc.* Suddenly, a picture flashed in my mind's eye.

I am helping raise a ladder next to a tall, stone block wall during a war. While climbing up the ladder in a heroic effort to go over the top, a spear is thrust into my chest. As the spear cuts through my stomach, I become horrified as my bowels let loose. My back twists as a result of these feelings, my life force abruptly starts to leave me, but somehow, I manage to thrust a spear into the heart of the person who has just killed me. I look at this person and recognize my mother from this lifetime.

After I became an adult, it never ceased to amaze me that I could not be in my mother's presence for four days without getting into an argument with her. As deeply as I loved her, I could never refrain from venting my opinions as she requested me to do anything which I thought smacked of "control." This pattern continued even during the last year of her life, after she had been diagnosed with ovarian cancer. I finally recognized that some of my intense "issues" with her stemmed from past lives shared with her; ones in which "control" was a major factor in our relationship.

Trust what you see in your mind's eye. It is there because it belongs there.

Does some past life trauma need to be cleared out of your energy field? Past lives can wreck havoc with our energy field which can affect our body.

March 20

Clearing Past Life Trauma (2)

Energy healing can occasionally lead to a "healing crisis." The new healing energy being given us is incompatible with the vibrations of the old energy which we are releasing from our body. This is why energy healing done slowly, over a period of time, is effective. Asking for more information, and attempting to process more energy through our body than our body can handle, is acceptable *only* if we fully understand the potential consequences.

On one occasion, after having cleared out an entire array of blockages, with full comprehension of the consequences, I had to stay in bed for four days since I could not move the first two days, and could barely move the second two. After that, I felt great! I had asked for the greatest depth of healing my body could tolerate. I fully understood what the consequences were, and was willing to pay the price – which was bed rest until my strength returned.

While I was on the table, having asked for healing on the deepest levels my body would tolerate, my teacher queried whether I was willing to go *deeper.* I was. The following vision occurred: *A miter's cap appeared, the kind a bishop would wear. The owner was a very wealthy cleric, who recruited young men – preferably from wealthy homes whose parents would sign over enormous amounts of wealth to the Church – to fight the holy wars for which he was pressing, all in the name of God and Holy Mother Church.*

The cleric lined his own pockets first. His personal wealth was swollen by the coffers of all those who died in battle. He did not share much of his wealth with the local villagers. Resentment against him grew, until the townspeople banded together and a few men, cloaked in black, stabbed him to death.

This lifetime of mine clearly showed an abuse of monetary power. In order to understand monetary power, we have to know it from all angles. We play the role of both the *just and powerful* as well as the *unjust and powerful,* along with that of the poor, the forgotten, the lonely, and the downtrodden. We also play the role of the middle class; the striver, the achiever and the self-motivated. Finally, we play the role of the very wealthy and the influential; those at the top echelon of worldly power. The same is true for any other attribute that we are "investigating" as a soul.

We must know power in every sphere, and from every angle, in order to understand that *we are power.* Power is not something that we take from an "other." The "old way" of thinking is: *I take from you, therefore, I have more and you have less*, or *you take from me, therefore, you have more and I have less.* The truth is different. Power is something that we *are.* It is a characteristic of our "Be"-ing. We don't "get it" from someone or something else. We *are it.*

In my young adult life, I would occasionally work with someone who absolutely hated me for no good reason. I did not know them, did not harm them in any way, did not provoke their agitation, and did everything possible to please them. Still, in the end, all that I could do was to stay away from those persons. I am now convinced that this type of attitude stemmed from various past lives in which I had abused them in some way or other. Some aspect of their soul recognized me from a past life, and then proceeded to *pay me back.*

In order not to generate karma or dharma for a future lifetime, the only thing I could do was to forgive them. From the perspective of today, I now know that my choice to forgive them their slights and injustices freed me from the wheel of karma; from having to repeat a lifetime with them where the issues may have been even more severe.

Are you willing to tolerate temporary pain for permanent release of pain when you "go deeper?" Healing takes many forms.

March 21

Focus and Concentration

One of the attributes of our power is our ability to bring into being that on which we focus and concentrate. So far, only a very few understand and know how to apply this universal law. However, millions around the planet are starting to awaken to it NOW.

We experience the effect of our power by understanding that we create that on which we focus and concentrate. Our ability to focus and concentrate on that which we *desire* to achieve is enhanced when we give ourselves enough time to *maintain* our focus and concentration. Our ability to manifest can occur *instantly.* We think of something, and presto, it appears! We are truly responsive to the creator "Be"-ings we are when we see an item come into form as soon as our thought about it occurs. When our focus is concentrated, we achieve our goals. If our focus is split and scattered between many things, our thoughts fragment and we do not achieve our goals.

We are a product of our thought systems. It is the concentration of our focus that brings us that which we desire. This concept is clarified in Napoleon Hill's book, *Think and Grow Rich.* I once heard a motivational speaker say that he did not "get it" until he had read the book eight times. I thought to myself, *that's my problem. I didn't* "get it" *either. I simply have not read it enough* (having read it only once). Midway through the second reading, I stopped cold. There was nothing to "get." The entire message of the book is in the title.

If we continuously think about nothing except growing rich, our entire focus and concentration will propel us to that state. If the single thrust of what we desire is to get rich, *we will get rich.* We may lose our health in doing so or lose the love of those whom we hold dearest. We may forgo any type of relationship with, understanding of, or joy from our family, who may grow to be total strangers to us. We may totally distance ourselves from our spouses or significant others. We may forever be haunted by a lack of trust from those around us. We may lose all our wealth after we accumulate it, and die bankrupt. However, we will indeed "get rich." We will receive that on which we focus and concentrate.

Wealth can be a blessing when it is shared, and a curse when it is hoarded. We live on such an abundant planet, with enough resources for every living being. No one needs to be deprived. The highest elation that our Spirit Self experiences is when we exhibit a willingness to help the less fortunate. Happiness comes from sharing wealth for the betterment of all, for it is *only in giving that we receive.*

As we check the focus of our thoughts, if we recognize that what we have chosen is not working out, we can make another choice.

On what have your thoughts been focused and concentrated? We "get" that on which we focus and place concentrated attention.

March 22

A Change of "Form"

A popular afternoon show featured transsexuals; men who had undergone sex change operations. One show featured a handsome young couple whose lives were flipped upside down when the husband finally went through with his decision to have a sex change operation. The resulting "woman" was very attractive. "His" former wife could not accept this new female form and divorced her former husband. She felt that she could not stay in a relationship that would essentially negate her heterosexual preference. Most of the show audience nodded in agreement. Her husband had known from the time he was four years old that he preferred to be a female and to have a female form. However, he did everything in his power to resist his own inner knowing, staying in a very "manly" profession and fathering several children.

Another show in the same series featured a male college professor, who, after having achieved many accolades and awards, undertook the process to become a female later in life. His employer and colleagues accepted him as a new female. He was able to remain in his job as a professor; adopting a female name similar to his male one. He continued with his teaching and publishing career.

A very important message came out of this show. The first man's daughter from a previous marriage – now in her twenties – said that she could accept this new "female form" as her biological father because *it doesn't matter what* "form" *Love takes.* The host agreed and said that the only thing that mattered was "who" loved you, not in what "form" that love came.

I especially felt grateful for the sensitivity and good judgment that was used when airing a program on a topic that other TV shows had sensationalized and stereotyped. Only Love is real. The "package" in which love comes doesn't matter.

I could only imagine what the difficulty of the struggle within me would be, if I had to accept with unconditional Love the desire of a life partner to have a sex change operation. I imagined the wrenching feelings that would wash over me when I fully comprehended what was happening to my marriage; facing a nightmare that I did not make but in which I was caught. I imagined feeling just as helpless as a fly caught in a sticky web. I imagined that even if I had a strong marriage in which my life partner was also my best friend, there would still be the incredible loneliness that I would suffer from having everything I loved ripped away from me. I imagined wanting to hide my pain from everyone to whom I was close, not knowing how to start sharing this new "event" in my life. To whom could I talk? Who would really understand what was happening to me? How could I explain this to my friends or to my children?

Somewhere, from deep inside of me – from a space where only God dwells – I would ask to summon the courage to face my future; a future that meant accepting the invitation from the "woman" who used to be my husband to meet "her" for lunch. I would summon the strength to bring JOY back into my life, as one of my best friends has done.

It all goes back to what is "real." Only love is "real." Only love prevails.

Is there an unexpected "form" that love has taken in your life? Only Love is real.

March 23

Stillpoint

With each breath we take, there is a slight hesitation, a fraction of a second *in between* each breath *in* and each breath *out*. That point of hesitation, the point where the breath changes direction, that fraction of a second is called the *stillpoint.*

We model our experience of the stillpoint after the Creator's experience, only cosmic time is not on the same scale as human time. The *stillpoint* – this fraction of a second in cosmic time – lasts approximately twenty years and seven months as measured in human years, according to the teachings from the Spiritual realms. We are currently in this period called *stillpoint.* It is happening *right now,* having started on 5/5/92 and slated to end on 12/12/12, after which time the reversal period begins, the out breath of God.

During *stillpoint,* creation goes into a "void." Just as we shift energetically, from an in breath to the out breath, so does the Earth shift the same way energetically. Throughout this period of time, *Earth changes* take place; from pole shifts, to earthquakes, to hurricanes, to typhoons and volcanic eruptions. During this interval, all manner of chaos seems to reign on the planet, from massive mudslides generated by too much rain to extremely dry conditions where sparks from lightening or the carelessness of man ignite fires over millions of acres. The deforestation of our rain forests, pollution of our waterways leading to the oceans, and smog clogging our air threatens the entire ecosystem this planet is dependent on and contributes to the instability of these times.

Furthermore, as we look around and bemoan the physical conditions of the planet right now, we also suffer from the massive financial corruptions perpetrated on an unsuspecting people. Knowing that the planet is in a void at this time brings little comfort to those who do not have the resources to meet basic daily needs, because their means of support have been ripped out from under them. People left in small towns throughout the United States watch helplessly as the owners move their factories overseas. These are hard-working people whose entire life has been spent pursuing a modest – but proud and independent – existence.

While the people from villages in "third world" countries *seem to* benefit due to the jobs created in their area, they are now condemned to sweat-shop existences for pittance wages and abysmal working conditions. All of this is for the sake of fattening the coffers of a few "owners." This is progress?

Natural imbalances and man-made imbalance are as harmful to each of us as they are to the planet. However, during this *still point* period, the massive physical destruction that has been predicted by many traditions over thousands of years has *not* occurred. Points of destruction have occurred, but nothing on the scale of the predictions in *Revelations* in the Bible.

Western cultures are waking up to their responsibilities to the planet and to its inhabitants. Recognizing our obligation to and dependence on the planet is no longer only the focus of indigenous cultures only. *We all* have a responsibility to the planet. *This is our home.* It is the only home we know, and we all have an obligation to care for it and its inhabitants *in its entirety.* We are not separate from our home, nor are we separate from any creation on it.

The *in breath* of the Creator – the period we have been in for millennium after millennium – is accompanied by thoughts of separation. However, the *out breath* brings with it thoughts of unification and agreement with the Oneness of all life. In addition, the *out breath,* which starts after 12/12/12, brings with it thoughts of peace, harmony, joy, and assistance for those less fortunate.

We each need to do our part in helping the planet, by working to upgrade the layer of thought forms surrounding it; the "collective unconscious." We assist, both collectively and singularly, through our music, art, writing, dance, meditation, or healing. The communion we inherently feel towards each other, and towards every bit of creation on this planet, cannot be eliminated, no matter who or what attempts to control us.

During this period of *stillpoint,* we are told to breathe deeply every chance we get. Our breath links us to the Prime Creator; to the Source, Pure Love, Pure Essence, to Spirit!

Breathe deeply. With each and every breath that you take, you will then get the maximum benefit of the air flowing into your body, which increases your connection to the Divine.

Can you sense that something is "different"
about this period of "time"?
We must each do our part to assist in
the change coming on 12/12/12.

March 24

Our Own Truth

We need to learn to live by our own truth; walk to beat of our own drum, uncover that which has meaning to us, and decipher our own individual and unique purpose for coming to this planet. We need to become authentic in our own sexual orientation, for to whom else can we be true but who we really are? We need to rethink our own priorities. It can be done.

If we do not live by our own truths, we dissipate our energies by attempting to hone in on someone else's parade. When we feel that the most we can do with our lives is to *be a participant in someone else's life*, then we let our own life forces drain from ourselves. Every time we surrender our lives to demands that are not our own (to the sitcoms on the TV, to glorifying the lives of movie stars or sports heroes, to neighborhood squabbles, to office tensions, to the needs of a co-dependent, to the pressures of our children, our spouse, significant others, or our co-workers), we become passive participants in someone else's drama, instead of actively participating in our own lives. When we do this, we do not have real lives. Instead, we become bystanders in someone else's "reel" life.

As we learn to become comfortable with silence, we commune with the spiritual side of our Self. We practice going within: we hoard "leisure" time for ourselves, become introspective, luxuriate in long walks in nature, and harvest the delights of each season. By attuning our awareness to the change of seasons and phases of the moon, we rejoice in each raindrop and each snowflake as they renew and refresh.

Even if we live to be over a hundred years of age, our days on this planet are numbered. Even though we have infinity, we do not have endless days and endless nights on this planet. By acting as if the number is shorter rather than longer – by acting now – we take the time and make the commitment to uncover the highest expression of our "Be"-ing. Each of us is connected to the Creator's voice. Each of us has a *direct connection to God.* Each of us can hear the guidance from Spirit to help us live our own authentic lives.

Nothing is ever as hopeless as it seems. Even if we are living our lives looking up from the bottom of a bottle, we can change our mind and start afresh. Even if we are hopelessly addicted, we can seek professional help. There are thousands of support groups around the world. Those emotionally close to us may not be able to help us because they may not understand the nature of addiction. However, there are others who can help us, no matter what our issues may be, and no matter what devastation we have wrought with our addictive behavior in the past.

In life, nothing is set in concrete. All is in a state of flux, all is mobility. When we are grateful in every moment for what we have when we have it, we move from our own truth into power. When we know that, on some level, we create what we have, we also know that we can *change* our creations or miscreation, if that is what they are.

We learn to live our own truths.

What is your truth?
We accept an authentic life for our self as we develop our Self.

March 25

Our Greatest Strengths

Your greatest growth in Spirit can look like your greatest failure on Earth. As *A Course in Miracles* states: "That which tries to defeat you the most can lead you to recognize the greatest strength about yourself."

Amongst my greatest strengths is that *I never give up,* even when the situation seems hopeless. One of the most terrifying moments in my life occurred when we had no money with which to pay our mortgage. The next day our mortgage would be *overdue,* and the fifteen-day grace period would be up. I prayed to God for a solution to this dilemma, and was given an opportunity *that day* which earned me enough money to make the payment. By making a sale on a home with an assumable mortgage (one for which no lender approval was required), I was able to secure an advance on my commission; sufficient enough to cover our cost.

In the 1980s, mortgage interest rates climbed to 17%. We could not *give* a house away; forget about trying to *sell* it. We had to close the doors of our small real estate brokerage firm. We had expended all our savings trying to keep our company afloat, had let all our part-time agents go, and had shut the doors to the office we had been in for eight years. We kept our fledgling property management department (thanks to the astute advice of our attorney), and re-licensed our real estate company out of our home.

My life was falling apart. My husband lost his job as Principal Broker, my mother was dying of ovarian cancer, and I was six months pregnant with my first child. We were supporting our home, subsidizing other rental properties, and sending money to my husband's mother to subsidize her meager retirement. There was scant income from sales. In fact, there *were* no sales. Even with our bills pared down, our only "guaranteed" income from the property management earned only 10% of what I needed to pay.

One of my best friends at the time said, "Why Alice, all you need to do is find another zero somewhere." Another zero indeed.

Life came crashing down on us as we closed the doors of our real estate company in the two months before our beautiful baby daughter was born. The next eighteen months were the leanest of all. My husband was able to secure employment that partially covered our needs. By reining in all of our expenses – no shopping trips, no restaurant outings, and limiting our meat to hamburger and chicken – all our bills were paid on time, even if that time came just before the grace period expired.

It was during this period that I shouted to the Universe, *I will not be defeated. I will not lose everything I have worked so hard to get.* That strength came from a voice deep inside of me that shouted: *NEVER GIVE UP.*

Only long after this period was over did I finally realize that Spirit had been trying to get my attention; cajoling to get me to change my life's direction. Because I was not ready then, I did not recognize all the guideposts, but simply kept thinking: *keep doing what I know best – list and sell real estate. Keep plugging away. Do not think about what has been lost; only move forward.* I ignored the tug at my heart guiding me to read spiritual literature, to study various spiritual modalities, and to open myself up to the many gifts of spirit, including healing with energy. It would be many more years before I would accept Spirit's guidance on those matters.

Right now, you may be experiencing the same kind of financial, medical, or emotional strain. You may have a hopeless addiction to drugs, to depression, or to alcohol. Your soul may be preparing you to help lead others out of addictive behavior or out of financial catastrophe in the future. Your experiences today would simply be paving your way; teaching you how to benefit others by totally understanding their situation. You will know how to help them because you will have personally experienced their pain.

Not too many years after my financial catastrophe, I helped my former sister-in-law by sending her enough money to pay for the taxes on her home (shortly before they became due). She, too, had felt hopeless during her time of financial distress. While taking a walk during her lunch break, she fervently asked God to help her. On her return, she found a message that I had called waiting for her. When I spoke to her of my offer, she started to cry softly; feeling as if manna had just dropped from heaven. The gift that was given to me, I passed on to another. When she was able, she repaid me at a time when, co-incidentally, I needed the money to re-pay a debt of my own.

Has any pain that you have experienced led you to have greater understanding of your spiritual side? Our lowest feelings of failure, rejection, abandonment, addiction, or hopelessness can be our greatest gift.

March 26

Our Massive Failures

I had another experience in which the foundation of my life was shaken, which I described in my first book, *God is the Biggest Joker of All*. In the late 1990s, I was asked by Spirit to give up my family. According to Spirit's guidance, at time when I was under extreme duress, I was to walk away from my husband, my children, my home, and all of my possessions and investments. I was asked to simply follow Spirit's path; to give up everything that made my life "secure." I had just begun group study of *A Course in Miracles,* and my spiritual work had become my top priority. I knew that if I did not pursue the path where Spirit beckoned, I would not die, however, would become very, very sick; of no use to anyone, since I would not be able to work.

The directive from Spirit was uncompromising. After receiving this instruction and mentally agreeing to follow the voice inside my head, I said goodbye to everything in my home. The hardest thing I have ever had to do in my life was to give both of my children a copy of the same letter that I gave my husband, a letter that stated that I loved them deeply, but I loved my God more.

I agreed to take nothing with me; just my clothes, my car, and a few personal mementoes. I was willing to give up every single thing that I had worked for my entire life. I had to do this to be able to breathe again. I could no longer live in the vacuum I had set up for myself.

Because I was willing to give up everything to do Spirit's bidding, I was able to keep it all. *I had passed the test of Abraham.* Fortunately, I had a husband who truly loved me. He was able to tolerate my need to follow the dictates of Spirit, even if he did not understand those needs at all. When I had an astrological reading done by Haloli Richter (since deceased), she asked me, "What happened around 1995/96?" My chart showed that indeed, there could have been a marital rift, had my husband loved me less than he did.

When I think back on these and other encounters I have had in my life (those which, to my ego self, look like "massive failures"), I see how closely aligned Spirit was with me. Spirit was always there; always ready to bolster me, which*ever* way I really wanted to go, even when I was *afraid* to go there.

Are some of your "massive failures" setting you up to experience your greatest successes? Our lifestyles change drastically when we can no longer follow the demands of our egos.

March 27

Miracle at Midnight

The following incredible story is recounted in a movie by Disney called *Miracle at Midnight.*

During World War II, the entire town of Copenhagen, Denmark, collaborated in giving the Jewish people a safe place to stay; an effort spearheaded by the chief surgeon of the hospital. The surgeon and his family hosted the betrothal party for his main assistant, a young nurse (a Jewish maiden), together with her fiancé and their families. Their own son, unbeknownst to them, was in the student underground resistance movement, which continuously put him in tremendous danger.

The Danes hated the Nazi occupation. Their government had a double agent working in collaboration with the Nazis, who discovered that the Nazis had broken into the Jewish Community Center and had stolen the membership list. They set Oct l, 1942 (the eve of Rosh Hashanah) as the date on which they were going to invade each Jewish home and transport them all out of Denmark – seven thousand, five hundred people in all.

Through this double agent, the Danes in Copenhagen received three days' notice of this event. They took it upon themselves to hide and transport every Jewish person out of Denmark, via small fishing boats moored at small fishing villages. The surgeon hid many Jewish people in the hospital. Records were changed; names were Christianized, and people were transported by ambulance vans to the departure points. At tremendous risk to themselves, the Danes hid, transported and sent to Sweden a total of seven thousand sixty Jews. Only four hundred and forty perished during the effort, counting the totally infirm, the disabled, and the suicides. At one point, the surgeon's wife was in danger as she became separated from her family, and was detained and questioned by the Nazis.

Not only did the Danes perform this heroic feat of transporting the Jewish people to Sweden, but (while these people were gone) they also took care of the shops, tended their gardens, and looked after the pets of their former Jewish neighbors. This incredible act of generosity displayed the finest of *man's humanity towards man* during World War II. The acts of the Danes showed the spirit of love and generosity of which the human is capable; the highest good coming out in every way possible.

Has there been a personal miracle within your family? Many families have exhibited the highest qualities of valor, honor, and quiet heroics toward each other.

March 28

Society of the Heart and the Rose

I would like to honor the efforts of the Danish people by publicizing their deeds during World War II – especially now, since there are still so many wars on this planet.

I propose a Society of the Heart and the Rose (SHR), with a dedication scheduled at the United Nations for any country that exhibits the highest humanitarian efforts to help the beleaguered and displaced. I propose that the Danish people be the first recipients of this award. I propose having one ceremony at the United Nations honoring the Danes, and another one in Copenhagen whereby each family that participated in the resistance be given a certificate featuring a heart and a rose acknowledging their bravery. If possible, a rose garden can be planted – as a living remembrance of their humanitarian deeds – in front of their government capitol building. Because both the rose and the heart are symbols of love, and the combination is an irresistible force to change the hearts of men, the Danes will forever be commemorated for the kindness of their hearts.

Most of the families who helped in this event were not identified in the Disney movie, *Miracle at Midnight.* They were simply nameless and faceless, but fearless, participants in this endeavor. I further propose a Special Day of Celebration on October I of each year, commemorating this event of selfless love and generosity of spirit; this *Miracle at Midnight.*

It is time for the Universe to take note of man's humanity to man. I propose that the people of Denmark be forever honored as the first recipients of this award because of their efforts *as a whole.* Certainly, there have been other incredible individual feats of heroism, but this award is to go to a country that acted as one – one mind, one heart, one Soul – beating to save those of their own. The people of Denmark must be exceptional, to have behaved in such a humane manner. As non-military people, they put their own lives at risk to save others; standing up for principle, acting on what they believed was right, and even dying while fighting for that in which they believed.

Furthermore, I propose that the Swedes be the second recipients of the Society of the Heart and Rose Award, since the Jewish people could not have been saved had the Swedish people not been willing to first accept them and given them safe harbor, then feeding and sheltering them. The people of Sweden, for their willingness to shelter and take care of their less fortunate fellow man, deserve to be honored as the second recipients of this award. This effort became a *fait accompli* only because the fine people of Sweden responded positively to the requests of the people of Denmark.

Is there a personal tribute that you are being guided to establish in honor of someone special? Life is a celebration and needs to be celebrated.

March 29

One Voice

I never ignore messages that come in groups of three. When I am uncertain about a course of action, I ask for validation from *three different sources*. When confirmation occurs three times from three different avenues, I am reassured that my course of action is correct. If a confirmation comes in a *fourth time,* that is simply Spirit's way of saying, *Just in case you missed the message, pay attention! This is what you are supposed to do.*

For years, the Voice for God woke me each morning; dictating various essays. Three mornings in a row, I was given identical information about the Society of the Heart and the Rose. Since I was awakened with the same words streaming through my head *three times,* that proved to me that this information was provided so that I and others could take action.

We each have a voice inside our head – speaking to us all the time – that ties us to the Creator. We are so darn afraid of admitting that we hear the Voice for God, because of what others think. Telling anyone that we hear a voice talking to us causes others to look at us in askance, as if we suddenly admitted harboring delusions that not only impact us but also, *might infect them* that instant – as if our admission was an infectious disease.

The Voice that urged Rosa Parks *not* to give up her seat on the bus helped to fuel the burgeoning Civil Rights movement in the United States. The same Voice that told her to hold fast to her seat also helped her override any fear that she might have felt, because she defied the standard practice of the day. Rosa Parks heard one Voice, and that Voice said "No" when asked to relinquish her seat. A Voice that strong can only come from one place, and that is from the Source.

One Voice *can* be heard. One Voice has *always* been a catalyst for change. One Voice can make a difference. One of the most important Voices – since the inception of our country – has been the Voice that gave us the *Emancipation Proclamation.*

"Your thoughts are given to you" says Mother Mary in *Mary's Message to the World*, by Annie Kirkwood. There is never a time when we are not aligned with God. That we do *not* pay attention is the by-product of our *free will.* While free will is our greatest gift – one which will never be taken away from us – it is also the reason that many of us choose not to align with Spirit. It is too darn hard; too controversial and too encumbering.

I'll think about that later, your ego urges and – of course – "later" never comes.

Spirit *does* have a sense of humor. The title of my first book – *God is the Biggest Joker of All* – brought me all manner of heartache. I felt the title was derisive of the Creator. Obviously, there are those who need to hear the message in that book who would never pick up a publication that had a "spiritual" sounding title. However, they *will* pick up this book simply *because* of its title.

The Voice for God binds all of us together, as one race, as we look out for each other.

Is there a Voice inside your head insisting on a particular course of action? We are each connected to the One Voice for God.

March 30

Asking for Spirit's Help

We can take control. It can be done! The first thing we have to realize is that we are never alone. Spirit's help is always there for us. All we have to do is *ask* for it.

Most of us are at war. Some of us are involved in a real war; one with bombs and tanks. Most of us, though, are in an imagined war: one involving our neighbors, spouses, significant others, children, relatives, friends, associates, acquaintances, and colleagues. Many of us are at war with ourselves, which is one of the reasons why addictions are so prevalent. Unable to achieve a *real* calm within, we seek to establish a surrogate calm by stuffing ourselves with addictive substances. This includes sedating ourselves with medication, so that we achieve a false calm; albeit only for a few moments.

By being totally immersed in and concerned with "damage control," we wonder how we can *possibly* do something positive or different with our lives. By surrendering our lives to circumstances that keep us tied up in knots, we do not have to move forward. In a codependent relationship, or a physically, mentally, or emotionally abusive one, we are constantly kept in turmoil. How can we, under such conditions, take control of anything?

When I was at my lowest ebb – when our bills were overwhelming and our income almost non-existent – I prayed for God's help. Help arrived in the form of books, gifts from my relatives, clients, and friends. It came in a steady stream of clients, and money that always seemed to materialize as we needed it. I knew I had to be strong. I had a beautiful baby daughter – a beloved first child – always looking at me; always smiling, always laughing. There was no way I was going to let her down. *NO WAY!*

Within three years, as our financial crisis eased a bit, our most engaging son was born. By his third year, we moved into a lovely new home in an area filled with young families. It is not that our financial crisis was over. Rather, we just kept chipping away at the debt load, and digging our way out of the mess.

The fact that you are reading this book is proof that you are open to Spirit's suggestions. Most of the messages in this book are spiritual. You are already much further along than you ever thought you were. You can take control and change the circumstances of your life. You simply have to accept a very simple principle: *You receive Spirit's help only when you ask for it.* YOU MUST ASK. That is the Law of the Universe. Your free will is never going to be usurped. You *must ask* for help.

Have you asked for Spirit's help recently? We receive all the assistance for which we ask, in order to take control of our lives.

March 31

Self Talk

We need to learn to quiet our ego selves in order to allow our Higher Self to become audible. Only when we quiet all the chatter from our ego selves, can our Higher Self be heard. Our Higher Self has always been there, but has been below the threshold of our awareness. The Voice of Spirit that comes through our Higher Self is a very small voice indeed, until it is *invited* to be a major participant in our lives.

We each have an internal cheerleader; the positive self-talk that we need to accomplish our goals and dreams. This internal cheerleader comes from Spirit. Only with our *invitation* can the Voice of Spirit – the Voice of the Higher Self – be heard loudly and clearly. This is the Law of the Universe. It cannot be usurped.

When we consciously listen to that which goes through our minds, we might be extremely surprised. We can start by listening to our self "talk" for a few minutes each day, and then increase that to a few hours. We can work at "staying tuned" to our self-talk for an entire day. To our surprise, we may find that which we say to ourselves is not the warm benevolence that we may have thought was there. How many times have we lapsed into judgment and criticism? How many times have we berated ourselves? Those closest to us? Our parents? Our co-workers? Our partners? Our spouses? Our children?

We bring about that on which we focus and concentrate. When we focus on negative self-talk, we manifest negative results. No structure, from the pyramids in Egypt to the Gothic cathedrals of Europe, to the Opera House in Sydney, Australia, was ever built by anyone who said it could *not be done*. Yet, by filling our minds with self-deprecating and self-defeating words, we set up the very conditions that we do not want. We broadcast the vibrational energy to bring more negativity into our life.

This is what my Guides have to say about us:

You are the most powerful creature ever created, yet you continue to dwell only on your littleness. You see yourselves as having to grapple for power. In that, you are correct. You are seeking only "false power;" the power of the ego. While the ego thinks its power is grandiose, it is but a thimbleful when compared to the magnitude of Real Power; the power of the Universe – the power that you really are. Yet you follow the dictates of your ego, since you think that is all there is.

In the meantime, this incredible part of you that is as vast as the Universe stays unbeknownst to you and not called upon. Do you not see how ridiculous that is?

We ask only to be a Voice in your lives, but we abide by your decisions to call us forth. We will not usurp your free will.

If you can remember that you are Spirit having a human experience, you can solve all the problems in your lives. You bring about everything that you desire through your thoughts. Each of your thoughts create some "thing" on some level of existence. Everything you think creates some thing, *somewhere.*

And so it is.

Amen.

What has your "self-talk" been saying to you lately? Only we can invite the Voice of Spirit to be a player in our lives.

April

Real Power – the power of Love – never hurries and never interrupts another, instead gives every other "Be"-ing as much time as is needed for the expression of self or Self. It chooses whatever major encounters it wishes to undertake toward spiritual mastery, then leaves the rest of the choices for the "personality" to select, for it knows that everything is choice. Real Power chooses peace over pain, and uses feelings as a gauge to help recognize where it is and where it wants to go.

Real Power – the power of Love – aligns with the Sacred and the Divine within, because it is the Sacred and the Divine within. Real Power considers everything Sacred, because it knows that everything is an expression of the One.

Real Power – the power of Love – never criticizes nor condemns, nor does it exclude, for no one is better than anyone else. It knows that all men are created equal. Each person on this planet is given the same spiritual gifts. It is up to each person to "uncover" them.

Real Power – the power of Love – recognizes that all time is NOW! It sees linear time only as applying to this dimension, since it knows that all time is NOW! Anything that has happened in the past or will happen in the future is happening NOW! Therefore, we can alter our past and change our future by the choices of NOW! We are not bound by the experiences of yesterday. It doesn't matter what happened to us before. Today, right this second, we can choose otherwise.

Create a Magnificent Life

All the ego stuff – around which we wrap our lives – continuously occupies our thoughts and keeps us chained to the lowest vibrations. It has no relevance or significance in our "real" lives; our spiritual lives. It may be hard for some of us to comprehend that the Prime Creator DOES NOT CARE what "drama trauma" it is with which we surround ourselves, from the time we are born to the time we exit this planet. This is because our outcome is assured: we all end up back with the Source.

Spirit is not concerned with all the nonsense that we perpetuate in our lives: our "stories," our excuses for not expanding into Self, our reasons for keeping ourselves limited and small, our petty squabbles, and our indifference to those whom we consider inferior to us. Spirit does not wonder what the fuss is all about. Spirit does not care!

Prime Creator sends us out as an aspect of Its Being and says: *Create as I create. Create the most magnificent life you can imagine for your Self. This is the Power that I give to you.*

Our Higher Self does its best to expand our awareness of the spiritual side of that which we experience. It is always there, helping us through the entanglements of this plane of existence. Only when we awaken to that which we really are, and align with Source, do we see miracles in our life. We move forward under the guidance of our Higher Self, for our ego selves hold us back, and keep us tied to the lowest vibrations, while our Higher Self encourages us to fly.

We can create anything that we wish – according to the desire of our free will – but we engender karma along the way. Our actions in this lifetime will help *us* determine what *we* wish to experience in the next lifetime. In conjunction with dharma (the cosmic order that applies to all living beings), we sort out and choose those lessons that advance the growth of our soul.

Oh yes, there is something else: There is a record of the sum total of every mental, physical, and emotional experience, as well as every thought that we have ever had, in every incarnation, in a book called the *Akashic Records.* This is not a *safeguard* that has been put in place as much as it is a *balance.* We will select another lifetime to be the balance for our current lifetime.

No one judges us when we transition from this plane of existence. *We judge our selves.* At the same time that we do our life review of the life we have just lived, we set up the circumstances for the next lifetime. We, together with our Higher Self, and our Council of Twelve, our Teachers-in-Spirit, choose the major events that we wish to experience in our next lifetime, as well as the people with whom we wish to experience these events. We then allow our "personality" selves (our ego selves) to fill in all the minor choices.

Are you living "responsibly" on this planet?
We are "tied" to every other creation on Earth.

April 2

Giving Up Attack

"Can attack in any form be love? What form of condemnation is a blessing?" asks *A Course in Miracles.* Attack in any form *cannot be* love. No admonition, no matter how gently administered, can come from unconditional Love.

How, then, do we live in this world, where attack is as common as breathing? We do so by somehow understanding that all is in Divine Order; that all is perfect. Possibly, the grown child who neglects us today is the same soul whom we neglected in a previous lifetime. If we can view the child's negligence from this cosmic perspective, can it ease our pain a little? Would we condemn a dearest friend today for the indiscretions of a previous lifetime? Of course not! Once we accept this manner of thinking, we can look beyond the problems that make us feel nervous, unsettled, hostile, and filled with pain.

Just as we cannot be “a little bit” pregnant, we cannot attack “just a little.” We have to give up all forms of attack, from now on and for all eternity. This is an all-or-nothing proposition. How do we do that? How is that possible? Through forgiveness! When any form of attack surfaces in our psyche, either as a distant memory or as a recent occurrence of pain, we can chose to state with firm conviction, *I forgive you.*

Once we start this exercise, memories will surface; ones that we have not thought of in years. These will include memories of people and events that we thought we had “put to rest.” As each memory arises, we must look it squarely in the face, acknowledge it, then state with equanimity “I forgive you for…”

How many seemingly small insignificant events in our lives are still lurking in our psyche, waiting to spring up and bite into our peace of mind? Attack is attack. Attack in any form will hurt us. While we still battle our egos for everything that our egos wish to attack, we have neither safety nor peace of mind. We must simply give it up!

Can you give up issues that you feel
are still worth attacking?
Through forgiveness, we can give up all forms of attack.

April 3

The Folly of Consensus Opinion

Popular opinion, also known as consensus opinion, changes on a whim. What is readily accepted during one era is disdained with contempt in the next. What is commonly received with approval during one period is considered quaint, outdated, or hopelessly old-fashioned in the next. Consensus opinion ebbs and flows like the tide.

Standard practices of different cultures around the world range in taste, varying from elegant to hideous. What one group of people readily consents to as commonly acceptable behavior is that which another group of people find barbaric. *So why do we so often live lives tied to consensus opinion?*

Consensus opinion commonly accepts killing another person in the name of "God;" by whatever name "God" is called. Consensus opinion readily accepts killing in defense of a country whose rights have been violated. This has been an accepted reason for war for millennia, and still is today. This is in direct violation and in contradiction to the creator "Be"-ing that we really are. We have to be trained to become killers; we are not that way naturally.

Being trained to become a killer is in direct contradiction to one of the tenements of Sacred Law, "Thou shalt not kill." Sacred Law is an integral part of the makeup of our "Be"-ing. It applies equally to what is visible as well as to what is unseen; to physical life and to non-physical matter. Since consensus opinion accepts killing under certain circumstances, but Sacred Law does not, should we wonder why the world is currently filled with such horrendous atrocities, just as it has been in the past?

Do we believe that the Sacred Law, "Thou shalt not kill," speaks to us only under certain circumstances? It would seem to be a matter of convenience that we justify who, what, and when we kill, regardless of our passing nod of acceptance to the Sacred Law that states "Thou shalt not kill."

How often do we diverge from this Sacred Law? What about killing the spirit of those with whom we disagree? What about killing cooperation in the name of partisan politics? What manner of killings do we accept, whenever we further the financial goals of the mega-gigantic corporations that plunder the world?

Do we not prefer to think that this law is speaking only to the *other, never to self?* No matter what our justification, what we do to another, we do to ourselves. This is because Self is All There

Is, for there is nothing outside of Self: *Self with a Capital "S" as an aspect of the Divine.*

The Christ Consciousness – the state of unconditional Love – trains us to "see" the world in a totally different manner than the way in which consensus opinion would have us "see" it. The Christ Consciousness (another name for unconditional Love, the love endowed upon us by our Creator) is in direct opposition to consensus opinion and gives us a new set of parameters with which to expand our vision.

Does consensus opinion or aligning with the Christ Consciousness help us resolve our differences? Give up the need to bend to consensus opinion.

April 4

Ridicule, a Tool of Consensus Opinion

We step out of that shell that binds us to littleness, for that little shell no longer suits us. It is not humbleness that keeps us small, *it is inertia*, which comes about when we listen to the *ridicule* of consensus opinion; the popular opinion of the day.

Four hundred years ago, the consensus opinion of the Roman Catholic Church was to put to death anyone who didn't believe that the sun revolved around the earth. For over three hundred years, consensus opinion led to burning millions of women at the stake for practicing "witchcraft," many of whom were healers, herbalists, or midwives successfully delivering babies.

With each succeeding generation, consensus opinion from the previous generation sounds "quaint." It shifts and sways like a reed in the wind, changing on a whim. Many times, consensus opinion is perpetuated by greed and profit for the very few who hunger for ego power. The masses are kept in check, as the needs of the planet are ignored and the Earth is violated.

Ridicule is one of the most powerful tools of consensus opinion. People would rather stay mute than to have to face an onslaught of ridicule, because it makes them feel as if they have to grovel to retain or regain their good opinion in the eyes of the "others." Ridicule is one of the most controlling aspects of FEAR: *False Evidence Appearing Real.* Since it warps the energy fields, causing an incredible drain on a person, an institution, or a nation, ridicule can lead to a *total* loss of power.

Ridicule is an extremely potent tool of FEAR, until we understand why it is being used. Then it loses its clutch on us. Ridicule is a favorite tool of writers, and masquerades under many guises, ranging from sarcasm to comic relief. At times, especially when we recognize it and know it for what it is, ridicule (hiding under the guise of humor) brings about positive change. If we can recognize it *as it is happening and refuse to be cowed by it,* we thwart its claws and retain our energy. Whenever we hear someone being ridiculed, or read about something that is being ridiculed, we can combat the effects of this ridicule by going to a place of stillness in the center of our heart. Then, by breathing deeply and straightening our spine, we allow maximum energy to flow through us. The talons of ridicule do not penetrate us. We can *refuse to be controlled* by fear of ridicule.

Ask Spirit for help each time the barbs of ridicule are thrust in your direction.

How has fear of ridicule controlled your life?
What is so highly ridiculed today may be
looked upon as sacrosanct in the future.

Attitude is Sacred

In the words scared and sacred, by rearranging the letter c, one word becomes the other. Move the letter "c" over one space and S C A R E D is re-arranged to read S A C- R E D. If we think that what makes us *scared* about spirituality is *sacred*, then we may be able to *shift our attitude* about that which scares us.

Our *greatest strengths* may come from our willingness to work to overcome the *greatest weaknesses* in ourselves or in those around us. It is our *attitude* that determines the direction which we take in our lives. We may not be able to control *what* happens to us, but we can definitely control *what we think about* that which happens to us. We can control whether the circumstances in our lives make us feel victimized and weaken us, or whether these circumstances strengthen us and spur us on. We may resolve to never make the same mistakes that our parents or caregivers made as they raised us. If our parents or caregivers demeaned or depressed us, we may recognize that as a way in which we *do not wish to live.*

When I was in the fourth grade at St. Isadore's Elementary School in Grand Rapids, Michigan, the nuns ran a raffle as a charitable event. Many beautiful treasures had been donated for the raffle. The chances were a nickel apiece, and I desperately wanted to participate. That was not possible, since even a nickel was more than my parents could spare on some "chance." Crestfallen, I walked to school each day, knowing that I did not even have a possibility of winning one of the delightful prizes.

That week, during my five-block walk to school, there on the ground lay a few blank slips of paper that were identical to the "chances" at school. I do not know from whence they came, but I picked them up, turned them over and over, and knew that I would use them, even though I did not have that right. With a pain of deceit tightening around my little body, I remember looking up at the sky, vowing, *I will never be poor.*

Very quickly and very quietly, I deposited those "chances" into the box and yes, I did win a captivating commemorative tin of English Toffee candy that day, with pictures of the coronation of Elizabeth II on it. My mother displayed this tin forever on an open shelf in the linen closet in the hallway of our home. It served as a constant reminder of the "way" in which I had acquired that box, and the vow which I had made.

That incident – my unwillingness to be poor – became the catalyst that cemented my attitude to always work hard and do my best to better my life. That sorry little incident became a lifelong motivator.

How is an attitude from your past affecting your life today? Only we can control our own attitude.

April 6

A Perfect Day

An instrumental of the song, *How Great Thou Art*, was playing softly in the background; a selection from *Celestial Morning,* a CD produced by a new friend, Henry Chandra. The morning sun splayed brilliantly through the east windows into the living room, its warmth penetrating my body. During my morning meditation, I saw galaxies being birthed.

Today's lesson # 267 in the *Workbook* of *A Course in Miracles* said: "My heart is beating in the Peace of God. It bathes me in its warmth and soothes my frazzled spirit. Surrounding me is all the life that God created in His Love. It calls to me in every heartbeat and in every breath, in every action and in every thought. Peace fills my heart and floods my body."

I finished reading the lesson, said my morning prayers, completed my daily journal, looked up, and smiled. It was time to start my day.

Why is it that the peace of God nourishes me so? Everything else brings such fleeting satisfaction. The material possessions that mean so much to me in one moment, I cannot even remember in the next, whereas "the peace that passeth understanding" fills me and sustains me; invigorates and energizes me. I need no other. The material things of the world lessen their grip on me.

During my morning prayers, I send light and love and Reiki healing energy to those around me, especially to those in pain. Recently, there have been many. Several of my friends have been diagnosed with liver or bone cancer; not exactly common ailments. Women who feel as if they should be in the prime of life are being prepared to leave the planet. A client who refrained from a lucrative legal career in private industry (because he felt so strongly that the Federal Government also deserved to have the best and the brightest minds working for it) was just diagnosed with liver cancer, and was told to put his affairs in order. A young grandmother holds tightly onto life so that she might see her second grandchild before she transitions.

It seems so unfair.

Yet, I have to remember that it is all in Divine Order; that there are no victims, only choices. I have to remember to live what I think and continue to bless this perfect day.

Can that which is so painful still bring peace into your life? Prayer can bring a benediction to the direst of circumstances.

April 7

The Peace Quilt

James Twyman, the "Peace Troubadour," brought the *Cloth of Many Colors* to the nation's capital in September, 2000. The idea for a "people's quilt," came to him one day during meditation. It was to be composed of bits of fabric from around the globe, and was to have symbols and words of peace on it. Knowing nothing about quilting, he told a female seamstress friend about his idea. She shared it with a few others and soon the word spread.

By the time it arrived in the nation's capital, the "Peace Quilt" was over five hundred yards long *and still growing*. Each of the sections was four feet wide and four feet long and most looked like artistic masterpieces. People offered a bit of their heart in their special tributes to world peace, sometimes including an article of clothing or a bit of artifact in memory of a loved one. Several schools sent white sheets filled with multi-colored handprints of their children. Some people embroidered words of love, kindness, and compassion on their sections; others artistically used puffy paint, glitter, sequins, or bits of lace to embellish their offerings. No two sections were identical, and each section exuded love.

As I approached the Capitol building – a powerful and majestic site – the early morning sunbeams radiated out to the right of this massive edifice, until the rays were too bright to allow my gaze to linger. Symbolically, these shining rays emanating around the Capitol seemed to say that even the Almighty was in agreement with what we were doing. The quilt had been laid out in long sections on top of plastic sheeting, in order to protect it from the morning dew. The warmth of the morn and the glistening dew were so inviting that even the grass begged me to take off my shoes and socks and rifle through it. Since there was almost a reverence in the air, I did not.

I photographed at least twelve sections of the quilt. One section in particular made a great impression on me. It portrayed our Earth floating in space, flanked on one side by a large dove holding an olive branch in its beak, while the other side displayed a rainbow emanating from our planet to the edge of infinity. This entire scene was set on a midnight blue background, a hint of stars in the void. Words such as *faith, charity, unity, tolerance, love, kindness, co-operation, compassion, and love* were embroidered onto its silken fabric. It set the tone for the quilt, and the tone for the ceremony later that day.

One (enlightened) Congressman, along with his assistant, showed up. He gave a brief speech to the circle of us who were holding the quilt and to the others who had gathered there. A large vortex of energy seemed to charge the air; perhaps from all the love and caring from those assembled, perhaps from the energy generated by the quilt itself, swirling around us as this sacred ceremony took place. At the conclusion, we were each given a small loaf of whole grain bread and encouraged to share it with someone less fortunate than us.

Were there other things that needed to be done that day? Of course! Did I feel as if my other obligations were more important than witnessing this tribute to World Peace? Not in the least! Somehow, I knew that this would be a life-affirming event that was not to be missed. And it was!

The greatest good comes from being able to see a world totally enveloped in peace. Peace in our day, peace in our night, neighbors living in peace, countries sharing borders in peace, countries honoring each other's diversities in peace. The next time you are given an opportunity to do something special in the name of World Peace, or anything that is important to you, take it. You do not know how deeply that event will affect you, or how much those who have organized the event will appreciate your being there.

Is there some ceremony for World Peace that you can think of for your community? Events celebrating World Peace offer balm for our Soul as they become available to us.

April 8

Our Sentinels under Siege

From space, we see our planet as a blue and white sphere. All of the green land is invisible, yet, our beautiful planet is under siege. The vegetation supplying us with the oxygen that we need to survive is under assault from every corner of the globe. Our soil is being fried by the chemicals we put on it. The rain forests are constantly being burned, in spite of the fact that the soil is not suitable for farming for more than a few years. Rows of trees along the major highways are turning brown. Trees are the lungs of the Earth. What are we going to do if the lungs of the Earth choke permanently?

Take a look at the barren wasteland on the surface of the moon, or the surface of Mars, and transplant that image to our entire globe. Is it impossible to conceive of an Earth as devoid of vegetation as those two spheres? Can humankind live on that type of surface?

Trees are the sentinels of the Earth. They are the largest of God's creation. Nothing speaks of their majesty more poignantly than the Giant Sequoias or the Giant Redwoods in the northwest part of North America. Standing under one of these majestic trees and looking up towards the sky is a very humbling experience. To think that it took the efforts on one man, John Muir, to save them from being extinguished by loggers takes our breath away. How could we even *think* of cutting them down? What effrontery! What arrogance!

Send thoughts of peace to those around the world who insist on destroying the rainforests, denuding them for farmland from which topsoil leaches away quickly. Send thoughts of peace to those who insist on denuding our forests on sides of mountains, leaving giant wounds on the Earth. Send thoughts of peace to the owners of the gigantic chemical plants producing products that fry our Earth. Send thoughts of peace to the farm conglomerates getting swayed into buying these chemicals in the name of increased production. Send thoughts of peace to those responsible for nuclear waste, so that they look for solutions that include bacterial consumption of these waste products.

The people of the globe can see each other as one large diverse tapestry; each interdependent on each other for the good of the whole. We can learn to work in harmony with each other for the good of this whole. Differences between cultures contribute to the beauty of the whole, just as differently-colored threads contribute to the beauty of a tapestry, which itself is a complicated composition of many small, colored, thread fragments. The people of the world are similar to those fragments of threads. All together, they make up one composition.

What greater gift can we give to each other than the gift of peace? As we find peace in our hearts and share it with each other, we bring peace into the natural balance of the Earth.

Can you send a thought of peace to the "hot spots" around the globe, in place of thoughts of frustration, hate, or war? The greatest gift that we can give the next generation is a planet filled with peace.

April 9

Flowers – God's Angels on Earth

Despite knowing that it will last for only a brief time, a flower does not begrudge its glorious form. From its tightly closed bud, it bursts forth into radiance with a magnanimous generosity of spirit. The layout of its petals may be singular or double: flat open or tightly closed, spiraling downward, swept upward, or in an intricate honeycomb-like structure. The petals may be pronged on the ends, flat and smooth, cupped, spiked, fringed, or frilled. What other creation shows off so many incredible variations to delight the senses of man?

The brilliant colors of a flower evince the full rainbow spectrum: from brilliant white through golden yellow to russet red, to sparkling orange, green, blue, purple, lavender, chocolate brown, and even "black." Flowers come in patterns and gorgeous color combinations: stripped with lavender and mauve, fringed in white with plum, or blushed with lemon fading into cream. Their sizes range from the smallest button speck to the size of dinner plates and beyond; their petals bursting forth in such a fullness of being.

Can you ever imagine a flower saying, *I am not going to bloom today, I have a headache?* Yet, they have every right to complain, since many of us don't give them the proper space, light, water or nutrients. They continue to bloom their little hearts out and raise their sweet little faces to an admiring sun. If a fragile little flower can make its "home" between the cracks of an asphalt driveway and the siding of a home, how much more can you do with the power that is bestowed on you?

The message that my Guides have given me to share with you is: *Take time, my dear friends, to admire a flower every day of your life. They are God's Angels sent here to lift your spirits and bring you serenity, joy, and peace. You so desperately need to nourish your Soul daily, if only for a minute. Take time to admire the beauty around you. Then, perhaps, you too will eventually see that only that which nourishes your Soul is worth pursuing. All the rest is bunk. But even bunk needs to be sorted, stowed, and carried out until it can be disposed of in the best possible way.*

I bless each one of you today: each thought, each deed, and each word that gets uttered. I am aware of your intention to be one with the Universe. I am one with the healing of the world. I walk in peace. I give love. I accept love. I radiate love. I have an open heart to all. I generate peaceful thoughts no matter how drastically the ego's eyes may revile against them or the ego's thoughts may fuss and fume over the injustice of it all!

May peace be with you. Let all joy be your joy. Let all peace and glory be yours. Amen.

Have you noticed the Angelic presences that flowers bring into your life? Let each flower we admire remind us of one of God's Angels on Earth.

April 10

Spirit's Perspective

The morning light had not yet broken through the curtains when I heard an encouraging voice. Yesterday could have been a day that crushed my Spirit, but it did not! Instead, throughout the entire day, I heard words of encouragement – words of calm explanation, words of soothing balm for my Spirit (the essence of my "Be"-ing), all coming from my Guides.

The crisis had come when a friend – one with whom I had worked professionally as a healer – discounted everything I had done for her so far. To make matters worse, the complaint came in a most unconventional manner; a letter. This was not the first time I had ever been rebuffed, but it was the first time ever in my professional life that a *friend* had complained. The protests were so vehement that I kept recalling the words of the two men listening to the Queen in Shakespeare's play, *Hamlet*, saying "The Lady doth protest too much, methinks."

I came into this lifetime to learn to be non-judgmental. So what kind of extended family did I birth into? One in which the members always had an opinion on everything that everyone else said or did. My mother always expressed great sorrow towards the "injustices" of the world. My father railed against the "Big Shots," instead of becoming one of them. An interesting group of siblings, uncles, aunts, and cousins were all assembled for the express purpose of teaching my soul one thing – Do Not Judge!

I now recognize, that, in my own way, I judged a lot. *This was right, that was wrong. This was good, that was bad. Do it this way, my way, or else.* Now I see that all dissatisfaction was simply dissatisfaction with myself.

Evaluating my current situation through my cosmic lens gives me a perspective that I never could have had earlier in my life. I am now able to dismiss the rantings of my friend, and know that her perspective *belongs to her.* It has nothing to do with me. It comes from baggage she is not yet ready to release; things she insists on hauling with her everywhere she goes. Her wounds give her an identity that she is not yet willing to relinquish. I am in the process of divesting myself of everything that doesn't contribute to my peace of mind, and thus am not going to take her baggage on as my baggage.

With the continued help of my Guides, I bring myself back to peace and center.

The next time a situation threatens to flatten you, ask Spirit to help you see the situation in a new light. How can an adjustment in our perspective help us regain our peace of mind?

April 11

A Changing Perspective

During my young adult life, I felt I had all the answers for someone else, but continuously seemed to fail in achieving my own goals. Despite having exceptionally high academic grades in the all girls' academy I attended, once I transferred to a co-ed High School, getting straight A's seemed impossible. A commitment of marriage from the person with whom I fell head over heels in love (from the age of fifteen to twenty-one) was not forthcoming. Not having the guts or the financial means to pursue the career for which I pined (drama), I majored in a subject (English) that skirted the periphery of that which I truly loved.

It was during this period that my ego self insidiously stated, *You will* ***never*** *get what you want, so settle for what you* can *get.* That belief, brought on by a sequence of events that started when I was only fifteen (even though it was subconsciously buried deep within my psyche) led to disastrous decisions as I went into adulthood.

However, in my early adult years, I projected an aura of confident sophistication while feeling both scared and indecisive inside. Both of my marriages came with some very painful karmic lessons. Through many tears – and with the help of God – I learned the lessons, mainly based on forgiveness. Divine Grace helped keep my second marriage intact, as I transitioned from an ego self-based mentality to a Higher Self-based mentality.

During this time, there were enormous upheavals in my work ethic. I had been a nose-to-the-grindstone career woman from the time I started my professional life: from my first professional job (as a first-grade teacher at Tri-Valley Elementary School in the Catskill Mountains in New York), through my employment as a Real Estate Broker/Owner and Property Manager (for our company in Northern Virginia). Nothing stood between me and my work: not my husband, nor my children, nor my health, nor even my God. My clients and my obligations always came first. The harder that I worked, though (and a sixty-hour week was *de rigueur* in my book), the less I felt my husband appreciated me, and the more my health deteriorated. All my priorities had to be violently re-arranged, and they were!

I stooped down to pick up a piece of paper and could not straighten back up. I was forced to walk at a forty-five degree angle. Five specialists gave me no relief. One of them questioned, "Why don't you slow down?"

I answered, "I can't. I have too much to do."

Eventually, the chiropractor and the osteopathic surgeon both performed their magic on me and brought me back to health and to my senses. During that period I was *forced* to slow down and to re-evaluate what was really important to me, and not keep doing what my ego kept pressuring me to do. I was in too much pain to do anything I did not "have to" do. Finally, I gave myself time to do some of the things I "wanted" to do, such as reading spiritual literature.

Thus, this period of intense pain led me to make choices that nourished my Soul and led to a path towards personal freedom.

Is ego's voice keeping you from that which nourishes your Soul? If we do not make time voluntarily, the Universe finds a way for us to make time for spiritual pursuits.

April 12

The Music of the Spheres

We can train ourselves to raise our vibrations. When we *are* attuned to the higher vibrations coming from the Divine Source we can hear, with our physical ears, the *Music of the Spheres*; the exquisite song that sings its praise of the Creator continuously on this planet.

This song of praise is sung all the time, in every place of the globe, by all of creation, but is heard only by those who are attuned to its vibrational level. I have heard it twice. Once, I was awakened in the middle of the night by the most beautiful singing coming from our cul-de-sac. I went to the window and looked out. *No one was there.* The cul-de-sac was empty, yet the exquisite vocals continued to radiate from the center of the street into that moonlit night. I kept staring out the window, totally mystified.

Fortunately, I already knew about the *Music of the Spheres,* so realized what I had just been gifted.

My next experience was different. Three of us were invited to hear the concert of one of our mutual friends whose exquisite voice was to be showcased at the Oberlin Chapel on the grounds of Trinity College in DC. She was one of two singers who were accompanied by a good-sized orchestra, which also played a selection of classical music. One piece was especially provocative. Filled with heraldry and pageantry, it brought to mind massive military movements and conquests by mighty rulers. While caught up in this piece, I heard powerful voices singing with such deliverance and determination, that it reminded me of the song sung at the end of *Les Misérables.* I kept looking for a source of the voices. *There was none.* So I relaxed into the sound of the movement and let it take me to the embattlements to which it seemed to be leading me.

At the end of the performance, I raved to the friend on my right, "Wasn't that singing incredible? Where did it come from?"

She looked at me strangely, "What singing? I didn't hear any singing."

The friend on my left started gushing, "Wasn't that singing amazing?"

I became excited. "YOU HEARD IT, TOO!"

She validated what I had heard. That two of us had heard the exquisite vocals was enough to make me feel as if I were floating for the next three days. Such a terrific gift from Spirit!

Later that night, I asked my Guides, *Who were those beings that we heard?* Their answer was: *Those were the Spirit Guides of the people who took part in the French Revolution.* No wonder that they sounded so intense, so passionate about their mission.

Nicole LaVoie, the creator of the tape series called *Sound Wave Energies*, recalls in her book, *Return to Harmony*, that she hears the *Music of the Spheres* at all times. What a gift to constantly hear the beautiful celestial music that graces our planet.

It was awesome to have heard music from the celestial realm, but the music that mortals have composed has also helped me dissolve time and space, and has taken me to faraway places; even through the birth of galaxies. I have heard the *Music of the Spheres* twice, but love Beethoven's *Jupiter Symphony* and Mozart's *Marches and Dances*, as well as works by so many of the other classical masters who bring the celestial realm to Earth, to nourish us for all time.

Can you stay open and receptive to a new experience that Spirit may send to you? The Music of the Spheres permanently changes anyone who hears it.

April 13

The Gifts of Spirit

Most magazines and newspapers inundate us with things to buy. Television programs are choked with commercials; articles, pictures, headlines, and ads all beckon us to spend, spend, and spend in our pursuit of "happiness." In the meantime, credit card debt is at an all-time high and savings accounts are at an all-time low. Despite all the consumer goods and technical gadgets that proliferate in our lives, there is no indication that we are the least bit "happier."

When faced with too many "wants" in my life, I take a deep breath and *Breathe…Breathe…Breathe…. This too shall pass.*

To start changing our material "wants" to spiritual "desire," recognize that no matter how many "wants" we put in place of the yearnings of our Soul, the chasm grows larger than we are able to fill. When we desire and ask for spiritual gifts, we receive them and feel fulfilled, because spiritual gifts are meant *for giving*, and as we give, we also receive. In Spirit's realm, receiving and giving are one and the same. There is no depletion or loss; there is only fulfillment and gain. For a rich and healthy life, we can choose amongst the following *desires* in our quest for happiness.

Breathe deeply when you say each phrase:

I desire Love, Joy, and Peace.
I desire Balance, Healing, and Well Being.
I desire Compassion, Tenderness, and Grace.
I desire Understanding, Enlightenment, and Unity.
I desire Awareness, Kindness, and Justice.
I desire Forgiveness, Tolerance, and Acceptance.
I desire Courage, Strength, and Confidence.
I desire Harmony, Hope, and Loyalty.
I desire Creativity, Inspiration, and Optimism.
I desire Calmness, Commitment, and Serenity.
I desire Clarity, Acceptance, and Abundance.
I desire Goodwill, Gentleness, and Respect.
I desire Warmth, Friendship, and Enjoyment.
I desire Trust, Thankfulness, and Sincerity.
I desire, Faith, Hope, and Charity.

That hollow rattled feeling will leave, and we will be filled with calm, peace, joy, love, and happiness instead of disorder. As we fill our Souls with all these gifts of Spirit, we fill ourselves with the greatest abundance ever.

Can the cavern of "wants" in your Soul
be replaced by the gifts of Spirit?
No amount of material goods will satisfy a spiritual hunger.

April 14

Living Consciously

Positive thoughts play a big role in the area of energy medicine, and are coming to the forefront of our understanding of how health connects to spirituality. When we treat only the symptoms and not the cause, we ignore the fact that the foods we eat, the water we drink, the air we breathe, the thoughts we think, and the way we move our bodies have anything to do with our health. Fortunately, more and more books, as well as magazine and newspaper articles, are being written for the express purpose of linking pure food, water, air, positive thought, and physical movement to our well being.

The most important facet regarding the thought process is to *live consciously*. We attract that which we wish to have in our life by living consciously; by knowing what it is that we are thinking and eliminating that which does not honor us and our fellow human beings.

Most of us create everything in our sphere by living unconsciously; by living as a *reactive* human being. We can change that NOW, by being aware of what it is that we think. What we think about is that which we will experience in our life. We can move from being a *reactive* human being to a *creative* human "Be"-ing. Both words are composed of exactly the same letters. Moving the letter "c" from its fourth position in rea<u>c</u>tive to the beginning creates the word <u>c</u>reative. One letter: two different positions, two very different meanings.

If we *do not like* that which we think about, we can always make another choice. Like attracts like. *We cannot experience a positive existence if our lives are consumed by negative thoughts.* It is impossible. The energy that we send out is the same energy that we receive. If we do nothing but send out negative thoughts, we attract negative feelings. Is it any wonder that we then become depressed or sick? Every thought that we send out into the Universe attracts similar thoughts to us. *We cannot think one thing and expect the opposite to appear in our life,* because we are a creator "Be"-ing; creating in the same manner that the Prime Creator does – with thought. The key is to live our moments consciously aware of what we are thinking.

There are consequences to our attempts to heal ourselves. Temporarily, we can become ill when we start removing negative thoughts (which preceded negative emotions) from our body; we can experience a "healing crisis." Yes, our lives can temporarily take a traumatic turn for the worse. However, nature abhors a vacuum. The space in which we once created the negative emotions can now become filled with positive emotions. Remember, if it does not come from Love, it comes from Fear. When we remove every vestige of Fear from our bodies, we start to feel better.

When our lives are spent consciously working with energy – sending and receiving energy, clearing energy in ourselves and others, balancing energy, and absorbing energy – we start to feel better. By clearing out negative emotions from our bodies, we re-establish the homeostasis with which most of us were born. Those of us who are totally out of balance can seek out energy healing practitioners to help regain balance.

By living consciously, we become fully aware of our spiritual nature.

How does living consciously attract what you wish to experience in your life? Living consciously with positive thoughts enables more positive experiences to appear.

April 15

Why Come to Earth? A Memoir – Part 1

If we are spiritual "Be"-ings choosing to have a human experience, why do we choose to come to planet Earth? There are easier places on which to incarnate; other planets in the Universe where Highly-Evolved Beings (HEB's) live, as described more completely in *Conversations with God (Book #3)* by Neale Donald Walsch. Why then, do we choose to come here; to the density of the third dimension with its respective dichotomy, with its pleasure and pain, its joy and sorrow, its sublime and ridiculous aspects?

When I thought about this question, I recalled several scenes from the birth of my daughter Elizabeth; my first-born. As I heard her first cry, a high "C" that could shatter crystal as she came out of the womb, I looked over in awe as the nurse whisked her away to weigh her. I remember her fierce penetrating look as she stared at us from across the room a few seconds after birth. The nurse deftly handled her, moving her here and there. Yet, almost defiantly, Elizabeth never took her eyes off us, only closing her eyes in sweet contentment as she lay on my chest. I caressed this little infant sleeping peacefully, choking as my eyes blurred. The nurse brought her to my room that first night, the low light illuminating that same fierce determination in her midnight blue eyes as she searched for me. Unsuccessfully rooting for my breast, her tiny mouth open, but not knowing where to stop, the nurse constantly helped me find a way to help her "get the idea." I remember her first tiny slobbering kiss on my face and the light in her eyes as she smiled at me the very night she was born.

Then I thought of the little beaded star Grandma Jones had sent that first Christmas. Elizabeth reached for it daily as she scooted toward the Christmas tree in her walker. The way she "learned" how to walk by reaching for M & M's being offered her in increasing distances by her Grandpa Joe and his brother, my Godfather Casimir. I remembered her grade school projects – *Under the Sea*, the *Mount Vernon Mansion*, the *Planets*, the *Caravan and Bazaar* – as well as the certificates, honors and accolades that make parents so proud. I recalled her constant and continuous creative ingeniousness.

Yes, I choose to come back here again. This is the place in which I can best serve the Universe and bring heaven to Earth. We have the privilege of raising our own children here. HEB's do have children, but someone else raises them; those who have a special inclination towards the maternal. I forever have my own experiences with my first-born. For me, somehow, it is well worth going through the pain descending into materialism, just for the memories that have so touched my heart. Spirit radiates nothing but Love, but can HEBs experience the same ecstasy that we receive from the love we share here? Someday, I will find out.

Do you have any special memories from this incarnation that you would not have wanted to miss? There are memories here that no where "else" can duplicate.

April 16

Why Come to Earth? A Memoir – Part 2

Not for all the enlightenment possible would I relinquish the memories of my second-born.

My son's birth came by C-section after a twelve-hour labor that seemed to stop as soon as I was given an epidural. When they finally operated on me and lifted him out, I held my breath and counted the seconds – sixty – before I heard his voice, this gentle muffled sound, and knew that he was breathing. He was a beautifully formed baby with a glorious shock of red hair, just as his paternal grandfather had in his youth. And so much of it! Because he had jaundice, he had to be put into intensive care for seven days, while I was sent home in five. To see him, I had to go to the intensive care unit where he was always asleep. Only on the third day did I see his beautiful sky blue eyes. On the seventh day, when I came to pick him up, I watched in horror as the nurse pricked his heel one last time to draw blood and *he didn't even cry.* I counted twenty-two pricks on the bottom of his heel. He must have resigned himself to the fact that this new "place" was a very painful place indeed.

The memories I recall are of an incredibly happy, contented baby; one who was a joy to be around, and one who slept through the night after only five weeks at home. Within weeks, he outgrew the cradle my first-born had occupied for months. He had to be placed into the "big bed," for he was already starting to turn over. His first attempt at pulling himself upright in his crib – when he was only eight months old – was captured on film; his little head turned toward me, his eyes dancing and brows slightly arched. Somehow, he knew he did something *special.* I remember the way he emphatically stated "NO WAY!" when we tried to put him upon the lap of a jolly fat man in a red suit and a white beard. I recall his boundless exuberance the first time he saw snow when we visited Grandpa's home in Grand Rapids, Michigan, exclaiming gleefully "NO, Daddy, NO" when his own father arrived. I remember his stubborn refusal to leave Grandpa as we were going home that year, and the way we had to tear him away as he wailed and cried, while we all silently wept. In Polish tradition, that was not a good sign. We took his refusal to leave as an omen that Grandpa would die within one year. He did.

I remember the little gurgle of pleasure that emitted from his throat as he discovered that his toes fit rather nicely into his mouth. I recall the excitement of his first tooth, his first step, and of all his successful other first attempts. His insatiable curiosity, extreme intelligence, and incredible strength form some of my most treasured memories of his early years. He was always looking for something new: a new toy, a new game, a new experience, a new hobby. When he asking me what "exposition" meant (when he was only four years old), he stopped me in my tracks, until I looked down and saw a headline on the *Washington Post* with the word "exposition" on it. His Montessori training had taught him how to break words down into syllables and "sound them out." Once, I looked up from my magazine at the beauty parlor to see twelve sets of eyes looking at my son and me.

One woman then asked me incredulously, "Does he always ask that many questions?"

For these and countless other reasons, I choose to come to planet Earth. These memories are mine forever, and I opt to come here again just for the privilege of experiencing them one more time.

What special memories have made your trip to planet Earth unforgettable? We have the privilege of enjoying our children each day for the special gifts they offer us.

April 17

The Circular Aspect of Choice

How can we all be so alike – genetically, we are 99% alike – yet be so different? Our personalities are all different, depending on how we each perceive and interpret events. Our preferences are different, depending on what resonates within us, which then determines that which we choose. What we choose determines that which we experience. What we experience determines how we feel. How we feel determines how we think. How we think determines what we prefer. We come full circle; from perception to preference, to choice, to experience, to feeling, to thought, to perception, to preference and so on. The consequences we experience determine the next round of choices that we make. The next round of choices becomes the next set of consequence. A circular pattern repeats.

We continue rotating around this same bubble, and continue making more of exactly the same bubbles, until we stop. If we think we are going around in circles, we usually are! We may find ourselves spinning our wheels – stuck on the same thought patterns – until someone or something comes along to give us extra leverage to get out; to thrust us forward or backwards. Until then, we continue digging ourselves into a deeper and deeper rut. That someone or something giving us the impetus to change can be outside of us, or it can be within us.

If we want different consequences, *we have to make different choices*; we have to look at our preferences. If we want different consequences, we have to reflect on that which we think about, and then recognize how we *feel* about the subjects of our thoughts. If we want different consequences, we have to determine that which we wish to experience, by looking at the choices that we make.

It all boils down to choice and it all boils down to self. We create the entire set of bubbles, the entire set of circumstances in which we find ourselves. One set of circumstances precedes the others in a round-robin fashion. Our choices come from our thoughts. Our thoughts come from one of only two places: our ego mind or our Spirit mind. Our ego mind shouts in a "loud shrill voice," which we have no trouble hearing. Our Spirit mind is the very *quiet voice* within. To hear it, we have to be willing to still our incessant thoughts and go into the silence.

I was firmly convinced that I could not do my spiritual work until we had paid off our mortgage. In evaluating what that would take, I deemed that impossible, so felt stuck in this rut of endlessly wanting something that I could not have. Eventually, Spirit set up a new set of circumstances for me, and told me to quit full-time real estate and work part-time instead. So I thought *Great! I will free myself from the property management and stay in full time sales and listing.* That is not what Spirit had in mind. Spirit told me to keep the property management, and give up full time listing and selling, which turned out to be the biggest blessing of all.

To give ourselves a new direction, ultimately, we must connect to our Higher Self; to our Spirit mind.

Have you been stuck in the circular aspect of choice? Learning to ask our Spirit mind for help gets us out of the muddles in which we seem to be stuck.

Step 3

Believe That It Is Possible

April 18

Aligning with the Mind of God

Why is it so difficult for us to align our thoughts with the Mind of God? We align our thoughts with the mind of ego readily and eagerly. What makes us think it is more difficult to align our thoughts with the Mind of God? The ego's voice is louder, that is all. Spirit's voice is quiet, gentler, more soothing. *It is still our voice.* They are both our voice. They are both our thoughts.

"It shall be done to you according to your faith." (Matthew 9:29) KJV It is always the dreamer who conceives the idea, who believes the idea, who can then achieve the idea, and have it become a reality. Most of what we have deemed "impossible" in the past is now simple fact. When we believe that it is possible – when we align with the mind of God – we open up a world of all possibility. Believing in the "impossible" (I aM POSSIBLE) helps us to evolve.

Think of the "flying machine" of which Leonardo da Vinci dreamt in Florence in the 1400s, and the hundreds of other inventions that had no "practical" application at that time. Think of Thomas Edison, who refused to accept the notion that a filament could not be kept alive, and that electricity could not be harnessed and transmitted across a wire. He did ten thousand experiments until he found the right workable combination. Think of Orville Wright, manipulating a box-like bicycle gear back and forth as he was pondered how to keep his glider in the air and land it at *his* will. This simple action led him to the breakthrough thought that he needed to become (along with his brother, Wilber) the inventor of the airplane. Where do you think their thoughts came from? Certainly not from the fear-based ego mind.

For those of you who do not believe you have a split mind – one that aligns with ego and one that aligns with God – did you ever have an experience where you were attempting to concentrate intently on some project, yet at the same time heard a song running through your mind, or had a niggling thought that kept distracting you? What do you think *that* experience was? Where do you think the simultaneous thoughts came from?

Our body is neutral. Our "ego" mind sends one message; our "Spirit" mind sends another. Both messages are received at the same time, and we actually hear both messages simultaneously. Since we can concentrate on only one message, the other distracts us. One message comes from Love – from All That Is – the other from fear.

Stretch your paradigm. "...You are part of God, Who is everything. His power and glory are everywhere, and you cannot be excluded from them...all strength is in God and therefore in you." *A Course in Miracles*

Can you notice the difference when you align your thoughts with the Mind of God rather than the mind of the ego? We connect to the Mind of God through our Spirit Self.

April 19

A Conditioned Mind

We have been *conditioned*, for thousands of years, to believe that we are nothing more than the products of our five senses. In this limited belief, our five senses *prove* who we are, what our limitations are, and define our total realities. This is utter nonsense. We are so much more than that! Thinking we are just a product of our five senses limits our perceptions. This makes it easy for others to control us. Authors have been trying to tell us that through their fictional writings for centuries.

Since what we *think* about brings the conditions that we experience into form, it is in the best interest of those who are in the seat of power to keep us thinking that we are *small and insignificant and of no consequence*. We raise less trouble that way. We can more easily be manipulated. Conditioning the group mind to go along with pack mentality does not take a great deal of work, if there is a vociferous leader at the head.

We do not have to reach very far back in this past century, merely to the early 1950s, to see the consequences of pack mentality in the giant witch hunt of the McCarthy era. People's lives, reputations, and ability to earn a living were ruined because one man's ego ran amuck. Senator Joseph McCarthy labeled anyone whom he saw fit as a *communist* (communism was the giant evil of the day) and consensus opinion – pack mentality – allowed him to get away with it. It took the courage of one man, Edward R. Murrow, a CBS news correspondent at that time (as courageously re-told in the movie *Good Night, and Good Luck*) produced and directed by George Clooney, to stop the witch hunt.

In a similar manner, it took the courage of one man, the mayor of the town of Salem when his wife was falsely accused of being a witch, to stop the witch hunt in Massachusetts in the late 1600s. It's interesting that Tennessee Williams wrote *The Crucible,* one of his most powerful plays recounting the Salem witch hunt, during the McCarthy era.

We obviously have not learned a great deal from either of these experiences, for the new buzzword today (setting up similar consequences) is *patriotism.* The same mentality that produced the McCarthy era in the 1950s exists today. *The players may have changed, and the words have changed, but the attitude is the same.* It is up to us to put a stop to ego run amuck.

We do not have to buy into the "littleness" that the factions who seek ego power impose on us. It is time for us to start aligning with our Spirit mind; to see ourselves as our Self, and to align with the highest aspect of our "Be"-ing; our Higher Self. We can be – no, *we are* – "powerful beyond measure," as Marianne Williamson claims in *A Return to Love.*

Do you go along with pack mentality just so you can get along with everyone? Ask our Spirit mind to help us discriminate for and align with our God mind.

April 20

Sound Creates, Sound Controls

"In the beginning was the Word, and the Word was with God, and the Word was God." In the opening sentences in the Book of John, by St. John the Apostle, the "Word" is thought and thought is sound; the sound inside the Mind of God. The Divine Source – the Creator – is *Sound*, tuned from the highest vibration, to the vibrations all the way down, to the vibration that we can *normally* hear with our physical ears.

Sound first existed as thought; as the "Word." Sound existed before matter existed. In fact, Sound created matter. From Sound came light, and from light came matter. I once heard the most unusual song emanating from a young Japanese woman, a series of long notes, some very high-pitched, others lower, all blending together in one harmonious whole. As I listened, in my mind's eye, I saw galaxies, solar systems and universes being birthed. It was one of the most amazing visions that I have ever had. After the performance, I approached her to tell her about my vision. She said the sounds she sang were given to her by God, and that the title of her song was *Creation.*

Sound can control matter, thought, and action. Because sound can control, the thoughts inside our head control our actions. The most important sounds that we hear are the sound within our own heads. We hear them both; the sounds from the ego mind, as well as the sounds from the Spirit mind, but it is our free will that chooses to which sounds we pay attention. It is the sound to which we pay attention to that sets our life in motion.

H. G. Wells, in his novella, *The Time Machine,* exemplifies how sound can control matter. Wells tells the story of a scientist who travels one million years into the future. He arrives in a place where the beings are divided into two types; the Eloi (who represent "good") and the Morlocks (who represent "evil"). The Eloi (blond, blue-eyed humans, dressed in pastel colors) survive by eating the marvelous bounty that the land provides for them. When a shrill sound emits from an enormous *sphinx-like structure* in their midst, this gentle race of people come out of their buildings, lemming-like, and follow the sound to an underground cavern. In this cavern, the Morlocks (a cannibalistic race) are ready to devour them. The shrill sound causes the Eloi to become mesmerized – not capable of independent thought – as they slowly file to their death.

The scientist finds a love interest amongst the Eloi, and is determined to help this gentle race. He enters the sphinx, but shields his ears from the piercing sound that has mesmerized these gentle people. He is able to break the Eloi out of their trance and discovers that fire blinds the Morlocks, which he then uses to defeat the cannibals.

The parallel in this story to our current situation is that light (represented by fire in the story) – the Light that we are – can overcome any situation, no matter how impossible it may seem. Just as the scientist put his hands over his ears to block out the sound of the shrill siren, we have to block out the sound of the "shrill shrieking ego" whenever we wish to accomplish something that no one else believes is possible. We have to block the shrill voice that says, *Who do you think you are to think you can change this?* We have to block out the sound that continues to say *No, you can't* every time we have an independent thought and think instead, *Yes, I can.*

Sound controls and sound creates. The most important sounds to which we are subjected are the sounds of our own minds; *our thoughts*. Our thoughts create our reality. Our thoughts create something on each level of existence. By monitoring our thoughts, we can choose thoughts to create that which we wish to experience. There is no "other." Any thoughts we think about an "other" are thoughts we think about ourselves. We need to choose our thoughts carefully; to choose only what we *desire* to experience. What we *see* in our lives is going to be determined by what we *think;* the sounds inside our heads.

Do you hear something within that is contrary to what everyone else says or believes? By monitoring the "sounds" to which we subject ourselves, we can discover what is for our highest good.

April 21

The Power of Sound on Water

Sound controls thought and action, because the crystalline liquid of which we are made responds to the vibration of sound. Dr. Masaru Emoto, a scientist in Japan, recently validated that words have energy, whether they are words we hear or the words we read, which become the words that we think. He did 10,000 experiments with water, taping a word such as *Hitler,* or *Mother Theresa,* or *I am going to kill you, Thank you* or *Love and Gratitude* over each vile of water. After freezing each vile, he filmed the water crystals under an electron microscope, which magnified the crystalline structure of the water a million times. The exquisite crystalline snowflake structure of water, photographed in its frozen state, was drastically altered by the types of words and by the types of music to which it was exposed, as well as the location from where the water came. Words which carried a loving connotation displayed a pure crystalline structure. Words carrying a negative vibration caused the water to look like a globular mess.

Dr. Emoto's patient diligent research validated that words do indeed transfer their energy to water. His research, which features splendid photography of his work, can be found in *Love Thyself: The Messages in Water III (v.3), The Hidden Messages in Water*, and *The True Power of Water:* ***H****ealing* ***A****nd* ***D****iscovering* ***O****urselves,* together with various videos published on YouTube. Dr. Emoto has also made various CD's that he has made of the music he used in his experiments. His work was also noted in the movie, *What the Bleep Do We Know?*

The scientific results of this massive undertaking are being promoted worldwide by Dr. Emoto, as well as being shown around the world via the internet. Since seventy percent of the human body is composed of water, his experiments have very far-reaching effects as to what type of sound is "healthy."

Do you notice how you feel after being subjected to different types of sound? Read the latest research of Dr. Emoto to discover the intricacy of his work.

April 22

The Effects of Sound

The sounds to which we expose ourselves – the sounds to which we listen – will make a difference on how we feel. Many of us eat with the television on. The vibration of the sounds emitting from the TV (discordant sounds) mixes with the vibration of the food that we are putting in our body. Since many of us eat heavy dense meals, laden with empty calories, is it any wonder that we do not feel good and that our bodies collapse long before we are ready to leave them? The sounds around us help deteriorate the vessels we use; our bodies.

Next time you eat, try this experiment. Choose a food that makes you feel great, arrange it on a *real* plate, and then take it to a place that makes you feel calm. Go outside, if that is possible. Use candlelight if it is evening, put on some beautiful music – something that soothes you internally and brings peace to your nerves – and eat the food slowly, savoring each bite. Note the effect this food has on your body. Do this for twenty-one days and keep a record of how you feel. Hopefully, the net result will be such that you will instill better eating habits for the rest of your life.

Notice how you feel after you read a newspaper filled with disaster upon disaster. Notice how you feel after listening to music that is jarring, or a radio or television program that brings only bad news with no solutions in sight or that has an argumentative news host. Notice how you feel after you visit an internet site that degrades the human condition, or play a violent video game. The energy field surrounding your body feels low and sticky. We carry that heaviness around with us – to bed and to our place of employment, or wherever we go – and wonder why we cannot seem to function at peak performance.

We can be driven insane by sound. By understanding the effects of sound (thought) on our bodies (physical body and subtle energy bodies), we can take precautions to protect ourselves from negative thoughts, which are *discordant sounds*. We must control our urge to think negative thoughts, for with such thoughts we wreck havoc on our own energy fields, the energy field of an "other," and the energy field of Mother Earth.

The sounds that we hear – that which has been said to us – can cause us anguish long after the words have been spoken. Our earliest memories can trigger some of our most painful wounds, for emotionally charged words carry within them an energy vibration that can hurt deeply. I have witnessed fifty, sixty, and even eighty-year old adults cry bitter tears over events that took place when they were four or eight years of age, because a well-meaning parent attempted to verbally invalidate their experience as a child; something they *knew* was true. The only thing they learned from that experience was not to trust themselves.

Becoming cognizant of the sounds in our living environment is one step towards improving the conditions that discordant sound sets up in our energy field. How close is discordant noise to us? Do we live close to traffic noise? An airport? A major highway? The subway line? A factory? A railroad? All of these can affect the way we feel.

Noticing how sound affects our lives is all part of living consciously.

Have you ever been aware of that
sound affects how you feel?
Becoming cognizant of how drastically sound
can affect us is part of living consciously.

April 23

Sound and Intelligence

Sound can help raise our intelligence level – the "Mozart effect." Teachers have long been known to play classical music to their students to help them attain greater concentration and better focus. Higher grades are the reward. New mothers play classical music to their babies *in utero*. If we can't afford to buy classical music for our personal use, we can borrow some from the library; from its assortment of recording and CD's. Many times, classical music is the *cheapest* music being sold. Request it as a gift.

Take every opportunity to be outside with Mother Nature. The sounds emitting from Nature provide the most soothing sounds of all, and are in harmony with our Spirit Self. Even a big city can offer natural respites. At the neighborhood park, the birds and squirrels chatter eagerly for any dry crust of bread we are willing to share with them. By being extremely patient, some people have been rewarded with birds feeding from their outstretched hands. Birds are always eager for a hand-out, and their joyous twittering at the treats we give them might be the happiest moments of our day. Plan a walk in Nature daily, even if it is nothing more than a walk around the block and look at the latest changes in the environment, no matter what the season. Note the weather, remember that rain and snow cleanses and nourishes.

Contemplation is a great tool to help us settle into our Spirit mind (which always helps us sound brilliant). Take a flower and stare at it for twenty minutes, really *looking* at the perfection of its creation. To expand into the Void and leave the emptiness behind, look up into the heavens at night, follow the phases of the moon, and contemplate the mysteries of the Universe. The same Universe that is *out there* is also *within* us. Not only will we feel calmer, we may also start to notice that we have greater ability to focus and concentrate.

Monitoring our minds for positive sound is just as easy as getting lost in a negative groove and continuing to think nothing but negative thoughts all day long. That is a choice we make. Just as we can think negative thoughts, we can choose to think positive thoughts. We can change the tape that is playing inside our head, even if it has been there since we were a child, or a teenager, or a young adult. At any moment, in any second, we can change our mind and choose to think positive thoughts.

Believe that any tape you play inside your head can be changed.

Does playing classical music to enhance your thinking ability appeal to you? We can attune to energies that raise our vibrations, not lower them.

April 24

Introduction to My Personal Guides

Throughout my life, with varying degrees of awareness on my part, I felt the presence of several beings watching me. I had the impression of a very patient loving being standing *outside* of me waiting for me to calm down and let go of my ego stuff. Another loving patient being *within* me also waited; calmly, lovingly, patiently while I drove myself in circles doing all the earthly things that needed to get done. The exterior being (one of my Guides) and the interior being (my Higher Self) had to wait patiently until my personality self was ready for their tutelage. They could guide me only when I was ready to listen.

What my Guides kept trying to reinforce is that we are not alone. We are never alone. We always have Beings-in-Spirit to guide us. Our Guides change as we grow and develop in our spiritual understanding. Some perform a specialized function. What we need in one moment, we may not need in the next. And we are never given a "cross" to bear larger than the one we are capable of handling.

Most of us have so many gifts that we allow to lie fallow because we are caught in the grips of fearful thoughts, such as *"What will people think?"* Ten years later, we kick ourselves because we did not act on our hunches, develop our talents, or expand our ideas as we see someone else come out with the same recipe, book, article, invention, store, restaurant, or program that we had been mulling around in our minds for years.

What will other people think? is the one of biggest hurdles that prevents most of us from giving form to our creative ideas. What we do not realize about other people is that *THEY DON'T CARE!* Once they give their opinion about the latest "news," they go on with their lives. If they pay us any more than scant attention, they have no life. We should be concerned about someone like *that?* Besides, if they like us, they will be happy for us – no matter what we do. If they do not like us, why should we care what they think?

So, let go of fear, and think only about "What would Love do now?" Let the path of Love be our guide when it comes to making a decision, whether it is for ourselves, our relationships, or a business decision. Let us make our decisions based on Love, not fear, nor on any of its attachments.

What will people think when they find out your "great idea" has succeeded? A decision based on Love rather than fear brings us peace of mind.

April 25

Message from My Guides: A New World Order of Peace

In the past, those who did not have pure intent – those who chose to exercise power in order to enslave humanity by following natural law – were able to tap in to the Source of Real Power by using the focus of their minds. As is revealed in the Old Testament about the plagues in Egypt, none of the high priests were impressed with what Moses did because they could do the same. They could turn the staff into a snake and back into a staff. They could put a swarm of locusts in the field. They could do everything Moses did, until it came to restoring life. They did not know how to restore life once it was taken away. They could not repeat that miracle.

But Jesus did! And he claimed that "Everything I can do, so can you. And more." *Jesus came from a position of love and compassion towards everything and everyone.*

What is to come is a New World Order of Peace – a new millennium of Hope, a new era of Love – dominated by the Oneness of which we are all part. We all serve the One because we all are the One. We will see no separation between self and our brother because there is no separation.

When we come in Love, that Love will be recognized and rewarded. When we come to unify – to heal, to balm old wounds – our vision is a world vision, and becomes the Vision of the Universe.

Do you feel called to be involved in community action for Peace? The pursuit of peace is vital to our hearts and overall well-being.

April 26

Message from My Guides: We are Your Teachers

We are your Guides – your Teachers-in-Spirit. We no longer need to incarnate on the physical plane, but in order for us to further ourselves along on our spiritual path, we assist you on yours. We are assigned to you at birth. We are each given one facet of your "Be"-ing with which to work and we try to reach you by whatever means we can. We will never stop in our efforts to reach you. Do not underestimate our power to contact you.

You think you are alone. You are not. You are never alone. You need to only call on us. You are the greatest creation ever made and you were given the greatest power – the greatest gift of all – the gift of free will. You are entitled to seek Love, or not to seek it; to seek the way back to your Source or not to seek it. It is all up to you.

We are always with you. However, we do not trespass on your gift of free will. It is only when you come to us, when you acknowledge us, when you ask for our help that we immediately come to your assistance. We are always there for you, but we never break the sacred bond we have with you.

When you calm yourselves down, only then are you able to hear the guidance that comes from your Self – your Higher Self and from all of us who are here for you. It is particularly difficult to get through to some of you. Some of you hear us and dismiss us constantly. You "get" the hunches we offer you and you dismiss them. You receive the messages, yet you turn away from them. Life becomes so much easier for you if you simply allow us to help guide you to a better way. You stand in such mire of confusion when you do not accept our help.

We love you with all our being and wish to extend that love to you. We can help remove some of the frustration and anxiety you go through so often. We help by bringing calmness and understanding. It does not matter who we are. We are legion. We are composed of both beings who have incarnated on the planet before and those who have not. Our only goal is to assist you to find your way back to the Source, to the Prime Creator, to wholeness, to the "Whole"-ey Spirit. Nothing more, nothing less.

Have you ever felt the presence of an unseen Guide around you? Our Guides are assigned to us at birth to help us navigate our journey here.

April 27

Message from My Guides: Filling Your Needs

You think you are alone. You are never alone. We stay with you till you come back to us in the form that we occupy. We are so grateful to be able to assist you, for it helps us in our development as creator "Be"-ings. It might seem strange to you that we also need to increase our abilities, but we do. We have needs just as you do, but they have nothing to do with the type of needs to which most of you are tied.

You think most of your needs are physical. In fact, most of you have every thing that you "need." Unless you are in a refugee camp or in the part of the world that is currently at war, your needs are exaggerated in your mind. You think, therefore you think you need. Most of you are trying to fill an empty cavern that simply will not be filled, no matter how many material things you put in it. But that cavern will be filled by the thoughts of Spirit.

We love you, we bless you; we give you guidance. We calm your fears, we still the churning waters of your mind. We bring you joy, love, and peace.

Hope is what some of you have lived for in the past two thousand years. But the fruit of that hope is LOVE. All will live in Love: Love of one another, Love of Self, Love of Mother Earth, Love of all Creation – the seen and the unseen.

Your Spirit Guides will be made visible to you and your energy fields will be made visible to you. You will have a sense of purpose unlike that of anything you have ever experienced before. The longing to do something else will have passed because you will clearly be doing the "something else." All of this will bring you peace; will bring you joy.

Can you hear your Guides?
Listen carefully for that still calm voice within.

April 28

Message from My Guides: Accepting Your Space Brothers and Sisters

Each of you has other aspects of your ego self and your Higher Self operating on all levels of creation. You will be able to accept your brothers and sisters from space and from the inner core of the Earth. They will not frighten you, because they are you!

There will come a day when you open the door, you will open the door to self and Self. Even though the being may look strange standing in front of you, you will feel a familiarity and a bonding with it. Know that it is you that you are looking at. On a soul level you will grasp that. Know it now. Be prepared, for all this is almost upon you. This phenomenon was first illustrated to saints, then to science fiction writers. So much of what is "fiction" *precedes* "fact," *as you will soon find out. Most great truths were originally looked upon as heresies, and the proponents of them punished accordingly, many times by having their lives taken away from them.*

We wait for you in glorious hope of reuniting once again with you as we have guided you from millennia to this point. Your Earth is ready for her new position in the Universe. Those of you who seek the Light are also ready to be part of her new ascended body. You have matched your vibrations with the vibrations of Mother Earth, which is what is propelling all of you to the new place of ascendancy.

What guidance do you sense is coming "through" you rather than "from" you? Our Guides help us connect to the stranger aspects of who we really are.

April 29

Message from My Guides: We Honor Your Efforts

Your enlightenment is our only goal. We – your Spirit Guides, the Angels, and the loved ones who have passed to spirit – all stand ready to assist you instantly, the moment that you call upon us.

Know that we are with you always. Call on us when you feel shaky, uncertain, or just in need of reassurance that you are on the right path. We stand ready to affirm whatever you need to guide you to the "right" *action and in the* "right" *direction.*

We love you. We bless you. We honor your efforts. We stand in awe of your magnificence. Recognize that. Recognize your power to "be" exactly who you think you are. Recognize your own glory, your own power, and your own free will to choose whatever direction you take. Whatever length of time you need is entirely at your behest. You are loved beyond anything you can ever imagine.

We shower you with love from all directions of the Universe at all times. Your gratitude shines back beams of light to us and shows us in Spirit that you understand who we are and what we do for you. We come to you in silence, mainly as balm for your frazzled souls. We smooth your ruffled edges and offer calm in the midst of chaos.

There is never a time that "you" *will not be* "you," *whether you are sitting in the arms of God – the I Am presence – or in any of the dimensions in between, and we are here to help you feel comfortable in your spiritual quest.*

Have you ever felt an unseen "helping hand?"
Our Guides open avenues that we might otherwise miss.

Message from My Guides: Go to Your Center Daily

We stand ever ready to assist you, to help you see that there are so many other parts of your Self that will not be seen – yet – for a little while. Spiritual sight is opening more and more. It is not yet the common sight, but it soon will be, as more and more of you open to the belief that it is possible. We love you. We cherish you. We give you as much support as we can without violating your free will. We will never trespass on your free will. Every era has its special charm. The New Age began two thousand years ago. The New Age was so threatening then. It is still threatening now, but the fear is losing its grip.

You have a center – the eye of the hurricane – where total peace resides. Reach that center daily. Go there in meditation. You can access it. You simply have to calm your mind. Release your anxiety about all you find so "important." What will all of this mean one hundred years from now? What will all of it mean a few years hence? What you deem so important today, you forget about tomorrow. Find not your happiness in things. It isn't there.

Find your happiness in relationships. Look around you and look at with whom you have peopled your world, since they are all aspects of yourselves. As you open your eyes to vision – the vision of the Christ Consciousness – you will see nothing but your Self because there is nothing else to see. Ask, "What would Love do now?" *when puzzled about a course of action.*

Find your voice. Speak your truth! Let them know exactly who you are, because who you are is a Magnificent "Be"-ing of Light. Who you are is a child of God, begotten of your Creator, endowed with the same gifts as your Creator, and able to extend Love as your Creator does in the form of miracles.

And so it is! Amen!

And so I Am! Amen!

Can you sense the presence of sentient Beings-in-Spirit around you? We have only to ask for the assistance and our Guides will respond instantly.

May

Real Power, the power of Love, is infinite. It always was and always will be. There is never an instant that Real Power does not exist. It has many expressions of its existence and uses the many levels, dimensions, and lifetimes in the third dimension as expressions of its existence.

Real Power, the power of Love, does not hurry and does not worry. It knows that it has an infinite supply of "time" in which to experience whatever it wishes to experience. It chooses what it desires to experience as a step towards spiritual mastery, and then leaves the remaining choices for the "personality" to select. It knows that everything is choice.

Real Power, the power of Love, knows that everything is an expression of the One, and holds every experience as a sacred expression of the One. Real Power, the power of Love, is something that we are. It is not something given to us. It is not dependent on our stature, education, age, development, or our profession. It is our Birthright! It is something that we bring with us when we agree to incarnate on this planet.

It is up to us to reclaim our power. It has never left us and is always there, waiting for us. Real Power, the power of Love, cannot be taken from us, because it was never given to us. It is who we really are.

As a child of God, we are the Universe.

Claim it in Love, for Love, with Love, by Love.

Be Love. Claim it!

May 1

Healing with Flower Remedies

> "And may we ever have gratitude in hearts that the great Creator in all His glory has placed the herbs in the field for our healing."
>
> Edward Bach, M.D.

Even though indigenous cultures and Eastern Europeans have used plant tinctures and teas to cure sickness for millennia, these were not common in Western culture. However, the idea that "if an ailment existed on earth, it could be healed by something present in nature" came to Edward Bach, M.D., a physician in England. This insight came to him while he was contemplating how to heal some of his more resistant cases. In the 1930's, he developed the *Bach Flower Remedies,* which treated illnesses originating from emotional distress.

When I was first introduced to the *Bach Flower Tinctures,* I was enthralled, since I had decided that I would take no pills, have no surgery, and undergo no invasive treatments to heal myself. Instinctively, because I felt that emotional unbalances were the cause of my problems, Bach flower remedies sounded like something I would be willing to try. After perusing the book, *The Bach Flower Remedies,* I started to check off the emotional ailments (listed at the back of the book) that bothered me, and found that most of my underlying emotions were feelings of bitterness, rage, resentment, frustration, and worry that "others" were blocking my path to "success."

This self-analysis revealed some very painful core issues, most of which made me look petty and small. Feelings of bitterness, rage, resentment, frustration and worry no longer fit the model of who I was becoming, but were exactly what I felt at that time. I did not like what was showing up, and had to rid my body of all the fifty-pound weights of negative emotions wrapped around me. They were drowning me! Four Bach flower tinctures showed up repeatedly in the columns of imbalances I had checked off: Willow, Cerato, Oak, and Agrimony. A combination tincture called *Rescue Remedy* (developed as a relief from *any* low-grade anxiety of unknown cause) became a staple in my repertoire of remedies.

Herbal practitioners have always known that tinctures, solvents, solutions, and teas brewed from various plants relieved various bodily malfunctions, severe burns, emotional crisis, and other types of distress. After all, where did indigenous people go except to the "medicine man" or "wise woman" when faced with a crisis in their body? Who were the healers before modern medicine came on the scene? Today, many medications come from the very plants that indigenous people have used, such as digitalis (foxglove) for heart disease.

Besides *Bach Flower Remedies*, there are those produced by the Findhorn community in Scotland and by the Perelandra Nature Research Center in Virginia. Many other herbalists and practitioners have sprung up around the globe, making essences which address the needs of people in their own communities. Choose one that resonates with you.

Could flower essences help you eliminate some emotional imbalances? Emotional imbalances can be the root cause of certain illnesses.

May 2

Healing with Essential Oils

The New Testament in the Bible tells us that the three wise men brought gifts of gold, frankincense and myrrh to the baby Jesus.

Everyone knows how valuable gold is, but what is known about frankincense and myrrh? How is it that the most valuable gifts the Wise Men had to offer included two essential oils? Both come from the resins of trees that grow in Asia and in Africa: frankincense from the Bursera family, genus *Boswellia*, and myrrh, also from the Bursera family, genus *Commiphora.*

Because essential oils address a vibrational pattern within our body, they can heal, calm, soothe, alter, change, and influence the way we feel. They help us to change our vibrational pattern by allowing their own vibrational pattern to mix in with ours. Essential oils are not only being marketed in their pure essence, but are also being added as a fragrance to sprays, candles, shampoos, conditioners, soaps, lotions, bath salts, sachets, and cosmetics. By looking at the list of ingredients, we can identify which products use pure essential oils.

We can also use essential oils to alter the environment around ourselves. Pouring a few drops of oil into a small attachment on a light bulb disperses the fragrance throughout the room and beyond. Blending a few drops of geranium oil, grapefruit oil, and lavender oil in a cup of distilled water, and spraying a fine mist, brings a harmonious air to our work or home environments. This can impact the quality of group dynamics, and tensions can melt.

The next time you anticipate a cantankerous group, spray an energy cleanser such as the one mentioned above, and witness the effect that it has. You may be pleasantly surprised.

The study of essential oils is fascinating. One company, Young Living, merchandizes an essential oil called *Thieves.* Its origin – an unusual one – came from an ancient formula used by unscrupulous men during the Bubonic plague. They were able to rob the bodies of people who had succumbed to the plague with no ill effects to themselves by protecting themselves with this specific formula, hence the name *Thieves.* It has interesting applications, include relieving gum disease. France has thousands of acres of lavender fields, yielding outstanding lavender oils used world-wide. A white rose oil from Bulgaria – one that I especially love – comes from one of our local practitioners mentioned in the Resource section of this book.

Essential oils can differ greatly in their quality. Experiment and see which ones you love best. You will be guided. Purchase the ones whose fragrances are "alive," permeating deep within your throats as you smell them. They can be purchased through health food stores or stores specializing in organic foods, through catalogs, through the internet and through local practitioners.

Is there a specific fragrance to which you are drawn? Look for products with pure essential oils as in ingredient.

May 3

Things Disappear

If you feel like Alice fast sinking down the rabbit hole – you are! Nothing is what it seems. You put something down, go back to retrieve it, and it is not there. You look. You know you had it a few minutes ago – you know you never left your work area – but the item is missing. You look again and again. It is not there! You take a deep breath. *You-know-it-was-there-a-few-minutes-ago.* So where is it now?

If it seems as if an object has been "lifted" into another dimension, it has. This is Spirit's way of reminding us that *we are Spirit having a human experience.* All dimensions exist at the same time and in the same place. This is just one of many strategies that Spirit uses to catch our attention. There are others.

Nothing is what it seems. Things are going to start disappearing; files on which we're working, boxes that we bring into the house, packages that we have in our hands. We might be using something and put it down or put it away, then go back to retrieve it and it is not there. Yet, we know we put it there a few minutes before. Then we spend the next hour and a half looking for it and still cannot find it.

We experienced two incidents recently. My son, during a college break, was in a hurry to leave the house for work, and asked me if I knew where his car keys were.

I answered, "No, I don't."

He proceeded to look a few minutes longer, rearranged everything on the kitchen table, and then gave up and took the spare set. I continued to set the table, and then sat down with my husband to eat dinner. As we were eating – within the blink of an eye – the keys that originally were NOT on the table, were now peaking out of the corner of the magazine; one that had been lifted up by my son during his search. No, I was not hallucinating. They had not been there. They had "disappeared" in this dimension and then were "returned."

I met a friend for lunch, took the glasses off my head, and threw them on the driver's side of the front car seat. When I returned, they were not there. Thinking they somehow must have slipped on the floor, I looked under both car seats, in between the seats and in the back seat. They were nowhere to be found. Six months later, as I was clearing the back seat, they casually rolled out from under the driver's seat as I looked on in astonishment.

Once, while sitting in my sister's car during a trip to Wisconsin, I was putting on lipstick and watched as the tube slipped from my hands and "disappear" in the middle of its journey to the floor.

Events such as these are being done to us on purpose to acclimate us; to turn our attention towards spiritual development. When we have seen enough of these types of events in our life, we start to pay attention. Spiritual development is to become our number one priority. Because of the shape the planet is in, we simply do not have the luxury of eons of time (as we have had in the past) to put off spiritual development any longer.

Have you ever experienced something disappearing and re-appearing recently? The veil between dimensions is thinning.

May 4

Working with Spirit

Spirit says all men are co-creators with the Prime Creator; One with all levels, all dimensions, and all creation, including the inanimate and invisible. Spirit tugs at our heart strings until we listen, because there is nothing else except Spirit.

Please remember that *spiritual* is not synonymous with *religious.* Through religious teachings we *can* reach spirit, but mainly the different dogmas of the various religions on this planet strengthen our idea of separation. *Spiritual teachings* are based on the concept of *unity*: *All is One,* that *We are all One,* that what we do to an "other," we do to ourselves because there is no "other;" there is only Self. As we open to Spirit's teachings, we learn about "Oneness." Typically, spiritual development has nothing to do with any dogma that the various religions teach around the world. Instead, truly spiritual teachings expound principles that apply to all human "Be"-ings, regardless of whatever "indoctrination" into which we were born.

Working with Spirit is exhilarating. Problems that seemed insurmountable are resolved, because we start to understand that within the problems lie the solutions. We will not be given a problem that we cannot solve if "within the problem is the solution." We will be given "clues" as how to solve the problem. We will be open to the clues or closed to them in direct proportion to how anxious we are to solve it. Once we understand that we "created" all of it, we will stop blaming everything and everyone else and start to look for the solution within our Self.

The solution may not be easy. We may have a health problem tied to caffeine consumption, yet the last thing we want to hear is that we have to give up caffeine. Our health problem may not be resolved unless we give up caffeine entirely, in spite of the fact that many merchants around the country are counting on our addiction to caffeine.

In the 1970s, I discovered that even one cup of coffee made me nervous. I switched to half a cup, then one-quarter cup, then to caffeine-free coffee. Nothing worked until I switched to caffeine-free tea. I used to love coffee, but my hands shook uncontrollably every time I drank even a little bit of coffee, so I gave it up entirely.

"Everything we need is given to us." Whatever problems we have are not insurmountable, no matter how severe we think they are. On a soul level, our Higher Self knows the basis for all we experience. Our Higher Self determines whether to or not to reveal that information to our conscious mind. Sometimes we may have chosen a severe situation for a karmic lesson. Sometimes, the fact that we cannot "see" that there is a solution to a problem is because we refuse to believe it.

One of the survivors from Hurricane Katrina in 2005 told a guest show host that, "I learned that I can live with nothing." There were many, rich and poor, who lost everything that they owned, except what they had on their persons. However, their lives were saved, so they could rebuild.

All "problems" are determined by you in conjunction with your Higher Self. Believe that you can surmount any problem no matter how dire it seems to you NOW.

Do you have a problem that seems insurmountable? Spirit is ever on the alert to help us overcome whatever problems we have.

May 5

Predictions as Possibility

Predictions are just that, a forecast of a "possible" course of action that may take place. There are as many possibilities as there are *thoughts* from the people on the planet. The possibilities therefore become endless.

Any prediction is true *at the time it is given.* Any possibility as a prediction can change, just as the thoughts of the people change. That is why predictions do not always come true. As long as people rigidly hold on to a set of beliefs, predictions do come true. As people change their previously-held beliefs (in spite of popular criticism or cynicism), predictions *do not* come true.

A commonly held belief that *one* person *cannot* change the world is not true. One person *can* change the world. There are numerous historical accounts of very humble people, who – despite what anyone else said or did – changed the course of mankind. Siddhartha Gautama known as the Buddha, Jesus the Christ, Abraham Lincoln, Thomas Jefferson (as the author of the Declaration of Independence), Mahatma Gandhi, and Mother Theresa are very well known individuals who have changed the course of events.

Other people – those who lead humble, unpublicized lives – have also altered the course of humanity. These are people who never receive any recognition or fanfare whose lives are making a difference in the course of human events. Their impact is sometimes recounted in human interest stories in newspapers, magazines, or television.

Countless people answer the call when crisis hits. International disasters from 2005 and 2006 have sparked the help of people from around the world, contributing to the relief of earthquake victims in Pakistan as well as the tsunami victims in the Asian Pacific. We do not know how many predictions of utter devastation have been thwarted in the ethers through the power of prayer.

One idea can change the world. A small example of this is the proliferation of magazines that do not take advertising, or use very limited advertising. Most of their cost is funded through *subscriptions.* Up until recently, this would have been thought to be impossible. Yet the magazines that are produced are not only delightful – with high quality pictures and interesting stories – but they frequently carry contributions from their readers, who also produce tidbits of information with excellent advice. These magazines are so well-supported by their subscribers that they are starting to expand. A magazine called *Taste of Home* (started by a group of grandmothers in Wisconsin), which features delicious, home-cooked recipes, has now spun off into a variety of companion magazines: *Birds and Blooms, Quick Cooking, Light & Tasty, Crafting Tradition, Country Woman, Farm & Ranch Living, Reminisce, Country Discoveries*, and *Backyard Living. All* were started without advertising, even though they did not stay that way. All of this happened because someone believed that it was possible.

Would anyone, twenty years ago, have dared make a prediction that a magazine without ads would not only be possible, but also thrive and multiply? I don't think so. Yet today, this approach it is not only commonplace, but is being imitated by those in more traditional venues.

Have you felt overcome by predictions of doomsday recently? Whatever dire predictions we hear can all be changed.

May 6

Simple Pleasures

I pray when I walk, which is why I prefer to walk alone. I love to admire the sky, tune into the birds, and listen as the sounds around me glorify God. The ability to focus on Spirit is lost when I am with someone else, since we rarely walk silently together. I love the ability to focus on my Self and my relationship with my Creator. I take my dog, Taffy, and off we go. He stops to sniff and mark his territory; I stare and wonder about the mysteries of the Universe. This is my decompression time.

Each new season brings its own special glory. It is hard to select a favorite, but if I had to choose, it would be spring. Springtime in Virginia is an absolute delight: so many new wildflowers peeking out along the route; gentle wild azalea and mountain laurel suddenly making their appearance, and such a riotous burst of color from spring bulbs.

Ahhh, bulbs! We have neighbors who rhapsodize about bulbs, planting delightful assortments of them: tulips, anemones, crocuses, hyacinths, and enormous varieties of daffodils, narcissus, and jonquils. All of these, whether multi-headed or with double or single trumpets, beam their sweet little faces to the sun. Just as a young nymph on May Day, garbed in a flowing skirt gently caresses her body, ribbons and wisps of hair flying everywhere as she dances lightly through the glen, I feel giddy from the intoxicating effect that all this color brings.

Divine pleasure comes to me as I turn a corner in the woods and see a lady slipper demurely looking around. She was not there a day ago! What delicate veining, how incredibly fragile; a flower that does not transplant successfully should anyone attempt to move her from the forest floor. Yet, how incredibly resilient she is. No matter what the weather, she stays in full bloom for about forty-five days before the blossom starts to shrivel and go into seed.

What a great joy it is to see a bluebird, or seven of them, as happened the other day, checking out the new nesting sites the Park Authority recently installed at Burke Lake. Each site is critically appraised and inspected. Three pairs of bluebirds agree on a new home and the seventh one flies away, in search of a mate.

Not one cardinal, but two, three, or four fly overhead, then flit from branch to branch as they lustily proclaim their song of praise to the Creator. A chance encounter of the quick dart of a hummingbird or of a gold finch both remind me of the faerie kingdom that seems slightly out of reach, but still so close.

Two fawns rest silently in the thicket, waiting patiently for their mother to come and get them. Further in the distance, a group of deer are feeding, utterly oblivious of those of us who gaze on them. It is amazing how close we can get before they catch our scent, raise their tails, and bound away. *Be gentle with your self* is their silent message, part of the native American wisdom related by Ted Andrews in his book: *Animal-Speak: The Spiritual & Magical Powers of Creatures Great & Small.*

Tuning into Spirit and learning the message behind each creation brings harmony to my heart, and heavenly hope to the rest of me. When I leave the forest and the neighborhood, every shopping center and strip mall, now bejeweled with pansies, tulips and daffodils, in groupings around every corner, beckons me to come by and BUY!

How would your life be enhanced if you continuously expressed feelings of delight about simple pleasures? Our awareness of our natural surroundings can enrich our lives.

May 7

The Power of Prayer

More things are wrought by prayer than this world dreams of.

Alfred, Lord Tennyson

If we understand that we exist within the Mind of God, then we can understand that every positive thought we think is a prayer. Prayers can be verbal or non-verbal. They can be simply nothing more than images of protection, a white light projected forward. When we have an atom bomb go off in our own life, we can insulate ourselves with prayer.

September is hurricane season in the Atlantic. Many time hurricanes reach the coast of the United States through the

Atlantic or the Gulf of Mexico and totally diminish or dissipate into a fraction of the force with which they are predicted to hit. I am convinced it is the petitions of the prayers of the people who live there that help keep the hurricanes at bay, keeping them from devastating the Eastern and Southern seaboard. Added to their prayers are the prayers of the many other relatives of those who live on the shoreline. All combine together to make an energy force that is more powerful than the 75-200 mph winds that threaten the coastlines.

Prayers can help overcome the most cataclysmic event from injuring us. During World War II, a newspaper picture showed a convent left standing in the middle of Nagasaki after the atom bomb was dropped on it. The nuns in the convent said a Rosary to the Blessed Mother three times every day. Everything else around the building was flattened, yet that convent was not destroyed. Similarly, when pictures came out of the devastation that the tsunami in Indonesia produced, one picture in *The Washington Post* showed everything flattened *except* a mosque, the only building that appeared to be standing for miles.

Gregg Braden, in his book, *Secrets of the Lost Mode of Prayer*, brings attention to a prayer of gratitude for that which has *already* been accomplished. This petition is made not *for* a future outcome, but in *gratitude* for the future outcome, *as if it had already been accomplished.* This lost mode of prayer brings with it a special grace which enables us to see through a cosmic lens; through the lens of the Mind of God.

Prayers have been published in the form of poems written by children; sometimes by very young children with crippled bodies, such as Matthew "Mattie" Stepanek. He had a rare form of muscular dystrophy (a condition that caused his lungs to fill with fluid), which prevented him from being able to get out of bed many days. He lived with this life-threatening illness from birth in 1990 until he died on June 22, 2004.

When Mattie was asked what he wanted to accomplish before he died, he said that he wanted to have his poems published. He was only eight years old at the time his first collection of poems, *Heartsongs,* was published in 1998, bringing worldwide attention to what he claimed was his life mission, to spread peace to the world, truly an inspiration for all of us able bodied, fully functioning, healthy human beings.

By 2003, Mattie had four additional volumes in print; *Journey through Heartsongs*, *Hope through Heartsongs*, *Celebrate through Heartsongs*, and *Loving through Heartsongs*, with plans for more, despite his being in the hospital sometimes four to nine months of the year. His poems read like short prayers, usually revolving around the theme of peace and love. By the time he died in 2004, he had befriended President Carter, his hero.

Mattie believed it was possible! So can you.

What have you prayed for recently that feels as if it were an impossible dream? Whatever love and peace we pray for can come into form.

May 8

The Anatomy of our Spiritual Energy Body, Our Light Body

Part 1: The Chakras

Part of our spiritual energy anatomy is an energy system in our Light Body called the chakras, a Sanskrit word (in the sacred language of India) meaning “wheel of light.” We have seven main chakras within our body, with an eighth activated not only within our body, but also connected to a place above our crown at the top of our head. These energy centers are funnel-shaped and resemble miniature tornadoes. They typically spin clockwise for the right-handed person (if the energy center is open), and counter-clockwise for the left-handed person (again, if the energy center is open).

The more open the energy center is, the faster the center spins; the more closed the energy center is, the slower that it spins. If something completely blocks an energy center, the spin can be reversed, be totally still, flow from right to left, or up and down. Each variation means something different within each person. Each aberration might mean a blockage, or that the chakra is resting or changing direction. We can test the flow of our chakras by using a pendulum, preferably a crystal one. A skilled practitioner can feel the flow of each chakra/energy body by sensing the direction in which the palm of their hand is moving.

Each chakra has a name and a specific placement in the body, together with a corresponding color, a vibrational rate, and a set of organs which are affected by this chakra. The major chakras are numbered one to seven starting with the first (the root chakra at the base of the spinal column) and ending with the seventh (the crown at the top of the head). An eighth chakra (the thymus chakra) is located above the head, but is connected to the thymus gland just above the heart. The eighth chakra – the seat of compassion – is just beginning to be activated in mankind.

The following chart delineates them in order:

No.	Name	Location	Color	Organs affected
First:	ROOT	base of spine	Red,	skeleton, skin, and muscles
Second	SACRAL	pubic area	Orange	reproductive system, and elimination system
Third	SOLAR PLEXUS	above waist	Yellow	stomach and digestive system, spleen and bile
Fourth	HEART	heart	Green/pink	respiratory and circulatory
Fifth	THROAT	throat	Blue	ears, nose, throat, thyroid

Sixth	THIRD EYE	forehead	Indigo	pituitary gland, lymphatic, immune, endocrine
Seven	CROWN	top of head	Purple	pineal gland
Eight	THYMUS	thymus and Above the head	Aquamarine	thymus gland

If we are healthy, happy, and positive, the colors of our chakras will be clear and glowing. Any disposition in our energy body that is not positive brings a murky color into our energy field, which can then look as if a grey cloud is surrounding us. People who can see the auric field can immediately note the clearness or denseness of our colors.

Each chakra affects its corresponding organs, and can be paired with another chakra. Chakras one and five can be paired, as can three and five, two and four, and three and six. Those who work with energy can sometimes see a bridge from one chakra to its corresponding pair. The first three chakras deal with the physical, emotional and mental issues of the body, and connect us to our ego self. The fourth chakra (the heart) is the gatekeeper to the upper chakras; the fifth, sixth, seventh, and eighth: the ones that connect us to our Higher Self.

Every day we have an unlimited amount of energy flowing into us; the energy from the Universe. This Universal energy surrounds us, as well as everything in existence. That most of us cannot "see" it yet does not matter, for there are many on this planet who can.

Have you ever felt your energy flowing within yourself? Knowledge of our energy system opens a whole new world for us.

May 9

The Anatomy of our Spiritual Energy Body, Our Light Body

Part 2: The Subtle Bodies

We each have an energy field, comprised of both our chakras and our subtle bodies; which in sum total is called our *light body*. Just as our physical bodies are composed of various distinct systems - respiratory, circulatory, digestive, reproductive, eliminatory, lymphatic, skeletal, muscular, glandular, and endocrine – we similarly have complex energy systems within our *light bodies*. These energy systems, attached to our chakras, are called *subtle* bodies. Conversely, each chakra is also connected to a specific part of our energy field; to a specific *subtle body*. Both of these systems taken together – the chakras and subtle bodies – comprise the *aura*.

The seven major chakras, along with the recently opened eighth chakra, are each attached to our physical body in their own special place, starting from the root (at the base of our spine) all the way to the top of our head (called the crown). Our total energy field – our aura – may be very close to our physical body, or may be very expanded. Normally, each layer is approximately six inches deep, but the first layer can be as close as three inches to our body's surface.

The first subtle body (attached to the first chakra) is called the *etheric body*. It is an *exact duplicate* of our physical body and extends anywhere from three to six inches away from our physical body. The etheric body is what we see whenever we "see" a ghost. The etheric body is the source of the "phantom pain" about which people complain when they feel pain in a limb that is no longer there, or feel pain in organs that have been removed. Even though the etheric body is perfect, because people associate with their physical body and have memory of what they had, they still feel "phantom pain" where their injuries would have been.

The second subtle body (attached to the second chakra) is the *emotional body.* Approximately six inches deep, the emotional body is a storage place of unresolved emotional issues. Many toxins are usually stored in this body, because of the damaged lives that many of us have led. This subtle body is very closely aligned with the fourth subtle body, another place in which emotions and feelings are held.

The third subtle body (attached to the third chakra) is the *mental body.* Also six inches deep, it can be a source not only of great energy but also of great pain. Since most people believe only in the physical aspect of their life, many stay trapped in their mental body, and never explore any higher aspects of self. In fact, most of the world's population lives in a combination of their first three chakras and first three subtle bodies, because they are trapped there.

The fourth subtle body (attached to our fourth chakra) is the first of what is known as the *spiritual bodies*. The spiritual subtle bodies are a much finer energy. Thus, they have a much higher rate of vibration. Each one of these higher subtle bodies is also approximately six inches deep. (A very spiritually-evolved person can have an expanded energy field that can go on for miles, but those people are rare.) The fourth subtle body is connected to the second subtle body, and is tied into feelings and emotions, as one would expect from matters of the heart. The fourth chakra and fourth subtle body together are known as the "gatekeeper," because they monitor access to the higher chakras and the higher subtle bodies. The fourth and fifth subtle bodies can often be felt by energy practitioners.

The remaining fifth, sixth, seventh, and eighth chakras and related subtle bodies are the *spiritual subtle* bodies. They each have to do with aspects of opening up to the Divine aspect of our Self. The fifth subtle body (connected to the fifth chakra) has to do with opening to Divine Will, and with acceptance of Divine Will as our will. The sixth subtle body (connected to the sixth chakra) has to do with right perception; with seeing through the eyes of the Source, or seeing as God sees, without judgment, and with allowance for the highest expression of our "Be"-ing. The seventh subtle body (connected to the seventh chakra) has to do with our connection to Universal life force; the unlimited supply of energy that flows all around us. The eighth subtle body (connected to the thymus gland on the physical body as well as to the chakra above the crown) has to do with the seat of compassion. Compassion, as an emotion, is rapidly opening up in all of humanity.

The first three subtle bodies, along with the remaining higher subtle bodies, compose the "aura" that is receiving so much attention these days. Many people are starting to see "auras" with their physical eyes; not only around humans, but also around other material things, since all things created have one or more subtle bodies around them.

If these are totally new concepts to you, please look in the Resources Guide for the titles of books that can lead you to more information about our energy systems. Belief that we can access them is the first step in awakening our ability *to* access them.

How can knowledge of your energy body help you? Our energy body is complex, but with effort, can be understood.

May 10

Our Energy Fields: Chakras, Subtle Bodies, and Distortions

Our energy fields, composed of fine esoteric material called "subtle bodies," exist as separate layers surrounding our physical bodies. Each subtle body corresponds to a specific energy center within us, which govern the various organs and systems within our body. The seven major energy centers within our body are called chakras, (a Sanskrit term, the sacred language of India) meaning "wheel of light." The Sanskrit tradition recognizes seven major chakras and three hundred-forty-two minor chakras. The Chinese and Japanese internal medicine traditions similarly identify both chakras and energy systems, although they have slightly different numbers and slightly different placements on the body.

Each chakra has its corresponding subtle body. The seven subtle bodies corresponding to the seven major chakras are the ones which receive the most attention. We are not limited to seven chakras, nor to seven subtle bodies. These are only the major ones existing within our physical bodies. Other chakras and other subtle bodies continue beyond our body towards infinity, but the energies become finer and finer as they expand into the Universe. Practitioners in energy healing are taught to identify all the layers of subtle bodies, and can feel the difference between them. They can feel where each layer stops and a new layer starts.

If we have no issues to work out on this plane, and if all our subtle bodies are healthy, they collectively form a beautiful *clear* oval around our body, commonly called our *aura*. When all our issues are resolved, our auric field is clear and glows energetically with white light or with white light tinged with gold, in the same manner in which saints are depicted in paintings from the Byzantine period through the Renaissance.

Most of us experience distortions in our energy field from unresolved problems, which come from many sources and wreck havoc with the vibrancy of our life. When the colors of the rainbow appear in the subtle bodies of our auric field, they identify issues on which we need to work. Very few people on the planet have resolved all their conflicts. Distortions can take many shapes: psychic hooks, tentacles, thin or thick prickly wires, gaping holes, large black masses, angry red clouds, dull gray wisps, or black borders. There are many other shapes. Distortions can also take the forms of ugly creatures that defy description.

Any disagreement, argument, or confrontation can have reverberations far beyond the sequence of events that occur, and can cause a warp in our energy field. A total separation of our auric field from our physical body is a byproduct of our desperation to disassociate from what is happening to us. The inability to release the trauma being inflicted can cause a separation or displacement of the subtle bodies from the physical body. This gives new meaning to the words: *I am beside myself.*

Energy healers may be able to see the distortions – or feel them or both – as they help bring about releases from the client. During a healing session, when my teacher and I worked on a client who had been diagnosed with psychotic tendencies, I felt small squiggly bursts of energy going through my hands that were releasing from his body. Later, when looking through the awesome book, *Sacred Mirrors: The Visionary Art of Alex Grey,* by Alex Grey with Ken Wilber and Carlo McCormick, I saw a picture of the very same distortions I had felt: small three-headed snake-like objects. My teacher identified these very same forms since she saw them within her mind's eye. They were not pretty.

Absorbing someone else's energy into our own energy field can be debilitating. It quickly drains our vitality, without our knowing why. We may not be aware that we have taken on another person's energy within our field, but we do know that we feel thick, gummy, sticky, or prickly inside, or that we feel heavy and bruised from the inside out. We may feel pain or pressure within various organs, an unquiet mind, or other body sensations that make us feel uncomfortable. All these are symptomatic of energy imbalances, and these drain us physically, mentally, and emotionally.

Energetically, we lose vitality through any part of our energy field that is sent out from ourselves to an "other," or from an "other" to ourselves, when unconditional Love is not attached to it. Whenever part of another person's energy is stuck in our energy field, it drains us, for its negative effects on us last far beyond the original events. Some people spend an entire lifetime carrying around someone else's energy without ever being aware of it.

Since most of us have no information about energy fields, we dismiss our feelings and continue trying to function in our daily routine. Yet, we cannot function properly. We feel weaker and weaker, go to a doctor who typically runs test after test on us, but finds nothing wrong. Sometimes psychiatric counseling or bed rest is recommended, or drugs are prescribed to us for depression. If we have an energy imbalance or an energy distortion, these will either not help us at all or provide only a temporary "fix."

I commonly see images in my mind's eye during energy healing sessions. One evening, an image appeared of a woman's head and feet buried into the third subtle body, with her backside sticking up in the air. The legs were covered with striped stockings similar to those worn by the wicked witch from the *Wizard of Oz*. I asked the client if she considered her mother "a pain in the ass." She did. Unfortunately, that "pain" was living within her third subtle body and draining her. Eventually, that "pain" would find its way into her physical body.

Two books from Barbara Brennen – *Hands of Light: A Guide to Healing Through the Human Energy Field* and *Light Emerging: The Journey of Personal Healing* – offer some of the most complete explanations about the human energy field, its composition, its reaction to events, and how the different healing modalities affect it. If you would like a more complete explanation of the human energy field or are being drawn to energy healing, these two books need to become a permanent resource.

More books are currently being written by gifted energy healers. Look for them.

Are energy imbalances making you feel ill?
Energy imbalances weaken us when no
probable physical cause can be sighted.

May 11

Our Energy Field: Chakras Further Explained

We fully understand who we are when we understand the electromagnetic power centers that exist in our body. These power centers are identified in the Eastern tradition by a Sanskrit term (the sacred language of India) called chakra, which means "wheel of light." Our body contains hundreds of chakras, but there are seven major ones running up our spinal column as well as an eighth major one above our head, all connected to our physical body. In addition to the major chakras tied to the physical body, there are many more chakras connected to our spiritual body taking us back to Source.

The chakras are spinning vortexes, like miniature tornadoes. Each one of them is connected to a specific set of vital organs and systems close to their location on the body. Each chakra is a funnel-shaped power center approximately six inches in length, with the small end of the funnel closest to our body and the wide end approximately six inches away. Chakras open both from the front and from the back of our body, the exception being the first and seventh chakra. The first chakra opens from the base of our spine downward towards the earth, but can also be sensed from the front and back as well as from the sides. The seventh chakra opens from the top of our head, our crown, upwards. The eighth chakra connects from the above the crown to the thymus gland just above the heart.

The chakras, when perfectly balanced, each radiate clear white light. When the personality has as issue on which to work, the chakras pick up a distinct color, aligning with the colors of the rainbow. Starting at the bottom: #1-Root is Red, #2-Sacral is Orange, #3-Solar Plexus is Yellow, #4-Heart is Green or Pink, #5-Throat is Blue, #6-Brow is Indigo, #7-Crown is Purple, Lavender or White, and #8-Thymus is Aquamarine. The colors vary, depending on the vibrational level and the issues with which the personality is concerned. Since most of us have issues on which we are working, most of us have chakras fracture into the colors of the rainbow. Many indigenous cultures hold the rainbow sacred with good reason.

An Ascended Master – a person who has completely integrated spirit into matter and matter into spirit, and who does not *need* to re-incarnate but assists other physical beings negotiate through their life on this planet – has chakras that radiate pure white light. In pictures, this is usually represented with a halo around the person's head or a glowing light around their body.

Distortions in our energy fields affect both the color and the *form* of the chakras, as well as the form of the subtle bodies which (together with our chakras) comprise our auras. A perfectly-formed chakra is a funnel-shaped spinning vortex of energy. Distortions can be energy flows that look like masses of angry clouds, balls of prickly arrows, sharp pointed tentacles, piercing thin or thick wire pieces, octopus-like appendages, black bands, iron gates, huge walls, or other convoluted shapes.

When our energy is not flowing correctly, instead of the chakra system resembling the colors of a rainbow, *one* color may be represented up and down the entire spinal column. The entire chakra system may appear to be yellow, if the person is totally consumed with mental work or the pursuit of one goal only, to the exclusion of balance in the physical, mental, emotional, and spiritual facets of life. Gray, brown, black, or angry red masses may also be present, or various objects may appear imbedded around our organs and can be felt as hot or cold spots. Distortions in our energy field show up first, before they appear in our physical bodies, for they represent mental or emotional issues which need to be corrected. Distortions in our physical bodies show up as illnesses.

Have you ever felt any disturbance around a person (bad vibes), without knowing what you were feeling? Learning about chakras brings the world of electromagnetic energy into our lives.

May 12

Our Energy Field: How the First Three Chakras Affect the Physical Body

The first three chakras – the *root*, the *sacral* or *sexual*, and the *solar plexus* – are the ones concerned with our physical bodies and our physical needs on this planet. When we live only in the first three chakras (which is where most of humanity lives), we are governed by either our emotions or our thoughts; the products of our emotional or mental body.

From an energy point of view: the first chakra – the *root* chakra (located at the base of our spine at our coccyx) – is our foundation. Its function is to *ground* us to this planet. If we do not feel the planet is a "safe" or "secure" place in which to live, we attempt to dissociate ourselves from our base. Most of us do this unconsciously to escape the pain which we perceive in our life. Any building that does not have a strong foundation eventually crumbles. The same thing happens to our physical bodies. Our bodies cannot continue to operate on this planet if our physical selves are always removed from our Spiritual Self. When we feel "flaky," we are temporarily not grounded. However, the problem becomes chronic when "flakiness" becomes a permanent condition.

Root chakra imbalances occur when we feel insecure all of the time, are not able to hold down a job, have no energy, or go through life with the impression that no one notices us. These symptoms all identify that we feel removed from our root. Attempting to blend into the walls (because we are not secure about being on the planet), and trying to mentally escape every chance we get are both examples of distortions in the root chakra.

The first chakra and first subtle body are linked to our fifth chakra and fifth subtle body. Distortions in one generally can be traced to distortions in the other. There is a bridge that appears between the two. Healing one will have some bearing on healing the other.

The second chakra – the *sacral* or *sexual* chakra (located in the area of our sex organs and our sacral distributor) – is the center of creation and relationships. Its function has to do with creativity, along with our personal relationships and our feelings. Any problems that we have with family issues (starting with the family into which we were born) are manifested here. The situations that cause us to feel loved or hated by an "other," the type and quality of involvement that we can have with an "other," and the feelings of being desired by an "other" – *or not* – are all stored here.

The second chakra is involved with the creative aspects of our lives and with how we express our creativity. Creativity, paradoxically, is one aspect of human life that can be highly rewarded financially by those courageous enough to exhibit it, and is encouraged by the most progressive teachers of our planet. Unfortunately, many educational institutions and teachers reward rote memory instead. We experience physical pain when we constantly "abort" our creative ideas before we give them a chance to "birth." Sadly, when we do this, we often do not know why we then feel so sick.

The second chakra and the second subtle body are linked to the fourth chakra and fourth subtle body. One is concerned with physical love and the other with spiritual love.

The third chakra – the *solar plexus* (located just below our navel) – is both the seat of our personal will as well as our gut instinct. Its function has to do with the self. Our personal ego lives here: how we see ourselves, what we believe about ourselves, and our ability to set and accomplish goals.

Our ability to tap into an energy that cannot be explained by logic alone also lives in the third chakra. Fortunately, we have a built-in safeguard for survival on this planet called our "sixth" sense; our intuitive sense, our gut instinct. This helps us identify things that are not in our best interest, when we are in danger, or when a different course of action is better for us, because, on some other level, we have already experienced it. This helps us "know" when someone is lying to us, since a part of us feels physical discomfort, no matter how cleverly or how sincerely the "other" tries to convince us. Our subtle body clutches when it hears an untruth, because what connects us to the Divine cannot lie. This chakra helps us navigate through this lifetime by helping us decide what is or is not in our own best interest.

The third chakra and third subtle body are linked to the sixth chakra and sixth subtle body. The third chakra and third subtle body enables us to connect to Divine intuition, even when our third eye (in our sixth chakra) is closed.

What are the names and functions of each of the first three chakras? Learning about the chakras and their effects on our body enables us to cope more effectively.

May 13

Our Energy Field: How the Fourth through Eighth Chakras Affect the Body

The chakras associated with the spiritual aspects of man are the remaining five chakras: four through eight.

The fourth chakra – the "Gatekeeper" to the upper realm – is called the *heart* chakra, and is also known as the Seat of Love. The function of the fourth chakra is to be the switch: the gatekeeper, the entrance to the higher realms. Love is the purpose for which we were created. We spring from Love. We are designed to manifest Love, to spread Love to whomever and whatever we touch on this planet. The fourth chakra helps us bring into form *our true purpose* on this planet. Lust and infatuation and all the other variations of romantic crushes all come from the second chakra. Unconditional Love comes from the fourth.

I have seen incredible blocks in the fourth chakra: huge padlocks, enormous boulders, giant screws, boards, iron bars, boxes, concrete forms, angry masses, leaks, holes, gaps, drainage systems, hot spots, prickly balls; all stemming from distortions in the fourth chakra. All were related to issues of Love.

The fifth chakra – the *throat* chakra, the seat of Divine Will – functions to connect us to our spiritual truth, and allows us to speak that "truth." This does not mean that we have now been given a license to be "cruel" to others in the name of speaking our truth, for Divine Will *never* harms. When we are truly connected to Divine Will, we are able to state our "preference" without fear of retribution for our statement. We state what we believe, but are not concerned with converting anyone else to our belief system and have no need to hurt an "other" if they believe otherwise. We simply state what our belief is, without looking to the "other" for validation. No "other" has the whole truth for us. Only we can determine that. Only we can know what our truth is.

When this chakra is activated, we are able to do the Will of God because our personal will is in alignment with Divine Will. There is no separation. Trust me, if we have been called to do the Will of God – which *is* our will since we are an *aspect of God* – Spirit does not back off. We are corralled into the work for which our Higher Self contracted, no matter how long it takes for us to understand our missions. This may upset all "others" in our life: our spouses or significant others, children, parents, best friends, fellow employees, business partners, and social groups; all because we have upset the status quo. However, we will not be released from our soul's contract until we complete it.

Millions of people are unwilling to share their experience for fear of ridicule, but that in no way changes the experience. This book is a prime example of both my speaking my truth and doing the Will of God. To fulfill my soul's contract, I had to overcome the fear of ridicule, which I did with the publication of my first book: *God is the Biggest Joker of All.* In that book, I made statements for which I felt "others" would criticize me – including the name of the title. I had to get over worrying about whether or not I would be ridiculed for these statements. Only after I received feedback from people had who thanked me for standing in my truth, did I realize that every person on this planet may have had an experience that they cannot explain but are not willing to talk about.

The sixth chakra – the *brow* – is commonly known as the Third Eye. It is our opening to the Higher planes (to our Spirit Self), and functions to strengthen our connection to the Divine. It is our "psychic" or intuitive chakra. "Perception" (which comes from the ego self) changes to "knowledge" (which comes from the Higher Self). It is through the sixth chakra that we are able to hear and understand our Guides, Ascended Masters, and Angels. These beings communicate with us at all times and in all places, but we often do not pay attention to them. It is through the opening of this chakra that we divest ourselves of the demands of our egos and give more credence to the instructions of Spirit. It is through the third eye in our brow chakra that we can see our Angels, our Spirit Guides, the Ascended Masters, and nature spirits as well as the other lower astral beings known as ghosts, along with other dimensional beings inhabiting the astral plane.

The seventh chakra – the *crown* chakra – is our connection to the Source. Its function is to unite us to the Divine; to the Source of All That Is. When we connect to the Divine aspect of who we really are, we flow as part of One design, One master plan, One functioning body. We are incapable of harming the planet or anyone or anything on it, for we know that we are only harming ourselves.

Through the crown chakra, energy healers are able to access all the information needed about a client, put energy into the entire physical body, and identify distortions in the energy field as well as illnesses in the physical body. Energy healers "see" distortions through their eyes, through their physical eyes, or through their third eye, located in the brow chakra.

Finally, the eighth chakra – the *thymus* chakra (located *above* the crown chakra but connected to the thymus gland just above the heart) – is the last major chakra to open. Its function is to be the seat of compassion. Compassion is tied to caring. This guiding force of compassion strengthens man's humanity to man, to the planet, and to all the creatures on the planet. The opening of this chakra in the many people across the world has lovely ramifications for the future of this planet. The underprivileged, inhabiting most of the world, benefit the most from the opening of the eighth chakra.

Can you summarize the function of the upper chakras; four through eight?
The upper chakras, associated with our spiritual body, set the future course of the planet.

May 14

Our Energy field: How Subtle Bodies Align – Chakras 1 – 4

Chakras are connected to layers of consciousness via an energy system comprised of subtle bodies. Each chakra has its own subtle body; an independent layer of consciousness with which we can communicate and which stores energy or a distortion of energy. Collectively, the subtle bodies form the *aura*; an egg-shaped mass of energy around our physical body.

Every one of the chakras is connected to another esoteric part of us, which collectively comprise our "subtle bodies." Each subtle body exists as an egg-shaped layer surrounding our physical body. Each subtle body has a name and a function, and is an independent layer of consciousness with which we are able to communicate. Through our subtle bodies, we can "feel" someone looking at us although our back is to them, can feel the "presence" of someone even when no one is there, can "feel" anger in a room (even when not a word is spoken), or can "feel" grief or terror in a room long after the incident happened that caused that terror or grief. Just ask anyone who has ever visited Auschwitz.

The first subtle body (an exact template of the physical body, and connected to the first chakra, the root chakra) is called the *etheric* body. Even if we lose a limb or an organ, our etheric body is still completely intact. This is the source of "phantom pain;" pain in an organ or appendage that no longer exists on our physical body.

The etheric body is also what we see when see ghosts; those beings who hang out in the astral plane of existence, which is so closely tied to the earth that most beings there still feel they are on earth. Their physical body is gone, but their etheric body is totally intact. In *their dimension* – in the astral plane – they appear to themselves just as solid as you and I appear to ourselves in our dimension. Since they have not committed themselves to the new spiritual dimension to which their soul *was supposed to go*, they stay caught between two dimensions and "haunt" this one. The movie *Ghost* (with Demi Moore and Patrick Swayze) effectively portrays the experience of being "caught" in the astral dimension. Another movie that captures this dimension perfectly is *What Dreams May Come* with Robin Williams.

The etheric body (approximately three inches to six inches thick), together with the other subtle bodies, can be "missing" from its correct placement on the physical body: it can be moved to the side of the physical body, completely deflated, or exhibit an assortment of peaks or valleys. Any displacement or distortion of the subtle bodies can cause problems to the physical body.

The second subtle body (connected to the second chakra, the sacral chakra) is called the *feeling* body and – if healthy – is approximately six inches thick. The second chakra is tied to our feelings about whether or not we are *lovable* to an "other," whether we feel we *deserve* to be loved, and whether or not we feel we are *capable* of loving an "other." Our hopes, dreams, and motivations live here, along with all the creations that we hope to birth.

The negative feelings that we feel "go" somewhere, and the second subtle body is the storehouse for many of them. Negative feelings make us feel so uncomfortable that we squash them into deeper and deeper layers inside our physical bodies. We think we have dealt with them in a positive manner. All we have done is temporarily remove them from our conscious mind. In the layers of energy into which they have sunk, negative feelings roam freely, affecting everything with which they come in contact. Also, they hurt whatever they contact. As we continue to further squash our feelings inside of us, we wonder why we hurt so much.

The third subtle body (connected to the third chakra, the solar plexus chakra) is called the *mental* body, and is also approximately six inches thick. Most of the thoughts we think throughout the day reside in this third subtle body. If we think positive thoughts throughout the day, we develop a healthy third subtle body. If we think mainly negative thoughts, all those negative thoughts eventually develop enough energy to become a "form" and *go somewhere*. They can end up as *negative thought forms* hosted in our feeling body. If we think them often enough, they can then become forms having *an energy, intelligence, and a life of their own*, which can wreck havoc with our energy field and our health.

Most of the people on this planet cannot get past the ego demands of the first three subtle bodies, and spend a comfortable or uncomfortable existence pursuing nothing but the demands of their egos during their entire lives. People obsessed with making money might have a mental body that expands and overshadows the rest of their subtle bodies. Thus, the yellow light of the third chakra overpowers the rest of the chakra colors. Many businessmen have that as their reality. Obsessions and compulsions live in the third subtle body. Overdrive and ambitions live here.

The fourth subtle body (connected to the fourth chakra, the heart chakra) is called the *emotional* body. When distortions occur in the second chakra and its associated subtle body, they often affect the fourth chakra and its subtle body. Just as one cannot separate the dancer from the dance, feelings and emotions cannot be separated. Our feelings cause our emotions to erupt, if they are not dealt with in a healthy manner. If we attempt to suppress our feelings, they may get buried deep within our layers of consciousness, but they do not go away. Neither do they disappear by themselves. Eventually, we have to deal with all of our "buried" feelings and emotions.

The density of the lower three subtle bodies is greater than the upper five, and can be felt quite easily with your hands. An exercise to help you feel your energy field is one I call *Pulling Taffy*. Rub your hands briskly, then bring them together as if you were holding a basketball. Very slowly move them closer together to the size of a large softball, then pull them apart again. Repeat and notice the sensation felt in your palms. Visualize this energy as a ball of light between your hands. Then rotate this ball of light. You should be able to feel the energy pulsating between your palms and fingertips.

Practice sensing energy often until you master it.

Can you feel the density of the first three subtle bodies? As we practice sensing energy, we become skilled at it.

May 15

Our Energy Fields: How Subtle Bodies Affect Our Well-Being

The names of the subtle bodies of the fifth, sixth, seventh, and eighth chakras correspond to the numbers of their chakras. The energy of the subtle bodies of the higher chakras has a much finer esoteric quality to it and, together with the lower subtle bodies, comprises our individual energy field; our aura.

Since the subtle bodies of the upper chakras are related to our spiritual development, as we open towards spiritual matters, our subtle bodies expand. Normal, healthy, well-connected subtle bodies in the upper chakras are about six inches thick, but will expand in proportion to the understanding of spiritual matters that the ego personality (self) exhibits. As each ego personality opens to matters of Spirit (Higher Self), the subtle bodies grow in proportion. Ascended Masters have subtle bodies that extend for miles.

Each subtle body is a separate layer of consciousness with which we can communicate. By practicing, we are able to feel the edge of the subtle body; the edge where the *matrix* exists; a uniformly-spaced set of communications lines that connect the different aspects of our individual energy field. In addition to the subtle bodies and chakras, there are also grid lines of communication running between each one of our chakras. These energy connections can be brightly lit or fully dimmed. This energy matrix, called the Fabric of the Universe, stores information for the Self and the planet, and is part of the Christ grid. We can tap into the same information about ourselves that a skilled energy healing practitioner is able access and read. All it takes is practice and persistence.

Each subtle body flows in a specific direction. If we are right-handed, the energy that comprises the subtle body flows clockwise; if we are left-handed, the energy that comprises the subtle body flows counter-clockwise. Professional energy practitioners check the flow of our subtle bodies by placing their hands over us and feeling which way their hands move naturally. When we have an imbalance, our subtle bodies will reverse their flow. When that happens, the subtle body feels irritating, in the same manner that going against the nap in a carpet feels irritating, as it drags against our palm.

A reversal in the natural flow of our subtle bodies signifies an imbalance or a distortion, and appears in our subtle bodies before it appears in our physical bodies. When distortions or imbalances move down into our physical bodies, they are called illnesses. When given enough energy – when the same thought occurs over and over again – distortions and imbalances in our subtle bodies sometimes appear as *negative thought forms*. Each of these will have an energy, a vitality, and an existence of its own.

Distortions and imbalances in the subtle bodies need to be cleared out on a daily basis, and can easily be done by each person. The best advice I was given by my teacher was to say: "clear, center, align, balance, and ground" at the end of each day and after working on each client. Some negative thought forms clear quickly; some take longer. Everything depends on how deeply imbedded the distortions and imbalances are. Distortions and imbalances can be hidden quite deeply, because the layers of consciousness in subtle bodies appear like layers of an onion. Even when one layer of distortions and imbalances is healed, another may be uncovered and need to be healed.

If people are in such a state of weakness and so depleted that they *cannot* help themselves, then they need to consult with a qualified practitioner. By being open to the guidance of Spirit, the right practitioner will be placed in their path; one who also can give them suggestions that will enable them to help themselves. Only the client can determine how many treatments they need beyond the first one. A qualified practitioner never suggests the amount of treatments, but instead allows the client to determine that. Some people only need one.

The energy field of a healthy person surrounds that person in an egg-shaped casing around the physical body, extending outwards to the tips of the fingers. A normal energy field feels "plump" and healthy and may even lightly "buzz."

If you are a person who has a displaced energy field, even if it is slightly *off to the side,* the area around your body will feel cold and *vacant.* No images or feelings appear for those testing you, for there is nothing "there" for them to feel.

Many people are totally divorced from their energy body system; their subtle bodies are displaced from their normal placement around the physical body. Their energy body is *off to the side* of their physical body, or has huge distortions in it such as gaping holes, leaks, blocks, tears, rifts, peaks and valleys. People who feel their lives are too difficult – that they are unable to cope with life on this planet – typically experience this. Most people have no idea about the makeup of their spiritual bodies, but do *know* they feel awful; that they are completely depleted of energy.

If you are one of those people who does not feel well – who feels that you are out of balance and out of energy – you may want to investigate energy healing further. Check the internet for someone in your area.

The subtle bodies of the higher chakras (related to the spiritual body, composed of finer esoteric materials) combine and extend into the Universe *ad infinitum*. We truly are unlimited "Be"-ings.

Do you experience low energy?
When our spiritual side is in balance, then
our physical body is also in balance.

May 16

Chakras and Subtle Bodies: Further Characteristics

As we mature, so do our chakras. According to Barbara Brennen, author of *Hands of Light* and *Light Emerging,* the chakras of babies are not as well defined as those of adults. They appear fuzzy and indistinct and their strength is diminished. They strengthen and grow as the baby strengthens and grows, exactly in keeping with the growth and development of the physical body.

Just as the health of our chakras and subtle bodies is determined by that which we create through our thoughts and feelings, our thoughts also put up blocks, barriers, and boundaries around each chakra, which in turn causes them to create distortions. There is a misconception that chakras close only when we are dead. This is not the case. Our thoughts cause our chakras and subtle bodies to change minute by minute. If our thoughts are negative, the strength of our chakras and subtle bodies is diminished, and if positive, strengthened. Testing the strength of our chakras with a pendulum reveals our thoughts only at the moment the test takes place. A change can occur as soon as our thoughts change.

Both our conscious mind and our unconscious mind are influential in the opening and closing of our chakras. Our conscious mind flits from topic to topic very quickly, and only we know if these thoughts are positive or negative. Our subconscious mind erects barriers in our conscious mind as a form of protection. We may be resistant to letting matters of Spirit unfold in our conscious mind for we may associate matters of Spirit with pain and death.

You may have had a past life where you were killed for being involved in spiritual matters, especially if you were female. Up to nine million women, over three centuries, were burned at the stake for being "witches." Many of these women were "guilty" only of healing with herbs, or of being a mid-wife. Perhaps you were once one of them.

If we are a spiritual seeker in this lifetime, the chances are that we were a disseminator of spiritual truths in "other" lifetimes as well. Alternatively, we may have chosen lives where, as a statesman or leader, we could pursue something higher than just the subsistence existence an average life allowed.

Many people still live in cultures where their lives are threatened if they disagree with group mind, which is not yet ready to accept information about the energy field. That situation is slowly changing, as information is disseminated via the media – especially the internet. Even the most remote outposts in the world can now be reached through technology. As the youth of each restrictive culture have access to more and more information, they refuse to bend to the norms which their government and religious leaders impose on them. Eventually, they will become the leaders of the countries that attempt to squash them now. As more and more information about the energy field is disseminated, group mind changes.

In each era, the danger of disagreeing with group mind lessened, just as the climate of fear generated once by the Catholic Church during the Inquisition has faded. Four hundred years ago, one of the most respected scientific minds in the world, Galileo, was a victim of the Inquisition. The power of the Catholic Church during the time of the Inquisition was power run amok. Views once held by the Catholic Church now look inverted; so contrary to reason that they are laughable.

As Galileo was forced to agree that the earth was the center of the solar system (under threat of losing his life), he muttered under his breath, "And yet, it moves."

None of the information on the energy field has to be taken on "faith." There are ways to see the energy field through the miracle of photography. The energy field – the chakras and the subtle bodies – can be photographed using Kirlian photography; a method of capturing the image of changing emotional states developed in 1939 by S. Kirlian, a Russian scientist. Any photographer who has Kirlian photography equipment has the ability to take a picture of your auric field. Because a photograph of your auric field changes each time you are photographed, this snapshot becomes a record of your emotional, mental, and spiritual states during various intervals in your life.

I once saw a picture of a woman whose auric field was totally green – the color of the heart chakra, typically associated with healing energy – yet she did not consider herself a healer. In fact, she was not even remotely interested in spiritual matters. Obviously, her Spirit was attempting to get that message across to her.

How can knowledge of the subtle bodies inspire you to change? The ability to feel or see our auric field can help open us to spiritual matters.

May 17

Healing with Light

When we become interested in learning to work with energy for the purpose of healing, we first learn how to *increase* the amount of light that we pass through our hands. We then learn how to pass light through our heart, through our eyes, and then through every cell in our own body. The healing that comes by touching someone else comes from the *Light* that we pass through our own self. We can heal another by sending light into them through any part of our body, but the most common is to send light through our hands. Energy healing has been practiced in the Eastern culture for millennia, but has been introduced to Western culture relatively recently.

"Man is the only one of God's creations who can pass light through his hands" spoke Jesus the Christ in *New Revelations for an Awakening Humanity* by Virginia Essene.

All healing starts with intent. First, we *state our intent to heal* as we place our hands on the person desiring the healing. By opening our crown chakra, we allow the *Universal life force* (light energy/ God's energy) to come into our own physical body, and pass through us (our hands, our hearts, our eyes, and eventually, every cell in our body) into the person to whom it is directed. *Universal life force* (a light esoteric energy flowing through everything on this planet) is Source energy from the Divine. We combine Earth energy (a heavier radiant Source energy emanating from planet Earth) with the lighter, finer Source energy (coming in through our crown chakra) for maximum healing energy. Earth energy is needed for grounding, for connecting us to planet Earth, and for healing issues related to family, origin, culture, and support. Source energy – connecting us to the Divine within – along with Earth energy, is used for healing mental, emotional, and physical imbalances, and for healing our sense of separation from the Divine.

The energies surrounding all beings – human, animal, mineral and vegetable – are layers of consciousness with which we can communicate. We witness each layer, with its separate function and different color, as it changes color, depending upon the physical, mental, emotional, or spiritual issues through which the personality is working. The spiritual gift of being able to *see* the colors surrounding a person's energy field – one that now only a few people possess – will soon be commonplace.

Healing with light reinforces the belief in our Self and in our Divine nature – that aspect of our selves that is connected to the Divine. Light is channeled through the chakras and the subtle bodies that surround the physical body; both inside and outside the physical body.

We are a more complex organism than biology and physiology books show us to be. We are composed of particles of light that respond to the *infusion* of new energy as well as to the *disbursement* of old "stuck" energy. Before ailments attack our physical body, they show up as distortions in our energy field.

New energy coming in disperses throughout the physical body and does not need us to focus and direct it. It knows where to go, for it knows what part of the body needs attention. The healing energy has an intelligence of its own and does not have to be "directed." It knows where to go and to whom. Should the recipient be closed to it, and not be willing to receive any energy healing, the Higher Self directs the energy to another who is receptive. Each layer of energy has an intelligence of its own with which we can communicate.

Since energy is not confined by time or space, *long distance* healing is also effective. Because energy is not limited by time or space, we can send it anywhere to anybody. Once we are "attuned" to the method of energy healing that we prefer, we can send healing energy to people and places around the world. It works because it is part of the *Divine aspect* of who we really are.

One of the best things that we can do is to send healing energy to the entire globe so that it can reach the "hot spots" of the world – the places where the most trouble "reigns" – and to the leaders of those areas who are responsible for the continuation of war, as well as to those in circles of diplomacy, who are the harbingers of peace.

There are many energy healing modalities available today: Reiki, intuitive healing, Healing Touch, Therapeutic Touch, Polarity Therapy, Zero Balancing, Quantum-Touch, cranial-sacral therapy, fingertip touch, reflexology, acupuncture, and the Feldenkrais Method, along with tai chi, qi gong, Falun Gong and Jo Rei. All martial arts programs utilize energy. Other modalities, such as feng shui, (pronounced "fung shway") also make use of energy as the underlying basis of their effectiveness.

By exploring methods of energy healing, ones about which we are drawn to know more, we open up a world of possibilities for ourselves.

Does working with healing energy appeal to you? Many health care givers have enormous healing energy in their hands.

May 18

Message from My Guides: Your Heart's Desire

You have such incredible power. You are such magnificent "Be"-ings, all hidden by your thoughts of littleness. If everyone simply acted on their "hunches," took stock of all their "coincidences," and did what their hearts desired – what they yearned for – there would be such a shifting on the planet. So much fear would be lifted. So much pain would be softened. So much anxiety would be eliminated.

You have no comprehension of the changes you can bring about by that one simple act: Do what your heart desires. Do what makes your heart sing. Do that in which you believe in the depths of your Soul. Do what you wish to do. That simple act will bring about peace to the planet faster than all the social programs you can implement. Follow the dictates of your heart; follow the whisperings of your Soul.

You are so much more than you think you are. In the words of Michael J. Roads, you are "Magnificent Majestic Multi-dimensional Metaphysical Beings of Light," just waiting for an opportunity to show your magnificence. You only have to take a chance to be who you really are. You don't have to wait to be given a chance. The Universe will open the space up for you. You must initiate the effort. This is due to free will and to choice. This is your right to be who you really are; the co-creator of your "Be"-ing. You simply walk into the space that is already there, waiting for you. Fireworks won't go off in the sky when you do that, but they will go off in your Soul. You will have a sense of calm, of destiny, of a job well done, and you will have just begun.

Believe that it is possible. Believe that your heart's desire is already there, waiting for you to claim it. It will manifest for you, as you believe it. The doors will open; the synchronicities will abound. All avenues will present themselves because you will be following the dictates of your Soul.

Believe in the "pull" on your heart.

Can you take the plunge to do what your heart pulls you to do?
When we follow our heart's desire without looking for assurance from others, we are guaranteed success.

May 19

Message from My Guides: Believing in Your Authentic Self

You have such incredible power, but it will only come to you as you believe. Believe in your smallness and you will stay small. Believe in your greatness and all power is yours: power to create, to manifest, and to achieve your dreams; to live – to really live. Everything will fall in place when you follow your dreams. Take no alternative path, no miss-step, and no vacillation in your journey to follow your dreams.

Your authentic Self is calling you home; calling you to be who you really are. S/he was always there within you – you have only to listen. Listen in the quiet of your mind. The seeds were planted eons ago; the sprouts are pushing through. The time is NOW; fertile ground for the plant to spring forth.

The seed doesn't question how it can possibly bring forth the plant that it will become. Nor should you question the manner – or how you possibly can – bring forth the dream of your heart. The means are beyond your comprehension for the moment. You are to simply relax into the moment of NOW! NOW is the time when all things come to you. NOW! Not yesterday, not tomorrow, NOW! Relax into the NOW. All means will be presented to you. They will come in many forms: a chance meeting, a message on a license place, the time on the clock radio, a snatch of a song, an invitation from a friend, a bit of a book review. They will all have meaning, once you align your ego self with your Higher Self, and let your Self guide yourself.

You have such incredible power to change the world, and NOW is the time. Relax into the moment. Watch for all the messages that are being hurtled towards you. Pay attention to the thoughts that come your way – what are they telling you? What is your guidance? Where are you being led?

Some think they have been "chosen." In fact, all are chosen. All have an integral part to play in the New World Order. Many won't act on the driving of their heart because of inertia or commitments to the old. However, many will take the call – will heed the trumpet sound that the beating of their heart has become – and will respond. You will see an upheaval such as you have never seen before. It is just beginning.

You come to us in prayer. We come to you in thoughts, in hints, in hunches, in messages openly given throughout the day. Nothing mysterious about it. Just be aware. Increase your awareness. Start to live consciously. Become conscious of all that is around you because it is all of the same God-stuff that you are.

You are part of the All, so is everything else. All is One. Recognize that – accept that – and you will lift the burden from your Soul that has lain there so heavily for eons. It will be gone in a flash. Hurt nothing because you only hurt yourself. Heal yourself and you heal the world.

We love you above all. Go in peace.

And so it is.

Amen.

Can you believe that the space for your heart's desire is already in place? We bring forth a new truth – a new paradigm – by choosing to be our authentic Self.

May 20

Releasing Fear of Ridicule

Ridicule is a favorite technique of the fearful. Ridicule and its companions – sneering, derision, mockery, contempt, scorn, disparagement, and sarcasm – all gang up against anyone attempting to break through the restrictive paradigm that holds our fragile societal *mores* in place. What people know as "truth" they are afraid to share, because of the barrage of criticism that they "know" they will have to face. So, people do not speak up. However, by staying mute, they stifle an essential part of their "Be"-ing. All the while, the ones who "know" nothing *shout* the *nothing* that they know from the rooftops.

Ridicule has squelched more attempts by Spirit to reach man than any other means. It was only when I was finally able to give up my fear of ridicule that I was able to do Spirit's work, and was able to find my authentic voice. I have taught classes on spiritual development which include Reiki and intuitive healing, have taught classes on a variety of spiritual subjects such as *Increasing your Intuition*, have given impromptu book talks, and have participated in a weekly lecture series in the Rays of Healing Church, speaking monthly. However, while I was still in the grip of the *fear of ridicule,* I could do none of the above.

Giving up the fear of ridicule frees us to do our authentic work. It does not matter *who thinks what* about our "crazy" ideas. The only thing that matters is what *we* think and what we do about it. Spirit would not give us the thought unless we were also given the means to bring the thought to fruition. Or, as an anonymous saying from the internet wisely states, "If God brings you to it, God will bring you through it."

Self-doubt is another method that squelches Spirit's voice, for there are more "great ideas" in Spirit than there are here on Earth. The upper planes are where all the ideas are conceived, but Earth is where the ideas are brought to form. If we *hear,* but *do not believe* what we hear, that is just as good as not hearing it at all. Jesus the Christ, channeled by Virginia Essene in the *Love Corps Newsletter,* reports that there are *two hundred people* contacted by Spirit with the same information in the hopes that *one person* will go public with it.

The next time you get a "great idea," do not bash it – for fear of being ridiculed – before you nurture it. Give it a chance to grow, to flesh out, and to develop, before you discard it as unworkable.

There are so many people out there who are "hungry" for Spirit's message. Be the one who gives it to them.

On the Thursday after Easter in 2003, the Dalai Lama was scheduled to speak at the Washington National Cathedral. No advance publicity appeared in the newspapers, but word spread by e-mail. With only three days advance notice, a crowd of over 7,500 people showed up. Fortunately, it was a beautiful day, and the overflow crowd outside was able to enjoy his words via loudspeaker. His message, one of compassionate tolerance, emphasized peace of self. When he left, people on the side of the cathedral pressed forward to get one last glimpse of him. It looked and felt as if a rock star was leaving. Here is one ambassador for peace who has never been afraid of being ridiculed.

Believe that you can overcome the fear of ridicule if that is a major stumbling block in your life.

Has fear of ridicule squelched your ability to express one of your "truths?" See ridicule and any of its companions for what they really are; FEAR of change manifesting itself.

May 21

Ridding Ourselves of Damaging Energies

Some of us are very weighted down with "things" that keep us a slave to the material plane. The most extreme case of holding onto "things" is the neurosis (bordering on psychosis) called "hoarding." This goes beyond stockpiling and amassing quantities of goods as a hedge against leaner times, or holding onto something for sentimental reasons. Hoarding involves the inability to release anything that comes into our possession, including that which could be recycled and that which is garbage.

People who insist on accumulating massive amounts of money (far beyond what they could possibly use in a lifetime) – and who do not share the wealth – have this disease as well. People whose only concern is to accumulate more money, and to keep that money for themselves (no matter what the cost to other lives and to the environment) exemplify hoarding at its worst. Accumulating massive amounts of money often involves damaging the planet, both in its physical body as well as its etheric body.

Another way to damage the etheric layer of our planet is to partake in energies that leave a muddy trail wherever they alight, such as gossiping. Some of us are sucked into it before we are even aware that it is happening. Pretty soon, we are riding a current so swift that events in our life are spinning out of control. We can learn to give up any need to partake in any gossip; to give up all the pettiness that may have tripped us up before. We do not need it.

We can also learn to release the fear of punishment for our "sins," real or imaginary. Sins are only "spiritual mistakes" according to the Divine Mother in *Mary's Message to the World,* by Annie Kirkwood. Since the soul continues to recycle in life after life, how can we possibly know what role everyone around us may have chosen in this lifetime, and how many "sins" that role includes? We may have been a saint before, and this time may have chosen to explore the flip side of saintliness – which may include committing a myriad of "sins." We do not know.

We can learn to release the feelings of guilt that bind us. We do not need them. If we feel we must do something for someone that we may not necessarily want to do, such as helping a person out during times of illness, we can do it from a place of compassion, not a place of guilt. Guilt and shame are the two emotions which emit one of the lowest vibrations on the planet. Why operate from such a low level of consciousness?

We only have to *believe it is possible to walk in two worlds* – the world of Spirit and the world of matter – and still function as a "normal" human "Be"-ing. Ask for spiritual help to stay in a space of awareness that keeps us in total peace, but still allows us to function in harmony with the third dimensional world.

If we can rid ourselves of these or other damaging energies, a certain lighthearted joy can replace the dull heaviness that accompanies our every movement. We can learn to flush out all attitudes that do not enhance our spirit. Release them. Let them go. We do not need them. Replace them with attitudes that better reflect who we really are.

Are you holding onto things that are crowding out your life?
Nothing is impossible to release for a child of God.

May 22

Then vs. Today

"You kill it," I demanded.

"No, you kill it," my husband replied.

"I can't do it. I can't kill something so determined to live," I shot back.

What were we talking about? A reptile? A rodent? Something repulsive?

No, a *plant* that had chosen the edge of our garage and our driveway to seed itself; so determined to thrive that it had pushed out the asphalt into an unsightly rounded cracked mound that made us wince every time that we looked at it.

Today, I am the type of person who captures moths in a glass and ants on my fingertips and escorts them out the door. I apologize to the nature spirits when I have to pull weeds out of my garden, and ask for their permission when I need to trim the shrubs. Today, I am very conscious of the "feelings" of both seen and *unseen beings.* My own feelings are becoming clearer to me.

Then, I would never have *intentionally* hurt anything or anyone, yet had hurt them *inadvertently.* In the past, I blasted out barrages of words without thinking of the effect the statements might have had on the recipient of my torrents. I felt it was a regurgitive reaction to what was said to me. Widened eyes stared back at me before we both set up the next round of attacks.

In thinking back on who I *was,* I wonder: *Who was that woman and why did she have to bring such drama into her life?* Even though some of the memories of who I *was* make me shudder, I realize that I needed to be *that* person in order to become the person I am today.

Back then, I always felt justified that I was "right," and used those feelings of being "right" as an excuse whenever I said anything that I would consider *hurtful* today. Then, I was immersed in ego. Today, I am immersed in Spirit. Then, I thought I *was* my profession, my ambition, my house, my clothes, my car. Today, I know that I am a spiritual "Be"-ing having a human experience. I come from a totally different perspective, and view life through a totally different lens.

Then, blocking out Spirit's attempt to reach me, I had a very limited view of who I was. In my youth and teenage years, I tried hard to be "a good girl" – to do what was required by my teachers, to never shirk my responsibility, to never make waves, and to follow all the rules. I tried hard to do what my parents expected of me, and to be helpful whether at home or in any organization I was involved. I bought into the paradigm that if I went to a great college and studied hard, I would have a good life; the promised "reward" for an upwardly mobile and ambitious youth from the lower middle class.

In spite of the fact that I made some disastrous decisions as a young adult – ones that affected the rest of my life – I fiercely held onto the belief that anything that I "accomplished" in life was up to me. For the first half of my life, those accomplishments had to do with "ego" pursuits.

No matter what heights to which my ego accomplishments brought me, something within me never felt quite right. However, I could not figure out what or why. I felt uncomfortable; ill at ease and out of place. Even though I tried hard to fit in, something within me would not stay settled. It was as if a malaise had taken permanent residence within my Soul. Nothing felt right; nothing fit right. It was this unnamed discomfort that caused me to feel as if *I just did not fit in.* Interesting that one of my parent's neighbor's made a statement when I was a teenager that he felt that every member of my family "belonged" in the family, except for me. He did not know from whence I came.

It was only when I made the commitment to engage in spiritual pursuits as the number one priority that my life started to feel "right" to me. In my forties, I felt a slight "buzz" whenever anything about spiritual matters crossed my path. My insides lit up, as if I were drinking champagne. Spirit was there guiding me all along, but it was up to me to recognize and to open to their guidance.

Spirit taught me to *go with the flow,* in order to handle the obstacles that crossed my path. Spirit taught me that in the middle of this swift flowing river we call our lives, there is a dock – a safe harbor, a resting place, a place to regroup and recharge – *and that place is within.*

Can you even recognize the person you were then? What we go through helps shape us into the person that we are today.

May 23

The Voice for God

The *Whole-ey Spirit,* the *Voice for God*, (the title of my next book) stays with us continuously and attempts to bring us back to our real home, where we return to each evening when we fall asleep. We go back to the place we *know* to *re-member* who we really are. Nothing and no one can hold us back. We are all things and we are No thing. We are pure essence and we are solid body and we are everything in between.

Only when I listen to and converse with the *Voice for God* does my writing take on a life of its own and everything "fits." At other times, I put my thoughts on paper, but the words neither please me, nor make sense to me; they neither amuse nor inspire me. Yet, when I *speak with* and *listen to* the *Voice for God*, I hear wisdom. My writing becomes very clear and defines the purpose of my life.

Everything in our lives can become a springboard to the *Voice for God*: a book we read, a study group we join, a snatch of a newspaper - carrying a pertinent message – at which we glance, or a person whom we meet; one who brings fresh meaning into our lives. All communications are designed to help us hear the *Voice for God.* All are there to assist us back to the Source of Creation. We need only to listen to that still quiet voice within our head.

All young children are connected to the *Voice for God.* Their pre-incarnation memories are still intact. They have memories of the place from which they came; either of Spirit or of past lives. It is only the constant denial by the adults around them that drive this memory from them. Ask any three-year old to tell you who they were *before they were born.* Just ask them! You may be surprised at their answer.

If we are an adult raising one of today's newly-minted souls, we need to ask our self if we have the *right* to drive memory from the mind of these precious "Be"-ings. Each new soul is a fresh slate with a unique perspective engraved on it that may be destined to change the world. Who are we to squash that perspective? Can we agree to nurture these fine young souls and help them develop their *authentic* talents, instead of shepherding them into a life of conformity and boredom?

Right now, whether we are taking care of a newly-minted soul or not, we may feel that we have too many things to do *all at the same time.* The harder we try to simplify our life, the more complicated it becomes, especially if we desire to follow a spiritual path. We have our distractions and our fears. However, we have all the time we need to do what we truly desire. Our *interest, attention,* and *intention* together send the vibrational energy spinning towards manifestation in form. By listening to that inner voice, that *Voice for God,* we can each receive guidance towards our individual correct path, and calmly say, *Today, I start the rest of my life.*

Believe that you can hear the *Voice for God,* the Voice of the *Whole-ey Spirit.*

Are you tuned into hearing the Voice for God? Directives from the Voice for God clear the confusion and clutter out of our life.

May 24

Energy Healing

Each morning, I state my intent to be one of God's healers; to heal through my words, through my writing, through my hands, through my heart, or through every cell in my body. *My intent is to heal.* To this, I dedicate my life.

This morning, during an energy healing session, I listened calmly to my inner voice, and then heard the opening prayer; each sentence flowing from the previous. Scanning my client's energy field, I checked to see whether the subtle bodies were all going in the same direction and where their placement was. Today, my client's mental body (the third subtle body) was reversed, with some resistance in her second body. Her energy was not flowing very fast. The fifth body was also reversed. The sixth body was sluggish. A reversed energy body "drags," in just the same manner that the nap on a carpet drags if it is stroked in the opposite direction from the way in which it lays flat.

While scanning the first subtle body, the first "change" I felt was in the ovaries. The client had taken hormone pills that morning on an empty stomach. She should have eaten. A banana cured that "alarm note." The next image I "saw" was the client's skeletal system. From there, the imagery moved inside to the bone marrow; to the production of blood cells. The message was that the red blood count should be checked by an M.D. The liver appeared to be dark greenish brown, with a small green bile duct on top. It did not look like a healthy liver, which is pink. Liver is the seat of anger and this client had anger issues to work through, related to both family and work. I channeled Reiki energy into her on the various places on her body, and sealed her energy field with the sign of the Infinity, which ended the session.

As we accept our part in energy healing, clients present themselves to us. Keeping our hearts open to those who *wish to heal* helps us keep compassion in our hearts for all of those who do *not* want to heal. There are many whose pain gives them a sense of identity. Giving energy to those who resist healing helps them to relieve their pain temporarily. Alternatively, it helps them with their transition, if they are getting ready to leave the planet but are reluctant to do so.

Those of us who come from purity of intent will be guided by the Light to the highest good. God helps all His "hands" on Earth. His hands are our hands. His head is our head. His heart is our heart. His Light is our Light. All hideousness will fade in the intensity of the Light. Those of us who stand in our truth and wish to be one of God's healers will be led by the Light to the right teachers.

Spirit works consistently at supporting each of us. The more we respond to Spirit's support, the more is given to us. The same holds true for spiritual *gifts.* The purpose of spiritual gifts is for healing. The more we use spiritual gifts *responsibly*; the more gifts we will receive. As we gratefully acknowledge and use the gifts from Spirit for healing, the more we will recognize *opportunities* for using the healing techniques.

Believe that you do God's work when you use vibrational energy to heal.

Are you drawn to energy healing?
Learning to heal by using energy is just
like any other technique we study.

May 25

Releasing Anger Permanently

Anger that has not been resolved piles back into our body into the organs that house the emotion of anger; the main one being the liver, but also the kidneys, bile duct, spleen, and gall bladder. Not releasing anger when it arises causes the eventual breakdown of these organs, deteriorating one's health. Items that are forgotten, but *not* forgiven, over time hide deep within the cell memory of these respective organs, which continue to deteriorate. *Releasing anger permanently always involves forgiveness.*

A few techniques – there are many others – for releasing anger are:

Identify the source of the anger. This is harder than it may sound if we are in denial. If we are not, it will be easier, but will still take a long time, since we will want to dredge up *every* incident where someone made us angry, and every incident in which *we* made someone else angry. Listen for the stories that keep repeating in our head, and become aware of the images that appear in our mind's eye. These all need to be identified and written down. During this period, we should set our intent *every day* to dredge up the memories of every angry episode, even if it takes months.

Make lists. For me, this became a four page "forgiveness list" of all the people who had hurt me. Then, I had another corresponding four page "forgiveness list" of all the people whom I had hurt. This took me several months to compile. Even though I never intended to *intentionally* hurt anyone, I had hurt them *inadvertently.* Each item became a one-line entry on a yellow pad. I stopped writing only when there were no more incidents coming up in my mind, either with pictures or with words. Only then was I certain that all the anger issues had released from my mind.

Mentally, dispose of the lists. Mentally take each one of the "hurts" and put them into a huge imagined bonfire comprised of a brilliant purple flame. This is the *Purple Transformational Flame of St. Germaine.* The purpose of sending all of these "hurts" through the purple flame is to release them to their next state of higher evolution. In this manner, we do not release them to clog the etheric body of Mother Earth. Since this is a spiritual exercise, we use spiritual means for cleansing.

Physically, dispose of the lists. This is a very important step. Prepare a "burning bowl." We want to physically remove all evidence of the anguished feelings that arose from the memories that we had to dredge up to make the lists. Take the lists and cut it into strips; one strip for each item of anger. Then take the strips and fold each of them into small pieces. Place all these pieces of paper into an enamel bowl, and very carefully ignite them and burn them until there is nothing left but ash. Throw this ash into the soil surrounding a living plant, where it can nourish the plant with the potassium released from this ash.

Last, offer a prayer of forgiveness for all parties involved. Prayer is important to seal our intent to forgive and to release anger permanently from our lives. This does not have to be elaborate. A simple prayer such as the following is sufficient.

I forgive you for all the hurts, real or imagined, that you caused me.

I forgive myself for all the hurts, real or imagined, that I may have caused you.

I send you to the Light, to go in peace and love.

And ask that that Light shine through me. Amen

The ceremony involved in this exercise is important to insure that we have totally cleared anger out of our energy field. There is something very purifying by "burning" every incident, both those that made us angry and those in which we made someone else angry. As memories continue to surface, this becomes a very effective tool to help rid our bodies of hidden areas of anger. It is important that we extricate ourselves from the emotion of anger for clinging to anger solves nothing.

Once we have completed this ceremony, if new situations continue to arise, we can ask what the lesson is that we have to learn from this experience. Then, we *learn the lesson, and move on.* We may find that for years after we have completed this exercise, new "items" may continue to surface. They need to be recorded and released.

Have you ever seen anyone permanently damaged because of anger?
Rid your body of anger permanently with this "burning bowl" ceremony.

May 26

Seeing the Aura

There are two Essene practices that can help you to see your aura. The Essenes were a reclusive sect of religious Jewish people around the time of Christ who lived in small, remote enclaves and who kept alive mystical traditions. To use the first of their techniques, first, splay your fingers against a perfectly neutral wall – black or white is best – then look beyond your fingertips at the wall. Eventually, a thin halo of light will appear around your fingers. For the second technique, begin by looking at a bright light *with your eyes closed*; then look up slowly. Then, very slowly, move into a horizontal position. You should see the colors of the aura on the ceiling. Eventually, a little blue light (the veil of Isis) will appear and expand. Do this three or four times a week for a short time.

Another easy technique is to look at someone against a white background and *softly defocus your eyes.* While looking at the other person, slightly cross both eyes and gaze towards the end of your nose. As you lessen the intensity of your gaze, a light should appear around the person. It can be bright or it can be dark. It can be different from side to side or from top to bottom. Many times, the aura around the shoulders and head of a person is the brightest. Do not be surprised if a figure or two or a symbol also appears in the auric field. This may happen. Just trust what you see. Practice and you *will* succeed in seeing the aura!

While listening to guest speakers, I have spent many hours absolutely fascinated by the "dancing lights" of their auric field. One spiritual speaker had a comic habit of mocking the royal family of England. Every time he made a joke at the expense of someone else, the intense blue light would pull towards his body. As soon as he changed the subject, the light would expand outward. Another speaker, an extremely generous person who gave away much information in order to help others succeed, had a soft – yet brilliant – golden glow around him; one that emanated warmth and kindness. Another had a bright orange glow emanating from him. Another – a great communicator and humorist – had alternating shades of light green and light blue. My meditation instructor had a thick golden band of light emanating from him whenever he started speaking.

Bright white, light blue, light pink, light green, brilliant gold and emerald green lights have also appeared around speakers to whom I have listened. The most unusual so far has been a brilliant green light, accompanied by the appearance of the Madonna and child, behind a woman who was leading a group of people who wanted to increase their speaking skills. I asked her about it later. She had no special connection to the Madonna and child, yet, the Blessed Mother appeared as her guide.

Practice the three techniques listed above and eventually, you will succeed in seeing the aura.

Have you ever seen an "aura" spontaneously appear? As we softly focus with total concentration on a speaker's face, an aura may appear in our peripheral vision.

May 27

The Reality Behind the Reality

It is very exciting to have spiritual experiences that expose the "reality" behind the reality.

Amongst the proliferation of worldwide spiritual practices that are having a global impact is the *World Peace Flame,* an idea that started with a group of college students led by Mansukh Patel – sometimes called the *new Gandhi* – a young man whose parents had been students of Mahatma Gandhi. These students wanted to do something to make a difference. The idea that ultimately came out of their meetings was to have a "live" flame, lit by a member of an indigenous culture from each continent, flown to London, and then transported to Bangor, Wales where all the flames from all the continents were to be put together into one giant *Peace Flame.*

The stories around this effort are filled with so many synchronicities that everyone associated with the project became convinced that a Higher Power was guiding the endeavor. The final obstacle was overcome when the Royal Danish Air Force stepped in to fly the peace flame lit by the Indians of North America when all commercial airlines, as well as the military transport of the

United States, refused to do so. The *World Peace Flame* came into being as a gift to mankind at the end of the twentieth century.

The first time I saw the *World Peace Flame* was shortly after it had been brought back to the United States. I listened to the story of the background information on how this flame came into being. As I continued to watch it and became mesmerized by it, this lovely little flame took the shape of a plump little angel, reminding me of the Fairy Godmother in *Cinderella.* Then the little elemental took her skirt in her hands and curtsied. It was the sweetest thing. This experience cemented my belief that the flame was a living being, and was one of many interesting "realities" that were being presented to me at that time.

Another exciting incident happened to show me another "reality behind the reality." One day, while intensely concentrating on my work on the computer, a vibrant blue halo appeared on the edge of the computer screen. Buddhist monks claim that everything on this planet has an etheric blue light around it, similar to the intense blue found at the base of candlelight. That color blue was the exact color I saw surrounding my computer.

A totally different experience occurred during a state of deep concentration when all awareness of sight and sound around me dimmed. The keys of the computer keyboard suddenly appeared larger than they were and seemed to come "alive." I was able to "shift" my focus (by blinking), and saw the keys as they originally appeared. Then, I blinked to shift "back" to this new dimension where they were larger, and continued to do this until I needed to resume my work. All it took was a blink.

Another time, while waiting for a friend in a restaurant, a small monochromatic pattern on a tablecloth – a field of small yellow daisies on a midnight blue background – took on a larger three-dimensional appearance. The field of yellow daisies "swam" in a "field" of blue that was "alive," as if it were plasma. Again, I was able to shift back and forth from this dimension to the next by blinking.

All of these experiences occurred spontaneously. I had no expectations and, in each case, was doing nothing to prompt them to happen. In the first experiences with the computer, I was concentrating intently. During the last, I was just sitting calmly waiting for my friend.

Trust what you "see." As the veil gets thinner, more and more "unexplainable" events will appear in your life.

Do you ever notice twinkling lights, especially during dawn or dusk, out of the corner of your eye? Lights or figures flitting through our peripheral vision usually signify an opening to spiritual sight.

May 28

A Secret Self

"You're very opinionated. Don't say you're not. You're highly opinionated. I've lived with you all my life and I know. Where do you think I get my strong opinions from? I raise my voice and speak in a highly opinionated manner. I've learned from you." Thus spoke my then sixteen-year old son.

He contradicted the statement I had just made, that "I didn't like to share my opinions with others because I don't like controversy." He slammed me for that one.

Sometimes, I feel as if I live in a world of contradiction. What appeals to me one moment and what I delight in sharing with one person, I loathe to share with the next. I am willing to be open and compassionate with one person, then pull the cloak of secrecy around myself with the next. I offer compassion, but nothing else of myself: what is important to me, what I hope to achieve, what my secret dreams are, the kind of world in which I desire to live. I simply say nothing, but continue to flip between these two personalities.

To my spiritual friends, I am one kind of person: comparing spiritual truths, finding mastery of Self, studying various techniques of energy healing, learning about other esoteric healing methods, and constantly looking to bridge the gap between matter and spirit. For the most part, my spiritual friends are my personal friends. It cannot be otherwise. I cannot have anything so dear to my heart and not share it with those I love.

To my business associates, I am another kind of person; answering their questions, drawing on over thirty years of experience in the business world to always find the best possible solution to the current problem. I have made deep and lasting friendships with the clients whom I have helped all these years, and cherish the long term association I have had with so many of them.

My family falls somewhere in between. I have to share selectively. Sometimes when I share my *truth,* I get slam-dunked as a *true believer,* for I come from an immediate and extended family whose members range from fundamentalists to non-believers. To some of them, I am a gullible foil for any new theory that comes down the pike, and am open to any new author who is trying to sell it. Sometimes they listen, take it in, and accept it. Sometimes, they just laugh at me or contradict anything I have to say. Other members of my family bristle when I speak out. They, more than anyone, have helped me learn *when* and *how* to *speak my truth* and yet stay true to my Higher Self. They, more than anyone, have taught me how to be non-judgmental.

Believe you can exist in this world, and cultivate friendships with those who are inclined to be both spiritual and non-spiritual.

Do you have to straddle two worlds, the
world of Spirit and the world of form?
Ask for Spirit's help to keep a toe-hold in both.

May 29

Lives between Lives

We each have a glorious mission to fulfill, even if it is to do no more than to rest and to observe. We would get awfully discouraged if each lifetime brought us only lessons. Every “role” has its own reward and punishment, a place to go and a place to stop, a castle and a dungeon. Some souls come strictly to observe, some come to rest, some come to learn. Some souls come to wreck havoc. We all create our own special “role” as threads in the whole tapestry of life.

After we finish playing our “role” on Earth, and transition to our spiritual forms, we may decide that the “roles” we played in the previous lifetime be reversed for our next incarnation. A spiritually enlightened person in this lifetime may choose to be a spiritually dense person in another lifetime. The glutton in this lifetime may come back as the starving child in the next. The saintly nun in this lifetime may come back as the prostitute in the next.

In spirit, once we transition from this plane, we evaluate the circumstances of our life on Earth based on the lessons we chose for ourselves prior to this incarnation. *No one judges us.* We each evaluate our lives and see how well we learned our lessons. The souls who commit suicide have a chance to see how “other options” might have worked out had they chosen to live. No, we will NOT be condemned to eternal torment if we commit suicide, but our Teachers-in-Spirit will express disappointment in us because each soul has a certain amount of “time” it agreed to stay here. Other people whose lives interface with the soul who chose to leave early expected it to fulfill a *full term.* We will discuss with our Teachers the options we took in this life where we could have made different (and perhaps more useful) choices; where we might have incorporated spiritual means to replace ego issues.

For further discussion of lives between lives, the books of Michael J. Newton, Ph.D., Richard M. Moody, M.D., or Brian Weiss, Ph.D., M.D. are indispensable. Each have practices whose clients have spontaneously led them to reveal information about lives between lives.

We are all connected. There is a web on consciousness that surrounds the planet called the matrix. We live under a matrix grid of unconditional Love called the *Christ Consciousness*. This matrix grid offers unconditional Love to each person on the planet, but *allows* us to develop from the state of consciousness with which we have incarnated. All is in a state of evolution. All come here – to planet Earth – to grow in the state of consciousness called unconditional Love. All have a place on this planet.

The state of consciousness of the souls arriving here varies from extremely light to very dark. There is no place where we are *not*. There is no place that is denied us, from the lightest to the darkest. As the light increases, so does the dark. *The lighter the light, the darker the dark.*

Believe that you exist now as well as between lives and that you are not judged by anyone else except yourself.

Have you ever had a sense of lives between lives?
Our consciousness exists permanently.

May 30

The Dearly Departed

Every time we think of a loved one in spirit, they are right beside us. The mere thought of them is enough to bring them to our side. When they are on the Spiritual plane, they do not stay "here," because they have their own agenda. They are by far too busy with their own "work" to constantly stand by our side.

But our very thought of them is enough to summon them, for we are communicating with them telepathically. They flicker in intermittently just to check up on us whenever we think of them.

Excessive grieving for a lost loved one brings them to us to try to comfort us. Excessive grieving may not good for the departed souls, since the souls continue to "stick around" just to try to help bring peace of mind back to us, rather than continuing their own work. They do their best to reach us telepathically, but just like us, they have their own agenda and a myriad of tasks to complete before their next incarnation.

Those trapped in the astral plane, which (according to Buddhist thought) is more closely associated with the Earth plane than with Spirit's plane, are those who have *not* made the commitment to align with Spirit. They have been trapped by *maya*; the illusion of *glamour* that the Earth holds for them, and cannot fully release to go to the next level of transition.

Ghosts who inhabit the Earth are in that category. *Ghosts do not know they are dead.* In their world, we are the ghosts; the interlopers in their reality. Communicating with them telepathically helps them transition to Spirit's realm; helps them release the ties to the astral plane of existence. It can be as simple as telling them to *Turn around until you see light in the distance. As the light comes closer to you, go to the light!* Or simply say, *Turn and go to the Light.*

A marvelous book, *The Boy Who Saw True*, is about seeing Beings-in-Spirit as recounted in diary form by a young lad in the Victorian era. Thinking that everyone could see the dearly departed just as he could, he kept being scolded for being "wicked" and for "making up falsehoods." His grandfather and his uncle came to him frequently, and occasionally he saw someone he called "Jesus." He called auras "lights," and saw distortions in the aura readily.

Fortunately, the boy was assigned a private tutor who was sympathetic to his gift of "second sight," and who recorded the instruction of his student's main Guides in shorthand, which then became part of his diary. After his tutor finished with his schooling, the boy (now a young man) continued writing in his own diary, but unfortunately lost a few volumes during a train trip across Italy. After his death, the young man's widow released the original diary for publication without releasing his name, since he would not consider doing that while he was alive, and would not wish to be identified after death. This book is a fascinating account about the auric field, along with people and animals existing on the astral plane as seen through the innocent eyes of a child!

Have you ever experienced a person in spirit? We can help someone trapped in the astral plane by sending them to the Light.

May 31

"Freed" Slaves

Freedom is an interesting concept that has recently been explored by the media in various shows. The Public Broadcasting Station (PBS) chronicled the lives of black people who were slaves, then freed, and who then *voluntarily* returned to the master's home to live in their tiny dwellings. They continued to work the fields, albeit for a small salary.

In the movie, *Shawshank Redemption,* one of the prisoners (who had been incarcerated for fifty-eight years) suddenly found himself set free as a seventy-eight year old. He ended up as a bagging clerk in a supermarket, in what he perceived was a frantic pace. He lived in one room, and spent most of his "free" time sitting on his bed staring ahead blankly. Ultimately, he ended up hanging himself from a beam in the ceiling, but not before he carved a message in the beam: "Murrie was here." Unfortunately, those who never learn independence skills are unable to handle freedom, and thus are "freed slaves."

Freed slaves exist anywhere at any time. Do you feel stuck by reacting to things in the *same* manner in which you have *always* reacted to them? If you feel that you have no control over your life – that you are always there for others, but nobody is there for you – you may be a freed slave. If you feel you can "act" only in a certain manner, "think" in a certain way, or "speak" according to the dictates of your social standing, you may be a freed slave.

I grew up in a household where Saturday was "cleaning day." We could not go out on Saturday until all the dusting, vacuuming, washing, and polishing was finished, which sometimes would take all day. My first husband insisted on following that same tradition. His job always kept him out of the home from early morning until midnight on Saturday. In defiance, I stayed in bed reading until 6 p.m., then got up and furiously cleaned and shined everything in the apartment, so that when he returned after midnight, everything gleamed. I could not give myself the freedom to go shopping, explore a museum, visit an art gallery, or to do an arts and crafts project. The only thing I could "allow" myself to do was to read because it required no effort, but yet satisfied my personal need for rebellion. I was a "freed slave" during those years. He never knew my *modus operandi*, because everything was exactly the way he wanted it when he came home.

Freed slaves exist everywhere. If we are reacting to things in the same manner we have always reacted to them, we may be a freed slave. If we have had a lifetime of always being told what to do, how to do it, when to do it, where to do it, how to feel, how to think, how to act, how to dress, and where to go, we may be a freed slave. It is time to break out of our box; time to take our first tentative steps towards freedom and declare our independence from the norm.

Examine what paradigms hold you back and where your frustrations lie. Believe that you can take the steps necessary to break through the chains that bind you and overcome the restrictions that keep you a "freed slave."

What societal constrictions have kept you a "freed" slave? Only we can allow others to eliminate our freedom to live a life based on our own guidance.

June

Real Power, the power of Love, never hurries and never interrupts another, but gives as much time as is needed for the expression of Self. Real Power, the power of Love, is non-judgmental and neither criticizes nor condemns, chooses peace over pain and uses feeling as a gauge to help recognize where it was and where it wants to go.

Real Power, the power of Love, never excludes. No one is better than anyone else. It knows that all "Be"-ings are created equal, from the highest to the humblest and not as a paraphrase of the words of George Orwell in Animal Farm states: "All men are created equal, but some are more equal than others."

Real Power, the power of Love, accepts all men as belonging to one race on this planet – called HUMAN. There are not five races according to the color of the skin and other attributes. There is but one HUMAN race on this planet. There are other races, but they are on other planets.

Real Power, the power of Love, increases exponentially when our vibrational level grows. As the vibrational level of man increases, the energy of courage increases.

Real Power is Love and comes from unconditional Love. Real Power creates only as It Self and extends only as It Self. Thus, the power of the ego self – superficial external power – is being withdrawn by degrees; sometimes unnoticeably, sometimes on a large scale. Just as the ocean recedes from the shore by degrees, ego power is receding by degrees.

Only that which is Love will increase and expand.

June 1

Just "Listen"

"You can wait, delay, paralyze yourself or reduce your creativity to almost nothing. But you cannot abolish it. You can destroy your medium of communication. But you cannot abolish it." states *A Course in Miracles.* Which is important to today's topic, because it involves us listening as our creative endeavor.

Listen to me, just listen! We wail inside our heads. The silent scream goes unheard. The world is not there for us.

Listening to someone else takes talent. Too many of us formulate the words for our next sentence, with only scant attention to what the person speaking to us is saying. Thus, our words become a *monologue* with an *audience,* rather than any meaningful dialogue.

We do not need someone to "fix" us. We *do* need someone to "listen" to us. If we are fortunate, we have friends and family members who are able to fill that role in our lives. If we *have to* turn to others, there are many professional listeners called therapists or counselors, and many social programs that sponsor them, some which are free.

When we choose to share with a group of strangers in a similar situation, there are at least three hundred different self-help groups alone, founded on the principles of the twelve-step program. The twelve-step program originated with Alcoholics Anonymous (AA) started by Bill Wilson in 1938. This self-help program was successful because it had no hierarchy, no bureaucracy, no dues, no real estate holdings, no religious affiliation, and no obligations except the intent of one person helping another, together with the willingness to accept a higher power working in our lives. Simple as that.

The fortunate among us find a circle of like-minded people, not to give us advice, but just to *listen.* People who are emotionally close to us often get frustrated and fixated on our pain, and sometimes rush to our aid with their solutions. Sometimes, they grievously insult all our efforts to help ourselves. We do not need either.

If you desperately need someone to listen to you, the best way to achieve that is to extend the grace of "really listening" to another, since what you give, you get. Perhaps, somewhere in that exchange, you will find that what *you* need to say will also come out. And you may help change the life of one less fortunate than you.

To increase our listening skills, we can find a group that is in harmony with the way we think, the way we feel, the way in which we are opening to new aspects of ourselves. We can each do what we *want* to do, not what we feel *obligated* to do. Acting out of a sense of obligation is acting out of a sense of fear.

If your world holds too many speakers and too few listeners, start your own group; one that is aligned with your needs. Believe you can find a group who will *really listen* to what you have to say, or have the courage to start your own.

When was the last time someone really "listened" to you? We may need to start our own self-help group if what we need does not exist in our community.

June 2

Home for the Holidays

Major holidays in the United States loom approximately every two months: New Year's, Martin Luther King's Birthday, President's Day, Easter, Memorial Day, 4th of July, Labor Day, Thanksgiving, and Christmas. Of course, the Irish will insist on including St. Patrick's Day, the day when everyone in the United States becomes Irish. We tip our hats to them; for their joyfulness on St. Patrick's Day, which is sometimes more important than their own birthday or Christmas. For the veterans, we also acknowledge Flag Day and Veteran's Day.

Many look forward to the holidays with love, but some of us look forward to them with dread. If we dread the holidays, something is wrong. *Going home for the holidays* has been parodied so often in the United States that the rest of the world must think that we have lost our sense of celebration. If we have nothing but "dysfunctional" family members to look forward to, no wonder we would rather stay at home.

But, if the *outer reflects the inner* – which it does – then who is *dysfunctional?* Why is the "other" always dysfunctional, never us? Are we willing to look at that? Are we willing to look at the fact that it may be "ourselves" who are "dysfunctional?" Or does that premise lie in the *field of impossibility*; where so many personal quirks are buried?

What happens when two people who are committed to each other each want to do something totally different to celebrate the holidays? Do we give each other permission to do what we each of us wants to do without attempting to lay a guilt trip on the other?

Do we have the right to choose with whom we will spend our free time, or do we sometimes have to make compromises for the betterment of the whole? Do we beat ourselves up for not choosing to act, think, feel or speak in a certain manner just to please the significant other in our life, then *rage* because we feel we have been *forced* to acquiesce?

Can we accept that *each* of us has the right to choose our path, and the "other" has agreed, on a soul level, to let us play out our drama, until we no longer need to have the drama in our lives?

What *are* the answers? When we come from a position of love in all that we say and do, even when it appears to be something unpleasant and distasteful, then everything else falls into place; everything else follows.

When we find that we are at a crossroads, and the paths leads in opposite directions, first and foremost, forgive. Forgive the other for not accepting everything we wish to do in the manner in which we wish to do it. Forgive the other for not agreeing with us every time we say something. We are, in effect, only forgiving our self. And when we can get over the concept of blame, we recognize there is *nothing* to forgive. But that may have to wait for another lifetime.

In the meantime, try to capture the sense of celebration that the holidays evoke. Helping someone else less fortunate have a good time may be the most satisfying thing that happens to us all year.

Do you look forward to going "home" for the holidays? Helping someone else celebrate a holiday may bring us the greatest joy.

June 3

Paths to God

There are as many *paths to God* as there are people on this planet. It is inevitable that *each* path leads to God because each path *is* God. No one person, sect, belief system, religious denomination, or culture captures the *one true path* to God to the exclusion of all others. This is fundamental nonsense, and meant to keep us limited, weak and small. All types of belief systems are exhibited on this planet. All beliefs are welcome, are acceptable, and eventually all beliefs lead to God.

Break the chain of any limiting belief which states: *This is the one true path to God, and should you not follow it, you will suffer eternal damnation.* Expand your paradigm. *Nothing can keep you from God.* Nothing can keep even the "lowest" person who has ever inhabited the Earth – a person considered to be the scourge of mankind – from eventually joining with the Source. That would be impossible, since the Source is who you are and the Source does not deny It Self.

All phases of belief, from atheism to fundamentalism to fanaticism and everything in between, are exhibited on this planet and all phases of belief *are welcome*. All beliefs eventually lead to God, since God – or whatever name we give a Higher Power – is All There Is. There is nothing else outside of God. It is all God, in different shapes, sizes, volumes, tones, vibrations, rays, molecules, photons, quarks, or beliefs.

Whatever we believe in is "true" for us. There are many things that are "true" that have nothing to do with "truth" since "truth" is the *same for everyone,* regardless of shape, size, sex, or religious affiliation. We lead our life in accordance to what we believe is "true." But we can change our beliefs as readily as we can change our clothes; we can change them *instantaneously* if we choose. It can be done.

If you change your beliefs, you are still on your path to God.

Do you have a path to God that is different from the people around you? All paths lead to God.

June 4

Experiencing What We Create

What we *experience* comes from that which we *create*. This is part of natural law; the Law of the Universe, the Law of Cause and Effect, which is where "karma" fits in. There are many simple passages that explain this law: "You reap what you sow." "Do unto other as you want it done unto you." "What goes around comes around." Karma is the Universe's answer to *justice for all.* "Reaping what you sow" simply means that if you are planting banana trees, *do not expect* to harvest mangos. Through the Akashic records, the Universe keeps track of all the "justice" or "injustice" you sow. Therefore, you do not have to do that.

To comprehend, even partially, the Law of Cause and Effect, is to understand why sometimes "bad things happen to good people." Some people suffer terrible ordeals in their lifetime – tragedies that might collapse another – yet, they find the strength to go on. On some level, their Spirit Self agrees to have this experience for the growth of their Soul, while giving them the strength *from within* to keep going in spite of what happens to them.

Personal tragedies are put in place for us to get through them to strengthen our Soul, not to collapse it. If we can get beyond the ego self and listen to the dictates of our Spirit, then we can get beyond the horror of all the suffering in this world.

No matter how grievous the offense, if we are experiencing it today, somewhere, on some level, we *may have* perpetrated it on someone "else" *yesterday,* even if the *yesterday* was millennia ago. That is why we have to understand that what we do to an "other" *we do to our self.* There is no "other."

Our Soul may have other valid reasons to experience "tribulations." It may be in preparation of a future lifetime, for the work we will do then, as a humanitarian, as a physician, or as a peacemaker. It may be to increase our understanding of senseless barbarian acts so we can learn how to teach others to raise their level of consciousness to a state of compassion, in which no one participates in any atrocities for any reason whatsoever.

Not only do people experience karma, so do nations. Famines, wars, catastrophes and retaliation due to hatred are staples in certain areas of the planet, while other areas seem almost idyllic. Pick up any major newspaper in the world and read about the atrocities that are being committed by all the different factions on this planet. Each perpetrator of atrocities, no matter what the "justification" for them, is setting up future karma for themselves.

Each nation that is perpetrating more atrocities in this lifetime would do well to luxuriate in the lap of *forgiveness*; the first step toward unconditional Love, the one sure way off the wheel of karma. Forgiveness is the key to stopping the world in its present cycle of *"an eye for an eye, a tooth for a tooth"* that persists on our planet, making everyone blind and toothless.

Believe that everything that happens on this planet is part of a Divine Plan in which we and everyone else have a "starring role."

How does karma explain why so many things can go "wrong" on this planet and still be "right" within the realm of Spirit? Every action we take can set up karma for a "future" time.

June 5

Take the Plunge

If Spirit wants us to move in another direction, one that is right for us but one of which we are afraid, we can either comply with Spirit's directives or we can opt for "inertia" because we are afraid of making a move. That ache in our heart, that squeamish feeling in our stomach, which always occurs whenever we have a "knowing" that the course of action is wrong (but our fear of change keeps us stuck in the same place) is there to alert us that a massive change is coming into our life.

We can either quit our existing job or Spirit will get us fired. The choice is ours. We have a choice: either leave our existing abusive relationship or land in the hospital, and then leave it. The choice is ours. We can continue wallowing in substance abuse to avoid facing our problems – to avoid finding solutions to our pain – or we can get *down on our knees*, and ask a Higher Power to help us. The choice is ours.

We may feel totally adrift in an ocean of uncertainty and indecision as we watch our life fall apart. We might feel we are a "good" person, yet lose everything we hold dear to us, and are totally mystified why so many "bad" things happen to us. We may lose our wives/husbands, our jobs, our children, our homes, our retirement accounts, or everything into which we've invested our energy, and wonder, *Why me?*

There may be a very good reason, in Spirit, for that which we are experiencing. There is a very important message waiting for us. We are never presented with a challenge which we cannot master. If we can *think* of it, it is within our sphere of possibility. We have the tools within us to make it happen, no matter what *it* is. *If we have been led to it, we will be lead through it.* Our Divine Self will guide us through all the obstacles we think hold us back. *Believing that it is possible* saves us much heartache and relieves us of the "fear of the unknown."

In 1988, when first told by Spirit that I was to teach about God, I did not believe I was qualified. In fact, I cried bitterly and convulsively, **"I CANNOT DO IT."** I was a real estate broker, with a demanding property management department that I managed solely; but I was *not* a minister, nor was I a minister's child or spouse. Furthermore, I had a reputation to protect.

In October, 1995, I went to weekend retreat on meditation taught by James L. Green, in Falls Church, Virginia. Two months later, after I joined *A Course in Miracles* study group, I fully committed to my spiritual path, and took my first Reiki attunement (a hands-on healing method) from Arlene Green, the wife of my meditation instructor.

Shortly after this, I met the woman who would teach me intuitive healing methods, Wanda Lasseter-Lundy; one of the greatest gifts the Universe ever presented to me. She opened my eyes to the healer potential within me and has taken me to greater heights in understanding than any other person. She embodied the Spirit of the Christ Consciousness, with an understanding of the human energy field surpassed by no one on this planet. Her patient and far-reaching instruction worked with my intuitive abilities and expanded my levels of consciousness that are so important to healing work.

My first client in 2001, a female accident victim, was my formal acceptance of my life's work as an energy healer. During an accident that occurred around midnight, the car she was riding in was totaled. The passenger in the backseat died, and she and the female driver wound up in critical care in a DC hospital. I came in to see her in the hospital for one hour each day to administer energy healing. Despite the multiple injuries that she had when she entered, my client was released from the critical care unit within four days, and released from the hospital in ten days. The driver, after thirty days, was still in critical care and ultimately moved with her mother to Brazil to finish her recuperation. My first attempt at energy healing professionally was amply rewarded.

There are others who have had big dreams who refused to be thwarted by popular opinion. One willing to take the plunge was a little poor, skinny, little girl from Mississippi with a big voice and a big dream, which was to become an opera star. Leontyne Price was told to *Forget it,* that there was *no way* someone from her impoverished background and her color could *ever* do that. She never let go of her dream and now is one of the brightest stars in the Metropolitan Opera headquartered in New York City.

Monty Roberts, author of *The Man Who Listens to Horses* (inspiration for the movie, *The Horse Whisperer*), had a fifth grade teacher who gave him an "F" for a project where he was asked to draw and describe the goal he wished to achieve for his life because she thought it was too "unrealistic." He was told to revise it downward to what was within reach for a boy from his modest background. He went home, thought about what the teacher told him to do, came back the next day and told the teacher he would *keep the "F" and keep the dream.* He is now living in exactly what he drew and described in the fifth Grade; a ten million-dollar ranch!

Oprah stated that the *only* reason she is where she is today is because she believed in the *possibility* of being there. She never wavered from that belief. She also said that God had a *bigger dream* for her than she ever did for herself.

My dream was to be on stage, but I never dreamed that it was for the purpose of being one of God's teachers. Yet, ever since I joined *A Course in Miracles* study group in 1995, I have been a teacher of God. The release of my first book, *God is the Biggest Joker of All*, cemented my declaration to the world that I was ready to fulfill my soul's contract to teach about God publicly.

Trust me, if Spirit can get through to *me,* Spirit can get through to *anyone.*

Is there a secret dream you are harboring; a wish that goes to the depths of your Soul? Do you have a desire that makes your heart sing, but which you are afraid of pursuing?

Take the plunge! Believe in your Self! Take the plunge and take the first steps you need to take to make "it" happen. *It will be done to you according to your beliefs.*

Is there a secret dream you believe as a "possibility" that you are holding close to your heart? We can each release to the Universe the dreams that we are holding closest to our hearts.

June 6

Intent

Intent sets the Universe in motion to get us that which we desire; the magnet that attracts what we are calling forth. Intent increases focus, sets the tone for the day, and sets the stage for our beliefs. Along with belief comes the *intent* we set for the day. *Intent* is so powerful, because *intent precedes belief. Intent* does it all!

What kind of picture do we get when our focus is not clearly set on our camera? A fuzzy picture! Intent *sets* our focus clearly. Intent is described as "firmly directed or fixed;" just as we might hold the hand of a child crossing the street. Let the child just try to get away. "Fixed" is "not movable;" similar to an iron peg that has been nailed to the ground. That is the power that intent brings to us.

What *is* the intent we set for our day? If we have none, what can we expect from the Universe? Since we are a creator "Be"-ing creating a fuzzy goal, the Universe follows suit. If we are *not* clear, the Universe, honoring our free will, does *not* clarify it for us. We can set our intent for the day as soon as we wake up. Resolve today: *I am writing the first page of my book*, or whatever goal that we have in mind.

Make each statement *in the first person, positive, and in the present tense*. The most powerful two words we can use are *I am*; the words that set the forces of creation in motion. *I am* aligns us with the Supreme Creator, since *I am* is another name for God.

From the time that I accepted my commitment to teach about God, I have started each morning with *I am a published author and a public speaker.* Every morning, as I awaken, messages stream through me. Then, I have to make a choice. Do I tend to everything else that is calling for my attention, or do I write down what I hear? If my intent is to be a published author and a public speaker, that intent helps me set my priorities. First, I write down the messages I hear, before any other chores are tended to. When those messages arrive at 4 a.m. or 5 a.m., so be it. I am grateful that they do not come in at 2 a.m. or 3 a.m., as they did for my first book. All my books flow out of my intent.

Why does the Universe respond to the intent we set for the day? Because we are the Universe! We are the All; part of All That Is. We simply have to re-discover who we really are. Intent provides the germination point for the idea to take hold; the starting point, base zero, the point of origin. We are all connected to the same matrix, an electrical system that binds each of us to each other. Intent is the springboard from which the motion begins. How important is intent? It is the first step in starting the other processes of creation in order to get that which we desire. Thus, it is important that we *set our intent each day.*

Every day, we choose that which we will be our focus. If we state our *intent* clearly, the Universe will comply, because we are a creator "Be"-ing and we create our own reality!

My intent is to remember my connection to the Source every moment of my life; to never forget who I Am, no matter what the circumstances are in which I find myself.

Believe that your intent sets in motion the forces of creation.

What is your "intent" for today?
Our beliefs come true based on the
intent we set for each day.

June 7

The Big Cheese

When we choose to incarnate on this planet, we take a vow that erases memory of our origins. We agree to a state of "forgetfulness;" a state of total amnesia about that place from which we come. This is critical to our nervous system; to our ability to stay grounded on this planet in order to experience what this planet has to offer. We have a choice about where we could go.

If we had memory of from whence we came, many of us would not agree to come here or to stay here. It would be too hard; the demands too great, the sacrifices too exhausting, and the challenges too threatening. Many beings-in-spirit consider coming here, but do not, for there are easier places in the Universe to incarnate.

There are still many remnants of *that which we are not* playing on this planet. It is a difficult concept; separating who we *are* from who we *are not.* We are not our body. That is the vessel contained *within* our Soul; our earthly space suit. We are not our clothes, our hair, or our makeup. These are things that either we put on or put up with. We are not our occupations, nor our jobs, nor our professions. These are roles that we play. We are not our names, nor are we our titles. These are identifications which we associate with our bodies. We are not our cars, our homes, our investments, or our boats. These are our possessions. None of these things come close to describing who we really are.

We ask: *If I am not my body, my name, my hair, my make-up, my clothes, my job, my profession, my hobbies, my possessions, my accolades, my leisure pursuits, than who am I?*

After all is said and done, there is only one thing left – *I Am*. *I Am* – the Big Cheese and the Cheese stands alone. *I Am* – another word for God. *I Am* is what is left, and that is BIG.

The spiritual energies now bombarding this planet are helping us to wake up; to re-member who we really are; part of the *I Am* presence; part of an aspect of God. When we distill away all the remnants of what or who we *think* we are – when we clear away all the debris from the fog in our mind – then we are left with the connection to all things. When we accept our *Oneness* with all creation, it is a powerful moment!

Believe that you are an aspect of The Big Cheese; the *I Am* presence.

How does the I Am presence reveal itself in your life?
We are part of something so much greater than ourselves.

June 8

Telepathy and Other Attempts of Spirit to Reach Us

An intuitive "knowing," cementing our understanding that all minds are in communication with each other, is telepathy. According to ancient Buddhist texts, the entire human race on this planet once experienced telepathy, and then forgot it. We can bring it back by practicing it. Telepathy – the journey of the mental body across space – occurs with increasing frequency as we perfect it.

Many of us send messages of love, hope, encouragement, safety and well being across the miles. Our prayers for the safety of our loved ones can be viewed as a form of telepathy. Many of us "know" when the telephone is going to ring, or "know" who is calling us; skills associated with telepathy. Many of us have a *sense of elation* before we receive good news and a *sense of doom* just before bad news reaches us. That is telepathy.

Occasionally, the phone rings and no one is there. One of our loved ones in spirit may be trying to contact us. They can get a phone to ring but cannot summon the "energy" to speak to us. Another common occurrence is to have lights flicker when members in the spiritual dimension are trying to contact us, or in my experience, the glass "pings" in a window.

When our Board of Directors was setting up the Constitution and By-Laws for the Rays of Healing Church, Inc. (the new church we had just established), at the precise moment we discussed certain issues, the lights started to dim and brighten, as if Spirit was registering their full agreement with what we were saying. We all laughed and acknowledged Spirit's acquiescence.

Many times my mother, who died in 1981, will get my attention by flickering lights, especially if I am doing something where my mind is "quiet" and I am receptive to her message. There are times when she will make a request – one she has made before – and I do not wish to honor her request and tell her so. Each of us has the right to follow our own guidance, regardless of what someone close to us feels is necessary, even if it is from the Spiritual realm.

We come from One Mind; from One Source. We are created as One Soul. We beat as One Heart; the heartbeat of Mother Earth. We have but one goal; to unite back to the Source from whence we came. According to *A Course in Miracles,* we can *delay* our understanding of Source energy. We can *deny* our understanding of Source energy. But we *cannot change* the understanding of Source energy. Eventually, we will all come to the same place of understanding.

Believe that all minds are One, and that you can communicate with loved ones in spirit.

What are your personal instances of communicating non-verbally? Telepathy is evidence of our ability to communicate through thought.

June 9

Telepathic Communication with Pets

I started to telepathically communicate with our captivating Corgi, Taffy, for the last three years of his life. I noticed how excited he got whenever I just "thought" about going somewhere in the car, or just "thought" about taking him for a walk, since he loved to go "bye-bye." Half of our "conversations" were telepathic at first, but before he died, most of them were.

Once, when I was crying over some frustration that took me over the edge, Taffy laid down, tucked his front paws together, rested his head on them and looked up at me with deep empathy, tracking me only with his eyes. Sympathy poured out of his beautiful brown-black eyes. He continued to send me messages of empathy and love, and didn't leave his spot until I settled back into harmony.

About a week after Taffy died, while sitting on the couch in the living room where I normally say my morning prayers, I started to cry thinking about him and all his funny antics. Within seconds, I felt him licking my face to comfort me.

Many pet owners of a beloved pet have had similar experiences. There was a charming story about a little Yorky who stayed at the feet of his master as he worked in his home office. The master, originally a non-lover of dogs, soon mellowed to the devotion this little Yorky gave him. He usually figured out exactly what the little Yorky wanted by the sound of the bark, whimper, or whine he made. When that did not work, he went through a list of about forty words until the Yorky started to yap excitedly at one of them. The master was always able to satisfy the need of his little friend.

There are countless stories about the ability of animals to communicate with those around them. The TV show, *Miracles,* portrayed the story of a man who had collapsed in his own backyard. His pet, a large pot-bellied pig – at risk to his own life – squeezed himself through a doggy door to get out of the yard, and lay down in the middle of the street to attract attention, in order to get rescue help for his owner. Each time a car passed him by and did not stop, he got up, squeezed back through the doggy door to check up on his owner, and then came back into the street to repeat the process, making himself bloody through this ordeal. Eventually, one sympathetic person stopped and followed the pig back to the yard where he found the heart-attack victim and called the rescue squad. That pot-bellied pig saved his owner's life.

When we communicate telepathically with our animals, plants, or minerals, we reinforce the knowledge that "We are One." We are all part of One system – One plan – that exists within the Mind of God.

Do you have a beloved pet with whom you communicate telepathically? Our beloved pets will be waiting for us when we transition to the next place.

June 10

A Little Willingness

We need but give the Holy Spirit *"a little willingness"* and the rest is done for us. "A little willingness" is the crack into the casing surrounding our heart. *Open the door a little*; that is all Spirit asks. While our heart is sealed shut, Spirit cannot enter. As we open our hearts a little, Spirit can.

Be forewarned. Once we open our heart to Spirit, *there is no going back.* Our commitment is firm. It is just like being pregnant; either we are or we are not. There is no "degree" of pregnancy. Similarly, there is no degree of commitment to Spirit. Open our hearts a little, and we will *see, hear, feel, and know* the changes coming to us that radiate from Spirit.

When you are firmly on the spiritual path, you will understand the phrase from *A Course in Miracles:* "You are host to God and hostage to no one and nothing." Even though you recognize and stay firm in *your* power, you can also allow everyone else to stay firm in *their* power. You do not have to accept their power as your power. You do not have to bend to the demands or needs of another, but can allow them to have their demands and their needs without judgment on your part. Then you start to own your power.

When we open the door to Spirit, we give up conflict, even to the point of surrendering our body – if necessary – because we understand that as a creator "Be"-ing, we can create a new body as soon as we choose to do so. We can stand in our own power, because we know there is no death, and death is what men fear the most. That we open our hearts and our minds to Spirit pays tribute to our level of *willingness.*

Rage happens in this world because of the prevailing attitude: *If this happens, then I will die. But in reality, THERE IS NO DEATH.*

When this concept is clear, then we step into the realm of God Power, the power of the creator "Be"-ing that we are.

Believe that your connection to your Spirit Self is entirely up to you.

How great is your willingness to align with Spirit?
Believe that "a little willingness" will align us with Spirit.

June 11

Holograms

Scientists have verified the holographic nature of our Universe. There are splendid videos on the market demonstrating how a hologram works. From the largest portion to the teensiest particle, each part keeps repeating until the entire hologram is duplicated. Each part starts with the most minuscule fragment, which grows into a large complete whole, and then shrinks back again; then the entire sequence repeats itself. Because of the musical accompaniment, the effect is mesmerizing. The images undulate and wave, expand and contract, and are so fleetingly beautiful that they easily take us into an altered state.

Since our bodies are holographic in nature, healing one part can heal the whole. One person having an "awakening" will change the whole for everyone. One person counts, because one person can alter the course for all mankind.

The closest that I came to seeing the holographic nature of the Universe was during the time when I was filling out a college application. I was typing so intently that the keyboard I was looking at instantly grew larger. The keys looked as if they were suspended in air, and the space in between the keys seemed strangely "alive." I blinked, and the keyboard resumed its "normal" size. I blinked again, and it enlarged. I continued this activity for about ten minutes before resuming my typing.

This holographic experience repeated during a time when I was idly staring intently at a monochromatic pattern on a tablecloth in a restaurant. Suddenly, the entire field of the tablecloth went into a three dimensional mode. The small yellow daisies grew bigger and looked as if they were suspended in a *fluid*, rather than a *solid,* navy blue field. As I focused and refocused, each time I blinked, the daisies on the tablecloth changed from regular size to a larger size. They seemed to float on the navy blue field, which resembled a pool of dark gently flowing plasma. The currents forming the plasma looked alive. Such observations are not easily forgotten!

We do not have to wait for any new holographic devices to be developed to allow us to communicate with Spirit. We are in communion with all minds at all times, through our God-consciousness. A meditative state can get us there.

Believe that most of this world exists in the "unseen" realms, rather than the "seen."

Have you ever had an experience that you would consider to be holographic? Study of the holographic nature of the Universe is a fascinating subject.

June 12

Calibration

David Hawkins, M.D., Ph.D., in his exceptional book *Power vs. Force: The Hidden Determinants of Human Behavior*, presents a body of work *identifying a map of consciousness.* He validates his premises with analysis of *millions* of answers, to questions posed to thousands of humans for over the past twenty years. The technique that he uses to validate his information is kinesiology; a method of muscle testing that validates whether or not a stimulus physically supports or weakens the body.

This method, first pioneered by Dr. George Goodheart of Detroit, Michigan, in the 1960s, eventually led to the formation of the International College of Applied Kinesiology. Goodheart's method, called *applied kinesiology,* was associated with *physical* stimuli. He proved, in thousands of experiments, that the muscles of the body went weak in the presence of harmful physical stimuli. Dr. John Diamond, a psychiatrist, further expanded the use of kinesiology to include *psychological* stimuli, such as art, music, facial expression, voice, or stress. It was his research that proved that clients went weak in the presence of *unhealthy emotional attitudes and mental stresses.*

Dr. Hawkins used kinesiology to map the levels of consciousness. He used a scale of 1-1000, where the level of integrity or truth calibrated at 200, which is the level of Courage. Every level below 200 had an element in it that *weakened* his clients. These included, on a *descending* scale from Courage-200: Pride-175, Anger-150, Desire-125, Fear-100, Grief-75, Apathy-50, Guilt-30, and Shame-20. The levels that calibrated above 200 *strengthened* his clients. These included, on an *ascending* scale from Courage-200: Neutrality-250, Willingness-310, Acceptance-350, Reason-400, Love-500, Joy-540, Peace-600, Bliss-660, and Enlightenment-700 to 1000.

The hundreds of thousands of experiments performed by Hawkins involved getting the calibrations of various emotions and attitudes; both positive and negative. He also calibrated countries, cultures, and professions, as well as former Master Teachers on this planet. He substantiated his assertion that one person of a higher vibration can overcome the effects *hundreds of thousands – even millions* – of people calibrating at lower vibrations. One person calibrating at 700 can counterbalance 70 million calibrating below 200. One person at 600 counterbalances 10 million people below 200. One person at 500 counterbalances 750,000 people below 200. Thus, people who engage in, focus on, and concentrate their energies on activities and thoughts that strengthen humanity overcome the negative effects of those who stay in the negative realms.

Since the late 1980s, humans, on the average, as measured by David Hawkins, have surpassed the level of 200 as a collective level of consciousness. This is significant, because 200 (the level of Courage) is a level of empowerment where obstacles are looked upon as *opportunities,* rather than as permanent *barriers.* Although eighty-five percent of the world's population calibrates less than 200, the remaining fifteen percent who calibrate over 200 make up for the eighty-five percent who calibrate less than 200.

There are places on the earth that calibrate at 40, the level of *hopelessness* – entire countries where the level of hopelessness prevails. Getting to a place of anger, which calibrates at 150, is an *enormous* improvement for anyone from an area that calibrates at 40.

The calculations are based on logarithms, and so convey the exponents of the number 10 raised to that power. An integer number on the logarithm-base-10 scale communicates the number of zeros (or place-holder numbers) after the first digit of a number. (For example, 1 is the logarithm (base 10) of 10, 2 is the logarithm of 100, and 3 is the logarithm of 1000.) This kind of logarithmic scale is often used to express the power of natural events; the Richter scale measures the power of earthquakes using the logarithm of the amplitude of seismograph waves. Thus even 41 (as a logarithmic scale) is a great improvement over 40. (41, compared to 40, is an effect that is *ten times more* than the effect at 40.) Whatever the beginning rate of calibration is in a person (in an average lifetime), the average increase is only *five points*, which explains why the consciousness of man evolves as slowly as it does.

Attending seminars or workshops that serve to expand limited beliefs, as well as reading spiritual material, can increase the calibration rate of a group. During the seminar Dr. Hawkins presented in Northern Virginia (just outside Washington DC), our group calibrated seventeen points higher at the end of the seminar than at the beginning; one of the highest increases he had ever recorded.

Believe that every attitude, every emotion, and every thought that carries with it a positive charge can strengthen not only you, but also can serve to strengthen all of mankind.

Have you ever had kinesiology applied to yourself or to another person? Kinesiology can help test our physical, mental, and emotional health.

June 13

The Light that You Are

You make incredible opportunities for yourselves through your Self when you are ready to stand in your own light. You are a child of God, a gift to the Universe. In fact, you are the Universe. All is within your "Be"-ing. You just have to know how to access it: through meditation, through the quiet within. Stillness is the path to the glorious part of your nature; to the God within. You access your light through meditation.

Everything that you bring into existence through your life is brought because you choose to bring it in. You have such glorious Souls; such brilliant light within that you never see and never acknowledge. You give so much attention to your little pains and insecurities that you never have the space and attention for the infinite part of your nature; the expansive part of you, the glorious Self.

Do not dim your light in order to make someone else feel good. That is the opposite of what Spirit seeks, which is to share your light. The ego tells you to dim your light so that the feeble light of others can shine. Spirit seeks to glow and shine. The ego tells you to diminish, contract, and dim. Spirit seeks to glow, shine, brighten, and transcend any blockages that come to the forefront.

You have such power to be anything you wish to be, if only you keep your focus and concentration on that which you wish to be. From thought to matter, through focus and concentration, matter comes into being.

If you have been given the thought, then you have also been given the means to bring that thought into manifestation. They go hand in hand. Thought is your inspiration, Thought is the catalyst for action. Thought creates. Thought brings form into being. God would not give you the thought without the corresponding power to bring it into form. This is your "creator potential." This is how powerful you are. This is the essence of who you are: a creator "Be"-ing; a GIT (a god-in-training). Believe you can change your thoughts to create whatever reality you desire.

Believe that the Light that you are knows no boundaries.

Have you repressed your "Light" in deference to someone else's insecurities? Our Light cannot be repressed any more than the sun can be kept from shining.

June 14

Changing Our Past

We can *change* the past, or we can *allow* the past to affect the present. We can release the past through forgiveness. Forgiveness is a terrific tool, but it is associated with blame. In order to forgive someone, we first have to blame that person for hurting us. Eventually, we release the entire concept of blame when we realize there is nothing to forgive, since – on some level – we *agreed* to all of it, whatever "it" is. When we release the concept of blame, and realize we have nothing to forgive, we are free from the cycle of blame and forgiveness and can go on to other facets of learning.

In the meantime, we may need to use other techniques. One of them is to alter the past, for by altering it, we change it. Whenever we enter a time or space that transports us to *another* time and space, know that we can *re-arrange it* in any way that we desire. We do this when we meditate or daydream. No matter what has happened to us – no matter how atrocious, how horrifying, how unjust – we can change the past. Our minds do not know the difference between a "real" experience and a vividly imagined one. We can place in our minds – mentally – all the images we feel would *now support* us without harming the "other."

We know what is *destroying* our peace of mind. Change it and replace it with what *supports* our peace of mind. We can go back through eons and change horrific ways we have died in a past life. The next time we feel "terrible" about something, take our self to a time and place where we could feel great about it. Sometimes, this means a simple alteration of the facts, sometimes a shift in attitude, sometimes an adjustment to emotional attachment. We are never a victim unless we choose to be.

We can change the past through our dreams. If we dream and *know we are dreaming,* it is called a *lucid dream*. Since we have full conscious awareness of the dream, know that we can change the dream. None of our nightmares, real or imagined, have to stay with us permanently.

A woman once described a dream in which she was frantically racing through the streets trying to run away from a bear. The bear finally cornered her and she asked, "Now what?"

The bear answered, "I don't know lady. This is your dream."

We have such incredible strength of character, and we each possess the means to be what we *truly* are. We are the God-Head sent down through the tubes to be a little child – to revisit creation on this – the most incredible level of existence – this awesome journey called life. Earth is the densest plane of existence, yet the most amazing. Because it has form and occupies space, we can see it, feel it, hear it, smell it, taste it, and love it. But since it is holographic in nature, we can change that form at will.

We need to do what is necessary to maintain our lives and our health in peak condition; to not undermine our lives with food that does not nourish us, with thoughts that pollute our energy fields, or with people whom we find are toxic. We can choose otherwise. As we seek our spiritual path, we need to have no regrets for what we do. We are children of God; each of us is Master of the Universe. All that is ours will come to us. All that belongs to us will be returned to us.

Believe that you have control over your past.

Do you feel the need to change something from your past? Our belief in our ability to change the past will free us from untold anxieties.

Step 4

Write It Down

Write the truest sentence that you know.

Ernest Hemingway

June 15

Why Write?

One consistent pattern in my life has been to record my thoughts. Even when I did not realize *why* I was doing it, I was writing. While some thoughts sounded brilliant, others were nothing more than a litany of complaints. Yet, I saw writing as a balm that soothed my Soul. From the beginning, somewhere in the back of my mind, the faintest glimmer of a thought about having my writings published gestated.

When I pressed a friend to edit some of my earlier writings, her only comment was: "Some writers keep journals just to see the personal growth they have made."

Why write? Writing was my way of expressing Spirit; that part of me that stood firm and unchanging. When I needed to vent, needed to express my extreme frustration over events spiraling out-of-control, and needed to sort through chaos to bring some semblance of order into my life, I turned to writing. Eventually, the effort became more and more consistent, until finally, ended up becoming a focal point of my life.

For years I had been awakened in the middle of the night by messages streaming through my head, *always about God.* It was useless to try to go back to sleep. The messages would not quit. *I had to get up, go to the computer and write down what I heard, or at the very least, record it on a yellow pad.* The computer became my ally; my faithful companion in the middle of the night when everyone in the house was asleep and everything was quiet. Eventually, the messages became a three-year journal that I called my *Angel Journal.*

I communicated with my Guides and with my Angels with such frequent regularity that this communication became essential to my existence – except that I shared it with no one. Not wishing to be subjected to quizzical looks, or worse, to ridicule, I kept these communications a deep secret; only speaking to a few select family members. I did not want my sanity questioned.

My husband and I owned a small real estate office; I headed our property management department and, for six years, belonged to a national real estate franchise for the listing and selling aspect of my business. I was totally grounded in the material aspects of the Earth. I even sold the stuff!

I started to feel like Dr. Jekyll and Mr. Hyde. During the day, I led a perfectly normal life as a real estate broker and property manager and took care of our children and pets. During the night, I communicated with my Spirit Guides and my Angels. Professional real estate broker by day; transmitter of spiritual truths by night. Could I share this with the world? Not very easily! I had a reputation to uphold.

The messages were fantastic. I filled reams and reams of paper with wonderful "stuff." Even though *I* was writing it down, these messages were coming *through* me; coming from a Source *outside* of me.

Write to record forever your thoughts about the experiences of your day.

Have you ever considered the possibility of writing or recording your thoughts daily? One hundred years from today, even our most mundane occurrences will be fascinating to someone.

June 16

Spirit's Directive

One morning as I was reading the Bible, a mandate came from my Spirit Guides: *You are to teach about God.*

The words were loud and clear and consistent. I protested, I cried. I wailed: *I can't do that! I am a real estate broker, not a minister. I have a degree in English, not theology. What is it, God, that You do not understand about my career?*

The voices were insistent: ***You are to teach about God.***

You are to teach about God.

You are to teach about God.

This was the end of the 1980's. I had no training in religious matters. *How could I possibly fulfill that instruction?* The Catholic faith in which I had been raised never encouraged us to read the Bible, preferring that religious instruction come from their dogma. Twelve years of parochial schooling and a smattering of Bible studies with a few couples from different faiths – Baptist, Methodist, and Catholic – certainly did not qualify me to teach about God. *What was Spirit thinking?*

I put my head down on the coffee table and cried convulsively, *I CAN'T DO IT!*

Spirit retreated, but did not rest. Eventually, after communicating with Spirit for three years in my journal, a new, and more authoritative voice awakened me on July 31, 1997, at 3:00 a.m. with the words, *Be still and know I am your God.* This conversation became the basis for my first book, *God is the Biggest Joker of All.*

The biggest joke on this planet is that we are separate from God. The title simply refers to *our insistence* that we are *separate* from our Source; that God is a Supreme Being "out there" rather than inside of us. No organized fundamentalist religion, no fundamentalist belief, no ideology, teaches us that we are *One* with the Source.

Has Spirit ever given you a directive you feel is impossible to achieve?
If God has led you to it, God will lead you through it.
(Anonymous)

June 17

Getting Started

Since Step #4, *WRITE IT DOWN,* is critical to ***Owning Your Power***, the first thing you that need to do is to purchase a package of yellow pads, or a tape recorder. You never know when you will receive a "brilliant idea." Having a blank tablet or a recorder ready to receive the messages from Spirit ensures that you will be able to capture every great idea that is given to you.

Keeping a yellow pad available in your kitchen, at your work desk or in your home office, your car, your bedroom, your briefcase, or in a large purse makes it convenient to record your thoughts. Yellow pads are bound together and do not fall apart. They are reasonably priced, enabling you to write on one only side of the page (critical if you wish to assemble your writings for publication in the future.)

Write the first thing in the morning, before you have even properly awakened. Take no food or drink (except water) do nothing to diffuse your energy field. Simply pick up a pad of paper and start to write anything that comes to your mind, or record whatever rambling thoughts come your way. Sure, you may have to get up a few minutes earlier each day, and some days you may not get to it at all. But make it an automatic part of your daily routine.

If you wish to become a writer, to get your creative juices flowing, "write three morning pages each day," states Julia Cameron in her excellent book, *The Artist's Way.* The most important thing you can do for yourself is to write three pages each morning *before* you do anything else The writing is just for you and no one else, so do not be concerned about editing it, or about the content matter. What is important is that you *write.*

Even if you do not wish to become a writer, composing three pages each morning may give you insights that you might have overlooked. You may be astonished as to what shows up in your daily journal. This is Spirit's way of getting your attention. You may have reams and reams of angry words that have been bottled up inside of you for years. This writing is for no one's eyes except your own, so you can be as forthright as possible. When the urge hits you, be it to vent or to write a cherished poem, as soon as inspiration comes in, *write it down.*

Gather together your writing materials today: your notepads, yellow tablets, fancy or plain journals; add to that an assortment of colored or plain pens, and some pencils as well. Put your thoughts down in notebooks, on yellow pads, or on the computer. Just write. It does not matter *what.* It only matters that you do it. Write even when you do not feel like it.

The theme eventually comes out. Once you start recognizing the *theme* of that which you write about, you will recognize what it is that *you* are all about. As you re-read what you have written, the pattern emerges. This gives you direction. If you are in the grips of fear because you wish to make a change in your life, yet do not know how, ideas may pop in to help you do just that: transform your patterns or habits into a new life.

As you write, put a date on each page to make it easier to track, should you desire to trace your progress and growth through a subject.

Have you ever felt the urge to write before but ignored it? Gather together all of your writing materials and do it now!

June 18

Write to Be Inspired

When my Guides gave me a strict format to follow: *write as soon as I get up, as many pages as I want, on any subject that comes through my mind,* I balked. I wanted to write "important stuff!" I had always written down vignettes that were bothering me, stories of events swirling around me, and emotions that I felt, but I wrote whenever I felt up to it; whenever I could squeeze it in, whenever I felt I had no one with whom to share my problems. When all other avenues of expression seemed inaccessible, I wrote. There was no pattern to my writing habit; no discipline. All I was doing was releasing energy, similar to the way in which we deflate an overblown balloon.

Following the advice of my Guides, I started to record what was happening in my life on a day-to-day basis. Mainly, I wanted explanations for things that I did not understand. For years, my *inner self* felt unsettled, in total contrast to what my *outer self* presented to the world. It was as if I did not fit into my own skin. Nothing seemed to go "right" in my life, in spite of the outward appearance of *success.* I felt weaker and weaker each day, as if someone were poisoning me in very small doses, yet I maintained an active schedule that could drain the life force of two people, much less one.

Over the months, my litany of complaints grew smaller and smaller as I communicated daily with my Guides. Pretty soon, there were no complaints. What remained were spiritual insights that astonished me: *advice for daily living, explanations for relationships that troubled me, soothing passages to ease the pain of what hurt me, calming explanations for what angered me.* These types of messages had been coming in all along, but my ego self had prevented me from hearing them. When I stopped *kvetching* long enough to *hear,* I was able to understand the wisdom of the words that were streaming through me. My first efforts, known as my *Angel Journal*, were written between 1993 and 1995. Even though the words still seem sacred to me, they, too, will need to be released to the Universe, for in releasing them, they pave the way for others to release their sacred messages. As I edit these words on March 19, 2006, I just realized that Neale Donald Walsch received his messages that became the book, *Conversations with God*, at the same time I received the messages that became my *Angel Journal.*

Sometimes it is important to write until we hit the vein of inspiration, "the ore that brings the riches" as Julia Cameron states in *Vein of Gold,* a further treatise on mining our truth. *Write – just write.* Follow through by writing each day *at the same time, in the same place.* The key is to be consistent. Writing a little each day eventually leads to all the treasure we desire.

Our thoughts and inspirations come in spurts; sometimes when we least expect them; thus, the importance of having pen and paper handy. Pretty soon we will have a yellow pad filled with loving words, with insights, with words of wisdom and words of praise, consistent with the goals our Spirit Self set for us at the onset of our journey here.

Start today.

Do you have any thoughts so sacred that you that you cannot share them, yet need to express them in some manner? Write them down!

June 19

Publicize Your Writings

When speaking about the book *The Celestine Prophecy*, written and published by James Redfield, I heard a friend say, "I could have written that book in ten minutes."

The truth is, she *did* write that book, only she did not *publicize* her writings. For at least twenty years she wrote for her own personal edification. No one knew anything about her writings. She felt her thoughts were too personal and too private to be shared.

We are the eyes and ears, hands and legs of Spirit. They give us hunches and encouragement; they put words in our mind, but we have to do the rest. They prompt us, but *do not do* our work for us.

James Redfield felt that he had an important message to share. He received enough rejection letters from publishers to paper the wall of his den, but did not allow the rejection letters to discourage him. He self-published, then went up and down the East Coast of the United States, talking on any radio station that would give him air time and selling books from the trunk of his car. Eventually, the sheer volume of his sales came to the attention of a large publisher and his book was released nationally. His career took off after he signed a contract with this publisher, and he has since become a nationally-known speaker as well as a published author of multiple books.

It takes a great deal of energy to go from recording "brilliant" passages to compiling them into a manuscript, editing and correcting the manuscript, sending out query letters to agents or publishing houses, waiting for a positive response, negotiating a contract, publishing the book, and then finally, to marketing the book.

Nothing will hold back what is supposed to be out there. As the Gnostic *Gospel of St. Thomas* states: "If you bring forth what is within you, what you bring forth will save you. If you do not bring forth what is within you, what you do not bring forth will destroy you. Those who have ears will hear."

If you have a message to share with the world, Spirit will pave the way.

Are you are a "closet" writer?
There may be someone else on this planet who desperately needs to read what you have to say.

June 20

You Need Do Nothing

When my Guides told me that my second book was almost finished, I answered in complete astonishment: *It is?* I had no idea that all my daily journaling from the previous two years – recording all these inspired messages about God – were to be compiled into a book. I thought the writings were terrific, but could not find the cohesive theme – since each day's writing seemed to be on a different subject.

While recuperating from a broken wrist during January and February of 2000, I would periodically be awakened by a phrase that kept repeating until I recorded it exactly as I heard it. Only then could I go back to sleep. Each phrase was recorded on the same sheet of paper and each phrase was underlined and highlighted, to underscore its importance. While this began in the early months of 2000, the entire process took about seven months to complete. A total of seven phrases came to me over this time.

As I started sorting out the writings I'd done from 1999 and 2000, I realized that the seven phrases that I had recorded in the middle of the night were the seven major themes about which this book is organized: *The Outer Reflects the Inner*, *Make Different Choices*, *Believe that It is Possible*, *Write It Down*, *Choose Your Self*, *Cocoon*, and *Connect to the Divine Source*.

There is a passage in *A Course in Miracles* that instructs [each of us to realize] "you need do nothing." If you take this passage literally, and indeed, decide to do "nothing," you may watch your world come crashing down around you. However, you receive all of the *spiritual assistance* to which you are open, which you can then use to manifest the *physical things* that you need to support your life and the lives of your fellow travelers on this planet. It is the *effort* that you put into your life that reveals to Spirit how you use the gifts given to you for the betterment of all.

I could claim that, indeed, *"I" did nothing* by accepting Spirit's *assistance,* which influenced every facet of this book. Spirit provided the inspiration, the words, and the major themes, together with guidance on publication and marketing. However, my receiving the messages was only a small part of the picture. I had to accomplish an enormous amount of work before the book was in anyone's hands.

What unique message do you need to share with the world? Keep focusing on the end result when working toward a goal of publication.

June 21

Asking Questions

The following is an excerpt of a “conversation” that I had with my Guides one morning when I felt particularly blocked. I did not feel my writings were going very well at all, and I needed answers. The answers I heard from my Guides are *italicized.*

“What is this all about?”

Your journey.

“Why am I blocked? Do I have ego issues to deal with?”

Plenty.

“Am I doing a good job of dealing with them to date?”

Better than before.

“Will I ever achieve my goal?”

It is just around the corner.

“When do I get to be the person I really desire to be?”

Look at yourself now. What does not serve you? Eliminate it!

“How do I eliminate that which I feel I am tied to but don’t want to be?”

Reorganize and eliminate all your clutter. Stuff is easy; get rid of it. People are another problem. Trust that all the answers are given you. It is up to you to hear them and to act on them.

"Did I forgive myself for all the transgressions I committed?" (This question referred back to my first marriage; a time that had caused both my parents and me a lot of heartache.)

Not completely. You are still carrying baggage from the past, but less and less all the time.

"What is the best way to achieve my goals?"

Discipline. Do the same thing each day till a routine is established whereby you achieve that daily goal.

"What do I do next that I have not done to date?"

Go into the computer and enter all of your writing on a <u>daily</u> basis.

"That's a lot of work!"

We know. We will help you do it. Transcribing and editing five hundred pages is not easy, but easier when assisted by Spirit.

"In the meantime, am I to continue as I have been doing?"

Precisely! You'll get further that way. No bellyaching, though! There is so much to do.

"Why did today's writings break down?"

They didn't. You broke down. You were distracted by other things: food, newspaper, and thoughts. Better to get those things off your mind – behind you – then continue.

The dialogue ended. I went back to the computer and continued to work. It would be several years before I committed fully to working *daily*, as I had been told to do several times.

Have you felt unable to move forward with a project dear to your heart? Asking questions of our Guides helps move us through any blockages that we may have.

June 22

Releasing Pit Bulls

Write! Write! Write! My Guides kept telling me. Easier said than done, when my heart and mind were being rent by an invasion of unsettling events.

At that time, I was wrestling with a very unruly client and a very demanding buyer. It was a very "hot" seller's market, and I was acting as a duel agent. The seller felt compromised and did not feel I had accurately expressed the current market conditions, which created an air of suspicion around everything that I said and did. I became afraid to check my e-mail for fear of seeing the seller's response to the latest demand from the buyer. It was a pathetic situation. During this entire transaction, I felt as if a pit bull was gnawing on my solar plexus.

I spoke to my husband and asked him for his advice, since his instincts always protected our family. He always had our best interests at heart, and I had learned to use him as my "base camp." A solid family man, he had always put family first, even when his temper invaded his better emotions. I had learned to check with him before I did anything. That had not always been the case. During the first part of our marriage, I used to plunge recklessly ahead whenever I felt my course of action was "correct," without bothering to consult with him.

When I described the situation to him, he immediately replied, "Get the buyer out of that transaction. I have always hated those homes. Twenty years ago, I worked on some of them and saw how shoddily they were constructed."

To everyone's relief, both buyer and seller were willing to get out of the transaction. Once the buyer realized that the seller would not make any concessions to his demands, he was willing to focus his attention on another purchase. End of problem. End of anxiety.

This was a lesson in helping me balance my emotions, which had always see-sawed before. I would get ecstatic when everything was flowing smoothly and free-fall when things were not. I was elated when I made a sale, and felt my happiness plummet when I did not. I had to learn to *go with the flow.*

Emotions are meant to flow through our bodies. Stuffing them back into their holding tank – the body – causes them to "back up" and start to negatively affect what they touch. It is almost as if they misfire and start to rot the organs with which they are associated.

I continued to write during this unsettling period, which helped bring a sense of perspective to that which I was experiencing. As soon as my husband said, "Get the buyer out of the transaction," I knew he was correct. I had faintly heard the same advice from my Guides, but was so preoccupied with the minutia of the transaction that I did not react to their guidance. So much of my energy had been spent on an internal dialogue, criticizing myself for having created this mess that I did not act on the message from Spirit. Spirit's suggestions come quietly, on angel wings. They are like the kiss of a butterfly: barely felt, but never forgotten. Writing everyday throughout this traumatic experience helped bring stability into what looked like a disastrous situation.

Write so you can hear the "quiet" solutions being offered you.

How can writing help bring clarity to your problems? Writing brings a different perspective to that which we are experiencing.

June 23

Personal Advice

The following personal advice came from my Guides following another stressful period in real estate. Some of you may see yourselves in a similar situation.

You have murderous thoughts about those who have "done you wrong." Until you expel this energy, you will be blocked from receiving positive new energy. Your left-brain needs to become quiet so you can give attention to your right-brain.

Regarding your being, you may need to write a manual – a left-brained treatise – in order to satisfy the left-brained nature of your being.

You need to rid yourself of negative emotions in order to bring stability and function back into your life. Bring stability back into your life through your breath. Breathe deeply every time you think a negative thought, at every opportunity. Most of the time, you are a shallow breather. You need to breathe deeply in order to have the right amount of oxygen reach your brain.

Rise above the occasion. Bring forth your deepest feelings of forgiveness, first for yourself, then for others. It will work in your favor. You will be able to get through any shock wave that hits you, whether it be verbal, visual, physical, or emotional. You have so much to offer humanity, and to do this, you need to be stable and sure footed – not a loose cannon.

You have tremendous potential to be a great teacher. You teach yourself first, and then you teach your fellow man. By learning how to take your consciousness into other people's realms, you will help them with the hidden crevices of their lives; the areas they are not willing to look at – just as there were areas you were not willing to look at.

Keep the faith, my child, and keep pulling this cart you call your life. Please look at all the lovely people whom you instruct in spirit.

There are choirs and choirs of them. They sit in rapt attention as you speak. You have tremendous powers of persuasion. Use it – for the Love of God – use it. You are cherished above all men. You walk in peace.

Please remember that we are behind you.

Have you ever written down the words of advice that you've offered to others? When we hear the advice being offered to us, then we can better advise others.

June 24

Prime the Pump

Daily journaling is needed to "prime the pump," says Julia Cameron. Journaling provides the little bit of water needed to "get the juices flowing." "You write to right," she writes in *The Artist's Way*: you write to get your minds into the right place – to place your mind into the space from which you create. Prime the pump by writing, even when you do not feel like writing. It does not matter *what* you write, just *that* you write.

In the depths of our hearts – deep within our psyche – is an authentic Self, yearning to get out. Not just a self created by ego who responds to our physical world, but a Self who is part of the Divine Source; a Self connected to Divine Inspiration, Divine Imagination, the All-of-Creation of which we are a part. "Priming the pump" gets us to that Source. It brings us right there. We uncover the themes that are important to us. After all the ego stuff is cleared out of the way, we find our authentic Self talking to us. Our authentic Self – our Spirit Self – can reach us only when we are primed and ready to listen.

Look at the subjects about which you write. What are your *main themes?* Did you ever wonder how some authors are able to produce an entire book by essentially saying the same thing over and over and over? The characters change, the plot thickens in different settings, but the theme is the same. Daily journaling is the method that they use. Writing before you have had a chance to eat, drink, or cloud your thinking puts you into a space where you reach the core of your "Be"-ing.

In my case, Spirit's words always talked about man's *connection to Spirit*; to the Divine Source, to the Presence within. Sometimes it came in the form of a prayer, sometimes a meditation, sometimes a blessing, usually a simple narrative about our connection to God. What *did* matter was that I wrote daily; that I was consistent.

When I got so busy with my life that I sloughed off and forgot the importance of daily journaling, I broke my wrist. Then the options for activity became very limited: sitting, reading, watching TV, or writing. Having no energy or interest in anything else, my life brought me back to the sphere of daily journaling. Something within me relaxed, and I became very content. I became ready to face each day, and wrote and wrote and wrote.

When the total goal of our life is to integrate Body, Mind and Spirit into One whole "Be"-ing, we do succeed; even if it is in a manner that we least expect.

Why is "priming the pump" – writing daily – so important? We need to prime the pump by writing, even when we do not feel like writing.

June 25

Influencing Unborn Generations

The written word teaches us on many levels at the same time. Since the written word survives the author, it is capable of influencing unborn generations. Therefore, it is critical that we *write it down.* By keeping a yellow pad on each level of our home, in our office, in our purse, briefcase, or in our car, we have paper handy no matter where we are or what we are doing.

When we record our "bright ideas," we get a sense of peace and joy as we recognize that we are aligned with Spirit throughout the day – we only have to listen. It does not matter that the message be mundane. It can be something as simple as a suggestion as to what to have for dinner tonight. If we are feeling lack because we do not have the money to buy something new or to go out to eat, even to a very inexpensive restaurant, Spirit may help us create a new dish by giving us ideas to use ingredients that we already have in our home. *Voila! The feeling of lack passes.* Spirit has rewarded us for paying attention.

Think back about the times in which you were so engrossed in a book that you could not put it down. Did *Gone with the Wind* rivet your attention, or was it one of the many new mystery novels coming out today? How many authors influenced the path along your journey? Think back about the times you were at your wit's end, stopped by a bookstore, and had exactly the right book fall in your lap or onto the floor, or catch your eye in a display. Is it not amazing that exactly the information you needed was presented to you?

We may think that what we write is of no importance or has no significance to an "other." We may feel that we do not have enough schooling or enough command of the English language to share anything verbally. Will anyone, besides our family, be interested enough to pause and listen, much less to buy the words that we write? Let Spirit determine that. If it is supposed to reach others, it will. If it is supposed to be contained within the perimeters of our home, it will be.

Living by listening to Spirit can become a very exhilarating experience. We start recognizing how exhilarating it is after we start recording it.

Can you possibly foresee how many unborn generations your words of love and encouragement might influence?

Did any favorite literature influence your growth and development? Words written by authors of long ago can produce the most profound effects in our lives today.

June 26

From Venting to Listening

My journaling, for years, took place in the middle of the night. Working a sixty-hour week, I was on such a treadmill that I could not possibly have eked out any time during the day to write. Thus, Spirit woke me up in the middle of each night with streams of messages coming through me. Trying to fall back to sleep was useless. It was impossible! The messages didn't stop until I padded downstairs, got on the computer, and wrote what I heard.

Many of my earliest writings were filled with passages of what was "wrong" in my life; my "daily lament." It was a good way to get it out of my system, because – at that time – it seemed as if *nothing ever seemed to go right* for me. I set very high goals, and did not meet them, then set other very high goals. Thwarted again! In the meantime, my health was deteriorating incrementally.

I strove to become financially independent, and we should have been, because we certainly earned enough money. Yet, somehow, I always seemed to be on the edge of financial disaster. What finally opened my eyes to Spirit's call were my last two years of full-time work in real estate. Despite my enormous earnings, I faced a huge credit card debt at the end of the second year of not listening to Spirit's demands. I figured it was just a matter of time before I would bankrupt us. Having no choice, I *had to* listen to Spirit's directive to work in real estate part-time, to free up the hours I needed to do my spiritual work in earnest.

The thought, *If I can just get through three months and pay my bills with part-time employment, I can get through the rest of my life* propelled me forward. Giving up full-time employment and becoming part-time cleared the space to hear Spirit on a more significant level. The messages coming in now had more universal application. These were messages that could be shared with all, not just personal messages to me about how to keep my life afloat. All because I chose to *write them down.*

I had used writing as a means of venting for nearly thirty years of my life. Now it was time to share some of the magnificent insights that came my way through this very personal means of expression.

Does all the venting that you are doing have a higher purpose? Never underestimate Spirit's reasons for guiding us to write.

June 27

Removing Chains of "Littleness"

Spirit will reach through and lead us to what we are to do with our lives with whatever means they have available. Spirit will reach through whatever it is to which we pay attention, to awaken us to our power; to the recognition of the magnificent majestic "Be"-ing of light that we really are. Light is at our core. Our bodies are frozen light.

So many of us think we cannot write; we may have horrible memories of being criticized for our attempts at expressing ourselves with the written word. We are blocked.

Remove the chains of *littleness* that bind you. Do not succumb to your thoughts of how insignificant you are. Do not allow your thoughts of lack of empowerment to strangle you. That is your ego talking to you. Remember that your ego is not your best friend. Allow Spirit to shine through you. Relax into the idea of writing. You are not producing this to be evaluated by anyone. You are producing this in order to make sense of your own world.

Write what comes to your mind. Breathe deeply, the thoughts will come. Nothing special has to appear at first. Everything special will appear eventually. If you have to lament about your life for years – so be it! This scribe did. After all the lamenting is done, then, and only then, will your real work shine through and make sense to you.

This is such a critical step to *owning our power.* We become authoritative as we witness the power of the written word and can say to ourselves, *I did it.* Eventually, all that we need to know will be told to us.

Everything that you need to know will be given to you. *Write it down!*

How can writing a list of laments help you clear your mind for bigger and better information? Writing helps remove the debris that clutters our mind.

June 28

A Personal Road Map

Write without question of how we *should* sound or judgment or criticism of what we *should* write. Our internal critic will immediately try to condemn or belittle our efforts. The key is to write without self-judgment. Whether we are able to put an outline on paper first, or start with thoughts in "balloons" - just tidbits of ideas floating through our heads – or use brainstorming (as teachers like to call it), the key is to *just write.* As soon as we come into consciousness when we wake in the morning, our first task should be to write whatever thoughts are streaming through our heads. We are being led to our authentic Self.

It does not take us too long to discover our themes: what subject matter consistently evokes our interest, what is pulling at our heartstrings, what needs to be expressed through us. Writing reveals to us who we really are by showing us that in which we are really interested. A pattern shows up. Writing expresses our "Be"-ing because it expresses what is going through our minds. Writing gives us a personal road map to follow that leads us to our authentic Self.

So many people say *I hate to write.* If we look a little closer, we might see such issues surfacing as self-pity, self-criticism, or a variety of other self-effacing emotions. Maybe we have never been praised for anything we wrote, or never been given a reward for our efforts, making the exercise seem futile. Being punished for our writings or seeing other people punished because of them (whether during this lifetime or another) may be impacting our psyche and may cause us to abhor writing.

If you have a learning disability, then perhaps a tape recorder to record your thoughts is the better solution. Your writing impairment becomes less of an issue.

In the early years, re-reading my writings produced only more confusion. My journaling (when it was ego-directed) kept me coming back to the feeling that something was being asked of me, only I did not know "what." The "what" became very evident as I continued to write and slowly recognized that all the writing had turned to spiritual matters: to the essence of Soul, of Spirit, to messages about God.

It seemed as if this little tugboat (my Spirit) had led this huge ocean liner (my ego) out into the ocean, when in reality, it was the other way around. Spirit (the little tugboat that never quit) with all its ramifications, its multi-facets, and its multi-dimensions, was something with which my ego self (my huge ocean liner) had to grapple. Spirit eventually won.

How can daily journaling chart out a personal road map for your next move? Writing clarifies and contrasts objectively all our options.

June 29

Opening to Spirit

When we ask, *Who am I?* we open the door for Spirit to enter. That is the only invitation Spirit needs. Spirit never violates our free will. We choose the entree point, even when we do not know we are choosing it. *Who am I? Why am I here? What is my purpose?* These are all questions that give Spirit the opening needed to reach us.

One of my earliest memories was looking up at the sky and asking: *Who am I? What am I here for?* During my young adult years, I was so busy with the rest of my life that I had "no time" for Spirit, but I had a nagging feeling in the back of my mind that all the ego "stuff" for which I was striving was not "enough," and certainly, not the "answer."

Today, my spiritual life consumes most of my thoughts. When not enveloped in thoughts about Spirit, or listening to what Spirit has to say to me, I busy myself with the other parts of my life that are important to me. I love being a mother, a minister, a healer, a friend, an author, a business woman, a gardener, a homemaker, a decorator, and a purveyor of gifts.

Spirit is not asking us to change the world. Spirit is asking us to change ourselves: one belief at a time, one attitude at a time, one habit at a time, one perception at a time. The world changes because we change. We change and the world changes.

It is through us that mass consciousness evolves. One positive thought helps to negate hundreds of thousands of negative thoughts. One positive statement helps to negate hundreds of thousands of negative statements. This is not wishful thinking, for it works holographically: one part replicates the whole, one part alters the whole, and each part is enhanced under Spirit's guidance.

Even when we cannot "see" Spirit, we can "feel" Spirit's presence in our energy field. We can sense that we each have a personal cheerleader always cheering us on, helping move us out of our "calamities" into our treasures. Spirit reaches out to us when we are *ready* to receive. Part of the brilliance of the Body/Mind/Spirit connection is that Spirit transcends all boundaries.

Writing is a way to open ourselves to Spirit in this lifetime. As we write about it more will come to us.

Have you ever asked: Who am I? Why am I here? What is my purpose? We control the opening to Spirit by our questions.

June 30

A Solitary Occupation

From the time my daughter was a pre-teen, she loved to shop and delighted in finding bargains. By judiciously sticking with expensive stores, her best buys were clothes reduced from 75% to 90% off the original price. Supplemented with clothes from thrift stores and vintage shops, she started to get a very reasonably-priced, fantastic wardrobe. When the sales rack produced yet another treasure, her delight in finding another "great buy" nourished her spirit. Shopping in thrift stores furthered her creativity, since she insisted on taking clothes apart and recombining them into unique garments.

In college, she steadily marched towards a career as a production designer in the film industry, working on set design and art direction as steps toward that goal. Her love of shopping helped her in the film industry, as she went about procuring the props needed. Purveying the merchandise, constructing it, and modifying it to get the look she desired has been done with the help of others, but her major creative activities – planning, researching, and drawing the sets – have been accomplished in isolation. So much of my daughter's *creative* life has been solitary.

So is writing. We cannot pull thoughts out of our heads if we immerse ourselves strictly in the world. We need to go quietly into a space that is strictly our own. It does not need to be an entire room, but it needs to be unavailable to everyone except us.

One friend had her husband carve a writing space for her out of her master bedroom closet. Her children knew that space was off limits to them. When mom was at her writing desk, all attempts to reach her had to wait.

Women, especially, do not feel the right to carve time out for themselves. They feel so committed to giving all of their time and attention to others: their family, their home, the workplace, or volunteer activities. Sometimes the attempts that working mothers make to carve out solitary space only makes them feel more fragmented.

Stop! We have the right to our own personal time and our own personal space. We need not collapse at the end of the day in utter exhaustion, with barely enough energy to crawl into bed. When we think back on all the yesterdays, how much of our frantic activities can we even recall, and to which purposes were they related? It is time to bring balm to our Souls, time to quiet the monkey-minds that keep us endlessly stirred up. Hurriedly running this way and that only serves to keep us scattered.

Write to carve out a space of your own, even if it is only in cyberspace.

Does the thought of solitary activity scare you?
Consider the time we carve out for our Self sacred time.

July

Real Power – the power of Love – is ours for the taking. First, we have to uncover it, then we have to accept it, then we have to own it.

When we tap into Real Power – the power of Love – we can tolerate any situation because we stand witness to all attempts of a "little shrieking ego" to control, belittle, diminish, or ridicule us and still keep our peace. The "little shrieking ego," whether our own or from an "other," eventually gives up. It runs out of steam because its source is fear and fear can sustain its energy only for so long. It goes back to the cavern it came from. We are able to stand firm because we know the Source of Real Power is unlimited. It comes from the power of Love, which never runs out.

When we come from a heart space, we come from the place where Real Power – the power of Love – reaches through into us. Our heart space has to be fully open to be able to accept it completely. But even if our heart space is open only a crack, Real Power – the power of Love – can be accessed by us. Eventually, all attempts by a "shrill shrieking ego" to keep the heart space from opening will stop.

When we understand that we can tap into Real Power – the power of Love – any time, any place, anywhere, under any conditions, then we know that we can bear any circumstance with dignity and grace, because the Source of Real Power is within. Even if we are in the middle of an impassioned plea and somebody cuts us off, we can still keep our energy flowing. We do not have to give away our energy, neither do we have to collapse under the burden of any imagined shame or guilt.

The Source of Real Power – the power of Love – is limitless and is within us. We do not have to let circumstance reduce our self to a shaking, quivering mass of jelly because another "shrill shrieking ego" has attacked us, under whatever guise the attack comes. All egos have agendas. There is no way of knowing what agenda another ego has when it attacks or what form that attack will take. It can come masquerading in the form of criticism or judgment applied in the most gentle and loving manner. It is still criticism and judgment. And all criticism and judgment come from the ego, which is based on fear.

July 1

Letting Go of Worry

Worry. Worry. Worry. That is a big one! Most of humanity expresses one big worry thought or another, many times about *there is not enough.*

But there is enough. This is a very abundant Universe and *there is enough* for everyone to have a share. Do you believe that? If you do, TERRIFIC!! If you do not, you will continue to worry about all the shortages and calamities in your life.

The best way in which we can identify what is worrying us is to simply write down the problem, then write down the *worst possible outcome* that could result, then write our reaction to the worst outcome. The chart looks like this:

MY PROBLEM WORST OUTCOME MY REACTION

Writing out the problems helps us to clarify them. We can see issues more clearly when we record them on paper, than we can if we just talk about them. Write out everything that is troubling us. The solution can only become obvious to us if we can see the problem clearly.

Within each problem is the solution. Somehow, in the *identification* of the problem is the *release* of the problem. When our minds churn relentlessly, they are in a muddle, and everything within them is clouded. Even mud in a pool of water eventually settles to the bottom and the water becomes clear again, provided that the water is not continuously stirred up. Our minds, with their frantic churning, do not allow us to see things clearly, because they keep stirring up the mud instead of allowing it to settle. *Writing it down* allows the mud to settle.

There is nothing more powerful than *writing it down* to help us clear our minds. By writing out the worst case scenarios and our reactions to them, we automatically lay out solutions for ourselves. When our minds are clear, the path to a solution can be seen, even when the situation seemed hopeless before. Whatever the issue – whether it is a financial, an emotional, a mental, or a physical problem – *writing it down* is the key to bringing clarity into our lives.

Whether related to spousal abuse, to financial support, to lack of achievement in school, to sexual abuse, to harassment at work, school, or church, to devastating news about our health or the health of our loved ones, to a sudden death, or to any crisis with our children, *writing it down* brings a solution closer to us than any amount of discussion will. There is something about seeing the problem on paper that gives us a perspective that words alone cannot.

When working with little children, especially those who do not yet have the benefit of written language, drawing a picture about the problem may provide insights to understanding what is bothering the child. It may be the key that unlocks the terror that the child is holding within.

Change your paradigm. Get out of the little box that keeps you stuck in the same worry habit. Let go of worry by *writing down* the problem and having the solution shine through.

What problem is keeping you paralyzed?
Writing it down will help lead to a solution of the problem.

Specialized Journals

An important step to *"Writing It Down"* is to do a series of *specialized journals.*

Keep a ***Synchronicity Journal,*** to record the events when synchronicities occur; all those lovely little "coincidences" that flock into our lives. Recording these events in a small pretty notebook or in a plain black and white composition book are equally effective, as is creating a separate file in your computer.

Synchronicities are the Angels' way of letting us know they are guiding us. Angels work so hard to synchronize events and we barely notice! They feel especially rewarded when we take the time to acknowledge and to record their efforts. As we awaken to the coincidences around us, we receive more of them. Angels attempt to reach us however and whenever they can. Please take note!

Another specialized journal is the ***Dream Journal.*** Dreams are like the kiss of a butterfly. They evaporate almost before we know they exist. By keeping our Dream Journal next to our bed along with a small flashlight, we can write in the middle of the night if necessary. We can capture our dream before we are fully awake.

If you have not captured the dream in the middle of the night, or whenever you have the dream, write in your Dream Journal as soon as you are able to. Very powerful dreams can come during short naps in the middle of the afternoon, so do not discard the "power nap" as a means used by your Higher Self, Angels, or Guides to reach you. Another possibility is to set an intention to direct a dream before going to sleep, or to ask for information to guide your life prior to going to sleep. These two methods work, even for power naps.

A third variation is the ***Gratitude Journal.*** A friend who had an aneurysm was told by her cardiologist to write down *fifty items* for which she was grateful before she went to sleep each night, even if they were the same fifty. Oprah Winfrey told her audience that the Gratitude Journal "will change your life." Meister Eckart, a thirteenth century monk said, "If the only thing you say is Thank You that will be enough."

Gratitude Journals do indeed change our lives. They help keep us focused on the positive things we have in our lives, and serves to uplift our thoughts daily. We have so many more things to be grateful for than we *ever* think about.

Other ***Personal Journals*** can be used to record an exercise program (calorie or carbohydrate intake, miles run, classes or workouts attended), arts and crafts projects, dinners we create for special occasions, or any other unique information that we wish to record and retrieve.

As we fill up all the journals, notebooks, or tablets, we discern which specific functions merit being recorded in their own journals in the future, or whether some of our journals need to be combined. It is amazing how good it feels to keep track of something that is important to us, rather than just to have a nebulous idea about it.

When you read what you *write* about, you recognize what you *are* about.

How do specialized journals keep you focused on the positive?
Specialized journals help keep us moving forward in our lives.

July 3

A Letter of Thanks

Four times I composed letters to a nationally syndicated talk show host, but never sent any of them. Somehow, Step #4 seems like the perfect time to express my thanks to that person.

Dear __________

Thank you for introducing me to the practice of the Gratitude Journal. You promised it would "change my life," and it has.

Thank you for your courage to speak your truth. As you speak your truth, you give us – your audience – the opening to speak our truth. As we speak our truth, so do countless other women and men also speak their truth.

Thank you for grappling with the issues of bigotry, prejudice, racism, and all manner of problems that many turn away from as too controversial. You show these controversial issues in the most positive light possible, showing solutions to problems, not just airing the problems, or making them into outrageous spectacles and shouting matches. You bring dignity and grace to some very difficult situations. You shine the light of exposure on some issues hiding in the underworld.

Thank you for emphasizing that there is only one race on this planet. It is called human. Thank you for bringing the issue of Spirit down from its lofty perch where it never wanted to be in the first place and into the hearts and souls of every human being. People are starting to understand who they really are and their connection to the Divine, thanks to you and some of your spiritually-minded guests.

Thank you for the sensitivity and good judgment you use when airing a show that could be sensationalized and stereotyped, such as the show you did on transsexuals. Once again, you proved that "Only Love is real."

Sincerely yours,
S. Alice "Alicja" Jones
Minister, Rays of Healing Church

The next time that you compose words of gratitude in your mind, write them down and send them out. The recipient may need to hear those words, for they may be the only positive words they hear that day.

Have you ever held back words of gratitude that you needed to bring forth? Someone's life may change because we have taken the time to write a note of gratitude.

July 4

Lessons from Drama Traumas

Coming home from the Philadelphia Flower show one March, I was driving with my sister to her hotel room. We came to a junction in the road, and I insisted that she take the north direction leaving town. From all her previous trips into the city, she *knew* that she had to take the south direction. Because I was so insistent, in deference to me, we went north and ended up in New Jersey. In spite of the fact that her guidance was to go south, she deferred to me and then became silently angry that we ended up in the wrong place. I apologized, felt her anger, and hoped that she could let it go.

I did not see the deeper message of that incident until that evening. I had previously had a similar incident happen to me on the way home from the 4th of July fireworks display in Washington D.C. To test the evacuation procedure from D.C., the bureaucrats decided to close most of the exits out of the city. *The Washington Post* had stated that only seven major arteries would be left open. (In actuality, only four major routes were open.) We left the city in record time due to the place that I had parked. In my friend's gratitude to me for showing her my "secret" parking spaces in D.C. and tips to exit the city quickly, she wanted to share some of her "secret" exits out of the city. As we were at the top of one of the overpasses leaving the city, my friend spied a short cut that she had used a number of times before. Since we were at a dead stand-still and that lane was totally open, she felt that this route would by-pass all the traffic and get us out quickly.

Against my inner guidance, I took it and found the entrance blocked. The irony was that, since there were no lights at that entrance, or to any other of the entrances to the major highways, there was no good reason for that entrance to be blocked. We were led to an alternative route and the entrance to the highway from that route *was also blocked.* We eventually got home, but all in all, the sequence of events added an extra hour to our trip; a small price to pay for attending the wonderful *Capitol Fourth* Celebration set on the grounds of the majestic Capitol Building – my first time ever!

Both incidents involved statements made by an "other," each insisting that they were correct. Both recipients, at the same time, had their own guidance that was different than what was being offered them by the "other." Both recipients did not follow their own instincts and were inconvenienced by the results.

Because of this event, I clearly saw the "lesson" in which I had agreed to participate, how the lesson is set up by the soul and how all the players who volunteer to partake in the lesson interact. Each soul lines up and plays its part. Each soul receives one side of the lesson involved; a mutual give and take. It is almost comical to see how clear it can be when one is determined to "see."

Happy 4th!

Do you recognize the little "drama traumas" Spirit sets up for you in which you participate? The major players in our "drama traumas" are usually those closest to us.

July 5

Venting for Clarification

Who am I? Who am I really? And what am I doing here? What is my purpose? Why do I keep writing, writing, writing? Is this just some delusional gibberish or will it really have some value? Will I fill this gap in my heart? Will I ever be able to get to a place where I can fulfill my life's mission? Please answer me. These were the words I recorded one morning when I felt less than content. Worse than that, I felt positively discombobulated and continued to vent.

I feel less than honorable each time I let myself down, when I don't follow the diet as one of the Masters instructed us: live foods only, two simple meals a day, no food before noon. It does not seem too terribly hard to do. But can I follow it? No! No! No! Two bananas and two pieces of cornbread have given me a bloated stomach. In fact, some wheat products produce residual bloating and are not much fun to contend with. Why can't I learn to stay away from what is not good for me, no matter how tasty it is?

Thus ended the denunciation of my current eating habits and personal attitudes that were vexing me.

We all feel down on ourselves at times and tend to mentally beat ourselves up. Sometimes, the last person we take care of is ourselves, especially if we are female. There are certain foods that will never be good for us, certain foods that combine together in our digestive system which cause distention and pain. We have to be strong enough to stay away from them, no matter how much we like and desire them.

One of those foods for me is the combination of cornbread and bananas. Another is chocolate, although I feel it is almost impossible to stay away from chocolate, since it shows up in so many forms, over so many holidays. White flour seems to produce an allergic reaction in my body. Whole wheat – especially the breads made with multiple grains – makes me feel great. *Essene Bread* in the freezer section of Whole Foods (made from sprouted wheat according to a process used thousands of years ago) may become a possibility. Any product with a concentration of sugar in it provides me a rush of energy, then a total let-down.

Too many foods recently have sabotaged my body and made me feel sluggish and weak, which, at times, is reflected in how I approach my life: a slow, sluggish, less than energetic response to everything with which I have to deal. But the ability to change all of this is within me. It is up to me to recognize what does not work for me and choose otherwise.

How can writing about the times that make you "whine" help you cope with those times? Keeping a list of negative reactions to food helps us to eliminate them.

July 6

Magnify Your Purpose

Earlier this morning, incredible messages streamed through, but I was not willing to get out of bed, and was not receptive to writing at all. Just could not seem to shake myself awake. So I rolled over, hugged my pillow closer, and drifted in and out of consciousness.

About an hour or two into this fitful retreat, I heard the words: *Magnify Your Purpose* – one of the names of the essential oils from *Young Living* developed by Gary Young – somehow, very appropriate to my current situation. I also heard, *You are an enigma. You say you want to do this work. You want material that can be published, yet you do not want to receive it when it is given.*

My Guides were right. Not only did I NOT want to write first thing in the morning as I had committed to, but also I was NOT available at twelve noon today – another time inspiration "hit" – due to errands that had to be run. Instead, I wrote in the middle of last night. My Guides had to adapt to my schedule, rather than me to theirs. Were they miffed? No! Rather patiently *at odds* with my schedule and my bratty behavior.

Is this an ego thing with me? Do I conveniently forget who I am and what I have agreed to do with the rest of my time on this planet? Yes! Do I stay connected to God at all times? No! I allow my three-dimensional world to take precedence over my spiritual world far too often. This has to stop. To honor the soul contract to which I agreed when I incarnated, I must teach about God. This work fulfills part of that contract.

Magnify Your Purpose – a lofty and noble sentiment – takes us on a mental journey to the pinnacle of the place where we work to accomplish the goal of our Soul. If we *know* there is *something else* being asked of us, we will feel unsettled about anything we do, no matter how high the accolades are. Until we get back to the "real" job which we agreed to do on this planet, that feeling will not go away.

One of the ways to do that is to write down what we feel when we feel "out of sorts." These feelings will hold at their core the work that we are supposed to do on this planet.

There were times I experienced despair when teaching elementary school, although part of that could have been the emotional turmoil of my first marriage. Nor did I sense that being a real estate broker was the culmination of my "Be"-ing on this planet. I never felt comfortable trumpeting my successes, which is part of the marketing scheme of all successful agents. Yet, when I give a spiritual or past life reading, it is effortless. When I talk about or give a speech on spiritual matters, it makes my heart sing.

Keep plugging and you, too, will be able to discern what work "honors" your purpose and what work dishonors it.

Can you see how writing, even when you do not feel like writing, magnifies your purpose? If our soul contract is to share our message with the world, only we can prevent that from happening.

Messages from My Guides – I: Paying Attention

If you only knew how we cheer you on to take our messages and improve your life. You hear our messages as hunches, and gut feelings. Most of you dismiss them, some pay attention, a very few act on them. More and more of you are listening now. There is a certain comfort in listening and acting on what you hear, and as you repeat the process, the level of comfort increases.

This scribe is completely aware when we break in versus when she is doing her own "thinking." She is not always happy when we come in at 2 a.m., 3 a.m., or 4 a.m., but that is when the voice of Spirit is most effective. The world is asleep. Your mechanical recording devices and all their distractions are quiet. You are extremely receptive at that time to hearing us. The next time you are awakened in the middle of the night, have a pad and pen ready and record everything you hear. You may be surprised at how appealing some of the thoughts are.

Listening to Spirit's message takes no more effort than listening to our mind prattle on. The difference is that messages from Spirit many times have *universal* application as well having *personal* application. Messages from Spirit that have universal application are meant to be shared with others. They are not just for our own edification. They *can be* that, but they also carry a universal theme that can assist all of humanity. When we write them down, we are able to tell the difference.

There are those who get messages from Spirit who would never dream of sharing the messages with anyone. This can be related to the fear of ridicule, or to sincere doubt that Spirit is indeed the Source of the messages. It can be related to fear of not being a good enough writer, to fear of being questioned about one's sanity, or to any other myriad of excuses the ego conjures up in order to keep the messages private.

One woman who has communicated with her Guides for over forty years has instructions in her will that all her journals be destroyed upon her death. This would be understandable if she did nothing but vent. However, if she received messages from Spirit from which the rest of humanity could benefit, what a shame it would be to never have those messages come to light.

The next time your ego gets in your way, ignore it and write down what you hear.

Have you ever been awakened with messages that you felt compelled to write down? Messages from Spirit could be more than just a wake-up call to us.

July 8

Messages from My Guides – II: Forgiveness

Spirit always waits for your invitation to come in. Spirit always wipes the slate clean each day. That is why habits that have been ingrained for thirty to forty years can change overnight. You can turn on a dime. You can become something that you are not simply with our help. Spirit always waits for an invitation.

We live in your heart. There is not a woman or man alive who exists without a heart. That is where we reside – not in your head as some would think. This is not an intellectual process. This is a process of accessing your heart space. Each day, you are given another chance. Each day, you have another opportunity to open the entrance to your heart space. Each moment is different than the one before it.

You access us through your heart. Forgiveness is the attitude that unlocks the door to your heart. You access us through forgiveness. Forgiveness is the key to most of what ails you. Since all others are a reflection of yourself, you only need to work on self: Higher Self will lead, ego self will follow.

There are two-hundred seventy-five ways to forgive listed in A Course in Miracles. We suggest you learn all of them. Nothing else you do is going to matter as much as this. Forgiveness of self allows all the other channels to open. Create a sacred space in your heart where you start to forgive every single person and incident that ever hurt you.

As you forgive, memories of old pain will continue to surface. As memories surface, recognize why they have surfaced. As you continue to run into people who annoy you, recognize why you keep running into them.

How many ways are there to forgive? As many as thoughts that go through your head; the list is limitless. You surmise so many justifications for withholding your love. Just look at your history. It is filled with innumerable atrocities. Forgive them all. They are all part of your evolutionary stature as a human race.

You need not feel that there is no way out. Even if you have lived with a pattern for ten, twenty, thirty, forty, sixty, or eighty years, you can be rid of it. You need not feel you are trapped indefinitely. You have the right to change your mind. You can choose to see peace instead of hatred. As you change your mind, you change your life. You open your heart.

Write about the messages of love streaming through your heart.

***Has your heart felt constricted?
Recording what our Guides say to
us helps us heal our heart.***

July 9

Messages from My Guides – III: Forgiveness (Continued)

What does it mean to forgive? Where do you start? Forgiveness means that you let go of the judgment of the action that happened, whether to you or to someone else. You suspend your "right" to pass judgment on it, to evaluate the "right" or "wrong" of it. You simply acknowledge that it happened, whether to you or to someone else, and move on.

There are many excellent techniques for moving blockages that bind you out of your body. They are all the same in essence. Here are several of them. First you have to recall the item that you have stored within your being. The best way to do this is to list all the people or events you perceive as having hurt you. Simply list them. This may take days, weeks, or months, depending on how many items you have buried inside of you.

Next, take the list and say to each item on it: "I forgive you for _________ and I forgive myself in my past, present or future for any participation in this event." If it gives you comfort to forgive each item individually, do that. Otherwise, lump the items together. Again, take as much time as you need to do this. You have spent a lifetime accumulating your grievances. You need to spend as much time as necessary relieving yourself of them.

Finally, mentally, place the list in the middle of a giant purple flame – the Purple Transformational Flame of St. Germaine – and purify the list with fire. Physically, burn it, or shred the list and mulch the earth with it, and ask the Ascended Master, St. Germaine, to help you release any last vestiges of resentment or ill will you may be harboring.

Writing a list of every person and every event that we have to forgive helps us to remove that person and that event from where they now live in our energy field. Some negative thoughts are so powerful that they have a life of their own.

How does writing a list help cement the forgiveness process? We forgive to free our own energy field.

July 10

Message from My Guides – IV: Opening Your Heart

You access us through your heart space, not through your head space. Don't come looking for us in your head. Don't think this is a mental exercise. It is not. We live in your heart. You hear us when you open up your heart. You pay attention to us only after your heart is fully opened. Until then, you simply think you have a "bright idea," which you typically file away and with which you do nothing. Look for us in your heart. Listen to us with your heart. You will find us there.

You can access us anytime you wish, once your heart is open. That is the doorway to working with us, your Guides. We only have your highest good in mind. We work with your Higher Self for the highest good of mankind.

This is not a power trip for the ego; quite the opposite. The ego says "This is for me and me alone. I don't care what anyone else says, thinks, or wants. This is mine."'

This type of thinking does not exist in Spirit. If it is not based on Love, it is not real. What stems from Love is Universal – for the good of all, because you are the All. There is not a thing in creation of which you are not part and which is not part of you.

You access the All with your heart; through us, through your Higher Self.

You are so much more than you think you are. You delve into littleness because that is what you have been taught. You are not the little beings you think you are. You are the most powerful of all Creation. There is nothing you cannot have dominion over, after you open your heart and learn the responsibilities of what it means to have dominion over something.

Access us. We are there for you. Call on us. Use us. In working with us, you also help us in our spiritual development. Our love for you is so great.

And so it is.

I Am.

Amen.

Writing down all the messages you hear captures them not only for yourself but for all posterity who need to hear the message.

How can writing about opening your heart space benefit you?
We write to capture the greatest thoughts that come through us.

July 11

Facing Anger

Certain behaviors may keep popping up over and over which negatively impact our present circumstances. If we recognize a negative behavior repeating itself in our lives, the Universe continues to put that behavior in our face until we learn to stop hating it. Making general assumptions about negative behaviors rarely teach us anything. When we learn to release our reactions to the behavior and let it go, the negative behavior recedes from our lives, and eventually vanishes.

In my case, the negative behavior was anger. The men closest in my life all had issues with anger, ranging from an undercurrent of it, to a smoldering volcano (ready to spew red-hot lava upon the slightest provocation), to a trigger-temper that could be set off without warning.

During *A Course in Miracles* meeting one night, a friend, listening to me complain about the latest outburst I had endured, asked: "Alice, what is it about you that attracts so much anger in your life?"

I was stunned. *I don't know*, I replied. *I will have to go home and think about it.*

I thought for two days. Then it dawned on me. I had a *judgment* about anger – that it was *BAD.* This judgment had to be released. Anger is neither good nor bad. *It just is.* When I learned to tell the Universe that I "preferred" *not* to have anger in my life, interestingly enough, most of the angry outbursts disappeared. Stating a preference rather than making a judgment changed my paradigm and the Universe supported me in that change.

Why does the Universe change its mind when we change our mind? Because, as Gregg Braden says, we *are* electromagnetic energy projecting forth onto an electromagnetic field of *all possibilities.* Every single possible outcome *already exists.* Whatever result we pluck out of the field of all possibilities is dependent upon that which we think we *can* pluck out. Each result is in line with the thoughts we think about it. It is all up to us. Yes, we are *that* powerful!

To further understand the electromagnetic field of *all possibility,* please read the books by Gregg Braden: *Awakening to Zero Point*, *The Isaiah Effect*, and *Secrets of the Lost Mode of Prayer.*

Write to understand any miscreation in your life.

How can writing about what brings you pain help bring more understanding into your life?
Writing clarifies all the issues with which we are dealing.

July 12

Heavenly Messages on License Plates

Shortly after I joined an *A Course in Miracles'* study group in December 1995, I changed my license plate to read MIRACLS. The little frame around the license place on the top said*, A Course In* and the bottom of the frame read *Teacher/Student*. This "vanity plate" expressed my joy at having found a spiritual group to which I could relate.

Vanity plates in Northern Virginia typically conveyed personal messages or something about the profession of the owner. Since I purchased my license plate and frame, there seemed to be a proliferation of spiritual messages in the Northern Virginia area.

My favorite were: ABELEVR, ADONAI, ANGELS 4, AL2GOD, AMZGRS, AWSMGOD, BLD2BME, BLESIT 1, BLESSJA, CHIME, DAWSUM1, DRE2BU, DVN LV, DVNLDY, ELOHEM, GD MAY, GDLVSUS, GDS CAR, GDS LV, GDS VUE, GDSFRND, GDSCHLD, GDSERVR, GLORYBE, GOD RLS, GODS 7, GODSRME, GODZRME, GOODGOD, GR8LFE, GR8-1-M, HELIVZ, HEZ LORD, INURDRM, JOY4ALL, JUST4GOD, JZSLVSU, ICQLORD, ILVGD 2, ILVGSUS, ILVLVN, KREE8IV, KWON YUN, L 2 GOD, LETLV 2, LORD I, LORDY, LUMN8R, LUV2LIV, LV2BME, LV4GOD, LV4U+ME, LV DVNE, LV IS AL, LV REIKI, LVUGSUS, LYTN UP, M8T4LIFE, NAGAPE, NFNITY, OPN MND, OSM GOD, PAX VO, PRAY 2 U, PRSGD, PSLM, 6-13, PSLM 23, PSLM 37, R LORD, SIMPLFY, SMIL2LF, SKYLVR, TALK2GOD, THNKFL2, URLVD 2, WELNESS, 23 EPHS, 73PSLM.

About two years went by before another proliferation of plates were seen: ANGEL 80, ANGELZ, B STILL, BE CR8TV, BLEST 3X, BLSSDBE, DEUSEST, DO PRAY, FLWRAVA, F8THFUL, G-PEACE, HEISGOD, IGO2GOD, ILVPRPL, KARMA47,

LEDITGO, LET GOD, LKUPWRD, MADONA, PCENOW, SMYLNQT, STR8PTH, TIS GOOD, TNKUGOD, TNKULRD, W AGAPE, 1AWSUM1, 1GD2LV, 3MRCLES, 4M2NJOY, and 4 SPRT.

When I saw the plate HEISGOD, my immediate thought was SOISSHE. But, so far, I have not spotted that rejoinder.

These may spur you on to think of your own spiritual message that is relevant to who you are today. Believe that it is possible to shift a paradigm. Believe that you can influence the little corner of your world when you follow your own truth. Write to capture these simple pleasures of our day to day existence.

What unusual avenues can you find to express the spiritual "Be"-ing that you are? Writing about small expressions around us that give us pleasure can have an impact.

July 13

A Morning's Delight

I walked amongst the plants in my garden last night, as I often do, and looked down. Three inch bell-shaped flowers hung gracefully from a one-foot tall sprig that shot up amongst an entire nest of heart shaped leaves rimmed with jagged edges. This lovely bell-shaped flower, in her delicate dress, just a peek of lace fringing her softly veined petticoat skirt with its lightly tatted edge, demurely continued looking down, completely oblivious of me. Like a colonial maiden in morning dress, she deftly went about her chores, waving in the light breeze.

I do not even know your name. I only remember that I received you from my Garden Club's plant exchange, went my silent reminisce, *but I am so glad you are here.*

I always feel the presence of God in my garden; a Presence more serene and peaceful than in any other space. Nothing made by man gives me the same feeling: no cathedral with its majestic spires and its hushed reverence, not the tallest buildings which seem to defy gravity as they shield celestial orbs from view, not the most tranquil village terraced into a mountain side, reflected in a lake. Although these too set my Spirit soaring, a walk through my garden several times a day settles me back into a state of reverence for all of God's creation: animal, plant and mineral.

Each new morning in the garden brings with it the possibility of a new "guest;" always invited, always welcome. Flowers, the physical representation of God's Angels on Earth, will – with any luck – stay awhile. How sweet to see them daily. Cicely Mary Barker's *A Treasury of Flower Fairies* (published first in 1923) charms people today, just as it did earlier. She illustrates each flower with its own attendant faerie along with a poem celebrating both the flower and the faerie. Delightful!!!

My mother loved the month of July, not only for the fact that it was her birth month, but because all the flowers were in bloom. She rimmed our home and separate garage with a profusion of annuals, perennials, bulbs, and tubers whose riotous color enhanced our home continuously, until a deep frost snuffed the life out of the beaming chrysanthemums. She never fertilized, but gave each plant plenty of love. She would bring home a dry rooted rose that she purchased for ninety-nine cents at the drug store, plant it in our front yard. Later, with no special care, it would produce the most spectacular roses. It was only after all my attempts to grow roses failed that I realized what a miracle that was.

Write to express the memories of special joys you have experienced.

How can writing about what you remember enrich your life?
We write to express the joy we feel in the moment.

July 14

S. Taffy Jones

Two little paws together in the prayer position – furiously moving back and forth, begging for a belly rub – bring me back down to earth. Clearing the sleep from my head, I stoop, rub his belly, rub it again, and again, till a little gurgle escapes from his throat. He is so happy! Mommy is paying attention to him!

Our Corgi, Taffy, constantly follows me from room to room, with a little *tap, tap, tap,* the click of his nails reverberate as they hit the hardwood floors. He feels he has no other "business" in his life except to "protect" those he loves. Should anyone approach the door, suddenly, he thinks he is a German shepherd. Since he became a member of our family, we have always felt secure, knowing that all thirty pounds of him would give up his life to defend ours. Should anyone *dare* to come in without being welcomed by us, his wrath would unleash enough fury to scare away even the meanest intention.

At other times, Taffy likes to show his domination over us, his family. This can get challenging, especially when we are trying to be heard by each other. His bark pierces through our conversation, and we cannot hear each other. Definitely the alpha male, he challenges any member of the family for domination. *Me too! Me first! Me too! Me first!* His incessant bark seems to proclaim, until one of us chastises him. He is jealous of any of us who receives more attention than he does.

Taffy constantly runs from room to room to be "where the action is." When our children's friends visit, he catches a corner of the carpet in his jaws and swings his head back and forth in a fit of anger as they leave the house. *How dare they go without me?* The teenagers escape, almost frightened of his wrath.

His exuberance for walks is boundless. He waits at the door patiently until I retrieve his leash, put a jacket on, and head outside. Even a *thought* of a walk sends him scurrying to the door, his head cocked, his eyes shine in anticipation. *Yay! We are going bye-bye.* Try and ask him, but most of the time he will not tell what he thinks about Mommy not walking him on time. His patience is endless, but even that has its limits. Occasionally, if his walk has been delayed, he barges into my office, barking his insistence that we leave *Right Now! COME ON! COME ON! COME ON!* His barks reverberate throughout the empty house, and do not stop until we are heading out the door.

When my daughter was little, she was always at the door to greet me if I got home later than she did. Now, Taffy is there to greet me instead; this little human on four legs, always ready to say hello, always quick to give me a kiss, always joyous that his Mommy is finally home.

After the children left for college and returned for assorted breaks, he would leap several feet off the floor in exuberance over their return, his long low body bent over backwards, his neck stretched high, smothering them with kisses. *My family's home! My family's home!*

Certainly, when our journey here is over, he will be there waiting for us, enthusiastic as ever, ready to greet us, to give us a million puppy kisses, to welcome us to our new "home."

In Memoriam
Saltwater Taffy Jones February 13, 1992 – August 19, 2003

How can writing about the special moments with your pets capture the fragrance of their charm? We write to remember the special moments that each pet brings into our lives.

July 15

An Outrage!

I am trying to see the perfection in all things, but this is bringing tears to my eyes, my outrage is so great. And I realize that on a scale of 1 to100, as far as global crisis is concerned, this rates a one, but here goes anyway: *THE DEER ATE MY DAY LILIES!*

I have been reluctant to use a deer repellent on the plants, because of the long list of caution warnings on the label. Such poisonous products must have negative effects on the soil, on the insects, butterflies, beetles, moths and other variety of bugs, worms, or reptiles that come to visit. I have asked co-operation from the Deva of the Deer: that they eat only 10% – which I thought fair and leave the rest for us to enjoy – to no avail. I have tried to rationalize that deer need to eat too. I am worn out from pleading, begging, and rationalizing. Today I am inconsolable!

Each plant had approximately ten stems on it with six to ten buds on each stem. The flowers that had bloomed to date were glorious lemon yellow lilies with fringed edges. Other clusters coming up had majestic blood red blooms, fully six inches across. THEY ARE ALL GONE. Just the nubbins remain; tall stalks bereft of their glorious buds, rudely severed by tiny teeth marks, awful reminders of their scalping.

How is it that when I spot deer in the woods feeding, I can stand for long minutes watching them with hushed reverence, marveling at the beauty and grace of these gentle creatures? Yet, when it comes to deer visiting my garden, I screech: *The audacity! The nerve!* Vile feelings of rage well up until my head feels light and unstable. There is a hollow pit where my stomach used to be, sawdust in my throat, tears in my eyes, and an incredible feeling of sadness at the loss of so much beauty. *For what?* A few tasty morsels, hardly even a mouthful for the deer, but such a tremendous loss of visual pleasure for us, another year gone forever!

Write to express the outrages and injustices in your life.

Have you ever felt that life is totally unfair? Write when we need to screech, even if only on a piece of paper.

July 16

A Solitary Journey

There have been times recently when I began to write in the early morning hours, even though I felt I had nothing to say. How totally different from earlier times, when my inquiring mind had a litany of questions, complaints, gripes, and heartaches that all needed to be aired to get them out of my body.

What a difference now – a clean slate. No grief, no heartaches, no gripes, just a clear place of acceptance, knowing that everything is perfect; is just as it should be. A great deal of effort has gone into getting me to this state of grace.

Spiritual books proffered by well-meaning friends, my sister Krystyna, and my Angels' guidance, have accompanied me on this journey of expansion into my Soul; into every new opening to Spirit. As my awareness has grown, my comprehension has grown. *A Course In Miracles* – a study of spiritual psychotherapy – has nourished me daily.

Yes, enlightenment is a goal. But, in the meantime, I am going to enjoy the journey; a *journey without distance* on a *road less traveled,* to quote the titles of two well-known books.

Since I started on my spiritual path, I feel that I am a real contributor to my own life, not just a passive participant or recipient of someone else's drama. No longer do sitcoms on television hold any fascination. My own life envelopes all the drama necessary and is more interesting than anything offered through the media. Not wanting to be just a participant, or a "viewer" in someone else's life, I prefer to be actively involved in my own.

Certain friends who have faded away are gone for good. The ones who have stayed, are here for good. New friends have replaced those who are no longer here. New opportunities for more meaningful friendships arise continuously, and I am calmer than I have ever been before.

A spiritual journey is a solitary journey; one that has to be taken alone *until* companions are put on the path. When the soul has outgrown its current situation, then the soul, as a student, looks for teachers. When the student is ready, the teachers appear, just as when the *teacher* is ready, the *students* appear.

Write to express the changes of the "current mood" in your life.

Is there a solitary journey that you have been putting off? We can write to clarify any new "direction" in our lives.

July 17

Archetypes

Caroline Myss's outstanding book, *Sacred Contracts: Awakening Your Divine Potential,* states that we all share in archetypal behavior. Each archetype represents a "pattern" that we have used from birth to help us navigate our journey through life on this planet.

According to Caroline Myss, four standard archetypes that we all share are: the *Child*, the *Prostitute*, the *Victim*, and the *Saboteur.* Along with these are eight other archetypes that we select to help us navigate our journey through our lifetime. Later in life, as we grow in spiritual understanding, the original eight archetypes can change when we no longer need them. They lose influence in our life and new archetypes take the place of the ones we have outgrown.

Some people may agree that they share three archetypes: the *Child*, the *Victim*, and the *Saboteur*, but may be outraged that they could possibly have a *Prostitute* archetype in their background. I certainly was. *Me? Never!* Yet, when reflecting on the circumstances of my first marriage, I realized that I married a man I did not know and could not possibly love – since I had no real concept of what it meant to love someone – simply because I felt I wanted to experience sex, and, being raised a good Catholic, sex only came after marriage. I did not know what to do with my life – where to take my talents – and so recklessly agreed to marry a man whom I had only met three weeks earlier, when he pressured me to do so. I "prostituted" all the future possibilities that could have been birthed, at that time, had I only the courage to take the time to explore them. I gave away my power to another person because of the lack of direction in my life.

How many people are trapped in a loveless marriage just for financial security, and suffer emotional, mental, or physical abuse simply because they do not wish to leave their beautiful home, or do not feel that they could support themselves? Spousal abuse transcends all class structures; a high income does not guarantee "living happily ever after" any more than a low income guarantees misery.

The *Prostitute* archetype, a pattern that is heavily influencing our journey, is alive and well. The current "gangs" that proliferate in our large and small cities, the "cliques" with which we align, the political parties with which we affiliate ourselves, and any institution which beats the drum of exclusivity as the "chosen" one of God, are all examples of the *Prostitute* archetype.

Other people may disagree that they share a *Saboteur* archetype with all of humanity. Yet, anytime they have a "great idea," the voice within their head showers them with ridicule. Pretty soon, no "great idea" surfaces because each idea is aborted before it gets a chance to gestate. Or, a person may be born into a culture that keeps them tied to a stratified class structure from which they cannot escape, and they are unwilling or unable to leave their native country to go elsewhere in the world where more opportunities abound.

The *Innocent*, the *Protagonist*, the *Judge*, the *Hero*, the *Villain*, the *Virgin*, the *Mother*, the *Sweetheart*, and the *Princess* are just a few models of the hundreds of archetypes that might be influencing us. When the pattern is with us from birth, or from our earliest memories, it is part of the archetypal group that guides us from our inception on this planet.

Archetypes control our actions subconsciously since they come from our subconscious mind. However, the influence of one particular archetype can be stopped. There is no need to continuously stay stuck in one mode or another. If we are trapped in the *Victim* mode, we cannot move until we do something to change our way of thinking. Caroline Myss admonishes us to recognize when an archetype is influencing our behavior, since they influence us *subconsciously.* To get control of our behavior, we have to start to live *consciously,* which means that we have to recognize when we are in the grips of a force outside ourselves, which has a *majority say* in our words and in our actions.

When I did the exercise to identify my archetypes, one of the names given to me by my Guides was *Keeper of Secrets.* This could be taken in two ways: a behavior that influenced my past lives or a behavior in the present. In addition to the serious work that I have done to uncover who I really am according to my Higher Self, I have also had a secretive side to my ego (personality) self. Interesting how the name of the archetype fits both sides of my "Be"-ing.

Write to recognize if you are in the grips of archetypal behavior.

Have you given over your power to a force beyond your control?
Comprehending archetypal influence over our behavior helps move us to another level of understanding.

July 18

The Vine, the Branches, and the Root

I am the Vine, You are the Branches. I exist as an embodiment of God. So do you. I heard these comforting words as I awakened.

The Christ Consciousness is the Vine. We are the Branches. Mother Earth is the Root. One is not more important than the other is. Without the vine, the branches have no support, without the branches, the vine dies, and without the root, nothing lives. All three aspects are equally important and all three aspects reside within the Mind of God.

For many of us, the root is askew. The root is our connection to Mother Earth, for the root is planted in Mother Earth. The planet is alive, just as much as we are. She has needs, just as we do. The trees and plants are her lungs. She breathes through them. The rivers, lakes, streams, and oceans are her circulatory system. They cleanse and rejuvenate her body with the water from the rains that fall and recycle back into her waterways. The terrain is her skin. Her soil and minerals, formed over billions of years, form her covering. Just as our skin covers our skeletal frame that encloses all our organs, so does the soil cover her frame and forms the foundation on which we live.

Why do we violate Mother Earth the way we do, by "bombing" her any place and any time we wish? Why do we poison her soils with our artificial fertilizers that are nothing more than harsh chemicals designed to burn her? Why do we smother her airways with our smog and emissions? Why do we pollute her waterways the way we do? Jacques Cousteau, the brilliant oceanographer, claimed in the early 1970s that *"one-third of our oceans were dying."* So what happened? They took his show off the air!

Just as our bodies are designed to be a self-cleansing and self-healing mechanism, so is the Earth designed to be self-cleansing and self-healing. But the planet cannot self-cleanse fast enough to counteract the effects of our lifestyle. Innumerable books, articles, and papers have been published about the deadly effects our waste products (resulting from our lifestyle) have on the planet. The pollution emitting from our vehicles alone staggers the imagination. So how do we respond? We build bigger and bigger SUVs and exempt them from emissions standard controls because we label them as trucks.

Are we so incredibly arrogant that we turn blinders to the needs of the planet for clean air, clean water and clean soil? Do we not realize that we are only hurting our future selves on this exquisite planet called Earth? Do we not comprehend that *we* are amongst those valiant souls currently standing in the wings waiting for their chance to express their Godliness through the vehicle of a body; that aspects of our Souls stand alongside the unborn generations who are waiting to come here??????

Once we make a commitment to come to Earth in the first place, we also make a commitment to *come back*. Will we be amongst those who finally call the insanity that currently inhabits this planet to a halt, and start the planet on the path to recovery? Hopefully!

Write to express your outrage about something you feel passionate about.

What do you feel passionate enough about to go on record?
Our opinions may be the ones to alter the course of the planet and save it for future generations.

July 19

Earth Energy

Life on this planet is a quest for balance. We come here to connect to the Earth as well as to Source. Since we have a body to maintain, by connecting to the Earth we are able to bring the maximum amount of energy into our body.

Some of the greatest healers on this planet are not connected to Earth energy at all. They "hang out" in higher dimensions. They do not value their "placement" here on Earth as much as their ability to access higher dimensions, thinking that higher dimensions are more "desirable." Yes, they are "light," but their light misses connecting to one of the major sources of energy; the Earth. Because they are not "plugged in" to the energy from the lower chakras, they lose their ability to receive energy from the Earth *as well as* energy from Source. Many have problems with their root chakra (the primary way to bring Earth energy into their body), and even displace their subtle bodies in their quest for *enlightenment.*

There are outstanding energy healers who deplete their bodies to the point of collapse; sometimes to the point of death. There are magnificent healers who almost lose their lives because they are not willing to let go of core issues. Because they are not willing to forgive the past, they stay stuck in their blockages and suffer tremendous bodily harm. This need not be.

One way we can bring energy from the Earth into our body is by visualizing roots growing from the bottoms of our feet and from the base of our root chakra (located at the end of our coccyx), and sending the roots down to the center of the Earth. Once we reach the center of the Earth, we visualize the energy coming up from the Earth into our body and circulating into our energy field. We do this by *breathing* through this process. It is through the breath that we connect to the energies that maintain our life.

We secure Earth energy into our body when we feel tingles up and down our legs, including the inside of our thighs. Every time we need to connect to Earth energy, all we have to do is *breathe* through the process.

We maintain the health of our own body by constantly replenishing our own energy. When we fully integrate the two suppliers of energy, Earth and Source, we replenish the energy we need to maintain our body in peak physical health. By utilizing both Earth energy and Source energy to heal ourselves and others, we become more effective healers.

Why is replenishing your energy so vital to maintaining your good health? Write to express concepts that help clarify new understanding.

July 20

The Christ Consciousness

Jesus is the man, Christ is the consciousness.

The Christ Consciousness, the aspect of God that that we call *unconditional Love,* accompanied Jesus all of his life. It was the Christ Consciousness that Jesus referred to when he talked about his Father's house having many mansions: there was room for everyone, no matter what their understanding of Spirit was during the time they lived on Earth. It was the Christ Consciousness – the embodiment of *unconditional Love* that Jesus talked about during his Sermon on the Mount – that brought hope to the masses of the downtrodden. It was the Christ Consciousness that Jesus tapped into, no matter who was clamoring to see him, touch him, hear him, or need him to heal them or members of their family. He never felt a separation from the Source of unconditional Love.

The Christ Consciousness grid surrounds the Earth; a matrix of white light to which we are all connected – a Unity Consciousness – part of a large group of matrices that surround every part of our being, both *in and outside* of our bodies. Through this matrix, the Divine communicates with each of us. This matrix is independent of our *acknowledgment* of it, our *acceptance* of it, or our *understanding* of it. We are all connected to it, whether we know about it or not. By the choice of our own free will, we each tap into this communication light source *both inside and outside* of our bodies that is available to each of us.

The Christ Consciousness is another name for unconditional Love, period. It does not expound *any* "dogma" from *any* religion, nor does it identify one particular type of religion or another. There are those who bristle at the very name of "Jesus" or "Christ." People who have had "JeeeeeZZZZuuuussss" rammed down their throat – those with only a fundamentalist background of what Jesus represented – may be very resistant to any mention of "Christ." Others cringe at the name of Buddha, Krishna, Mohammed, or any other founder of the twelve major religions.

The purpose of Jesus' life on earth was to teach us about *unconditional Love*, and that the *consciousness of the individual survives death*. No matter how badly they mutilated his body, they could not kill him for his essential nature was Spirit. He further taught us not to amass great earthly power, great wealth, and control of the masses. None of his teachings were intended to establish one particular type of religion or another. That was man's invention.

The Christ Consciousness did not start with this planet, and is not exclusive to this planet. It is an inter-galactic understanding. The role of unconditional Love permeates this Universe. Unconditional Love is where we come from, and is that with which we seek to reunite. Words of unconditional Love are a reflection of our God Mind. It is our ego-mind that insists that we are separate from God.

When I write about the possibility of unconditional Love, I write with all the power and majesty of the God within.

I am within God.

God is within me.
There is no difference.
Where I walk, God walks.
When I talk, God talks.
What I see, God sees.
Where I go, God goes.
What I do, God does.
There is no separation.
It is only my ego that insists that I am separate from God.
There is only GOD.

Overlaying the layer of the *collective unconscious* that Carl Jung identified is the Christ Consciousness; the layer of unconditional Love that comes from the God Mind. This layer is accessible to us at all times. Our free will decides whether or when we choose to tap into it.

Write in order to sort out that which comes from your God Mind, versus that which comes from your ego mind. Start by recalling a story about something that is troubling you. Ask God to help you see the situation differently. Ask your Spirit Guides to bring information forth, to help you understand why this is in your life

Did you know that you can tap into the layer of unconditional Love at any time? Our God Mind keeps our consciousness open to the Christ Consciousness.

July 21

An Expert Organism

We are an organism composed of up to one hundred trillion (100,000,000,000,000) cells: cells that re-invent themselves hourly, daily, weekly, monthly; cells that operate in perfect harmony with each other, cells that consistently slough off and renew themselves in an endless dance of "being."

Does one cell ever say to you, *I am not going to follow my cycle today, you hurt my feelings?* Not a chance. All move in a rhythmic progression from birth to death, all with the grace of the Living God. Without any complaints on their part, they take partake in the journey of life. They all do their part.

These cells are specialized and become the systems that maintain our life. The heart pumps gallons of blood throughout our body each day. The lungs filter enormous cubic meters of air each day. The kidneys flush gallons of liquid out of our body and we also eliminate water through our sweat glands. The endocrine system processes hormones throughout our body. The lymphatic system, with its hundreds of glands, is found in nearly every organ of the body that contains blood vessels. New cells replace the old ones, to continue the process of life. Within seven years, almost every cell in our body has changed and our body has totally renewed itself.

What do all these cells that make up *us* ask *from* us? Clean air, clean water, and food without chemical residue to fuel the body. What do we offer our body, instead of what it asks of us? Many times, we overwhelm it with the amount of sugar, fats, chemicals and caffeine we deposit into it, or with the drugs and narcotics we inhale and ingest.

The miracle is that our bodies function as well as they do, considering what can go wrong with them. Pick up any copy of a *Medical Family Guide* and study the diseases that can develop. It is a miracle that we stay as healthy as we do. Peruse a copy of *Gray's Anatomy* with its 780 illustrations, and its minutia of detail, to get a much deeper appreciation of what is involved in the make-up of the human anatomy. This appreciation and understanding of our body can help us take better care of it.

Anyone who has studied microbiology intently can identify the minute parts of the cell as well as the atomic particles and the function of each particle. They can describe how each particle takes its place in the "dance of life," but there is not a single person who can identify any one particle and call it "life." That is up to the Soul. When the Soul departs, the life force is gone.

Spiritual anatomy is another story. Very little has been published about the human energy field, but that is starting to change. New books are reaching the market every day to expand our paradigm of the components of our spiritual make-up.

When was the last time you perused a biology or medical book? We write to keep track of the changes in both our physical body and spiritual bodies.

July 22

Patterns

What patterns follow us? The families from which we come, the cultures to which we are born, the society that we keep, the jobs or professions that we choose to pursue, the leisure activities and hobbies in which we delight, the sports or exercise regimens in which we partake, and our religious affiliations all form the patterns in our life that fill up most of our waking hours. The thoughts that fill our minds during the times our minds are *idling* further identify patterns that are important to us.

Lay out the threads of your life and see what pattern they make.

1. FAMILY: Are you a family of one or do you have a myriad of relatives around you? Your soul contract may have you immersed in a group of strangers who become closer to you than any other "family" members. Your "spiritual" friends may become your

real family, taking the place of blood relations who are spiritually distant to you. They become your "family of choice."

2. CULTURE: You may have opted to incarnate in an Eastern European culture, with its rigid mind set. You may have picked to incarnate into an indigenous culture – a native culture with its reverence for the Earth – or into a very materialistic and militaristic society, or a culture where woman are subjugated or revered, or a very aggressive, highly competitive culture.

3. SOCIETY and SEXUALITY: You may have selected to experience extreme wealth or extreme poverty, to experience celebrity or to live anonymously. You may have preferred a male lifetime with all of its ramifications or a female one, or have preferred to experience this lifetime as a homosexual, bi-sexual, lesbian, transsexual or transgender or mixed gender.

4. JOB/PROFESSION: You may have committed yourself to pursue professional goals only, or preferred to immerse yourself in family life. Or you may have combined the two options, and pursued both family life and a career. You may have decided to go through adult life independent of anyone else supporting you or you may have chosen circumstances where you feel inadequate about providing for yourself. You may be completely optimistic in your thinking, or hopelessly depressed in pessimism, or somewhere in between.

5. LEISURE TIME/HOBBIES: You may be very creative with your leisure time. You may have a wonderful talent with Nature, planting splendid gardens, arranging beautiful flowers, or creating fanciful wedding cakes, set designs, or furniture displays. Or you may be a total dud, feeling no creative juices flowing whatsoever and aborting every creative idea that comes to you.

6. SPORTS/EXERCISE REGIMEN: You may be very athletic or very inept with sports. You may have opted to pursue an Olympic dream, or to play sports professionally, with all of the ramifications

of that experience. Or you may think that a simple walk is beyond your endurance level.

7. RELIGIOUS AFFILIATION: You may have picked to incarnate into an Eastern religion with its emphasis on mysticism, opted to become part of the nation of Islam, a Sufi, a Hindu, or a Buddhist. You may have chosen a Western religion immersed in dogmas and fundamentalism, each proclaiming to be the one true religion. Alternatively, you may have chosen to experience both sides, opting for one in your youth and another in your adulthood, or have turned your back on religion or spirituality as having no meaning in your life.

In relating what choices we have made, we are going to find a pattern evolving. When we are able to identify that pattern, we get a better idea of what we are all about.

Write about the patterns in your background to get a better understanding about who you are.

What patterns have you evolved into or are you following? Our patterns will reveal deeper and deeper aspects of our "Be"-ing.

July 23

Multi-Tasking

Eke out a space for my children drummed through my head daily, together with *give me the luxury of a few leisure activities.* What I yearned for – time to read books that nourished my Soul and leisure time with my children – I did not have. Most of the time, I felt numb, rushed beyond belief, always late for their "little shows" during pre-school, doing one last chore before I left the home so I would not have an idle second. Always, I had a disturbed feeling of neglecting my work when I was with them; always a pre-occupied feeling of neglecting my children when I was working.

One memory of my daughter at eight-months of age haunted me. Because she was a very slow eater, I left her in her high chair in the kitchen, with her baby bottle, a large hole poked in the nipple so she could get the milk and cereal combination out faster, propped up under her chin while I went down the hall back to my home office to finish some real estate work. Looking back at that beautiful baby girl in that empty kitchen, bottle propped under her chin, expecting her to feed herself, left a pit in my stomach for years.

When my daughter was thirty-four months old, I gave birth to a beautiful, gentle nine-pound four-ounce baby boy. He had to stay in intensive care with the preemies in the hospital for seven days because he had jaundice. The same day that we brought my son home from the hospital, I went back to work, even though he had been delivered by C-section and I had neither the strength nor energy to do anything "extra". My youngest sister, who arrived shortly after his birth, left the same day we brought him home. With no additional help, I did what I thought was right at that time. Thinking back, I realize the insanity of those actions.

I had both a toddler and a newborn to care for, a growing property management business, and more work than could be completed in any twenty-four hour day. Spirit quietly waited for me to come to my senses. Spirit, being patient and kind, waited till I got all the quirks out of my mental body that demanded acknowledgement, yearned for recognition and awards for the amount of real estate sold, and the pride I felt as *Principal Broker*; the head of our small business.

Self-help, spiritually-based books, and seeking the power within all had to wait. I had work to do! Then, they called it "multi-tasking." Today, I call it *nuts.* I have forgiven myself for this desertion of my good sense, since it was all I knew at the time. Then it seemed right. Now, it seems so limited.

Write to sort out the memories that make you feel uncomfortable.

Have you been trying too hard to be all things to all the people in your life? Multi-tasking constantly may be the wake-up call we need to re-evaluate our lives.

July 24

Finding My Self

Nothing was working in my life. Nothing! No amount of business (busy - ness) would fill the emptiness I felt inside of me. To the outsider looking in, I looked like I had it all: a high powered job, a "million dollar" family (daughter and son), a husband who loved me, was faithful to me and proud of my accomplishments, an impressive home set high on a hill on an acre of land, a new car, a beautiful wardrobe, and time to pursue some arts and crafts projects. To the outside world I looked like a success story. *So why was there a hole in my heart?*

During a week at the beach in the mid-eighties for a quick summer break, I left the two children with my husband in our rented condo and sat down on the sand, feeling very forlorn and alone, having escaped the wake of yet another argument that periodically flared up in our life. Feeling this pit in my stomach growing into a cavern, I kept thinking, *What will it take to make me happy?* Oblivious to the sand pipers, the tiny sand crabs, an occasional road runner, and the rhythmic beating of the surf, all I could tune into was my own misery. Barely aware of the sun gently setting in the distance, only one thought kept ruminating in my mind,

I…have…to…find…my…self.

Only I did not know where to look, or even how to begin. This feeling of emptiness swamped over me, engulfing me, sucking me down into despair.

Turning to the only piece of paper with me, a bank envelope with scribbling on one side, I started to write what I wanted out of life. *Twenty-five* items appeared rather quickly on the back of that envelope, all the things that were important to me. Later, when I re-examined what I wrote, I saw that *twenty-three* of them were *spiritual:* Number one on the list was: *Peace of Mind,* Number two: *To See Things Clearly.* I possessed neither quality at the time.

These two qualities became the driving force of my Universe. Whenever a mental plateau interfered with my ability to function, *Peace of Mind* and *To See Things Clearly* became the focal point of my existence. No matter what I did, these two qualities, acting as two sentinels, accompanied my thoughts and guided my actions.

Write to help understand Spirit's guidance to the authentic purpose of your life.

No matter how busy and successful you are,
is something missing in your life?
Writing out what it is that makes us happy
re-establishes our priorities.

July 25

Peace of Mind

I had no peace. I had a small business out of my home, fulfillment (so I thought), responsibility, some satisfaction, varied successes, a certain amount of flexibility, occasional spurts of joy, *but No Peace.* I lived a life regimented by a *TO DO List*, always putting out "brush fires." I did my very best to increase our property management accounts, and listed and sold real estate to bring stability back into our lives, in the hopes of ultimately achieving financial freedom. The real-estate meltdown that occurred in 1981 shook our foundation to the core.

Working towards my goal of financial security seemed natural, since it was my job to help people achieve their American dream of home ownership. Helping them buy their first home, guiding them through the entire process, and advising them on how to put together a down payment became the mainstay of my existence as a real estate broker. When I changed focus by going after more expensive listings and sales, working with people who had purchased up to six, seven, or eight homes – some of whom were only interested in the amount of money they could squeeze out of each transaction – Spirit decided to start squeezing me.

In 1986, I had already experienced feeling constricted. Each succeeding day, I became more and more tired until one day I could not breathe! In a panic, I called my husband for help. He recognized my symptoms. My two children experienced Mommy, who was always in such control, looking wildly at them, breathing into a small brown paper bag.

"Hyperventilation" is what the emergency room medics called it. In the hospital, they put me on oxygen for several hours until I stabilized, and that was that! I went home and continued to do the same things I had been doing. Nothing changed! No awareness came into me that my *lifestyle* was destroying my *life.*

Another incident, in 1989, was even more severe. I stooped down to pick up a piece of paper, and then could not straighten up again. Bed rest did no good. I still walked at a forty-five degree angle. Consulting the expertise of five specialists, the best help I received was from my chiropractor (who helped me externally with his adjustments of my spinal column) and from an osteopathic surgeon (who helped me by stretching an internal muscle). The combined efforts of these two specialists brought me to health.

During this incident, one of the medical doctors I spoke to suggested, "Slow down."

I can't, came my reply. No follow-up, no counseling, no further query as to why I was running so hard on empty.

Eventually, after the second incident, I realized I was running from myself.

Do you scurry around each day dowsing brush fires that have no purpose in your "real" life? We write to discover what the hidden meaning of all our frenzied activity is.

July 26

Finding My "Real" Purpose: The Angel Journal

During the early 90s, I would be wakened many nights between 2 a.m. and 4 a.m. with messages streaming through my head; messages about God. Always about God! Reams of messages would stream forth. A voiceless voice was using me as a conduit for information; spiritual truths were coming through me as a conversation from Spirit.

I would come downstairs to the computer in my home office and start to type. Either it would still be black outside, or the rays of the sun were just starting to color the sky, when I finished and crawled back into bed for a "nap" before I began my day, staying in a perpetual state of exhaustion; never feeling quite rested, yet never feeling so depleted that I could not put in a full day's work.

The list of what would make me happy stayed nestled in my night stand as a reminder of what was really important to me: *#1. Peace of mind, #2. To see things clearly.* These middle-of-the-night sojourns on the computer seemed to be an exercise related to both of these qualities, but especially the second item – *To see things clearly.* Since each day's communication was filled with explanations of spiritual matters, the experience of writing these communications down gave me not only peace of mind but also provided answers to questions that had been stored up in me over a lifetime.

What began as a journaling exercise became a daily communication with the Angels and my Guides, which I called my *Angel Journal.* All this eventually led to a conversation with God, which became the basis for my first book, *God is the Biggest Joker of All.*

A product of my imagination? Some would say that. A serious journey into Self? Absolutely! The Higher Self is the connecting link between the lower self (the ego self) and God; a union which gave me access to the higher realms of "Be"–ing.

Write to excavate your way into your authentic Self.

Are you being led on a journey to your "real" purpose?
Spirit will pave the way to our authentic life.

July 27

Messages of Peace

By seeking peace within ourselves: within our thoughts, within our feelings, within our physical body, within our subtle bodies, we collectively bring peace to this planet.

The Apostle Paul, in his second letter to the church at Corinth, states: ... *be of one mind, live in peace; and the God of love and peace shall be with you.* (2 Corinthians 13:11)

This message of peace was offered by a German friend of mine:

Wo Glaube da Liebe	"Where there is Belief	there is Love
Wo Liebe da Friede	Where there is Love	there is Peace
Wo Friede da Segen	Where there is Peace	there is Blessing
Wo Segen da Gott	Where there is Blessing	there is God
Wo Gott keine Noth	Where there is God	there is no Want"

Those who work with Angels know that the Angel of Peace can be called upon at any time there is strife, whether it is on a personal, local, national, or international level. There is no place and no person that is immune from the reach of the Angel of Peace. Merely invoking the Angel of Peace into your life, or into a situation, changes the vibration of that person, place, or thing.

We should never lose an opportunity to say an affirmation invoking peace into our lives. As we invoke peace on a personal level, we change the vibration towards peace on a global level, on a planetary level, on a galaxy level, and on a universal level. Our thoughts reach out to the farthest corners of the Universe, since we are one with all that is.

An outstanding way to spread thoughts of peace is through songs. One of my favorite songs written about peace is, *Let There be Peace on Earth, and Let It Begin with Me*, by Jill Jackson Miller and Sy Miller, written in 1955. This song is the entrance hymn for the ordination ceremony for the Rays of Healing Church, of which I am an ordained minister. Another favorite song is based on the prayer of St. Francis, *Make Me a Channel for your Peace.* Just thinking about these songs brings more peace into my day. Just thinking the word "peace" can change the energy of our day.

Write to clarify the ways in which you can bring more peace into your life.

Is there a favorite method to restore peace into your life when all is chaotic around you? Writing about all the ways we can bring about peace can serve to anchor it into our lives.

July 28

Changes

Writing is a solitary occupation. If we immerse ourselves in the material world to the exclusion of all else, chances are we will not pull spiritual thoughts out of our head or our heart, even though they are being given to us at all times. We focus on either the Spiritual realm or the material realm. We do not do both.

Right now, the material world seems to have won, since there seems to be a concentration of only material thought rummaging through my brain rather than the spiritual thoughts to which I have been attending.

Let's get back to the itinerary I have set for myself: Yoga, Prayer, Meditation, Writing, Computer Work, and Breakfast.

I sit alone, mulling over thoughts of this day, wondering how the months and years could have gone by so quickly: One child in college, right now upstairs in her bedroom, is sorting and deciding what to take and what to leave behind as she prepares for her second year; one child in his junior year in high school, taking the SAT, is thinking about the selections in his near future. One pet bird is anxious to go from his perch in the kitchen to outside on the porch, one dog is chaffing at the bit to go for his walk.

Not much assistance was needed to help my daughter get ready for her sophomore year at New York University. Packing for school was simple; my daughter did it all over a three day period. As she brought her possessions down from her bedroom, the living room became filled with boxes, bags, clothes, and art items. It never ceased to amaze me that no matter how many items she brought down, my husband was able to find room for them in the rental van, even if he had to place something on our lap after we were all seated. My son will be much easier. His needs are simpler, yet there are many things he will need to get, the most important being an upgraded computer.

The next few years will bring massive changes to our lives. The past twenty-two years will come to a close. No more children's schedules that need attention and concern; just their college bills. Their needs are changing so rapidly, so are their interests. Hopefully, they will appreciate what we as their parents have provided them.

Write to help yourself to remember the little details of the milestones in your life, or in the lives of your family members.

Have you ever regretted not recording something special in your life? Writing helps us to recall the details of our day's activities before they go into the ether.

July 29

A Creative Life

Only after my daughter, Elizabeth, went away to college did she recognize the value of the care the family gave her. She pressured herself to get good grades, which were always high, and strove for excellence in everything she did. Not once did she slack off, even if it meant staying up all night to finish a project or a paper.

I asked her if we had adequately prepared her for her college experience. She said "No." We should have made her fend for herself a little more, taught her how to balance a checkbook, made her clean up after herself, made her get the items necessary for all the "projects" she produced. At college, it was a real shock to find the glasses and dishes she left the night before still there the next morning. Her father had always done a sweep of the home to pick up used dishes and glassware each night before he went to bed. Miraculously, every time she needed any supplies for any project, they were there, with no effort on her part.

Elizabeth attended New York University in the "Big Apple," a perfect place for a person with her vision, her insight and love of all that is unique and different. Almost everyone who knows Elizabeth well knows that she makes a very special mark in this world. Her creative talents parallel none. She is unique unto herself. She has a vision that she pulls from a wellspring deep within her Soul; one that seems to draw appreciation from all of those with whom she works.

Since she decided to major in film production, I once suggested that she use her talent to document abuse of some kind. I felt she could bring a unique perspective to whatever subject she decided to "expose."

She looked at me strangely – as if I didn't even know her – and said, "That is not me, Mom. I find beauty in everything I do."

I recognized that statement summarized her life. She had indeed found beauty in everything she put together. For her senior art project, she took a roll of duct-tape, black plastic bags, black construction paper and miniature white Christmas lights and transformed them into a diorama to display the fifteen pieces of artwork she chose as representatives of her style. This included lining a ten foot "background" with black plastic bags, then framing her "studio area" by hanging crushed black construction paper piped with duct tape around the entire section. Miniature white Christmas lights were hot-glued to the entire recessed "frame," which became the perfect setting to display her fifteen pieces of artwork. Burns from the hot glue gun did not deter her from getting the look she was after: a completely black enclosure with a black and silver "puffy" frame, accentuated by twinkle lights. The diorama was stunning in its simplicity and beauty!

She once mentioned that when she felt blocked, she would lie down on her bed until an idea came to her; until she felt inspired. My daughter lives where God lives; in her imagination. She is always creating; always has a new project sifting through the filters of her mind and heart in areas that only she can access. She knows her Higher Self intimately. She visits there daily.

Write to help you recall small, but important facets of your children's lives, or the lives of those important to you.

Did you ever find a scrap of memory tucked into a book somewhere that helped you recall important but forgotten events? Writing helps us to recall the details of the fragments of our lives that will be gone forever unless we record them.

July 30

The Truest Thing We Know

Ernest Hemingway told us to "write the truest sentence that you know."

The truest sentence – the truest *thing* – is what comes from our authentic self. What I *know* is all about Spirit, since I "know" I am Spirit having a human experience. For me, life is very simple. Everything exists within the Mind of God.

Did you ever consider writing about your experiences? Who can express your life better than you? What problems have you had to which you found unique solutions? Can you help someone else going through a similar experience?

The truest experience is our personal experience. We bring an inimitable perspective or a singular solution to a problem that no one else may have thought of when we survive an event that may have crushed the spirit of another. Some personal catastrophes are shared catastrophes. Others are not. No one else can come from our unique perspective, because no one else sees life through our lens. For example, who can better write about addictions than one who grew up in an addicted household, or one who has conquered an addiction? This similarly holds true for those who may have had a compulsive obsessive disorder, or binge eating or purging, or frantic anxiety, or any type of phobia.

My addiction was to work. There was a time when all the meaning of my life was through work. Work came first: before God, before family, before my personal needs. I felt this need to work hard, but also wanted people to be aware of my diligence, ambition, dedication, prowess, and earning power.

What did I discover? They did not even notice! Some may have felt sorry for me as they saw my physical body break down, my lips tremble or my hands shake. Did *I* see that happening to myself? Of course not! I only saw the goal ahead of me, but it was achieved with such difficulty. So much was sacrificed to achieve it and in the end, I, the giver, stood empty.

How did I feel through this entire time when ambition and hard work were the keystones of my life? I started to begrudge the leisure time of the people around me. Sure, the professional people with whom I dealt all worked as hard as I did, but most of them did not have young children the same age as mine; theirs were mostly out of the nest and launched into careers. Mine were at home and needing my attention. My fragmented self started to revolt. My physical body could no longer keep up. My Spirit Self kept finding any wedge to reach me – a crack, an opening, a willingness to listen – and patiently waited for me to come to my senses.

It was through writing that I finally saw where my life was taking me. Writing continued to be the mainstay of my existence; no longer used primarily to vent, but instead used as a means of expressing my authentic Self.

Write to set a new course or direction for yourself; to find your Self.

What is the "truest thing you know" that you can share with another today? We can write to find the benefit in that which appears to be negative.

July 31

Advice from My Guides

It is 3 a.m. and I have been awakened again, as I have been each morning with *words, words, words,* flowing through my mind, *always about God.* Words of advice to my fellow man, words of advice to me, to show me how to live a better way! This is my time to come forward; my time to become who I really am, my time to step into the role for which I signed up prior to incarnating on this planet.

The following words came as a direct order from my Guides: *Here is an assignment with your gatekeeper; the heart chakra. Ask for a whole-ey relationship with your Self. Not holy, but whole-ey. Ask to be connected to the "whole" of who you really are. This is the planet of free will. Until you ask, you will not be able to enter the door. The door is free will: to choose or not to choose.*

My Guides told me to connect with the Higher Self, which is the basis of this book. But what is this *"whole-ey" relationship* of which they speak? *A Course in Miracles* speaks of a *holy relationship*; one where the "other" is looked upon through the eyes of the Christ Consciousness – through the eyes of unconditional Love – in contrast to a *special relationship,* where the "other" is accepted only for what can be gained for the ego self.

A *"whole-ey" relationship* is similar to a holy relationship. According to Webster's New World Dictionary, "whole" means "in sound health, not diseased or injured, healed, intact, entire." A *whole-ey relationship* is a relationship where the lower self (the ego personality) is not separate from the Higher Self. It is *intact.* It is *entire.* It is a *healed* relationship, where misconceptions no longer exist. Nothing is held back. All are accepted as part of the One on our path to personal and world peace.

The *door* to a *whole-ey* relationship is free will. The greatest gift we are given as a human race is free will. It is also the gift that gives us the most trouble. Since we can choose *any* path that we wish to follow once we get here, it doesn't matter how much preparation we are given in Spirit to find our way back to Source. While on earth, we can stumble about wildly, put blinders on to all things spiritual, and aggressively, voraciously destroy all of our conscious access to Spirit. Or, we can enhance our lives, the lives of others, and the life of the planet Earth by the actions of our free will; by the spiritual choices we make.

Have you heard any advice recently that you have chosen to ignore? Writing it down will keep it fresh in your mind.

What words of advice do you need to keep hearing? Writing down advice that we hear from our Guides helps us to remember it.

Step 5

Choose Your Self

Who are God's Teachers? A teacher of God is anyone who chooses to be one.

A Course in Miracles

August

Real Power – the power of Love – stands in its truth. Consensus opinion never sways it. It stands firm in its own knowledge of what "is," since it calls on a higher truth. It doesn't need any one or anything else to validate it.

Real Power – the power of Love – does not reach out its hands and say "Love me, Love me, Love me or I shall die." Real Power reaches out to love, not to be loved. It has no "neediness." It has no need to be authenticated by someone else, because its authenticity does not come from the outside. No one can destroy its authenticity because its authenticity does not come from the outside; it comes from within.

Real Power – the power of Love – does not crumble when someone from the outside withholds their love, but instead, waits patiently – for eons if necessary – until an adjustment in attitude is forthcoming. It does not crumble when someone from the outside withholds their love because it subscribes to "unconditional Love."

You can deny Real Power – the power of Love – or can procrastinate learning about it, for you have free will. You can attempt to cover it with the endless boxes of emotional trauma into which you immerse yourself. You can pretend it is not there. You can ignore its attempts to influence your actions. However, Real Power – the power of Love – cannot be crushed, nor diminished, nor extinguished, nor eliminated, because It comes from the Source – and that Source is Love, and that Source is infinite.

When you arrived on this planet, you came in knowing you were perfect. Everybody since then has told you that you were less than perfect and you bought into that. You forgot you ever thought you were perfect. You bought into what the fear-based egos said about you. Now is the time to shed that.

To access Real Power – the power of Love – get back to the same thoughts you had when you arrived here, when you were aligned with unconditional Love; with the perfection of the Universe, with God.

Protecting Our Energy

The Vampire archetype is alive and well in the Universe. There are people out there who are *energetic* vampires. Fifteen minutes in their presence and we are fully drained. They suck all the life force out of us. We feel it in our solar plexus. This is more than just knowing when someone is having a bad day even before we start talking to them. We can feel our energy being sucked out of us as if we were an open spigot. Their energy fully drains us as they pull energy out of us, leaving us limp and depleted.

One time, as a fledging real estate broker, another agent asked me for help in getting her home ready for the market. By the time I left her home six hours later, I felt as lifeless as a washcloth wrung dry. My life force, usually on energetic overdrive, was entirely drained out of me. The only thing I could manage to do was to drive home and lie down. Since I knew nothing about personal energy at that time, I could to do nothing to counteract the effects of energy drain except to sleep.

Since most needy people do not know how to pull energy from the *unlimited Source,* they pull it from each other, which robs the "other" of personal energy. Pulling energy from an "other" causes distortions in the energy field of both people. Each distortion has a distinct form and a distinct feel. They can look like cords, hooks, electrically charged wires, angry arrows or diffuse clouds. Barbara Brennen's book, *Hands of Light: A Guide to Healing through the Human Energy Field,* displays some excellent examples of distortions in the human energy field.

When necessary, we can protect ourselves from energy drain by putting our shields up. We visualize shields surrounding our physical body which cause our energy fields to become impenetrable. No energy can be pulled out of us. We can also enclose ourselves with white light surrounded by a mirror reflecting outward. The person sending negative energy towards us has it deflected back towards their own selves. This technique works both in long distance healing as well as hands-on healing. Wrapping a blanket of white light protection around an "other" helps insulate them from energy leakage. Working with white light is the only "defense" we need. The human energy field is the strongest field created and the human energy field is composed of white light.

We can choose a variety of ways to protect our energy field. However, there is no way that anyone can suck energy out of us without – at some level – our permission. When our own vibrational energy is high, no "protection" is needed. Negative energy may visit us, but does not stay.

There is no need to pull energy from an "other," for there is an unlimited supply of energy from the Source. There is no great mystique about pulling energy from the Earth or from the Source. Simply ask for it in meditation and prayer. A guided imagery meditation using the sign of infinity (which helps us receive unlimited energy from the Source) is the following:

Visualize roots going from your feet and your first chakra (your root chakra) down, down, down, to the center of the Earth. Stop there momentarily, gather the Earth energy through your breath, and bring it back towards yourself.

Then, visualize a swath of energy (the size of your head) exiting the top of your head at your crown chakra, going up, up, up towards the Central Sun in the center of our galaxy. Breathe in that energy and bring it back towards yourself through your crown.

Visualize the two energies meeting in the center of your heart; mixing in your heart and becoming one.

Then, visualize the energy flowing up through your crown, separating above your head, then flowing down either side to below your feet, then back up through the center of your body, in two continuous unbroken circles. You are now balancing the energy from the left side and the right side of your body. Breathe in that energy. Expand that energy to become a sphere, and see that sphere grow and grow and grow. You are now surrounded by white light and are connected to Heaven and Earth. Breathe through that connection. You now have an unbroken stream of energy connecting you to the Source of all energy and to the Earth. Stay there in the comfort of that light as long as you wish.

When you choose to come back, know that every time you consciously take a breath, you connect to the unlimited Source of energy.

Some churches, synagogues and mosques get kudos for recommending prayers for people, both living and deceased. Prayers are energy being sent to the recipient through our *intention.* Those who have died need additional energy to help them cope with situations in their new state of existence. If you do not know any prayers, send white light. Encase each person you think of in white light. It accomplishes approximately the same thing.

We have all the means within us to be able to access and utilize the maximum amount of energy each day. There is a part of us that knows it all. We simply have to remove the blockages to what we already know.

Have you ever felt energetically drained in the presence of someone? We can choose to utilize the Source of unlimited energy.

August 2

Buying Organic

I awakened, stretched, and got out of bed. Went into the shower and used some cocamidopropyl to wash my hair. Took my favorite bar of triclocarbon to lather myself down. Noticed some spots on the shower stall and swiped them with sodium hypochoride. Dried, dressed myself, and put on some propylene glycol and came downstairs for breakfast. In the cupboard, I selected a snack bar of cyano cobalamin. Thought I better take my whey lecithin with me since I would not be able to stop for lunch. Put some 3-hexenol on my hands before I left for work.

Drove to work, but not before I noticed the haze in the air. Stepped outside for a breath of fresh air and noticed the haze had not lifted. Made an engagement for dinner. At dinner, put monosodium glutamate on my salad. We talked. We laughed. Got caught in a traffic jam behind a truck spewing out fumes into the air. Came home. Took a little monocalcium phosphate and enzyme as a snack before I went to bed. Didn't feel so good. Didn't look so good. Didn't sleep very well.

I encourage you to go into your pantry, cupboard, and refrigerator and look at all the chemicals listed on every product you consume. If you cannot pronounce it, do not use it.

That was when I decided to go strictly organic. I wanted to eat real food (not chemicals), to wash my body and hair with soap and lanolin (not chemicals), to wear fragrances made from essential oils (not chemicals), and to breathe fresh, clean air. Fortunately, I can make and adhere to these choices.

You may be fortunate enough to live in an area of the country where the air is relatively clean, or you may live in a large city where the quality of the air – while not desperate – leaves a lot to be desired. Even though you seem to have adapted to it, your body still pays a price.

We long for peace of mind, yet stuff our bodies with all sorts of chemicals (instead of nourishing live food), slather chemicals on ourselves for cleansing, and then deodorize and perfume ourselves with chemicals, when we could be using natural ingredients instead. We inhale carcinogens into our body by smoking and by breathing the air our gas-guzzling vehicles spew forth. Do we really need such behemoth all-terrain vehicles – ones that, due to their classification as trucks, do not have to meet emission standards – when all we drive on are level city streets? Then we wonder why our bodies start to fail when in our forties and fifties.

To bring our bodies back to homeostasis, we need to get rid of all the chemicals with which we have been surrounding ourselves. We need to wash our bodies, hands, and hair with pure soap (not a bunch of chemical thrown together that resemble soap), drink pure water, eat pure foods (not chemically processed ones), and eat as many live, organically-grown foods as possible. By learning about food combinations, we learn which food should and should not be eaten together.

Edgar Cayce, the "sleeping prophet," had much to say about the subject of pure living. His entire body of work is available through A.R.E. (Association for Research and Enlightenment) in Virginia Beach, Virginia, which also carries the largest library of metaphysical materials in the United States.

To learn about body types and what foods are right for our blood type, an excellent reference is *Eat Right 4 Your Type: Complete Blood Type Encyclopedia* by Dr. Peter J. D'Adamo with Catherine Whitney. When we listen to our body, we recognize what foods make us feel energetic.

Can you commit to keeping your life as chemically-free as possible? We can choose to eliminate one item each day that is not beneficial.

August 3

Dream Interpretation – Part 1

Dream interpretation is not difficult. However, we do have to trust the messages given to us by our Guides. This dream took place one evening and the interpretation from my Guides follows.

Scene One: I am attending some type of healing seminar where a man appears, first seated in a wheel chair, then lying on a stretcher on the table, then lying on a pallet on the floor. I feel compassion for him as he seems rather helpless.

Scene Two: I turn to say something to him and watch as he stands up tucking his shirt into his pants. No signs of any ailments, deformity, or disease.

Scene Three: Before I leave, my gaze travels back into the room. The man is standing at the window, surrounded by his wife and five children. I feel rather surprised that he has such a warm, loving family around him. During our initial meeting, he had presented himself as totally alone and relying on the generosity of strangers.

Interpretation – Scene One: I see only the outward physical appearance of the handicap, represented in three stages: wheelchair, stretcher and pallet. I feel compassion, am about to give him some words of encouragement, and am seeing only through the eyes of perception; through the eyes of the ego.

Scene Two: I am not aware of the inward, spiritual reason for the handicap – the gifts that the handicap brings with it – represented by both his ability to take care of himself and his independence in dressing himself.

Scene Three: Reiteration of what was established in Scene Two: nothing is what is seems. His wife and five loving children represent the reality of his situation, no matter what the outward appearance may be. Originally, I did not recognize the gifts around him – gifts that were supporting his life – presuming that he was helpless because of his external circumstances. The reality is that no matter what the external circumstances show, on some level, the person chose to have that experience and that choice is fully supported in Spirit.

Have your dreams ever clarified spiritual issues with which you may have been struggling? We are best at interpreting our own dreams.

August 4

Dream Interpretation – Part 2

Same night, Part Two of the same dream:

Scene One: I am back in the same Baroque-styled opulent hotel with its twenty- foot ceilings and multiple levels. As I head back to my room, I meet my neighbors (who are also running late) at the elevator.

Scene Two: After looking at my key card, I cannot remember my room number, because one number flashes on the card and another number flashes in my head.

Scene Three: I am winding through corridors in the hotel that start to feel as if they are a maze, and keep admiring the opulence as I wind through the bar area, several dining rooms, courtyards, and the swimming pool area.

Scene Four: I stop and ask the hotel personnel for directions. A man pretends that he is writing them down for me, and then ignores me. I keep asking him where the lobby is, so that they can read my card and give me the correct room number. In frustration, I hit the man over the head with a briefcase, and find my way back through the dining area and back to the elevators, but still there is no lobby in sight.

Meaning of the dream – Scene One: Opulent hotel with its many passageways represents the material world that holds many distractions, empty promises, and pretenses, but is ultimately just that – a distraction from my real purpose in life.

Scene Two: The two different numbers mean that the material world will hold out a different direction than the one the Spirit gives me, which is the number in my head – the flash of insight. Spirit's intuitive help – flashing through quickly – which (if I follow this guidance) will ease my way. If I ignore it, I continue to wander down blind corridors in my journey through life. Gifts from Spirit come in a flash – a quickening pulse, a hint of a scent, a sense of direction to follow – which I heed quickly, because they disappear in an instant. Use them and the path is eased.

Scene Three: There is no end to the distractions that come from material things; they just keep coming and coming. The material world beckons with its blind alleys and its futile promises. They are all part of the glamour of this world, and have to be released before the gifts of the Spirit will manifest in my life.

Scene Four: There are those who pretend to have the answers for me. In the end, I have to find my own way – through my own guidance – to the right path for myself. No one can give me the correct "directions" except my Higher Self. Eventually, I find myself back to the correct starting point – the elevator – which will take me where I need to go when I "remember" where that is.

On the surface, this seems like a dream of futility and frustration, but it is not. It clearly shows all the distractions that the material world throws us. I had to continue to choose my path to higher knowledge, which is where "home" – represented as my "room" in the dream – really is.

Has the well-meaning advice of others ever conflicted with your own "inner" guidance? We can each choose to follow our own path.

August 5

The Gift of "NOW"

NOW is the time to understand who we really are. NOW is the time to be one with God. NOW is the time to heal our sense of separation; to give up our feeling that we are separate from God. In truth, nothing is separate from its Creator; not one thing. All exists in the Mind of God. All exists as the Body of God. All exists within the in-breath and the out-breath of God. NOW is the only time we have.

Staying in the NOW brings a sense of balance and harmony into our energy field which, in turn, affects the energy fields of everyone with whom we come in contact. NOW is where the great intelligence of the world exists. NOW is the realm of Divine Spirit; the *I AM* presence. It all exists in the NOW.

We create everything that we experience in the present moment; the NOW. The past is gone, the future has not arrived. We only have the NOW; we create in the NOW. By continuously dredging up the past or by looking forward to the future, we eliminate the only time that we really have; the moment. By staying in the moment, we truly exist.

To give some semblance of order to the third dimension, we choose "time" and say that there is a past, a present, and a future. Outside of the third dimension, there is no "time." Backwards (the past), or forwards (the future), means nothing. *All time is One.* Everything that has happened millions of years ago is happening NOW. Everything that will happen millions of years into the future is happening NOW. All of creation exists in an infinite NOW. We exist in an everlasting NOW.

Those who have vivid experiences during shamanistic journeys know that what is perceived as a *long* time may be *no* time at all. Henry Wesselman, in his book, *Spirit Walker: Messages from the Future,* takes a shamanistic journey five thousand years into the future and sees a North American continent by far different than the one that exists now. Each journey that he takes covers many years, yet the clock on his dresser registers that only twenty minutes has passed. Eventually, the person whose "self" he occupies five thousand years in the future actually becomes *consciously aware* of him; aware that there is another presence behind his mind who is observing him and guiding him. This book (along with its corresponding audio tape) is a fascinating odyssey into expanding consciousness.

The gift of NOW is the gift of Creation. We create in the NOW through our thoughts. Our thoughts become our words, become our actions, which becomes our "history."

Have you caught yourself living only in the past or in the future? Choose to stay in the NOW.

August 6

Choosing Our Self

We are the creators of the choices that we make. We are the master of our destiny, not its victim. If we become tired of our chosen role as victim, then perhaps it is time to clear that role out of our "Be"-ing. When we fully tire of being a victim, we will choose otherwise. The one who torments us the most on earth may be the one who is our best friend in Spirit. If we are able to get past the perception of being tormented (which exists on the ego's level), then we can tap into the cosmic realm (which is Spirit's level).

In the path to God – the path of Spirit – we do not have to wait to be chosen. We choose our Self. There is a Biblical passage which states: "Many are called, but few are chosen." This statement implies that God is elitist and discriminating. *A Course in Miracles* rephrases this statement to: "All are called but few choose to listen." (Text, Chap. 3, Sect. IV, Par. 7, Sent. 12) There is a huge difference in these two statements, both in content and in intent. In the first statement, "Many are called, but few are chosen," the power is not with the chooser, but rather is delegated to someone "else." In the second statement, "All are called but few choose to listen," the choice is made by the chooser, thus allowing the chooser to stay empowered. Whether we choose or choose not to choose, we have still made a choice; the choice "not" to choose. We have expressed our desire. No one selects or eliminates us. We chose that for ourselves.

The ability to *choose our Self* is explained in the *Manual for Teachers* from *A Course In Miracles:* "Who are God's Teachers? Anyone who chooses to be one." (Teachers Manual, Sect. I, Par. 1, Sent. 1) Who chooses God's teachers? We do. We are not "chosen"; we choose our Self. Our own willingness empowers us, enables us, and sets us free from the restriction of having to wait to *be* chosen.

From Spirit's perspective, more often than not, the messages that Spirit sends forth to humanity lie fallow simply because the recipients do not act on them. The recipients often dismiss them, do not believe anything will come of them, and bury them in the dust of their dreams where thousands of other "messages" have been buried alive.

Once you connect to your Spirit Self and know that only perfection exists, you may realize that you chose victimhood to help someone else learn their lesson.

Can you see the importance of choosing to give voice to Spirit's promptings? We can each choose to publicize our own truth, not just the truth of others.

August 7

Facing Discrimination

Is there a soul on this planet who has not suffered discrimination of one type or another? When we sift through our grade school or high school experiences, how many of us still carry scars from being the last one chosen for an athletic event, knowing that the leader of the team reluctantly accepts the fact that s/he was saddled with us? What about auditions for the drama club? How about the boyfriend, or girlfriend, or our *best* friend, who let us down? How about the promotion we did not receive; one that went to someone we thought less qualified? Or the nagging feeling that our mother or father favored one of our siblings over us? The list is endless.

In the sixth grade, I was just coming into mastery as a budding artist. I loved to draw and color, even though supplies were very limited. I took great pride in my skill as an artist, was praised for it, always compared my art work against other pieces and silently blessed the fact that mine was "the best." It was a source of high self-esteem for me.

Two experiences in the sixth grade helped crush the budding artist's spirit within me. Once, after I had labored lovingly on a picture of autumn leaves, I did not find it on the bulletin board where the "best" examples were. Instead, my paper was a crumbled ball in the waste basket because I had forgotten to put my name on my paper. I felt just as crushed as that piece of paper. The second incident centered around being selected to work on a special art project in the library. I was not the first one chosen, nor the second, nor the third, but instead somewhere between the fourth and sixth. It did not matter. Slowly my interest in art diminished, so that I never seriously drew or painted anything beyond the tenth grade.

During my senior year in high school, I toyed briefly with the possibility of majoring in art, but the sting of the discrimination inflicted on me in the sixth grade helped to persuade me to pursue a Bachelor of Arts degree with an English major, redirecting a career choice I might have made. For many years – until I completed the forgiveness work regarding that teacher – the smarting pain of those two incidents brought tightness in my stomach, despite all my effort to release its negative energy.

The sting of discrimination can stay with us for a long time, but it need not be permanent. It is up to us to let this pain go. Discrimination comes in many forms, and touches many aspects of our being – even when it is the result of our own competitive nature. Regardless of where its tentacles have reached into our lives, we can give it all up.

You can release all the chains that bind you to the past and hold you back from becoming what you desire for yourself.

Are you still holding angst about being discriminated against ten, twenty, thirty, forty, fifty, sixty, seventy, or eighty years ago? We can each choose to let go of all feelings of discrimination as being no longer relevant to our life.

August 8

Joy is Our Birthright

One if the most exhilarating passages from *A Course in Miracles* is, "Joy is your birthright." Joy is not reserved for those who *get it* or *won it* or *deserve it* or *earn it*. Joy is our birthright. It belongs to all of us. We have the "right" to joy by virtue of having incarnated on this planet. Our inherent "right" to joy comes from our Creator.

A heavy heart cannot be joyful. A burdened heart cannot be joyful. A hardened heart cannot be joyful. While we concentrate our attention on only the pain in our lives, we cannot have that which is our rightful inheritance – a state of joy. Joy is ours, no matter what the circumstances of our lives may be, or where on the planet we live. No matter how much pain we continue to witness, we can still call joy into our hearts, for the only thing over which we have total control is our attitude. Yes, we can choose to go through the rest of our lives feeling rueful about all the circumstances that have caused us pain. Alternatively, we can give up the need to stay in that state. It is up to each of us.

One way to bring joy into our lives is to become *consciously aware* of the beauty around us that is ours for free. So much joy can be found in the natural world, if only we take the time to look. By becoming aware of the gift of each morning's sunrise and the changing phases of the moon, by witnessing the varying seasons that alter the terrain around us, by hearing the chirping of birds, the buzzing of insects or the scampering of squirrels amongst the leaves, by really looking at every flower that appears (no matter how small), by tuning into the sound of the ocean or a small meandering brook, by noticing the rolling hills, misty mountains, or the favorite tree or shrub in our yard, we can shift the entire experience of our existence. The exquisiteness of Nature is all around us. We just have to become aware of it.

We can choose to start our day by acknowledging and recognizing the beauty of Nature and of the role the sun plays in our lives. Everyone on this planet receives the beneficence of the sun: saint and sinner, friend and foe, terrorist and patriot. We can choose to spread sunshine wherever we go – to all we meet – by finding the benefit in that which we are creating. We may change the direction of someone's life by bringing a ray of light into their life. Then, joy comes into our own.

No one, nothing, no barrier whatsoever can stop you from having that which is inherently yours. Come forth and accept the joy that rightfully belongs to you.

What brings you joy and enhances your life? We can choose to live in a state of awareness of how much we have to be joyful about.

August 9

The Infinite I

No obstacle can keep us from being able to access Spirit, our Higher Self, our true purpose on this planet, our "grandest vision," our highest level of "Be"-ing. No degree or lack of it, no class structure, no inheritance or lack of it, no work ethic or lack of it, is going to keep us from accessing who it is that we "really" are and why we are here. It does not matter how many lifetimes we repeat our journey. Ultimately, we will recognize the spiritual aspect of our "Be"-ing and our acceptance of the role we chose to play on this planet.

Sometimes, a person chooses to incarnate into what is called a "victim" soul. S/he may have an adult body and the mental capacity of a three month old. These are usually very old, very wise souls who "know" exactly what they are doing when they choose to incarnate into those conditions.

No barricade can stop us from doing our spiritual work, if that is part of our soul's contract. It does not matter how successful we are in our career, or how many financial obligations we may have. If we have agreed to align with Spirit on this life's journey, we will do so eventually, if only on our deathbed. If our soul's contract is to teach about God, no matter how unqualified *we think* we are, Spirit will show us the way. Spirit is relentless in pursuing us; a "hound of heaven." Spirit teaches us how to reclaim our Real Power – the power of Love.

While our body is a temporary vessel that can be changed as necessary, our consciousness is ours into infinity. Even if the lifeblood from our body is forcibly taken from us, our consciousness never dies. It is there regardless of how many times we change the "space suit" that we occupy on our journey through the Infinite Mind.

You will always be "you," even when your form is pure Spirit and there is no physical demarcation. Can this realization help you stop being so concerned for the temporal, and help you accept the eternal gifts that are yours for the taking?

There is never a time when "you" will not be "you."

What is it about aligning with the Spirit Self that seems so out of reach? We can choose to give expression to the spiritual side of our "Be"-ing as often as possible.

August 10

Rescue Work

John L. Brooker, a member in the Spiritualist Association of Great Britain for over fifty years and a minister for over twenty years, has written two enlightening books about his work with those souls who have not quite successfully transitioned to the Spirit world: *Darkness into Light: Rescuing Souls on the Other Side* and *If Heaven is so Wonderful… Why Come Here? How to Discover Our Whole Being.* John describes the rescue work in which he participates to get souls to leave the astral plane and go to the Light. The first of the two thin volumes, *Darkness into Light,* ends with the souls who are victims of the terrorist attack on the World Trade Center. He describes his encounter with some of these souls who were killed in the attacks (including one of the perpetrators), but who do not know that they are dead. He gives each one of them instructions on how to "go to the Light," and how to help other souls – equally confused – transition to the Spirit world. They are all stuck on the astral plane.

He describes various Beings-in-Spirit – some who had recent lives on earth – who help others on their journey. Nothing is left to chance in the Spiritual realm. Every step of a soul's journey is guided by various Beings-in-Spirit. Even the most fearful and the most hysterical souls are calmed down and guided to "go to the Light."

According to Buddhist tradition, the astral plane (which is the realm to which most of the souls leaving the planet Earth transition) is considered part of the Earth plane, rather than the Spiritual plane. It is a plane of existence where each person manifests exactly what s/he thinks immediately. All those who die together may find themselves together, but their surroundings are going to be exactly as each person's imagination creates; thus each person's "surroundings" can be different. This is why it is so important to understand what happens to us when we transition from this plane of existence.

Authors who have the courage to write about their spiritual experiences, such as John Booker (who has spent over fifty years of his life doing psychic research and has taught classes in psychic and spiritual development), help promote understanding of our "real" nature as spiritual "Be"-ings.

Are you familiar with rescue work or any other aspect of the astral plane? We can deliberately choose to increase our knowledge of the various planes of existence.

August 11

The Light of the World

"You are the Light of the World." Those words, spoken two thousand years ago, remind us to recognize our Self as a Christed "Be"-ing. When we recognize our own light, we are able to step up to the level of mastery that we need to accomplish not only what it is that we desire, but to help others achieve what they desire. No one can stop us. Our intent – our focus, our concentration – is a laser beam that cuts through anything that keeps us from recognizing who we really are and from recognizing the ability of Real Power in our "Be"-ing. We just have to accept the Light within for ourselves.

What is it about accepting the Light within us that frightens us? Is it the amount of *responsibility* that comes from *accepting* that light? Are we afraid we will have to *act* on that light? Do we feel we must give up all the feelings of littleness and insignificance, feelings that – although they are disturbing – have settled into our bodies and fit like comfortable robes around our beings?

Why do we shrink from accepting light over darkness? Why do we keep feeling that we are so defective? We need to stop reading all the advice from all the experts who keep telling us how to improve ourselves, and start listening to that voice within to guide us to the next level of understanding; to the magnificence that is our "real" self.

Self-examination and self-acceptance are not mutually exclusive. Self-examination, if conducted under the guidance of our Higher Self, will bring us to the center of our heart; to where God lives, to the Source of our Light. For each of us, the center of our heart will show us the truth about our Self; that we and every being on this planet are composed of the same "stuff." Each of us, at our core, is composed of the same Light. It is all the *blockages* that our "personality self" puts in place that differentiate how fast we grow in consciousness and acceptance of who we "really" are.

The Source of Light is within *each and every one of us,* not just *one* chosen "Christed" human being who incarnated two thousand years ago. We are all composed of the same Light; *the Light of the World.*

Why should we feel inferior to anyone else when we are made of the same "stuff" of which everyone else is made? We can each choose to accept our Self as "the Light of the World" and act accordingly.

August 12

Our Passion Will Guide Us

We choose our Self. No one chooses us. Nor does anyone keep us from doing that which we wish to do. We keep ourselves from it. Whatever our Higher Self has designated for us as a life's goal, our abilities will unfold as our consciousness of Spirit grows.

Once you accept that you choose your Self, then, what do you choose? Choose what makes your heart sing! What is it that you truly love? What causes your breath to pause as you listen to it? What makes your heart beat rapidly as you witness it? What stills all the chatter in your mind and prompts it to become perfectly quiet and enter another stream of consciousness? What dissolves time for you? What places a bubble of energy around you as you enter your sacred creative space? What makes you feel One with all creation?

We can bring all our feelings to the forefront of our lives, and use them to guide the next step of our lives. These feelings *are* our guide. These feelings are our clue that things are different than they have been before. These feelings take us into our God space.

What is your passion? Can that eventually evolve into a career for you? Can it lead you to another "lifetime" within this lifetime? Your life is more than the sum total of your "to do" lists and your responsibilities. Responsibilities will always be with you. Bring your passion to the forefront of your life. Focus and concentrate on giving expression to your passion at least once every day, even if only for fifteen minutes.

What a colossal waste of energy to use our life force trying to escape from this Earth. If we give as much energy to exploring our passion as we give to trying to escape from here, we will be well on our way to a self-fulfilling career.

Focus and concentrate your energies on that which nourishes you, not on that which depletes you. As you follow your passion, your Higher Self will guide you to the highest reaches of your Soul.

Have you wasted the moments of your life force on that which is of no importance? We can choose to use our "passions" to energize our life force.

August 13

Just Ask

As we become adept at choosing our Self, we start to recognize that we have all the answers to our questions *within* us. All that we need to do is ask.

"Ask, and it shall be given you. Knock, and it shall be opened unto you. Ask, and you shall receive." These are terrific recommendations from the *New Testament* of the Bible! Why so much emphasis given to *asking*? We never receive something for which – at some level – we have not asked. We only get that for which we ask.

When we were building a new home in Northern Virginia, our down payment was forty thousand dollars more than the proceeds of the home we were selling. I counted on earning enough money from future sales to cover the difference, even though settlement was to be in four short months. Because of the building boom at the time, settlement was delayed another six months from the time that we had originally expected, which helped immensely. However, within fourteen days of closing, two of my settlements had been delayed, and we were still ten thousand dollars short to close on our home.

About this same time, my father – in a magnanimous fit of generosity – announced that he would give a gift of ten thousand dollars to each of his children if they would just *ask* him for it. He made the stipulation that we would have to *ask*. I could hardly get the words out of my mouth, since I valued my independence so greatly, but I did manage to tell him that *we, indeed, did need ten more thousand dollars to close on the home we were building.* And he gave it to us.

Just ask! Spirit stands ready to assist us, may throw hints our way, but does not enter our life without our permission. By asking, we open the way to receive guidance and all the good that is coming our way. A lovely lady from one of the spiritual groups in which I participate signs all her e-mails: *All good is coming to me.* What a forthright statement of expectancy of nothing but good!

More importantly, ask to receive answers *from* our Highest Self, *for* the highest good. We *do* receive an answer to every question, which may not be the answer that we wish to hear. It may not be remotely connected to what we think we "want" in our lives, but when it comes in under the guidance of our Higher Self, it will be for our greatest good, whether we think so or not. Eventually, this routine of asking and listening will lead us towards the path that we have selected for ourselves in this lifetime.

Is it at all possible that Spirit will let you down? Never! Your ego may think so. What your ego judges as a success, your Spirit may evaluate as failure. As stated in *A Course in Miracles*, "Some of your greatest advances, you have judged as failures, and some of your deepest retreats, you have evaluated as success." (Text, Chap. 18, Sect. V, Par. 1, Sent. 6) The ego has one agenda. Spirit has another. Sometimes the gifts for which we ask while in Spirit are gifts that our personality self feels are abominations, but our Spirit Self knows are *exactly* the challenges that we need to grow in spiritual lessons. This is a difficult planet on which to live, since most of the gifts from Spirit on this planet revolve around "forgiveness."

I constantly berated myself for not being a published author, because originally, I had given myself two years to be published, and here it was (many years later) and nary a publisher in sight. Yet, Spirit kept insisting that I write. Sometimes, I became so discouraged that I refused, went into a funk and sulked! But, somehow, the pull to write won out, and I resumed my writing. Every day, before my session began, I would say a prayer to my highest Guides – my Angels and Archangels, the Highest Beings of Light, and my Higher Self – that I be given the right words to fulfill my mission that day.

Each day is another chance at a new beginning and we receive only that for which we ask.

Does asking for spiritual help intimidate you?
We can choose to live by the guidance of
Spirit by asking for help every day.

August 14

Your God-Mind

You are trying to take a thimbleful of knowledge and call it an ocean of knowledge. The thimbleful of knowledge can indeed be expanded into an ocean of knowledge when you tap into your God-Mind. However, you do NOT tap into your God-Mind with your existing ego-mind. As Einstein said, "We can't solve problems by using the same kind of thinking we used when we created them."

You have to step out of your existing ego-mind and all of its restrictions and step into your heart. When you can do that, you will look at everything through the eyes of compassion – you will look at what you have created through a different lens. Then you will see as your Mother/Father God sees.

As you merge your heart with your mind, you will become One with All of Creation, which is what you really are. You will become what is the "essential" you. You will get closer to the core of your reality; the real you. You are such incredible "Be"-ings, but you see yourselves as so little and insignificant. You see yourselves as separate because you have separate bodies. You see yourselves as wanting and lacking in many basic needs; grasping for the right to even a bare minimum existence.

There are a few amongst you who know the power of your thoughts and the power of your consciousness. Those who are in physical power do their utmost to keep the rest of you ignorant of your own power. They want to keep control by keeping you ignorant of who your really are, so they are able to continue their mad dream and keep you as their pawns. Fortunately, enough of you are waking up and are credible enough to spread the word to the rest of the world.

You are such incredibly powerful beings with powers beyond your wildest imagination. You have all the power within you to be who you really are. You will access this power through only one means: by going within. This is the authentic power of the Soul. This is not the external power of the world. Two thousand years ago, Jesus said to you, The kingdom of God is within you. *By going within, you will uncover who you really are, will discover your authentic power, will step into the realm of your true authority, and will access your Divine Self.*

And so it is.
I Am.
Amen.

How does applying your God-Mind to your problems change their perspective? We can choose to step into our God-Mind whenever something seems "unsolvable."

August 15

A Fail-Safe System

You are here by Divine Request. As you learn, so shall you teach.

You have not been allowed to develop as freely as you should have. Had you been able to do so, your evolution would be greater by now. You have had interference from other planetary beings who have used you for their own benefit. But your evolution could not be thwarted – no matter what efforts were used to hold you back – because you were created with the greatest gift of all; that of free will. Keeping you at the same level was not possible for any length of time, since your free will can override anyone's attempt to stop your evolution.

You are free to destroy your bodies if you choose, but you are not free to destroy your planet, as this has already been done in your planetary system – with serious repercussion to the rest of the planetary realm. The shock wave sent out with the destruction of that planet – which exists in the form of your asteroid belt – caused incredible reverberations throughout the Galaxy. That is not to be the fate of your planet. It will not be allowed to happen anymore.

You have all that you need right now to be the magnificent majestic "Be"-ings that you really are. You simply have to accept this role for yourselves. You have to believe. You have to trust. You have to desire to be who you "really" are. The differences you exhibit on the surface are just that; superficial irrelevancies. You belong to one race. It is called human. You exist in one mind; the Mind of God.

Trust in God. Trust in your Divine Power to be who and what you really are. Trust that you are guided. Trust that yours is a fail-safe system.

Do you realize that you cannot fail at what you set out to do as guided by Spirit? We have the free will to choose to follow the guidance of our Spirit Self.

August 16

Trust Your Feelings

You will be as happy or as sad as you choose to be. You are a creator "Be"-ing. You have a built-in mechanism that is a guiding light for you; your feelings. You have to learn to trust your feelings to guide you.

If you are relentlessly pursuing the goals that you have set for yourself and your life is not working, stop and examine: *Why not? What is wrong? Where am I going that I am not supposed to go?* Trust your feelings – your inner connection to Spirit – a fool-proof guidance system. Most of the time you ignore your feelings, or you discount them as irrelevant. Then you get a wake-up call that flattens you.

When you no longer feel good about doing the job that you do, all the signs may point to your having to move out of one career and into another. Yet, you may choose to stay in a career that no longer fits the person you have become, and thus continue to live in misery. You may have to get hit by a figurative two by four (or even a two by ten) to take the action needed to move on, especially if inertia has you in its grip.

If you are in a relationship that does not honor you, get over the feeling that this is the best that you can do; that you do not deserve any better. You are a child of God. Your acting small is not honoring the highest potential within you. As a child of God, you each have the "right" to the greatest possible existence this planet has to offer. You each have the right to live with dignity and with purpose. You have the "right" to claim that for yourself, and only you can claim that for your Self.

Trust your feelings. Your feelings come from your Creator and are endowed with the Power of Love. Love is the Power that fuels the Universe. Eventually, all will turn to love. Now, only the enlightened do.

Do you allow the expression of your feelings to guide your actions? We can each choose to allow our feelings to be our guide.

August 17

An Expression of God

You have so many gifts that can be used to heal men's minds about the idea of separation. That is the only "sin" on this planet. You think you are separate from God. You are not.

You are no more separate from God than the dancer is separate from the dance, than the wave is separate from the ocean, than the valley is separate from the mountain, than the hollow is separate from the tree, than the petal is separate from the flower. You are simply an expression of the God within, just as they are.

Don't succumb to the "littleness" in which your ego keeps you bound. The little ego is nothing more than a "small shrill voice" shrieking in the wilderness; one that keeps being replaced – lifetime after lifetime – depending on what you have chosen to co-create on the planet. Co-create is what you do, because co-creator is who you are. Co-creation is your function, your mission, and your goal.

When you align with your Spirit Self, you express God. You give form to God's thoughts. Your thoughts are God's thoughts. You think as God thinks. You are one with the Divine Source, the Prime Creator, the All. Rise to your own power. Shine with the magnificence that you really are. You are the most powerful being ever created. Rise to that creation. Choose your Self.

What new expression of God can you create through your distinctive talents?
We can choose to express God in the unique way that is given to each of us.

August 18

Creation or Miscreation

According to *A Course in Miracles*, "God did not create this world. You did. You also created all the other 'worlds' that you inhabit. However, you did not create yourself. God did." You did not create yourself any more than you created your parents. But you have been endowed with the same attributes that your parents have, by virtue of the fact that you chose to incarnate through your parents.

In the same manner, God chose to experience physicality through His creation – You! God created you in His image and likeness, and you created everything else. As such, you have to take responsibility for everything around you. Some of what you have created, you do not like. They are your miscreation.

God created only perfection; only Love. All else, we have created. God created a holy space. Man created density. Volumes have been written about the "fall" from grace, whereby man has been accused of disobeying one of God's commands. The *fall* simply means the lowering of vibrational energy. The fall is our belief that we are separate from God. God does not see us as separate. We do.

We see ourselves as separate from God and justify all the atrocities that we commit to each other because of that belief. Furthermore, we perpetrate atrocities on each other in the name of God. What arrogance! Whenever we insist that *My God is the right God – the only God* – and use that as the justification to ridicule, exclude, maim, torture, or kill, we operate out of a state of imperiousness.

How often have we heard, *How can God allow such atrocities to take place?* What happens on this planet – including the weather – comes through the design set forth by our free will. Atrocities are not committed as part of God's will. God simply waits for us, as planetary beings, to grow up! God waits for us to act with wisdom, and wisdom has nothing to do with age, since some of the most enlightened people on the planet are the youngest. Neither does wisdom have anything to do with publicity, since some of the most enlightened people on the planet are those unknown to anyone, except to their closest companions. God created man and gave man free will, and then effectively *sent man out to play – in order to experience It Self.*

When *we* take the responsibility for all *our* creations, then we understand one tiny facet of the nature of God.

What have you created in the holy space that you call your life? Choose to create only that which honors life and which brings peace.

August 19

Our Outcome Is Guaranteed

Since we *are* eternal "Be"-ings having a human experience, our eternal nature is always connected to God: indeed, it *is* God. On some level, we have never left the Mind of God; we are always *with* God and thus, our outcome is guaranteed. We get back to our Source, no matter how we live our lives and what experiences we choose to have on this plane of existence.

When we choose to come to Earth, we choose to experience a situation from *every* facet. There are roles that we will take that do not feel good. There are situations we get into where we are not the "hero." There are lifetimes that will be a retribution for a karmic debt and there are lifetimes where we will "rest." It would be too discouraging if we only had to learn hard lessons here. Each lifetime is designed by us to further our understanding of the Whole; the Source from which we came.

We can drift through our learning, or we can absorb it. The choice is ours. We can blame others for that which goes wrong in our lives, or we can choose to let our experiences guide us in a better direction; to a better choice. We can stay grounded as we go through our existence, or we can choose to live outside of our bodies. The choice is ours. We can choose to always be in dire straits, or we can take responsibility for our creations and choose a different path. It is all up to us. We can choose to feel "poor" no matter how much abundance we have around us, or we can choose to be grateful for that which we have, and share our excess with others of lesser means. We can choose to incarnate in dire poverty but revel in the richness of the environment.

Regardless of the way in which we act towards each other, our *outcome* is assured. We have never left the Mind of God. There is nothing for God *to do* about the perils that we get ourselves into, for we return to the Mind of God instantly through our awareness of the same.

It is our choice, whether or not we accept our Divine nature.

How do your choices affect the outcome of your life?
We can each choose to see the outcome that we desire.

August 20

Facing Our Fears – Part 1

Face your fears. Stand squarely in front of them and look them in the eye. Embrace them and love them. Then they will disappear.

Turning points in our lives have often been the lowest points in our lives. Mine certainly were. Somehow, somewhere, I dipped into a well so deep that the reserve on which I pulled was beyond my ego's comprehension. The reserve came from Spirit and carried me through. I refused to accept defeat! In retrospect, many of my setbacks were minor, a mere sniffle, in contrast to the setbacks that other people have chosen to experience.

Just as the pioneers moving West against great odds – establishing homesteads, surviving bitter cold, drought, scorching heat, insects, Indian raids and incredible loneliness – were given a reserve from Spirit that enabled them to persist, so have we been given reserves that find their way into our being, if we just open to them. The important lesson has always been to *never give up.*

In the summer Olympics in 2004 hosted by Greece, the world witnessed the memorable feats of Paul Hamm, the gymnast from Wisconsin. He fell off of the parallel bars, plummeted into twelfth place, came back and gave two outstanding performances that gave him enough points to become the overall champion.

He proclaimed to the world that his coach encouraged him to continue to do his best and not to take anything for granted, that "anything can happen out there."

When asked what lesson he learned from this, Paul answered, "Never give up."

As I write these words, I grapple with the fact that yesterday my computer inadvertently swallowed the past thirty days work on this manuscript. What I (as a writer using today's technology) feared the most was exactly what had happened. I came downstairs, turned on the computer, opened my working title, and looked at a blank screen. Nothing! Nada! Zilch! What greeted my gaze was a blank screen with a blinking curser, which seemed to say: "Where is it?" "Where is it?" "Where is it?"

I had been warned about the possibility of this. My husband had repeatedly warned me to save each day's writing in a different folder with a new date. Others had recommended breaking each chapter into different sections, and to backup my work incessantly. The caution was all there. I did not pay attention. Now all I that had was a pit in my stomach and an aching feeling throughout my body, as I looked at that blank screen and blinking curser and thought about all the hours of the past month that had disappeared into the ether. My husband helped as much as he could, by finding the last version that he had backed up. A total of one week's work was gone; not the thirty days that I had envisioned.

It does not matter how low this blow feels; I will go on. I have come too far with this manuscript to quit before it is finished.

What are some fears that have spurred you on to make changes in your life?
By choosing to face our fears, we continue moving forward with our lives.

August 21

Facing Our Fears – Part 2

Some people are incredibly fearful, even though their fears have never come true. Their fears live inside their head, but never materialize. Maybe the situation has never been that serious in the first place. Maybe they belong to a culture that makes a practice of complaining about all manner of fears, and of exaggerating all aches and pains because they are so into victim mentality. Then there are others who can take the worst situations and still find something about which they can laugh, as Mark Twain did with his comments to hundreds of thousands of people. He entertained people around the world with his "common folk" wisdom.

Every major fear in my life came true. I was afraid my first marriage would fall apart. It did. I was afraid our small business (a real estate brokerage company that I jointly owned with my second husband) would close its doors. It did. I was afraid that my mother would die before my first child was born. She died eleven days prior to the birth of my daughter. I was afraid that I would not be as financially sound as I hoped to be before I began my spiritual work in earnest. True again.

The irony is that none of these fears mattered in the long run. I have felt the presence of my mother many times, have felt the presence of my Angels supporting me, and am in better shape financially than I was when I was working a sixty-hour week in real estate.

Some of my worst fears have never materialized. I was afraid that I would live and die as a real estate broker, while feeling in the pit of my stomach that there was something else that I was supposed to do. Spirit answered that feeling. Spirit gave flesh to those dreams that refused to go away, regardless of how far back in my mind I tucked them. No matter how deeply I buried them under mountains of busy work, they refused to die.

Somehow, I always felt that I was giving up on myself; that I was not following the dream of my youth, even though that dream seemed totally impossible to achieve, and – at the same time – so utterly ridiculous; the product of a teen-age ego. That dream held such a strong grip on me – to be on stage. Now, I am on stage, in front of a group of people, except that I am not reciting someone else's lines, I am reciting my own, as assisted by Spirit.

The attributes that I picked up in my real estate career are still with me. I *love* to sell and feel that I am a salesperson to the core of my being – a salesperson for God! I sell a God-of-All, a God without condemnation, a God without judgment, a God who accepts all nationalities and all creeds, a God of all that is, a God of ONENESS.

What fears have you tied up in knots, even those left over from childhood? By choosing to see the illusion of our fears, we allow ourselves to move forward.

August 22

Awakening to Spirit

There are two of "you" living inside of you; your lower ego self and your Higher Spirit Self. The ego self speaks to you in a "shrill shrieking voice" and *demands* your attention. The Spirit Self speaks to you in a gentle low voice – almost inaudibly – an *impression* rather than an actual sound, and gently nudges you in the right direction. You have to be very vigilant to hear the voice of Spirit.

Normally, it might take a person until their forties, sometimes called the "mid-life crisis," to start awakening to the Voice of their Higher Self. It is often in their forties that people wish to be connected to a job with a "purpose," and that purpose is not to just earn more money to buy more "things." It is at this juncture in life that a person starts to examine and question everything that s/he has valued up to that point.

The Voice of the Higher Self cuts through all classes of society. People who enjoy high status in a white collar career might find their jobs becoming empty shells. They lose their joy. The massive homes, cars, boats, luxury apartments and entertainment centers that their high-paying jobs afford them no longer have any meaning to them. They opt for a much simpler lifestyle; choosing to work with their hands, pursuing more environmentally-sound positions, or becoming responsive to the needs of others through social work or charity work. If they are financially independent, they may even choose to "retire" at a very young age, pursuing volunteer work in inner-city schools, working with troubled or high-risk youth. When their former lifestyles no longer support the needs of their souls, they transform themselves by seeking employment that brings more meaning into their lives. They transform their careers into ones that bring joy and well-being into their souls.

Some people make such a huge impact that they receive publicity for their actions without seeking it. One such person is Rafe Esquith, an educator with underprivileged children. His remarkable book, *There Are No Shortcuts*, recounts how he inspires his inner city students and challenges the rest of the education process in America.

Another such person has been Jeremy Fischer, who as a sophomore at Walter Johnson High School in Bethesda, Maryland, demanded an accredited course on peace studies. There was no one person or committee at his school who was willing to create the course and he was told that if it was to be created, it was up to him. According to the Washington Post: "He endured brush-offs, runarounds, frowns, yawns and countless can't-you-see-I-am-busy looks from big desk rajahs."

Jeremy did not quit, he did not go away, he did not give in. By the time he became a senior, he had the course in place and convinced Ty Healy, a faculty member at Walter Johnson High

School, to teach the class. Jeremy hit a home run through a huge amount of persistent effort by designing a course in peace studies that hopefully becomes a model for other high schools.

George Mason University (in Fairfax, Virginia) offers a Master's Degree in *Peace and Conflict Resolution;* one of the few colleges or universities in the *world* to do so. That is so far-sighted that it is in the stratosphere of innovative degrees. Along with the accreditation of formal peace mediators will come the resolution that *there are better ways* to resolve our conflicts than with bombs and guns.

Many hearts and souls are awakening to Spirit's message and are shifting paradigms that were once considered sacred cows.

In what form does Spirit constantly beckon to you?
We can choose to live with awareness of
what the voice of Spirit is saying to us.

August 23

Spirit's Call - Part 1

During the 1960s, at the start of the Aquarian age, a huge and widely-publicized crisis blasted through the youth in America: flower power and the drug culture. Searching for more meaning in their lives, they were rejecting the programming that bid them to walk lock-step into the future; taking matters into their own hands through non-violent or semi-violent means became their entire focus. They were looking for something more. At the forefront of their protests was the word "Love." They had the right message, but many used the wrong means to accomplish their end.

There was a time in the 1960s when I thought the whole world had gone mad. The student riots, the Vietnam protests, the civil rights demonstrations, the race riots in California, Michigan, New Jersey and Washington D.C., the massacre of four students at Kent State University in Ohio, the cross burnings and arrests of peaceful demonstrators (whether white or black), the assassinations of our President John. F. Kennedy, of civil rights leader Martin Luther King, and of presidential candidate (as well as being the brother of the assassinated president) Robert Kennedy, together with the murder of Ernesto "Che" Rivera (who had championed for rights of the poorest in South America), caused us one heartache after another. This, following a decade of negativity that included daily news about the Cold War, nuclear holocaust, and bomb shelters, shattered any sense of peace and stability that we had thought possible. Yet, in spite of all that swirled around us, we moved forward with our lives.

The irony about the untimely deaths of those who were assassinated is that they joined the league of legends. The legacy of their work lived on and became stronger and more effective. Their legacy spurred more social legislation to be passed than had been possible before their deaths.

There was a giant awakening to all matters of Spirit. The Higher Self was making its voice heard to those in their teens and twenties, and was affecting every manner of "status quo." Bastions of ideology came tumbling down. Civil rights legislation may have cost the Democratic Party the break-up of the "solid south," but who would have wanted to continue living in the United States as it was, dotted with signs of *For Colored Only.*

Those who were in their teens and twenties in the 1960's are now in their fifties and sixties; an excellent age in which to introduce and support legislation that responds to a higher social consciousness. The search for new meaning by the youth of the 60's has never gone away. Rather, it has stayed within their energy field, continuing to motivate these same people towards what is right and what is good for the whole, not just for the individual self.

On a metaphysical plane, the intense feeling of rage at social injustices in the 1960's coincided with the opening of the eighth chakra – the energy center which is the seat of compassion. The eighth chakra (located above the crown chakra at the top of our head) bridges the space between our physical body and our spiritual body. While each chakra is a bridge between the physical and the Divine, the eighth chakra does double duty in the sense that its physical location is above our heads, but it connects to our bodies at the thymus gland, just above the heart. It seals our connection to the Divine within us.

Eastern religions became popular during the 1960's. The Dali Lama, having been thrust on the world stage by the Communist regime, began to be recognized as the spiritual leader that he is, and his teachings about compassion became more well-known. The Beatles studied in India, and spread the message of what they learned there when they returned home.

Have you lived through any frightening times that ultimately became the catalyst for change? We each have the right to choose to live by that which nourishes our Soul.

August 24

Spirit's Call – Part 2

There are a few things that each of us *knows:* what our full name is, where we were born, who our parents are, who our siblings are, who we married, who our children are, where we have lived. These are indisputable facts that we know.

What we have to accept as a "knowing" – with that same degree of certainty – is that *we are spiritual "Be"-ings having a human experience.* It is then that we find our purpose, whatever that may be.

I *know* that I am to share the same information that I learn from the Spiritual realm. I *know* that I receive a steady stream of information on a regular basis. I *know* that when I quiet my mind and allow Spirit to come through, reams and reams of information enter my sphere; important stuff that will help to change the paradigm that binds men to smallness; to their *little* minds, to their loss of power, to the giving away their power.

I do nothing on my own. I just sit quietly and listen to the impressions that come into my mind. When the impressions stop, there is nothing more to write. They just stop, in the same manner as does the television station when it reaches the end of its scheduled broadcast. My mind hears that same static when Spirit's "transmission" ends.

Earlier in my career as a writer, words came streaming in between 2 a.m. and 4 a.m. When I would rather be sleeping, a stream of thoughts awakened me, and would not quit until I came downstairs, opened the computer and started recording what I was "hearing" inside my head.

There is nothing either mysterious or mystical about the force that comes through me. I do nothing to induce it. I do not go into meditation or a trance, nor do I use any special means to contact Spirit. Spirit contacts me. My part is effortless. That is the way it is; that is the way it always has been. When I say my morning prayers inviting Spirit to be a part of my life – to assist me to that which is for the highest good – I become one with the *flow*; that wonderful force that moves me along effortlessly.

I now pay attention to what Spirit says. Before, I was too busy. As long as the information comes, I record; when it stops, I stop. I can now set a designated time during the day or receive impressions as I ask for them. I simply have to remember what time has been set apart to receive and be ready at the pre-designated time. Impressions have come to me for years, much of it strictly personal. However, universal truths are to be shared.

If you have a sense that you are being called to do something other than what you are doing, quiet your mind and tap into the flow of your spiritual truth. Who knows where your path will lead? The world is waiting.

Are you being tapped by Spirit to share spiritual truth? We can each choose to follow the lead of our own heart, rather than the scolding in our head.

August 25

Creation and Miscreation

The hardest thing that we will do on this planet is to step into our power. We think we are so little. Our greatness has been squashed out of us through condemnation, ridicule, laughter, teasing, mind games, and death. Little minds with enormous egos have done their utmost to keep us submerged. It is up to us to get out of the depths of the ocean; to rise above the currents that buffet us and fly up into the air.

You are made of the same "stuff" of which God is made – Light. You come from Light and return to Light. Your bodies are "frozen Light." God is an energy; a Divine, Intelligent, All-Encompassing tapestry of energy. You are a thread within that tapestry. Think of yourself as a single thread within a gigantic tapestry of light and sound. Every single thread adds to the whole, yet the whole is not dependent upon any single thread. A single thread can unravel, yet the whole is unaffected. God is unaffected, because God knows the outcome is assured.

You come from God – from the Source – and go back to God; to the Source. The whole is guaranteed. Your validation is not "out there." You are great because you are God. That is who you are. That is what you are. God is an energy and so are you. If it is too difficult for you to accept that you are God, then call yourself a G-I-T (a God-in-Training) or an aspect of God. If it makes you feel better to keep yourself below the Creator, then do it. You are not the Supreme Creator any more then you are your parent. However, you are endowed with the gifts to create in the same manner as does the Supreme Creator, and you are given the right to create as you will.

No one has to give you power. You *are* power. You are all-powerful in the same way that your Creator is powerful. Your Creator extends His love through you. You extend and reflect the power of your Creator in your creations. Even through your negative thoughts – your "miscreation" – you are still creating. You may not like how your miscreation feels, but you have the freedom to create whatever you focus and concentrate on, as well as the freedom to choose otherwise.

Though you cannot "be" the Prime Creator, in the same way that you cannot "be" your parents, you can create in the same way your Creator does – through thought and sound. Through your thoughts, you create that on which you focus and concentrate. Where your focus and concentration is determines that which you see in your life. If your thoughts are negative, your thoughts will bring about miscreation, and you will not like what you see in your life.

If you are not living consciously, you may feel that you have nothing to do with what you see in your life. Not true!!! Everything you see in your life – on some level – is something that you (through your Higher Self) have placed there for your learning.

Have your "creations" been positive or negative lately? We can choose to live consciously so that we are each aware of what we are creating.

August 26

Spirit's Voice

The ego screams. Spirit whispers. Learn to differentiate between the two voices. They are always present within us. The loud and brash voice of the ego is easy to hear. It dictates to us all manner of unnecessary stuff that leads us to keep our self bound up in knots. Once we enter early adulthood, scant attention is paid to any other voice, for the voice of the ego is so abrasive and so clamorous that it drowns out all possibility of hearing Spirit's voice.

Most children, especially up to the age of sixteen, are connected to Spirit's voice. Spirit taps the young, simply because they are receptive to it. Not only do young children hear Spirit's voice clearly and distinctly, many of them also see forms from the spiritual plane – whether they are Angels or beloved departed members of the family. Children may also see their Spirit Guides, power animals, beings from other dimensions, or the beings who are still trapped in the astral plane.

Any mention by children to parents about hearing or seeing Spiritual Beings usually sends the parents into a tailspin, and the parents quickly give a *poo-poo* to the spiritual occurrence. Parents simply cannot accept the fact that their children see something that they themselves cannot see or hear. Other parents credit their child's experience to an overactive imagination, and do not wish to hear any more about it. Children learn from that early dismissal not to trust themselves. Eventually, spiritual sight diminishes and goes underground, but the ability to see and hear Spirit is never extinguished.

As the child grows (all too quickly), worldly concerns kick in. Apprehension of various question abound: *How am I going to make a living? What kind of career will I have? Who will I marry? Where will I live?* Any possibility of hearing Spirit's voice fades as the ego spirals endlessly in circles. Any attempt to share Spirit's voice with another – be it a friend or family – is met with resistance. Thus, the voice dies down, goes underground, and diminishes, but is still very much there. However, Spirit's voice is very, very quiet for it does not override free will. Only when we become receptive to it, does it resurface to guide us again.

We have to invite Spirit in for this assistance to come into our lives. We have to *ask* for spiritual help. Our free will cannot be violated. We have to be open and receptive to Spirit's assistance and as we become open and receptive, we will receive all the help for which we ask.

The assistance that we seek, if it is only to further ego needs, *may never be* forthcoming. Spirit knows the needs of our Soul and we receive their assistance accordingly. Our Higher Self always knows what is best for our spiritual evolution and advancement. Our ego may shrink from what is laid before us, and rant and rave that God does not hear us, is not listening to us – but Spirit knows best.

Our prayers are *always* answered, regardless of what our ego thinks.

When are you most receptive to hearing Spirit's voice? We can each choose to take the time and the effort to listen, really listen, to the voice of Spirit.

August 27

Authentic Power

Today, our search is for *authenticity.* Everywhere we turn, we hear about being authentic: expressing our authentic selves, displaying authentic behavior, waging authentic power. Mountains of words are being written and spoken in every media about being *authentic*, and how it is necessary for our very survival.

And so, we continue on our quest for authenticity. But who else can we "be" except who we "really" are? Why do we keep this charade going – *that we are separate from God?* It is this single concept that causes more grief than any other concept that we have. Our idea that we are separate from God distorts our thinking and feeds our egos to justify all manner of barbarian actions, all aberrations to well-being. We self-righteously point to our sacred books and scriptures and proclaim that not only do we have the *right* to kill in the name of God, but we have a sacred *responsibility* to do so.

How much longer do we have to buy into the boorish attitude that we need to fight *wars* in order to bring *peace*? How many more times does Mother Earth have to be violated by the bombs that we set off in her body? How much more blood has to be spilt in order to promote freedom? How many more lives have to be strained to the breaking point before our collective consciousness cries, *ENOUGH!!*

Why does our population keep being influenced by those who make the news? Why do we allow others to continue to pull a cover over our consciousness? This is similar to the way in which a Silkie (in Irish folklore) pulls the skin of a seal over herself and returns to the ocean, the "real" home from which she came. Can we step outside of our self-imposed barriers that prevent us from seeing who we really are? We have lived with these barriers for millennia, and each artificial barrier has about the same substance of which our dreams are made. One big… POOF…and they are gone.

Can we surround ourselves with stuff that uplifts us rather than drags us down? We have plenty of that which drags us down. In the meantime, there is a veritable paradise out there that we ignore. Just as people who have been subjected to living in a blackened room their entire lives – thus seeing only darkness – might be resistant to and actually frightened of sunlight, we are resistant to adjusting to our authentic power.

Just because we have not been exposed to Spirit does not mean that Spirit does not exist, anymore than the person deprived of living in sunlight can say that sunlight does not exist. It is time to come out of our self-imposed graves, and revel in the Light – the Light that we are –and accept the power that we have as well.

The incredible power that governs the Universe is called LOVE, and is ours *for the taking*. It is up to us to accept it for ourselves!

Does claiming authentic power for yourself seem like a choice that you can make? "Teach only Love because Love is who you are." (A Course in Miracles)

August 28

Balance

Life is about balance. If we are doing something only out of a sense of obligation, then we are out of balance. The effort that we expend keeping everything functioning smoothly might start to split at the seams, and we find that our lives are falling apart. Eventually, we crack. We can have a "mid-life crisis" while in our sixties or eighties just as easily as we can in our thirties or forties.

Regardless of the roles that we have chosen for ourselves, any one of us may feel like a slave – or an *accessory* to a life – rather than a partner or a co-creator of a life. If our lives consist of nothing but work, we are out of balance. If we are working a full time job, or even a part-time job, unless everyone else around us pitches in to help us do the things that support our life, we can be on overload. Because it takes so much effort to maintain a life on this planet, if we are trying to do it all ourselves, we are out of balance.

One way to achieve balance is to eliminate clutter. Just keeping up with clutter can be a full time job. Rather than continuing to organize clutter, eliminate it! If you cannot find it, you do not need it. Except for tax receipts, most of the time, if you have to file it, you will probably never look at it again, and you do not need it. Except for seasonal items, if you have to store it, you do not need it. Let it go. If your desk keeps getting messy, no matter how many times you expend effort to keep it straight and clean, your life may be out of control. From Spirit's perspective, what is external to you signifies problems with the internal you. Clean up the externals and the internal will also straighten up.

If you are in the "career mode" and give 110% effort to your job (at the expense of all other facets of your life), then you are not in equilibrium. No matter how much diligent effort and attention you give to your career, you may not be rewarded for it. You may have a soul contract to do something other than what you have chosen for yourself, and Spirit will not allow the Universe to reward you for your efforts, no matter how intensely you seek such a reward.

We get into balance when we pay equal attention to the four parts of our energy being: *physical*, *emotional*, *mental*, and *spiritual*. If attention is lacking to any one of the four parts, then we have shortchanged a portion of our essence. Just as attempting to do our work while standing on one foot would feel horribly uncomfortable, we experience a similar effect if we attempt to focus our lives on one area only. Energetically, if we ignore any *one* of these parts of our energy being, the rest of our being suffers.

Give equal attention to all four parts of self – physical, emotional, mental, and spiritual – to reach a state of balance.

Are all four parts of you – physical, emotional, mental, and spiritual – being given equal attention? We must each choose that which is necessary to bring ourselves into balance.

August 29

Knowing That We Are Perfect

When we arrive on this planet, we come in knowing we are *perfect*. However, everything that happens to us since our birth tells us that we are *less* than perfect, and we buy into that. We forget that we are perfect. We accept what all the other fear-based egos say about us. After all, they are the adults and they should know. Right? Not so!

Now is the time to shed all these feelings of imperfection. Go back to the same thoughts that you brought with you when you arrived on the planet; thoughts that aligned themselves with Love, with the perfection of the Universe, and with God. Go back and concentrate on your spiritual growth.

If you are a young parent raising a family, you may feel you do not have the time to spend on spiritual growth. This may be the exact opposite of what your children need, especially today. Your children are souls who bring with them the wisdom of the Universe, because many of them have been given a special dispensation which enables them *to remember who they really are and from whence they came.* They *know* that they are *perfect.* They do not buy into anyone telling them otherwise.

In the past, well-meaning parents squashed the gifts of their "special" children, for they did not want them to be different. They wanted them to "fit in." They felt that theirs was a contractual obligation to discipline each child to be just like everyone else.

That is the same premise that originally gave rise to our education system: homogenizing all talents, and demanding that all children pass a set of standardized tests (which gave no distinction or allowance for each child's individual preferences). According to our education system, every squirrel would flunk swimming and every duck would flunk storing a hoard of supplies for the winter ahead. I am not sure what is worse: those who feel that they have wasted their lives running through the gamut of our education system and graduating after twelve years of pain, or the bored-of-education goof-offs who run amok and bring chaos into the lives of dedicated students and teachers. Does anyone ever ask the teachers what is in the best interests of the students, and how their individual talents could best be developed?

On a soul level, if we have agreed to be the parent or grandparent of a child, we have also been given all the "tools" within ourselves that enable us to fulfill our contractual obligation to that child. We have been given the correct life situation, together with the right words and the patience to comprehend the needs of our child or grandchild.

If we stay open to Spirit's guidance, we can bring harmony and balance into our lives and into the lives of our children through the choices that we make.

Has a new soul chosen you to guide them through this lifetime? We are very fortunate if we have been chosen to shepherd a child through life.

August 30

Changeless and Eternal

We are not our jobs, whether our job is as an aviation specialist or as a zoo keeper. It does not matter how intense our responsibility, how deep our commitment, how much time or effort we invest in our job; no one ever takes their job with them when they transition from this planet.

We are not our homes. The owners of the most expensive mansion on this planet cannot take the bricks, mortar, mirrors, and gilt with them as they leave this plane of existence. A desire to be surrounded by exquisite objects is fine, as long as we realize that these do not define who we really are. No amount of "wishing it were so" will make it otherwise. The many artifacts that were given to the Pharaohs in their tombs for use in the afterlife remained in the tombs, until grave robbers or archeologists discovered them.

We are not our clothes, our cars, our hair, our grades, our possessions, our professions, or our companions. All of these things are subject to change.

Who we are is changeless and eternal, subject to no fluctuations of temperature, nor to any state of being – living or dead. We are as vast as the Universe, and beyond. We encompass all things, behold all things, and create all things. We are all that is, without limitation, without restriction, without qualification.

We manifest things *unconsciously*. The key is to manifest them consciously.

Are you choosing "externals" to define who you are? Choosing to understand who we "really" are holds the keys to an existence beyond time and space.

August 31

G-I-T, God-in-Training

Both in the *New Testament* of the Bible and in many New Age sayings the statement appears: "You are God." If you take exception to that and simply cannot accept that for yourself, you can say, *I am a GIT*; a god-in-training. Just as a baby is not an adult, but has the seeds of the adult programmed within its being, you also have the seeds of the Creator programmed within your Self. You are not the Supreme Creator any more than you are your parents. However, you have all the same characteristics of the Supreme Creator, just as you have the same characteristics of your parents. You play a "role" while fulfilling your journey on this planet, just as your parents did. In this role, you are the producer, director, star and main attraction.

The role that we play is determined by the choices that we make. We have been given the greatest gift that any creature has, that of free will. We can make a choice to do whatever it is that we choose to do. We create our life by the choices we make. We create our reactions. We create our reality. Our reality is unique unto ourselves and, yes, we *are* the center of our Universe. Our life is spent maturing into becoming God/creator/"Be"-ing. Please be assured that whatever role you have agreed to play on this planet, you will be given the strength to bring it to fruition. Whatever strength you need to follow through with your "assignment," you will be given.

Sometimes the role that you agreed to step into is a very difficult one. If your soul's contract is to enact prison reform *from within*, you may enter a role in which a number of people die because of your actions and you are sent to prison for what you caused to happen. You had no intent to murder anyone, yet inadvertently people die from actions you set in motion. Only from within the setting of the prison system can you fulfill your soul's contract, yet your ego and the egos of others may be screaming at what a bad person you are.

Should your soul's contract be to help battered women be released from prison for having killed their spouse due to the extenuating circumstances of their lives, the best way to understand their story may be to hear it from within. If the best way to achieve your role is to be confined to prison, then you will commit an act which will land you in prison, and will be given the strength of character to fulfill that role.

The mishaps that people experience – ones that the ego considers to be tragedies – may be the very things that Spirit considers the greatest triumphs. A Sufi saying, "What the caterpillar considers a tragedy, the Master calls a butterfly" proclaims this insight succinctly.

First, we need to break through the illusion of what we are NOT. We need to break through the illusion of limitation, that which holds us back from our own full potential. Our fears, doubts, anger, injustices, outrages, pitfalls, and all of our other negative creations are here to teach us to let go. By going to the center of our "Be"-ing – in stillness and quietude – we are able to access the directives that we need in order to make the decisions that are right for us. We do that when we cocoon.

What is the new role you are being challenged into as a G-I-T?
We can each look for evidence that our life is changing.

Step 6

Cocoon

In this context, cocoon means to isolate oneself; to leave the cares of the world behind and enter into that private, sacred space of our hearts.

September

Real Power – the power of Love – is not something that you get from another. It is something that you are. The Source of Real Power is the same Source whose sound hurtled galaxies into being.

Real Power – the power of Love – honors the "Be"-ing that you are and applauds all your steps toward spiritual mastery. It does not try to push you out of the way, hurry you along, or cut you off. It never judges and never cloaks its "judgmental" statements as Love.

Real Power – the power of Love – is not given to you. It is not something you have to earn, nor is it something that you have to master. It does not come after a certain age. It is not something that can be taken away from you. Even if you are forced – against your will – to surrender your body, you still have Real Power.

You never stop being you. You always have consciousness of the essence of the Light that you are, even when you are combined with the essence of everyone else's Light. Real Power is who you are.

When you accept your power, you recognize that you have the power to "channel" energy; to be the instrument that directs healing to others, the instrument who allows the healing energy of the Universe to pass through you. To accept your power, you need to simply believe in it. You are a healer if you choose to be. You come to this planet in order to heal yourself, then to accept yourself as the instrument through which others can heal. You use the same energy that Christ used to heal. No different. Christ was a clear channel for Divine energy; so are you becoming the same – the Christ Consciousness.

September 1

The "Stillpoint"

There are certain things we have to do by ourselves. *Cocoon* is one of them. Yes, we can *cocoon* with another, but we do not receive the same degree of learning as when we choose to cocoon by ourselves. When we are totally by ourselves, we are able to go into the silence – into the stillness of our own Soul – to expand into our *stillpoint.* It is in the stillness that we are able to communicate with our Higher Self. Within this stillness lies the "peace that passeth all understanding" (from Philippians 4:7). Reaching this place is possible only when we *cocoon.*

We can each learn to access the *stillpoint* within our being; the point in the center of our Soul where we can hear Spirit, where we can see Spirit. We reach a *stillpoint* every time we inhale and exhale. That briefest pause at the end of the in breath, before the out breath occurs, is called the *stillpoint.* For a brief fraction of a second, everything is held in suspension. We already have practice in reaching the *stillpoint*; the only thing that we have to learn is how to expand the time that we stay there.

An easy technique to expand the *stillpoint* is to practice the art of contemplation. Contemplation is the art of looking at an object intently – with thoughtfulness, with complete focus and attention – allowing no other thoughts to enter.

Contemplating a flower is one of the easiest and most pleasant ways to connect to the Source. Gaze on a flower intently for twenty minutes. Keep your mind focused solely on the various parts of the flower: the petals, the stamen, and the sepals *to the exclusion of all other thoughts.* Really look at the way the flower is constructed; the way the petals are arranged around the stem. Notice the geometric patterns that are created by the various parts of the flower. Appreciate the magnificence of its color as it reflects the sunlight. The radiance that comes from this most fortunate of creations reflects the Angelic Being that makes up a flower.

After I did this exercise, I can still recall every nuance of the daffodil I selected: how its ruffled edges curled over the side, the brilliance of its coloration from intense yellow to deep orange, the way the trumpet sparkled in the sunlight, the manner in which the petals overlapped at their attachment to the base of the stem, and the way the sepals and stamen held on to their pollen.

Another item to contemplate is to use a match head. When my meditation instructor, James Wyche Green, Ph.D. distributed match heads and told us to stare at them for twenty minutes, I thought he was kidding. What fascination could a match head hold? How could there possibly be enough to look at for twenty minutes? It took me a full five minutes to settle my mind down, to turn off the chatter, to "relax" into this contemplation. Only then, did its purpose come through.

To my amazement, the contemplation of a match head opened the door to the value of contemplation, to the value of removing all extraneous thoughts from the mind, to quieting the constant chatter, to reaching the *silence* within. That is what daydreaming is all about – entering a time and space where time and space do not exist.

We can do this same simple exercise with any piece of mineral, rock, stone, crystal, or grain of sand, or with a fragment of fabric, a leaf, a sliver of wood, ceramic, glass, or with virtually anything that resonates with us. The important thing is to keep our focus and concentration on the item that is the focus of our contemplation. By not allowing our attention to wander away, or intruding thoughts to cause us to lose our focus, we enter an altered space in which time means nothing. We become so engrossed that we feel as if we have contemplated this item for hours rather than the twenty minutes that have just passed.

To access the stillpoint within your "Be"-ing, practice this at least once a day.

How can going into the stillpoint shift your awareness of who you really are? We can each learn to practice the art of contemplation daily.

September 2

We Are All One

If a mirror splinters into a great many shards, each shard is still a "mirror." If one Soul splinters into a great many pieces, each splinter comes from one Soul. It does not matter how many divisions into which the Soul has splintered, or how many "forms" it wishes to occupy. *We are all one.* We came from One Source, One Heart, One Mind.

Let us concentrate on the Oneness of All – the Oneness of God – and think of ourselves as having one heart, one mind, one Soul. When Neale Donald Walsch asks God, in *Conversations with God, Book III,* how many souls were created, God answers "One." He repeats the question, as if God did not hear him clearly the first time. The answer is still "One." *We are all One* is a common belief in most metaphysical practices today.

Other animals besides birds sing about their union with the Source. Various audio engineers have experimented with slowing down recordings of crickets chirping, scaling them to "human lifetimes." (An internet search using a key phrase such as "crickets chirping slowed down" will yield several recordings.) When slowed down to the same frequency level as the sound of the human voice, the sound of the crickets chirping becomes *identical* to the sound of humans singing, but *feels* as if it were coming from the Angelic realm. *We are all One* takes on a special meaning after listening to these recordings. The goal of each inhabitant on this planet – be it animal, vegetable, or mineral – is to return to the Source.

The animal kingdom never forgets its connection to the Source. According to those who telepathically communicate with animals, no "loss" occurs when an animal surrenders its body. If an animal is killed or dies, it goes back into the realm of "Be"-ing; to the stream of consciousness that represents its own genus. When each animal belonging to its specific genus "loses" a body in this realm of consciousness, they meld back into the realm of consciousness from whence they came.

Thus, our beloved pets – while a tremendous loss to us when they die – blend back into the realm of consciousness of the Devic kingdom from which they came. According to the animal communicators, animals have no trouble with the concept: *We are all One.* There is no feeling of separation from the Source.

This longing to go back to the Source – this search for *Oneness* – expresses itself in many different ways, one of the most potent is singing. Who can listen to Handel's *Messiah* and not feel a stronger connection to God and to the Angels? The *Hallelujah Chorus* alone is enough to make us feel that we stand alongside the Angelic realm.

By cocooning – going into the stillness of our hearts – we increase our understanding of metaphysical concepts such as: *We are all One.* When we become open to the mysteries of the Universe, mysteries reveal themselves to us.

How many times have you been able to connect with the Oneness of your pet? We can each notice how many times "We are all One" appears within our sphere.

Eliminating Wrath

We cannot eliminate wrath on a global scale until we eradicate it from ourselves. Just for today, pay close attention to the intensity of your wrath; to the times that you lather yourself into a fury about this infraction or that inequity, this transgression or that tyranny. Focus your awareness on how often you allow wrath to bubble up into your life.

Place a stroke on a sheet of paper every time you catch yourself getting furious about all the injustices that occur. "Fine" yourself a dollar for every "infraction" – for each time you go into a state of wrath – whether physically, emotionally, or mentally. Repeat this exercise until you are aware of how often wrath controls your life. What might seem "outrageous" is how fast your "fines" increase. If *wrath* is not your game, employ the same technique on other *negative thoughts*.

Cocooning with our results prevents us from feeling the burden of being "judged." This is meant for our eyes only. There is no necessity to share our efforts with anyone. Doing this exercise privately makes it that much easier to go back to it every time that we slip and allow wrath or negative thoughts to control our actions. Our efforts to expand our awareness about how we are subconsciously controlled *increases* our level of consciousness. We are working on our ego self to reach into and blend more with our Higher Self.

What we bring into existence through our thoughts and reactions affects every part of creation. The more that we focus our thoughts on the *negative* around us, the more we pollute the etheric body of Mother Earth, and the more healing and cleansing we both need. Why would we hurt one another? We are only hurting ourselves. Why would we do injustice to another? We do injustice only to ourselves. Why do we think ill of someone else?

Our ill will is heaped upon ourselves. Each one of our negative thoughts and reactions *goes somewhere*.

Did you ever notice how *heavy* you feel after each negative episode? The next time that you feel like exploding at someone because you feel you have been slighted, think about the possibility that you are only heaping your wrath upon yourself. As you increase your efforts to eliminate wrath, ask Spirit for the ability to comprehend that you are part of a Whole. What you do, and how you act and re-act, affects the Whole.

When we do anything to heal ourselves, we heal the Whole. Isn't that a comforting thought?

How quickly does wrath deplete you?
Eliminating wrath helps advance us on the
physical as well as the Spiritual realm.

September 4

Going Within – Part 1

We come to know who we are by going within; by our willingness to cocoon to access the innermost part of our being. We accomplish this through meditation where we learn that we are as our Creator is: complete, whole, and indivisible.

To reach the Supreme "Be"-ing within you, establish a routine; a quiet time in which you will not be disturbed. Begin by quieting your mind, only achieved through practice, practice, and more practice. Be still. Allow yourself the time and luxury of doing nothing for twenty minutes each day. Expand this to two times per day. Set aside the same twenty minutes at the beginning of the day and at the end of the day. Do not get discouraged over every thought that invades your "quiet time." As you continue to practice, your mind will start to calm down even *before* your quiet time, because you are reinforcing a new habit. Your mind accepts your determination to go within, and starts to settle down as your "quiet time" approaches. The goal is to get your mind into a theta state: a stage of drowsiness leading into semi-consciousness. The active mind slows down and allows other images to enter.

Prior to starting your meditation, several techniques can help calm you down: saying a special prayer, ringing a bell or chimes, listening to soft, voiceless music, lighting some incense, or using essential oils. Then begin. Sit in a cross-legged position either on the floor or on your bed, or sit in a comfortable chair with a small pillow supporting the lower part of your back, with your feet squarely on the floor. If you choose to lie on your bed, make sure that you are not so tired that you fall asleep. Wear loose comfortable clothing, nothing binding anywhere, and place your hands either in your lap or at your side, palms facing up or down; whichever is most comfortable.

Begin your meditation by closing your eyes <u>or</u> keeping them open and relaxing your facial muscles. If you keep your eyes open, place them on a focal point and *keep them there.* Let your jaw sag. Tell *every* major part of your body to relax, starting from the bottom of your feet upward or from your crown downward. *Your body will do as instructed.* After you finish the relaxation technique of telling every part of your body to relax, you should feel as limp as a rag doll. The key is to relax your body in order to calm your mind – to go into nothingness – with your eyes closed or with your eyes open.

Quiet your mind by whatever means you wish. Some people become more distracted with their eyes closed because too many visual images crowd into their mind. Others can meditate *only* with their eyes closed. If you keep your eyes open, fix your gaze on *one object only* during the entire meditation. You will soon know what is best for you.

Two meditation techniques are recommended by Mietek Wurkus, a nationally renowned energy healer:

1. Lighting a candle and staring into the flame, or
2. Staring at a large orange dot on the wall (make the dot from construction paper, about four inches in diameter, and place it six inches from the ceiling).

Various Buddhist traditions recommend saying a *mantra,* a word or phrase repeated for the quality of its sound. Some well-known mantras are:

OM (pronounced: *oh-mmmm* – translation: the sound of creation)
AUM (pronounced as three syllables: *ah*, the sound of God and *oo*, *mmm*)
OM MANI PADME HUM (I am the jewel in the lotus of the heart)
OM NAMAHA SHIVAYA (Thought and Infinite Spirit are manifested)

A mantra does not need to be in a foreign language. Any word or phrase that has special meaning to you will do. During one group meditation, one of the young participants chose the word "dance" because of its importance in her life. She was a budding ballerina, later to play the title role of Clara, in Tchaikovsky's *The Nutcracker.*

Should you feel that you need assistance, there is an exquisite recording of *Om Namaha Shivaya* by Robert Gass and the renowned singing group *On Wings of Song*.

You have such grandeur hidden from your Self. Uncover it. Lift the veil. Cocoon to go into meditation. Be not afraid to discover who you really are, where you really come from, and what power you really have.

Have you ever attempted to meditate?
We can each discover a huge difference in our meditation process after we relax our bodies.

September 5

Going Within – Part 2 - Techniques

Several types of beneficial meditations are: *Breath Work, Creative Visualization,* and *Daydreaming*. In the first, *Breath Work,* breathe slowly and rhythmically. Be aware of nothing except your breath going in and out. Become oblivious to everything except the awareness of your breath going in and out … in and out … in and out. Focus on the breath; just the breath. Feel the breath sinking into your feet, to the end of your toes. Feel your legs getting heavier and heavier, and the inside of your thighs tingle. Feel the breath going down your arms and into your fingertips, until your fingertips pulse. Feel the breath going up to the crown of your head and down the central core of your body. Focus on the breath, nothing but the breath.

Eventually, your breathing will enable you to sink deeper and deeper into the void. Learn to become an observer; a witness to whatever feelings, colors, sounds, or visions come up on the movie screen inside your head. Allow whatever visions appear to arise and fade as they please. Do not get involved in any "chatter" about them. Leave your active mind outside.

If we consistently set the *same* time each day for meditation to connect to the Divine within, our body will "get ready" to meditate quicker. In the beginning, it might take us a full twenty minutes just to calm down; what I call *getting ready to get started*. Soon we will become calmer more rapidly, so that we can begin immediately, with little effort.

When we do the breath work, our feet become heavier and heavier, as if they were made of lead. We connect with the energy of the Earth. By drawing this energy up into our body, we help our body stay connected to the Earth and receive the maximum benefit for the day's activities.

This leads into the second type of meditation: *Creative Visualization.* We think of a series of mental pictures to help us align with the sacred within us. There are thousands of possibilities for creative visualization. Anything that we love can become a focal point for creative visualization. We can purchase someone else's tapes, or create and record our own.

The following is a creative visualization that I love: Visualize your feet becoming heavier and heavier. Then, visualize roots growing down from your legs and down from the base of your spine. Send these roots down slowly into the central core of the Earth. Visualize the roots filling up with energy. Bring back all the energy from the core of the Earth into your body to fill your lower three chakras; the lower three energy centers: the Root, the Sacral and the Solar Plexus.

Next, visualize a central core of light about the width of a tennis ball, which you will eventually expand to the width of a basketball. Take this core of light and send it out of your crown chakra slowly to the Central Sun in the middle of the Universe. When you connect to the Central Sun, gather the energy there and return it to expand your core. Bring the energy back down through your crown. Mix the energy from the Earth and the energy from the Central Sun in your fourth energy center (your heart chakra), for distribution to your entire body. Visualize the blended energies circulating out of your crown chakra (the energy center at the top of your head), descending down both sides of your body to below your feet, then returning back into your body through your roots. The energy now fills the entire core of your body. You have formed two gigantic angel wings around your body, with the energy from the Earth and from the Central Sun. Feel how good, how full, and how protected that makes you feel.

Daydreaming also falls into the category of meditation. How many daydreams precede the "brilliant idea" that provides the very breakthroughs that we need in our lives? How many daydreams forecast the direction of our lives? How many times do we receive a "brilliant idea" while in the shower? My husband is a master at this. Perplexing work problems often resolve themselves as he is showering.

How many times has a person gone to sleep puzzling over a problem, and woken with exactly the right solution? Thomas Edison, an inventor, would work around the clock and fall asleep on the couch in his studio whenever he was tired. A short nap refreshed him enough to begin another marathon round of work, often providing him with the very solution to the problem on which he was working. He had more patents to his name than any other human being in the United States.

Practice any meditation technique for twenty minutes per day, two times per day, *at the same time of day and night*, and notice a remarkable change in your outlook on life. When we do this, we feel more rested, refreshed and relaxed. The tension lines on our faces soften. Our eyes take on a brilliance that was not there before, as they reflect the Light that fires up from within our Soul. Small or large upsets seems insignificant. Any edginess in our demeanor calms down. Our nervous system relaxes. Whatever meditation technique we practice for at least twenty minutes per day brings us enormous benefits.

Experiment with various meditation techniques to find one which resonates with you. In all meditations, you must cocoon and allow yourself the time to connect to the spiritual part of yourself.

When can you fit meditation into your routine?
We can each choose to cocoon and meditate
to reach the innermost core of our being.

September 6

Going Within, Part 3 – More Techniques

During the times that our egos makes us feel as if we are on a raging torrent – totally out of control – meditation helps us enter the eye of the hurricane; helps bring our peace back to our center. To bring peace and understanding into our lives, we *must calm* ourselves down. We do this by retreating from the demands of the world. We can connect to Spirit by going within, into a cocoon of our own making. Since our mind races through a good number of thoughts *per minute,* it is difficult not to become scattered and fragmented, especially given the complexity of the demands on our waking moments.

Meditative states are also possible through *movement exercises,* such as tai chi, qi gong, yoga, walking, or stretching, and are an excellent way to reach the Divine within. It is up to us to find the method that suits us best. During movement exercises, no words are spoken – except the ones that we hear in our heart. Eastern culture has promoted various movement exercises for millennia; Western culture is just catching up. Fortunately, the number of people willing to *teach* what they have been practicing for years is expanding. Movement exercises are being offered in every locale by skilled practitioners in formal studios, in school settings, in adult education classes, in recreation facilities, in churches, and in private homes. Ask around to find a program at an affordable cost.

Guided imagery (a series of visual pictures that bring more energy and balance into our energy field) – while not a "true" meditation – can get us into an altered state and can provide access to the Divine within. This can be done either alone or with a group. A proliferation of guided imagery meditations are offered in many books, one of my favorite being *Ask Your Angels* by Alma

Daniel, Timothy Wyllie, and Andrew Ramer. They offer over forty guided imagery meditations, each one building on the previous, and all serving to increase our understanding of the Divine within.

By meditating, by calming ourselves down, by sifting past the layers of thoughts that keep us agitated and upset, we get closer to the essence of who we really are. We change our minds about the way we act and react towards others. It is entirely up to us how much effort we put into doing this.

We cannot do this work with anyone else. We need to cocoon to get into our own space.

Is there a raging torrent inside of you that is keeping you agitated? We cocoon to calm ourselves down.

September 7

Seeking Quiet

When we have nothing but commotion around us – when the mood of calmness is broken – *retreat.* There is always a quiet place to which we can go; we simply need to find it. We have to be alone to follow our spiritual path. Even though we are surrounded by others, as often as possible, we need to cocoon. Whenever thoughts of child care, family matters, relationships, work, and responsibility ruminate through our mind with their burdening demands, we can retreat to a quiet space to be alone. Then the Voice *for* God – the Holy Spirit – can come to us, or rather, we can hear it; since it is always there, however soft spoken it may be.

Even though distractions make up the bulk of our time on Earth, we must eke out a space and time for ourselves to hear what is being offered us by Spirit. While our mind is churning, we are unable to hear Spirit's suggestions. We may feel so alone, that the Universe does not support us, or that there is nothing out there to help us. That is not true! We are never abandoned. We are never alone. Our prayers are always heard, but sometimes, we are too agitated or too busy to hear Spirit's message.

When we discipline ourselves by setting aside a specific time each day and night, we are able to communicate with our Source. We receive all the guidance that we need for the pressing matters of the day. We have a choice – we always have a choice. We can stay mired in our busyness or we can choose to go into our quiet space. If we choose our quiet space, by recording what we hear, we have a permanent record of the advice given to us. Clarity comes through sorting out our options. When we look at what we have written, a course of action may jump out at us. Our options become clearer, and we feel less likely to continue rummaging around in circles.

We may claim that we never hear Spirit giving us any guidance; that our prayers are never answered. That is not true. Spirit always listens to every request that we make, and our prayers are *always* answered, although they may not take the *form* that we want them to. Spirit never stops talking to us; never fails to assist when asked.

We can each learn to cocoon, in order to enter that quiet space in which we can listen to what our Higher Self has to say about the direction our lives should take. Our goals may change drastically from what they were when we started our adult lives. If we have a soul's contract to step into a new role on this planet, our Higher Self will not release us. We will feel an uneasiness – a restlessness, a discomfort – in spite of all the seemingly positive directions of our lives. Accolades will be meaningless, huge earnings will not satisfy; and emptiness will be pervasive no matter how many tributes are paid to us. The heaviness continues until we answer Spirit's call. If our Higher Self oversees a soul contract for us that is different from the one that we are currently playing, our Higher Self *will* get through to us by whatever means possible.

At the start of my real estate career, my goal was to own a successful real estate brokerage firm with my husband. Having five successful, thriving local offices seemed exactly right! I thought I would go to my grave listing and selling real estate and doing property management. I never envisioned another life for myself. My ego enjoyed the accolades associated with sales production, such as Million Dollar Sales Agent, or the title of Principle Broker (when I started a property management company with another partner). However, that is not what my Higher Self had in mind for the rest of my life. All of my original goals had to be released and permanently let go.

From the beginning, all things "spiritual" made my heart sing. I tried to find the spiritual message in every seminar, every contract, every client, and every event. Spirit knew what I had come here to accomplish, even though my ego resisted it vehemently. Eventually, I aligned with Spirit's goal; the goal of my Higher Self. My goal now is to be a channel for Spirit, for whatever truth Spirit wishes to share with humanity. To do this, I need to cocoon. Writing is a very solitary occupation, so that fits in perfectly with Spirit's plan.

We can experience advancement while participating in group activities, but most of our personal growth will come from doing our work alone--by entering a cocoon.

Are you on the cusp of a change in the direction of your life?
We must each take whatever time that we need to retreat from our responsibilities into our personal quiet space.

September 8

Sinking to Delta

We have incredible powers that are hidden from our ego self that are only accessible through our Higher Self, because our ego self is not willing to investigate who we really are. The ego self is petrified that should we reach any state of being outside of what "it" offers; this will be the death of the ego. It does not realize that "it" (the ego) will be elevated along with every other facet of our being. As we enter through the door within, we find a world more fantastic than we would ever be able to imagine – worlds within worlds, dimensions within dimensions, Universes within Universes, throughout infinity.

These concepts only have meaning when we choose to explore who we really are. We do that by going within; retreating into our cocoon, silencing ourselves, calming our mind, stilling our thoughts, and sinking from alpha and beta to delta – a state of relaxation that emulates the same brain wave activity as when we are in deep sleep. For most of us, this is extremely difficult, because we automatically associate delta with deep sleep and wonder how we could get to that state and still stay alert and awake. It seems impossible but it can be done, by applying whatever meditation technique appeals to us.

There is plenty of literature that offers to teach us, but as the bulk of the work is experiential and has to be done by cocooning. There are many ways to get into a deep meditative state, but the quickest way to sink into delta and still stay *alert and awake* is through music. Pieces featuring exquisite harp and flute music will open you to outstanding possibilities. Mietek Wirkus, an energy healer, gives each of his students a copy of *Spirit Wind. Hemi Sync* music selections (by Monroe Products) offer contemplative music to help balance the left and right brain. Bookstores featuring metaphysical products can also help. Many book and gift stores demonstrate different pieces of music throughout the day. Larger bookstores each have a metaphysical section called New Age, while some of the smaller book/gift stores are *all* New Age. There are so many possibilities out there. Look for them.

Continuing practice increases our ability to access the deepest part of our being. As we practice these techniques, we increase our level of ability to reach delta. While we practice, it is important that we do not chide ourselves for all our failures. Our introduction to reading did not start with the *Encyclopedia Britannica.* We had to learn to recognize the sounds and shapes of the letters first. That took practice. To chide ourselves about our inability to be *perfect* – while we are in the growth and expansion stage – is not productive, just as lamenting that a first grader cannot read the *Encyclopedia Britannica* is not productive. We increase rapidly, provided that we are consistent in our practice sessions. If we practice every day, even two times per day, we notice how much "better" we are in reaching deeper and deeper levels of consciousness.

If this is your lifetime to expand in spiritual understanding, nothing in the material world is going to provide permanent satisfaction. You will seek something more. Your descent into the material realm is part of a grand experiment in which you agreed to partake. The time to access who you really are is at hand. You are awakening to your own potential as you read these words and other works similar to this one. You have all the tools that you need to excavate yourself and extricate yourself from the pit you think that you find yourself in, and Spirit assists you with all you have to do to access the greater part of your "Be"-ing.

You do not have to *become* anyone special, because everything that you could possibly be, *you already are.* You simply have to open yourself up to the wondrous possibilities of what you "really" are. Expand your paradigm to accept this new image of your Self.

Have you ever tried to access the delta state of mind while alert and awake? We cocoon in our efforts to reach the deepest part of our "Be"-ing.

September 9

Continuing to Still Our Minds

To bring balance to the "inside," we need to learn how to meditate in order to get answers about the idiosyncrasies that make our lives feel like shipwrecks. To meditate properly, we need to blank our mind and think about nothing. This is not as hard as it seems. There are many techniques to help quiet the "monkey mind" within.

To still your mind, find a quiet time at the *same* time each day – preferably just before you get up – to go within. If you are adventurous and would like to experiment, do not set an alarm clock. Simply ask your Guides to wake you at whatever hour you wish to rise. You be awakened. Sit up in bed, or on a comfy chair, and prop a small pillow behind your back. Get very comfortable.

Think of nothing. Just focus on your breathing. Think of nothing (no thing). This is the time to reach the center of your "Be"-ing. Continue doing this exercise daily, whether you "feel" that you have any results or not. The results are not for you to judge. You have spent a lifetime looking "out there" for answers. Now is the time to look within.

Quiet your mind by focusing on a flower; appreciate its beauty and thinking of nothing else, looking at each petal, concentrating on nothing but the petal. Blank your mind to everything else. Sink into the feeling of the flower. Connect with the consciousness of the flower. This is easier than you think.

You can accomplish the same by looking at a match head for twenty minutes. This might make you very uncomfortable at first, but eventually, you will feel an incredible peace as you blank your mind to all external thoughts and focus and concentrate on that match head.

Light a candle and stare at the flame until you feel your eyes start to get heavy. When your eyes close totally, allow the heaviness to help get you past the alpha stage; the normal waking stage that keeps your mind in a frenzy. Continue to breathe rhythmically and steadily. Keep your eyes closed and wait. You may see images, you may see colors. You may see bright lights. You may see nothing at all. Don't put any significance on what you see or do not see at first. That will come later. Right now, ask to quiet your mind.

Allow your lids to become very heavy as you softly de-focus your eyes. Light a candle, and look at the candle by looking at the end of your nose until the image of the candle splits in half. Watch as the candle disappears. While many of you may not have a mystical experience immediately, some of you may.

Allow the comfort of the situation to guide you. Simply sink into the comfort of Mother Earth. Sink down, down, down until you feel completely supported. Let go of all the feelings that bind you. Let go of the pain, the restrictions, the guilt, the blame, the endless "stories" that you tell yourself about yourself. Let go of all the wounds that others have inflicted on you. Let go of the pain of the memories that belittle you or dishonor you.

"Let Go and Let God." As we enter into the stillness of our inner sanctum, we feel the surrender that accompanies that feeling. Allow the sanctity of that "Be"-ing that we are – our Higher Self – to come to the forefront to guide us. Let go and enter into *a timeless realm* where all possibilities exist, including the possibility of calm to our hectic lives; totally achievable when we cocoon.

Why is calming our mind so important?
"Seek and you will find" has been
promised us by many Masters.

September 10

Calming the Ego Mind

We have a split mind – an ego mind and a Spirit mind – and both are available to us at all times. The ego mind speaks to us with a very loud voice. It is loud, brash, insistent, and consistently keeps us thinking about the same thing over and over again. It does not let us rest. It offers no solutions, simply repeats the same thoughts over and over again. It keeps us jangled and uncomfortable, offering us no way out of our problem, keeping us mired in the same hopeless thoughts minute by minute. It makes us feel trapped, endless spinning in the same groove. Yes, we are moving as fast as we can, but where are we going?

The ego mind feels trapped and takes it out on us; its host. It can only exist as we exist, but, according to *A Course in Miracles,* "prefers us dead." The ego mind, despite all its bravado, does not realize that if we die, *it* dies along with us, since it cannot exist outside our body.

The trick with the ego mind is to get it into a state where "it" will not think that "you" are "its" enemy. This can be complex. You have to soothe your ego and give it the attention that it craves until it calms down. Eventually, the needs of the ego sublimate to the needs of Spirit, for Spirit is who you really are.

Spirit mind is quite the opposite. It exists not only in every cell of our bodies, but also in every cell of creation. Spirit communicates with all of creation. Thus, when we truly understand the power of Spirit mind, we realize that we can communicate with everything that is around us: the air, the wind, the water, and all material possessions on planet Earth.

Since Spirit mind is changeless and eternal, it has no boundaries. Since it is not bound by our body, it is available to us in whatever state of existence we are residing, in whatever dimension we exist, in whatever Universe we inhabit. "It" is *here.* "It" is *there.* "It" is *everywhere.* Who else does that sound like a description of?

Both minds are present and accessible to us at all times. However, Spirit mind has a very quiet voice. To access our Spirit mind, we must quiet down, calm our senses, remove ourselves from stimuli, and leave all ruminating thoughts at the doorstep.

Be still. Calm the torrent of thought that flows within you so that you can hear the words of the Voice within. You can only do this when you cocoon. Then you are able to access going home – the home of the true Self, the "Big I" versus the "little i" of the ego – while still in full consciousness of your surroundings here.

Why does "ego" mind compete for our "life"?
Spirit mind patiently waits for us to get into a calm state.

September 11

Finding God in a Flower

I now recognize Spirit's hand in every facet of my life. I constantly look for the Divine within every aspect of the people, places, things and events around me. My life's service is to teach people how to integrate Spirit into matter; how to bring heaven to Earth through my writing, my teaching, and my public speaking.

During one lecture of the *Service to Spirit* offered by the Rays of Healing Church, the topic was *What Makes Us Happy?* Our Senior Lead Minister asked us to speak about what *nourishes* our Spirit. One thing that nourishes my Spirit – more than anything – is looking at flowers, whether they are in a garden, a store, a vista overlooking a valley, or on the roadside. I feel that flowers represent God's Angels on this Earth, so I chose to speak about one particular experience that I had with a flower.

During a period of contemplation, I once dismembered a daisy and discovered the sacred geometry within. Each surface of the daisy brought a new revelation. There were two layers of petals around the rim of the center. Two lower petals were equally spaced underneath each of the top petals. Each petal was exactly the same width throughout the entire rim of the flower. Each petal had exactly the same formation: one long central indentation, with parallel lines of veining.

The center – the head of the flower, from which the seeds would form – felt velvety smooth. Each potential seed – which would eventually turn black and hard – was now filled with pollen – soft and yellow, resembling a minuscule fleshy flute with a flayed edge – and was easily removed. The removal of each tiny seed head revealed yet another miraculous layer underneath. Hundreds of perfect hexagons appeared, each bearing an indented center! I started to pick at the edge of the layer of hexagons and discovered yet another perfect layer of hexagons underneath the first layer, except that they were rotated at a slight angle to the first layer.

The underside of the daisy brought more perfect form to light. The back of the daisy formed a cap over the front side and held it in its protective grasp. From the base stem, a perfect swirl of fleshy parts emerged, with identical spacing between each one of the pieces. Six raised ribs, each having two tiny leaves protruding from them, resembled the craggy flesh of dragons. Even though the underside of the flower was craggy, it was faintly reminiscent of the whorl at the top of a baby's head.

This entire exercise lasted no more than twenty minutes, yet I felt as if I had witnessed the hand of God within this creation. As with any other type of deep reflection, I had to be alone to do this; to cocoon.

I encourage you to do the same. As you gaze on anything, please see the Maker's hand in every form. It is there. All you have to do is look around and start to see how things are put together, especially in Nature. Sacred geometry is everywhere.

Can you believe that God is present in all of creation? Sensing God's presence in all things helps us have respect for all things.

September 12

A Message from the Heart

The next time you read a "spiritual" book, as you go into that solitary space, evaluate that book's content not only on the scholarly references that it cites but also on the way it makes your heart feel.

After reading a book on spiritual matters by a well known author (a scholarly work with many citations and references), and then reading another book by a less well-known author (but one who was speaking from his heart), I recognized that there are some books that nourish my Spirit and some books that do not; no matter how well-written they are, and no matter how "high" their intent. In the former, the authors may be very well educated, and their publishing company may promote the book around the world. The books may come highly recommended by other authors held in high esteem by many. Yet, in the latter case, a book written straight from the heart – containing no research but guided by Spirit's message – may have more depth and more meaning than any spiritual book written as an *intellectual* treatise. No book, not matter how polished, gives as much comfort as the one in which the author's direct communication with Spirit is *felt* by the reader.

Paul Ferrini is an author who speaks to me from the heart. While he does not call it "channeling," he has aligned with an energy identified as the Christ Consciousness and has written a series of books about the Christ Mind. His four simple little books: *Love Without Conditions*, *Silence of the Heart*, *Miracle of Love*, and *Return to the Garden*, all subtitled *Reflections of the Christ Mind (I, II, III, & IV)*, lead the reader into a timeless realm, one in which total peace, joy and love live in harmony with the material world. His words bring balm to the Soul because there is Truth in them – Divine Truth.

We each hold a space within our Soul that *knows* when we hear Truth. We cannot be talked out of this *knowing,* nor will any amount of ridicule change our mind. We also hold a space within our Soul that *knows* when someone is lying to us, no matter how strong the justification. Why do people in certain professions have a hard time retaining any type of credibility? We can *feel* when they are lying. No matter how carefully worded their proclamations are – no matter what "spin" they put on the subject – we "know" that they are not telling the truth.

While books on meditation practices speak to my heart when they relate (through the author's words) direct communication from Spirit, there are also books that treat meditation as if it was an *intellectual pursuit*. Such a personally *spiritual* practice can be made to look as if it was an *intellectual* exercise, in order to increase the number of people who might be interested in the practice of meditation. A book on meditation as an intellectual exercise can be made to appeal to those who are deeply entrenched in ego; those who allow their "logical" mind to control them. If that is what it takes to get the message past the left brain, then so be it!

Stories have been written for millennia that contain messages from Spirit. God always sends His Masters to this planet to educate us about the spiritual side of our nature. We gladly embrace our human aspect, but have such difficulty in accepting our Divine aspect. Yet, it is from our Divine aspect that we achieve the freedom, the joy, and the peace we so desire as a race.

What "spiritual" messages have started to appear in your life? Some messages, no matter how sincere, no longer represent who we really are.

September 13

Eliminate Guilt and Shame

If you feel trapped between guilt and shame, please know you can make a conscious decision not to accept them as your reality any longer. Whatever it is that you may have done *at any moment* may have been for someone else's lesson. Unless you know your entire past, present, and future, you do not know the full meaning of the "story" in which you have been participating. Free yourself from the guilt and shame that binds you. You can eliminate every negative emotion in this lifetime – including guilt and shame – no matter how deeply they are entrenched in your psyche, no matter how heinous the "crime" you may have committed, no matter who may have suffered at your hands.

Have we evolved in consciousness enough to let go of stories of guilt and shame that control and paralyze us, whether these "stories" come from our family, our peers, our work, our government, our media, our religion, or our culture? It is up to each of us to evaluate the message from these "stories" and decide whether we feel they have application to our life. The era in which we automatically have had to accept all the limitations, from the all the "stories" with which we grew up, is long gone. In its place is a new era of inquisitiveness.

Do we still need stories that contain elements of guilt and shame in them, or can we throw them out? According to David Hawkins, M.D., Ph.D., in his splendid book: *Power vs. Force*, guilt calibrates slightly higher than shame, but both calibrate at the lowest level of all the emotions. Is it any wonder that these emotions make us *feel* so bad? Guilt and shame have been used as forces to control the populace since the inception of this root race, but then so have pride, judgment, and separation from the God within. Get beyond all of these limiting stories. Let them go. Get rid of them!

Guilt and shame are two emotions which have run their course over the millennia. Say goodbye to them. You no longer have to be attached to them. Say goodbye. A lovely metaphysical practice is to send them out of your body into the *Purple Transformational Flame of St. Germaine*. Visualize an enormous neon purple flame that descends on all the negative forces that bind you. This lovely purple flame will escort all negativity to its next place of evolution. Go into a space deep within the center of your being to eliminate negativity from yourself and your psyche. In its place, ask for *understanding* of the part of the Divine plan to which your actions are related.

Are you participating in a "story" about guilt and shame? It is up to each of us to eliminate that which controls us.

September 14

Indigo and Crystalline Children

If we want answers to the unknown – the mystical – we can ask our babies. The most enlightened beings coming to the planet are the newest ones arriving – the infants – for they are coming in with *memory of that from whence they came.* They completely understand that *they are Spirit having a human experience.* They are the Indigo children, arriving here since the 1970s, and so named because of the large amount of indigo in their auric field. (Indigo is the color of the sixth chakra, the brow chakra.) Others, called the crystalline children, have been arriving here since the 1990's, and are so named because they come in with memory of the crystal palaces where all their learning took place before they came to the planet Earth.

Because they do not accept all the limitations that our culture is attempting to impose on them, many of them suffer frustrations about the wrong information and restrictions that are being thrust upon them by unwitting parents and teachers. Many of these children are being mislabeled as having ADD or ADHD. Sometimes seen as rude, incorrigible, and unmanageable, they are also not allowing themselves to be controlled in the way that other generations of children have been controlled.

Lee Carroll and his wife, Jan Tober (one of the first authors to write a book about Indigo and Crystal children) go into depth about the characteristics about these remarkable children in their book, *Indigo Children: The New Kids have Arrived.* They give detailed first-hand accounts from parents who are enlightened enough to recognize the gifts of their exceptional children, and offer insights from the private teachers and private schools that are in place to teach these unprecedented new souls.

Some of these children have written about the sense of isolation and alienation that permeates their lives from their earliest memories. Many of these children know their purpose for coming to this planet. They are aware of the divine plan for humanity, live only in the NOW, and are so in tune to the truth that they can immediately sense when anyone is lying. They refuse to follow the restrictions placed upon them by well-intentioned adults who try to rein in and control their energy. They are more attuned to the creative aspect of their being, and rebel against the rote memorization that passes for "education" in our society today.

If your child displays wisdom far beyond his or her chronological age, shows evidence of being able to see Spirit or energy fields around humans or anything else, consider yourself blessed. Not only have you been chosen to guide this incredible child into adulthood, but you are also up to the challenge, or you would not have agreed (while in Spirit) to be a caregiver to such a gifted child.

Cocoon, go into the center of your heart, and ask for the guidance that you need to help such a special child come into maturity.

Does your child represent the characteristics of an Indigo or Crystalline child? You are capable of it, if you have agreed to guide and Indigo or Crystalline child to adulthood.

September 15

Change the Dream

Only the Christ Mind is real. Only that which spreads love in its wake is real. All the rest is a dream – some would say a bad dream - which we have made up. It is up to us to wake up from that dream. It is up to us to create another dream, another reality which will reflect who we really are.

The denseness of our vibrations has led us down this path for so long that we can no longer sustain ourselves, much less this planet. Every year on April 22, we celebrate Earth Day. Occasionally, some drastic action takes place on the planet that draws attention to a horrendous injustice. For two years, a woman called Luna lived in a tree in one of the last stands of virgin forest left in the United States to save it from logging. She drew attention from around the world, and yes, she did save her forest and her tree.

Some years, barely a whimper comes from the conventional press about what we can do to help the planet. Some years, the front page of our local paper makes no mention of Earth Day, and the rest of the paper barely gives a whisper of coverage to the needs of this planet. Yet my personal e-mail is deluged with dire news about global warming, and terror to the wildlife and the land due to drilling in the Alaskan National Park system. News also comes in about the catastrophic conditions of the waters leading to the Atlantic Ocean, since the rivers and tributaries on the East Coast are some of the most contaminated on the planet.

In the meantime, we are being inundated with news about saving the "life" of a woman who has been in a continuous vegetative state for the past fourteen years. The front page of the press shows men straining every fiber of their being – praying with feverish intent – to keep others from "pulling the plug" on her feeding tubes, for they fervently believe that every "life" is worth saving,

Why is the same sense of outrage not applied to the loss of "life" of the thousands of soldiers who have been commanded to go halfway around the world to fight a senseless, unprovoked war? They become a two-second blip on the TV screen on those few programs that choose to honor their memory. When there have been enough fatalities to fill two pages, our newspaper, *The Washington Post*, honors their memory with a small color photo, their name, rank, serial number, where they came from and a small citation about the cause of their death.

Where is the sense of outrage over the thousands of soldiers who have become permanently disfigured? Once in a while a human interest story appears on how they are coping with their loss; their recovery, physical therapy, and problems with adjustment to this new phase of their life.

Why has diplomacy not been ranked as the first and only solution to all problems? Why not a choice to talk, talk, talk, talk, talk until the offending parties come to a resolution to which there is mutual agreement?

War has never solved any problem on this planet, yet men continue to justify its use as a means to resolve conflict. It has never worked before, and it does not work now, no matter how much the military protests about their "smart" bombs, or how many reasons the heads of government gives as justification for it. Only we can eliminate the insanity of using war and violence to bring about "peace."

As Dr. Martin Luther King, Jr. said, "We can change the dream" to help the survival of our planet. Change the dream to encompass peace throughout the different cultures, the different religions, the different nationalities. Change the dream to include the environment, the plants and the animals as all interdependent on one another. Know that there is a space deep within from which we can all change the dream from the fear and violence that seems to control this planet to one of harmony and peace.

We are all in this together. As we abuse one aspect of our being, we affect all aspects of our being. We are not separate from the plants and the animals. We are not separate from other cultures and other nationalities. We are all just "different." We can change the dream from one of "domination over" to one of "stewardship of" the planet.

What "dream" pulls your attention towards it? By applying our energies to that which attracts us the most, we can change the dream.

September 16

Puncturing Beliefs

Several things happened during my young adult life that started to puncture my belief in the organized religion into which I was born. First, I married in a civil ceremony outside my "faith." That in itself was enough to condemn me to hell. I gave up that belief and eventually found a priest who agreed to marry us again in a Church service, since that was incredibly important to my parents.

Regarding the issue of having children, my faith condemned any type of birth control. Again, I found a priest who asked me *when* I planned to have children. I answered, "When I am financially able to," and that seemed to satisfy him. Every other priest whom I approached in 1966 labeled any type of birth control as a "mortal sin" and under no circumstance was to be practiced.

Another precept of the Church of my fathers was that only those who are members of my faith will go to heaven. At the age of fifteen, when I attended Mount Mercy Academy (an all-girl's high school in Grand Rapids, Michigan), I was moved with a mixed sense of pride, relief, and comfort by the fact that I was born into the "one true faith," and felt so privileged to be one of God's *chosen* people. As I entered young adulthood, this sense of privilege and well-being started to make no sense.

Shortly after I married my first husband, we moved into the Catskill Mountains of New York for his schooling, then secured summer jobs in one of the local resorts; the Windsor Hotel. The owners, a delightful Jewish family, took such great care of their guests that no matter how outrageous the request, it would be met. How in the world could such a loving, giving, conscientious, kind-hearted, and generous family be condemned to hell because they were *not* part of the faith of my fathers? Another chink in the armor of my "faith" appeared.

Years later, I discovered that the teacher of my son's CCD class (religious instruction designed for children who did not attend parochial school) kept rebuffing his requests for more information, sending him back to his desk and telling him to be quiet. Since this child had an inquisitive mind about everything, it was no surprise that he would question the premises that the teacher was advancing. To rebuff his questions seemed unconscionable.

All too often, I would sit through Sunday Mass and idly daydream rather than feel it was nourishing my Soul in any way. It was almost as if I were responding to programming within, rather than a desire to be a part of a community of Spirit. I would feel uncomfortable and not know from whence this discomfort came.

These incidents and others continued to bring fissures into the faith of my fathers. Eventually, I was forced to go deep inside of myself and think about the tenets of my faith, to see how well they fit with the person I was becoming. No longer did the excuse of being "too busy" to think about these matters suffice. The flagrancies were too great for me to be able to continue to overlook them.

I was forced to cocoon and open a space deep within me that allowed the thoughts of my Spirit to percolate through.

What disillusions about your beliefs are presenting themselves in your life? Each collapse of our old beliefs clears the path to new ones.

September 17

Spirit's Wake-up Call

While I was teaching first grade in the Catskill Mountains in New York State, I went to confession at my local church and started to cry that I was not doing enough to help my fellow man. The young priest was astonished, and did his best to soothe me by saying that, "Teaching little children was certainly helping my fellow man." His words appeased my distress somewhat. However, the emptiness did not go away.

In the early seventies, we moved from the Catskill Mountains to Northern Virginia. In those years, since teaching was a coveted career choice, there were six thousand applications in the Fairfax County school system and no jobs, and the following year, ten thousand applications and no jobs. Unable to stay in the teaching profession because I did not have a degree in education (having graduated as an English major with a Liberal Arts Degree), I gave up that noble pursuit and abandoned pursuing a Master's in Reading Specialization, settling for several mediocre jobs until real estate came along.

Once I got into real estate, professionally, I felt as if I had found my niche. I discovered that I *love to sell.* Every time a new client or customer appeared, the hunt was on. While guiding a seller to do what it took to maximize profits, I helped more women become pristine housekeepers, if only for a fraction of their life. Sellers took my advice seriously and, unless the listing was grossly overpriced in a very sluggish buyer's market, took handsome profits from their home, no matter what the general climate of the market was at that time.

For a buyer, the challenge was even greater. After listening to their needs, the list I pulled off the computer contained an average of two hundred houses. Then came the weed-out. I knew that somewhere in that list of two hundred homes, the perfect home for my buyers was to be found, and it was up to me to find it. Because I listened closely to what the buyers said they wanted, at times, we found their perfect home the first day out. If they could not be convinced to buy it and lost the home due to their procrastination, sometimes the next nine months were spent trying to duplicate the "perfect" home that they had lost. One client took two years to buy, since he was a single, very fearful man. Eventually, the market slowed down to where his procrastination paid off. The home did not sell while he was "thinking about it," and he was able to purchase the home he had once again selected.

Although I would not recommend this technique today, in the early seventies, the entire office would gladly canvass a neighborhood door-to-door to see if anyone was interested in selling. I canvassed door-to-door sporadically for several years (occasionally with retired military officers next to me, occasionally by myself), until my sales increased to a point where canvassing was no longer necessary.

Originally, I thought I would live and die as a real estate broker, since I saw no other choice for myself. Spirit had another idea. Spirit knew my soul's contract; the agreement my soul had made prior to incarnation – my reason for coming to this planet at this particular time in the planet's history. Although I had come well-prepared to pursue the role my soul had selected to play, it was hard to convince my ego. Spirit had tried to reach me since I was eight years old. Even though Spirit made a big push for me to wake up to who I really was in the late sixties, it would take many more years before that happened. But Spirit did not quit! Circumstances forced me to look to the Spirit within to see what it would take to make me happy.

No matter how firmly we are entrenched in our profession – no matter how difficult it is for us to give up coveted notions about ourselves – if we have a soul's contract to do *God's work* on this planet, Spirit will have its way. Spirit will not give up.

Are you being hounded by a sense that you should be doing something different? Our current choice of a career may not be the permanent choice for our lives.

September 18

Going into the Void

If we need an ego trip, we will be sent one. If we find ourselves surrounded by every material advantage – with the freedom to pursue our own personal interests, but are still not happy – we may be on the edge of the Void; a place to which spiritual seekers go.

One of my friends recalled that as a twenty-seven-year-old songwriter, he had two gold labels to his name, drove a big fancy car and wore finely tailored clothes; flashy expensive suits and shoes that now made him shudder. He had every possible material satisfaction, yet nothing made him happy, and he did not know why. Only after he sank to his knees and asked for Spirit's help did he come to the edge of the Void and into the Light. All this on the streets of Manhattan!

What is it inside of us that pushes out of us? What force dominates our feelings, to cause us to feel so unsettled – no matter how much is going right in our lives? This is the force of Spirit; the call of our Soul to take us to a place *consciously* where we go unconsciously each night. If this statement confuses our ego, our Soul instantly understands.

Nothing is what it seems. Everything that shows up in our lives means something. Dissatisfactions come in large and small packages. Sometimes the smallest trigger can set off a chain of events that will change the direction of our life and lead us to where we are supposed to be.

I remember becoming bored with the endless repetition of identical real estate questions posed by clients and customers. On the way to an appointment with a new buyer, I remember thinking: *If I hear that question one more time, I will just scream.* Of course, the client asked *that very same question*, which made me feel as if someone was dragging fingernails down a blackboard. Slowly, dissatisfaction was creeping into every corner of my real estate career. My voice reflected my increasing angst. It became increasingly dull. As one of my buyers said, *I lost my smile.* No longer did I have the same degree of enthusiasm for this career choice that I did in the beginning. I started to avoid clients who had become friends. I did not want to share my increasing unhappiness with anyone. Only on the edge of the Void was I ready to listen to what Spirit had to say.

When Spirit gave me the directive that I was to pursue real estate only as a part-time career, I thought that meant giving up the property management, since that took up so much of my time with less monetary reward. Just the opposite! I was to give up listing and selling on a full-time basis, since that part was much more demanding of my attention. I had to free up enough hours in each day in order to pursue my spiritual work. Financially, I thought that decision was a disaster, since listing and selling provided 85% of my income, but I was willing to follow Spirit's demands. With every change in direction, Spirit guided my steps. When I was ready for something new, Spirit presented itself into my life.

Regardless of how unsettling it was to give up full-time brokerage in real estate, there were other aspects that helped make that transition palatable. Writing has been the one stable factor throughout my life. No matter what happened to me, I always wrote. Each word seemed to flow from the next, as if an inner voice was guiding the words. It was by re-reading the earlier writings that I recognized that *something was being asked of me,* only I did not know what. I had been in the Void a very long time.

When my first book was rejected by main-stream publishing companies, I asked *Why?* and heard the voice inside me say: *There is something you still have to learn.* That "something" was energy healing. I had to learn how to heal by using touch; by channeling universal energy through my body, sending it into another person, either physically or long-distance.

Only by tuning into the quiet within – listening to Spirit's directives and allowing events to unfold as they may – was I able to step out of the Void and into the next phase of my life.

Are you feeling unhappiness with your career choice? Signs will appear that identify when we are at the edge of the Void.

September 19

Goals

In my early years, and throughout my life, I had always been fond of making lists of daily goals. I was also fond of crossing off items on my list. With a great sense of accomplishment, I stroked a bold line through a listed item, At times, I even listed something I had already finished just so I could cross it off, similar to April in the movie *Pieces of April*, starring Katie Holmes. It felt like a reward for a job well done!

Then, in the early 1980's, a new element was added to my list making: itemizing goals under specific headings, such as Personal, Social, Financial, Physical, and Spiritual, and laying out a life plan. On top of daily goals, there were weekly goals, monthly goals, and lifetime goals: a one-year plan, five-year plan, ten-year plan and twenty-year plan. Wow! I dutifully stated all my hopes, dreams, and perceived needs for the next twenty years of my life and filled in all the slots as requested.

Reviewing my lists several years later, I discovered that my precious little daughter – a toddler at that time – fascinated with her first pair of craft scissors, had somehow found the booklet in which the goals were listed, and cut all my lists to shreds. Was that to be the metaphor for my life – my goals in shreds? That event turned out to be strangely prophetic. Most of my stated goals in those years had to do with material possessions – what I wanted to have after twenty years, and how hard I had to work to get there. This was not exactly what Spirit had in mind for me, and certainly not what was in my soul's contract.

Invariably, every goal-setting schedule included a slot for spiritual development. Somehow, that slot always placed at the bottom. Yes, it was important, but not just yet. I would get around to it – sooner or later. *What constituted spiritual development anyway? What did it really mean to me? Would I have to renounce everything I loved in this world to be close to God? Were all the sacrifices absolutely necessary, as the Catholic Church claimed they were? Did I have to give away everything I loved? If God was All-loving, then why was He called a judgmental God in the Bible? Why was I told that God was someone who kept score and sent His children to hell for their transgressions?* Maybe, I could think about it later, much later – after all my other goals were met. Still, there was this tug in my heart that pulled me toward Spirit. But I wasn't sure that I wanted to devote the time needed to think about it just then.

It was not an enormous catharsis in my life that propelled me toward spiritual development. Rather, it happened in small degrees, just as the minutes of each day come in sixty-second increments; a little at a time. Spirit would not be put on hold indefinitely, nor was spiritual development something to be addressed at the end of my life – when I was teetering close to the final chapter. This was NOW! Spirit made its presence known in my life in every way possible: through my friends and clients, through my readings and writings, and through the thoughts that kept leading me back to the Divine. Spiritual development rose to the top of my priorities; all else fit underneath.

While being interviewed on the Phil Donohue Show in 1987, John Bradshaw stated: "You are Spirit having a human experience" – words that flipped my world *right side up.* That single statement opened the floodgates to the torrent of questions racing within my mind, and brought me answers that finally made sense.

My job in this lifetime is to bring Heaven to Earth. *Thy will be done* because Thy will *is* my will.

Which of your life goals is tugging at you, demanding to come to the top? Spirit has a way of re-arranging our priorities.

September 20

A Triumphant Day

A day that began like any other turned from triumph to disaster to triumph before it was over. This day took me on a roller coaster high, sunk me to the depths, but ended on another high.

The day started with the presentation of a full-price contract on a home that I had fully renovated for the landlord; a home that commanded and received the highest price on the market to date for that subdivision. That gave me great satisfaction, for the landlord had accepted my entire request for the renovation items, and when he put the home on the market, it looked as if it were brand new. *Yay!*

Then my son, who was on a summer break from college, left for a week to help his sister in a film production in New York City. Soon he called to say that his car had been stolen. In the car were his brand new EZ Pass and his entire assortment of Blues CD's that he had carefully collected for years, ranging from musical pieces from the 1920s to the latest offerings. *Bummer!*

Next came news that a lot survey for which I had been patiently waiting had been sent, not to me as requested, but to the escrow agent's office. *Bummer!* After driving through fourteen miles of slow traffic to pick it up, the copy of the survey had only a small portion of the seal showing. Upon inquiry, the office manager stated that the copy of the survey was being given to me in the identical manner that had been sent to them. I knew this would cause problems in the government office to which I had to take the survey, which it did. *Bummer!* But eventually the imperfect copy was accepted. *Yay!*

Early in the evening, attending yet another meeting on a neighborhood consolidation project (currently in its seventh year), a major decision was made by the homeowners to sign a document that virtually tripled the value of the homes. *Yay!*

Just after coming back home, my son called to say he found the car. *Yay!* At first, the insurance company did not think the car was covered for theft. *Bummer!* But the next day, a second agent called who claimed it was. *Yay!* Even though we did not need the theft coverage at that moment, it was nice to know the car was covered.

Throughout the day, no matter what was thrown to me, I kept myself in balance; not succumbing fully to the depths, while still being able to enjoy the highs. Even though I felt the elation, it was not so high that I came crashing down with each bit of bad news. Every time the emotion switched from high to low, I turned to the God within to help me stabilize and help me cope. It was the constant reminder of the fact that *I am Spirit having a human experience* that helped even out the flow of emotion; leveling out the eruptions and filling in the valleys.

Someone stated that the reason men make war is that they are bored with a state of bliss. The ego loves war; Spirit loves bliss. By aligning with our Spirit Self, we will not be bored with a state of bliss. We can maintain our highs, balance out our lows, and still enjoy the process in the meantime.

Thank you, Gary of the National Speaker's Association, whose suggestions to say *Yay! Bummer!* Lightened my life.

Do you vacillate from triumph to tragedy in your daily life? Learn to balance out the highs and the lows, and enjoy the process in the meantime.

September 21

Seeking Balance – Outside

We cannot control the events in our lives, but we can control our *attitude* towards them. We can control how we react to the events that cause us to become unstable, even if that instability has its roots shrouded in mystery. We may not know the origin of what makes us react the way we do. Why do we lash out when people start to sing in unison around us, or when they start to clap in congratulations for something that we did? Where did these feelings of instability originate? Why do we feel terror about going into a group of people that we do not know; feeling as if we are going to burst into tears? Where do these feelings come from? How can we begin to understand some of the things that bring us out of balance?

Psychiatrists would put us in therapy for years, in their attempt to uncover items from our past to give us insights. New Age therapists would find origins that extend beyond this lifetime, and would delve into past lives for answers. In some cases, what started as traditional psychotherapy evolved into a search for meaning from past life. Books written by the psychiatrists Raymond Moody, M.D. and Brian Weiss, M.D. have attested to this; both of these psychiatrists had thriving careers using traditional psychotherapeutic techniques. To their amazement, several therapy sessions took bizarre twists. In each case, these two men were hesitant to write about what transpired. Both of these men waited a long time to reveal what had happened, because both had reputations to protect in their field. In the end, their need to share the information was too great; the news too important to keep under wraps.

Fortunately, thousands of others have joined in the march to offer alternative means that can help bring us into balance. Reiki practitioners and other energy healers bring our chakras and subtle bodies into balance after removing imbalances in our auric field, both within and outside our bodies. Tai chi instructors help us balance our chi; the energy that flows within, around, and through our body. Yoga teachers guide us in stretching *all* of our muscles to free the tension stored in them and remind us to stay in the NOW. Myofacia release therapists ease us into relief by working with fascia (the inner membranes connecting all of our cells), and cranial-sacral specialists help mobilize the fluid up and down our spines, and find the natural and gentle rhythm pulsing in each of us from our sacrum up to our cranial area. Therapists who work with Zero Balancing or Polarity Balancing bring the right and left hemisphere of our brains and our right and left sides into balance.

Other energy treatments have become increasingly powerful tools. Reflexologists massage our feet to free up imbalances, knowing that all the organs of our bodies are connected to the bottoms of our feet. Hand therapists use acupressure to connect to all the organs of our bodies as reflected in our hands. Acupuncturists use a series of fine needles on our bodies to get our chi (the energy both within and outside our bodies) flowing freely again. Massage therapists and Rolfers massage our bodies with different degree of intensity and help to relax all the tightness and stiffness that we are holding within, since massage and acupressure can be applied to the hundreds of chakra points throughout our bodies. Whatever our ailment, there is a solution for us. These therapists help us connect to our entire energy field to find answers to our problems.

We discover an enormous assortment of energy healing techniques when we start looking for them. Any store that carries metaphysical books, health foods, or metaphysical gifts, crystals, or minerals may be a resource center for alternative healing information and spiritual classes. The internet is a wonderful resource.

We receive the information on which we focus and concentrate. As we seek alternative solutions for an ailment, we find them.

Have you needed energy treatments to bring your body into a state of balance?
We can do whatever it takes to bring ourselves into a state of balance.

September 22

The Energy of Words

Words carry energy. Words annoy and words thrill. Word crush and words elevate. Words enhance our energy or they drain it. Words have an energy that can stay in our bodies long after they have been spoken. Just ask anyone who has been harmed by words when they were growing up.

The kindly words of a therapist can bring a renewal of optimism to the victims of child abuse or spousal abuse, who so often heard only words of derision and anger and blame. Sadly, endless sessions of therapy have stalled because people cannot get over what has been said to them in the past. However, kind words spoken to anyone, under any circumstances, can soften the cruelest intention.

Words can elevate the most despairing moment and bring consolation where there has been none. People's lives have been changed by the effects of words. The words of Winston Churchill and Franklin Delano Roosevelt during World War II are perfect examples of words buoying up a nation, bringing fragments of hope to a populace starving for encouragement.

Words can be used to shore up the most desperate of circumstances.

The last words my mother spoke to me before she died were: "May God help you."

Those were the most trying times in my life. All our savings had been depleted, trying to shore up a small but previously-thriving real estate company which was struggling through market reversal and 17% interest rates. In those days, it was almost impossible to sell a house, and many agents resorted to forms of "creative financing" that were legal in other parts of the country, but unheard of in Northern Virginia.

My mother could not have chosen a greater goodbye to me than "May God help you."

My desperation was so deep those days that God's help was the only help on which I could rely, and the strength that I received from the Spiritual realm pulled me through.

Recognize the energy of the words you use and carry in your mind.

Can you remember a specific incidence when kind words spoken by a well-meaning person changed your life? We will be given whatever words we need to support our journey on this planet.

September 23

Accessing Calmness

I am no different than any of you reading these words. The impressions that I receive are the same that you receive. The only difference is that I am *aware* of the impressions that I receive. I *acknowledge and trust* the impressions that I receive, while you may doubt them.

This awareness, acknowledgement, and trust did not happen overnight. I had to become ready to acknowledge Spirit, just as you have to become ready. The fact that you have selected to read this material proves your readiness to enter into a new paradigm.

Come along on the journey that is "without distance" – the journey within – which may be the most important journey of our lives. It may be a "journey without distance," but it is one that takes us to the farthest reaches of the Universe and beyond. It exposes us to dimensions beyond our comprehension, delights us with the magnitude of all that is yet to be discovered, thrills us with the beauty of the ride, cajoles us to expand our paradigm to include the *impossible,* and exhilarates us beyond anything that we have ever experienced.

We are never alone, for even when we find ourselves physically alone, a Spiritual Guide arrives to lead us as we step into the void. As we journey within, the Guide can be seen, heard, felt or impressed in our minds.

We are not going to be able to "turn off" our outside influences overnight, or even with the first, second, or third try. We will turn them off by degree. Each degree will take us to a greater place of peace and calm, and with each new degree of calmness, a greater feeling of satisfaction emerges. Calmness is something that most of us have forgotten. It is there, buried deep within our cells. We can access it, but we need to do so slowly in order to do this effectively.

Be patient with yourself. You have spent an entire lifetime frantically scurrying about in the external world. Give yourself a chance to *relax*, which is the only way you are going to be able to explore your inner world. This cannot be rushed, any more than the exploration of any unknown territory can be rushed. Each bend, turn, and twist of the experience needs to be examined, and this can only be accomplished s-l-o-w-l-y.

Practice bringing calmness into the chaos at least once per day. The next time that you feel especially frenzied, deliberately stop what you are doing, isolate yourself, and draw calmness into your sphere. Breathe into your body until you feel a state of undisturbed placid peace, as if you were the surface of a mirror lake. See the situation from a state of self-composure rather than frenzy. Become the peaceful, tranquil self that you desire to be.

You are only able to go within when you cocoon.

Have you ever tried to become calm in the middle of chaos before?
We can bring calmness into the most frazzled day.

September 24

Developing Calmness

You will never find that for which you are looking "out there." There is no thing "out there" that will ever fully satisfy you. There is only within. To find out who you really are, go within. To find the essence of your true Self, go within. To see what it is that you are all about, go within. To re-arrange all your frenzied activity into a state of calmness, go within.

Your lives are all tied up in such "busy"-ness that calmness is totally foreign to you. Yet, it is in and through the calmness that the door to eternity lies – the eternal that is within you, the eternal that is you – your Divine Spirit; your Higher Self, your connection to the Source, your I AM presence, the Real you. This is your true Self; the seat of your power. You access this Self through calmness.

Practice becoming calm daily. Never miss an occasion. Set aside a time when you will not be disturbed. At the beginning of the day, middle of the day, end of the day, it does not matter, but do your best to practice at the same time each day. You may wish to rise earlier or go to bed later. This journey into calmness is a solitary journey; no one can do it for you. You take this journey not in a rush, nor do you ask anyone to accompany you. You are on your own.

Set the stage. If possible, go to a favorite place – indoors or outdoors – and begin by breathing deeply. Breathe until you feel the breath reach your outer extremities, the tips of your fingers, the edges of your toes. Feel the breath fill your lungs. Feel the breath fill your cells, feel the heaviness of your limbs, feel the muscles on your face loosen. Breathe so that your chest goes up and down and relax. Relax the muscles of your face, your neck, and your shoulders. Relax your torso, your arms, and your feet. Relax into the pillow you have chosen to support your lower back. Relax into the seat on which you are sitting. Relax into the Earth. She supports you.

As you breathe, visualize your breath going up out of your crown, then circulating back through into the bottom of your feet, and back up again. Feel the energy in your body. Form angel wings outside your body with your breath. Do this repeatedly until a state of calmness comes into your body. In your mind's eye, see what images come forward. Just observe them, do not think about them, comment on them, or wonder what is coming next. Just observe them as if you are a witness to the scene, much as you witness the events on a movie screen. If you record your experiences in a small journal you will have a permanent record of your ability to expand calmness in your sphere.

(I just did this exercise and a delightful selection of cherubs appeared. The calmness was pervasive. It spread deep into my core and then to the outer layers of my body. It felt great!)

You are going to go on the most important journey of your life, one breath at a time. Sustain the deep breathing for at least a minimum of twenty minutes. If you become distracted, quit for the day. Resume the same steps the next day at the same time, sinking deeper and deeper into relaxation. Repeat the following day, and the next, and the next. When greater vistas open, your own inner voice will guide you and assure you that you are "safe."

As you breathe, you will sink into a void, and your mind eventually will go blank. Until you get to this void, to this sense of blankness, you will not be ready for step two. Even if it might take a month or two, you will get there. You are undoing the habits of a lifetime; habits that bind you to chaos.

Give yourself a chance to heal. Give this exercise the same consideration that you would give a broken bone. You can stare at a broken bone all that you want, but the bone will mend at its own pace. No amount of wishing is going to rush it to mend sooner.

And so it is. I AM.

Amen.

Can you expand your sense of calmness to permeate your life?
We can train ourselves to develop a sense of calmness.

September 25

When to Make a Change

How do you know when you are ready to change jobs, your chosen career path, your current life partner, or any other major part of your existence? The clues are all there.

What gave you pleasure before will no longer satisfy you. What made you feel good about your efforts, no longer has any meaning. A vague uneasiness creeps into your mind that you are missing out on something; that there is something else you should be doing. Similar to the scent of stale smoke which permeates everything it touches, a feeling of unsettledness inhabits your body, penetrating into your very Soul. You become more concerned with the meaning of life than with earning a living. You feel a longing within that cannot be diminished, no matter how much food you stuff into your body or how much work you cram into your hours. You have to look elsewhere for satisfaction, and that elsewhere is within.

When you are being nudged in another direction, Spirit will be gentle at first, then will come on a bit stronger. You are given directives throughout your journey here and now. Spirit presents you with signposts nudging you towards the correct path. It is up to you to notice them. You have to move into the direction of your Soul's calling eventually, even if you are in mid-life or old age. It does not matter. Change is not just for the young. Change is for all to experience, even those who hate change. It might take months, or even years, to effect the changes that you need to implement in your life, but you can begin NOW.

There is a very good reason why you are being asked to make changes in your life. You may have a soul contract to step into a totally different role than the one that you are currently playing. The role may be one you have prepared yourself for in other lifetimes, but which now feels a bit foreign or downright scary.

Know, however, that if the change "feels right," then it is right. Know that if you have the "desire" to effect the change, then it is right. You are not given an idea that you cannot bring to fruition.

You may have chosen to help shift the paradigm of humanity. You may feel as if you have been asked to buck the trends of the world in which you live. You have been! Do not worry about it, though, because you have the entire force of Heaven and Earth behind you. You have the assistance of legions of Angels, Ascended Masters, and Spirit Guides within who present you with the knowledge of the ages; who instruct you each day and each night as to the next step of your journey. You are not alone. You have never been alone. You are being guided every step of the way.

Some of you are meant to live your lives in solitary isolation; some are meant to live in front of the public eye. Whatever the new role is that you are being asked to play, you are also being given all the tools that you need to play it, just as you are given the thoughts that precede the lines that you have to say. When you tap into your Spirit Self, you are given the abilities to accomplish all the goals and dreams that float through your mind.

You are the eyes and ears, hands and feet of God, and are the means through which God moves forward in a continuing spiral of evolution. There is nothing (no thing) static about the Universe. Everything is in a constant state of flux; continuously expanding. You are part of that expansion process. You are the ways and means committee; the power that puts all into motion. The power comes from the Source, and nothing is impossible for God. If God is able to keep the Universe from spinning out of control, God can certainly help you sort out the steps that you have to take to fulfill the role that you assigned to yourself on this planet.

Trust in God.

Are you being nudged to fulfill another role than the one you are currently playing? Trust that you have all the means to fulfill that role.

September 26

Heal by Connecting Back to Source

Caroline Myss stated that in the mid-1980s, the common complaint that she heard was, "I have tried every healing modality known to man. Why am I not healing?"

Why indeed?

Perhaps you are attempting to heal, but are not paying attention to the changes that you have to make to keep that healing permanent. Even if you are given a miraculous healing – what the medical profession calls a "spontaneous" healing – but do not change the thought pattern from which the malfunction arose, then the ailment of which you have been healed will return.

"Go and sin no more" can be interpreted as a directive to "not" repeat the same thought pattern that put the illness in the body in the first place. It need not apply solely to moral transgressions. Much of the advice from the Masters who have visited the earth has been misconstrued in order to lay a guilt trip on the people of this planet. Efforts to control the people of this planet have been legion, as recorded in *Hidden Mysteries: ETs, Ancient Mystery Schools and Ascension*, by Joshua David Stone, Ph.D.

Yes, there are serious medical illnesses that arise from chemical imbalances, or are due to bad diet, lack of exercise, and stress; there are genetic factors, miasmas (energy patterns coming from group thought), and environmental conditions. But emotional thoughts circulating in our personal energy fields – both inside and outside of our bodies – contribute to an overwhelming amount of illnesses that our bodies experience.

The "disconnect" we feel from our Source only exacerbates the problem. The only way that we can truly feel empowered on this planet is to ignore most of that which we have been told is "true." Conventional "wisdom" – the consensus opinion of the majority – only serves to weaken us. Governments, religious institutions and schools are only interested in getting us to acquiesce to the lowest common denominator. There is no allowance given for free thought; for thinking outside the box. Creative solutions to massive problems are not only discouraged, but are also considered downright dangerous.

Healing is a function of finding your way back to the Source. All too often, you are trying to heal in isolation from who you are. You are trying to heal separated parts of yourself as if those parts did not belong to the whole, in the same way that you store parts of food in containers in the refrigerator.

You cannot heal in isolation from the Source. The whole of you needs to be healed at the same time. The whole of you needs to find your way back to the Source. You have tried all the external means; now you must try some internal ones. External means are fine – they can assist you – but they are not the entire answer.

You must look to who you really are. You are *One* with your Creator. You must go back to the Source. You do this through silence and meditation. You do this by quieting your mind; by giving up external stimuli and going into a gentle space. Find the time to meditate; to go within. All answers are found inside of you. It is all within.

You need more quiet time to go within; more time to cocoon.

How can connecting back to the Source
bring healing into your life?
We must each take whatever quiet time that
we need to connect to the Source.

September 27

Disaster Bringing Compassion

A massive spiritual presence blanketed this planet in the 1960s. Unfortunately, it broke to the surface as the drug culture, and expressed itself on the physical plane in all manner of aberrant behaviors. Those infused with spiritual longings often used the wrong techniques to manifest their desires. They had the right idea, only they found the wrong means to fulfill their longing for Spirit.

Massive infusions of Spirit's presence continue to shower us today. Look at the contents of some of the current woman's magazines. They are often filled with articles about healing. Ten years ago, they were filled with anything but. Even trade journals – those magazines that cater to a particular industry and have no circulation outside their industry – offer articles that smack of spirituality. Spirit is penetrating into all the institutions on this planet, through every possible avenue.

While the events of September 11, 2001 changed the culture of the United States (some believe for the worse), that event awakened the seat of compassion in people around the world, as did the tsunami that took place off the coast of Indonesia in 2004. Both of these events bought an overflow of compassion to the surface of this planet, as has never been seen before.

At the edge of the World Trade Center, St. Paul's Chapel (the oldest surviving church in Manhattan) miraculously survived intact on 9/11, with the exception of a large sycamore tree at the edge of the property that was struck by a steel girder. The chapel was continuously manned by volunteers for nine months afterwards, and became a haven for the firefighters and the demolition crews who used it as a sanctuary for rest, shelter, and food. Hundreds of thousands of meals were served free of charge, thanks to the contributions of area restaurants and to assistance from area residents. Pillows and blankets were laid out on the pews, and cots flanked the walls to offer a place to rest to those who were too weary to go home after their twenty-four hour shifts.

The massive iron fence and gate around the chapel property became an instant memorial site as tributes of encouragement arrived from around the world, along with the flowers, candles and pictures and mementoes of those lost in the World Trade Center. The chapel became a rescue site and a haven for all those involved in clearing the World Trade Center area, as well as a memorial shrine to those who had died.

All of those visiting the site of the World Trade Center today can stop by the St. Paul's Chapel and watch the videos of the rescue operation and see the many mementoes that are still hanging in tribute on the wall. Two steel girders in the shape of a cross stand on the apron of the property itself. It no longer looks like the gaping wound that it once was, but there is still an atmosphere of quiet around it, as if to honor the memory of all those who lost their lives there.

Compassion overflowed from people when the news of the 2004 tsunami in Indonesia instantly spread around the world. People responded with kindness and generosity, their compassionate thoughts accompanied by kind deeds. After the tsunami hit, many left the comfort of their own homes to volunteer in helping the surviving victims to rebuild their lives. Many others, including small children, organized contribution events to collect money for the victims. Retailers that normally may not have been involved offered collection options at the check-out counter. Many large and small corporations had their employees contribute deductions from their paychecks. So many people offered to contribute in some way to help the less fortunate.

Along with the normal sense of horror or fear, these two disasters brought an outpouring of compassion from around the world, upgrading the collective consciousness of the people on this planet who united in helping and comforting the survivors. This compassion has been repeated time and again whenever disaster has struck in the world.

As we respond to our national and international disasters, we also learn to weather our personal disasters.

Can you remember the good that may have come from a disaster that you personally experienced? Disasters may be the opening to a paradigm shift.

September 28

Becoming the Oneness – A Message from My Guides

Look within. All your guidance comes from within. Each one of you is connected to the Source. Each one of you is a piece of the Source. It cannot be otherwise. You are just as we, your Guides; only we vibrate at a different rate than you. Our vibrations are much lighter than yours.

It does not take much effort to hear us. You have to be open to it. But to hear us and to act on what we suggest; that is another matter. You all hear us. There is not a one of you who does not react when given a spontaneous idea for healing. However, most of you dismiss these ideas as being too hard, too uncomfortable, too threatening to the status quo, or too upsetting to the routine. In plain words, you do not want to do anything about your situation. You have to be willing to do the "tough stuff" as well.

There are moments when time and space suspends; when you enter a realm of total peace, when you know that you are part of something bigger than "you" are. These times come when you least expect them. Temporarily, you suspend your belief that: "This is not possible, this cannot be."

That you can "be" elsewhere, whether it is past, present, or future, is absolutely possible. An overwhelming sense of Oneness rushes in and overtakes your thoughts. No separation exists between your body and your mind as you melt into this new state of awareness. You are One with everything. Your thoughts cannot contain you. Your body is not a barrier.

You have the means to heal yourself completely from all your ailments. It is a foolproof method. It is tapped by your willingness. You need to stop and pray and ask for help. Ask for guidance. All will be given to you as you ask. Prayers are simple. A conversation will do. Nothing formal is needed. Everything depends on your willingness. The effort comes from within. All the power is within you.

Music can transport you to this place on Oneness. So can art, so can working on any project with total focus and concentration, whether it is constructing something in the machine shop, making a dress, preparing a meal, or working on the computer. Writing can take you there. Looking at a candle and abandoning yourself into its light can take you there. Sound, vibration, and light all take you there.

This place of Oneness, where all "laws" of physics are suspended as you gently bask on an endless beam of pure "Be"-ing, helps you lose track of the placement of your physical body. You cease to be concerned about where your feet and hands are placed. You have slipped into a void in which physical laws no longer exist. You have entered a state of Oneness.

Have you ever experienced a state of Oneness?
Know that it is possible to enter into
a state of pure "Be"-ing.

September 29

Effecting Change

Take the time to stop and stare into a candle flame for twenty minutes each day, and feel how this helps calm the restless spirit within you. Twenty minutes might seem like a long time, until you compare it with the time that you spend being agitated and aggravated. Release the ties that bind you, and start to restore yourself to the state of perfection from whence you came.

It is from within that we pursue Real Power. We have all the "time" in the world and as many lifetimes as we need. It is our free will "to do" or "not to do." It is totally up to us. While the crises of this lifetime seem so important, each lifetime – as my son says – is like "a tick the width of an atom" in the total scheme of our evolution.

"You need do nothing" except give a little willingness to Spirit, according to *A Course in Miracles.* Spirit will enter when and where invited, even if the invitation merely opens a crack in your consciousness. The statement does not mean that Spirit will do all of your work for you. Sitting back and expecting results while doing nothing about it (because you take these words literally) is an abdication of your life force. You are meant to do your own work, and more.

Thoughts precede deeds, but thoughts without deeds can be very weak. Deeds are the visible manifestation of our thoughts. Deeds show our character to this world. We can think about desiring a career as a public speaker, a published author, a singer, a rock star, or a dramatic artist, but until we get up each morning and practice our art, put forth our articles for publication, take voice lessons, or line up auditions for performances, our thoughts do not manifest themselves into form. Instead, they stay in that amorphous place where thoughts live rather than propel us forward as the instrument of change.

Very few have chosen lifetimes of solitary meditation, as have certain orders of Buddhist or cloistered monks or nuns. When the Dalai Lama had to flee Tibet for fear of his life, it seemed to be an abomination of his life force. However, his exposure to the rest of the world – to the cultures that have welcomed him – has been the greatest gift to this Universe at this time. Wherever he speaks, he is treated as a rock star; people hang onto his every word, so hungry are they for his message. Through his teaching of applying peace and calmness, he has become an instrument for change that has been universally accepted throughout the world.

The late Pope John Paul II was the most traveled pope in history. He made his life a mission for good, extending a branch of reconciliation to the different faiths and apologizing for the transgressions that the Church committed to various cultural groups in the past. He always taught peaceful means to accomplish change, and was the quiet force behind the Solidarity movement in Poland. He loved young people, and organized a World Youth Day for young adults. On the average, his path took him outside the Vatican every ten days. He was beloved by many people around the world, both inside and outside his religion. Through it all, he kept an abiding faith in the rituals of the Church, continuously saying the rosary in his devotion to the Blessed Mother, whom he credited with saving his life.

Pope John Paul II forgave the man who tried to take his life and visited him in prison, thus becoming a model for forgiveness. He led his congregation until the very end, even when his body was crippled with Parkinson's disease, and long after he could have justified stepping down for health reasons. He felt he exemplified Christ's mission on this Earth, and those who saw him felt the same. During the week of tributes paid to him, many came forth with stories of how contact with Pope John Paul II changed their lives.

Needless to say, we do not need to be a high prelate to effect change in our lives. We simply need to follow the dictates of our hearts. We evolve into the greatest potential possible when we follow our inner voice; all possible when we cocoon.

What can you do to effect change in your life right NOW?
Only we can take the necessary actions
to bring our thoughts into form.

September 30

Witnessing Wisps

Three candles are burning, their fragile trails fluttering across my page, misty shadows formed by the essence of the smoke. These ethereal billows cannot be seen with the visible eye, looking more like jellyfish in the ocean rather than smoke, their moves more closely resembling movement in water. Their shadows dance, twist, turn, and pirouette on the paper, thanks to the sunlight streaming through the window. Nature spirits associated with fire are called salamanders. What an interesting way to see them, as they reveal themselves as wisps of smoke.

The candles barely flicker, yet the air moves in a continuous flowing rhythm, like a long, diaphanous chiffon scarf flying in the breeze. Just as a scarf weaves back and forth and folds in on itself, these flickering candles have their own dance of life, completely oblivious to those who observe them. Can the dancer be separated from the dance? Can one exist without the other? Is one not the physical expression of the other?

Everything sings a song of praise to the Creator, even the candles that I witness. Lost in their own rapture, they send forth streams of air plasma in perfect rhythm to the exquisite music filling the room. Had a sunbeam not cast its light through the window, I would have missed this glorious joyous tribute to the Creator this morning. Leaping, flowing, furling and unfurling air masses emitting from three flames, all to a secret beat; a mysterious crescendo that waxes and wanes to the rhythm of its own heart wafting in glorious tribute to its Maker.

Thank you, sunbeam, for allowing me a glimpse of yet another one of Mother Nature's great mysteries.

Do you take every opportunity to witness the beauty of Nature? Never miss a chance to see what Nature has to offer.

Real Power – the power of Love – is ours for the taking. We have to own it, accept it, uncover it, and use it. When we tap into Real Power, we can tolerate any situation. We can stand witness to all attempts of the little "shrill shrieking ego" to control, belittle, diminish, ridicule, bypass, cut off, or eliminate our power, and still let it go. The little "shrill shrieking ego" eventually gives up. It runs out of steam because its source is fear and fear can sustain its energy only for so long. Then, it goes back to the cavern from which it came. We can stand firm because we know that the Source of Real Power is unlimited.

Real Power – the power of Love – is ours NOW. We are always present in the NOW. It is we who takes our consciousness into the past or into the future, as if they were more important than the NOW. Some of us do not pay attention to the NOW, for we seek answers for the future. A few of us have a gift of prophecy where we can accurately predict the events of the future. However, should we give all our attention to the future and ignore the NOW, we miss the essential element of our lives. By giving our focus and concentration to the NOW we see the miracle of change that we so desire in our lives.

Through our free will we can deny Real Power; the power of Love. We can procrastinate in thinking about it. We can cover it with endless boxes. We can bury its light within the depths of our being, but we cannot extinguish it. We can pretend it is not there. We can diminish its attempts to influence our actions, but we cannot eliminate it, since it comes from the Source.

October 1

Undines

Whatever else awaits me today can wait for the moment. By listening to the same CD each day, I am transported into an altered state; a place of calm and peace that forms in the central core of my being. Right now, I am very still, lost in wonder, enjoying the music *Celestial Morning,* composed and performed by a friend of mine, Henry Chandler, certainly appropriate for my mood this morning. The melodies are very pastoral, very quiet, very contemplative, except for one song. Sprite and lively, it brings to mind sunbeams dancing on water, just as they do at Lake Idlewild in Pennsylvania.

During one magical part of the day – a few hours before the sun sets – a thousand points of light, each one riding a lick of a wave, gently come to shore. One of my favorite spots in the entire world, the edge of Lake Idlewild, revels in its role as the gathering spot for undines – the nature spirits of water. Each element of the Earth has its corresponding nature spirits, and the undines belong to the element of water. This is the kingdom to which mermen and mermaids belong – the magical kingdom of the sea that exists in another dimension, only occasionally offering a glimpse of its mystery to some lucky human who traverses between dimensions.

Within my reverie, I am transported back to the shore edge. All is still on the lake now, but an occasional laugh from the other side wafts across; a child's whoop, a distant roar of a motorcycle, or zoom from a passing car. No jet skis, no outboard motors, no water skiers. Nothing to mar the compacted stillness except a tiny flip of water as a fish breaks through to catch its targeted fly. The luminous little undines – the water spirits – dance just under the surface. A thousand specks of dazzling lights ride toward me, laughing lightly, dancing, darting, and undulating, all caressing the surface of the water, each bright little face tasting life.

The water lilies in the far corner are totally oblivious to this wondrous delight; this feast, this spiritual banquet that has been laid out for anyone wishing to take the time to witness it. Their petals are firmly shut – their glory closed now – as they prepare for the end of the day. The pads sit silently, gently rolling as laps of water break from a passing wave. Even the frogs are quiet; no croaking their message to life, no acknowledging their joy to the Creator, the Maker of Life.

The fishermen, nodding their heads in acknowledgement of one another while giving homage to each other's privacy, practice their art, perfecting their skills, while occasionally teaching a youngster how to cast properly or how to bait a hook.

All is quiet now. My Soul slips into tranquility as I sit on the edge of the dock, silently observing the sweetness around me and feeling so grateful to have this time to myself to nurture my Spirit.

Do you have a favorite spot of retreat in which you can refresh and renew your Spirit? Take every opportunity to revitalize your Spirit, if only in your mind.

October 2

Strings of Things

I used to marvel at how absolutely insistent my daughter was about purchasing a favored treasure when she was younger. Because she took very good care of her possessions, she knew that I would buckle under and get her what she wanted, and she acted as if her heart would break if she did not get the coveted toy, piece of clothing, or accessory. The new item would receive special attention for many weeks or months, then the coveted object would be relegated to a spot on her shelf and left forgotten as a new article seized her attention and affection.

My son went through the same phase, only his devotion lasted from a few weeks to a few years, depending on his continued interest in a subject. Once time, coin collecting became his obsession, and he received all the official folders needed to get started. His interest waned in a few weeks, before he filled up any of them. He went through the normal litany of items that interest boys: *Richard Scarry* books, *GI Joe*, baseball cards, *Star Wars* cards, pogs, puzzles, board games, and trucks in all shapes and sizes. However, the *Games Workshop* toy armies became an obsession that lasted for years. He spent thousands of dollars and hundreds of hours painting his "armies," and setting up strategies for each new game.

I was no different. In any plant section of a big-box store or nursery, I coveted new perennials, new bulbs, tubers or bedding plants. What excitement to go outside every spring morning to see which new "babies" had appeared – those perennials that had become a permanent fixture – along with concern when some became so aggressive that they eventually became invasive. The only plants that I finally relinquished were house plants, keeping only the "survivors;" those plants which could go outside all summer, make the transition to indoors in the late fall, and could survive indoors with a minimum of attention during the winter and early spring, or those that never went outside – which simply resigned themselves to their very boring life indoors.

This seeking also applied to my spiritual pursuits. Going into any metaphysical bookstore or gift shop, I coveted a new crystal for its healing properties, or yearned for a new book for its ability to expand my Soul. No matter what condition my budget was in, if I was truly interested, I found a way to afford another class on spiritual awareness. Expanding my intuitive abilities was of utmost importance to me, until I learned that there is nothing *out there* that would or could permanently fill my hunger. I had to learn to go within.

We keep looking for something *out there* to calm our restless souls, but there is nothing *out there.* It is all *within.* We have to go within to get in touch with who we really are; to get in touch with our essential Self. Nothing *out there* is going to bring lasting peace; lasting satisfaction. All "things" *out there* will parade endlessly in front of us, changing shape and dimension. One "thing" will be replaced by another "thing," in an endless string of "things," till some of us tire of them all, weary from our search and blasé about each new offering that presents itself.

Even though we use "things" to enhance our lives, when we use "things" to try to fill an empty hole in our hearts, none succeed. Things are only temporary. What make us deliriously happy one moment is forgotten the next. The only *City of Joy* that we find is the one where nothing ever changes; where truth stands alone. We may plead piteously to empty air, but no "thing" will ever be there for us *permanently.* No "one" will ever be there for us *totally.*

We have to learn to rely on our Self; that inner core of our "Be"-ing that is unchanging, that part of us that is connected to the Divine Source.

Have you ever tired of the endless string of possessions with which you fill your life? Bringing more "things" in our lives is not the answer.

October 3

Surviving Joyously

Pansies, planted in the cool months in the fall, learn to weather the winter, blooming whenever the least bit of sunshine coaxes them out. An innate joyousness bursts from within each group of pansies; their little faces beaming up amiably to the onlooker. Even when the face is "missing," the pansy still looks like a face.

No grouping of flowers brings forth more vibrant hues than do these lovely little testaments to God's creative genius. Velvet to the touch – a perfect blend of hue and symmetry – an exquisite range of colors exists in this species, from deepest violet reminiscent of regal robes, to cornflower blue, burnished red, cantaloupe orange, sunny yellow, and seafoam white. What secret mysteries do they hold within themselves? While the rest of the earth is still asleep, pansies present their faces straight to the sun and proclaim joyously: *I am glorious!*

Another survivor species are the violets, whose tenacious blooming – without the least bit of care except from the nature spirits – brings admiration from almost everyone who sees them. In the woodland, they burst forth as soon as the Earth is pungent with the smell of spring. A friend once said that when she was in high school, the only flower she that ever wanted for a corsage – which she never received – was a little bunch of violets. Perhaps she will get her wish one day.

A shady spot in our back yard is covered with moss, along with a prolific spattering of violet leaves. The heart-shaped leaves, growing parallel to the ground below them, resemble café tables set in a moss-covered dance floor. I have often called this area our fairy nightclub, since the presence of fairies is so strong in that particular spot. Before leaving this plane permanently in this lifetime, I pray to be able to see with my physical eyes – what I see so clearly in my mind's eye – the activity that transpires there when no humans are about.

Snow drops, heads bowed, will open even after having survived rain, sleet, or an onslaught of snow during the night. The new light of day is enough to coax them out of their sheltered state where they stand firmly clustered together, heads all bowed in unison. The smallest hint of warmth from the sun relaxes their tight buds, and each one opens a bit, looking like the tiniest bit of angel wings.

Just as persistent are the crocuses, which will bloom peeking out of the snow. No matter how dreary the day or night has been, a bit of bright light is all they need to open their petals and go full throttle into the day. The cold of the night can flatten them, yet even the barest hint of warmth finds them standing bright and firm.

I stand in awe of all of these plants, willing to bloom or to stay in bloom despite inhospitable conditions, proclaiming their joyous right to survive in their brief explosion through life. Some are proud, some are humble, some are brazen, some are bold, and some are just plain survivors. Which are you?

Which flowers draw your attention?
Take every opportunity to admire
flowers, God's Angels on Earth.

October 4

Heart Meditation

(Do this meditation very, very slowly.)

Close your eyes gently and softly.

Take a deep full breath in. Breathe in Love.

Pause four seconds. Exhale all tension, worries and fears.

Take another full deep breath in. Breathe in Joy.

Pause four seconds. Exhale all frustration, regrets, and worry.

Take a third full deep breath. Breathe in Peace. Pause four seconds.

Exhale anxieties and anguish.

(Repeat as many times as necessary.)

Move with the rhythm of your breath, and focus your attention on your heart. Enter into your heart space and look around. See what a majestic instrument your heart really is.

Feel your breath coming in through the center of your heart. See it expand through your arteries, through your veins, through your capillaries to every part of your being. See your heart expand until it is the size of your body. Feel the outer shell of your being melting away. Feel your heart expand to fill your room. Feel your heart expand until it fills your building. Feel your heart expand until it fills your community. Feel your heart expand until it fills your country. Feel your heart expand until it fills your continent. Feel your heart expand until it fills the planet. Feel your heart expand until it fills the solar system. Feel your heart expand until it fills the galaxy. Feel your heart expand until it fills other galaxies. Feel your heart expand as it travels into the Void. Feel your heart expand until it reaches the Central Sun in the center of our Universe.

As you reach the Central Sun, know that you are One with All That Is. Feel your heart mix with the energy of the Central Sun. Rest in that energy for a few minutes, and know that all you are is All That Is. Know that you are One. Know that you are Joy. Know that you are Peace. Know that you are Love. Know that nothing will be kept from you. Know that nothing will be denied you. The power, the majesty, the All of Being is in you. Feel your "Be"-ing filling up with the energy of the Central Sun.

Take another deep breath and gently start to return. See your Self coming back from the Central Sun. See your Self coming back through the Void. See your Self coming back through other galaxies. See your Self coming back through this galaxy. See your Self coming back through this solar system. See your Self coming back through this planet. See your Self coming back into your continent. See your Self coming back through your country. See your Self coming back into your community. See your Self coming back into your building. See your Self coming back into your room. See your Self coming into your body. See your Self coming back into your heart, until you are fully integrated. Rest a moment with these feelings.

Know that you have total freedom to recall the feelings of joy, peace and love whenever and wherever you wish.

Does your sense of calm and peace expand as you work with this meditation?
We use our breath as the instrument to transport ourselves into a state of joy and peace.

October 5

Love, the Power Within

Hope looks outside and waits.
Love looks within and finds the Power of Self.
Anonymous

What can be more empowering than that simple statement? Love, the guiding force of our life, looks within and finds what? Power! Where does that Power come from? Self – the Higher Self that exists in alignment with the Creator! Love stands alone as Master of the Universe; the strength of all who see it, touch it, taste or smell it. We have the power to "be" Love because, in effect, we "are" Love.

The ancient Greeks have thirty-eight names for the word "love," each describing a different state of being. Strangely enough, we have one – "love" – which stands for everything from an esoteric state of ecstasy to the erotic in the physical; from our love for our Creator, to our love for our perfect mate, to our love for a piece of chocolate cake and everything else in between.

How strange our notion of love: we wish love would *befall* on us. Romantic love – love that gratifies the sexual desires of our nature – always yearns for an "other" or needs an "other" to complete it. The Greeks called this form of love *eros*, which forms the root of the word *erotic.* But there is so much more to love than eroticism.

There is brotherly love, or what the Greeks called *agape. Agape* described a brotherly love that had nothing to do with eroticism, and everything to do with fairness and kindness; a moral way of acting toward our fellow man. We were told to "Love our neighbor just as we love ourselves." We learn in metaphysics to love our neighbor because our neighbor *is* our Self.

Once, when I was listening to the sixth presentation of the identical speech in my attempt to gather enthusiasm for selling an independent long distance system – the income which my ego self claimed I needed before I could do my spiritual work – I escaped for a moment and went into the ladies room. Inside, there was a group of young black women who looked so radiant, so polished, and so alive that I asked them what they were there for. They said they were a part of *Agape Ministries* that worked with the poor and disadvantaged. Their brightness only served to increase my sagging Spirit as I left the ladies room and continued to listen to the same dreary speech that I had heard before. No amount of sincere enthusiasm by the presenter made any difference to me. I left the workshop that day, and started to do my spiritual work in earnest. I quit trying to sell the long distance service and quit the real estate franchise to which I belonged. Those ladies in the restroom, *who gave from what they had,* shined from within. I, trying to pursue material riches in order to do spiritual work, was a lost soul. That day stamped itself indelibly on my psyche. Whenever I felt I *did not have enough* money to continue pursuing my goals of following the path of Spirit, the memory of that day would sneak into my mind to help me realize I had everything that I needed.

Sometimes, we trip on our journey through life, stumble and fall, or put a foot out to cause others to stumble and fall, all part of the same effort of *self* to experience *Self.* The biggest joke on this planet is that we think we are separate from God, but God has the last laugh. We are not separate from our Creator, any more than we are separate from the genes that each of our parents contributed to form us. We are one and the same; vested with the same Power, created of the same "stuff" that our Creator is/was/always will be.

We can allow our conscious mind to reflect on what our Spirit mind already knows: since all exists within the mind of God, we are One with God and can simply accept that as our reality within the stillness of our "Be"-ing.

Have you tapped into the Source of Eternal Love within your life? Love is the secret power within each one of us.

October 6

The Power of Music

Most classical music transports me to a different place. All boundaries dissolve. A soft soothing space surrounds me as I enter another time, another place. My body drifts off into a dreamy state, filled with soft clouds and comfort. No stress here. No worry, no constraints, just freedom to express and to be who I am: pure Spirit. No constrictions anywhere, no feeling in my feet nor in my hands, only a feeling of floating in an outer space joining the inner space that connects me with *All That Is*.

Each note dissolves into the next one, transporting me to other places in the cosmos. The notes merge with the molecules of my body as if the notes were salt crystals dissolving in water. Music helps me let go of boundaries; the limits to who I think I am. As my molecules merge with the notes of the music, I am more expansive, more diffuse, more in tune with my "I Am" nature than at any other time. I am "here," yet I am "there"; different, yet still the same.

When salt dissolves in water, the water looks the same but the salt crystals change entirely. The crystals separate into positive and negative ions, which move throughout the water. The water may have a slightly different color, and a different flavor, yet still it is water. What happens to me? As I float out into the Universe, my consciousness is all that reminds me of "me," and I feel a part of *All That Is*. There are no delineations; no "them," no "me." It is all the same. I seem to be holding my breath. I cannot feel the sensation of taking in or expelling air, yet I am fully aware of who I am as I merge into this other state of consciousness, this other state of "Be"-ingness.

Listening to fine classical music has other benefits. A dear friend practices seeing auras while listening to chamber orchestra. She discovered rather quickly that these musicians have very bright auras, and because they are seated against a neutral background, their auras light up rather dramatically. By soft focusing her eyes, she is able to see their auras quite easily.

Teachers have long promoted classical music for its "Mozart effect"; producing brighter minds. Not only are students able to concentrate better, they produce more creative work, solve problems quicker, and respond in a more positive manner.

The next time that you feel absolutely dreary, play a sprightly selection of classical music. You will find your mood changing as the molecules of your body enliven and energize you. Use music not only to entertain yourself, but also to expand into your Higher Self.

Have you noticed how music can alter your state of consciousness? Music is a powerful instrument for expansion.

October 7

A Wrap on the Window

A rap came at the window that roused me from the light sleep into which I had fallen, but no one was there. Was this rap to remind me of my "promise" to say the rosary? During this period each night before I went to bed, no matter how tired I was, I got down on my knees in the guest room – which is set up with a meditation altar and has one of the most peaceful vibrations in our home – to say the rosary, my contribution to expanding peace on this planet. Where did this knock come from, which roused me out of a state of slumber? Could it be the deep yearning of my Soul to be who I really am: a teacher of God, teaching others who they really are? Is this Spirit's way of getting my attention, helping me bring my focus back to what is really important in my life?

There have been other times when Spirit has attempted to rouse my attention, sometimes rather dramatically. I can remember sitting at the computer, typing my first book, when time and space suddenly suspended as I went into an altered space. In my mind's eye, I saw a shroud of linen cloth – loosely wound into a rope around my body – unwrap itself from around me. This continued for about twenty minutes. I sat perfectly still and could not move even if I had wanted to, while this shroud of dirty linen rope unwound itself from my body.

After the experience was over, I asked: *What was that all about?*

The answer was: *Moldy feelings. Feelings trapped within you that no longer serve you. Feelings that have to be released and let go.* I felt a sensation of lightness after these moldy feelings released from me, and was able to continue typing as if nothing had transpired.

Another strange event occurred in the late 1990's. The day that I met Wanda Lasseter-Lundy (the woman who would become my mentor and teacher), she noticed a negative thought form that was suspended in my mental body; a dense cloud of debris suspended within the right side of my energy field. After being told about it, I worked very hard to clear that negative energy out of my energy field, always paying attention to any negativity that would creep into my thoughts and counteracting it with a positive statement or feeling. Each time she saw me she would comment that the negative thought form appeared less dense.

One night, I had barely fallen asleep when I bolted upright in my bed after something went *POP!* The door of the bedroom opened from the inside, and instinctively I knew that the negative thought form had left for good. The next time that I saw Wanda, I asked her to look at my energy field. She did and exclaimed: *It's not there!* My efforts to keep myself positive had cleared the negative thought form from my energy field entirely. I do not know how long it had been there, but probably for a long, long time.

Although my home resonates peace, beauty, harmony, elegance and abundance – fruits in the kitchen and family room, flowers, angels, pictures, plaques, figurines and crystals throughout the home – the most important décor is the décor of my own Soul. Through breathing and setting intent, I do my best each day to clear out the debris within my energy field that may have accumulated during the day in my interactions with others. You can do the same, through deep breathing exercises and by setting your intent. Set aside a time and space for yourself to align with Self; a time and space where you will not be disturbed, where you can cocoon and get into a private place, where time stands still and effort becomes effortless. Do this every morning before you start your day, and every night before you go to bed. You will notice a great difference in the way your day flows.

Have you ever made an effort to clear yourself from the debris of the day? The greatest feeling of all is to go through life "lightly."

October 8

Sacred Geometry: A Point of Light

A point of light radiated out from the Mind of God: the radius was formed. From the edge of the radius, the point moved around three-hundred-sixty degrees, until it returned to the starting place: the circle was formed. The radius looked back over itself beyond the original starting point: the diameter was formed. Two diameters crossed at the center: a cross was formed. The point of light moved out to the edge of the radius and moved three-hundred-sixty degrees around: two circles overlapped each other where their radii touched. After the two circles overlapped each other, the process was repeated until four circles overlapped each other, then twelve circles overlapped each other, then one-hundred-forty-four circles overlapped each other, until the flower of life was formed: the most magnificent symbol of all, because all form originates from it. Thus, sacred geometry was birthed, that which has been called the *Language of Light*; the mysterious, unique, omnipresent connection of all things – the patterns that keep repeating in Nature.

The centers of three circles were connected: the *triangle* was formed. The centers of four circles were connected: the *square* was born. The centers of six circles were connected: the *rectangle* was formed. The centers of five circles – each equidistant from its neighbor – were connected: the *pentagon* was formed. The centers of six circles – each equidistant its neighbor – were connected: the *hexagon* was formed. The centers of eight circles – each equidistant its neighbor – were connected: the *octagon* was formed. The process repeated itself until all the forms of the world came into existence.

Another fascinating form is the *Fibonacci sequence* discovered by the monk Leonardo Fibonacci, who lived his life in a meditative state two hundred and fifty years before Leonardo da Vinci was born. Interesting how they both chose the same first name. Could there be a connection between these two souls? Leonardo Fibonacci noticed, on his walks through the woodlands, that the same numbers kept repeating themselves in flower and leaf petals: 1, 1, 2, 3, 5, 8, 13, 21, 34, 55, 89, and so on. Adding the first two numbers gives you the third number. Adding the second and third numbers gives you the fourth number. Adding the third and forth numbers gives you the fifth number. Adding the fourth and fifth numbers gives you the sixth number, and so on.

These numbers, known as the Fibonacci sequence, when drawn out on graph paper become the *Fibonacci spiral*. There is a corresponding male and female part of the spiral. The male is composed of the square lines, and the female derives from the curved lines connecting the edge of each square. There is another variation of the male and female. If the first line drawn starts at the top of the first square and goes down, then it is known as male; if the first line that is drawn starts at the bottom of the first square and goes up, then it is known as female.

Thus, the spiral would produce the same shape but in a different position.

The *Flower of Life* – the symbol that is the basis of all of all sacred geometry – began its existence as a *point of light* that became the line that moved out from the mind of God, spun into a complete circle, moved to the edge and gave birth to multiple circles, to the cross, to the square, to the rectangle, to the triangle, and to every form in existence, all connected to each other. The *Flower of Life* was formed from a point of light in the mind of God and became the sacred symbol from which *all* life was formed. Multiple *Flowers of Life* are placed in a specific order, with connecting lines between them: the *Tree of Life* was birthed. This sacred symbol is placed over the body to identify the different energy centers of the human body.

Jewish mystery schools use the symbol of the *Tree of Life* to promote their understanding of the *Kabbalah*; their most sacred mystical interpretation of the texts of their religion. Those who studied the Kabbalah in the Jewish mystery schools learned about the characteristics of God. In the past, permission was given only to a few male students; to those specifically selected for their ability to absorb esoteric information. Now, that information is available to all who seek it.

The Kabbalists place within the *Tree of Life* ten characteristics of the quality of God:

Sphere One: the **Crown** (Hebrew name: *Keter* or *Kether*),
Opening to the Will of God.

Sphere Two: **Wisdom** (Hebrew name: *Hochma* or *Chokmah*),
Connecting to God through intuition and synchronicity.

Sphere Three: **Understanding** (Hebrew name: *Binah*),
Reining in the logical mind through discipline and persistence. Spheres Two and Three are connected on opposite sides of the axis

Sphere Four: **Mercy** (Hebrew name: *Hesed* or *Chesod*),

The forbearance to forgive and to be compassionate and kind.

Sphere Five: **Severity** (Hebrew name: *Gevurah* or *Geburah*),

Encompassing strength, decisiveness, and energy.

Spheres Four and Five are connected on opposite sides of the axis.

Sphere Six: **Beauty** (Hebrew name: *Tiferet* or *Tiphareth*),

The energy of Love, balance, and the Christ Consciousness.

Sphere Seven: **Eternity** (Hebrew name: *Nezfed* or *Netzach*),

Relationships bringing energy into being.

Sphere Eight: **Splendor** (Hebrew name: *Hod*),

Communication along with magic.

Spheres Seven and Eight are connected on opposite sides.

Sphere Nine: **Foundation** (Hebrew name: *Yesod*),

Blending the energy of sex, death to the old, transformation to new.

Sphere Ten: **Kingdom** (Hebrew name: *Malkhut*),

The force of the material world granting what your heart desires.

All matter starts out as a point of light; as a beam of consciousness from the Source. All consciousness is connected, thus all matter is connected, since all matter comes from the Source. All form came from the initial point of light that formed the flower of life; a variation of the straight or curved line.

We are Light, and to Light we shall return. Each day brings another opportunity to get closer and closer to core knowledge. Many Spiritual Masters say: *You know all of this. You just have to remember it*, or as Neale Donald Walsch, the author of *Conversations with God,* phrases it: *re-member it.*

Do you hunger for new knowledge that was not readily available before? We can each open ourselves to receive whatever our own hearts validate as right for us.

October 9

Resilience and Rebounding

No parent should have to endure the loss of their child. No human should have to endure the loss of their own home. My parents endured both.

A year after they married, my mother gave birth to a lovely little boy; a child so sweet and so gifted that at the age of eleven months, he played a little tune on a harmonica placed to his lips. This was at the start of World War II, and my parents lived in a small village known as Tomaszów Lubelski in Poland, in the home of my father's parents. During a bitter winter day, his mother and his oldest sister insisted on bathing the baby *against* my mother's wishes. The baby caught pneumonia and died.

My mother never got over the death of her infant. Until the day she died, tears would come into her eyes whenever she spoke of him. Regardless of the pain from the memories of her first-born, the kindness she always exhibited to her mother-in-law and her sister-in-law planted the seed of forgiveness in me.

Shortly after they celebrated their twenty-fifth wedding anniversary, at a time when their lives were comfortable enough that they considered buying a little vacation home on one of Michigan's many lakes, they were the victims of a land subsidence.

At 3 a.m. on a September morning in 1965, a huge sound – similar to a car crash – woke them up. Frantically, my mother rushed to look down towards the basement, which was starting to cave in. She rushed outside, trying to wake the neighbors. They thought something was wrong with her. No one heard anything. She rushed back into the home to get everyone out of the house. Within less than a minute after my grandmother was outside, the front stoop dropped three feet. Miraculously, no one broke a leg. All six of them – mother, father, two sisters, one brother and a grandmother – were all standing outdoors in the cold damp air, numb, barely able to comprehend what was happening to them.

The ground continued to subside until a cavern – thirty feet deep and twenty feet wide – opened up. They had to relocate to a home in the neighborhood, and became tenants for the first time in their lives in America.

More bad news was to come. The insurance company refused to pay any of the cost of transporting the home to another lot, or to help them build another home, because they said it was *An Act of God,* which would not be covered under the policy. The home that they owned – a home that my father had built on land that another member of his family had purchased for investment – had originally been a landfill for the city of Grand Rapids, Michigan. At my father's funeral, one of his neighbors told me that as a small child, they called that lot the "mystery spot," because anything that they left on that place disappeared. Each item placed on the spot was never there when they came back the next day to check on it.

To add insult to injury, the town of Grand Rapids – which had sold the lot to the developer for one dollar, stipulating that it was sold *at your own risk* – insisted that my father continue to pay the taxes on the property at the same rate at which the other homes were taxed, as if it were a valuable piece of land. He kept it mowed and cleared, and periodically had to put more fill dirt in as each new fissure opened up.

One week after the original fissure opened up, I came home from the University of Michigan, walked into the kitchen and witnessed my father sitting at the kitchen table, not saying anything, a distant look on his face. He looked like a tired old lion, wondering what to do with the devastation around him. He had always resembled Cary Grant, but not now. He looked ten years older than the last time I had seen him, just a few weeks before.

It took my parents a full year before they were able to move back into their own home. Through their own efforts, they transported their home to a new lot, and eventually recovered not only the value of their home, but built two more new homes – the last one a brand new, full brick home in a lovely location on the gentle crest of a hill on the west side of town. One of my mother's life goals had been to own a full brick home. She happily lived in it for two years, before she died of ovarian cancer at age fifty-nine.

Once, she was lamenting her fate that she did not listen to her inner voice that had kept telling her to "uciekaj z tego domu" (*run away from this home*); a warning which began within six months after the family moved in.

I asked her what she would have done had she sold the home and this same thing happened to the new owners. Would she have given the money back to the people who experienced this?

She answered: "Yes."

She never raised the lament again, realizing that she would have been victimized one way or another.

Through it all, their faith sustained them and gave them both the endurance and the resilience to continue. Except for a thousand dollar offering from the collection taken at the local church, my parents only had each other to rely upon, and they had to rescue themselves.

There are daily examples in the media of people who lose all, but who still rebuild. Some have massive financial aid; some have none. Those who recover their lives without any financial assistance at all – or with a pittance of aid as my parents did – find an inner reserve that pulls them through.

From the determination that both my parents exhibited to NOT allow this incident to crush them, the seed of resilience and persistence was planted in me. No matter how bleak a situation was, I learned to continue moving forward; to continue to work, put new in place of the old, salvage what I could, and dig out from under – no matter what. From my parent's experience with their home, I learned to never give up. I learned resilience, resourcefulness, and rebounding.

Little did I know how important all those virtues would be in my future.

Have you had a life experience that felt as if it would devastate you? Our greatest strengths come through our lowest points.

October 10

Turning Inward

There is a little known part of our energy anatomy that my teacher, Wanda Lasseter-Lundy, introduced to our ministers. These little known mechanisms are called "receptors," and they exist in our energy field, encircling the brow area. To those who can see the energy field, these receptors resemble small discs which circle our head approximately three inches away from our physical bodies, and are attached to points in our crown. These receptors can be turned inwards or outwards, upwards or down, and can be willfully controlled by the direction on which we focus and concentrate.

When our receptors are turned inwards, we receive messages from Spirit about ourselves. We turn our receptors inwards to receive the message from our own Soul to bring peace and calm back into our lives. To turn inwards, we need to go into a quiet space – no phones, no faxes, no meetings, no agenda – and simply retreat away from all the noise, the commotion, and the clamor that the world throws at us, in order to bring clarity into our lives. We practice doing this by visualizing it.

When our receptors are turned outwards, we receive messages about everyone else. To receive information regarding others, the receptors can be turned outward and up for information about the future, outward and forward to receive information about the present, or outward and downward to receive information about the past. Again, we do this through visualization.

Whether we turn the receptors inward or outward, whether we receive information about and for ourselves or for another, the one who guides us is our Higher Self. How do we learn to trust our Higher Self? By listening to the dictates of our own Soul – our own Spirit, our own heart – when it guides us with messages of unconditional Love. Much to the chagrin of our egos, our Higher Self encourages us to act with unconditional Love.

When we allow our Higher Self to guide us, we will always be in conflict with our ego selves. What we hear may come from Higher Self and may be for our highest good, but it will not be what the ego self wants to hear, for the guidance often will ask for a course of action that is extremely upsetting to our ego. What we hear may not be easy, but may be best for our spiritual development. What our ego self considers to be our greatest disaster, our Higher Self may consider our greatest triumph.

In the third dimension, we experience a complete feeling of separation from our Creator, until we decide to experience something else. Our earliest actions are generally guided by the ego, since most of us have no memory of our union with our Creator. The evolutionists, in conjunction with scientists, are in disagreement with the creationists. However, individual theories are starting to link back together towards Divine Intelligence; a natural order of existence on this planet, similar to what various Masters (including Pythagoras) proclaimed all along. There are many other *truths* that Masters have brought to Earth – spirited away in monasteries and in caves around the world – which are now slowly surfacing; truths all celebrating the oneness of all things.

We think that we are all separate from God. We are not. We think that we are alone. We are not. We think that we are material matter only. We are not. *Love is what we are.* Love is what we were created from. Love is what we were created by. The Source of All Creation is pure Love. We are so much more than we think that we are. We are One and we are All; both at the same time. We are a little piece of the whole and we are the whole, just as in a hologram.

By turning inward – forming a quiet space and noticing the perfection there – whatever rattles and upends us can be smoothed out. We can bring ourselves back to homeostasis with our intent to do so.

Start to set aside a certain time to cocoon – to commune with the interior of your own Soul – the same time each day, for at least twenty minutes,

When is the last time you set aside time for your own Soul? We must do whatever it takes to free up some moments to commune with our Self.

October 11

The Master's Lesson

Dry your tears and blow your nose. You are okay. You are safe. The world cannot hurt you. Even if someone or something else takes away your ability to function in your earth suit (your body), you will get another one whenever you choose. You do not leave this plane one second before your subscribed time. Nothing is by accident; nothing is by chance.

The Master certainly proved that to you. That was the message of his life: no matter what "they" did to mutilate his body, "they" could not kill him. His Spirit lived and he materialized another body to be with his disciples for a while. You, too, eventually will learn how to live according to the laws of Spirit, and you, too, will learn how to manifest another body at will. You can take as many lifetimes as you wish to learn these lessons. And until you learn the lessons of Spirit, you can choose to be in any drama that you desire, until you no longer desire it.

Shed the guilt, the anger, the bitterness, the sorrow, the hurt, the sense of injustice and outrage. Shed all the negative emotions that you use to keep yourself bound in chains. Shed all the pain and resentment against which you rail. They are only mirrors to you, to show you that which is still unhealed within yourself. Shed them all.

Shed all attempts by the "others" to keep you small and insignificant, and step into the greatness of who you really are. Do not cower under criticism and ridicule. Criticism and ridicule are only ploys by others to mask their insecurity, which stems from fear. Do not allow the fear of others to dictate limitations to you, or keep you from exploring your highest potential. No one else can make these fears miraculously go away from you, but you can make them miraculously go away from yourself.

All of the named and unnamed fears are symptoms of an underlying fear that you are not loved. That is at the base of all of your fears: that you are not loved and are not lovable.

No matter what role you have chosen for yourself on this plane, each of you is an expression of the Divine; the Creator experiencing It Self. Each of your creations – the light and the dark – no matter how much the ego wants to judge the dark as "bad," are part of an expression of the Creator. It is all God. You choose the dark expressions in order to illuminate them; to bring them to the Light. If they do not make you feel good, then, hopefully, you will not choose them again.

When you fully accept that you are a creator "Be"-ing, then you realize that you create everything that is in your sphere. You have control of your attitude about what you create. Your attitude determines whether or not to do something about your negative thoughts or the negativity that you witness. Your attitude determines whether or not you will stay stuck in negative emotions, or will move forward in positive emotions. Your attitude determines your course of action towards negative deeds; whether or not you wish to get involved.

Can you accept both the light and the dark as part of the same God? Accepting all the lessons of our lives brings us into a calmer state.

October 12

Message from Your Guides

We, your Guides, are doing our utmost to help you recognize the truth of your "Be"-ing. We are bombarding you with spiritual messages, but are doing it observantly so as to not overload your circuits, which have to be "seasoned" carefully. In the same manner in which you acclimate a plant into a new environment, you acclimate yourself into the higher vibrations of Self – a little at a time. Otherwise you go on overload and do not know how to utilize the information that you receive. You misinterpret the messages that you receive, and look for sources outside of yourself to fill the needs of these messages. You look to "others" to fill the needs of your Soul, when all you need to do is to look within.

When you fully activate your Light Body, you can spread out energetically for miles. Right now, you have just stepped out of your cocoon and have just started to spread your wings. They are barely dry, but you already are noticing that there is something different about you. You are no longer bound to the Earth; trapped in this chunky body. You recognize that your energy field can change shape, can become clear or fuzzy, can be a well-defined exterior or can twist into tentacles that seek to wrap themselves around an "other." Your control over your energy field comes from your thoughts.

Your new sleek and slender body has appendages fastened to them. And Yes! They are wings. You are going to learn to fly. Also, you do not have to spend your lifetime alone in a cave on top of a mountain to do it. You have already done that. That lifetime is behind you. You are going to learn to fly at the same time that you are tending to your ordinary work at home, at the office, on the farm, or in the factory. You are going to learn how to fly because somewhere in the back of your mind, you know you can! You know that the limitations that you place on yourself come from nowhere else except yourself. Thus, you are going to shed those limitations just as easily as you shed a coat when it gets too warm. You simply take it off.

It is your intent that sets the tone for your day; your intent to see all of humanity as brothers and sisters, no matter what. Everything that you set in motion, you do with intent. Set your intent for the highest possible outcome for the highest potential that you carry within you for this lifetime. Then, do the work that is necessary to achieve that intent.

Nothing can stop you. You are on a roll. The period of initiation is ending. You are stepping out with your newly-formed bodies – the cells that are awakening to who you really are – and you are glorious! And with these newly-formed bodies, you set the intent to reach your highest potential, and only you know what that is.

A new day is dawning. With each ray of increasing light, your awareness is growing. You are Love. You embrace Love. Nothing else matters. Not judgment, not ridicule, not debasement, not rage. They are all manifestations of FEAR (False Evidence Appearing Real), which you are shedding. You are also shedding all manifestations of EGO (Edging God Out).

You are on a roll!

May Peace be with you.

You are on a roll!

Have you noticed any changes in your life recently; changes elevating you? We can consciously choose to become aware of the momentum for change around us.

October 13

A Change of Perspective

Some days we feel that everything has conspired to irritate us. While some irritants need to be removed immediately, others can produce items of great value. While a grain of sand in our eye needs to be flushed out as fast as possible, a grain of sand in the oyster eventually becomes a prized possession to man. When irritants seem to fill our day, please consider that just as the oyster produces a pearl because of an irritant, so can something magnificent – or inspiring, or life-altering – be produced from the things that irritate us. We have the option of staying in pain from our irritants, or of asking to see the benefit.

Did you have a mother or father who belittled you every chance s/he got? What conceivable benefit could come to you from that type of behavior? Did their entire lack of consideration for your feelings help make you into a kind and compassionate individual? Possibly you learned how *not* to treat your daughter, your son, or anyone else.

Perhaps you had just spent a previous lifetime filled with your own self-importance; one in which your ego needed to be stroked for everything that you did. Perhaps you criticized the actions of all those around you. Maybe your power base was so strong that no one dared cross you. What better balance than to choose a lifetime where someone close to you – someone who should be loving and nurturing – does nothing but belittle you? This change of perspective can free you from future traumatic lives, when you have such horrible memories of your past.

Did the person who belittled you so cruelly in this lifetime become dependent upon you at the end of their life? Maybe your soul decided you were ready for a plethora of spiritual gifts before your former tormentor left this plane. Possibly your soul had chosen additional lessons in *forgiveness*, along with *tolerance*, *compassion*, and *understanding*. Is it possible that you came from the Angelic realm to have an earthly experience? Did you choose to come here to anchor more light on this plane?

Perhaps the person whom you married criticized your every movement, action, and spoken word to the extent that you began to doubt your own sanity. Could it be that one of the virtues that you wished to strengthen for yourself in this lifetime was *to set boundaries*? If so, this may have been an area in which you were previously weak.

Had you agreed, before you entered this lifetime, to be a *mirror* to someone else? Possibly all the criticisms that were ladled on you reflected the insecurities and fears that the "other" had; insecurities and fears they could not accept about themselves. Your spirit knew that the strength of your personality would be able to ward off the blows of the criticisms of others. A change of perspective could now help you get beyond the immediate issues of what went "wrong."

Sit for fifteen minutes with the image of the oyster and the pearl that it produces as the result of its "irritant," and listen for the messages from what irritates you. Evaluate your life from a higher perspective. Ask for help from the Angelic realm to see things differently. Maybe all the pain that you feel was for reasons that have eluded you before, but will now make sense to you.

Can the irritant in your life help you bring forth your greatest gift? Evaluate "opportunities" as they present themselves, and see the hand of God in them.

October-14

The Lost Mode of Prayer

More things are wrought by prayer than this world dreams of.

Alfred Lord Tennyson

In *The Lost Mode of Prayer,* Gregg Braden spoke of a prayer of gratitude for what is *already* accomplished, rather than what was wished to be accomplished. He told a story of one of his friends, a Native American, who performed a ceremony thanking the Great Spirit for the rain *that had already fallen* in an area where there was tremendous draught. And, miraculously, after the ceremony, it poured rain until the ground was saturated. This young Native understood the concept of gratitude for something *as if it were already an accomplished fact*. In effect, he practiced the "Lost mode of prayer."

When we pray, we change the energy of that for which we pray. If we pray with gratitude for the abundance in our lives even when we do not feel abundant, we bring the abundance forward by our very ability to be grateful for it. The same rule applies to everything else. The lost mode of prayer can be applied to anything that we wish to manifest.

In Spirit, all communication is telepathic and there is no time. The yogi masters understand this. Indigenous people understand this. Mastery of this concept is the mastery with which miracles are accomplished. If we can understand the lost mode of prayer, and pray for that which is – on some level – already an accomplished fact, then we, too, can see miracles in our lives.

There are other modes of prayers. Most of us pray for something or someone at some point in our lives. We are all familiar with *Prayers of Petition*. These are prayers asking for that which we want to happen or to have. We perceive a lack, in our own situation or in that of others, and we wish for that lack to be corrected. Prayers of petition are pretty common, for we learned these prayers from the time that we learned how to pray. Then, there are *Prayers of Gratitude.* In these prayers, we open our hearts to express gratitude for that which was received, what was avoided, and what was accomplished. We express gratitude for our station in life, our blessings, our life force, our energy, our goals, and our heart's desire. We express gratitude for our health, for our daily lives, for the people who support our lives (the invisible people behind the scenes who make our lives work), for our safety and for the comfort of those whom we love. We express gratitude for this beautiful planet that we call our home, and for the Universe as we know it.

There are *Prayers of Acceptance*, when we did not receive that for which we petitioned. We ask to be able to look at situations differently; to come from another perspective. We ask to be enlightened about our blockages; to see things clearly. We ask not to be resigned to accept things as they are if we are able to change them, and ask for the courage to make the necessary changes. We thank God for the compliment when we are sent bigger burdens than we think we can bear. We ask for the strength to go on in spite of major setbacks.

Other very powerful prayers are the *Prayers of Adoration*, *of Joy*, and *of Exultation* to the eternal Spirit from whence we came. We express bliss to the Divine for the state that we are in. We acknowledge God in all of the forms in which God manifests, and ride a wave of joy into all phases of our lives.

Communing with Spirit through various modes of prayer brings us the greatest joy, the greatest freedom, and the ability to release the confines, restrictions, and rules that man imposes on us. Ultimately, we learn to sit in silence and to communicate without words.

Why is the Lost Mode of Prayer so important?
Prayers bring us comfort, joy, solace, and gratitude.

October 15

Stepping into Power

(Dream Journal 7/13/00)

I saw the seven dimensions of the planet Earth as I traveled on a laser beam of light with a friend who has shared my path. Each dimension held a different color. First, there were hints of color; light-hued shades of green and blue that affected what we saw. The light changed; became more intensely golden, white gold, then white. The gray cloud encompassing us was parted by the laser beam. Each dimension was in the same space, yet each dimension was separate.

The laser beam was the vehicle that we used. Our consciousness intact, we moved forward on that laser beam of light. We kept examining clouds, other areas of light, and some scenes from the planet; all of which are lost to me now. The dream ended.

Some dreams bring insight and clarity into confusing aspects or our lives; some bring more mystery. This dream seems to be a validation of so much of what a group of my friends and I have been talking about recently: seven dimensions of planet Earth, all existing at the same time and in the same place. Recent programs on television about string theory have aired this very possibility.

Does this not encourage me to stretch my concept of who I am and why am I here? I, the human, am the most powerful of all the beings that have been created. To paraphrase Marianne Williamson: *It is not my littleness I fear, it is my power.* Power brings with it responsibility. As long as I subscribe to "littleness," I have an excuse; a reason to be small. By accepting my power, I have to step up to the podium – up to the plate – and prove myself. When I connect to and acknowledge my power, I enter a new place of responsibility.

Why do it? Why take a chance? Why leave for the public arena instead of staying in my nice private comfort zone? What if I do not measure up? But what if I succeed? What if I step up to the podium and discover that I meet the challenge? What if I step up to the plate and hit the home run? With Spirit on my side, all my efforts are *assisted*; are guided, are validated, and are confirmed. I have all the power to be who I really want to be!

So do you! You do have the capability to reach out beyond what you thought was humanly possible. Your limitations are self-imposed. Your fears are self-inflicted. You do not need to bow to the crucible of commonality. Your Spirit is not homogenized; neither do you have to be.

Every day brings a new light and new opportunity. Start NOW.

Why is it so difficult for us to accept the powerful part of our selves? Power brings responsibility.

October 16

Expanding into Spirit's Work

During my fourth energy healing session, my teacher/healer said to me, "Now, you do me." I got up off the table and stood behind her as she lay down. She guided me and had me say a prayer for assistance from the Spiritual realm. She asked me to "open" her up etherically, and told me where to place my hands and proceeded to guide me through my first healing session.

I proceeded to tell her what I saw and felt. It never dawned on me to say, *I can't do it. I don't know how. I don't know enough.* I continued to work with her for the next half-hour and felt very settled, as if I knew exactly what I was doing. On some level, I had done this work many times, and was simply tapping into the cell memory of what had happened in the "past."

My Higher Self knew it was not restricted by time and space. Rather, it unceasingly existed in an everlasting NOW! No barriers here. Fortunately, I had been in communication with my Higher Self often enough to know that when I got up off the table to work on my teacher/healer, I never questioned whether I could do the work. I just did it. I simply asked her to guide me, to tell me what I was to do next, which she did. Now, as I think back, it was an experience of amazing grace.

Outside of this dimension, there is no time. Everything exists in a continuous NOW. Therefore, the past is the present is the future. We are able to tap into the resources of what we have learned in the past since it is all part of our cell memory. We are able to tap into whatever skills we learned along the way. Nothing is lost. It is stored away for reference anytime we wish to retrieve it.

Within each of us is a low flame that will not go out; an eternal flame that is being kept alive by the feeling that we are to make some notable contribution to humanity on behalf of the Spiritual realm. This feeling is stronger in some than in others. For some, this translates into being of service; ministering to the physical needs of mankind. Others feel led to give healing ministry to the mental, emotional, or spiritual needs of mankind, possibly to speak in front of groups sharing the message of Spirit, to write books to inspire others, or to record music or messages of inspiration. Each responds to their call to service in their own way.

Some people agree to work with those of a lower vibration; with those who have given up on the goodness of life – people who have been imprisoned in a life of crime and violence, people who are stuck in addictions which erupt in savage behavior, or with people who commit reprehensible acts. Others choose to work with people of a higher vibration; one that will raise the vibration of all who come in contact with them. Either choice is good. Either choice raises the vibrational level of the recipient, who can then, in turn, raise the vibration of all those with whom they come into contact.

The best advice that my sales manager - who ultimately became my second husband - gave me when I was a fledging real estate agent, was: "No matter how little you think you know, they know less."

As a new agent, that advice served me well, until my confidence grew as I learned more and more about the many aspects of my business. This and other advice he gave me impressed me enough to later become his wife.

When teaching about the Spiritual realm, I have to remember that my Higher Self is always prepared. I am taking the plunge, just as I did in real estate in 1972. The message that Spirit conveys to me, which I wish to convey to everyone else is: *YOU KNOW IT ALL. You just have to remember it.*

Today, there are many out there who know much about the Spiritual realm and energy healing techniques. New energy healing modalities are being re-discovered continuously, and you may be one of those who has special insights to share. If you find yourself bobbing your head in agreement, or disagreement, with what is being said by the instructor of a class that you are attending, then it is up to you to share what you know. If you know as much, if not more, information as the instructor does, then it is time for you to seek the podium and get up to the front of the group. It is time for you to become a *teacher of God.* Regarding the question of "who is a teacher of God?" the *Manual for Teachers* in *A Course in Miracles* states "[a teacher is] anyone who chooses to be one." Someone does not choose you. You choose yourself.

If you are learning to live consciously, and find yourself repeatedly getting into situations that strengthen conscious living, then you may need to share those techniques with others. If you find yourself struggling, constantly pulling yourself up and forward, refusing to give up, you may need to share those lessons and those techniques that sustain you so that others may learn from you. The time to bring newcomers into the realm of spiritual development is so short. It is time to *re-member*, not only for your personal enrichment but also to share it with your fellow travelers on this planet.

There are so many who hunger for word about Spirit as they awaken to an inner knowledge through revelation. So many are accepting their role as a "spiritual 'Be'-ing having a human experience," and are doing whatever it takes to find their spiritual roots in a world that seems hostile to them. The Bible succinctly states: "Man shall not live by bread alone, but by every word that proceedeth out of the mouth of God." (Matthew 4:4), but it does not clarify that the *word* is within. Eventually, though, every man will awaken to that understanding.

We need to nourish our spiritual bodies as well as our physical bodies since a much greater part of us exists in Spirit than exists in physical form. Our physical body is the tiniest part of who we are. Much of the time, we keep our physical body busy to the point of exhaustion. I certainly have. The time for that to stop is NOW. By alternating between the items that enrich our life spiritually as well as physically, through our focus and concentration, we can bring harmony and balance into our lives.

Do you feel that you have too much to do with your life to waste it keeping it busy doing things that no longer enhance your spiritual growth or the spiritual growth of others? Are you keeping yourself "busy" to the point of exhaustion? The time to stop that is NOW! Leave time daily for that which enhances your Spirit.

Are you being shifted and called to do Spirit's work? Only we can allow our new interests to root and grow.

October 17

Release and Restoration - a Visualization Technique

Why is it so important that we learn about visualization? Outside of this dimension, all communication is telepathic. Creation comes into being through visualization. Everything that we create outside of this dimension is done through visualization. Just as quickly as we imagine it, it appears. All the work is mental.

I have read that there are souls in other dimensions who beg to come to this dimension to "get a break" from all their creations because they continue to create at the same vibrational level that they created with while on this Earth. Since most people seem to concentrate on the negative, when they leave this dimension, they continue to create negative situations around themselves in whatever dimension to which they go. If they are continuously surrounded by negativity, is it any wonder that they beg to come to this dimension to get a "break" from their creations?

Release and Restoration is a visualization technique that we can use to bring the maximum amount of spiritual energy back into our bodies. We can tap into the realm of all possibility, and focus and concentrate on that which we wish to accomplish at the moment. We can learn to clear our ego selves from all negative thoughts lurking within our energy fields through the visualization technique called *Release and Restoration:*

Start by bringing in a mental image of the spinning vortexes within you; the energy centers that fuel you – the chakras. See each chakra stacked one on top of each other, from the crown down to the root. Release debris from your chakra column by bringing in a tornado of brilliant white light down through your crown chakra, down through your brow chakra, down through your throat chakra, down through your heart chakra, down through your solar plexus chakra, down through your sacral chakra, and down through your root chakra. Watch as all the specks comes flying out of each chakra. Release all the debris that may be hiding from the events of the day, events from other dimensions, other time frames, or events from parallel lives in this dimension.

The white light spins very fast and can move as quickly or as leisurely as you desire, down through your chakras. The debris that is loosened and spun out is gathered and transported out of this dimension by the *Purple Transformational Flame of St. Germaine*. See the debris being escorted to its next level of evolution. Then ask that the maximum amount of energy your body can hold be given to you during this period of restoration.

I had to clear negativity out of my energy field, for it was holding me back from doing what I knew to be my soul contract: to teach about God. The first time that I spoke from my heart to a general audience at the National Speaker's Association, D C Chapter, I was so scared that my hands shook, since my topic was about being a Spirit having a human experience; sensing energy and chakras. It was way too broad a range for a five-minute speech. A deathly quiet permeated the room when I finished, but soon three people rushed up to talk to me.

The comments on my feedback sheet ranged from: "You are an Angelic Being, to: What was your point?"

I get up with such aplomb now, for the audience at our church, Rays of Healing, is very recipient to hearing about messages of Spirit. Every time I step up to the center stage, my confidence increases, for each subsequent teaching and coaching session has given me more maturity and clarity. I have learned to accept the words that come to me as divinely inspired, to trust the images that come into my head, to trust the feelings that come through my hands, and have learned how to direct the flow of Divine energy that flows through me into the person on the table. Trust in God increases when clearing techniques such as release and restoration are applied to clear blockages, for we learn through necessity.

I trust God and I trust my Higher Self. My ego self – my personality self – has learned to follow. When my ego self merges with my Higher Self, I have a perfect day, no matter what hassles, what problems, or what anxieties are thrown my way. My Higher Self knows what to do; my ego self follows and all is in harmony. When my personality self gets rattled, when the situation merits super-human coping strategies, I bring Spirit into matter by clearing, centering, aligning, and balancing my inner being. The process of visualization helps me move forward, and brings back a sense of equilibrium, peace and calm into my body.

Through the process of *Release and Restoration*, our bodies can get back into equilibrium. We can bring Spirit into matter.

Have you needed help for recent challenges? We can trust that Spirit is guiding us to the right events for maximum growth.

October 18

Unconditional Love

Unconditional Love states: *I love you no matter what.* I love you no matter how much you earn, who you date, who you marry, what your choice of career is, where you live, what color your skin is, whether any of your teeth are crooked or missing, what your religious preference is, what teams you follow, how much you weigh, what profession you hold, whether you are educated or not, or what you did. *No matter what, I Love You.*

Unconditional Love states: you do not have to agree with me, follow my belief patterns, look like me, act like me, think like me. You can be exactly who you really are because who you are is perfect.

Unconditional Love accepts all things as part of the Divine Plan and above all, does not judge. Unconditional Love accepts any path that we take to God/Source/Prime Creator as valid. Our path is assigned to us by our Higher Self before we incarnate on this planet and our outcome is assured. Whatever path we take to God is perfect. Unconditional Love states that there are as many paths to God as there are beings on the planet, and each path is the "correct" one.

Look at the word love, reverse the letters of the word and add another "v" and "e" at the end. We have just created the word "evolve." When we love, we evolve into something bigger than what we are right now. To practice unconditional Love is to expand into the aspect of the Divine that is much bigger than the personality self through which we experience our lives.

The Master who came here two thousand years ago taught unconditional Love and changed the course of history. A few in the world were ready for him then, and a few more are ready for him now, despite much evidence to the contrary. Yet, unconditional Love seems to be a foreign concept to most of the cultures of the world. The prevailing mentality of the world says that I love you only if you agree with me. I love you, therefore, I can control you. I love you, therefore, I am right and you are wrong. I love you and I am in charge of you – body and soul. Very few cultures encourage unconditional Love between the races or even between the sexes.

The pets that we cherish teach us about unconditional Love. Eventually, all people will turn to unconditional Love as the guiding force in their life. Now, only the enlightened do. Remember, the only four letter word we need to know is LOVE.

Can you accept that unconditional Love is part of who you really are? Practice unconditional Love towards at least one family member.

October 19

Co-incidence

A friend called me today, and I greeted her with this message:

"I was just talking about you to a fellow minister who is very close to Mother Mary. I gave her a picture of the Blessed Mother of Emmitsburg, and suggested that we go to the Lourdes Grotto at Mt. St. Mary in Emmitsburg, Maryland. I told my fellow minister about the picture that I had given you, and how much you liked it. After presenting her with a picture of Our Lady of Emmitsburg, I told her about you and your family and the ordeals two of your sons had gone through."

My friend kept exclaiming: "Oh my God! Oh my God!"

The reason that she was calling was to invite *me* to go with her to Emmitsburg; to the church where the Blessed Mother had been appearing.

That was exactly the way I had opened my conversation with her. Now it was my turn to say, "Oh my God! Oh my God!"

The two of us were having identical conversations; mine out loud and hers in thought – an interesting co-incidence. Co-incidences are "God's way of staying anonymous" – a piece of wisdom (anonymously) stated by one person and shared by many through the web.

This neat co-incidence of intention led us to select going to Emmitsburg on November 11, Veteran's Day. Who knows? Maybe there were some veteran souls who needed extra prayers. The Catholic Church petitions us to pray for the souls of those who have left us. How many veteran souls, from how many wars, could benefit from our prayers? Was that just a cosmic co-incidence to have us send the veteran souls light and love; to help them move on to their next state of cosmic evolution?

My friend spoke of many things, and coincidences were among them. She spoke of how things were disappearing in her home; things that she knew were there. Try as hard as she might, she had no explanation for what disappeared.

I felt those disappearances were Spirit's way of trying to get her attention. I had had similar experiences, but some of my things disappeared, then re-appeared. As each thing disappeared, I became annoyed, but heard the "voiceless voice" inside my head state: *Everything that is yours will be returned to you.*

Totally true. A pair of glasses – ones that I threw on the front seat of the car once I had arrived at my destination – were nowhere to be found upon my return. They disappeared, but then gently rolled out on the floor of the back seat over a year later. However, not everything that has ever belonged to me has yet shown up. While I was riding with one of my sisters, a tube of lipstick disappeared in mid-air as it slid between the car seat and the floor of the car. No matter how carefully we looked, no tube of lipstick was ever found. It has yet to re-appear. Currently, my sunglasses are missing. Just as before, I will get them back as soon as the world of Spirit is ready to release them.

Watch for the co-incidences that appear in your life, and the messages that accompany them.

Have you had an interesting co-incidence recently? Co-incidences are Spirit's way of getting us to pay attention.

October 20

Trust Your Feelings

You have a built-in mechanism that is a guiding light for you: your feelings. Trust your feelings; your inner connection to Spirit, your foolproof guidance system (FGS). Most of the time, you ignore your feelings, discounting them as irrelevant – until you get a wake-up call that flattens you. If all the signs are there for you to move out of one corner and into another, you have to learn to trust your feelings to guide you. When you no longer *feel good* about the situation you are in, move on.

Your feelings come from your Creator, and are endowed with the Power of Love. Love is the Power that fuels the Universe; the glue that keeps the Universe together. You tap into that power when you trust your feelings.

You cannot control the circumstances when remarks from a "shrill shrieking ego" are being hurtled at you. But you can control your reaction to them, by drawing on Real Power. When an event happens that cuts you off at the knees, the fabric of your energy field is ripped open. When you recognize that you are losing power to a circumstance, a remark, or an event beyond your control, let it go! Let it all go!

Let the feelings that are welling up inside of you go; feelings of insecurity, shame, bewilderment, guilt, rage. Let them *all* go! Do not stuff these feelings back into yourself. As you let the energy of these negative feelings go, you will feel a release of energy that can sometimes be rather dramatic. You may feel a POP out of your body, you may feel drained, or you may feel lightheaded.

Feelings are energy, and they bring dis-ease if they are not released. You release these negative feelings by allowing them to course through your body. It generally takes twenty minutes. If you stuff the feelings back into your body, or deny their existence because you are not willing to give twenty minutes of expression to them, then you set yourself up for all manner of future problems.

By letting the feelings run through your body, you allow them expression of being. *Your feelings are your feelings.* Not allowing yourself to feel them brings rage within your body; rage that will come spewing out at a future date. You cannot deny your feelings. By giving them expression for twenty minutes, you release them.

Even if you are publicly chastised, reprimanded, or humiliated, you will survive. Trust me. You will not die. Public censure does not mean the end of your being. You can continue to stay in your power! When you feel battled and bewildered, let the feelings course through your body, then bring the energy of Real Power down through your crown chakra to stabilize your emotions. You are able to survive any situation by drawing on Real Power; the power from the Divine Source, the unlimited power of the Universe. Once you calm your frazzled self down, you will feel – through your energy field – the energy of Real Power.

Spirit reminds us to give back to Spirit our feelings of littleness, our fears, our doubts, our insecurities, and our feelings of inadequacy to be transformed for us. We are asked to send these feelings through the *Purple Transformational Flame of St. Germaine*, which transmutes and sends them onto their next level of evolution. As these feelings rise up in us, do not stuff them back down – this is the natural tendency – but rather move them out.

As we *feel* our feelings and move them out of our bodies, we feel entirely lighter and clearer.

When was the last time you allowed the full expression of your feelings? We can each give ourselves every opportunity to rid our bodies of negative feelings.

October 21

Emotionally-Charged Energy

Everything has energy. You co-create by harnessing energy. In order to think, you harness energy. In order to speak, you harness energy. If you are speaking in what you perceive is an emotionally-charged situation, you rein in even more energy. The energy that you employ then has to be dissipated. You either send it out of your body, or you internalize it. If you send it out of your body, it may end up in your energy field. You are still not safe, because that energy can work its way down the different layers of your energy field into your physical body, and eventually become disease. Dis-ease produces disease.

If you are speaking and your ability to speak is cut off, you may feel as if you have been attacked in your solar plexus; in your third chakra from which your third subtle body (the mental body) emanates. An emotional attack on your solar plexus can be equally as painful as a physical attack. The energy that attacks you can cause you to double over in pain, in much the same way that a physical blow can cause you to double over in pain. Furthermore, the fifth chakra and fifth mental body can also feel attacked, since the chakras are linked to each other. You feel you are not being heard; that no one is willing to listen to you.

If you are attacked emotionally, energy can leak from you in the same manner that it would if you were physically cut and spouting blood. In addition, the fabric of your energy field can be *ripped,* which can be very painful indeed. Your ability to function "normally" – when your energy field is ripped – is severely impaired. Furthermore, you go into a state of shock. In your effort to stabilize yourself, you may say to your ego self that what happened "does not really matter." You try as hard as you can to convince your ego self, usually without much success. So, you bury your hurt and pain under another layer of "protection" as you go about doing your best to bring equilibrium into your body. And you wonder why you do not feel so good.

Whether you have a fragile ego or a huge ego, when you prevent yourself from saying what you feel, you go into a state of shock. Your emotions well up within you. You may start crying. You may start shaking. You may turn on your heel and punch the wall, or you may bury the pain in a little box in a cavern deep inside yourself, where you try to hide all your wounds. The problem is that the energy in that little box is *alive. All energy is alive*, and will not stay put forever, no matter how deeply you bury it within yourself. With a will of its own, the energy comes out of its cavern and affects the organ or system or gland to which it has attached itself.

Have you ever experienced a painful memory from your past; one that you have not thought about in years – until it suddenly surfaces again? It may even be an issue that you thought you had dealt with totally and dismissed. But *here it is again!* Have you ever witnessed grown wo/men cry over something that happened when they were only four years old? If it is an emotionally-charged situation, *it is an emotionally-charged situation!* No amount of protesting or pretending that it has no effect on you is going to make a difference. If you stuff your emotional baggage into little boxes into compartments within yourself, no matter how deeply you bury them, they will come out! All unresolved issues produce an uneasiness (dis-ease), which, in turn, produces disease.

Wounds are wounds, whether they are produced emotionally, mentally, or physically. Wounds are energy and all energy within your body requires your attention. When the wounds comes up, they *can* be released, but they have to be *felt* first. Neurotic behavior comes from your unwillingness to feel pain. You develop neurosis to mask pain, to help deal with pain, to help get rid of the pain. In the process, you bring *more* pain into your life. All you have to do, first, is to *feel* your pain. *Acknowledge* it, *feel* it, then let it *go*.

Into my thirties and forties, unresolved pain had such a grip on my being that I felt as though I was trying to swim with a fifty-pound weight tied to myself. Each day brought a new reason why I should "drown."

I have used visual imagery to help myself deal with pain. Depending upon what seemed appropriate for the type of pain that I was trying to excavate out of my body, I saw it encased in a variety of images. I saw the pain leaving me as a huge snowball racing down a mountain, or being thrown overboard in the wake of an ocean cruiser, or being consumed by a huge bonfire. I also saw the pain being shredded like paper or being dissolved in a brilliant white light or purple flame. If the pain came from another human, I would shrink them and make myself into a giant and totally ignore them. I would see them the size of a gnat when I was my normal size. This is just a small list of the endless possibilities that we can use to help us rid ourselves of pain.

There is a remedy for all this pain. We can fill ourselves with universal energy through our breath. It is free and available to us at all times. We do not need to get anyone's permission to use it. We need only to recognize our own power to take it each minute, each hour, each day. We can take as much energy as we need from the universal Source, the universal supply. We need not take from anyone else's energy field. We have an endless supply from the Universe and can always have all the energy we desire.

What area has the most painful energy
that still lives within your body?
We can remove all residue of painful energy, layer by layer.

October 22

Words to Re-mind Us

Some of the most exquisite music on this planet comes from *The Phantom of the Opera*, by Andrew Lloyd Webber, which was made into a movie after being a huge success as a theatrical play. The heroine, Christine, is dogged by the Phantom, who insists that she be his. She has already fallen in love with a beautiful young man; one more suitable as her husband than the Phantom. Because the Phantom is determined to make her his, he threatens the life of the man she loves. Ultimately, she is willing to make the greatest sacrifice – to give up her freedom – to save the life of the man she holds most dear.

This is the type of movie that has to be viewed at least three times, once for the beauty of its songs, once of the story line, and once for the higher meaning. Viewings after that will reveal other subtle meanings present in the story. The visual effects are stunning, the singing unearthly, and the storyline implausible, yet it eloquently speaks about the power of love that transcends time. God speaks through Christ (Christine) who reminds us that Spirit (the Phantom) lives *inside our minds.* The exquisite lyrics concern themselves with matters of the flesh, but as they wash over us, they take our spirits soaring to the highest pinnacles. The *words* reach deep within our core to nourish our Soul.

God sends us *words* as messengers to remind us (or, as Neale Donald Walsh says in *Conversations with God,* to "re-mind" us) of our spiritual connection, using any means possible to reach us. How many times – in our endless stream of ego thoughts – are we interrupted with a little nudge from Spirit by a tiny vignette to jolt our memory back to that from which we came? How many times does a thought float inside our head that makes us wonder: *Where did that thought come from?*

The last time that I hosted a dinner party, I was sitting quietly observing the men and women talking to each other when a thought invaded my mind: *Isn't it amazing that* "she" *is at your table.* The "she" referred to was a guest whose permanent home is on another continent, but who lives in Virginia with her husband while he completes his assignment here. I presume that I had a strong, rather adversarial relationship with this woman in a past lifetime. Today, she is one of my best friends, and is one of the people in my healing circle whom I most admire.

How many times have we felt a special kinship towards a person whom we've just met? How is it possible to feel such warmth in our hearts for a total stranger or a brand new pet? How many times have we read about friendships that developed at a supermarket check-out counter, a deli, at a craft demonstration, a do-it-yourself frame store, or a special event that was attended? These little nudges prompt us to live consciously; to connect to the Divine within.

How is it possible that we can look across a room, and say to whoever is listening: "That is the man I am going to marry."

When one of my friends made that statement to those around her, one of her friends questioned: "Well then, would you like to meet him?"

Love at first sight is not only possible, it can – at times – turn into a very successful marriage.

Verbal reminders (*re-mind*ers) from God are around us continuously. It is up to us to listen, and to be aware when God is tapping us on the shoulder to: *Pay attention, this is important.* It is up to us to learn to live consciously.

Can you think of any occasions that have led to greater relationships?
We can look for hidden meanings in the events in which we participate.

October 23

Hugs

When it is needed and *wanted,* there is nothing more comforting than a hug. From the time that we are born, we seek out the comfort of the human touch, and hugs extend that comfort until the day we die. Unless we have been violated, every person on this planet responds positively to a hug. If we have been violated, we can be so closed within ourselves that positive feelings from hugs are blocked from reaching us. When we hug, we willingly share our energy field with another.

The groups that I have always enjoyed the most are the ones where we hug each other when we come in and when we depart. As long as we give each other permission to do so, hugs extend a feeling of belonging. Hugs say, *I accept you exactly the way you are.* Several groups in which I participate always hug both upon entering and leaving. What a lovely glow of acceptance envelops the group as we acknowledge each other with a hug.

A common practice of signing XOXOXO after a name has always meant hugs and kisses. The circle is the perfect symbol for a hug, since we encircle someone when we hug them. A friend of mine always signs her e-mails with "Hugs," which never fails to bring joy to my heart. One of the sweetest images ever came from the internet: two preemies, siblings in the same incubator, their tiny arms extended across each other's back. Some very sick people have been healed just by being hugged continuously. Research has shown that hugs help heal post traumatic stress disorder (PTSD).

One time, when my teacher was stressed out over all the things that she was doing, and feeling that she was not getting the help that she needed at that time, I thought, *This woman needs a hug.* Instead of being sucked into the energy of her words of frustration, I got up and hugged her, and gave her exactly what was needed to dispel the air of frustration that had been dispersed in the room at that moment. The rest of the meeting was conducted in peace and harmony.

There have been times when I can actually feel the hugs of the Angelic realm; feel their wings enfold me, feel their gentle brush against my cheek, a slight pressure around my shoulders, and a warmth within my heart.

A smile lights my face and I know that all is well.

Hugs make me feel good,
Hugs make me smile;
Hugs tell me, I like you –
Stay awhile.

Is there someone who might really need a hug today? Never miss an opportunity to offer someone a hug.

October 24

Replenishing Energy Loss

If we feel that we are living like squabbling monkeys, either warding off blows from those around us or administering them, then we need to reassess. Many of the blows are verbal. Nevertheless, these verbal blows leave devastation in their wake, equally as painful as physical blows. Every time that someone verbally assaults us, there is a loss of power. Energy starts draining out of us just as quickly as water drains out of an open spigot.

We may not be able to see the energy, but we certainly can feel it. We feel it immediately, because it alters our ability to respond. We become "different" the minute that we are verbally assaulted. We enter into a "fight or flight" mode. It may take a while to stabilize our emotions, but we no longer act the same in the presence of the person who verbally assaulted us. We become passive or aggressive, or are always "on guard," and we stay "on guard" subconsciously, even after we stabilize our emotions. We put the past behind us and try to act normally, but there is a part of us that remains sensitive; always tuned in, always ready to ward off another attack, which – consciously or subconsciously – we know will come.

We live our lives in this mode – attack/defend, attack/defend, attack/defend – and totally give away our life force, our energy, our power. Our energy leaves us, flows out of us, and our personal life lies in a shambles around us. Yet, because we "look" perfectly normal and act as if everything is normal, we may even hold a responsible job. But as our energy leaves us daily, we eventually feel that life is not worth living, and go into crisis mode: emotional, mental, or physical breakdown.

It does not have to be that way. It can be different. The inexhaustible supply of energy – the energy of the Universe – is all around us and is ours for the taking. We are blind to it because we cannot see it with our physical eyes. However, it is there, and it is ours for free. We just have to learn to access it.

Fortunately, the entire energetic climate of the world is changing. Most of us may not be able to see energy (yet), but we certainly can feel it. By feeling it, we can learn to work with it. When we learn to work with our energetic subtle bodies, we learn to bring an inexhaustible amount of energy down into our ego selves from our Higher Self. We learn not only to keep our own energy flowing, but also to energize others and to teach others to maintain their energy levels and not give their energy away.

These exercises are designed to bring more energy into our sphere. They all involve breathing and visualization. Learn to breathe as deeply as possible and as consciously as possible. We can each learn to take ten minutes every day breathing deeply into all the cells of our bodies.

Visualize all the organs of your body filling up with oxygen. Start at your feet, and breathe energy up into your crown. Take each breath as deeply as possible, while keeping your focus and concentration on your own body. Feel your feet becoming like lead. Visualize your feet sending roots down to the center of the

Earth, and pulling up the energy from the center of the Earth. Bring that energy into your body through your breath, and mix it with any energy that you have taken in through your crown. Visualize your breath coming in down through your crown. Mix the energy from your roots with the energy from your crown in your heart. From your heart, send it to the rest of your body.

Do this exercise for ten minutes each day, or whenever you feel you lose power. You will be astonished how good you feel, and how fast you can stabilize yourself.

Do you recognize how quickly you lose energy? We can breathe deeply to replenish the energy that supports our lives.

October 25

Removing Fears

What is this still gnawing inside of us? Fear? Doubt? Uncertainty? Ennui? Boredom? Anxiety? What is this that keeps us cooling our heels while we watch all others having an "authentic" life, while our own seems to be on hold?

Each of us who are afflicted with many known and nameless fears know how we are affected by them. These known and nameless fears are numerous enough to fill volumes of books and countless essays in magazine articles.

Society preys on our fears. We are told how to act, what to think, how to guard ourselves, how to behave, what to wear, how much we have to earn, what places we should go to eat, where we should live, where our children should go to school, what clothes will give us status, what cars will make others envy us, what cosmetics will make us more "desirable," ad nauseam. We vex ourselves trying to meet the standards of that "someone" else.

However, there is a problem. That “someone” always changes the ground rules. We are trying to hit a moving target. What is desirable at one time becomes very passé the next.

Much of the energy on this planet is spent consuming items that will make nary a difference. One hundred years from now, most of that which we fret about now will be meaningless. Few of us will leave behind a legacy that positively affects mankind, and all the fretting in the world will not matter, except to pollute the etheric body of Mother Earth. It does not have to be this way. There is a better way to live.

Much of the personal energy on this planet is consumed in thinking about “things” that have no real meaning. These “things” simply serve to distract us from the true goal at hand – learning who we really are. Throughout this entire journey on the planet, we never stop thinking, and our selection of focus for our thoughts is the most important thing we do, for what we think about is that which we create.

And, yes, we do take it with us. We take our fears, our phobias, our prejudices, our bigotries, our dread, and our anxieties with us, but we also take our loving kindnesses, our tenderness, our compassion, our benevolence, our mercy, our openness and every positive gesture and virtue that we have mastered.

Why is the Spiritual plane so desperate for us to learn how to think positively while we are on this plane of existence? Our thoughts make all the difference in what we create once we leave this plane, for we create that which we think about. When we recognize that the core of our “Be”-ing is an aspect of the Source, we are able to align our thoughts with the Source and keep our thoughts positive.

Our lives become infinitely easier when we are willing to bend towards the positive with everything that we encounter on this plane of existence.

How do your fear thoughts control what happens to you? Positive thoughts will bring positive actions into our spheres.

October 26

Our Sentient Plants

If you are amongst the millions who look upon plants as if they were inanimate objects, then resurrect a copy of *The Secret Life of Plants* by Peter Tompkins and Christopher Bird. Originally published in the 1960s and now available under a new imprint, it is worth your while to find and read this book. You will never feel the same toward any plant again, and will start to treat them as the sentient beings that they are. Not only can they feel pain, or even the threat of pain, but they respond emotionally to your thoughts of love about them.

The Secret Life of Plants documents examples of thousands of experiments, completed by scientists around the world, done with plants to verify these points. However, we – in our supreme arrogance – pretend as if these experiments never existed and constantly say: *Show me.* The scientists do, and we focus lavish attention only on the latest developments, then barely give a glance to that which has been so painstakingly researched and developed in the past. One scientist in China patiently documented over ten thousand experiments, yet his research is barely mentioned or publicized.

Many of the experiments were made by hooking up a plant to a lie detector. One plant was threatened verbally with being cut and it "fainted" in horror of the thought of what was going to be done to it. Again, hooked up to an emotional detector, another plant consistently showed excitement around the time that the owner was coming home, even though that "event" was about forty-five minutes in the future. Still another perked up and bloomed profusely after it was threatened with extermination if it did not bloom by a frustrated owner who watched it send up copious amounts of leaves year after year with no blossoms.

Plants react to loving words just as much as we do; with awareness and grace. How many little old ladies have been laughed at because they talk to their plants? Yet, the plants in and around their homes are lush and green and bloom in profusion. Instead of giving any of her plants fertilizer, one of my friends administers Reiki; an energy healing modality. Her African violets, lush and vibrant, bloom continuously.

We have such a large body of evidence that plants are sentient beings, yet we consistently abuse them. We continue to harm them by smothering them with chemical fertilizers rather than the natural fertilizers that are readily available in the form of cow, horse, or chicken manure, or our own compost from kitchen waste. We asphalt over our wetlands to build more houses and commercial buildings, or import topsoil so that we can plant more crops instead of bowing to the intelligence of Nature that uses the wetlands as a filtration system. Tropical forests are the home to over ***eighty percent*** of the current wildlife species on the planet, along with ***fifty percent*** of the vegetation, and are not suitable for planting crops. Yet we burn down our tropical forests, then watch as the topsoil erodes away within years, which renders the site useless for planting. To ignore that which has been in place for millennia is the height of arrogance.

Those who work in co-operation with Nature – those who co-create with the Devic kingdom such as the community of people in Findhorn, Scotland, or Perelandra, in Northern Virginia – know that they do not need fertilizer to keep their gardens happy, healthy and productive. They simply need to honor Nature in her myriad of forms and know how to co-create with Nature. Without any harmful sprays, they are able to produce all the vegetation that they need to make all the products they desire. These are sacred places indeed, and draw attention from people around the world.

One of the most pleasurable publications to hit the newsstands in recent years is *Birds & Blooms,* started by a small group in Wisconsin. This little treasure features birds, butterflies, gardens and flowers, and celebrates daily life in the gardens around the United States. The contributions from its readers illustrate experiences in their own backyards resulting from the owners' never-ending efforts in their gardens. *Birds & Blooms* illustrates creative birdhouses and bird feeders produced by the readers, together with pictures of family members and wildlife enjoying nature. There are so many exquisite pictures published in the magazine that many readers have found extraordinary ways to use them. Pure joy!

Do you have a special place in your yard, home, or patio for plants? Flowers are reminders of God's Angels on this Earth.

October 27

Knowing versus Perception

A Course in Miracles provides many lessons teaching students the difference between *perception* and *knowing.* The *Course* claims that perceptions come from the ego, and that the ego is insane. All perceptions come through the filters of the person speaking. These filters can relate to control issues, fears of abandonment, quests for self-reliance, lack of abundance, feelings of low self-esteem, a gnawing sense of insecurity, a need of approval, or any one of hundreds of other discords that people bring with them into incarnation on this planet.

The *Course* teaches us that since perception comes from the ego, we do not have to accept the perception from another, no matter what their comment is; no matter how self-righteous they think they are, no matter how attuned to Spirit they feel that they are, no matter how much they claim that they are correct in their statements. There are myriads of issues through which perceptions percolate.

Whenever we accept someone else's perception as truth, we are denying the aspect within us that is connected to the

Divine. There is a *knowing* within us that is right for us, and that *knowing* is that on which we have to rely. That *knowing* may get us into trouble with our family and friends – who are usually more interested in preserving the *status quo* – for our *knowing* may be taking us to greater heights than the people around us. We *know* when something is not right for us, since *what we know* comes from the Divine. When we cannot accept the statements from another that are hurtled at us that damage us, then we have to go into the silence of our own hearts and run it by the *knowing* that lives there. We have everything we need within us.

We cannot control what happens "out there," but we can control how we react to it. When we are wrong, we can choose to apologize. When another rejects what we are saying, we can choose to stand firm and not cave into their fears. Their comments and accusations come from their perceptions. We can choose to run their comments and accusations by our *knowing*, and honor what we hear and what we feel from within.

Once, I was accused of having "too much light in my eyes" when speaking about my teacher, because I mentioned that she is the person closest in alignment with the Christ Consciousness that I have ever met. The person listening to me speak saw the light in my eyes as "adoration," and felt that I was lavishing a feeling of adoration on my teacher that was not merited, since I have everything that I need within me, and that feelings of adoration are something reserved for the Divine. I was so stunned, I did not know what to say. Part of me stood firm, an iron peg firmly planted in the earth; another part of me felt as if someone had punched my solar plexus and all the air had drained out. This was a clear case to demonstrate my *knowing* against someone else's perception.

When we are able to recognize when someone is coming from a *fear* space, even though they may vehemently protest it is from a *loving* space, we can "know" that it is acceptable for them to do that. We can also "know" that we do not have to accept the other person's words as Truth. What may be "true" for them, may not be "true" for us. Many items are "true" that have nothing to do with Truth. Truth is the same for each person on the planet.

If it contains a variable depending upon race, culture, religion, education, marital status, political affiliation, gender, or sexual orientation, than it may be "true" for the person perceiving it, but it has nothing to do with "Truth."

Learning to stand in your own "Truth" connects you to your Source. Recognizing the difference between *knowing* and *perception* depends upon the level to which you have evolved.

Have you been targeted recently by someone else's "truth?" Learn to recognize the difference between knowing and perception.

October 28

What Are You Creating?

If you are pleased with what you are creating in your life, terrific! If you feel you are creating nothing but messes in your life, ask your Higher Self: *Why?* Listen for the answer. You may be surprised by the answer you receive. You will always receive an answer, but you may not be ready for it, especially if you are playing the blame game. If you are in victim mode, then everyone else *except* you is responsible for your fate. Even though the Universe is neutral, your Soul is going to gently nudge you to take responsibility for what you have created, even if it takes your entire lifetime or many lifetimes to recognize it.

If we presume that a certain person is going to *bite us* every time we encounter them, they will – until we drop that presumption. The Universe is neutral. It will reflect that which we put there. It does not judge our creations. It simply puts into place that which we have created. The Universe repeats *Uh Huh* to everything we create.

Consider that certain people are going to be disgruntled with whatever you do, and that this even includes those who are working with the Spiritual realm. The message is: *DON'T QUIT!* When you feel that you have to ward off blows from those around you who disagree with or disparage you, or who are even downright mean about what you are doing in your pursuit of increasing your spiritual life, *do not quit*. This may be the Universe's way of testing you; testing how sincere you are about following the path you have chosen for yourself. Many say that they want to increase the spiritual aspects of their lives, but at their first setback, they fall back to their old habits. Do not let setbacks upset your path. See them for what they are; an opportunity to solve a problem. *Do not quit*.

When circumstances repeat themselves, and we see the same situations over and over, we can recognize that we have not yet learned our lesson. Possibly we are being guided to move into a new career, possibly a change of marital status, possibly a total change in the direction that we have been taking our lives. Our souls may allow us to pursue one thing for a number of years, then suddenly ask us to change directions because we have a soul contract to do something drastically different from our current pursuits. Our Soul path is being altered to match that which we had agreed to do while in Spirit, prior to our incarnation on this planet.

That happened to me. I thought I would live and die as a real estate broker. No such thing. My Soul path was to teach about God. In the late 1980s, I was utterly horrified by the insistence of my Guides that I teach about God. I felt so unqualified. Today, since I teach about God daily, that distance memory seems almost ridiculous.

In attempting to figure out how I could best serve humanity, in October of 1995, I took a weekend meditation class, which led to an introduction into energy healing by the instructor's wife, who attuned me to Reiki I. Eventually, I became interested in learning about energy healing in earnest, took additional Reiki classes, received my Reiki Master Teacher attunement, and continued to take additional Reiki classes to perfect my teaching skills. Since my first introduction to a group study class of *A Course in Miracles* (in December of 1995), I have been on roller skates; my Soul leading me down an accelerated path of spiritual events.

Spirit sent me a teacher and mentor, who saw a healer in me. Her vision, while she was still working for the federal government in another state, was to establish a non-denominational metaphysical church, healing center, and educational center, together with a library of metaphysical books and a full ministerial community outreach program. That vision expanded to include a world-wide web-based virtual site, with virtual churches around the world.

I have since become an ordained Minister of Healing and am on the Board of Directors of the Rays of Healing Church, Inc., the church started by Wanda. We currently have active ministers in five states, and aim at becoming a true cyber-church; a nice start to Spirit's directive.

What are you creating with the actions in which you have recently chosen to partake? We can learn to recognize when our Soul has shifted the path that we have been taking.

October 29

Finding Solitude

Since fifty percent of the people disagree with us no matter what we do, what leads us to maximum growth is to follow the dictates of our own hearts, no matter who or how many disagree with us. To learn what the dictates of our heart are, we need solitude, so that we can hear our own inner voice. Permanent change comes when we give ourselves the gift of solitude, and take the time to think and connect with our Higher Self, which usually means cutting back on something else that we are doing. We learn to trust in God and God's directives as our Spirit unfolds, and we learn this in the quiet.

Just as we encounter space and light as we traverse the cosmos, we also encounter space and light as we go deep within our physical bodies. Our essence is light. We came from light, we return to light. We access that light through meditation. A good way to start is to set aside a twenty-minute session every morning and another twenty-minute session every evening *at the same time,* where we connect with God, our Guides, the Highest Beings of Light, our power animals, and other amazing creations.

Sometimes, the only way to get the solitude that we so desperately need to enrich our Soul is to go away on a spiritual retreat. This can take many forms, from exotic to local: it can be a yoga retreat in Costa Rica. It can be a journey to sacred sites in the British Isles, or to the pyramids of Egypt, or to sacred Buddhist temples in the Far East, or it can be a backpacking expedition across a continent that we have not previously visited, or a silent retreat at a local monastery. It can be time that we eke out for ourselves in our local park or in one of the pews of a vacant church, or even simply sitting in a comfortable chair in our homes or in our own back yards. The choices are endless.

The secret recesses of our Soul, generally not accessible to us in the hub-bub world, are revealed to us during solitude. The world is built around frenzied activity, most of which is designed to drain our power. When we heap worry, anxiety, frustration, and anger on top of that, we have a recipe for general collapse: mental, emotional, physical and spiritual. Solitude brings us to the still point within our being, to the core where stillness reigns supreme, to a point where we can access God.

When we are free from the distractions of the outer world, we go within to the core of our being and access what is beyond our imagination. We might see colors, images, geometric symbols, points of light; we might see nothing. Accept whatever comes. Whenever we are ready for more, more will arrive. Giving ourselves adequate time each day to be still and quiet, and to record and interpret what we see during our internal journey, is essential.

When we get closer to the core of our "Be"-ing, we may even be able to identify who our Guides are. By doing our spiritual work in earnest, we open up new worlds to explore, even if it means getting up in the early hours of the morning to work on our spiritual path.

What is your favorite place of solitude? We can each enter into the quiet of our own Soul by cocooning.

October 30

Embracing Solitude

You do not have to go to exotic places to reach the still point within your mind. Try your own backyard. During a walk around your home or garden, your silent observations may reveal something that you never noticed before. Watching Nature interact with itself, seeing cloud formations form and dissolve across the sky, and looking up to see the phases of the moon against a clear starry night all enhance that sense of wonderment that will sooth and calm you.

What was not here before, even for a faint second? Was there a wisp of a feeling of your hair being lifted, without any wind around? Did that tiny speck of light in broad daylight slip into your sight, seemingly coming from nowhere? How did that leaf seem to bend down and brush against your face, or the butterfly wings whisk against your cheek? Who spoke to you faintly above a whisper, to cause you to turn your eyes to look at the lady-slipper demurely waiting on the forest floor – not one, but five of them!

What made you look up just in time to see the hummingbird whiz by? Or another, and another?

Walking my dog down the bike path next to Burke Lake has always enriched my life. Once, a convoy of seven bluebirds appeared, all chasing each other; playing tag. I smiled the rest of the day. Shortly after we moved into our new home, four bluebirds appeared around the back yard, flitting around my four-year old son who was out there with his toolkit to "help" construct the porch that was being added. Once, on my birthday, one bald eagle, then another, paired together and circled overhead. What an incredible tribute to my special day. I smile to this day recalling those memories, but what if I had been "too busy" to make note of these tiny occurrences?

Everything we see in the animal kingdom brings a message to us from the Spiritual realm; gifts that increase our level of consciousness. Along with *Animal Speak* (a treatise filled with Native American wisdom on the meaning of animals, birds, insects, and reptiles that cross our path), Ted Andrews has published *Enchantment of the Faerie Realm: Communicate with Nature Spirits & Elementals.* At daybreak and dusk, the veils between the Universe in miniature and our Universe are the thinnest, and God's magic increases. We have to be silent to even notice. When we give ourselves the gift of solitude, we come closer to the place where our Soul resides.

Solitude is a gift that we can access daily; a treat that takes us into an invisible realm in which all possibilities exist. All we need to do it is to will it. On some level, everything that *was* still is, everything that ever will be *already exists.* Outside of this dimension, a timeless realm exists. Solitude helps us gain access into it.

What places around you help bring solitude into your sphere?
We can explore all the areas of our lives in which solitude exists.

October 31

Spiritual Pilgrimage – Part 1

Sometimes we just need to get away. After my last birthday, I felt the need to finally complete what I had been planning to do for years: go on a spiritual pilgrimage. I chose Scotland in mid-September, starting it as a solitary journey, hooking up with a spiritual pilgrimage group, and then ending it as a solitary journey.

My first stop was Inverness, a charming town located on the Ness River, a quiet exquisite area in the Highlands and five miles north from the Loch Ness, where all good monster seekers go in hopes of catching a glimpse of "Nessie," as she is affectionately known. I never did get to the Loch Ness, but did have a delightful sojourn along the Ness River, admiring the homes and buildings that cropped up against her banks, and then crossed over the Ness Islands, enjoying more of the wilderness of the river. The untamed part of the riverbank burst with energy that only the faerie kingdom can provide as they tend to every tree, shrub, and plant along this naturally-wild area. One solitary little old lady walking her dog, "Kit," smiled as I sailed by. My spirit soared, and I smiled back, feeling so safe and comfortable in this place.

The next day, after a brief stop at Forres, (the flower capitol of Scotland) came Findhorn, an internationally known community whose members work in conjunction with the nature spirits. It was started by Eileen and Peter Caddy, as publicized in Dorothy McLean's book, *To Hear the Angels Sing.* Findhorn Bay beckoned me; the beach strewn with a myriad of multi-colored rocks where I was told to take only *one,* that there would be many more for me at Iona, the final leg of my journey.

After arriving in Edinburgh by train, I hooked up with the spiritual pilgrimage. We started by going to Rosslyn Chapel, built in 1446 by William St. Clair, the third and last Prince of Orkney. His grandiose expectations of building a full-fledged cathedral stopped with his death, but he left one of the most intriguing chapels of the medieval world. Rosslyn chapel is totally shrouded in mystery, especially since it has always been associated with the Knights Templar, and the plunder from the Temple of Jerusalem is supposed to be buried there. Despite repeated diggings, no one has yet to find an entrance into the underground vaults that they know are present in the Chapel. One of our guides took us to a stone near the edge of one wall, stomped on it, then stomped on an adjoining stone. One rang hollow, the other did not. Mmmmmm! Such intrigue.

To further the mystery, Rosslyn Chapel has some of the most exquisite stonework in Europe; the Apprentice's Pillar and the Master's Pillar stand highest among the treasures of stone carvings in Europe. Other carvings around the chapel include plants from the New World – carved well over a hundred years *before* Columbus' journey – as well as one of the largest representations of the "Green Man" – the five-story male figure totally covered in leaves or other foliage, sometimes seen at the edge of the forest.

Unfortunately, prior attempts at preserving the Chapel – a limestone wash that was applied in the 1950s – have caused extensive permanent damage. The beautiful sandstone is deteriorating from within. A scaffolding cover put over the top of the chapel in the late 1990s simply keeps the elements off, so the façade is difficult to see. According to one guide who has lived in the area for over fifty years, unless any real attempts at restoration are done, one of the most beguiling medieval buildings may soon lie in ruins.

The Glen behind the chapel offered a magnificent foray into Nature. The river that gave Rosslyn Chapel its name formed a narrow rocky gorge called the Esk Valley. Rivulets gurgled sweetly as they wound their way down the gorge, their little tunes in harmony with the collective breath of Nature. The entire glen throbbed with life. While even tiny wildflowers poked their heads out wherever they could, one incredibly impressive stand of plants – four feet wide and eight feet tall – looked like giant rhubarb leaves. Breathtaking foliage enhanced the outcroppings.

Fallen trees everywhere were deeply covered with moss, lichen, and ferns, in their firm resolution to be of use to the forest faeries. Ferns of every shape, size and variety crowded into each space, sending up their fiddleheads to proclaim new territory. The foliage, glistening from Scotland's almost daily mists, shone brightly – each little mirrored fleck reflecting tiny glints of light.

I had been introduced to tree people and stone people by one of the members of our pilgrimage. With her gentle instruction, I was immediately able to see the eyes, nose and mouth that are found in trees and rock formations, if we only take the time to look for them. Some were so prominent; they looked as if they had been carved by man. Others were more subtle, yet welcomed any recognition of their being. Still others looked like an apartment complex: two, three, four, or five faces stacked one on top of another. Another magical journey, but all too soon, the next part of our pilgrimage beckoned: Glen Lyon.

Prior to reaching Glen Lyon, we stopped at a sacred stone circle and a grove of giant oak trees spreading their limbs out to the sky, as if they were proclaiming a special welcome to our group. As with each place we visited, I could have stayed there longer. Before we left, we hand-fed a few of the sheep and goats behind the barbed wire barrier that edged this sacred space, who eagerly took our meager offerings of grass even though they had plenty of green pasture to feed from. It almost felt as if they were hungry for human contact. Finally, we made a quick stop to a perfect little gift shop filled with Scottish artifacts called Glen Lyon Arts, owned by George Brettell. George collected stones from around the nearby mountains and had one set up at the entrance that eerily resembled a hooded monk. He said *at night that stone seemed to have a life of its own.* Even though he had been offered several hundred pounds for it, he would not part with it.

A little further down the road, we stopped at the Fortingall Church, where the five-thousand years old Fortingall Yew Tree lives, and is said to be the oldest living tree in Europe. According to a plaque at the site, it originally had a girth of seventeen feet across, but was pillaged by souvenir hunters in the eighteenth century, and set fire to by children. It now consists of three remaining free standing trees – all remnants of the original tree – and is surrounded by a protective stone wall offering a few grated "viewing" areas. Somebody had hung a little elephant ornament from one of its branches, which seemed oddly symbolic: the largest animal on terra firma paying homage to one of the oldest living beings on the planet. We all touched a part of the limb that had grown close enough for us to reach it, shiny from so many fingertips having reached up to rub it in honor.

At Glenlyon, we stayed at the comfortable Invervar Lodge, nestled on the side of a crystal granite mountain. The massive gathering areas for kitchen, dining, and evening community enveloped us in peaceful contentment and each bedroom, with its rustic décor, emitted warmth and coziness. One of the owners was due to deliver a baby in a few weeks, but remained very accessible to our group.

During the evening, we were delighted in a concert by Fiona Tualach. She was a young woman, a member of an old Celtic group called the Culdees – a group with an ancient tie-back to the druids – who played the Celtic harp (smaller than a regular harp), and sang sweet lilting ballads of an era long gone. At the end, she was joined by Gabriella Kapfer, one of our leaders, who played the cello. As we listened to the entrancing music, we forgot that there was a world out there beyond our four walls. These enchanting sounds wound their way into the very cells of our being that night. The full moon appeared, as if on cue and seemed to smile, as if satisfied with the performance we had just witnessed.

During our stay at Glenlyon, on a solitary quest to meditate in the drizzling rain, I ended up on the uppermost peak of Fire Mountain, and was able to see seven cloud covered peaks, all shrouded in mist. I stayed there for hours, and eventually noticed two little clouds close by that seemed to appear out of nowhere. Turning to look at the expansive sheep ranch below, I made a deep promise to myself and to the countryside, *I shall return.*

Happy Hallow's Eve.

Is your soul's journey calling you to do a pilgrimage? As we honor the requests of our Spirit, we nourish the infinite part of our Self.

Step 7

Connect to Your Divine Source

You did not create yourself.

A Course in Miracles

November

The power of the Universe is within us. There is nothing outside of us that will ever give us that which we need. Everything we need we already have. We simply have to accept it, harness it, and use it for the betterment of mankind. To harness Universal Power/Energy/Love is to learn to love unconditionally: no strings attached, no personal agenda, no massive ego cloaked in the guise of spirituality. We have to let all that go.

We do not need to be anywhere special to start to own our power. Unless our heart directs us otherwise, where we are is where we are supposed to be. We start to own our power when we can accept who we really are: an aspect of the Creator; a co-creator "Be"-ing.

If we have asked for spiritual mastery in this lifetime (and many of us have), then we have to be able to withstand the lessons that spiritual mastery brings. To our ego self, any attempt to reach our Higher Self is a disaster. Higher Self does not give ego self any credence, and ego self only has a vague notion that Higher Self exists. Eventually, Higher Self prevails, because Higher Self is All There Is. Ego self keeps being replaced by personality after personality, depending on what we choose to co-create on this planet. Co-create is what we do. Co-creator is who we are. Co-creation is our function; our mission, our goal – unless we have chosen this lifetime to simply be an observer.

November 1

Spiritual Pilgrimage, Part II

Our final destination was Iona, a sacred isle; the burial site of Scottish, Danish, and Swedish kings from the medieval ages, the site of druid activity, and the first landing place of St. Columba (the Catholic missionary who converted the Highlands to Christianity). Here, I was further introduced to "dragons" – visages that appear throughout the massive green hillsides composing the island – hillsides that look just like dragon heads.

Iona has many enigmatic parts: the mists of Iona – gently swirling rain which mysteriously seems to swirl *against* the current of the water, with the water receding as the wind blows toward the visitor on the shore. Wondrously variegated stones, rounded by eons of being tumbled within the Gulf Stream, are spit up on the shores of the island; irresistible "collectibles" by both locals and visitors to the island. Sacred stone temples – quiet edifices that once housed the powerful – now beckon silently. Faerie rings so prolific that I called them faerie condos; twenty, thirty, forty mushrooms in dizzying circles over here! Over there! Everywhere! The winds – alternately whistling and howling – constantly admonishing everyone to *Listen, Just Listen.* Ancient stone crosses and the tall Benedictine abbey settled and impressed themselves into a crevice deep within my Soul.

Our first outing was to St. Columba's Bay, the exact place where St. Columba was thought to have landed in 563 AD. Here, I collected a fair share of Iona stones with their intricate markings; some composed of compressed coral, some slate grey with veins of white quartz in intricate patterns, some in variegated shades of green reflecting the countryside, and others in a myriad of colors. One of the members of our group (who lived and worked on the island during the tourist season) told us to rub them with our fingertips moistened by our own saliva to bring out their shine.

Various places on the island were identified as chakra points; energy centers on the island. The stone temple area had been identified as the throat chakra. St. Columba had a circular stone hut to which he retreated, known as the *Hermit Cell* (probably the site of druid activity before his arrival on the island). Another larger stone edifice affixed to a hillside was set a little further back, which prompted the organizers of our pilgrimage to rename the area the *Temple Stones.* I had been warned to ask for permission to enter this larger sacred stone temple.

When I did, it silently answered, *Welcome Sister.*

Angels have a special way of visiting on Iona. In fact, the heart chakra of Iona is called the *Hill of the Angels.* While sitting on a ledge overlooking St. Columba's Bay, four tiny tide pools flanked me, each containing the visage of an angel. Another splendid angel appeared to be carved from the ledge of the stone outcropping facing me.

Another day's outing took us to *Dun I,* the highest point on the island, known to be the third eye or brow chakra. Here the wind was so strong that my *jeans* were flapping. Gabriella introduced me to a special secluded spot at *Dun I* where she had previously experienced a rebirthing.

My solitary journey led to the crown chakra – the northern-most point of the island where white sand beaches crest the point – a welcome relief from the stone outcroppings that circle the island. Just prior to reaching the beach on that isolated northern point, dozens of faerie ring circles from three feet in diameter to twelve feet in diameter appeared in the short stubby grass – hundreds of mushrooms ... thousands of mushrooms – circles of six to eight mushrooms across. *Faerie Cities!* No faerie rings ever seen before could compare. What a special gift!

On the way back from the beach area, there was just enough time to see the Abbey, a non-denomination Church, originally a St. Columba monastery of the 12th century, then replaced by a Benedictine Abbey. The Abbey (currently maintained by Historic

Scotland) sat alongside St. Oran's Chapel and St. Martin's Cross; a venerable monument distinguished by the fact that it was over one thousand years old.

Even when following a group to a special site, there was time to be alone, and I used every opportunity to be one with Nature. Since we all walked at our own pace, we soon found ourselves separated from each other. In every direction we went, the highest point beckoned me and whispered its quiet messages into my Soul. No call to return would hasten my descent; too much unbridled beauty to feast on.

Every vista offered a mystical view; miraculously captured by the owner of the local Art gallery in his painting and pottery. The local jewelry shop owner (a young woman) copied Celtic patterns from thousands of years ago, forging them into stunning high quality sterling silver bracelets and earrings.

The isle of Iona honors many religious and indigenous traditions, all of which are sacred in their own distinctive way. Thanks to our splendid guides, De Fano and Gabriella Kapfer (who have discovered all of them), this pilgrimage could not have been more special.

What sacred journey, which sacred site, beckons you? That which nourishes the Divine within us supports us.

November 2

By Special Invitation Only

You are here by Special Invitation. Lighten up. Don't take yourselves so seriously. Find Joy in your life. Find the joie de vivre in your daily actions. Nothing is worth being so serious about. You have so much to look for. To laugh for. To love for. You are so alone in your pursuits. Think Community. Think Love. Think laughter. Think I Am "Be"-ing. What is life but the expression of Love? Live life to the fullest! Waste not your most precious moments on Earth. You have a finite time here. You live in infinity.

Give me your attention when you are lonely, afraid, depressed. I will transmute it for you. You need only to ask. I will not violate your free will to choose. The right to choose will always remain with you. You have choice in the many things that you do/think/speak. Choose wisely. Choose consciously. Think about the effects of your choices. Your choices reverberate throughout the Universe.

You think you are so powerless. You are, instead, the most powerful "Be"-ings in the Universe. Have faith that you are guided toward your truth. Trust in your Self. You each have a fail-safe system within you.

You are each here on Earth at this time by Special Invitation Only. You have so many levels to your understanding – it is no wonder that you feel that you are fragmented at times. All the pieces will start to fit, and to fit tightly. You will soon be able to understand concepts that you have never before understood. You have to come with me when I call, or you will continue to feel disappointed and out of sorts. You are me and I am you. You see only your surface imperfections.

We see you as you really are; perfect in every way. Seek not the things of this world, but seek only the Kingdom of God – because that is where your peace lies.

And so it is!

Amen.

Do you feel "invited" to receive guidance from Spirit? If Spirit is pulling, set aside a special time each day to commune with the Divine within.

November 3

Have Faith and Trust in the New World Order

You are so afraid of silence. You are afraid of Love. Love might just reveal to you the magnificence of who you are. It is much easier to you to accept yourself in your limitations than to accept yourself in your magnificence. Your magnificence scares you.

Each of you stands on the brink of a New World Order. I assure you that each of you has prepared yourself through many lifetimes and many experiences to be able to step into your power. You are not floundering out there alone: without guidance, without tools, without instruction, without teaching, without the power to do that which you know you must do to achieve the New World Order.

You do have to have faith. You have to trust; you have to believe that who we send to assist you is there for you to do what you need to do when you come up to bat. You simply have to ask for that assistance, since your free will to choose will never be violated. Your entire support system is there waiting for you to ask for it.

Surround yourself with Light and with that which brings the Light to your Self and to others. You have all you need within you to do exactly that which you have contracted for in this lifetime. Each one of you is more brilliant than the finest diamond ever discovered. You simply need to be polished to bring out your brilliance. You do that by your efforts to learn the spiritual facets about yourself. All the effort comes from within.

You do not need all the books in the world to teach you how to communicate with Spirit. You just need to listen to the Holy Spirit. The Holy Spirit – the Voice for God – is the answer to all your needs while on the Earth plane. That voice is not out there. That voice comes from within. Listening to the Whole-ey Spirit will bring each of you back to wholeness; will help you anchor Spirit into matter, will help you ascend matter into Spirit.

As you listen to the guidance from the "Whole-ey" Spirit, you notice that you become stronger in your beliefs. Someone else's beliefs are not able to sway you as quickly as they once did. You have more confidence and more self-assurance. You are more firm about your own convictions, since they come from within you. You are able to withstand the barrage of nonsense that is thrown at you on a daily basis, and are able to step away from other people's efforts to influence your decisions. You are firmly planted within your own power.

And you realize that you simply have to forgive – since everyone else means well, but is coming from a sense of lack and limitation within themselves, even though they may be ignorant of that fact. As you forgive the other, you also forgive yourself for buying into lack and limitation. You also forgive this third dimensional Universe, until you realize there is nothing to forgive, since it is all a role that you assigned for yourself prior to coming on this planet. As you change yourself, you change the Universe. All is contained in one. One is contained in all. That is part of the holographic nature of the Universe: All is contained in the One: One is contained in the All.

It all comes back full circle; to faith and trust. Trust that which is given you by Spirit: the guidance, the hints, the messages, the feelings, the sense of what to do. That takes faith!

Has guidance from Spirit come to you recently? Having faith and trust in what is given to us by Spirit eases the complexities of our lives.

November 4

Instructions for These Times

My beloved child, you are so blessed. You third eye is opening up to see into other realms of existence. You need only have courage to step into that realm. You hold back yet as an observer, not as a participant.

Lavender oil will assist you in the transition. Keep some close by at all times. Essential oils support this part of your journey. Their molecules mix with the rest of your molecules to enhance the work that you have to do. Close one nostril while inhaling the scent from the essential oil to increase the volume within your lungs, and to spread it more quickly to the other parts of your body. (Lavender oil is a general healing oil, known to have many benefits, including healing burns.)

Leave plenty of time for silence and meditation. We know you are confused about meditation, but make your life a walking meditation. As you go about your daily chores, totally concentrate on each one. You will soon see that they are accomplished quicker and with more harmony. That is staying in the NOW. Eliminate and resist any attempt on yourself to feel pressured and overwhelmed. Stay calm, stay cool and stay collected. We will assist you from our realm to harness your energy, so that you can work in an efficient and abundant manner.

Honor the Earth. She is your Mother. She supports every facet of your life and well-being. Walk gently upon her. Walk purposefully. Enhance her. Re-use her bounty by recycling and composting. She only wants you to learn to love her as she loves you. Acknowledge her. She is your Mother. Would you pass by your own mother without greeting her? Set up a time each day when you acknowledge and greet your Mother Earth. She will welcome you and expand your good wishes exponentially.

Acknowledge the little people; those who serve her and you – the unseen miniature race on this Earth. They abound around you. They undo the damage that you inflict on the Earth – your Mother. Just like a good Mother, she is very tolerant of you and your abuses, but even she has a limit. There is an entire Universe in miniature that surrounds you. When your third eye is fully open you will see this race of creation. Right now, most of you have to be content simply to know that it exists. Be content with that flash of light you see from the corner of your eye. You will see this entire miniature kingdom of light when you are ready to not get caught up in their drama.

Accept one another. You are all aspects of the One Source. You have so many differences that you cannot seem to resolve amongst yourselves. Those differences are meaningless. You are all cut from the same cloth, regardless of what you may think. You all have the same gifts and you choose how to develop these gifts. The only limitations that you have are those that you place on yourselves. Any disadvantage with which you were born, or which you choose to experience later in your life, has been chosen by your soul for the growth of your soul.

Hurt no one and no thing. You only hurt yourselves. You are all part of a seamless whole. All bad things are there by design. No matter how self-righteous you think that you are, you do not know the real meaning of all the bad things that happen for which you dole out punishment. Rather than living your days in judgment of everything around you, send light to the subject, which brings illumination from within.

Relax and have fun: schedule time for merriment, joy, rest, and relaxation. Laugh, above all, laugh. Laughter is the music of the Soul. Not snickering, nor sickening humor, nothing that puts anything or anyone down. Your older comedians, many of whom have passed in spirit, knew it best. They knew what was genuinely funny. They had humor down pat. Encourage the studios that own them to resurrect their shows. They are magnificent.

Joy is your birthright, yet you never seem to turn there. Learn to live your life with joy in your heart. The sun shines on saint and sinner alike. Thus, too, you can bring joy into your being and into the hearts of those around you. There are so many things about which you can be joyous, yet you barely notice them. The natural beauty around you falls into the category of that which is taken for granted. Learn to focus on the natural beauty that each passing day offers. From the rays of the sun to the twinkling of the stars and light streaming from the moon, there is natural beauty that feeds your Soul. By keeping your home in order, you add to the beauty and harmony that is so craved by your Soul.

Call on us. Just ask for help. I love you. We love you. We all stand ready to guide you. Ask for clarification. Ask for the meaning of what you see, hear, smell, taste, touch, experience. Just ask. We will rush to your side to give you the knowledge that you need to go forth to the next stage.

We Love You.

Namaste.

How can asking for Spirit's guidance bring calmness into your life? Spirit brings us that which we need exactly when we need it.

November 5

Choosing to Hear

Spirit's voice is a very quiet one. It is entirely your choice whether or not you wish to tune into Spirit's voice. It is always there. It never leaves you. You have total free will to choose to hear or to choose not to hear. Spirit is completely undemanding of you; totally patient, totally kind. How many lifetimes you wish to waste on ego-driven matters is entirely up to you. Your free will is never going to be overridden by Spirit. You are free to choose to connect to the Divine Source or not to connect. It is entirely up to you.

You may be inspired to connect to the Divine Source or you may choose to ignore your inspiration. Your inspiration (in spirit), comes from understanding who you really are: a Spirit having a human experience. You are both human and you are Divine. You are subject to the laws of man, but you are also subject to the laws of Spirit. It is up to you to determine which set of laws you allow to influence you the most. Everything you do, everything you are, is guided by the voice of Spirit, but it is always your choice where you put your attention.

Your connection to God is not something that you established. However, you are free to deny it if you wish; free to deny the existence of God, or whatever name you call the Supreme Being, in whatever culture you have chosen to express your personality in this lifetime. What name you call the Source is not important, be it God, Allah, Buddha, Krishna, Brahma, Jeshua, Jesus, Great Spirit, Oneness, or any other of the myriad names that have been given to the Supreme Being. They are all identical. They all address the same "Be"-ing.

Your expression of the ego self is not to be misunderstood as your expression of the Higher Self. They are not the same! Any attempt to insist that they are gradually leads to a hole in your heart, which eventually needs to be healed. Nothing will work for you; not your addictions, your denials, your obsessions, nor your attempts to fill that hole with busyness of any kind – constructive or destructive.

You can deny the existence of God for as many lifetimes as you wish. You can continue in the drama trauma you have established as "your life" for as long as you wish. When you tire of seeing all of your ego plans fall apart, then you will turn to peace and understanding, because they go hand in hand. Peace comes linked with understanding. When you seek peace in your heart for yourself, you seek it for All.

Eventually, over the course of your full existence, you become one with the Source, since that is from whence you came. This is why God is unconcerned about your drama traumas. It is all God, so ultimately it all comes back to the Source.

You are part of It. It is part of you. It is who you are.

Are you choosing to hear the guidance from Spirit? We can deny that which is given to us by Spirit, or we can choose to listen.

November 6

Being One with the All

As Spirit, you are connected to everything else. There is no separation, no distinction, no other. There is only your Higher Self as an expression of All That Is. Higher Self came into "be"-ing as an expression of the All. There is no one else, there is only Self. You are All That Is.

If this sounds too confusing, think of the ocean. Every drop of the ocean is still a drop and still the ocean. We can isolate one little drop and call it a little drop, but it is a little drop *of the ocean.* When we put the little drop back in the ocean, we clearly see it as the ocean. However we choose to view it, *it is still the ocean.* We can take the drop and let it dry and separate it into its essential parts: sodium chloride (salt) and H_2O (water). The water can become vapor, and the salt can stay behind; they are still components of the ocean. When we reconstruct these components back into liquid form to recreate the drop, *it is still the ocean.*

We cannot say that a drop of the ocean is *not* the ocean because it is merely a drop. No more than we can say that we are not part of the All – part of the Whole – because we are just an isolated little being. We *can* see ourselves that way if we choose, until we *tire* of seeing ourselves that way and accept the magnificence of who we really are.

We choose whatever way we wish to view ourselves: as a "magnificent, majestic, multi-dimensional" *"Be"-ing of light*, or as an insignificant little human being. The more that we choose to tune into Spirit, the more that we align with the "magnificent, majestic, multi-dimensional" *"Be"-ing of light* that we really are, we ease ego out of the picture. As we choose to live by the rules of Spirit, we choose to let most ego issues move out of our energy field. That which used to "bug" us so much before now scarcely receives a passing glance. When we tune into the higher aspects of our *"Be"-ing*, we become a kinder and gentler human. We have more tolerance, more patience, and more benevolence towards our fellow humans, and we choose to accept only peaceful solutions to outstanding problems, no matter what the issue.

When we live by the rules of Spirit, we live by rules that man is commonly unable to accept. The current climate in the ego world is to pass judgment on everything in every way possible. This does not bring us peace. We recognize we are better off to leave the judgment to One who knows the entire past, the entire present, and the entire future of the thing or person being judged. Instead of passing judgment on something in which we do not wish to participate, we can learn to say: *That is not for me.*

Is your "sense" of being One with the All increasing? Aligning with the Oneness within brings us peace.

November 7

From Pain to Wisdom

Wisdom needs a very quiet space in which to nest, and is oftentimes preceded by pain: painful events, painful bodies, and painful lives. Pain is like a traffic cop. It stops us dead in our tracks and makes us pay attention. We have to obey. It can, because of its intensity, absolve us of responsibility. While we stop to nurture ourselves, we cannot possibly take responsibility for others. We have limited resources on which to draw, and we cannot get well until we pay attention to our limitations.

Pain may sometimes screech us to a halt. We can no longer do that which we have been doing, and can no longer think that which we have been thinking. However, we always have the option of changing our behaviors and thinking new thoughts. We can change our minds about our priorities. As we differentiate between our ego mind and our Spirit mind, we learn to distinguish between that which was important *then,* and that which is important *NOW.*

How many of us lament that we would delve more deeply into spiritual matters, if only we had more time? Pain gives us that "time," since often we cannot do anything else as we recuperate from a debilitating illness or injury.

Ask the pain: *What are you trying to tell me? What is the purpose of this pain? Why is it here? Is there a new direction that I should take?* You may be astonished by the answer.

Pain connects us to Spirit quicker than anything else, if we listen to its message. Pain gives us access to our Spirit mind and allows us to hear that which previously we may have been unwilling to hear. To access our Spirit mind, we have to be *out of* our "ego" mind. According to Spirit, what the ego may see as the greatest tragedies, are in effect some of the greatest growth spurts that we experience. Nothing is a tragedy. There are no victims. All is part of a grand Divine design of cause and effect. Our Spirit mind recognizes that.

Pain gives us a different perspective about the "hits" in our life: those comments, people, and events that used to make us feel uncomfortable and unstable. We learn to handle the "hits" differently. We understand that everyone comes from their own perception. We cannot alter someone else's perception, but we can expand our own. We realize that what we thought was important is no longer important, and we choose to put greater emphasis on that which *we* value and cherish, rather than that which other people think, say, or do.

When ego "hits" come forth, what has changed NOW is the way I react to them. They do not ruin my day, my night, my sleep, or my special event. Yes, I have changed! I used to get sucked down the rabbit hole every time anyone looked at me cross-eyed, since I always felt that *I* was doing something wrong. My personality went into a sulk and did not come out for several days. I accumulated hurts along the way, and stuffed them back into my body. YUCK! What a sad way to live.

This has all changed. Now I simply chalk off the "hits" as belonging solely to the person speaking. I allow the other person to be in the space in which they are, and continue to stay in a space of peace and compassion. I do allow the "hits" to flatten me or to cause me to feel off balance.

Pain is the ultimate healer. We have three choices. We can heal ourselves by turning a new corner in our life, or we can continue to do what we have been doing all along and live a life of debilitation in body, mind, and spirit, or we can die. Since there is no death, this is the ultimate healing. We return to our real home or to another plane of existence; to whatever level of consciousness that we have created for ourselves to continue our journey towards the Source.

Even when we are recuperating from an illness or from some tragedy that has gripped us, we are capable of experiencing peace. Peace, understanding, and wisdom are all points in our crown; the area of our energy field where all virtues reside. Peace (one of the by-products of wisdom) may enter our mind, even under the most trying circumstances. Where peace lives, wisdom and understanding also reside, since they are companions of peace. Pain can lead us there.

Have you had an opportunity to experience wisdom as a result of pain?
Pain can play a great part in bringing us to wisdom.

November 8

Breathe Deeply

Learning to breathe deeply enhances your Spirit "Be"-ing as well as your health, and increases your energy level since it allows you to expel toxins from within. On top of calming and centering you, it is the one thing you do that immediately connects you to Spirit. Every living thing inhales and exhales. Breathing deeply helps you to focus and center, and guides you to a meditative state which helps you connect to your Divine Source.

There are many different types of breathing techniques. The best is the simplest: *increase the number of seconds* you breathe in and breathe out, reaching for the length of time that a Master can use for an extended breathe-in/breathe-out cycle; approximately three minutes. As you breathe in, feel the breath circulating into all the extremities of your body; from the top of your crown, to your fingertips, to the tips of your toes. Breathe deeply and expand your lungs so that oxygen can reach into the minutest parts of your bronchiole; to enter into every cell of your body.

Practice different breathing techniques.

Instructors of yoga teach us to close one nostril and breathe *out* through the other, then inward through that same nostril, and then to reverse the procedure, calling this alternate nostril breathing a "cleansing" breath.

Lamaze instructors (whether the mother elects to have childbirth without anesthesia or with) teach pregnant women to manage their contractions with short *panting* breaths, while looking at one particular spot – a focal point – which both helps distract from the pain of the contractions and rids the body of toxins. This is also an especially useful coping technique after receiving any news that seems to suck oxygen out of our body.

Walking briskly, swinging our arms and inhaling deeply as we walk, increases our body's capacity to take in oxygen.

Concentrating on our breath – as it goes in and out of our body during meditation – calms us down, and helps us drift into the void where no thoughts exist. This attention to our breath allows our thoughts to sift to the bottom of our mind. We stay in the NOW.

Focusing our attention on a painful spot in our body increases blood flow to that spot, and the extra oxygen helps us to manage the pain.

Notice when – without realizing it – you are *holding your breath*. You may stop breathing for any number of reasons: sometimes during the most exciting parts of your life, sometimes when listening intently, sometimes because no one taught you to "check in" on your breath, and sometimes when under great stress.

If you give up lung capacity to cigarette smoking or because you work with airborne hazardous material, you take the risk of considerably shortening your life. Your lungs are such a gift from your Creator. Honor their capacity to work as well as they do by not filling them with carcinogens.

Take every opportunity to breathe clean, fresh air. Find a friendly tree that appeals to you and spend some time under it; especially important to those of you who live in the city. Most cities offer multiple park areas for a brief respite from the concrete and asphalt. Many major cities have planted trees that not only survive vehicle pollution, but also thrive within that atmosphere. Many communities are rimming their trees with flowers, a mute testimony to God's Angels. Trees belong to the lung supply of Mother Earth. They inhale carbon monoxide and exhale oxygen through a process called photosynthesis. Without plants, the atmosphere surrounding Mother Earth would be similar to the atmosphere surrounding Mars.

Our breath connects us to our Creator. Humans have been known to live for months without food, for weeks without water, but only for minutes without breath. Honoring our capacity to breathe brings us closer to the Creator.

Why is breathing deeply so important?
We increase our energy by applying
different breathing techniques.

November 9

Ego Mind vs. Spirit Mind

The ego mind, in contrast to what we may believe, frequently tells us why we *cannot* do something. The ego is not our best friend.

However, as one of my friends states: "It sometimes gets a bad rap."

Yes, we do need a full healthy ego to get us to a certain point in life. After arriving there, though, we need to start dismantling our ego to lessen its grip on us.

The ego mind concentrates on *fear*, *scarcity*, *loss*, *separation*, and *death.* It feels as if everything on this planet centers around fear; the mainsail that guides us throughout our journey here. This morning, I woke with the phrase *Face your Fears* ringing in my ears. There is not a single facet of the three-dimensional world that does not attempt to strangle us by laying multiple layers of *fear* upon us.

Pick up any newspaper in the world and count all the "bad news" versus the "good news." Listen to any news show and evaluate that which they select for their discussions. Browse through any woman's magazine, and see how many ways they offer to "improve" us to make us more desirable; keeping women fearful of how inadequate we (presumably) are. The Washington D.C. area – the hub of this nation's political arena – is rife with fear. The first sign of a snowflake causes pandemonium. The ego mind thrives when it can share any bad news.

Another favorite theme on this planet is *scarcity*, which dampens whatever shred of abundance we feel. Listen to all the commercials and see how many of them offer us a solution for that which we "lack." No matter what we have, someone else has it better, and if only we would "do this" or "buy that" can we possibly join the ranks of the "in crowd." The "must have" of the moment is never something that we already own. Feelings of scarcity are a favorite tool of the ego mind.

It is natural to grieve *loss*. It is only when the grieving is excessive or out of proportion to the loss that it wrecks havoc in our lives. When we choose to place our possessions ahead of our relationships, we tip towards the edge of excessiveness. When our pride gets hurt and we lash out at someone over loss of "face," we may be setting up the next round of karma for ourselves. It is only on the occasional talk show or on a few gifted family-oriented TV shows that *loss* is looked upon as a means of strengthening our resolve or our character. The ego mind hammers loss into our psyche, until we buckle under its strain. Paradoxically, if we live our life without fear and without expectation of the outcome, all that is ours will be returned to us. No matter what we may have "lost," if it is truly ours, it will be returned to us.

The ego mind loves to prey on our fear of separation. My teacher, in her quiet gentle manner, likes to state that our feeling of being *separate from God* is the only thing for which we have to forgive ourselves. We feel that God has abandoned us; that we are flailing – alone – in this wilderness of a planet, that we have been isolated and must make our way alone through this veil of tears. Yet, from the reports of those who are able to receive messages from loved ones in spirit, once we leave this plane of existence, we recognize that the only thing that is "real" is Love, and that we are indeed one with our Source.

In the Western culture, *death* is looked upon with grim-faced horror. There is nothing good about death. Yet, in the Eastern culture, death is seen as a reunion back to the Source; back to that from which we came, back to the essence of who we really are – a blessing rather than a curse. Death is the ultimate terror to the ego mind. Because we in the Western culture have such an inordinate fear of it, our ego mind can easily be manipulated when it comes to issues of death.

Spirit mind sees only Love; only abundance, only gain through our efforts to reunite with Source. Spirit mind says we receive that which we give and *only that* which we give. Spirit mind opens us to unlimited potential; no matter what our circumstances, no matter how dire our situation. Spirit mind constantly gives us gentle reminders of why we are here, what our sacred contract is, what we chose to work on, and how to access our Higher Self. Spirit mind always supports us and exhibits itself in those *quirky little hunches* that we think just might work out.

Spirit mind comes in a flash of inspiration which may fade quickly but which never leaves entirely. It merely submerges until we are ready to pay attention to it. Conversely, ego mind comes and stays and stays and stays, just like yesterday's newspapers. Even if we read them from cover to cover, we can never quite remember what was in them, but still do not feel right about throwing them away.

Spirit mind always encourages us to see our unlimited potential, and gently reminds us of our Oneness with all of creation. Spirit mind enables us to expand into the outer reaches of the Universe and says, *Here, I will show you how. I will hold your hand.* Spirit mind helps us answer the question: *Who am I?* I am not a body, not my possessions, not my goals, not my intellectual pursuits, nor the sum total of all of my achievements. I am Spirit having a three-dimensional jaunt into material space. I am Love in form. I am the Will of God. I am God's Grand Design. I am Spirit in human form.

Why is differentiating between the ego mind and the Spirit mind so important? Learn to listen and understand the difference between Spirit mind and ego mind.

November 10

Love is the Glue

Everything on this Earth needs love. Every crystal, mineral, animal, vegetable, and human living creation needs love. Yes, even stones need to be loved. Go to some of the oldest buildings in Europe that have been *continuously occupied*, and witness that – no matter what their age – they are still standing and thriving as homes, government buildings, castles, or places to visit. Next, go to any building that has been equally well constructed and equally as old, but somewhere along the line, has been abandoned. Its ceilings have caved in and its floor now plays host to a beckoning sky. Its walls are covered with vines, inside and out. Why do abandoned buildings collapse, but not the ones that stay occupied? Abandoned buildings have no one to love them. They have lost human contact.

Love is the glue that holds the Universe together. Love is what created it. Love is what sustains it. Love is All That Is. Anything that exists outside of Love, as Marianne Williamson so poignantly states, is "a call for Love," or "a cry for love."

When we look at our surroundings through the eyes of Love, we start to heal ourselves and everything around us. How can this be done? By changing the lens in the filter through which we view the world. By clicking on the filter of *compassion,* we grow in understanding of our Spirit mind. We recognize that there is a huge difference in the rate at which each person vibrates. If their vibrations do not match ours, we feel a sense of imbalance. Yet, by looking at them through the lens of *compassion,* we lessen the rage that our ego mind might feel. Rarely are two people in the same household on the same vibrational plane. Looking at them through the lens of compassion helps us to retain our balance, while not upsetting theirs.

We reflect what we have created. We can deny the existence of Love, close our eyes and all our senses to Love, and follow practices that dis-connect us from Love. But we cannot eliminate it. We all re-turn to Love eventually because Love created us as It Self. No matter what our choices have been in the past, at any given moment, any one of us can choose differently. This is the true meaning of redemption.

A Course in Miracles expresses it best: "The meaning of Love is the meaning God gave to it … God loves every brother as he loves you; neither more, nor less." (Chap 15, Sect V, par 10, sent 3 & 5.) No one person, and no particular religion or religious practice, has an "exclusive hold" on the love that comes from the Creator. The idea that this could be so is fundamental nonsense.

We are all cut from the same cloth. We all share equally in the Love that comes from the Creator, for that Love forms the essence of who we are. We cannot separate something from its essence, anymore than we can separate our energy fields from each other because they overlap each other *ad infinitum*. We go back to the Source through the entirety of our energy fields.

Our founding fathers tapped into a Universal truth with their statement: "All men are created equal." All men *are* created equal, since they are all created with the same spiritual gifts. It is up to each individual to uncover them. That is what spiritual development helps us do: uncover our spiritual gifts.

How many ways do you manifest Love in your life? Witness to Love as often as possible, the glue that holds the Universe together.

November 11

Multiple Layers of Existence

For those of you who think that you came from nothing and to nothing you shall return, get over it. There will never be a time when you will not be you. You will always be who you are even when you become part of the group consciousness of the One.

The multiplicity of layers of who you are is beyond the current level of human comprehension. You have so many more levels to your "Be"-ing than you can comprehend. Just know this: they all exist at the same time and in the same place. You exist in the past, in the present, and in the future, all at the same time because – outside of this dimension – all time is NOW.

Ask for help with concepts that seem to bog you down, and do not succumb to ridicule from others for attempting to understand esoteric concepts – since ridicule only comes from fear. Learn to think for yourself.

The Earth simply represents another dimension of that which is, which consists of things far beyond what you think it is. The instruments that you use now to measure time and space are so incredibly primitive. You are on the cutting edge of where your civilization once was, and are just cutting your teeth on the instruments that can carry you to the farthest reaches of space. You have so much more to learn. New information is being given to you slowly, so that you do not abuse your planet and sink a continent as you once did.

What is visible on the third dimension is only a tiny fraction of that which exists. What exists is part of the Whole, which is All That Is. All contains all. Every particle contains the whole. That is the way it is and the way it always will be, since you are a holographic Universe, which is why cloning is possible; every cell contains the whole. Since all form is holographic in nature, the pattern continuously repeats itself.

You are a creator "Be"-ing; part of a network of creator "Be -ings. Each of you has the same capabilities as the whole. A mirror can be shattered into a trillion shards. Each shard is nevertheless a mirror. Each shard can be brought back together to re-create the whole, because each shard is part of the whole.

The Universe is vast. There is space for all my creations. As you learn to live in peace, they will be made visible to all of you. They come in peace. The come only to serve you and the whole of Creation.

And so it is.

Amen.

***Do you have a sense that* nothing is what it seems?**
As we learn more, we come to accept
God's holographic Universe.

November 12

Assistance from Spirit

Many of us, in our self-absorption, feel so alone and so forgotten. Extending beyond ourselves – taking one step toward an "other" – helps us to feel better. If a sense of alienation and depression has settled in because we feel that our family and friends have forgotten us, we can take one step forward by helping a stranger.

Fortunately, some progressive communities have learned how to team the needs of children (who benefited from the extra attention only an adult can provide) with the needs of their senior citizens. Several decades ago, one housing community in Florida set its homes as if they were spokes of a wheel, with each home leading to a central courtyard. The seniors in each hub greeted the children off the bus and provided the day care after school. Both benefited: the children's grades improved due to the help of the seniors with their homework, and the seniors received joy and blessings as they felt a renewed sense of purpose in their lives.

The most hardened exterior melts if we shower it with love, as is brilliantly exhibited in a movie with Kirk Douglas, *The Bird Man of Alcatraz.* His love of canaries inspired all of his fellow prisoners to take care of these creatures with such love that it brought out the best in his fellow prisoners. To this day, his research on the diseases of canaries is one of the most extensive ever developed on the ornithology of that precious species.

Allow yourself the right to *feel* the spiritual assistance and incredible protection that surrounds you. Your loved ones in Spirit constantly try to help you. If you feel that you have no loved ones in Spirit, then you may have come here to break through that limited belief. You may have rejected another's attempt to love you in other incarnations, or spent lifetimes pursuing a person who was already committed to someone else. Now, you experience a solitary existence until you recognize the value of a union solely with one who is able to be totally committed to you.

The Soul knows that we *get* only that which we *give* – for *getting* is for *giving*. What we *give*, we *get* – for *giving* is *getting.* Ego mind tells us that as we give, we have less. Spirit minds says that as we give, we give from an Infinite Source that never runs out. We replenish everything that we gave and receive even more than we had in the first place. When we give attention, we receive attention. It cannot be otherwise.

You expect the Universe to function backwards from the way it is organized. Reverse your expectation. What you give – you get.

What prevents you from feeling Spirit's assistance?
We can ask for Spirit's assistance
whenever and wherever we need it.

November 13

The Power of Thought

There are no accidents. All is part of a Divine Plan of Oneness. We are all part of the plan; a shard of a mirror that comes from One mirror and ultimately goes back to the One. We are all One "Be"-ing; One manifestation, One Creator God. Prime Creator experiences through us. The Source of All That Is splintered into an infinite number of pieces in order to experience Him/Her/It Self. While the Prime Source stayed as Prime Source, no experience was possible, just a *knowingness.* Prime Creator *knew* but did not *experience,* then breathed forth a Universe through thought in order to experience.

As the Gospel of St. John states: "In the beginning was the Word and the Word was with God and the Word was God." *Word* is thought. The beauty, the joy, the wonder, the glory, the primal awe of creation, burst forth into form *from* thought. Breathing something into existence through thought is the power of the creator "Be"-ing that we are; an aspect of the Supreme Creator. Embrace it or not, that is our choice. The power remains.

We are the "Be"-ings of creation who can align our thoughts with the Supreme Creator. Our power comes from who we are. We are created in the "image and likeness" of our Creator. We are created similar to the Creator "Be"-ing from which we came. What we think, we bring forth, just as our Supreme Creator does. We, too, create with thought. We think, therefore, we create.

We are creator "Be"-ings not creator "Do"-ings. As an experiment, take something simple that you wish to manifest in your life and think only of bringing that item, value, or goal into your life. Hang a picture of that which you wish to bring into form in an area of your home that you see every day. Think of it as a *fait accompli,* an accomplished fact. See how long it takes for that item to become a reality in your life.

Without realizing it, I manifested the home I always wanted to live in by simply never giving up on the dream of where I wanted to live. At the time of my second marriage, I told my husband that I wanted to live in a three-level four-bedroom colonial with a full basement, first floor family room, large kitchen, and a two-car garage. I never wavered from that description. A few days prior to our marriage, we purchased a three-level, colonial-styled town house. Three years later, we purchased a bi-level that looked like a colonial; it had majestic pillars and was ensconced on an acre of land. Ten years after the purchase of our second home – thirteen years after my original statement and in spite of the financial crisis we had endured six years earlier – we moved into the home that I had described from the beginning. My thought turned into form.

Just as no amount of dissuasion could get me to change my mind about wanting to graduate from the University of Michigan, no lack of resources could prevent me from wanting to live in the home that I chose for myself. The power of thought was behind me.

Do you give sufficient credit to the power of your thoughts? We can each recognize how powerful our thoughts are.

November 14

A Sense of Urgency

Think beyond human, beyond the limitations of body and mind. Align your thoughts with Spirit, which exists before the body and mind were formed. Our bodies are lifeless without Spirit, for it is the infusion of Spirit that gives it life.

No matter what curve balls life throws us, as we each keep our mind aligned with our Higher Self, we bring stability and joy into our life. The body is neutral; body does not dictate to the mind, mind dictates to the body. The body will react to whatever instructions the mind gives it. Mind goes along with the dictates of either the ego self or Higher Self. To keep peace within our selves, keep the mind aligned with the Higher Self. We may feel that our parents, our children, our friends, our peers, our colleagues, our religions, our financial institutions, our governments, or our culture put parameters around us that keep us little. We have such incredible power to do and to be whatever it is that we think about, but ignore most of our power as we respond to the commands of others, which entrap us. We react or respond. We do not create our heart's desire because we succumb to the bonds of fear which control us and hold us prisoner; chains of fear that keep us from meeting our highest potential.

Lyndon Johnson had a saying that served him well during his career in the United States Senate: "To get along, go along." That same premise applies to most of the people on the planet right now. Do not make waves. Do not become visible. Do not become a trouble-maker by swimming against mainstream thought, for fear that you make someone uncomfortable. Besides, it is too difficult. Go along with what everyone else believes. It is much easier that way.

Whoa! Stop! Re-evaluate! Is this what you want for the rest of your life? To be an expression of *someone else's* will?

Wake up! Wake up!! There is no time to waste. We have so little time to express unconditional Love; the unconditional Love from which we came. We all have to *be* our part; that part of the Creator Self that exemplifies who we *really* are. We must stand up and express our highest potential. We have so little time to fulfill our soul contract; that which we came to achieve for the Creator Self that we really are.

Major changes have been effected because of the gestures made by people who had had enough: colonists in Boston throwing barrels of tea overboard (cargo that had been levied a tax by their governing body), Mahatma Gandhi urging passive non-violent resistance to free his country (of over three hundred million people) from the bondage of another's rule, Rosa Parks refusing to give up her seat to a white man because she was tired, thus risking the indignity of a jail sentence. Actions – both large and small – changed the direction of prevailing thought.

A Master appeared on the planet two thousand years ago, refused to answer the charges hurtled against him, and was condemned to death as a common criminal. Many fear that if they speak out, they will meet a similar fate. That is not to be. The consciousness of mankind has reached critical mass. More and more people have courage enough to stand up to the commonly-prevailing thought. They will not allow the jealousy and short-sightedness of others to stop them.

Maybe we stay invisible because we recoil from experiencing the "tuff stuff" which causes us to reach deep within our Soul to stand up to life's buffeting. Perhaps, if we stay invisible, the Universe will make no demands on us; will forget that we are here, and will allow us to stay in our littleness – pursuing our own pleasures, not having to face any challenges.

How many times do we witness a fellow human being lament, *Just let me get through this day, Lord*, and shrink as we hear that? If we want our experiences to be soft, pleasant, and undemanding, then we certainly do not want any spiritual growth. When we look upon difficult encounters as a pariah – when we want no sense of urgency in our lives, just nice, soft, complacent places on which to land – we miss the best part of what it means to be human. Spiritual growth comes on the heels of sometimes excruciatingly painful experiences. When we get through them with our sanity intact, we have just forged the steel in our lives that had to be subjected to 2,000 degree heat in order to become what was its destiny.

No matter what "form" our experiences take, if it is a *major* life experience, then – on some level – we agreed to it before we came to Earth, even if it seems *unbearable* to the ego mind. Whatever our soul contracts to work on, we – along with our Soul Group – agreed to it during our incarnation between human lives. Nothing major happens to us by chance or by accident. All co-incidences and synchronicities have been put in motion by the Angelic realm, and are part of a Divine Plan to which we agreed before we came here.

Minor life experiences are a result of the choices that we make during this incarnation, but minor choices can change the destiny of this planet. Due to free will, our choices are endless. No matter what injustice we rail against – ones that we feel we are powerless to change – think again.

Muster all the courage within, and ask for the assistance of Spirit to help you. That minor choice may be part of a major issue on which your soul agreed to work, just as was that simple gesture of refusing to give up a seat on the bus.

What sense of urgency are you experiencing in your life right now? We can pair our "forms" with our choices.

November 15

Our Filters

This following little pep talk came this morning from Archangel Michael: *Courage, my child, courage! Tap into courage to anchor and align with the Holy Spirit. Spirit is giving you all the energy you need. You have deep rest when you sleep. You wake up refreshed and are ready to start. You simply have to get out of bed and begin.*

Each one of us "hears" Spirit through our filters. We could each be given the *same* message, but that message is going to be interpreted differently by each of us. We are each going to hear our *own* message, based on our beliefs.

If you have been raised to believe in guilt and sin, or believe in sin and guilt as an adult, your *message* will contain words of guilt and sin. If you have been raised to believe in a judgmental God, your message will contain words of judgment and condemnation. If you have been raised to believe in unconditional Love from a Loving Creator, than your message will be one of a loving, giving, non-judgmental Creator. Your filters will allow the words to be interpreted to comply with your belief system.

The Blessed Mother has been appearing in many places all at the same time. She says that she delivers the same message to each person to whom she appears. However, her messages all sound different. When asked why, she states that each person interprets her message through their own filters. Those who have been raised in a predominantly Catholic country will hear a message that is different from those who have been raised in a less fundamentalist religion, or raised agnostic, or atheist. Those raised in a home where fundamentalist religion is practiced – no matter what the name of that religion is – hear a message laced with sin and guilt. An atheist, raised with no agenda or fundamentalist belief system, brings a totally different slant to Mary's message.

Each one of us has a certain role to play on this planet, although some of us have chosen multiple roles. If our role is to disperse spiritual truth, the messages from us will reach everyone who needs to hear them, provided we get out and deliver those messages. Given the variety of temperaments, drives, desires, goals, and pursuits of the individuals on this planet, the messages delivered from our filters will be perfect for someone who aligns with our energy level. There is always someone around who needs to hear our message, whenever we are ready to deliver it.

If we feel stuck in a certain place, remember, as Einstein said, that "energy cannot be destroyed, it is just transformed." We are a very complex energy system. We cannot be destroyed. We are just transformed.

Please do not feel – if you have a spiritual message to share with the people of this planet – that you will be destroyed, as you may have been in the past. That is behind you. However, the remembrance of being tortured, mutilated, burned at the stake, beheaded, or killed in some other abominable fashion may still be stuck in your cell memory. Use any energy cleansing method that you need to help you clear that fear out of your body.

How have your filters affected your choices?
We can give ourselves the gift of freedom
to change our filters at will.

November 16

Waving Goodbye

Two cute children grace the shelf of my china cabinet; a little boy and a little girl standing close together, waving goodbye, handkerchiefs flowing in the wind – my only Hummel figurine.

When I purchased this figurine with the two children, one of the little "waving hands" had been broken off, and was taped to the figurine's side. This brought the cost down to a fraction of that for an undamaged figurine. I brought the piece home, repaired it with glue, and was pleased with the result. The broken hand, once mended, never showed a sign of a repair.

One day, though, I saw that the *other* little "waving hand" had been fastened to the little figurine with scotch tape. My cleaning lady had broken it, could not bring herself to tell me, but also she did not surreptitiously mend it in hope that I would never notice. So, out came the glue again. Again, the mend could not be seen. It was as seamless as if it never happened.

It seems as if those two little hands waving handkerchiefs, with the faces uplifted to an unseen viewer, represent what I have done all my life: wave goodbye to those whom I have loved. I was a restless youth, always wanting more experiences than my humble beginnings allotted me; always wanting to go somewhere on the weekend. Instead, I was expected to clean our home on Saturday, bake a dessert for Sunday's dinner, rest a few hours, take a bath and be happy with the results. Sunday meant going to church, followed by my mother preparing a delicious Sunday dinner, and my Godfather driving our family to the closest local park; a routine which bored me to tears. Lake Michigan, with its lovely beaches, enormous sand dunes, pavilion, and ample opportunity to meet someone of the opposite sex, was only thirty minutes away – but might as well have been thirty hours. My uncle (the only driver available, since we had no car) – as well as my parents – felt that the park was good enough, and they were not inclined to go to the beach where I desperately longed to go. Many times, I cried bitterly from the sheer boredom of my life.

Once I left home for good, boredom has never been a factor again. Overwork, yes. Boredom, no.

When I was young, I did not appreciate having a loving family around me. Only after moving ten times in five years, following my first husband to wherever his whim or employment took him, did I appreciate the environment in which I had been raised: the intense love that my family had given me. It was the memory of that love that sustained me through the many years of anxiety from the new experiences I had created.

Ultimately, strangers became friends and took the place of family in my life. Fortunately, the Universe had another gift in store for me. A second marriage – a union with a man who loved children – provided us with two loving souls who agreed to be our children. My husband and I wondered how we could have been so lucky to have two such gifted, creative, inventive, illuminating, brilliant lights come into our lives. We felt so blessed to have been their parents.

Since both children now live in another state, my fondest dream is one in which I am able to visit them on the occasions that matter the most: birthdays, holidays, and special events. Neither am I in close proximity to my sisters, brother, in-laws, nieces and nephews, cousins and their children. I do try, whenever possible, to share in the major festivities of their lives, and am eternally grateful when an important event coincides with a planned trip to visit my family.

Now, though, when I wave good-bye, it feels more like saying "sayonara," "we will meet again."

Does saying good-bye to family
bother you or free you?
We can learn to relish each moment that
we spend with family, for we may be
separated from them in the future.

November 17

From Worry to Wisdom

I have lived my life in so many moments ahead of their time, worrying about events that never materialized. Empty shadows, never coming to pass. Empty shadows crossing each other in space. Bare whispers ... veiled truths ... wisps of smoke ... clouds ... streams of air ... nothing of any substance.

Mine has been a strange life; one not lived authentically because I was afraid to acknowledge what I really wanted to do as a youth; afraid to pursue the path that made my heart sing. Worrying about: *What will people think?* haunted me and created chains of imprisonment which coiled around me and prevented me from taking actions toward my heart's desire; a tragic fear which led to some awful decisions.

When we look at our worries, we have to decide: *Which are real? Which are fragments of fears that have magnified themselves in our imagination?* Do we worry about *all* the possibilities of what could happen? The possibilities are endless. Worry never accomplishes anything except to draw more worry to it. Our energy field attracts that which we present to the Universe.

Spirit has many portals – ways in which they offer assistance – to support our journeys through life. We decide when and where to enter. When we are ready, we go through. No prompting from anyone else gets us through. Spirit's door always stays open and ready to receive us whenever we decide to walk through, which we do when we *ask* for help.

Once we have entered through their portal and have asked to receive Spirit's help, the drama traumas that show up in our lives are ours. We can choose to use them to help ourselves learn to love unconditionally, or to discard the lessons as we wish. Whatever it is that we *have to learn* will be made clear to us. Those whom we are to teach will surround us. Those who are ready to hear will be drawn to us. "Whoever has ears to hear, let him hear." *(Gnostic Gospel of St. Thomas).*

Fortunately, events in my life beat the superficial stuffing out of me. The pain of my worries about career path, marriage partner, and financial stability eventually sank me to my knees trying to figure out: *What would it take to make me happy?* Because of my pain, I wrote out a list of what it was that I really wanted out of life, and figured out what was truly important to me. Life had a way of introducing its blows, then showing me that, *Yes, I am strong enough. Yes, I have courage enough to withstand my fears.* I increased in strength each time I withstood the blows that came along the way.

Living life and loving every minute of it is my goal; staying in the moment, having nothing but moments to enjoy, to relish, to roll around my tongue, savoring each special fragment, beholding each moment with beneficence, regardless of the opinion of my ego.

Are you even aware of how much worry you call forth in your life? Asking for spiritual help frees us from the coils of worry.

November 18

Validation

If you are still waiting for any*one else* to validate your experiences, you will wait forever. Your authentic Self does not need validation from an outside source. You already *are* everything you need to be. You *authenticate* your *Self.*

I once witnessed a grown woman cry burning tears because her parents insisted on invalidating an experience she had as a little child. When she was four years old, this precious lady – who resembled an elf herself – saw a three-foot gnome with his rotund belly straining against a tightly-belted green outfit, topped with a straight red pointed hat, bounding across her parent's garden. Of course her parents did not believe her, and kept persisting that her vision was only a product of her imagination. She kept insisting it was not. Now in her late sixties, and still with much sorrow, she viewed this incident as an invalidation of her own mind. She still did not believe that she could trust it. Fortunately, she learned to heal her inner child during the workshop we attended.

Our need to receive validation from others must come to an end. Our resolve to stand firm in our own validation is going to have to take precedence of other self-effacing beliefs that we have had in the past. Our authentic Self is going to become our grown-up self.

There are many changes taking place on this planet and Mother Earth will need all the help she can get. The next few years are going to be critical because man has put the planet into crisis mode. In preparation for the Earth ascending to a higher dimension, the veil between dimensions is thinning. Every time we experience something that we feel is just *too weird,* know that what used to be considered weird is now *normal* to the elevated vibrations of this planet. We must recognize Mother Earth as the living being that she is, and use her natural resources for the betterment of all – not to just assuage the greed of a few. We should neither despoil her with our discards nor poison her with our chemicals, nor strip her of her trees as we pave her over with asphalt and concrete, nor willfully strip the natural resources that she has put in place for our use. We all need to assist, not just a few environmentally-conscious people.

This planet is capable of sloughing off every living thing on it. Currently, we are choking and poisoning her at such a rapid rate that she is using natural forces to retaliate. Too important to become victim to the foibles and power struggles of the power seekers, unless co-operation amongst all the nationalities and cultures of this planet is achieved, she will continue with her upheavals of Nature: hurricanes, typhoons, volcanic eruptions, tidal waves, tsunamis, massive winds, and fires that rage out of control. The wars that we wage (resulting from nationalistic pride or greed) – dropping bombs into the bowels of the Earth – *must end.* Those who harvest natural resources at the expense of the Earth – putting the profits into the hands of a very few – *must stop,* for the violations to the Earth produced as a result of these actions are an abomination.

It is no mystery as to why "the meek shall inherit the Earth," for the meek are the caretakers of the Earth. They do not despoil it. They understand that *it is their home*; that they are the temporary guardians of a land that is to be used and enjoyed for their lifetime, and to be left in pristine condition for the generations that follow. The meek fully comprehend that there is not a person on the planet who does not bear some responsibility for her condition.

Fortunately, Mother Earth is receiving help from the newest souls arriving on this planet. These gifted children – the Indigo, Crystal, Rainbow, and Children of the New Consciousness – are coming into incarnation with memory from where they came and they will *not* be dissuaded from their spiritual sight. Hopefully, they have selected their parents carefully; ones who will support their spiritual journey here.

If you have been chosen to be the parents or grandparents of one of these special children, be open to receive whatever they are willing to tell you. If their demands puzzle you – or worse, frighten you – please ask for spiritual help to be able to understand the experiences that these newly-arrived souls share with you. You have been selected because you are ready to hear their message of oneness and peace.

These newly-minted souls are powerful because they need no validation for their spiritual experiences from the moment they come onto this planet. Because their *knowing* comes from within, they do not heed the efforts of others trying to dissuade them from their experiences. By tapping into their own resources, they *know what they know,* remember where they came from, and stay connected to their Source.

We are to follow *their* advice, not vice versa. We are energetic beings composed of energy, both visible and invisible. What we *see* is a fraction of what we *will see* once we train ourselves. The new children arriving on this planet will help us in that training, the most important of which is to honor the Earth.

Tap into your own inner knowing to validate whatever it is that you know is truth. Learn to rely on your own validation.

Why does waiting for validation from those around you feel like bondage?
Ask for validation only from our Higher Self or our Highest Spirit Guides.

November 19

The Voice Within

As soon as you are open to me, I guide you. I am the little voiceless voice within that stands ever patient; ever ready to assist you. You simply have to open to me from within. Give me a little bit of willingness to hear my voice, and be quiet. Still your mind, clear the mental chatter in which you find yourself enmeshed.

When we learn to still our mind, we hear the voice within; the voice that is only heard in the quiet, in the stillness. That voice can have a name – or it can have none. The name of the voice within is not important. Just know that it is there.

This inner voice is part of our *Internal Guidance System* (IGS). Instead of blindly accepting what is being offered, we can turn to our *Internal Guidance System* (IGS) every time that we are asked to do something with which we are uncomfortable; every time we are asked to accept something that makes us squirm inside, every time we hear anyone – no matter how lofty their position is in the material world – justify yet another atrocity in the name of freedom, or patriotism, or religion. We are well-equipped with our own evaluation technique.

Some of us claim we *never* hear the voice within; that Spirit has passed us by. The small still voice is there, but our mind is too busy rummaging through the maze of thoughts that we filter through it; many thoughts per minute. With the possibility of a good fraction of our thoughts being negative, and all those negative thoughts being thrown into the collective unconscious, is it any wonder that the Earth is in such a mess?

We can learn to become a witness to those thoughts by sending our consciousness outside of ourselves and learning how to stand aside and watch ourselves thinking those thoughts. It is a marvelous experiment. If we play a negative tape over and over in our mind for whatever reason, we can change that tape.

We are not a victim of our circumstances unless we choose to be. We can change the effects of whatever happened to us by changing the tape that plays within our head. Even the results of the most wretched experiences can be altered if we only learn to forgive. It is all our choice.

Internal chatter can be eliminated by whatever means appeals to us: soft music, candlelight, staring at a crystal, looking at a beautiful vista, staring at the ocean or any other body of water, resting next to a stream or river, walking in nature, gardening, cleaning out our drawers, cupboards or closets, or painting. Any one of these experiences can put us into an altered space in which we can hear the voice within and stay permanently connected to it. We do not have to set aside a special time or a special place to hear the voice within. It accompanies us wherever we go.

We have another device to turn to: our feelings. Our feelings are our *Direct Connect to God* (DC to G) just as the voice within is our *Direct Connect to God*. Memorize *I am a DC to G,* until it becomes automatic. We can learn to stay on automatic pilot and can stay tuned into God throughout the day and night.

If the word *God* makes you uncomfortable (because of a fundamentalist upbringing that claims that there is only one Son of God and you are not it), then substitute any other name that is appealing. Please do not get hung up on labels. Use any word that works: Supreme Power, Primal Energy, First Cause, Prime Creator, Source, Eternal Power, Divine Infinite Spirit, the Light, Eternal One, Oneness, All That Is, I Am That I Am, I Am, or any other generic name that makes you happy. If the word God, Jesus, Krishna, Buddha, or any other name with a "religious" overtone makes you feel curdled inside, then blank it out and substitute whatever is appealing. The important thing is to connect with a Higher Power, even if that Power is called "Dance" or "Oak."

We are free to do whatever we wish. If we identify the Highest Being to be someone who lived on this planet, so be it. All is acceptable. Again, do not get hung up on labels. We access the voice within by calling forth the name that we have chosen as we connect to the spiritual aspect of ourselves.

Own your power; the unlimited supply of power you already are.

DO NOT GIVE YOUR POWER AWAY.

When do you feel your Direct Connect to God is the strongest? We can learn to tune into our feelings as our Direct Connect to God.

November 20

Reflections on the Christ Mind

Those of us who study *A Course in Miracles* know that we are in a safe place. In our group, we share intimate details that increase our vulnerability, sometimes crying; shedding tears of joy or weeping silently. We laugh as we quietly and gently support one another, by sharing our pain and listening to each other. We know that we are protected from the force of a negative mind.

We open ourselves to the Christ Mind, and allow the Christ Mind to come into our consciousness; to guide our thoughts and our words, and to harmonize our energy field. As we build community – a community of Spirit, a sense of Oneness – we remind each other of our connection to the One. We are One: One Soul, One Spirit, One consciousness; the product of One Mind.

We come from One Supreme Being who splintered into as many pieces as S/He/It desired in order to experience life; to go beyond the knowingness into experiential. We never cease to amaze God as we continue to create according to our Divine Plan. We have total freedom to pick and choose our experiences, just as we have total freedom to pick and choose our thoughts. From our thoughts, our plans arise, our experiences unfold, our goals are met, and our lives are enriched – or not – as we choose. We are learning to create just as our Creator does: through our thoughts. We bring all into being, first through our thoughts, and then into form. We have everything within to create either the heaven or the hell that we see around us.

We constantly delight ourselves when our plans stay positive, and bog ourselves down when our plans turn negative. We recoil from all the negativity around us because our vibrations are changing, and what we could once tolerate at a lower vibration, we no longer can tolerate in the higher vibration.

We are aligning ourselves with the vibrations of the Mother Earth. She is getting ready to enter into a timeless realm, so time feels as if it is speeding up for us. A month now seems like two weeks. Even the youth are noticing how fast "time" seems to flow. We come from a timeless realm, and we are learning to adjust our vibrations into order to go back into the timeless realm while still in the third dimension.

This is all illusion is a common prevailing thought in the metaphysical community: only Spirit matters, all the rest is illusion. But when are any of our experiences, on any plane, in any dimension, *not* an illusion? Until we join into full union with the Source, what space do we enter into that is not a product of our thoughts? When we leave this plane, we communicate telepathically, so we constantly create the new reality we are experiencing – again, a product of our thoughts. Is not our state of *knowingness* just an elevated state of thinking through the Mind of God? Do we ever get away from thinking?

As we study *A Course in Miracles* (a course in spiritual psychotherapy that teaches us to connect to the Christ Mind – the level of unconditional Love), we learn that everything that we thought to be "true" before is not. We learn to discern and discriminate between the fundamental nonsense ("none sense") that has been thrown at us in order to control us. We learn to give up all ego investment in separateness; that all we need is within, and that everything that we need will be given to us.

We learn that there are both light and the dark aspects of self. The light is called the Higher Self; the dark the shadow self. They both exist within us. One is not better or worse than the other; they are just different. If we have come here to experience the "dark" aspect of ourselves, there is nothing wrong with that; simply a choice that we made while still in spirit. In the next incarnation, we may choose to experience the light. In this manner, the saint becomes the sinner and the sinner becomes the saint.

What an interesting world we have created!

Are there any new teachings about unconditional Love that appeal to you? If we feel that we are being strangled by the teachings of our birth, we can change them.

November 21

Gifts from God

The *Declaration of Independence* states: "All men are created equal, that they are endowed by their Creator with certain inalienable rights, among these are Life, Liberty, and the pursuit of Happiness." *A Course in Miracles* states: "All of its gifts from the peace of God are given everyone, and everyone unites in giving thanks to you who give, and you who have received." (Workbook, Lesson 188) Neither message states that some men are smarter, cleverer, more important, or more equal than others. These scribes for God both state, in one sense or another, that: "All men are created equal."

When the *Course* states that we are all given the same *gifts,* it refers to spiritual gifts. No man has been given any spiritual gifts that another has not been given. What one man can do – no matter how enlightened it seems – every other man can also do. The lives of the Masters who have walked this planet are quite remarkable and their message is the same. *Everyone who lives on this planet can do the same as I do.*

The gift from Self is that all "Selves" are created equal. Not one "Self" is given any gifts that another "Self" has not been given.

It is up to us to excavate those gifts. They are all there – all within us – just as the Master from Nazareth reminded us 2000 years ago; the *real* start of the New Age.

Yes, some of us do choose an exceptionally difficult path to negotiate through this lifetime; i.e., to be blind, deaf, quadriplegic, to have a rare genetic disorder, to be mentally slower than others, to be addicted, or to experience any one of hundreds of different challenges, but that is the choice of our Soul – to fulfill a soul contract about which only we and our Soul know.

All men are created equal; however, they chose to play different roles. The roles change polarities, for a role chosen in one lifetime can be reversed dramatically in the next. Thus, the saint becomes the sinner, the cloistered nun becomes the prostitute, the bigoted human becomes the oppressed minority, the self-absorbed becomes other-directed, and people who previously were totally ignored choose to be a celebrity in this lifetime. In this manner, the Soul can examine *an aspect of behavior* from all sides, which assists in its own evolution. Eventually, the Soul no longer needs to do this, because it has evolved enough to move off the wheel of karma.

See the beauty of role reversal. Think carefully about how we are using our roles in this lifetime, since we are building up lessons for another lifetime with every thought and every action. How boring to do otherwise. What would there be left to learn if we stayed in the same role over and over again, each time we chose to incarnate on this planet?

One man choosing to play an exciting role at this time is Dr. Masaru Emoto of Tokyo, Japan. He calls himself a water researcher. While not trained as a scientist, his finding, his experiments with frozen water crystals are influencing the way in which humans are accepting the effects of their thoughts on their own bodies and their surroundings. His research with water, documented in his self-published books (later published by major houses such as Hay House and Simon and Schuster-Atria) have reached *New York Times* best-seller status. Some of his books include *The Hidden Messages in Water, Love Thyself: The Message from Water III (v. 3)*, and *The True Power of Water:*

HADO Healing And Discovering Ourselves. These books show the exquisite crystals that form when water is exposed to words that carry a positive meaning, versus the grotesque forms that appear when the water is exposed to words that have a negative connotation. All the findings in his books show the vibrational effects of words on water, with a correlating effect that words may have on the water in our body, since our bodies are about seventy percent water at birth and fifty to sixty percent water as adults.

His experiments with HADO, the energy vibration emitted by water, showed the impact of prayer on pollution. Dr. Emoto led a group of participants to pray over the highly polluted Fujiwara Dam. The ice crystal formed by the water photographed prior to the prayer looked like a grotesque face in agony. The ice crystal photographed after the prayer was so exquisite that it was chosen for the cover for his fourth book: *The Hidden Messages in Water.* He displayed the results of words on cooked rice: one sample that had words of love spoken to it, one sample that had words of hate hurtled at it, and one that was ignored. Interestingly enough, the one that was ignored rotted faster and was more foul-smelling than the one that was subjected to negative comments. A bit about his research was illustrated in the movie, *What the Bleep Do We Know*; a movie well worth owning.

We each arrive on this planet with the same *gifts,* but we each arrive with *different agendas.* We are here to mine the fullness of insights from the roles that we have chosen for ourselves.

We are so much more than we think we are, or as in the words of Michael Roads, we are each a "magnificent, metaphysical, multidimensional Being of Love/Light." What we *see* is just the tip of the iceberg; the two to ten percent that is above the surface. Most of what we really are is hidden to us, until we are ready to uncover it.

Look for all the gifts that your life has brought you.

What are the gifts you have received from Spirit?
We can opt to use our gifts for the betterment of mankind.

November 22

A Resting Life

We all know them – the golden people – those who seem to never have to weather any crisis, whose lives are exemplary, whose finances are always in order, who are surrounded with luxury and freedom of movement, who have vacations whenever they want or need them, together with great health, advancement in business, and bright, successful children dedicated to building their own futures. This may not be your case in this lifetime, but it is always a choice for another lifetime – *a resting life.*

Some lives are meant to be a breathing space; a period in which to relax and rejuvenate – a resting place. Those lives are not just shining rewards for a job well done. They are circumstances that we have chosen for ourselves, to give ourselves a break from all the other incarnations where have we had many lessons to learn; many difficulties to overcome. As in every other major happening in our lives, we may sometimes choose a *resting life.*

Not every life is designed for crisis management and growth. That would be too difficult. We would be reluctant to come back to this plane of existence for any more *experiences.* Every once in awhile, we select a resting life for ourselves; one that is relatively free from difficulty and pain, one that flows smoothly, one in which we are comfortable and safe and secure, one where we live in the eye of the hurricane – the calm center – while everyone else is dealing with the buffets of the storm.

If a resting life is not your current experience, do not be envious of those who have it. Know that you can choose it for yourself the next time. Do not go around bemoaning to yourself or to others that life does not treat you fairly; that all the others have all the breaks. Instead of being envious of what others have, choose to develop your own gifts, to bring out the best in what you have to offer.

Look at what is showing up in your life constantly, for it is probably an issue on which you have to work. What circumstances keeps following you around like a little puppy dog?

If you notice a theme threading itself throughout your life, pay attention to what that theme is attempting to tell you. Chances are that is the issue that you came to excavate, to explore, and in which to participate – until you no longer need its lesson.

One of my issues dealt with ridicule. In elementary school, I overheard a fellow student call someone else a vulgar name heaped with ridicule, and I vowed that that would never happen to me. That vow had a disastrous effect on my life. Too often, my actions were stopped by the thought: *What will they think*? I never realized that *they don't care*; whomever it was to which that mysterious *they* referred. This thought of wondering: *What will they think?* strangled me; it kept me from pursuing a spot in the limelight, kept me invisible so as not to attract attention. It was only after thirty years of having my religious – then my spiritual – beliefs ridiculed by those who loved me that I realized that ridicule was no longer an issue in my life.

A friend of mine related how she experienced the theme of abandonment. Her father never came back from World War II, for he died on the battlefield when she was two years old. During her first marriage, her husband found someone else to whom he preferred to be married, and her mother died at a time when she felt vulnerable and alone. Other issues with family and friends heaped lesson upon lesson on her, to the point where she finally "got it."

When my friend spoke about all the conflicting circumstances surrounding her life, another one of her friends listened in quiet wonderment. This woman managed a horse farm, tended to her animals, took care of her loving, supportive family, and lived in splendid isolation; all free from pain and misunderstanding – a *resting life.*

A simple truth states: "What goes around, comes around." To anyone experiencing a resting life: Enjoy! Your time to experience "lessons" will come whenever you choose them for yourself.

Does your life qualify as a resting life? Prior to incarnating, we choose the type of life that we wish to experience.

November 23

Assistance from Spirit

Some souls choose to never incarnate, feeling the Earth plane is too difficult. Instead, they assist from the Spiritual realm and become our spiritual cheerleaders; staying in Spirit form, cheering us on, urging us forward when we feel that we have lost all hope, encouraging us when odds seem totally stacked against us. Those in the Spirit realm assist us by placing aids which help us through our perils: books, friends, and the physical, mental, and emotional support we need.

Pioneers received tremendous doses of spiritual assistance during the hardships that they endured across the mountains and plains of this country, as they continued their trek against incredible odds. George Washington lost the majority of the battles he commanded and was on the brink of despair, when he was visited by an Angel who showed him a vision of the future of the new country that he was helping to form. With a renewed ability to rally his men, he won several decisive battles that turned the tide for the cause of freedom. During the framing of the Constitution, when it seemed as if no compromise was possible from the southern states who insisted on their right to retain slaves, St. Germaine appeared and offered advice that broke the stalemate and allowed the northern states and the southern states to accept terms that guided this fledging country. These are not "facts" that appear in history books, yet somehow make themselves known.

While in crisis, how many of us experience a sudden burst of illumination which somehow manages to pull us through at the precise moment when our lives look as if they have collapsed around ourselves? *The Power of Positive Thinking*, by Dr. Norman Vincent Peale, helped me move me through my lowest financial ebb. Re-reading a paragraph, a page, or a chapter at the end of each night re-energized my depleted spirit bringing peaceful sleep, with Dr. Peale's words of wisdom floating in my head.

An invitation to join *A Course in Miracles* study group came from one of my tenants after a brief talk about the spiritual truth that *there are no co-incidences.* The *Course* introduced me to my spiritual family. From the moment I arrived, I felt I had come home. Several years of Bible study with an ecumenical group of Baptist, Methodist, and Catholic participants no longer calmed the restlessness within me, nor provided me with answers to the questions that kept morphing within my mind.

Besides the Spiritual Beings who assist us, sometimes there are those who lead lives only to serve others, such as Mother Theresa, the Dalai Lama, the late pope John Paul II, or Dr. Martin Luther King. When Mother Theresa visited Washington D.C., she saw a need to establish an orphanage and said she wanted it fully operational by the time she left the area *three days later.* No matter how vehemently everyone protested that was IMPOSSIBLE, due to all the forms, permits, construction, preparation of building, procurement of supplies, hiring of personnel, selecting the participants, she stood her ground. Three days later, upon her departure, that orphanage was in place and ready to accept its first occupant.

When he visited the Washington D.C. area, the Dalai Lama spoke in his own gentle voice, repeating his message into his native tongue so that his fellow monks could understand what he was saying. His message was brief and consistent with the main themes in his books: peace, co-operation between all nations, and reconciling conflict through diplomacy. Yet, throngs of people who had waited hours to see him treated him with the same enthusiasm teenagers offer a rock star, albeit much quieter.

Because the late John Paul II loved young people, he established a forum where youth from around the world would gather for a one day discussion about World Peace; a tradition continuing under the pope who was his successor, Benedict XVI. John Paul II continued to travel beyond the time his physical health made it comfortable for him to do so, and was treated with homage from all factions around the planet – even from avowed atheists.

Even though the aforementioned people led very visible lives, this world is filled with unacknowledged "saints" – people in every profession, in every walk of life, from the youngest to the oldest – who inspire us to do more with our lives. Every community has them; every town, village, and city. Usually the most exemplary lives come to light only when there has been an untimely death, before they have lived what the ego feels is a "full" life.

There are those who – when looking at what they consider is only a life of sacrifice – are horrified, never considering the possibility that they may be choosing that very manner of expressing their next incarnation.

How does inspiration and assistance from Spirit reveal itself in your life? We can each become aware when Spirit is infusing us with extra help.

November 24

Eradicating Negative Attitudes

Excavating and eradicating negative attitudes from our minds frees us from the bondage of other people's opinions; from the control other people have on our actions. Amongst the most controlling and damaging negative attitudes are:

BLAME: Once we comprehend that we are part of the One, we realize there is no one to blame, because there is no one outside of self. There is only self. Every time we blame another, we blame our "self." Blame and its fellow companions, shame and guilt, when tested by David Hawkins, M.D., Ph.D. (as described in his book, *Power vs. Force*) calibrate at the lowest levels of consciousness. Not exactly the best bed-fellow with which we want to hang out.

SHAME: In spite of this being an effective tool used by communities for eons, a human revolts against shame. Energetically, shame presses one's face towards the ground while the human's natural inclination is to stand upright. Shame builds rage within the body; an explosive anger that does as much harm to the body as it does to the mind of the victim it violates.

GUILT: While it is a totally useless emotion designed only to keep us small, weak, and paralyzed, guilt is a favorite mechanism of fundamentalists, and is used to control us since it is usually paired with blame, judgment and threats of burning in hell. Once we understand that we are only playing a "role" on this planet, we can rid ourselves of guilt. When we recognize that we are attempting to control members of our family by applying guilt, we can eliminate it from our repertoire of behaviors.

JUDGMENT: Unless we know a person's entire past, present and future, we cannot judge. We do not have all the "facts." Only the Supreme Creator knows the entire past, present, and future of anyone. Besides, our future is guaranteed, since ultimately we return to the Source, as does everyone else. In the meantime, we can choose to play all the "roles" that we desire for ourselves: light, dark, animal, vegetable, mineral, or human, in whatever dimension or whatever Universe our soul has selected for its growth.

SELF DOUBT: There are a great number of thoughts racing through our brains every minute. It takes our body hours to recover from just a few minutes of negative self-talk. We must remove those thoughts that do not make us feel good about ourselves. *If we can think it, and believe it, we can achieve it*, or we would not have thought it in the first place. If God brought us *to* it, God will bring us *through* it. We achieve freedom from self-doubt when we learn to align with our God Mind, rather than with our ego mind. Life is so effortless when listening to the inner voice of Spirit, and so painful when listening to our own "inner chatter" of self-doubt. Since we have so many thoughts running through our brains every minute, why not make them positive thoughts?

If you only recognize your real power, you would not doubt your ability any longer. You are a creator "Be"-ing. What you think about is what you bring into your life. Your self-doubt prevents any good from reaching you. The most important things in your life – a sense of peace, well-being, and happiness – elude you.

WORRY: If we keep track of that which we worry about, we discover that most of it never happens. We tie ourselves into knots over events that live only in our imagination. Our energy field is electromagnetic. We attract to ourselves exactly that which we think about. Our worry thoughts are simply setting up a field around us that is going to attract more worry. For a more effective way to live, we can bring into our minds only the *results* that we wish to see happen in our lives.

Many times, we cannot control the outer circumstances of our lives, but we can control our attitude about them. Those who were captured as prisoners of war or those thrown into concentration camps during World War II could do nothing about their confinement, but *only* the ones who were *determined to live* did. When a person gave up, there was nothing anyone else could do to encourage the discouraged one to live.

We lose power in direct proportion to how much we allow ourselves to wallow in negativity. All the aforementioned qualities are negative attitudes that serve as blocks to our understanding of who we really are. By eliminating every one of them from our thought system, and allowing our self the luxury of thinking differently from the way in which we have previously thought, we allow the Light to penetrate our minds. While we hold onto old negative attitudes that no longer serve us, we keep ourselves from experiencing the freedom that is so rightfully ours.

Eliminating blame, shame, judgment, guilt and self-doubt or any of the other negative attitudes can shift the paradigm on the planet from violent to peaceful. Changing our thinking can shift the planet to a peaceful place; a true Heaven on Earth. Currently, the etheric body of the planet – the collective unconscious of which Carl Jung wrote so often – looks as if it were thick grey smoke; it is so congested with negative thought forms. Even though Light workers around the world are energetically cleansing it, we can help by discarding negative attitudes as soon as they occur. By using the spiritual gifts we have been given, we can eradicate from our hearts and minds negative attitudes that have prevailed for millennia; attitudes that no longer serve mankind.

Let go of all the fear that has manifested itself into bundles of hatred, insecurity, self-doubt, misgivings, worry, judgment, blame, and guilt. Letting go of these negative attitudes will release us to accept joy, light, blessings, and good feelings into our lives.

This is the time of clearing. One way we learn to let go of negative attitudes is to bombard them with positive attitudes until we release the negative ones. Karmic release comes when we can experience something with which we no longer feel comfortable, and let it go instead of stuffing it back into our bodies, usually accomplished through forgiveness. When we are no longer interested in what we previously accepted – such as judgment – we are on a path to wisdom.

Do negative attitudes keep you bound in a little place, unable to move forward? We can eliminate all the negative attitudes from our thoughts and our behaviors.

November 25

One Soul

God created only one Soul and that one Soul fragmented into a great many personalities.

In his book, *Conversation with God, Book 3,* when Neale Donald Walsch asked God how many souls God created, God replied: "One."

Neale repeated the question, God repeated the answer: "One."

Even though one Soul splintered into a great many personalities, within this splintering, a natural progression occurred. In the early 1900's Alice Bailey brought to the planet, from the Ascended Masters, knowledge of the anatomy of the Soul: the I Am Presence (God) split into the Monad, the Monad split into twelve Souls, and the twelve Souls each split into twelve soul personalities. Thus, at any given time, there are one hundred forty-four aspects of our "personality" into which we can tap; one hundred forty-four aspects of our self that align together to share learning experiences.

If we all come from One Soul, how did we get so many forms? That is the gift of soul personalities. Each soul personality occupies a different form (a body). We each see our body as separate from everyone else's body, but we do not yet see the soul and how each soul is connected, both to each other soul and to Source. We will. We are formed from white light, and to white light we shall return. We are light snowflakes – no two of us are alike.

If this seems complicated, it is, but not beyond comprehension. As a multi-dimensional "Be"-ings, we defy time and space. Since all matter is composed of light and space, the smallest components of the physical body are also comprised of light and space. Is there any way that we can separate those minute components of light that make up our physical selves? If our body is frozen light, and our energy field is electromagnetic light, is there any way to separate out where our energy field ends, and where another's energy field begins? No, there is none, giving credence to the fact that we are one Soul.

Furthermore, since we all burst forth from the same Light and energetically occupy the same space, we can all communicate with every other "form" of creation telepathically. It is a built-in characteristic of our creation as "Be"-ings of light.

How does our auric field get to be so many different colors? A prism is clear glass cut on an angle. Only when the sun shines through it, can we see the beautiful colors in that clear glass; fractured bands of light forming the colors of the rainbow. Our core is a column of white light, and our chakras, if fully balanced, are also white light. However, if we are still working on issues related to the different rainbow colors of the chakras, (which most of us are), the bands surrounding our body – our subtle bodies – are multi-colored. When those issues have been resolved, we blend back into white light, reflecting the brilliance of the sun. When all our issues are resolved and we are fully balanced, we reflect that which is in our core; white light.

We come here to witness experientially for the Source; to be the eyes, ears, nose, throat and tongue for God, to be a songbird for the Spiritual realm, to proclaim our Selves as part of the great I AM.

Where do we begin and someone else ends?
We are part of One Soul splintered
into a great many pieces.

November 26

Thanksgiving for an Abundant Universe

Fall is the season of harvest, and the season when we thank God for all of our blessings. While other countries have their special day of Thanksgiving, ours happens to fall on the fourth Thursday of the month of November, somewhere between the 22nd and the 28th of the month.

We thank God for this abundant Universe. There are over *three hundred thousand* species of beetles alone. The Blue Ridge Mountains, forming a long ridge framing the Shenandoah Valley, contain *nine hundred* species of wildflowers and over one hundred species of trees. There is so much beauty on the planet that is abjectly ignored every day. Each season brings its own special magic show, and some of us do not even recognize when one season has passed and another one has begun.

It is in the Spirit of Thanksgiving that I would like to offer this blessing:

We thank you, God, for our health, just as we try to help those whose health has collapsed.

We thank you, God, for our healers, for their work in helping to restore bodies to their original vibrancy, and ask that Your healing energy revitalize them also.

We thank you, God, for our gift of voice, that we are able to say whatever we think, and ask that You send an extra dose of tolerance to those people who stifle any voice they consider the opposition.

We thank you, God, for our soil; for while grain is the staff of life, the soil is its foundation through which grain comes to life, and we humbly ask that the chemical companies see the wisdom of processing and selling natural fertilizers.

We thank you, God, for our trees – part of the lungs of Mother Earth – for supplying us with the oxygen that we need to sustain life on this planet.

We thank you, God, for the domestic animals that surround us; for their loyalty, their affection, and we also give thanks for the wild animals and insects; for their place in the cycle of life. We ask that our eyes be opened to the wonderment of Mother Nature.

We thank you, God, for the love around us; from our families, our friends, our co-workers, our compatriots, our service personnel, from those who repair our defects, and from those who keep our country running smoothly.

We thank you, God, that we can choose among the endless varieties; not only that which nourishes us physically, but also that which nourishes us spiritually.

We thank you, God, for the invisible Universe; for all the help we receive from the inhabitants of this realm – more than we will ever know – until we, too, join them.

We thank you, God, for enfolding us in Your Divine Grace and Divine Mercy.

Have you counted your blessings recently? We can become consciously grateful for all the abundance that surrounds us.

November 27

Releasing Old Paradigms

One of the limiting beliefs that was thrust on me (due to my Catholic upbringing) was that only those who were members of the Catholic Church went to heaven. At the age of fifteen, during the time I attended Mount Mercy Academy in Grand Rapids, Michigan, I felt so special that I was one of the "chosen ones."

That same belief stayed with me until the summer of my twenty-second year, when I worked for a lovely Jewish lady; an owner of a resort in the Catskill Mountains of New York, who embodied such thoughtfulness, care, consideration, kindness, understanding, and had only the best at heart for her family, employees, and clientele. In spite of all her positive virtues, *she was condemned to hell by my religion because she was not a member of my faith!* How could that be?

That question chinked the armor of control the Catholic religion had on me. Because I could not understand how it was possible that this lovely lady be condemned to hell, I shelved the thought. Simply buried it. *Do not want to look at it, examine it, study it, or think about it. Too busy.* Other more pressing matters took precedence, such as trying to earn a living while traipsing around the country, looking for a place to call home.

Eventually, the question would no longer stay dormant. It roused its red flag each day, nagging to get my attention. Finally, I had no choice but to address it, as well as the other questions that the dogma of my faith said I had to accept – or be condemned to hell myself. Something very disruptive lived within my mind, unsettling my body – nothing would stay still, and no amount of busyness would quiet the feelings and make them go away. No longer could I ignore the questions in my mind as they paraded out each day, leaving me feeling agitated.

Finally, instead of ignoring these questions, I went back in my mind to the time when the questions began, starting with my experience in working for the Jewish hotel owner. I began re-examining my beliefs from that starting point, which eventually led me to a study of comparative religions, where some astonishing facts came to light. The core of spiritual beliefs in the world religions, while not identical, is similar. However, the matters of dogma are wildly divergent, with most religions condemning the other groups to hell (except for the beliefs of indigenous people, which are more inclusive). Sifting through metaphysical information, I discovered that many of the major religions had the same "root," which would be a shock to the major world religions if they were able to accept that fact.

Contemporary religions, starting with Martin Luther's Reformation, were attempts to free themselves from the controlling aspects of other groups. These new religious groups then immediately put their own controls in place, in order to stifle opposition within their own group. Some sects had such strict limiting beliefs that they extinguished themselves. Some religions were perpetuated as a means of keeping financial control vested in the hands of a central enclave, not to be relinquished lightly.

Throughout the years, I had witnessed those who, while professing deep religious beliefs of their own faith, insidiously or overtly mocked the beliefs of others. I kept quiet. They would not understand, and besides, I could not change their minds, so (I felt) there was no sense in making waves.

Ultimately, I chose to accept those facets of religious beliefs that worked for me – centering on love, compassion, tolerance, divine mercy, and grace – and chose also to abandon the rest. My studies centered on spiritual truths, not dogma; lessons of unconditional Love and how to apply them in the world situation. Thus, I released the limiting beliefs with which I was raised, and stepped into an expanded version of my Self.

Do the paradigms within you serve the type of person you have become? If they do not, change them. And, no, you will not be condemned to hell if you do. When can you release certain restricting paradigms with which you grew up? When they no longer *feel* right!

Is blind acceptance of dogma causing you to be restless with your faith? We can bring all the questions regarding our faith to the surface for careful examination.

November 28

The Carpenter's Lesson

The tone adopted by a humble carpenter from Nazareth two thousand years ago, as he ushered in the New Age, used simple words set in a very simple style. Nothing about what he said was above the common man's ability to understand. Yet, so much confusion and dissent has arisen from his words of unconditional Love that wars have been fought –and are still being fought to this day – over their meaning. He spoke of basic truths; all relating to love, peace, and forgiveness. Both then and now, his words have been taken and used to justify the most outrageous acts of violence, torture and war. His message was one of love and peace, yet men used this message to escalate hatred and vengeance.

This all has to stop. Mother Earth can no longer sustain the atrocities that are being heaped on her as retaliation for another's religious beliefs. The time of war – that most barbaric act – has passed. Mother Earth can no longer sustain the energy of war and the hell and misery that spreads with it.

The entire message from Spirit has been altered. Man's hatred stems from *pride,* a level of consciousness that is *below* courage; the level at which (according to David Hawkins, M.D., Ph.D., author of *Power vs. Force: The Hidden Determinants of Human Behavior*), man sees problems as opportunities rather than as obstacles. The level of courage is the first level of consciousness that sustains life; one that brings us to a state of power. All the levels below it do not.

Before we let another season pass, let us lay down our arms, extinguish the hatred that suffocates us, and return to the place we came from; a place of love. The season ahead – the season of Christmas – is an excellent time in which to start. Even the most embattled groups have been known to lay down their arms and enjoy camaraderie with the enemy on Christmas Day; playing soccer and sharing food and cigarettes with the front line opposition. What we can do for one day, we can do for a lifetime – one day at a time.

No man can make another "pay" for some atrocity from the past. However, each man can forgive. The words *forgive*, *forgiveness*, or *forgiving* are mentioned 2,878 times in *A Course in Miracles.* Through forgiveness, each man regains the power that he so blatantly gives away.

Forgiveness wipes the slate clean and allows us to move ahead. Forgiveness brings light into the darkness. Forgiveness removes us from the wheel of karma.

Has the thread of a need for forgiveness
woven its way into your life?
Every Master to this planet expresses forgiveness
as an aspect of unconditional Love.

November 29

God Power - Keys to Understanding

We are learning to bring Heaven to Earth; to anchor Spirit into matter, to merge with the Divine. We do this by increasing our level of consciousness. Every time we become aware of Spirit contacting us, we merge with the Divine. Every time Spirit sends us a synchronicity and we acknowledge it, we merge with the Divine. No fireworks have to go off, no esoteric visions have to take place, no Beings of Light must come to us in the middle of the night. We simply have to stay tuned into that still small voice within ourselves; one that has been with us forever. That still small voice guides us.

And the Word was made flesh (John 1:14) is no longer a mystical thought – beyond our comprehension – to be accepted only on faith. The Word (the expression of God) was made flesh (material man). The essence of God became expressed in human form. The mystery is solved. Nothing is beyond our comprehension. Nothing has to be taken on faith because we cannot comprehend it. It is comprehensible. We can understand it because we understand who we really are – an aspect of God experiencing matter – a lower vibration of a Higher Being; All and Nothing at All rolled into One.

We are looking at alternative forms of ourselves when we look at all the different forms of man that we see. We are all One creation, split into a great many different forms. We come from One Source, contained in one essence of "Be"-ing. We see our self as different, but only the shell we inhabit is *different.* The essence is the same.

The essential you is identical to everyone else. The essential you is Love. You came from Love and you go back into Love and so does everything else. You are not alone. You have never been alone. Just as your Father/Mother/God has always taken care of the least amongst you, so will S/He/It take care of you. God is pure energy, and as such has no sexual nature. It is your civilization that continuously endows a gender to the Divine Infinite Spirit.

Go beyond your finite mind into your infinite mind. It is present in every cell in your body. When you access your infinite mind (as you grow in spiritual understanding), the silver thread inside your core grows. Even if it starts out as the most slender thread, as you fulfill your soul contract on this plane, your core grows. As you accept all aspects of the Creator as One, your core grows. As you grow into a place of unconditional Love, your core grows.

Everything that you need is given to you; every lesson, every material advantage or disadvantage, every person, ever situation in your life. Prior to incarnating, you and your Higher Self meet with your Soul Group, and you choose the major life lessons on which you wanted to work. You came here to reach your highest potential within the framework of the situation that you selected for the growth of your Soul.

The key is to stay connected to the Source; the God-force which powers you.

When do you feel connected to your God Power?
Nothing can prevent us from being One with our Source.

November 30

The "Word"

> *In the Beginning was the Word, and the Word was with God, and the Word was God.*
>
> *The Gospel of St. John, 1:1*

The Word is thought.
Thought is All There Is.
Thought always was, is and will be.
Thought is God, And Sound. And Light.
Thought and Sound and Light is God.
Thought and Sound and Light became Man.
But how?
Sound begat creation.
Light produced the Great Rays.
Thought was the Mastermind.
What is matter?
Frozen Light!
What is man?
Thought and Sound and Light
Solidified.

Thought and Sound and Light
The Holy Trinity.
Each combined together
Indivisible, yet Separate.
Amen.

What meaning do you give to the "Word?"
The Word is thought.

If we understand that we can tap into Real Power – the power of Love – any time, any place, anywhere, under any circumstances, then we can bear any incident with dignity and grace, because the Source of Real Power is within. Even if we are in the middle of an impassioned plea and someone cuts us off, we can still keep our energy flowing. We do not have to give our energy away, neither do we have to collapse under the burden of any shame or guilt because someone has cut us off.

The Source of Real Power – the power of Love; our power – is limitless. We do not have to let circumstances reduce us to a shaking, quivering mass of jelly because another ego has attacked us.

All egos have agendas. There is no way of knowing what agenda another ego has when it attacks, and what form that attack will take. Another ego's agenda can come masquerading in the form of a criticism or a judgment, applied in the most gentle and loving manner. It is STILL A CRITICISM OR A JUDGMENT, *and as such it comes from the ego and the ego is fear-based. We cannot control the circumstances that permit the remarks from an ego being hurtled at us. However, we can control our reactions by drawing on Real Power; the power of Love.*

When we come from a heart space, we are coming from the place where Real Power – the power of Love – reaches through into us. Our heart space has to be fully open to be able to accept Real Power. Eventually, all attempts by the little shrill shrieking ego to keep the heart space from opening will stop. Right now, that is not the case.

Accept Real Power – the power of Love – for yourself, because it is who you really are.

December 1

A Better Way to Die

"Everyone has to die of something!" a neighbor's mother once protested.

Not so! There is a better way. We have the ability to choose when we exit this planet from this great adventure that we call "life." We can learn to make other choices, and those choices will set us free. There is a better way! A better way to live and a better way to die. What is death anyway, but transitioning back to the state from which we came; transitioning back to Spirit.

Knowing how to die is important, but knowing *when* to die is the answer. Most writers extol a better way to live, but *how do we find a better way to die?* If we have lived our life to the fullest and are at the end, is there a better way than lying in a hospital bed, tied to a tangle of tubes while everyone involved feels as if they are quietly being sucked dry?

Fifty percent of the bankruptcies filed in the United States are due to hospital bills. Most hospitals extend life for an average of two weeks. Thus, fifty percent of the bankruptcies filed are due to someone *trying to extend another person's life for two weeks* – a life tied to tubes.

Look at the patient. Wired, miserable, helpless. Tubes everywhere. Poked, prodded, pricked and pushed. Life force ebbing away, drifting in and out of consciousness. The atmosphere heavy with fear!

Let us contrast this with *choosing* the time at which we are going to leave this plane, and *dying peacefully in our sleep* – knowing that whatever it was we were supposed to do is over, knowing that we are ready to leave. Taking the time and having the ability to say goodbye to those we love, calling everyone together for a big final dinner; a final farewell. Leaving with no regrets. Leaving because we choose to. Leaving because we know that the body that we inhabit is a temporary "space suit." Knowing that when we are ready to create another adventure, we will receive another body; another vehicle with which to work through our mission. Knowing that we can choose to incarnate with the same souls with which we surrounded ourselves with in this lifetime (if that is what we desire), or with other souls to which we may have become attracted, but who were on the periphery this time around. Alternatively, we can choose to surround ourselves with entirely different souls from those we met in this lifetime. We and our Higher Self choose whatever scenario we wish to experience.

How much more serene and peaceful is this?

Contrast dying tied to tubes to dying peacefully in our sleep. Dying peacefully in our sleep is a choice. And we can make it happen. Somewhere, deep within our core, we *know* that this possibility exists, just as we know the next breath we need is going to be there for us to take.

Hospice has partially answered the need to allow people of this planet to die with dignity. Patients are given all the pain-killing drugs, in whatever form they need, in order to manage the pain with which their body is wracked. Friends, relatives and neighbors come in to say their final goodbyes, without having to witness anyone writhe in agony. Fear of dying is lessened. No "heroic measures" are made to resuscitate the body. No feeding tubes are installed to keep a body alive when the mind no longer responds. Volunteers who serve in hospice come in the last month. Trained in helping the patient transition from this planet, they read to them, talk to them, and administer to their requests or just hold their hands. The patient is never left alone.

When we learn to live our truth, we learn to die the way in which we choose, not the way in which we have been programmed. Within the deepest part of our "Be"-ing is our connection to our Source. That never leaves us, and no one can ever take it away. It is there by choice and by Divine decree. Not the most wretched condition on the face of this Earth can prevent us from connecting to our Divine nature.

Sometimes, it is just before we leave this planet that we open ourselves up to the Divine within. Dying peacefully in our sleep is a subject that has not been commonly explored before. Now, however, it is. Consider it. There *is* a better way.

Why does so much fear exist around dying? When we learn as much as possible about the dying process, it helps to eliminate our fear.

December 2

Real Eyes ** Realize ** Real Lies

Eventually, we are going to stop lying to each other. Why? Because we are going to be tired of being sick. And tired of watching our babies die of cancer. And tired of watching our children die through senseless acts of violence perpetuated by monstrous egos who mean well, but who get way laid by political and military agendas. And tired of being rushed to hospitals tied to an endless array of tubes, when there is no possibility of resuscitation. And tired of being tired.

We are being fed a bunch of lies, and our bodies are revolting. Our bodies are saying STOP! There must be a better way! To re-program ourselves, we implement slowly, we start in moderation. One step at a time.

A good place to start is to read about the dying process, as written by those who are not horrified by it. Without parallel is: *The Tibetan Book of Living and Dying* by Sogyal Rinpoche; a treatise about ancient Buddhist traditions that can help us with every phase of living and dying. It gives us a new perspective about why we choose to come to this planet. It walks us through the process of life and what each process means; the karma and dharma of the choices we make. It offers several meditation exercises to open our channels to our Divine nature. It speaks of the evolution of the Soul and bardo, that mysterious process that threads all our lives together.

It teaches us to develop a relaxed and comfortable attitude around death and dying, and gives us the means to teach others to do the same. It takes us through a near-death experience, and shows how our every feeling, thought, emotion and action is influenced not only by those around us (whether we know them or not), but also by the environment, air and animals on this planet. It shows us how we are all interconnected to everything else; that all our thoughts go *somewhere.* It takes us through the entire dying process; what happens minute by minute as the four elements – air, water, earth, and fire – separate from the body.

You get all the spiritual help for which you ask. Always ask. If death is something that you greatly fear, ask for help in understanding it; for help in releasing yourself from the fear that you feel associated with it. Unless you reach Master level in this lifetime, as described in *Autobiography of a Yogi,* by Paramahansa Yogananda, you cannot escape death. But you can make it no more fearful than the process of, as the Dalai Lama says, *changing your clothes.* You change your earth suit for a spiritual suit.

No longer are we satisfied with the lies perpetrated on this planet; that death is something to be dreaded, that we will burn in hell if we did this or did not do that, that we will go to a place of NO HOPE for accepting beliefs outside of the faith of our parents, or of our culture. When we transition, we *go to* the place that we have *created* for ourselves on this planet. We can ask ourselves: *What am I creating here?*

As we learn to align with our Divine nature, we learn to fear no more. Upon our transition from this place, should we find ourselves trapped in a shadowy pit with vile creatures tearing at us, we know that we *can* transport ourselves out of it if we *pray.* We draw the Light of the Christ Consciousness to ourselves when we pray. The Christ Consciousness lets us know the level of unconditional Love; that anything outside of Love is illusion.

Have you thought about what happens to you when you die? Learning about the entire dying process frees us from misconceptions.

December 3

Where Did I Go? Vision of the Elements of Air, Earth, Water, and Fire

Where am I? I came into consciousness with a vague sense of an ethereal place; soft rounded edges, misty, as if wisps of a gentle fog have settled in, licking into every corner. Some areas shine luminous despite the fog, and I have a vague recollection of Light "Be"-ings speaking to me; giving me instructions, all gently allowing me to assess where I am in my process.

I remember thinking that *nothing is what it seems.* I must go back to that from whence I came. *Who is that Majestic "Be"-ing sitting on the throne?* I sense that it is an aspect of me, but it is so far removed from what I am experiencing that it is almost amused by my concerns. *What is the real power behind my throne?*

This place I am in pulsates with life. I first become aware of the metaphysical element of *air*, as even the *air* around me is charged with a vibrancy that I do not ever experience on the planet I call home. The molecules are electrically charged; the spaces in between vibrate with life. I sense bustling activity taking place all hidden behind this gentle fog.

But wait, the scene keeps changing. First, coming through the mist, massive, ancient tree trunks come into view and are speaking, slowly, with a sense of ponderousness that is befitting their stature as the lungs of the Earth. With grave sincerity, they speak of our need to clean up the *air* on the planet Earth. The atmosphere is being choked by the fumes that we throw into it. Their dire message: *You are choking the lungs of the Earth; her ability to breathe is being stifled!!* They slowly retreat.

Next, I am drawn towards experiencing the metaphysical element of *earth*. A massive interior appears with very high ceilings. Pictures of *great acts of kindness* are displayed on the walls, one at a time; not the usual display of conquering civilizations, or scenes from epic battles of war that adorn the important buildings on our planet. These acts of kindness come from every culture, every age, and every walk of life. It is through these acts of kindness that the consciousness of man elevates. It is through these acts of kindness that the *Earth* stays alive. It is these acts of kindness that nourish the Earth and give it the strength to keep going.

Then, *water* arrives; a vibrant cobalt blue streaked with lighter blue. The vessel of water holds myriad life forms – all thriving from the sun, food and oxygen on which they rely for their growth. From the cobalt blue of the deep ocean to the turquoise green blue of the shoreline, the water is clear, healthy, and alive. All of its life forms increase in volume; all is in balance. The oxygen in pure water sustains life; the life forms multiply and propagate themselves.

Finally, *fire* arrives, its massive sphere blazing red and orange; its great flaming tongues consuming whatever approaches. I stand in awe of this mighty force that can reduce all to ash. Even rocks melt and surrender their form. Its majesty is surpassed by none. It is from fire that we are formed. The simplest part of our "Be"-ing is the fire of light. We are the spark of life. At the elemental level, we are pure white light.

Thus ended the vision. I slowly come to full consciousness and continue with my morning writing, recording all that I just saw, heard and felt.

Are you having visions that you vaguely remember, whether awake or not? Change comes from conviction that nothing has to "stay" the way it is.

December 4

Opportunities to Heal the Planet

Healing comes in many forms. The next phone call you take might be an opportunity to heal someone. Not only you do have an opportunity to soothe a troubled soul, but in a very gentle way, can steer the person to a place of gratitude, serenity, or peace; to a safe harbor; a sheltered space – away from the turbulent mind that is common to most people. A gentle touch, a smile, a soothing comment becomes the balm that soothes the troubled waters of the soul. Never underestimate your power to change somebody's day; to change their life, to keep them from checking off the planet.

So often, people have such deep currents of unrest that they do not even know what is troubling them. They are uneasy, but from what? These currents of unrest are the Soul searching for a way to express Itself; its Higher Self, its God Self. You help free the unrest of the Soul every time you stop and offer someone a helping hand; a smile to lighten their day, a change in the direction they were heading.

It is your kindness that is going to change the world, not your stature. Your random acts of kindness are setting in motion a vibrational wave that is affecting future generations. Your prayers are cleaning up negative thought forms that pollute the planet and choke it. Your reverence for everything "natural" is spreading a love and respect for the planet that only the indigenous people have carried in their hearts.

Your violent natures are turning gentle. It is that softness that is changing the vibrational patterns that millennia of war-mentality put in place up until now. Slowly, man is sensing the futility of war and is seeking peaceful means to put an end to conflict; to reconcile differences. Many are now seeking diplomatic means instead of violent means to secure compromise towards the ends that each side demands.

More than anything now, the planet is in need of healing. Do not be in such a hurry to ascend off this planet. Instead, help anchor the energy of Spirit into matter. Practice your ascension techniques, but do them as a means to balance the planet to the perfection she once knew. You are always "somewhere." Any other place to which you go can sometimes be no different than this place, except that you instantly manifest that which you think about in the other place. Here it is a bit slower. There is no such thing as an extinguishment of being. Matter does not extinguish itself; it simply changes form. Matter cannot be destroyed. It can only be transformed.

What are you doing with all the matter you find here? Concentrate and focus on removing all the violations heaped upon this planet. Stop torching her tropical forests. The land that you claim is fertile only for a very short time, then the topsoil erodes. The soil designed to support tropical forest roots cannot support grassland. Trees are needed to anchor that soil to the earth. Nothing else will do it. Topsoil washed back into the ocean is of no use to you. Stop applying all the chemicals that you use now – especially those of you who have such a love affair with grass. These are chemicals that run-off and clog the streams and tributaries. All those chemicals eventually run into the great rivers; the bays and the oceans. Use only natural fertilizers. Cow, horse, and chicken manure are plentiful. Apply them directly from the pasture to the plot, or convince your chemical manufacturing plants to process them for home use.

Compost, recycle, and reuse. Do whatever is necessary to recycle and remove trash from your environment, especially the plastic that you discard by the mountain-full daily. Plastic does not disintegrate, ever! A million years from now, that plastic will still be there. Harness the "free" energy of the Universe. The technology is out there.

Send your healing thoughts to the planet as often as possible. The Spiritual realm can assist you, but cannot do your work for you. Stop fretting about not being able to do anything that makes a difference, and stop pretending that what you individually do does not matter. IT ALL MATTERS!!!!!!

What part of the planet needs healing around you?
Use every opportunity to heal the planet.
She needs it desperately.

December 5

A Leap of Faith

Before I came into consciousness this morning, I had two visions, one which was a repeat. First, I saw my Higher Self surrounded by rays of light; two radiating from the heart, one from each hand, a group from the crown chakra, and several more from the feet. Behind the vision of my Higher Self was a brilliant light that I sensed was God. This beatific vision showed me how we are seen by Spirit, and reinforced how powerful we really are. The energy of the Great Rays and the Christ Consciousness radiate from us as we tap into Real Power. When we lift the veil of our littleness, we see ourselves as part of the great I AM.

I cannot remember the second vision, but do remember it was a repeat of one that I had had prior. I don't remember who was speaking to me when I wrote the words that I received during this vision. However, after the vision faded, I wrote the following words: *I will forever carry your testimony to your faith in my heart. The turbulent waters that you encounter here are nothing more than surface "stuff." You have sunk your roots so far into your faith that no matter what happens, you will be anchored.*

It is visions like this that have always guided me towards the next step, and kept me from straying from my determination that I could do something else with my life besides selling real estate. Reminders such as this have kept me tethered to my computer, writing day after day, editing and re-editing, proceeding forward with hope that what I am recording can make a difference on this planet.

Since we have been given the greatest gift of all – the gift of free will – we can deny who we really are. We can spend lifetime after lifetime stuck in whatever drama we create, which keeps us convinced of our littleness. Alternatively, we can accept our brilliance and move on and harness our real power, take our place alongside the great Masters, and play our new role with great compassion and love for those who continue to stay in the same place of penury.

Stepping into our new role takes a great leap of faith. We accept on faith that our process will be supported; that we will have shelter, food, and clothing, that all our bills will be met. Some of us are told to change our lifestyles drastically; to leave the employment to which we cling (even though it does not nourish our Souls), to leave our spouses or our life partners, to change localities and move across the continent, or even to another continent. We are asked to accept on faith that what we are being guided to do *is correct,* even when marching forward with these new instructions might be edged with trepidation. It takes great courage to follow our inner guidance against the will of others, and we become all the stronger for it.

Uncover your gifts, uncover your essential nature, and uncover your true Self. You are "you," no matter who you think you are. You can stay in your little box, tethered to the familiar routine with which you surround yourself. You have free will to do that. Or you can expand to the size of the Universe. It is all your choice. Little box or the Universe. It is all still "you." Light or dark – still you. Big or small – still you.

Before he transitioned from the planet, Christopher Reeve wrote an autobiography entitled *Still Me*, which made me smile when I saw the title. The healing work he started in helping people who have had severe spinal injury walk again is his legacy. Many will credit their new-found mobility to his persistence to bring movement back to where there was none. His leap of faith in never denouncing his fate – and never bemoaning *Why me?* – came to fruition with all the technological innovations with which he experimented in his effort to heal his injury. He paved the way for more research. Christopher Reeve played his role magnificently on this planet, and fulfilled his soul contract with excellence. He shined his light into every corner of his work. He did not just fade away into oblivion after his injury. In fact, he had more attention given him rather than less.

Where does the light go when you hide from it? Still there! The fact that you hide from the light does not extinguish it. You have simply chosen not to see it. Your choice. The fact that you shut your eyes to the light does not diminish the light, nor extinguish it. You have chosen not to see it. Your choice. Free will is yours and will never be taken away from you. It is your special gift for having incarnated on this planet.

Send Love, because Love is what you are. Send Light, because Light is what you are. You will always be "you." It is not your willingness that makes it so; it is your willingness that uncovers it for you.

Have you ever had to take that great leap of faith into something totally new? The next time we are given an opportunity that we have never had before, we can each take the leap of faith.

December 6

Asking for Spirit's Help

Spirit is always willing to give us all the help for which we *ask*. Asking is the pre-requisite, we have to ask. The greatest gift that we have is our free will. Spirit may have great compassion for us, but will never override our free will.

Should you transition from this plane of existence and find yourself in any kind of horrible place, know that all you have to do is to pray and ask for Spirit's help. It will never be denied you. No matter how horrendous the conditions, no matter what the beings surrounding you say to you or do to you, no situation is hopeless. Just ask for Spirit's help, and a point of light will arrive. That light is a Spiritual Master who comes to assist you to a better place. Turn to the Light.

Be open to receiving. That is Spirit's way. Never feel that your situation is without hope; no matter what the conditions are, no matter what you may find happening to yourself, no matter how adamantly your belief system insists that you are being "punished" for your transgressions. Ask for help and it is given to you. You receive that for which you ask. Do not leave this planet feeling that you are stuck in any situation in which you find yourself, or feel that this is a permanent condition. Ask for help, and it is given to you instantly. The Master that arrives starts out as a pinprick of light speeding towards you. Follow the Light. Always go towards the Light. You are never bereft of spiritual help. All you have to do is ask for it.

Hospice workers, relatives, and friends of those in their final hours sometimes witness the patient's face light up with recognition of loved ones who have died years before who now surround their bed, or an Angel or saint from their religious belief system who has come in to help with their transition. Those who "come back" describe Beings-in-Spirit who have come in to assist them in their final hours. These visions give the dying person comfort, to know that someone is waiting to escort them to the next plane of existence.

While on this plane of existence, send all your fears up to the Light; putting them into the *Purple Transformational Flame of St. Germaine*. Those fears will be escorted to their next state of highest evolution. Let the Angels and other Spiritual Beings take those fears to the best place for transformation to their next place of evolution.

St. Germaine has a special commitment to assist the United States in progressing in its spiritual development. He has been here from the beginning, encouraging our forefathers during the writing of the Declaration of Independence, and in framing the Constitution, as recorded in Joshua David Stone's material in *The Ascended Masters Light the Way: Beacons of Ascension.*

There are many Highly-Evolved Spiritual Beings waiting to assist us. Besides the ones mentioned in the *Complete Ascension Manual* series by Joshua David Stone, Ph.D., others are written about in *Archangels and Ascended Masters: A Guide to Working and Healing with Divinities and Deities*, by Doreen Virtue, Ph.D. Highly-Evolved Beings-in-Spirit can help us with even the most mundane matters on this plane. They can ease our way through problems that seem insurmountable, sometimes by offering suggestions for a solution where there seems to be none; they plant a thought in our mind, a "whacky idea" that just may work.

Spiritual help knows no boundaries and is only a thought away. Use it.

Do you think about asking Spirit to help you?
Use the Purple Transformational Flame of
St. Germaine to help clear away fear.

December 7

Ego Issues

"The ego makes no sense and the Holy Spirit does not attempt to understand anything that arises from it." (*A Course in Miracles*, Tt, Chap. 9, Sect. III, Par. 3, Sent. 3)

The ego makes no sense because the ego operates under the guidance of *perception.* What it perceives to be true, what it thinks is true, *is* true – to the ego.

But if what one ego *sees* or *thinks* is not what another ego *sees* or *thinks*, each ego will argue their position to the death, arming themselves with all kinds of *proofs.*

When we live *only* in the first three chakras, we negotiate a path through this planet that looks solely through the eyes of the ego. We arm ourselves with all manner of justification for whatever atrocities that we wish to heap on others or on the planet, because we feel we are armed with "truth," and that "truth" *has to be* accepted by all.

When we believe we have the *right* to impose our *truth* on somebody else, we will stop at nothing to force our belief on the "other," even to the point of torture and death. Not only do we believe that we are right, but we also believe that we have a *Divine right* to *impose* our view on the "other." This is what leads to war.

Wiley, a nationally syndicated cartoonist, in his Sunday column of *Non Sequitur*, stated that *war* is an acronym for *W*e *A*re *R*ight. Is it any wonder that this planet has had only twenty-nine years of peace since recorded history began (according to the World Fact Book), or that at any given time, forty wars are being waged around the globe?

This all has to stop. The Earth is worn out. She can no longer fight off the atrocities that are being heaped on her by those who gut, slash, burn, and poison her and her atmosphere. She is beleaguered to the point where her nature spirits can no longer undo the harm that man has heaped on her in the name of "truth" or their rush to "progress."

We can no longer afford to claim that we are innocents and that all this is happening *to* us. We are part of the group consciousness. Everything that happens has collective conscious energy behind it. It exists in thought form first, before it anchors into material form. When the collective consciousness for war no longer exists, war will no longer take place.

What can we do? We can elect new leaders. We* can* refuse* to* fight. We can respond to all the attempts by the select few who take away the rights of the masses under the guise of "freedom" by voting them out of office. We can educate ourselves as to where all that chemical discharge goes, where the nuclear waste is buried, why the Chesapeake Bay is dying, why our oceans are dying, why the polar ice caps are melting, where the discards from our insatiable consumption are congregated. We can find out the sources for all the topsoil that fills up the deltas of major rivers around the world. A world without topsoil is barren. Just look at Mars. We can find a better way!

What else can we do? We can use low wattage incandescent or florescent light bulbs. We can stop applying poisons to our lawns and shrubs. We can compost. We can ask to be taken off mailing lists for junk mail. We can recycle *everything:* glass, paper, plastic, aluminum, and other metals. We can purchase hybrid autos that have high gas mileage, because of their combined use of electrical and gas. We can build homes that incorporate energy-saving techniques, and use appliances that have maximum efficiency ratings; small steps that make a difference.

What else can we possibly do? We can envision a world in which we live in harmony with the needs of the planet; in harmony with all the animals, plants, and other life forms on it – where small communities of diverse people group together for the benefit of all, where each person's talents are honored and diversity is acclaimed; where our needs are met through thought (the precursor to form), and where all energy is free – harnessed as a gift from the Universe.

We can envision a world in which all needs are met through loving kindness, where the Oneness of all of creation is acknowledged and glorified, where *any type of control* is considered barbarian, and where war is a distant memory fought by a primitive people.

We can envision a New World Order; one run in co-operation with the Spiritual Beings who assist us and this planet to maximum expression of our talents for the benefit of all.

How does seeing through the eyes of ego limit you?
We can each expand our sight to include spiritual sight.

December 8

Internal Power

Why do I wake up with all the wonderful words flowing through my mind, and then when I get up to record them – Nothing!!

What part of me still doubts? I ask my Guides.

My ego, is their reply.

Why does my ego still doubt? I query.

They answer instantly: *Your ego will always doubt. It wants to control your life. You have to relinquish control and become part of the Divine Will in order to come fully into your power. The Divine Will is your will. You just don't see it that way yet.*

This book is about *limitless power*; the *power* that we are, the *power* contained in the essence of our "Be"-ing. *Limitless power* to create according to Divine Will, for the benefit of *all,* not just to enhance the might of one person or one nation. *Limitless power* to *accept* the Oneness of all creation – acknowledging the rhythm, harmony, and intrinsic value of creation – not power to abuse, to crush, conquer, and vanquish a people, then divide the spoils of war. *Limitless power* to honor the sacredness of all life, to walk gently upon this Earth, with purpose and reflection; not power that terrorizes whatever it touches while attempting to expand dominion over everything else. *Limitless power* that acknowledges the right of all Earth inhabitants to partake in the abundance of this planet; rather than power which hoards wealth to keep it in the hands of a very few.

Unlimited power comes with you when you choose to incarnate on this planet. As *A Course in Miracles* states, "It is your birthright!" This power sustains you as you rise above all adversity, no matter how bleak the situation appears at the moment. This power causes your heart to open no matter what the experience you have had growing up, no matter how impoverished your upbringing was. This power supports your efforts to *get over* issues that need your forgiveness, because ultimately *you know there is nothing to forgive.* You know all circumstances have been chosen *by you* for the lessons that you wish to learn, and that your Soul Group (chosen by you) assists you in these efforts, each member playing their role magnificently to help you evolve.

Limitless power opposes nothing, because it knows that nothing means anything on this plane; that all things only have the meaning we give them. As Shakespeare's Hamlet said, "There is nothing either good or bad, but thinking makes it so." This is the power that *encompasses* all because it *is* all. This is the power that we *are.* Recognize it.

Where has limitless power appeared in your life?
The power within is limitless power.

December 9

Changing Negative Concepts

If you think you have only one shot at life and this is it – you either earn your heavenly reward or your eternal damnation by what you do in this lifetime – get over it. You have been here before. You'll come here again. You re-cycle through this dimension as often as you choose, until you learn to see all things through the same eyes as your Creator; with unconditional Love, with no judgment, with complete gratitude, with total blessing, and with complete acceptance – the Five Attitudes of God.

When my son was nine years old, a group of us were all standing in the kitchen, talking about matters of Spirit.

He pointed to an area about fifty feet long and said, "If you take this length and call it eternity, then my lifetime occupies a space about the width of an atom. Why in the world would I be punished for all eternity for something I did during a time that was so small?" Why indeed?

Throw out the concept of punishment for deeds ill done. Think about the possibility that the highly negative role – according to the world's judgment – that you may have chosen to play was for someone else's lesson. Certain souls have agreed to play the role of the "heavy" – the negative roles that this world judges to be wrong. It takes a very bright Being-in-Spirit to accept a highly negative role on Earth, since so much abuse is heaped upon the memory of that soul.

Betty Eadie recalls a near-death experience in *Embraced by the Light*. First, she is shown a vision of a drunken bum on a street in New York City, then sees that same person's Highly-Evolved Spirit – flashing brilliant colors of light – and sees how respectfully he is treated on the Spiritual plane. She recognizes from that vision the impossibility of imposing judgment on anyone.

Throw out the concept of victimhood, and replace it with the idea that every negative person and situation in your life is one that you have placed there as the "abrasion" that you need to rub up against, in order to change your mind about the way you think and about the way you act. Eventually – hopefully – you will get tired of playing the victim, and will find the inner strength to release that role and go on with your life.

In place of punishment and victimhood, substitute karma and karmic balance. The controller returns as the one being controlled. The abuser returns as the one being abused. The glutton returns as the one who starves. The greedy person returns as the one who is penniless. The slave returns as the master, and the master slave owner returns as the slave. All plays out in an endless cycle, until—we—let—it—all—go. The scenarios in which we have agreed to participate on this planet have been chosen *by us* for our own specific learning.

When we are involved in highly charged *negative* situations (which usually signify powerful lessons in forgiveness), generally, a group of souls (who are often best friends in Spirit) agree to come together and take their respective "roles" for the desired outcome. Consider the possibility that those who are our greatest enemies on Earth are often our greatest friends in Spirit. Only those who love us dearly in Spirit would agree to take such a harmful role on Earth, all for the lessons that we have chosen for ourselves. All is for our learning to make other choices, to choose otherwise.

Ultimately, we come to experience the *grandest vision* of our Self; to develop our highest potential, to fulfill our impossible dream, to accomplish a goal that is essential to the core of our being – yet seemingly *impossible* by our estimation or by the standards of the world. Nothing can hold us back: not time, not money, not educational degrees, not government restrictions, not family ties, not social status. We throw overboard previous entanglements, engagements and enterprises, and start a new journey in line with the dictates of our Soul.

When we follow the dictates of our Soul and fulfill our soul's contract, doors that were previously closed to us now open. By choosing to accept our soul's contract as our life work, we receive dispensation to reap the highest benefits in the third dimension. Our choices to follow the dictates of Spirit align us in all other dimensions on which we exist, and further enhance the evolution of the one hundred forty-four soul personalities of which we are a part. Our path is assured by our own willingness to follow Divine Will.

What are the negative events in your life revealing to you? Learn to take the negative events and turn them into positive results.

December 10

Take a Chance

God spoke to me today through my Self as I was reading a book, *Communion with God*, by Neale Donald Walsch. I felt only the gentlest tug and heard a little murmur in my heart space that spoke to my heart: *I am OK! I am right on. I am to go ahead with my special project in my little corner of the world, for I am that I am. I am all that is. I am one with the Creator; one with God, one with Self, one "Be"-ing, one aspect of Divine Truth, one little step of mankind, one little truth to be shared, one ounce of kindness to be spilt out of the vessel it is contained in. One.*

So let it begin – the long journey to my way home – this journey that began fifty–five years ago when two big beautiful blue eyes first opened and beheld her new home on a new planet; this place called Earth. From the Cosmos I came; a long way away, a gifted Soul, a Highly-Evolved Spirit, subjected to temporary amnesia.

Now, I step forward to my rightful place in the Universe, along with a chorus that continues to swell out to the heavens:

Let it be me, Lord.
Let it be me and me and me.
Is it I, Lord?
You want me?
Who am I?
The great I Am?
Take a chance, My child!
For God's sake, take a chance!

Where are you being asked to take a chance? When nothing seems to work, sometimes we need to take a chance towards a new beginning.

December 11

Beauty and the Beast

Many have been entertained by the movie and the stage production of *Beauty and the Beast*. However, this delightful tale suggests a deeper meaning: Beauty is Love, Beast is all the ugliness that can be transformed by Love. Because of her love and affection for her father, Beauty is willing to sacrifice her normal existence to save her father's life; to trade her confinement with the Beast for her father's freedom. No matter how frightened she is, she chooses to stay with the Beast. Over time, Beauty (Love) sees the goodness in the Beast and extends her love to him. In doing so, she is able to free this handsome young prince from the tyranny of the spell that changed him into a frightening-looking Beast.

Everything is transformed by Love. All is conquered by Love, because there is a spark of Divinity in all things – no matter how imperfect they seem to be as perceived by the ego. Because perception *changes* with each perceiver, perception is a fruit of the ego; not Spirit. Love is a gift from Spirit; a gift from the Source to all creation. Love brings out the perfection in all things, just as Beauty, through her love, released the perfect human being trapped within the form of the Beast.

How can we apply this tale to our lives? According to *A Course in Miracles,* since we do not know the true meaning of anything, we are asked not to judge even the most atrocious act or the most heinous crime, no matter how brutal the attack. We are asked *not to judge*. Most of the events that we witness today have had their origins eons ago. *Nothing is what it seems.* Deliberate acts of misbehavior, violence, and corruption that have been set in motion in the prior week may have had their origin in previous millennia. Since we do not know the origin of events, we are asked not to judge.

Life is about learning how to see the perfection in all things. Life is about learning *how to love* when we would prefer to *hate* instead; to *reconcile* when we would prefer to *divide;* to *reconsider* when we would prefer to *dismiss;* to *accept* when we would prefer to *reject.*

In 2005, *The Washington Post* carried an article about a young woman who, as part of a prank to get back at an old boyfriend, set on old mattress on fire on his balcony; a fire that then smoldered and later spread out of control in the middle of the night. It was instrumental in killing four young people who were sleeping in the complex. The young woman was identified, sentenced to life in prison, and was extremely remorseful for the pain she had caused three families – one of whom had lost twin daughters in the fire. She vowed to spend the rest of her life helping woman in prison reconcile the issues that caused them to get thrown in prison in the first place. In the meantime, one of the men who had lost a daughter started to visit her in prison, because she reminded him of his child, and because he believed in the newly-found work she was doing with female prisoners.

As I read this story, I received an inner vision of this young woman's karmic mission. Her soul contract was to help female prisoners from *within* the prison setting. While in Spirit, she willingly agreed to participate in an action that she knew would land her in prison, just as the four souls who "died" also willingly agreed to participate in their role of "victims," and their parents chose to receive lessons in forgiveness.

As this entire scene in Spirit was revealed to me, I felt wonderment in the perfection of the Divine plan. The father willing to visit her in prison had chosen to forgive her, thanks to his Higher Self prompting him to understand the nature of his soul contract; revealing a glimmer of it to help him with the forgiveness process.

Even though something to which we may have agreed to participate looks *beastly,* when we recognize the aspect of it that is part of the Divine plan, we see nothing but the *beauty* in it.

Has something that has horrified you initially ultimately offered you a benefit?
Ask to be shown the relevant part of the Divine plan in "difficult" situations.

December 12

You Are What You Fear

"The only thing we have to fear is fear itself." words chosen by Franklin D. Roosevelt in his first Inaugural Address, and designed to encourage and to help extricate a nation gripped in the fear precipitated by the Great Depression.

You have heard the phrases *you are what you think* and *you are what you eat.* Now, expand this further to include *you are what you fear.* The sum total of your energy field – the invisible part of you that influences how your body feels – is directly affected by that which you fear, because that which you fear sets up energy blocks which prevent the free flow of energy from the Divine. The core of you then becomes muddied and constricted. The energy field around you becomes filled with darkened clouds of debris. Your matrix grid – both inside and outside your body – becomes twisted and tangled, which prevents energy from moving smoothly throughout your body. The intersecting points within your matrix grid no longer communicate with each other. The "lights" are out.

These blocks are created within our energy field each time we that experience something that causes us to trap fear within our bodies. Should we have experienced drowning in one lifetime, something about the experience – whether it is the fear of water filling our lungs and choking us, or the fear of losing control, or the fear of going into an abyss – becomes a fear that is trapped in our cells. This sets up blocks in our cell memory. These blocks – *issues we feel that we cannot face* – start at the highest level in our energy fields and filter down to each successive level and do not go away until we release them. Only by releasing them can we each free the energy in our field; allowing it to flow smoothly and freely.

We may have called into our sphere several attempts to release the blocks by reconstructing the experience of drowning in this lifetime. This is one of my core issues. I have always been uncomfortable in deep water, even aborting an attempt to learn how to swim after being told that we would be asked to hold our breath while sitting on the bottom of the pool. Not me. I almost drowned as a child but an adult was close enough to rescue me; was "rumbled" as a young adult during an outing at the ocean, but again, another person was close by and pulled me from the surf; and always hugged the side of the pool when in deep water.

When past life experiences prevent us from enjoying deep water, then we still have to learn that we are *not* our bodies. Only when we remove the blocks, can we be on our way to understanding *Who We Really Are*.

Is Love stronger than Fear? That is the only question that we have to answer, for our answer will determine which side we are on; Love or Fear. It will decide what our priorities are; how much peace we wish to have in our lives, how we conduct our business, and how we react to everything that we perceive in our lives. When things go *wrong* (as they surely will), whether we choose Love or Fear will determine everything we think, say, do and feel in our lives. We may feel the need to pray that we choose the right side. However, *there is no wrong side.* Whatever side we choose simply reflects where our Soul is in its evolution.

When we can fully accept that "the only thing we have to fear is fear itself," then we are on the way to healing the constricted parts of ourselves.

Do certain fear issues continue to appear in your life? Recognizing your fears is the first step to removing energy blocks.

December 13

Facing That Which We Fear

What we fear the most is what we will have to face – eventually. We can face it in this lifetime or in another; the choice is up to us – but face it we must in order to release it. When we are able to go into *the belly of the fear* – whatever that fear might be – we will find that we are still OK. Our consciousness is intact. We have survived. We are whole and complete. We have come out the other side.

Neuroses are methods that the ego sets up to escape facing fear. Psychoses are means to block fear to the extreme. Once we go into the belly of the fear and come through the other side, we are never the same. We come through with a state of grace; a sense of peace, a sense of accomplishment – but most importantly – a sense of the Higher Self that we really are.

How do you journey into fear? Very simply. Start by making a list of your fears. As you continue to write them down, more will surface. This might take days, however you will get to the next point in time whether you do this work or not. The days will pass anyway without you having done this work, and you will be no better off than you are right now. Do it now! Start today! Start to list your fears.

Next, lie quietly on your bed, and *starting with your earliest memory,* recall the things that you fear the most. It may be the fear of punishment, the fear of retribution, the fear of attack, the fear of choking, the fear of heights, the fear of being ridiculed, the fear of a person, a particular animal, object or act. It does not matter. Each is equally important. None are insignificant. Recall the fear and bring up the entire emotion that sent you into a tailspin: the shortness of breath, skipped heartbeat, choking sensation, lightness, vertigo, sweaty palm or forehead – all the sensations that you have been stuffing back into your body all these years. Whatever you fear – no matter how big or how small, how important or how insignificant it is – call that fear into consciousness. It is only by facing your fear that you can eradicate it from your energy fields, both inside and outside your body.

See yourself approaching your fear; standing at the edge of it. *Breathe deeply!!!* See yourself entering that fear; standing in the middle of the "belly of the beast" – totally enveloped in it – until the fear passes, probably about twenty minutes. *Let the feelings course through your body*; again, this entire process of bringing the fear to full consciousness and letting the feelings course through your body takes about twenty minutes. The feelings will move through each cell of your body; from the bottom of your soles, to the top of your crown, to the tips of your fingers – through every bone, through every pore, every membrane, and every organ. It is only by going through the emotion that you release it. Nothing else will do. You *have to feel it* and allow it to flow through you. Tackle one fear a day until all are released. Release, Release, Release.

Once you begin, you continue because it feels too good to stop. You feel a sense of freedom such as you have never experienced before. The net effect is the feeling of *Whole-someness*. You start feeling *whole* again.

Think of how much energy we have spent keeping fear from surfacing throughout the years. Think of how many times – and in how many ways – the emotions have surfaced anyway. They *will not* be held back. We keep building bigger and bigger blocks to hold the emotions back. The blocks become walls, and soon we are imprisoned in a prison of our own making; one which keeps us from enjoying life, engaging our passion, and living joyously. Sadly, we do not have a clue how we got there.

There is nothing to fear. We have made it all up anyway, and we can unmake it. We are never stuck – we only think that we are – no matter how vile the situation in which we find ourselves.

Above all, ask your Angels to help smooth the way to clear out the psychic debris and replace it with white light.

What is the greatest fear that you are not willing to face?
Facing our fears helps eliminate them from our energy fields.

December 14

The Biggest Burdens

The most enlightened souls take on the biggest burdens; the weight of which would crush newer souls. Sometimes the "newer" souls are those who create huge burdens for the older souls who have agreed to journey with them. Newer souls do not have the wisdom to discern the repercussions of their actions. They may succumb to the temptations that this planet has to offer, and have not learned to act responsibly as they will learn in future lifetimes.

Sometimes a soul is not certain that it wants to come here, or once here, not sure that it wants to stay. According to metaphysical teachings, SDS (sudden death syndrome) occurs when the soul of the infant changes its mind about staying on Earth. This creates an enormous burden on the parents or caregivers of the infant, who invariably fall into blaming themselves or seek to blame others for their baby's sudden demise.

Sometimes a soul is "hitchhiking" through the galaxy, and decides to investigate planet Earth to see what living on the third dimension is all about. They may not be happy with what they find here, but once here, decide to stay. The lives of such souls, and the lives of all whom they affect, may be filled with high drama, for they are not yet used to living in the third dimension. The full impact of the calamity caused by the "hitchhiking" soul may be felt for generations by their progeny on this planet.

Parents who have agreed to give birth to handicapped children, as well as the children themselves, are all advanced souls: the parents for taking on the caretaker role, and the child for agreeing to the mental, emotional, or physical challenge. A soul who wishes to become a teacher to others (in the same situation, but in the next lifetime) may use the handicap in this lifetime to fully understand the challenge, for deeper capability in the next. Experiencing the deficiency first-hand in this lifetime plants the information into their cell memory, while releasing karma from other lifetimes.

The parents who experience extreme pain in the third dimension, because of the suffering their child goes through – parents who agree to nurture a child through a coma, a debilitating illness, a heart condition, paralysis, muscular degeneration, terminal cancer, or an early demise – are also advanced souls, because only advanced souls would agree to such a mission; the newer souls would be crushed. Sometimes the soul of the child is of Angelic origin. They have asked for the experience, to learn what it means to be "human." Sometimes, both parent and child are of Angelic origin.

The physical being that you are may belie the spiritual "Be"-ing that you are. You may have been subjected to someone who did not seem to have your best interests at heart on the Earth plane; someone who may have physically, emotionally, or mentally abused you. While your Spirit Self welcomes that treatment, your ego self derides it. You may spend an entire lifetime getting over the effects of the conduct to which you have been subjected, but once you do – and are able to forgive the perpetrator – you have lifted a huge weight off your physical body, and come out of this lifetime with a radiant triumphal color band added to your Spirit body.

Engulfed by a very dense layer of consciousness (which must be cleared before Mother Earth can move on to her next place of evolution), this planet is a very difficult one to which we must adjust. Anyone who comes in from a lighter plane is necessarily going to feel like a misfit, especially within their own body.

One way to cope on this plane of existence is to shift back and forth from the physical plane to the Spiritual plane, while in *full consciousness*. Do what is necessary to sustain your earthly life – perform your responsibilities here fully and completely – then retreat to your spiritual life. Through the assistance of all of your heavenly helpers, you can learn to stay connected to Spirit at all times while still performing your earthly chores.

We are never given a burden that we cannot carry, and we agree to our chosen tasks and roles while still in Spirit form. Asking for all the spiritual assistance available helps us to carry our burdens with dignity and grace, even when we feel overwhelmed. We receive that for which we ask.

Have you agreed to carry an extra burden on this plane of existence? Asking for grace helps us with the life challenges to which we have agreed on this plane.

December 15

Staying in Tune

People say that they *never* get any spiritual messages. That is not true. They are bombarded with spiritual messages, but refuse to listen. They may hear a spiritual message, but doubt what they hear. They may be given intuitive "hits" over and over again, but refuse to act on them. Instead, a person may may close their third eye and shut down their solar plexus, so as not to see or feel what is coming to them from Spirit.

Messages come in many forms. When the person who became my first husband entered my room in the middle of the night, asking me to pay him back the few dollars I had borrowed from him so he could leave town that night, my roommate suddenly bolted up in bed, horrified – she that dreamt there was a snake in her bed. As he continued to talk to me – keeping me up all night, telling me that he was leaving for good from the resort where we were working for the summer – the door to the bedroom suddenly swung shut, and I had a sense that someone had left the room. Before the next day was over, I was married, and frankly did not even know how I got there.

Did I receive any messages? I received, but did not hear. Had I listened to the "warning" omens, the trajectory my life's path took would have been far different. But Spirit had something else in mind; helping me evolve into a person of compassion and forgiveness.

What if you had agreed to become a metaphysical teacher during this lifetime, but now are bombarded with self-doubt about all the messages you receive? This leads you to become a prolific student of the metaphysical – taking one class after another – until you are a virtual repertoire of metaphysical knowledge; receiving certification after certification from each class. Yet, you continue to harbor doubts about what it is that you know. Your doubts propels you to seek out yet another class; another certification. Has Spirit contacted you? Yes, but your doubt gets in the way. How very beneficial to mankind, when you finally take a stand and become the teacher that you contracted to be.

I never saw myself as a healer. Writer, yes; speaker, yes; but *healer?* Yet my teacher, Wanda, saw a healer within me. A talent for healing was also confirmed by an astrological reading that I was given by a gifted astrologist of German parents, Haloli Richter. Born in Austria, she practiced for over thirty years, and only towards the end of her life used the computer to make her charts. She stated that I should be on the cutting edge of healing modalities; that everything the *farthest out* was within reach for me. I accepted both of their assessments of my ability to channel healing energies, and incorporated healing into my lifestyle.

Writing was not a problem, since I was constantly bombarded with messages from Spirit and continued to record what I heard. To open to my healing Self, I signed up for all the classes that my healing teacher offered, then went into a mentoring program with her, was ordained a minister, and served on the Board of Directors for the Rays of Healing Church that she had started. Only grace helped me accept *healer* as part of who I am.

My role as teacher of God began in earnest after I became a Reiki instructor and a speaker in the lecture series offered by the Rays of Healing Church. I have taken my place as one of God's teachers; a role that seemed *impossible* for me to play when my Guides first told me (in 1988) that I was to be a teacher of God.

Even though I have always received messages from Spirit, the task of how to distribute these messages frustrated me. My earliest overture to a newspaper about writing a metaphysical column never materialized. My first attempt at being published by a mainstream publisher resulted in self-publishing. When I asked my Guides *why*, they answered: *There is something else that you have to know.* That *something else* was healing work.

As I continued to write, I continued to receive enough material to produce more books. But more importantly, finding the courage that was lacking in the earlier part of my life is no longer a challenge. What do I have to lose? *A reputation?* That is intact, for some clients have stayed with me for decades, while others have fallen away. Those who were meant to stay did; those who were meant to leave, did.

Heavenly muses align with me in the morning as I receive inspiration from within. My Angels are a constant part of my life, and never leave my presence. I call upon them in gratitude many times throughout the day, especially when my fingers fly across the keyboard. They implant within my mind that which I have to bring forth.

I stay in tune with my heavenly Guides, and encourage you to do the same. As you continue to develop your spiritual talents, you bring forth that which is in your soul contract. The fact that you are following the monthly meditations in this book confirms that you are open to guidance from Spirit.

Have you been receiving spiritual guidance to which you have not paid attention? We all get bombarded with spiritual messages that we ignore.

December 16

Recipient vs. Creator "Be"-ing

There is a difference between thinking we are the *recipient* of our lives, to thinking we are the *creator* of our lives. Even the most enlightened humans can fall into the trap of saying: *This too is perfect*, or *All is as it should be*, or *See the perfection in all things* – all the while surveying devastation surrounding themselves. Then, even as they are making these statements, they may *still feel* as if they are the *recipient* of everything that has gone wrong. Somehow, they do not recognize that they have *created* the devastation. They think of only *receiving* it as their lesson.

If we can recognize that – *on some level* – we create everything that we experience, then we can release the feeling of victimhood. Even if we do not think of ourselves as a victim, if we do not recognize ourselves as the *creator* of all that we experience, on a subconscious level we may still feel victimized. As long as we continue to see ourselves as the *recipient* of all that we experience, we absolve ourselves from any role in its creation.

The most commonly prevailing thought on this planet is that *things happen,* rather than that *we cause them* to happen through our group consciousness. In the 1980's, world leaders were spiraling out-of-control in their haste to escalate and stockpile nuclear arms. These actions were leading us closer and closer towards nuclear annihilation, until groups of concerned people around the world declared: *This is madness. What are you doing?!?!?!?!* Many common people spent their life force trying to get countries to stop the nuclear arms race called *Star Wars*, and despaired that their efforts made a dent. Priests and other consciousness-minded adults were willing to risk being jailed for their anti-nuclear activities, in their efforts to bring a level of awareness about the idiocy of a nuclear arms race. And slowly, their efforts paid off. The madness subsided.

The rest of us whistled while we worked, for we went about our daily lives as if nothing different was happening *out there.* However, group consciousness changed and we stopped marching lock-step into the arena of nuclear stock-piling. All those who spoke against the build-up of nuclear arms *did* make a difference.

The group consciousness that had once leaned toward annihilation has softened, and today speaks of peaceful resolutions framed in diplomacy; of continuing talks until an agreement has been reached. Too many people have recognized that this planet is by far too important to be blown up by savage power seekers – motivated by greed – who have only their own interests at heart.

Past successes between two sides of thought – originally separated by a chasm of differences – have shown the world that we *can* meet in the middle. The peace accord negotiated by President Jimmy Carter in the 1970's changed the mental climate of this world, and brought a new paradigm to this planet: *Peace is possible through negotiation.*

Group mentality composed of mostly negative thinking (the "collective unconscious" described by Jung) hangs as a thick dense grey layer in the etheric body of Mother Earth. Light workers around the world, in their effort to shift the collective consciousness of man, have been working to clear this thick dense grey layer of negative thought forms. When the pressure becomes too great, she clears herself by using the forces of Nature: typhoons, hurricanes, tidal waves, tsunamis, volcanic eruptions, and fires that rage out of control.

According to the teachings in *Autobiography of a Yogi* by Paramahansa Yogananda, our physical universe hangs like a small bubble at the bottom of a huge astral plane. On the astral plane (which is the closest dimension to planet Earth), that which we think about, we create *instantly.*

That is why we should monitor our thoughts so carefully while on the physical plane; to keep our thoughts focused only on that which we wish to see in our lives. It is our thoughts that create our reality. Thus, it is critical to learn how to think positively on this plane of existence. Since our "creations" are slower to arrive here, we have the leisure to *undo* our creations. In other dimensions, our thoughts manifest instantaneously, and we are caught in a web of our own making – often not knowing how to extricate ourselves.

One of the most damaging "creations" on this plane is prejudice. Prejudice and its cousins – bias, bigotry, intolerance, and ridicule – stem from fear; the *fear that the oppressed will become as powerful as the oppressor.* Fear did not originally govern this planet, and it has just about run its course. Brandishing fear in order to control is slowly shrinking, as people around the globe recognize that all fear stems from the ego and that (according to *A Course in Miracles*) "the ego is insane."

However, there is still much resistance, by those of the lowest vibration, to letting go of fear as a control tactic. All those in power who operate from a place of fear are right now making the loudest noise on their way out; screaming obscenities as they are being ushered off the planet. They still think they are in control.

To achieve peace, whatever fear that we have created must be released from our lives. As we release the lower vibration, finer higher vibrational patterns arrive to replace the denser lower ones. Whenever we come from a position of love, we look around at our new creations, and recognize that we are operating from an elevated position and that this is good.

Whenever fear rears its appearance in our lives, we have the option of taking it firmly by its haunches and escorting it out the door. By eliminating it from our energy fields and from all that surrounds us, we create a new dynamic of love.

You are a Creator "Be"-ing. Recognize it. Accept it. Assimilate it into your being.

Can you accept all the ways in which you are a creator, not just a recipient, in your life? Pay attention to how the planet clears out debris from our negative thinking.

December 17

Chipping Away at Chains

By recognizing your Self as a creator "Be"-ing, you are more able to remove the etheric chains that block your understanding, your creativity, your joy, and your expression of Self. You are as vast as the Universe, yet you settle for a grain of sand. Chip away at the chains that block you, but chip away in love; not in frustration, not in anger, not in spite, not in hatred, and not with wrath. These are all manifestations of fear. Chip away with love; with joy, with whole-some-ness, with happiness, and you will restore your well-"Be"-ing.

Take responsibility for all you see in your sphere; knowing that you put it there. The Universe truly does revolve around you. You have put into it everything that you see; you and no one else. Recognize that, accept it, embrace it, and you will see the chains that bind you fall away – just as the shadows fall away when the sun come out. Chains are no more than shadows, nothing. The only meaning they have is that which you give them.

To see the how the chains within our current political climate block us, go back to the founding of this country. Our forefathers sought for us a new world summarized by three lofty goals: *Life*, *Liberty*, and the *Pursuit of Happiness*. They placed our future within the hands of God, as written on our dollar bill: *In God We Trust.* Somewhere, along the way, we seem to have lost those goals, since we are being told that we cannot handle even the most basic elementary freedom of planning *our day*, much less *our lives*. We are being subjected to huge restrictions in the name of freedom, while at the same time, our basic human rights are being eroded daily by those who control through the use of fear. We need to go back to the ideals that our forefathers had in mind for the future of this country; to the writings of Thomas

Paine on which most of their idealism was based, and to the scriptures – to view them as our forefathers did – not to control, but to guide.

Many of us, after viewing the events that pass as daily "news," rant and rave at a glowing TV screen, then go about our business as if nothing has happened. As we break through the chains that attempt to limit our understanding, we see that we have the power to send Love and Light to any place in the Universe through our hearts, our minds, our eyes, and through every cell in our bodies. Nothing can stop us from sending Light and Love, and it is that Light and Love that will melt the most ingrained fear. No circumstance can take that power away from us.

When we recognize that the chains that bind us are just shadows – merely thoughts within our minds that constrict us – we can re-direct our paths towards personal *freedom*. We can bring forth a new paradigm: the thousand year's peace that we have been promised on this planet. As we establish this new paradigm for ourselves, we prepare to emerge in a new form, just as the newly-transformed butterfly emerges from its cocoon and quietly waits to dry before spreading its wings and taking flight. When we break free of our limitations and quietly go about our work spreading Light and Love, we see that we, too, can fly.

What thoughts do you need to change, to help bring about the thousand year's peace that this planet has been promised? By sending Light and Love through our thoughts, we can make a difference.

December 18

Your Thinking Makes It So

What one person sees as a gift, another sees as a judgmental act. One nationally-known speaker claims that each morning, he and his spouse partake in a ritual exchange as a re-affirmation of their love and commitment towards each other, and assert that it strengthens the bond between them. Another might look at that ritual and find it to be self-demeaning, draining, and judgmental.

It is whatever we think it is. When we hold reservations about another, because we think that at any time we have contact with them, they will "bite" us – they will. Our thinking makes it so. If we expect an insult, we will get one, because our expectations make it so. The irony is that our *conscious mind* may *not* expect an insult, but we get it anyway – for our *subconscious* belief (the underlying belief below the threshold of any consciousness) *does not believe we are worthy*. The electromagnetic energy field that surrounds us attracts whatever beliefs we hold. If we have low self-esteem, then all things that *lower* our self-esteem come flying towards us.

When we gather in a social situation – be it for work or for play – if we think that we will be attacked, then we will be. Our thinking makes it so, because – ironically – we will choose the one phrase – the one sentence, the one utterance out of the conversation – and see it as an attack; an insult, a prejudice against us, something that undermines us. Our thinking makes it so, and all experiences in our lives align to make our beliefs a reality.

It is whatever we think it is. Whatever paradigm we set up for ourselves, we will find an "other" who will engage with us in the dance of life to affirm our beliefs, no matter what those beliefs may be. The limiting beliefs on which we have come here to work will present themselves in our lives over and over again, until we can let all of them go.

To learn what limiting beliefs you have set up for yourself in this lifetime, evaluate all the circumstances in your life. What pattern or thread keeps repeating? These patterns will point you to the restraining beliefs through which you have to burst. Talk to your paradigms and ask that you be given to tools to help expand them – whatever those tools may be: spiritual classes or books, psychic readings, energy healing, volunteer work with terminal patients or children with cancer. Be flexible! Evaluate what shows up, and choose from that menu of offerings. Life is very boring when you continually select to eat the same things or wear the same clothes. Experiment! Consider doing something that you might have never dreamt of doing before.

Instead of going along with group mentality, start to think for yourself about what is right for you. Thinking about that which you *do not desire* only serves to bring *more* of that which you do *not* desire into your life. "*What you think about is what you bring about,"* as Zig Ziglar astutely states. What is it that you think about all day long? That is what you are creating in your life.

Taking a look at our "creations" will reveal our thoughts to us, since they are the manifestations of our thoughts. What manifests in our spheres is that which we put there through our own thoughts. As we examine our thoughts, we begin to understand our lives.

Categorize the duality of your thinking:

Optimistic	Pessimistic
Truthful	Deceitful
Hopeful	Despairing
Joyous	Sorrowful
Generous	Miserly
Beautiful	Macabre
Sensuous	Lustful
Prosperous	Impoverished
Courageous	Cowardly

Do your thoughts cancel each other out because they are equally positive and negative, or are they concentrated on one theme? When you categorize your thoughts, you sort out your life. You sit in the center of your being, and distinguish what is driving you – where, how, and when. Eventually, you hit the "mother lode" – the core issue on which you come here to work.

How do your conscious or sub-conscious thoughts control that which shows up in your life? Our paradigms expand as our thinking changes.

December 19

We See That Which We "Think" We See

There is a lesson in *A Course in Miracles* that states: "My thoughts are images that I have made…the thoughts you think you think appear as images…You think you think them, and so you think you see them." (Workbook, Lesson 15, Par. 1, Sent. 1-2)

I received a vivid illustration of this lesson one day during an appointment at the acupuncture's office. After my treatment, I was led to a room and told to lie down in a bed. Because I thought the room was empty, I did not see the other person lying there, even though she had on a bright red sweater and dark blue jeans. When the doctor came into the room, I thought he was arriving to check on me. Instead, he walked over to the other bed. Only then did I "see" the patient in the other bed. My expectation of an empty room had "created" an empty room.

Another story illustrating how we see only that which our expectations allow us to see is attributed to a conquistador's rounding Cape Horn in Africa: when the explorers landed on the shore in the small boats from the galleon that had brought them there, the shaman of the tribe that was gathered on the shore figured out a way to ask them, *How did you get here?* Since the natives had no concept of a galleon, they could not see the galleon. Only after the shaman was able to "see" the galleon himself, was he then able to communicate the idea of that massive ship to his fellow natives.

This was further illustrated by a study done by Harvard graduate students on kittens raised in a horizontal world. From the moment of birth, they were subjected to an environment of broad bands of black and white stripes laid out horizontally. Then the kittens were introduced to a vertical world; broad bands of black and white stripes laid out in a vertical pattern. In this vertical world, they constantly bumped into walls, and were generally disoriented. They "saw" only that part of the stripe that fit into their original horizontal paradigm.

Whether psychologically, or neurologically, we "see" what we *think* we see. If it does not exist within the model imposed on us by society, we do not "see" it. To help us "see" more clearly, studies are made, studies are repeated, and studies are forgotten. Hopefully, experiments such as those with the kittens make a dent in the way man views his world, and can help erode the fear that still grips this planet.

This is the time of remembering that from whence we came and what our real purpose is for coming to this plane of existence. This is the time of unity; not divisiveness, harmony; not discord, kindness; not greed, and gentleness; not harshness. This is the time to share the bounty of the Earth with *all* of its inhabitants – not just a grabby few hoarding all the wealth for themselves.

This is the time that all those who control through fear lose their power on this planet, as men recognize: *Yes, these times are different!*

Have you ever experienced seeing something that was not there originally? We "see" whatever we put there.

December 20

Extricating from Ego Self

Our ego wants us to think that we are a glass jar encasing a drop of water which has been thrown into the ocean; buffeted by the waves, thrown up against the rocks, tossed, twirled, blown by the wind and subjected to the changes of tide. The sole function of our jar (representing our ego mind) is to protect this tiny drop of water (representing physicality – our personality self) to keep the jar from breaking; to keep it from merging with all the other drops of water that make up the ocean. One drop, protected by the jar, is the limit of what our ego mind thinks that we are.

We do not see that by opening the jar – by using the power of our Spirit mind – to empty the water into the ocean – to Spirit – we can merge with and become part of that Great Force that surrounds us; that indeed *is us*. We keep our individual personality so tightly encased in that jar, that we cannot possibly conceive of the idea that we each have the same power as the whole. We limit our consciousness to a tightly constricted view of life.

When our consciousness is confined to that which our physical senses reveal to us, some of us who think we are very small and insignificant live lives of despair; no hope, no future. We accept the blows that life delivers and brace ourselves for more to come. We think that we are merely recipients on this journey through life, and cannot conceive of having anything different from that into which we were birthed. To accept another reality for ourselves is too outrageous. So, we stay stuck.

Others, led by massive egos, think that we must grab all for our ego self and leave nothing for another, even when we are surfeited. The larger the ego, the bigger the grab. It does not matter how much money we have; we want more. It does not matter how many corporations we control; we want a bigger share. It does not matter how horrid the effects of our undertakings are to the natural environment; we stomp over the cautions touted by environmentalists and scientists around the world, and hurtle forward with our next project in the name of "progress." We ravage the Earth to fill the cavernous needs of our egos.

Our ego self thinks only in terms of duality: too weak, too strong, too big, too small, too important, too insignificant, too anything else. Our ego self does not allow us to think that we could possibly be part of One seamless ocean of energy. Only our Spirit Self allows us to accept that we are One drop that is part of the Whole – One drop that has the same characteristics as the Whole. One drop can accomplish what the Whole accomplishes by merging with the Whole – by allowing ourselves to be One with the Whole. We are sacred because we share the same characteristics as the Whole.

It is not our bodies that enslave us. It is the ego part of our minds, that part of our consciousness that insists that we are separate from the Whole. Our bodies are neutral. Our ego consciousness keeps us imprisoned (encapsulated in the glass jar), until we extricate ourselves from its grip, and give ourselves the freedom to merge with the Whole.

We do this by exercising our free will to choose to listen to the Voice of the Whole-ey Spirit who speaks for God; who speaks to us daily, in a very quiet Voice so as not to usurp our free will, who speaks quietly to re-mind us who we really are and what we really are about.

By letting go of our need to be separate, we merge with the greater part of our "Be"-ing. There is only of us – one ocean, composed of droplets beyond measure – all moving together in one vast plasma of Being-ness. Instead of holding fast to the idea of separateness, we "Let Go and Let God." "Let Go" of our need to be separate, and "Let God" help us merge with the vastness of who we really are.

We receive the gift of *grace* when we go about our daily efforts connected to our God mind. How effortlessly the day seems to flow. How effortlessly our work seems to flow. When we open ourselves to our Spirit Self, we see the vastness of our connection to the all, and become One with the All.

Have you exercised you free will to choose Spirit Self over ego self? When we let go of our need to be "separate," we merge with the Whole – yet still retain our individuality.

December 21

The Realm of all Possibility

All That Is (God) manifests all that is (all of creation). All That Is magnifies all that is. Life is a series of spirals linked together; a giant slinky in an endless chain of possibilities. The consciousness that you call "you" in this lifetime is a tiny blip on that endless spiral of possibilities. Because there are other tiny blips of "you" in other dimensions on that endless spiral, the collective "you" is a giant tuning fork reverberating throughout each of the dimensions at the same time. Every one of your collective thoughts influences each of the dimensions simultaneously; all orchestrated by your Higher Self. Since you are the possibility of everything about which you think, the possibilities that manifests in your sphere in *this* dimension may be accomplished facts in another dimension.

Gregg Braden, in one of his lectures on *The Isaiah Effect,* showed us a chart filled with a series of wavy lines banded in the colors of the rainbow called "the band of all possibilities." Each thought that we think taps into this band of all possibilities somewhere, but *all* possibilities exist for our choosing at all times. As we choose, we then experience the results of our choice. However, that does not preclude us from choosing differently the next time around.

I would like to take his "band of all possibilities" one step further. Since the color bands are identical to the colors of the chakras, all possibilities are related to the same issues that the chakra colors represent. Our thoughts continuously flit from color to color, as we "think" throughout the day. All of our thinking happens in split second "sound bites." All possibilities are open to us at all times, but let us look at an example featuring the first three color bands of the chakras: red, orange, and yellow.

Our first thought centers on the root (the first) chakra, colored red. The issues related to the root are: our family history, our country of origin, and the societal and cultural restrictions that we have chosen for ourselves. Let's examine how our thoughts and chakras interact in an imaginary scenario. The holiday season is approaching, and certain family members request that we spend the coming holiday with them. We decide that we have had enough of family, and are going to spend the holidays at home by our self.

The next thought, concerned with the sacral (the second) chakra, is colored orange. Issues concentrated on the sacral are: our relationships, how we view our interaction with those around us, our loved ones, whether they are close to us or not, and all issues with our emotional body. We think about how sad other family members will be about our choice to stay at home by our self during the holidays. We decide that, regardless of how other family members feel, our decision to spend the holidays at home by our self is right for us. We consider the consequences, and know that we have the right to make a decision based on our own needs.

The third thought is attached to the solar plexus (the third) chakra, colored yellow, and is also associated with the third subtle body (the mental body), together with our personal needs in the total make-up of our energy being. We consider the logistics of taking one more trip during the holiday season; the traffic tie-ups, the delays at the airport, the tired feeling that we have when we arrive back home to face the mountain of work there, and decide positively that we will stay at home for the holidays.

Suppose, in this imaginary thought-scenario, that we are recuperating from a debilitating illness and have more treatments to go after this intense period of activity is over. That would certainly determine how much energy we would be able to put forth for the holidays. Our mental body will put brakes on our enthusiasm to "celebrate," in order to preserve our strength for the upcoming treatments. We claim our right to make the decision to stay at home without any feelings of guilt, but feel compassion for the disappointment that everyone else will feel. We come into our power as we accept our right to make the decision that is best for ourselves.

When we fully understand and accept our self as our Self – as One with All of creation – everything that we think about has spiritual overtones to it. We tap into the purple band (the crown chakra); our connection to the Divine. As Spirit overlays our thoughts, our connection to the Divine expands and expands. Our decisions are based on the highest good for our spiritual development, thus contributing to the highest good of all mankind.

Can you believe that all possibilities are available to you? No matter what possibility shows up, we can choose another.

December 22

Core Issues

One of the core issues that we all ultimately have to face is *who we really are.* We have forgotten who we really are.

Your core issues are the items that you have extracted from the nucleus of your Soul, prior to incarnating on this planet. You have chosen to work on eliminating certain limiting beliefs that held you back in prior incarnations. If you incarnated to overcome the feeling of abandonment, from your earliest age, circumstances in your life led *towards* feelings of abandonment. Your father died and your mother died long before you were ready to let them go. Your spouse left you and your friends let you down. You were afraid of crowds, because of the impact that other people's energy had on you. Relationships continued to reinforce your belief that this planet is an unfriendly place; that no one has fully supported your journey here. Slowly, everything you held near and dear evaporated from your sphere; all issues which dealt with abandonment.

When you decide abandonment is no longer an issue, the scene changes. Friends and family call, invite you over, and solicit your advice. Your home becomes filled with people who relish your company and provide you with a sense of purpose and merriment. Your new friends support all the activities that you dearly love. Your spiritual path shifts to incorporate different modalities than those with which you had previously been familiar, and you find a spiritual activity to which you can relate; one that brings joy and meaning into your life. You have come full circle from the space that you were in before.

If your core issue is rejection, then you have a haunting feeling that somehow people do not like you. You are not able to secure the affections of those you consider the most special to you. Teen-age "crushes" break your heart. Your family seems foreign to you. You just do not seem to "fit in." Some of your co-workers act as if they hate you. You are unable to keep a low profile so as not to draw attention to yourself, because so many things call attention to you. Your relationships fizzle and your marriage ends in disaster, since you married for all the wrong reasons. You do not even know your own mind.

When you give up the idea of rejection, you meet the person who then brings completion to your life, is able to support you, and together you establish a family that is the love of your life. You succeed financially and prosper. Your life is by no means without stress, but the stresses help you grow into the person that you were meant to become. They become the catalysts to catapult you into your life's work. You see them for the blessings that they really are.

If your core issue is low self-esteem, your spouse or life partner may abuse you physically, mentally, emotionally, or verbally. All the people who are significant in your life do not appreciate your efforts, no matter how hard you strive. You are convinced that you are the victim of all the disasters in your life, because somehow every major decision rests on your shoulders. Your economical set-backs are rampant. Your friends may be very limited or non-existent. You look around and realize you have no one in whom to confide or with whom to have fun. You feel that your life is filled with excuses and complaints, and a general feeling of ennui sets in.

As we give up the feelings of abandonment, rejection, or low self-esteem, we see our lives changing in such a dramatic fashion that it barely resembles the lives that we used to live. When we learn to stand on our own two feet instead of leaning on another, we achieve mastery of self, which leads to Mastery of Self. When we have reached Mastery of Self, we recognize that nothing has "happened" to us to which we did not agree while still in Spirit form. We accept our role as creator "Be"-ings, and know that we have worked very hard to clear out any remnants of fears that held us back in the past. We are now free to go forth and bring out the highest potential in our Self.

Some who incarnate here have one core issue; others more than one. Some of us - those who have chosen to receive spiritual mastery in this lifetime – have chosen to clear out *all* the remnants of debris trailing over from prior incarnations that may still live in our energy fields.

When we recognize that we are the creator of our own reality, we then recognize that we can change our reality to whatever we wish.

Have you uncovered the core issues of your life yet?
Core issues must be examined before
we step into Self-Mastery.

December 23

Natural Law: Intention

We used to marvel at my Aunt Mary. She was a Bingo aficionado and she consistently won!

Whenever we spoke to her about her incredible "luck," she would say, "I always win."

There was something about her self-assurance that reverberated in my mind. I theorized that her *intent* was to win every time she played, and decided to test this theory in the simplest way possible. A neighborhood dice game called *Bunco* proved to be the best venue. After silently proclaiming *I always win* I noticed how many times I did indeed come home with a prize. Law of Chance stated that I would win once every eight months. After saying *I always win* for approximately six months, I averaged a win once every two months – and sometimes every month – a fairly nice increase. I thanked the Universe and I thanked God.

Now my husband thinks I should start buying Lottery tickets.

The Law of Intention is one of a series of Natural Laws that governs this planet. When we set our *intention*, we then focus our *attention*. Interesting how these words break down:

Intention IN tension

Attention AT tension

These two little words, with their very slight difference of meaning, can sometimes be interchangeable. *Webster's New World Dictionary, Third College Edition* offers the first definition for *in* to mean "contained or enclosed by" while *at* means "on, in, near, by." When we are "in" some place or state of "Be"-ing, we are also "at" some place or state of "Be"-ing.

Our intention sets the focus for our creations. That on which we set our *intention* is that on which we focus our *attention*. That on which we focus our attention is that about which we think.

That which we think about is what we manifest. All of creation rests on a foundation of the twin pillars of intention and attention, expanding from there. All work together in a logical progression from inward to outward.

If we do not set our intention each day for that which *we* desire to manifest, we are subjected to the desires of other people. We are pushed and pulled into the giant wave of collective consciousness that can overtake any personal will of ours, because we have not expressed any personal will. Other people decide for us how we are to think and what we are to do. They have their own agenda, and we are part of it, to help them get what *they* want. That is – until we tire of this situation, and take the reins back into our own hands.

Our lives do not have to be a giant stagecoach, running out of control. We can take charge of the reins, and bring circumstances back into harmony. No, we do not have to be in therapy for years. It can happen instantly.

Simply change your mind about the way you think. One place to start is to give up your feelings of victimhood, forgive, and move on. Another can be to *act* on your “great idea” – to find the logical progression to bring it into form, and to take each necessary step to bring your “great idea” into reality. A third can be to ask for the courage to extricate yourself from group mind and stand in your own truth about “what is.” Set your intent towards manifesting what *you* desire in this lifetime, and bring your life back into control.

Each person on this planet has had an experience they cannot explain, but which they refuse to share with others for fear of being ridiculed. Each person acquiesces to group mentality, because no one wants to stand out as being “different.” Group mentality is herd mentality. Set your intent to extricate yourself from the group.

Some of us have more “drastic events” in our lives than others. We can take our guidance from Nature. Even the giant wave produced by a tsunami recedes immediately. An earthquake’s aftershock may yield another earthquake and another wave, but nothing similar to the magnitude of the initial earthquake that caused the first wave. Nature shakes things up dramatically, then immediately restores calm. No matter what the "drastic events" may bring into our lives, we can restore calm to ourselves. We can clean up the mess left behind by setting our intent to bring more peace, calm, and harmony into our life.

As we seek to master the Law of Intent, and learn the importance of setting our intentions every day for everything that we wish to manifest, we learn to live consciously. Miracles unfold in our lives daily. They are called coincidences; *God's way of staying anonymous.* Paying attention to all the coincidences in our lives – becoming aware of their synchronicity and the messages they bring us – helps us to achieve our heart's desire.

Become attuned to receive Spirit's message, but do not misunderstand it. If we ask for an abundance of money or a new job, a new home, or other material benefit, Spirit may send us an *abundance of energy* so that we can do what is necessary to achieve our heart's desire. Should we squander that energy on useless pursuits that have nothing to do with financial gains, then we are misinterpreting Spirit's message. If we have received Spirit's help, but not in the manner for which we had originally asked, we are being honored for our position as a creator "Be"-ing. Spirit is willing to "assist" us, but will not do our work "for" us. Should we misuse Spirit's assistance, we reap the consequence; the effect of another natural law – the Law of Cause and Effect.

How does the Natural Law of Intention manifest itself in your life? Intent is one of the Natural Laws that govern this planet.

December 24

Christmas Eve – Amazing Grace

Had the Grinch stolen my Inspiration for the Christmas letter that I kept trying to compose? Nothing that I wrote sounded right. The Angels and Guides all patiently waited while I listlessly plodded forward. Nothing seemed to come forth as a theme for this year's letter until I silently heard the words … *Amazing Grace,* then thought about what those words meant to me.

Amazing Grace held me in its embrace during my 20's, as I struggled through my first marriage (with ten moves in five years), and then with several favored careers that came to a screeching halt, and finally through the last move to Virginia; the "deep south" (or so I thought).

Amazing Grace paved the way to a new life; a new career in real estate which has lasted all these years, a new husband, two beautiful children and three moves that landed us in South Run in a home that I envisioned from the moment that we bought our first home. It helped me stay continuously employed while raising my children; two beautiful souls who developed their own interests and pursuits. It sent me a husband who always willingly pitched in wherever work was needed to be done, which then gave me the freedom to pursue the "something more" for which I searched.

Amazing Grace promoted a change in the make-up of my life, prepared me for spiritual pursuits, helped me to self-publish my first book, and opened me to the wonders of the metaphysical. It filled every facet of my life: cementing new friendships, assisting in developing my intuitive and Reiki healing and teaching skills, perfecting new techniques, and enhancing old ones as we worked with patients who had cancer and other debilitating illnesses. It helped me witness innumerable kindnesses: spoken words that felt like feathers across my Soul; healing hands that healed broken hearts as well as broken bodies; and smiles everywhere.

Amazing Grace has given me the fortitude to nurture and enjoy two very independent, very creative entrepreneurs: Elizabeth (www.ElizabethJonesDesign.com) now works in films, commercials, and print media in New York, and David (www.SetsandEffects.com) does woodwork and set production, and also works for films, commercials, and print media in New York.

May your life be filled with *Amazing Grace* to soothe the rough spots, enhance the joyous one, and provide you with the peace that you richly deserve.

When has Amazing Grace silently appeared in your life?
Recognize Amazing Grace every time it enters your life.

December 25

Christmas Day -Gifts that Money Can't Buy

Once again, another year looms to a close. This year, I thought of the words of a friend of mine. She was talking about her brother-in-law's ministry and how, in this season, he counsels grown men who weep because they cannot *buy* all the things that they feel their loved ones want for Christmas. This started me thinking about all the gifts that money *can't buy* – Gifts from the Heart, Gifts of the Spirit – and I would like to share these gifts with you.

From my parents, I received the gift of learning to *Trust* God – that He had a plan for my life. When I saw only the shadows, He saw the Grand Design. From that, I learned to trust myself, my husband, my children, my friends, my clients, and my life. I have never been disappointed. When I *forgot* to trust and my life felt like it had turned upside down, then I learned that I simply had to see things from a different perspective, had to put a different lens in my camera.

From my parents I received the gift of *Compassion* – to share what I had, to be kinds to others, to never look down on those who wore dirty tattered clothes, to treat each person with a sense of dignity and respect, and above all, not to gossip. This sense of compassion has served me well. I look each man squarely in the eye. No man is beneath me, but neither is one above me. God gives the same gifts to each of us. It is up to us to lift the veil.

From my family I received the gift of *Love* – a love so deep that it seemed to come from a bottomless well. But it was from my mother-in-law that I learned about unconditional Love. I watched her with her schizophrenic son (my husband's brother); her endless patience, her simple acceptance of whatever small triumph the day would bring, her incredible sense of joy and good humor, and her stability. She loved without expectation of anything in return from him – ever! Through watching her, I, too, learned the meaning of unconditional Love.

From my parents I received the gift of *Vision* – to see not just what was in front of me, but what *could be.* And I learned to ask for *Amazing Grace* when my vision dimmed, the grace to accept all of God's creatures and all of God's creation, no matter what they looked like.

And finally, from my parents I learned to *Forgive* – as they did – for all the slights, injustices, ridicules, hurts; real and imagined. I learned that when people are not coming from a position of love, then they are coming from a position of fear. From my parents, I learned to for*give* and to for*get*, because what I *give*, I *get.*

I have watched people receive a myriad of "things," when all they *really wanted* was a hug – and someone to listen to them. This year I share these "gifts" with you because I know that you have shared these same gifts – or better ones – with those you know and love.

What gifts have you shared with others that have nothing to do with money? The greatest gift that we can give someone is the gift of our time.

December 26

Nothing but Angels

The Angels and I would like to share the Gift of New Life, the Gift of Tolerance, and the Gift of Adventure this holiday season.

The Gift of New Life –

"Every baby born into the world is a finer one than the last."

Charles Dickens

I can honestly see now why people look forward to being grandparents, if only to a pet. There is nothing more exciting than to look into the light of new life, whether it is a plant, a pet, or a person. When we clear away the old to make room for the new, we look at the light beaming forth from what we have birthed. Within the sparkle of that light is the promise from the Creator that all life is forever. Somewhere deep within us is the knowledge that we are all connected to the Source of all Light, the Divine Creator.

The Gift of Tolerance –

"I may not agree with what you say, Mom,
but I will defend your "right" to say it
with my life, because that is the American way."

E. David Jones

David's statement emphasizes a very tolerant point of view as we are called upon to extend tolerance every day of our lives:

- Tolerance for those on the "other" side of the political process, promoting *co-operation* between disagreeing factions as the *only* way to get things done.
- Tolerance for the bigotry and prejudice that organized religions sometimes expound in the name of "God." Remember, to a cannibal, "God" is a cannibal.
- Tolerance for those in need, whether it be mental, emotional, or physical. Sometimes offering the gift of our time to a friend or family member is the greatest gift of all; sometimes offering the gift of our time to a stranger makes the difference between whether they choose to live or choose to die.
- Tolerance for those whose choices society judges to be "wrong," whose lives – in the cosmic scheme of things – may have been dedicated to helping someone else learn a lesson in forgiveness.
- Admiration for those who toil away in the bowels of the "system," never receiving any specific recognition or awards, yet always doing their job quietly, efficiently, and correctly, and who themselves show tolerance for those who, higher up *or not,* take the credit for their work.
- Tolerance and compassion for those whose grief overwhelms them *during* the holidays.

The Gift of Adventure –

"Life's a banquet, and most poor suckers are starving to death!"

Auntie Mame

Auntie Mame is totally into finding adventure wherever she goes or in whatever happens to her. We can do the same. From wide open spaces to hidden inner places, sometime the greatest adventure of all can be found from within. By stopping all the frantic rushing about, and taking the time to share an intimate moment accessing the God within, we look at all the beauty that surrounds us. From the first rays of sunrise to the last glow of moonbeams, each moment brings its own special joy.

May the Angels gift you this holiday season all the blessings that your heart desires of new life, tolerance and adventure.

How has adventure, tolerance, or the gift of new life shown up in your life lately? Sometimes accessing the God within bestows upon us gifts beyond measure.

December 27

Restoring Mother Earth's Original Intent

We agree to come to planet Earth to advance in spiritual mastery, *not* to accumulate all the wealth, land, possessions, or tea cups that we covet. When we learn the purpose for our placement on this planet, we stop the horrible misuse of Mother Earth's resources. We flagrantly disregard her needs as a living being. We send sound waves into her ionosphere and into her oceans through HAARP (the High-Frequency Active Auroral Research Program) in our effort to alter sound patterns. We shrug our shoulders pretending to be mystified that her gentle caretakers – the whales and dolphins – end up beaching themselves on the shore with massive hemorrhages in their brain.

We explode atom bombs into her bowels to test their "effectiveness" so that we can heap more and more destruction on her creatures on the Earth. We continuously drop bombs on her soil in our puny little power wars, waged with such righteous indignation.

We destroy hundreds of thousands of acres of tropical forest to raise more crops, and watch as the top soil blows away in a few years because soil that supports a rain forest is not suitable for farming. We straighten out her rivers and construct dams where it is convenient for us to have extra water, and pollute her water supply with all our chemical run-off, then watch as the marine life within her tributaries, streams, rivers, and bays dies and her water supply becomes undrinkable. We alter her deltas in the name of housing or entertainment, and pave over her wetlands which are her natural sponges, then decry her attempts to reclaim them.

Then, we sit back and wonder: *Why is she blowing her top? Why all the massive volcanic eruptions? Why the intensity of the earthquakes? Why so many hurricanes and tsunamis? Why the fierceness of the forest fires raging out of control?* Why indeed! All is cause and effect. We put the natural disasters into motion by our outrageous neglect of the needs of the planet.

Mother Earth was *not* created to be in the mess that she is in. She was *not* created to be a haven for hoarders, for power seekers, for those who have utter disregard for human, plant, or animal life. Darker and denser planets were created as havens for the denser impenetrable energies and people matching *those* vibrations land there. All life on this planet is being re-evaluated, and those who cannot subscribe to her lightness of being are destined to be ushered off the planet to be matched with the denser, darker energies with whom they vibrate.

Mother Earth is being restored, replenished, and returned to her original intent as a planet. To return to her *birthright* – to regain her original state of "Be"-ing; a state of pristine beauty, a true Garden of Eden – she is being assisted by those in physical body called the Light workers, who, in turn, are being assisted by the Galactic, Angelic, and Devic realms for this mission, all overseen by the Beings from the Central Sun.

Two thousand years ago, a Master taught the *Beatitudes* in the *Sermon on the Mount*, promising us that "the meek shall inherit the Earth, for they are the children of God." Through *calmness* and *meekness,* which adds to and helps Mother Earth increase her vibrational level, she is being elevated to the pristine state of her original being. As this planet returns to the state she was at the beginning of creation, only enlightened beings are slated to live here. The great experiment – the total forgetfulness of that from whence man comes – is almost over. Her intent is to be a planet for enlightened beings, and she is reclaiming her original design.

Mother Earth's destiny is for her to take her rightful place in this quadrant of the galaxy to be – as Barbara Marciniak states in her book *Earth* – the "living library" that she is; a repository of all of God's creations.

Have you thought about the "needs" of the planet? Light workers share their light to help the planet regain her original stature.

December 28

Our Path Is Ours Alone

Since the evolutionary path to Spirit is unique to each person, each of us is in a different place from our spouse, child, parent, friend, or business associate. What resonates with us simply reflects where we are on our evolutionary path. We are not "equally matched" with anyone. That is why sharing our own spiritual truths with those we love may not work. The poem: "Don't try to lead me, I may not follow. Don't try to follow me, I may not lead. But walk beside me as my friend, my lover, my compatriot." reflects this truth. We each have our own work to do. We walk *beside* those whom we love.

Each soul decides what it needs for its growth, understanding, and completion. Each soul seeks to complete its "chosen" mission in this incarnation, which may be to bake the best chocolate pie. Nothing more, nothing less. The soul may be in a "resting" life. The soul may be here only as an *observer* of the planet Earth; not needing to contribute anything to further the growth and development of mankind. The soul may be a “new” soul, not heeding the normal paths of growth, and those attached to the “new” soul may feel their lives are totally out of control.

Alternatively, the soul may be an “old” soul with blockages to clear; one who sets up circumstances to help it burst these blockages. A person connected to an “old” soul who is clearing out blockages may feel victimized as they become entangled in daily drama traumas, forgetting that – *on a soul level* – they each agreed to the circumstances in which they now find themselves. On a personality level, they may begrudge what is happening to them.

This is why it is so critical not to judge. Even the most heinous amongst us fits into the Divine Plan. We are not the *puzzle maker* any more than we are our parent. We are simply a *piece* of the puzzle. Underlying everything is All That Is! We each have our own work to do. Our work is unique to our self and unique to our Self. The (ego) self has an earthly plan to complete; the (Higher) Self has a spiritual plan. We are each part of the Whole; in effect the Whole-ey Spirit.

Where we are *is where we are*. When someone tries to force learning down our throats when we are not ready, it is like trying to feed steak to a baby. It does not work. The baby does not have the mechanism to swallow the piece of steak. It is not that the mechanism isn’t there. It is. It just is not developed enough at that age.

We each have the means within ourselves to achieve the highest connection to Spirit, but most of us have to develop that mechanism over time. Through our free will, we can *keep it from happening.* That mechanism, *our spiritual anatomy,* is composed of an entire grid-work of energy connections that is *identical* in each person. Our egos throw up blockages to understanding energy connections to the Divine, in order to keep our personality from developing its full potential as a “spiritual” “Be”-ing having a “human” experience.

As we receive new information and become open to the gifts of Spirit, we each then expand our spiritual core and expand our energy field. Only after we are "ready" to receive information about our spiritual anatomy can we reach our full potential. Our level of understanding depends on how open we are to new information. For many of us, the path to wisdom is paved with pain, and we have to sink to our knees before we are ready to receive spiritual advice. Those of us who are destined to do so eventually take our place as one of God's teachers.

Spiritual age has nothing to do with chronological age. Many of us are still in infancy when it comes to spiritual maturity. Some of the oldest beings on the planet may be the least evolved. Our Souls may push us toward spiritual interests, but we may ignore their urging because we are consumed with raising our children or are in the middle of material pursuits; seeking status and financial gain. When we are ready to accept new information, we will be given it. If we subscribe to the same limiting beliefs with which we grew up, and are happy in the place that is exactly right for us in this lifetime; that may be as far as we are willing to evolve.

If we examine our Soul's needs and recognize that we need "something more," then we are given new information to help us rise to a higher state of evolution.

Are you here for your own learning or are you here to be a world teacher? "Forcing" our belief system on someone else simply does not work.

December 29

The Power Within – I AM

If we think that the Spirit who connects us to the Source of our "Be"-ing – the Source of our power and self-worth – as being *outside* of us, then when the events of the world come punching, we lie contracted on the floor; an empty shell, a balloon that has been deflated flattened, defeated, without hope. We cannot cope.

When the Source of our "Be"-ing is *within* us, and the world throws its punches, we become a roly-poly. We can be hit and may briefly touch the floor, but cannot be knocked down permanently. We bounce right back. When our power is *within,* even when circumstances seem to take away everything that we hold dear – as the hurricane victims in Louisiana and Mississippi and the tsunami victims in Indonesia experienced in 2005 – the Source of our strength is replenished. Hope is restored, and we find the will to go on.

After we release all the pain, all the injustices, all the unfairness, all the hurt, all the grief, and all the agony from our lives, and we stand naked in our vulnerability, what do we have left? After we release all the categories that we think identify who we are, there is only one thing left – *I AM.*

We stand in our *I AM* presence when we give up all ego issues, and return to the inherent "Be"-ing that we are. We stand without our defenses, our procrastination, our ego mania, in all our vulnerability. We give up everything that our ego has once held dear, yet we gain back the world. We are introduced to something deeper than we had ever before believed possible; a deeper faith, a deeper hope, a deeper sense of fulfillment, a deeper commitment to pursue that which is important to our Soul.

To help us find the Source of our power, we have to think differently than we did previously. We are going to have to believe that it is possible. Only then will circumstances change around us, which will then indeed change our lives. We will see it as we believe it.

There is no better teacher than Higher Self, because nothing exists except Self. All is a reflection of Self. All else mirrors Self. The people who are in our sphere reflect Self. The environment in which we have chosen to live identifies Self. The work in which we have engaged copies Self. The illnesses that we have drawn to our body imitate Self. This is the one concept that we cannot accept about our Self: that we have created everything that we see around us, that we are a creator "Be"-ing, that there is nothing outside of Self. It is all up to Self, because Self is all there is. There is nothing outside of Self.

We incarnate here with no set of instructions. We use the writings of those who have gone before us to pave the way until we learn to listen to the Inner Voice of our own Souls, the guidance that comes from Cosmic Source to guide us, to help us step onto the path that our Higher Self has chosen for us prior to incarnating here.

At your most vulnerable, have you learned to turn to the "I AM" presence within? We can access our "I AM" presence instantly.

December 30

Volunteering for Change

Our Souls know the missions for which we volunteer when we agree to come here. If we have a higher purpose for our life on this planet than our ego minds would lead us to believe, we can either accept all the accoutrements that go along with our ego lives and stay there, or we can balk. We have a choice. We can be the catalyst for change and willingly accept the higher purpose for which we came here, or we can wait until an atom bomb goes off in our lives, which sinks us to our knees and makes us more receptive to hear Spirit's message. Those of us who have agreed to be a catalyst for change come in many shapes, sizes and circumstances.

How many employees in the World Trade Center looked out the window shortly before the planes hit on September 11, 2001 and knew with complete certainty that this moment on Earth was going to be their last? How many were resigned to that fact, yet survived against all odds; were led down stairways that they never noticed before, escorted to safety by personnel who appeared from nowhere and who seemed to know exactly where they were going, even though it was pitch black? How many employees did not even know what hit them? However, *their souls knew* they had volunteered to be part of the group who had perished.

How many people were not at their desks as they were supposed to be, and thus were spared? How many were late that morning, due to the tiniest detail that skewered their plans: missing trains, car-pools mysteriously not showing up, having a sick child who could not be left alone, inability to find a child's shoes that caused delays in leaving home, getting a last minute a cup of coffee around the corner. These and hundreds of other minutia were reasons why people were not at their desks in the Twin Towers when the planes hit. Obviously, these were not part of the group who volunteered to leave.

How brave were those souls who volunteered for that mission; to be the catalyst for change for the world. No matter who they were – passenger, flight attendant, captain, perpetrator, hijacker, rescue worker, security guard, policeman, firefighter or employee – all were very courageous souls who would have gone on with their lives had their souls not made a choice. What a special brand of courage it took to be part of changing the energy of the world. What a special brand of courage it took to be part of the clean-up mission at Ground Zero, laboring for nine months without stopping to clean the area of all the debris. Similarly, others became the support personnel who volunteered their time and skills to help the clean-up crew.

Our world, being what it is, grieves for those who died in the events of 9/11, and for all the loss that they represent in our lives. We have forever been changed by their courage. No one has been unaffected, down to the smallest towns in the United States, and also in many countries around the world, as all the commemorative services, church services, and various types of financial assistance have shown support for those affected.

Whatever major events to which we have been agreed to be a part that have brought grief into our lives, we remember that nothing will ever be the same. We remember through our tears; *nothing will ever be the same.*

Have you been asked to be a catalyst for change in your life? Accepting our soul's contract increases our spiritual vitality.

December 31

Finally, Guidelines from the Source

Let Love be your Guide. Only Love.
Ask "What would Love do now?" when puzzled on a course of action.
Look on all as brothers and sisters.
You have one race on this planet.It is called HUMAN.
You will be introduced to other races from other places.
They, too, are aspects of your Self.
Refrain from harming even the smallest creature on the Earth.
Instead, guide them back to where their life is most suited.
Tread upon the Earth softly. Be gentle with your Mother.
Everything that you need to sustain your life is available here.
Honor the Sun. You are as the Sun.
He shines in the heaven to remind you of who you are.
The brilliance of his light discriminates not; neither should you.
Honor the Moon. The light from the moon affects all the water on this planet.
The moon guides your way.
The Darkness is there simply to remind you to rest.

Even I rested when I blew forth the Microcosm that became the Macrocosm.
Remember that: We are all One:
One with Me, One with the Source,
One Universal energy that is forever expanding and contracting,
One Love, One Mind, One Whole.
Happy New Year!

Make one resolution only.
Listen for the resolution that Spirit offers
for the next year's mission.

Bibliography

Andrews, Ted. *Animal-Speak: The Spiritual & Magical Powers of Creatures Great & Small.* Woodbury, MN: Llewellyn Publications, 2002.

-- *Enchantment of the Faerie Realm: Communicate with Nature Spirits & Elementals.* Woodbury, MN: Llewellyn Publications, 2002.

Anonymous. *The Boy Who Saw True: The Time-Honoured Classic of the Paranormal.* Reprint, New York: Random House, 2010.

Bach, Edward and E.J. Wheeler. *Bach Flower Remedies.* New York: McGraw Hill, 1998.

--*Heal thyself: an explanation of the real cause and cure of disease.* 1931. Reprint, Healdsburg, CA: Pilgrims Publishing House, 2008.

Barker, Cicely Mary. *A Treasury of Flower Fairies.* New York: Penguin-Warne, 1992.

Braden, Gregg. *Awakening to Zero Point: The Collective Initiation,* 2nd ed. North Palm Beach, FL: Sacred Spaces Ancient Wisdom, 1997.

-- *Secrets of the Lost Mode of Prayer: The Hidden Power of Beauty, Blessings, Wisdom, and Hurt.* Carlsbad, CA: Hay House, 2006.

-- *The Isaiah Effect: Decoding the Lost Science of Prayer and Prophecy.* New York: The Crown Publishing Group-Three Rivers Press, 2001.

Breathnach, Sarah Ban. *Simple Abundance: A Daybook of Comfort and Joy.* Reissue ed. New York: Hatchett Book Group-Grand Central Publishing, 2009.

Brennan, Barbara with Jos. A. Smith (Illus.). *Hands of Light: A Guide to Healing Through the Human Energy Field.* Reprint, New York: Random House-Bantam, 2009.

-- *Light Emerging: The Journey of Personal Healing.* New York: Random House- Bantam, 1993.

Brooker, John L. *Darkness into Light: Rescuing Souls on the Other Side*. Nevada City, CA: Blue Dolphin Publishing, 2001.

-- *If Heaven Is So Wonderful… Why Come Here?: How to Discover Our "Whole Being."* Nevada City, CA: Blue Dolphin Publishing, 2004.

Carroll, Lee and Jan Tober. *Indigo Children: The New Kids have Arrived*. Carlsbad, CA: Hay House, 1999.

Cameron, Julia. *The Artist's Way: A Spiritual Path to Higher Creativity*. New York: Jeremy P. Tarcher-Perigee Books, 1992.

-- *The Vein of Gold: A Journey to Your Creative Heart*. New York: Tarcher-Putnam, 1996.

Cayce, Edgar. *The Power of Your Mind: An Edgar Cayce Series Title*. Reprint, Virginia Beach, VA: A.R.E. Press, 2010.

D'Adamo, Peter J. with Catherine Whitney. *Eat Right 4 Your Type*. New York: Penguin-G.P. Putnam's Sons, 1996.

-- *Eat Right 4 Your Type: Complete Blood Type Encyclopedia*. New York: Penguin Putnam-Riverhead Books, 2002.

Daniel, Alma, Timothy Wyllie, and Andrew Ramer. *Ask Your Angels*. New York: Random House-Ballantine, 1992.

Eadie, Betty J. *Embraced by the Light*. Reprint, New York: Random House-Bantam, 1994.

Emoto, Masaro. *Love Thyself: The Message from Water III (v. 3)*. Carlsbad, CA: Hay House, 2006.

--with David A. Thayne (Trans.). *The Hidden Messages in Water*. New York: Simon and Schuster-Atria, 2005.

-- with Noriko Hosoyamada (Trans.). *The True Power of Water: Healing and Discovering Ourselves*. Trade Pbk. ed. New York: Simon and Schuster-1st Atria Books, 2005.

Esquith, Rafe. *There Are No Shortcuts*. New York: Random House-Pantheon, 2003.

Essene, Virginia and the Christ. *New Teachings for an Awakening Humanity*. Austin, TX: Bookpeople, 1994/1995.

Essential Science Pub. (Compiler). *Essential Oils Desk Reference*. 4rth ed. Essential Science Pub., 2007.

Ferrini, Paul. *Love Without Conditions: Reflections of the Christ Mind.* Greenfield, MA: Heartways Press, 1994.

-- *Silence of the Heart: Reflections of the Christ Mind – Part II.* Greenfield, MA: Heartways Press, 1996.

-- *Miracle of Love: Reflections of the Christ Mind – Part III.* Greenfield, MA: Heartways Press, 1997.

-- *Return to the Garden: Reflections of the Christ Mind – Part IV.* Greenfield, MA: Heartways Press, 1998.

Findhorn Community. *The Findhorn Garden.* New York: HarperCollins, 1976.

Foundation for Inner Peace. *A Course in Miracles.* Reprint/ Combined ed. Foundation for Inner Peace, 2008.

Grey, Alex with Ken Wilber and Carlo McCormick. *Sacred Mirrors: The Visionary Art of Alex Grey.* Rochester, VA: Bear & Company-Inner Traditions, 1990.

Hawkins, David R. *Power vs. Force: The Hidden Determinants of Human Behavior.* Revised ed. Carlsbad, CA: Hay House, 2012.

Hill, Napoleon. *Think and Grow Rich.* Reprint, New York: Tribeca Books, 2012.

Jolley, Willie. *A Setback is a Setup for a Comeback.* New York: Macmillan-St Martin's Griffin, 2000.

Jones, S. Alice "Alicja." *God Is the Biggest Joker of All: Awesome God, Book I.* iUniverse, 2002.

Kirkwood, Annie. *Mary's Message to the World: As Sent by Mary, the Mother of Jesus, to Her Messenger, Annie Kirkwood.* Grass Valley, CA: Blue Dolphin Publishing, 2005.

LaVoie, Nicole. *Return to Harmony: Creating Harmony & Balance Through the Frequencies of Sound.* Sound Wave Energy Press, 2000.

Marciniak, Barbara. *Earth: Pleiadian Keys to the Living Library.* Rochester, VT: Inner Traditions-Bear & Company, 1994.

McLean, Dorothy. *To Hear the Angels Sing: an Odyssey of Co-Creation with the Devic Kingdom.* Hudson, NY: Lindissarne Press, 1980.

Meyer, Marvin W., with Harold Bloom. *The Gospel of Thomas: The Hidden Sayings of Jesus.* 2nd rev. ed. New York: Harper Collins-HarperOne, 2004.

Moody, Raymond and Elizabeth Kubler-Ross. *Life After Life: The Investigation of a Phenomenon – Survival of Bodily Death.* New York: Harper Collins-HarperOne, 2001.

Moody, Raymond. *The Light Beyond.* New York: Bantam, 1989.

Myss, Caroline. *Sacred Contracts: Awakening Your Divine Potential.* New York: Crown Publishing Group-Three Rivers Press, 2003.

-- *Why People Don't Heal and How They Can.* New York: Crown Publishing Group-Three Rivers Press, 1997.

Newton, Michael. *Destiny of Souls: New Case Studies of Life Between Lives.* 2nd ed. Woodbury, MN: Llewellyn Press, 2000).

-- *Journey of Souls: Case Studies of Life Between Lives.* Woodbury, MN: Llewellyn Press, 1994.

Nightingale, Earl. *Lead the Field.* Thousand Oaks, CA: BN Publishing, 2007. (Earlier work in audio format.)

Northrup, Jan. *The Promotable Woman: Have We Come a Long Way Baby?* Glendale, AZ: Management Training Systems, Inc., 2007.

Peale, Norman Vincent. *The Power of Positive Thinking.* Reprint, Japan and Mountain View, CA: Ishi Press, 2011.

Prophet, Elizabeth Clare. *Violet Flame to Heal Body, Mind, and Soul.* Reprint, Summit University Press, 1999.

Redfield, James. *The Celestine Prophecy: An Adventure.* 1st ed. New York: Warner Books, Inc. (now HBG), 1997.

Reeve, Christopher. *Still Me: With a New Afterword for this Edition.* New York: Random House-Ballantine, 1999.

Rinpoche, Sogyal. *The Tibetan Book of Living and Dying: The Spiritual Classic & International Bestseller.* New York: HarperCollins Publishers-HarperOne, 2002.

Roads, Michael J., & Genevieve Wilson. *Talking with Nature and Journey into Nature.* Novato, CA: HJ Kramer-New World Library, 2003.

Roberts, Monty. *The Man Who Listens to Horses: The Story of a Real-Life Horse Whisperer.* Reprint, New York: Random House-Ballantine, 2009.

Simmons, Robert, & Naisha Ahsian. *The Book of Stones: Who They Are & What They Teach.* Berkeley, CA: North Atlantic Books, 2007.

Skutch, Robert. *Journey Without Distance: The Story Behind a Course in Miracles.* Foundation for Inner Peace, 2004.

Stepanek, Mattie J. T. *Heartsongs (1st Edition)*, *Journey through Heartsongs*, *Hope through Heartsongs*, *Celebrate through Heartsongs*, and *Loving through Heartsongs.* New York: Hyperion, 1998 & 2002, 2002, 2002, 2002, and 2003, respectively.

Stone, Joshua David. *Hidden Mysteries: ETs, Ancient Mystery Schools and Ascension (The Easy-to-Read Encyclopedia of the Spiritual Path, Volume IV).* Flagstaff, AZ: Light Technology Publishing, 1995.

-- *The Complete Ascension Manual: How to Achieve Ascension in This Lifetime (Easy-to-Read Encyclopedia of the Spiritual Path).* Flagstaff, AZ: Light Technology Publishing, 1994.

-- *The Ascended Masters Light the Way: Beacons of Ascension. (The Ascension Series).* Sedona, AZ: Mission Possible, 1995.

Tolle, Eckhart. *The Power of Now: A Guide to Spiritual Enlightenment.* Reprint, Novato, CA: New World Library, 1999.

-- *Stillness Speaks.* Novato, CA: New World Library, 2003.

Tompkins, Peter and Christopher Bird. *The Secret Life of Plants: a Fascinating Account of the Physical, Emotional, and Spiritual Relations Between Plants and Man.* Reprint, New York: Harper & Row, 1989.

Virtue, Doreen. *Archangels and Ascended Masters: A Guide to Working and Healing with Divinities and Deities.* Carlsbad, CA: Hay House, 2003.

Walsh, Neale Donald. *Communion with God.* New York: Penguin-Berkley Trade, 2002.

-- *Conversations with God: An Uncommon Dialogue (Book 1)*. Reprint, New York: Penguin-G. P. Putnam's Sons, 1996.

-- *Conversations with God: An Uncommon Dialogue (Book 2)*. 1st ed. Charlottesville, VA: Hampton Roads Publishing Company, 1997.

-- *Conversations with God: An Uncommon Dialogue (Book 3)*. Reprint, New York: Penguin-G. P. Putnam's Sons, 1996. Charlottesville, VA: Hampton Roads Publishing Company, 1998.

-- *The New Revelations: A Conversation with God*. New York: Simon and Schuster-Atria, 2002.

Weil, Andrew. *Eight Weeks to Optimum Health, Revised Edition: A Proven Program for Taking Full Advantage of Your Body's Natural Healing Power*. New York: Random House-Knopf (Ballantine), 2007.

Weiss, Brian L. *Many Lives, Many Masters: The True Story of a Prominent Psychiatrist, His Young Patient, and Past-Life Therapy That Changed Both Their Lives*. New York: Simon and Schuster-Fireside, 1988.

-- *Only Love Is Real: A Story of Soulmates Reunited*. New York: Hachette Livre-Grand Central Publishing, 1997.

-- *Messages from the Masters: Tapping into the Power of Love*. Reprint, New York: Warner-Hachette Livre-Grand Central Publishing, 2001.

Wells, H. G. and Stephen Arata (Ed.). *The Time Machine (Norton Critical Editions)*. Reprint, New York: W.W. Norton & Co., 2008.

Wesselman, Henry. *Spirit Walker: Messages from the Future*. Reprint, New York: Random House-Bantam, 1996.

Williamson, Marianne. *A Return to Love: Reflections on the Principles of A Course in Miracles*. Reprint, London, England: Harper Collins-Harper Paperbacks, 1996.

Wright, Machaelle Small. *Behaving As If the God in All Life Mattered*. Warrenton, VA: Perelandra, Ltd., 1997.

Wright, Machaelle Small, and Elizabeth McHale (Ed.). 3rd ed. *MAP: The Co-Creative White Brotherhood Medical Assistance Program*. Warrenton, VA: Perelandra, Ltd., 2006.

Yogananda, Paramahansa. *Autobiography of a Yogi*. Reprint, Nevada City, UT: Crystal Clarity Publishers, 1995.

Referenced Audio & Video/ DVD Resources

Almine, *The Power of Silence* (Audiobook). Spiritual Journeys with Almine, 2006.

Arkenstone, David. *Spirit Wind.* Windham Hill Records, 1997.

Arntz, William, Betsy Chasse, and Mark Vincente, Drs. *What the Bleep Do We Know?* 2004. Independent feature film, now available as CD and as a book.

Chandra, Henry. *Celestial Morning*. Private release;

Crichton, Charles and John Frankenheimer (Dirs.). *Birdman of Alcatraz*, 2001.

Irving, Judy. *The Wild Parrots of Telegraph Hill.* 2007.

LaVoie, Nicole. *LifEssence Series - Sound Wave Energy,*
-- *Sound Wave Energy - Spiritual Series*
-- *Physical Series (each a 12 CD set).*

Gass, Robert & On Wings of Song. *Om Namaha Shivaya*. Audio CD, available online.

Kapfer, Gabriella. *Sacred Passage*,
--*Dance of Light*,
--*Remembering the Promise*, and multiple other audio CDs are available online.

Wirkus, Mietek. *Basic Level Training Course in Bio-Energy.* (6 CD Set.) Available from www.mietekwirkus.com.

Referenced Tools and Other Resources

Bach Flower Remedies are available in many health food stores and metaphysical stores. See also: www.bachflower.com.

Birds & Blooms Magazine is available in select stores and online at www.birdsandblooms.com/.

Love Corps Newsletter, Share Foundation Network, written and edited by Virginia Essene

Hemi Sync, produced by Monroe Products. (www.hemi-sync.com,

White Rose Oil from Bulgaria is available through various online sources, it may also be available in certain metaphysical and health food stores.

Young Living Essential Oils are available through the internet and at certain stores. Youngliving.com

Acknowledgments

I wish to thank those who have been part of my journey:

My eternal gratitude to God, the Angels, Archangels, Ascended Masters and Reiki Masters, and other beings in Spirit who constantly guide my thoughts, words, and actions.

On the human side, Alianna Maren who was my copy editor for many years, my sister, Krystyna Sweeney, and Barb Maloney, who very carefully read and corrected *Own Your Power,* Leonard Rosenbaum, and his editorial skills and ceaseless helpfulness, and Betty Yeary for her assistance and encouragement.

The staff at Balboa Press, who made this dream a reality.

My husband, Bob, my biggest cheerleader, who patiently assisted me with the computer every time there was a glitch.

My children, Elizabeth and David, who were the inspiration for some of the meditations.

Wanda Lasseter Lundy, my mentor and teacher, who saw a healer in me from my first professional foray into spiritual work.

The Rays of Healing Church, the ministers for all their help, and all others associated with it, for the wisdom and understanding that constantly comes from the lectures presented there.

My *A Course in Miracles* family, Gerda vonder Oelsnitz and Joanne Taylor, for their wisdom and understanding.

The *Sisterhood of the Solar Cross*, my writing group, but especially Elizabeth Cho, Donna Bright, and Sandra Weber who are a delightful part of my support team.

Sacred Circle, Tom and Anysia, and all their employees who provide such a loving environment to promote my spiritual work. To all the fellow seekers who attend my "A Course in Miracles group at Sacred Circle.

Mountain Mystic, Jerry and the healers and participants in Front Royal, VA.

My sisters, Mary Czarnopys and Krystyna Sweeney and brother, Tony, Czarnopys for their unflagging support.

My dear friends, Susan Withe and Mary Jane Banks, for their steadfast wisdom and friendship and love.

My beloved pet corgis: Taffy, Sampson "Sammy" and Delilah, affectionately known as Ms. D or Misdeed. They, too, were influential in my writing.

About the Author

Alice "Alicja" Jones is a Psychic, Medium, and Intuitive healer who gives Spiritual and Past Life readings and healings. She communicates with the Angels, Archangels, Ascended Masters, and Reiki Masters and other beings in Spirit to help bring spiritual, mental, and emotional transformation into your life. She works with energy healing and was given a specialized healing method from Archangel Metatron that affects your subtle bodies (your auric field). She calls it Metatron's Healing Method.

She is a Reiki Master, teacher/practitioner and a licensed Minister at Rays of Healing Church in Falls Church, VA.

She lives in Fairfax Station, VA with her husband and corgi, Sammy.

She is available for speeches, readings, and healings:

Contact: www.alicjajones.com
e-mail: alicejones7@verizon.net